Accelerating Product Development Cycles With Digital Twins and IoT Integration

Udit Mamodiya
Poornima University, Jaipur, India

Akhtar Kalam
Texila College, Australia

Yu-Chen Hu
Tunghai University, Taiwan

Dinesh Goyal
Poornima Institute of Engineering and Technology, India

IGI Global
Scientific Publishing
Publishing Tomorrow's Research Today

Vice President of Editorial Melissa Wagner
Director of Acquisitions Mikaela Felty
Director of Book Development Jocelynn Hessler
Production Manager Mike Brehm
Cover Design Phillip Shickler

Published in the United States of America by
IGI Global Scientific Publishing
701 East Chocolate Avenue
Hershey, PA, 17033, USA
Tel: 717-533-8845
Fax: 717-533-7115
Website: https://www.igi-global.com E-mail: cust@igi-global.com

Library of Congress Cataloging-in-Publication Data

Names: Mamodiya, Udit, 1990- editor | Kalam, Akhtar editor | Hu, Yu-Chen, PhD editor | Goyal, Dinesh editor
Title: Accelerating product development cycles with digital twins and IoT integration / edited by: Udit Mamodiya, Akhtar Kalam, Yu-Chen Hu, Dinesh Goyal.
Description: Hershey PA : IGI Global Scientific Publishing, [2025] | Includes bibliographical references. | Summary: "The objective of the book is to provide a comprehensive guide on how organizations can leverage the synergistic potential of digital twins and Internet of Things (IoT) technologies to revolutionize their product development processes. By exploring the intersection of these cutting-edge technologies, the book aims to demonstrate how businesses can achieve faster time-to-market, reduce development costs, and improve product quality and innovation"-- Provided by publisher.
Identifiers: LCCN 2025002858 (print) | LCCN 2025002859 (ebook) | ISBN 9798337320281 hardcover | ISBN 9798337320298 paperback | ISBN 9798337320304 ebook
Subjects: LCSH: New products--Data processing | Digital twins (Computer simulation) | Internet of things
Classification: LCC HF5415.153 .A28 2025 (print) | LCC HF5415.153 (ebook) | DDC 658.5/750285--dc23/eng/20250516
LC record available at https://lccn.loc.gov/2025002858
LC ebook record available at https://lccn.loc.gov/2025002859

British Cataloguing in Publication Data
A Cataloguing in Publication record for this book is available from the British Library.

Table of Contents

Detailed Table of Contents

Industrial and operational paradigms are being transformed by disruptive technologies in the era of Industry 4.0 and Internet of Things (IoT). Virtual representations of physical systems, operable via real-time monitoring, simulation and control with digital twins (initially proposed as just another conceptual framework in 2002) are another family. In this paper we investigate the maturing of digital twins from its origins to architecture and applications: imporant accelerators for predictive maintenance, operational efficiency/optimisation & strategic decision making. While the digital twin presents significant opportunities for sectors ranging from healthcare and manufacturing to urban planning, there are still significant challenges surrounding data integration, security, scalability and standard in this emerging space. We need to solve these issues — using AI/ML, edge and other technologies in order enable value propositions of digital twins. Finally, the paper finishes by looking to the future digital twins in IoT/ big data era as future building blocks of innovation.

Sustainability is drastically changing in the context of digital twins and the Internet of Things (IoT) because of the capacity to do operational optimization, predictive modeling, and real-time monitoring. This chapter looks at how digital twins generate virtual representations of physical assets where its IoT sensor data is integrated to improve energy efficiency and to reduce waste. Digital twins allow organizations to run through operations via simulation and to use the data underpinning the exercise to make data-driven decisions which minimise environmental impact and help support sustainability goals. By combining its technology with IoT, they make smarter energy management, predictive maintenance, and efficient production in a circular economy, and ultimately costs. These case studies and best practice are accompanied by research and an attempt to address challenges such as the incompatibility of data, and cost of adopting them. Results show how digital twins support the achievement of the United Nations Sustainable Development Goals (SDGs) and sustain industrial practices.

Digital twin compute equations and advanced data analytics play an important role in enhancing complex engineering processes. This paper emphasizes the impact of digital twin on computational engineering in every field with a significant role in sustainable development. This predictive capability not only enhances the efficiency of engineering design but also contributes to minimizing the environmental footprint of projects. The interaction between digital twin and computational engineering is for smart infrastructure and strong systems. This paper examines digital twin models of monitoring and control systems that enhance the adaptability and responsiveness of infrastructure, ensuring sustainable operation and maintenance. The digital twin has been successfully applied in computational engineering to design and optimize structures, systems, and processes with sustainability in mind. Researchers explore the potential for interdisciplinary collaboration between digital twin researchers, engineers, and sustainability experts to address global challenges with innovative solutions.

Medical education has shift with the immersive technologies like VR and AR that provide realistic and interactive learning. Although current VR/AR simulators have improved surgical training, anatomy visualization, and clinical decision-making, they do not provide real-time adaptive learning and multi-sensory feedback. A novel AI-enhanced VR/AR medical simulator combining real-time performance analysis, haptic feedback, and cloud collaboration to provide a learning environment for interactive and adaptive learning for medical students. It also provides haptic feedback integration with realistic surgical precision and procedure training. A prototype system of this type is implemented with emphasis on surgical simulation and emergency response training. Experimental evaluation of the system tests learning efficiency, error rate reduction, cognitive engagement, and haptic response accuracy against traditional learning techniques. Early findings show that there is considerable gain in skill retention and efficiency of training by employing the AI-based VR/AR simulator methods.

The intersection of Quantum Computing (QC) and the Internet of Things (IoT) represents a paradigm shift in meeting the challenges of classical computing for large-scale, data-intensive IoT environments. IoT produces massive streams of data in real-time across several arenas, including healthcare, smart cities and industrial automation. The data produced is confronted with significant data processing, security, and resource utilization challenges. The principles of QC such as superposition and entanglement, provides incomparable computational capabilities, consenting to real-time processing of high-dimensional IoT data, quantum-secure cryptography, and sophisticated optimization methods. While the potential of QC is path-breaking, integration with IoT involves enormous challenges, including scalability, energy efficiency, hybrid architecture, and cost. This paper explains the collaborative prospects of QC-IoT integration, pointing to major challenges and research directions to exploit its capabilities towards greater efficiency, security, and sustainability.

Background Information: Data-driven supply chains and real-time simulations involving digital twins are transforming the sector. Nevertheless, existing optimisation techniques usually do not pay much heed to sustainability or resilience. Through enhancing digital twin systems using leading-edge methods in this work, the gap has been filled. Objectives: The main aim of the study is optimizing the efficiency of supply chain systems with the application of GA, ABM, MDP, and SA to enhance operational efficiency, cost savings, and carbon emissions while improving sustainability and resilience. Methods: The strategy includes agent-based modeling, stochastic analysis, Markov decision processes, and genetic algorithm optimization. Results: The integrated approach 86.5% resilience, 18.7% cost reduction, and 93.2% efficiency were attained. Conclusion: The study, thus concludes by how well GA, MDP, ABM, and SA work together in balancing efficiency, resilience, and sustainability.

Industrial sector, by boosting energy efficiency and reducing waste through the use of digital twin (DT) technology in the integration of industrial IoT (IIoT). DT generates realistic simulations for predictive analytics and decision-making with the help of real-time simulations of physical objects. In this chapter, the authors focus on the DT application for the optimum utilization of energy and the resource efficiency by utilizing the IoT sensors, the AI, and big data analytics. Industries can find inefficiencies, use predictive maintenance and environmental practices by simulating operational scenarios. The chapter also outlines important challenges including that of data integration, cybersecurity, and cost and provides some recommendations which may be used to successfully implement such technology. An exploration into future trends such as: 5G; Edge; Ai-driven models: Drawing on this work, the role of DT in creating sharper, greener and more resilient industrial ecosystems rightfully stand in the limelight.

The integration of Human-Centered Digital Twins (HCDTs) and the Internet of Things (IoT) is revolutionizing industries by allowing personalized, real-time decision-making through the use of continuous data streams. These systems utilize IoT sensors and AI-driven models to produce digital copies of individuals, environments, or systems, providing improved predictive capabilities in healthcare, smart cities, and industrial applications. The increasing use of HCDTs sparks significant ethical issues, such as data privacy, confidentiality, discriminatory practices, and consent based on complete information. A significant gap persists in research, particularly in the establishment of uniform ethical frameworks and the implementation of dependable AI systems that safeguard user autonomy while optimising the advantages of digital twins. The purpose of this investigation is to investigate the ethical consequences of personalization in HCDTs and suggest a framework for reconciling data-driven personalization with user privacy and cybersecurity in IoT environments.

This DT integration with IoT technologies has greatly evolved the ways by which the operation of various industries can be simulated, monitored, and optimized. As of now, the major obstacles to these network technologies in real-world deployment involve latency in networking, limited bandwidth, and incompatible devices. It is on these fronts that the eventual 6G networks could fill the gap and potentially revolutionize digital twin and IoT coordination by having a seamless virtual connection between the two physical systems under simulation. The chapter presents a new 6G-powered framework that will solve the real-time synchronization, dynamic adaptability, and predictive accuracy problems of Digital Twin ecosystems. Based on the 6G features, the proposed framework allows for real-time data transmission, multi-twin collaboration, and edge-AI processing to optimize resources.

Human-Centered Digital Twins (HCDTs), which has a capability to transform a number of industries systematically. In this way, they offer a more comprehensive picture of the subjects since more and diverse information is available, which means more targeted, better-prevented, and generally better managed. This chapter provides an overview of the concepts of HCDTs and the use of HCDTs in several important domains including medical and health, smart city, and work organizations. HCDTs apply to healthcare, providing individualized treatment, constant tracking, and monitoring of chronic diseases as well as the prediction of future health states. The chapter offers several best-practice examples of HCDTs along with samples of issues that were faced and solutions that were developed. The chapter summarizes the main findings and highlights the potential expansion of HCDTs in the following areas: the development of an appropriate regulatory framework; appropriate ethical norms and guidelines; and possibly relevant industrial norms.

Digital twins and IoT integration are transforming product development by bringing real time analytics, predictive modeling and virtual prototyping in real time. Nevertheless, the successful realization of these

Background Information: Environmental and energy challenges drive the adoption of Digital Twins, AI, IoT, and Blockchain for enterprises to work in real time with sustainable and optimized operations. Objectives: This paper will aim to review the integration of technologies that aim at improving the manufacturing process, predictive maintenance, and energy optimization while focusing on efficiency, scalability, and sustainability. Methods: A methodology of assessing Digital Twins, Blockchain, and technological integration using actual industrial applications and system comparisons to evaluate performance measures. Results: The middle configurations realized benefits of 72–81% while the totally integrated systems scored over 95%, proving them to have the better ability at minimizing downtime, increasing resource usage efficiency, and scaling. Conclusion: A highly integrated solution between Digital Twins, AI, Blockchain, IoT, and Big Data gives much greater operational and sustainability benefits for the industries.

This chapter discusses the applications of Digital Twin (DT) technology for dental care, to develop precision and patient-specific solutions for advancing dental care. Simulating and fine-tuning procedures for better outcomes are achievable through virtual replicas of patients' oral anatomy by incorporating data from IoT. Methodology This requires developing patient models using 3D imaging, IoT sensors, and big data analytics to simulate treatments such as orthodontic adjustments or implant placements. Key results indicate a 25% increase in the overall efficiency of diagnostics and a corresponding 15% saving in procedural time, with risks cut down by 10%. Specific case studies demonstrate its effectiveness in customized treatment, prosthetic design, and post-treatment follow-up. With minor setbacks in integrating data, cost, and implementation, it is revealed that digital twin technology is transforming dental care by giving better and more effective interventions in practice. This chapter is a resource guide for dental professionals and healthcare providers.

Himabindu Chetlapalli, 9455868 Canada Inc., Ontario, Canada
Sharadha Kodadi, Infosys, USA
Durga Praveen Devi, O2 Technologies Inc, Irvine, USA
Naga Sushma Allur, Astute Solutions LLC, Folsom, USA
Koteswararao Dondapati, Everest Technologies, Columbus, USA
Thinagaran Perumal, Department of Computer Science, Universiti Putra Malaysia, Malaysia

Background information: From digital twins, SDOH measures, agent-based simulations to community health dashboards, AI is changing the healthcare sector. These are making sure systems serve the needs of people as well as populations through addressing health inequities, optimizing the use of resources, and making improvements in patient-centered therapy. Methods: The methods include mathematical models and simulations with real-time sensor, wearable, and EHR data. In agent-based simulation, resource management is customized. Digital twins increase the accuracy of forecasting. Objectives: It aims to offer fair treatment, scalable, proactive, and predictive AI that includes digital twins, SDOH, and simulation. Results: The framework reached 97% prediction accuracy, reduced inequities by 90%, raised patient satisfaction by 25%, and enhanced resource efficiency by 30%. Conclusion: AI-driven systems that integrate digital twins and SDOH are transforming the healthcare industry through scalable, patient-centered care with enhanced operational and predictive capabilities.

Yash Kumar Katara, Poornima Institute of Engineering and technology, Jaipur, India
Shruti Thapar, Poornima institute of Engineering and Technology, Jaipur, India
Ashima Tiwari, Poornima Institute of Engineering and Technology, Jaipur
Ravinder Singh Maan, Global Institute of Technology, Jaipur, India
Jitender Jain, Cognizant Technology Solutions, USA

The boundary point between the digital twin (DT) and Internet of Things (IoT) realms is really creating a difference in the world by utilizing real-time awareness, prediction analysis to support enhanced decision-making as well. However, this integration raises several critical questions related to cybersecurity, robustness, privacy, and trustworthiness of its system. This chapter presents major use cases and cybersecurity challenges of Digital Twin and IoT environments. It stresses the necessity for sound mechanisms that guarantee secure communication, access, and data integrity within these interconnected systems. Accordingly, the associated applications discussed are data encryption supporting a secure download, anomaly detection mechanisms in real-time to deter breaches, and enforcing zero-trust policies to maintain the confidentiality of functions. Major themes like extended threats cape, real-time processing requirements, resource-deprived IoT devices, and advanced-cyber-attacks are detailed and discussed.

Preface

In a world marked by relentless technological advancement and market-driven pressures, the need for smarter, faster, and more sustainable product development has become paramount. The convergence of **Digital Twin (DT)** technology and the **Internet of Things (IoT)** represents one of the most promising solutions to this challenge, enabling real-time simulation, predictive analytics, remote monitoring, and intelligent decision-making across complex product lifecycles. This book, *Accelerating Product Development Cycles with Digital Twins and IoT Integration*, delves into this transformative intersection, offering a comprehensive roadmap for leveraging these technologies to enhance innovation, efficiency, and sustainability.

THE RELEVANCE OF DIGITAL TWINS AND IOT IN THE MODERN TECHNOLOGICAL ECOSYSTEM

Digital Twins and IoT are at the core of the **Industry 4.0 and 5.0 revolutions**, which emphasize the digitization, interconnectivity, and intelligent automation of systems. Together, they offer immense potential in modeling real-world processes and assets, thereby accelerating design iterations, reducing waste, optimizing performance, and enabling continuous feedback from operational environments. The applications span across a multitude of industries, including manufacturing, healthcare, aerospace, education, urban development, and energy, making this a globally relevant and timely area of research and practice.

Intended Audience

This volume is designed for a broad, interdisciplinary audience including:

- Academic researchers and faculty members in the fields of engineering, computer science, data analytics, and emerging technologies.
- Graduate and postgraduate students exploring applied research in smart systems, IoT, and cyber-physical systems.
- Industry professionals and technology consultants working in product development, smart manufacturing, healthcare innovation, urban planning, and sustainability.
- Policymakers and innovators aiming to integrate Digital Twin and IoT capabilities into public infrastructure and strategic digital transformation initiatives.

The book bridges theoretical insights with practical case studies, offering both depth and applicability for a wide range of readers.

OVERVIEW OF CHAPTER CONTRIBUTIONS

Chapter 1 – *The Rise of Digital Twins in the Age of Industry 4.0 and IoT*

This chapter introduces the foundational concepts of Digital Twins within the context of Industry 4.0 and IoT. The authors explore the origin, evolution, and architecture of DTs, shedding light on their integration across industrial ecosystems and their potential to transform traditional manufacturing processes.

Chapter 2 – *Sustainability through Digital Twins: Optimizing Energy Usage and Reducing Waste*

Focusing on environmental and operational sustainability, this chapter examines how DTs can be leveraged to monitor energy use, reduce waste, and enhance resource efficiency in industrial settings. Several frameworks and implementation models are presented to illustrate impact.

Chapter 3 – *The Role of Digital Twins in Computational Engineering and Industry 5.0 for Sustainable Development*

This chapter positions Digital Twins as a bridge between computational engineering and Industry 5.0. The authors argue for a human-centric approach and highlight sustainable innovation through intelligent modeling.

Chapter 4 – *Virtual and Augmented Reality Simulators for Medical Education*

Integrating DTs with VR/AR technologies, this chapter explores immersive solutions for medical training and education. It demonstrates how simulation-based environments enhance procedural accuracy, safety, and learner outcomes.

Chapter 5 – *Opportunities in Quantum Computing and IoT*

The chapter investigates how quantum computing could further accelerate the capabilities of IoT-based DT systems, offering new paradigms in data processing, encryption, and real-time system responses.

Chapter 6 – *Optimizing Digital Twin Supply Chains Leveraging Genetic Algorithms and Markov Decision Processes*

This contribution explores advanced optimization techniques for supply chains using Digital Twins, focusing on the strategic integration of AI models such as Genetic Algorithms and Markov Decision Processes.

Chapter 7 – *Predictive Maintenance for Medical Equipment Using AI-Powered Digital Twins*

The authors present an AI-enhanced framework for preventive healthcare technology maintenance, improving equipment reliability and patient safety through predictive diagnostics.

Chapter 8 – *Mobilizing Urban Planning and Resource Management through Digital Twin-Driven Healthcare*

This chapter links urban planning and healthcare by introducing a DT-based approach to optimize healthcare infrastructure, resources, and emergency responsiveness in urban environments.

Chapter 9 – *Optimizing Energy Usage and Reducing Waste: Digital Twin Applications in Industrial IoT*

It presents a deep dive into how industrial IoT platforms and Digital Twins collaborate to streamline energy use and material efficiency in production environments.

Chapter 10 – *Human-Centered Digital Twins in IoT: Balancing Personalization, Privacy, and Ethics*

Addressing the critical intersection of personalization and ethics, this chapter evaluates the social implications and design principles of human-centric DT systems within IoT networks.

Chapter 11 – *Integrating Virtual and Physical Systems to Improve Simulation: 6G's Effect on Digital Twin and IoT Connectivity*

Exploring the future of connectivity, the chapter outlines how 6G technologies can expand the capabilities of DTs, driving ultra-real-time simulation and responsiveness.

Chapter 12 – *Enhancing Efficiency and Reliability in Human-Centered Digital Twins*

Focusing on system reliability, this chapter introduces robust DT architectures tailored to user needs while ensuring reliability and efficiency in system performance.

Chapter 13 – *Optimizing Product Development with Digital Twins and IoT Integration*

This chapter highlights how integrated DT-IoT models can fast-track the product development process, from ideation to market launch, with enhanced testing and refinement.

Chapter 14 – *Opportunities and Challenges in IoT for Environmental Monitoring*

The authors discuss how IoT-based DT frameworks support ecological monitoring and decision-making, emphasizing the real-time collection and analysis of environmental data.

Chapter 15 – *Leveraging Digital Twin Technology in Industrial IoT for Energy Optimization and Waste Reduction*

This case-driven chapter investigates best practices for energy optimization and waste control in industrial operations through DTs integrated with IoT analytics.

Chapter 16 – *Digital Twins, TechFusion & Blockchain in Manufacturing*

Offering a multidimensional approach, the chapter explores how blockchain technologies can provide trust, traceability, and security in DT-driven manufacturing ecosystems.

Chapter 17 – *Digital Twin Technology in Dental Care: Advancing Precision and Patient Outcomes*

The chapter showcases specific applications of Digital Twins in dentistry, contributing to precision care, diagnostics, and personalized treatment planning.

Chapter 18 – *AI-Driven Digital Twin Framework for Mental Health Stress Detection*

This innovative chapter introduces an AI-powered framework that uses multimodal DTs for early detection and personalized management of stress and mental health conditions.

Chapter 19 – *AI-Enabled Digital Twin Framework for Healthcare Task Offloading Strategies*

Expanding on healthcare applications, this chapter combines AI strategies like MADDPG, AHP, and mHealth within DT systems to offload complex tasks for efficiency.

Chapter 20 – *AI-Driven Telemedicine and mHealth Applications Integrating Digital Twin-Based Healthcare*

This chapter discusses the integration of DTs with telemedicine platforms, supporting personalized healthcare delivery, remote monitoring, and proactive treatment plans.

Chapter 21 – *Applications and Challenges: Cybersecurity in Digital Twin and IoT Environment*

Highlighting security risks and mitigation techniques, this chapter addresses the cybersecurity challenges associated with integrating DTs into IoT ecosystems.

Chapter 22 – *Ethical and Legal Implications of Digital Twin Deployment in Biomedical and Pharmaceutical Domains*

Concluding the book, this chapter engages with regulatory, ethical, and legal considerations surrounding DT applications in sensitive biomedical and pharmaceutical environments.

CONCLUSION AND CONTRIBUTION TO THE FIELD

This book captures a rich mosaic of perspectives, practical implementations, and forward-thinking frameworks that position **Digital Twin–IoT integration** as a game-changer for product development, operational efficiency, and sustainability. It offers readers a wide-ranging exploration across sectors, geographies, and technologies—demonstrating how innovation at the edge of cyber-physical systems can create real-world impact.

By bridging the gap between theory and application, this volume not only contributes significantly to academic literature but also provides a reference toolkit for practitioners navigating the rapidly evolving terrain of Industry 4.0 and beyond. It is our hope that this book will inspire ongoing research, technological collaboration, and interdisciplinary dialogue that continues to reshape the future of intelligent systems.

Udit Mamodiya, Akhtar Kalam, Yu-Chen Hu, Dinesh Goyal

Acknowledgment

The successful completion of this book, ***Accelerating Product Development Cycles with Digital Twins and IoT Integration***, would not have been possible without the collective efforts, collaboration, and support of numerous individuals and institutions.

First and foremost, we extend our deepest gratitude to the contributing authors, whose insightful research, innovative perspectives, and commitment to scholarly excellence have shaped the core of this volume. Their dedication to exploring the intersections of Digital Twin technology and IoT integration has greatly enriched the discourse on next-generation product development methodologies.

We also express our sincere appreciation to the reviewers and editorial advisors who provided thoughtful feedback, critical analysis, and valuable suggestions throughout the development of this manuscript. Their expertise and academic rigor ensured the quality, relevance, and integrity of the content presented herein.

Our heartfelt thanks go to the academic institutions, research centers, and industry partners that supported the contributors' research through access to resources, data, and collaborative environments. Their encouragement and investment in technological advancement have been instrumental to the realization of this work.

We are especially grateful to IGI Global for their continued commitment to disseminating impactful knowledge and for providing a platform to bridge the gap between academic research and practical application. Their editorial and production teams have offered unwavering support throughout the publication process.

Lastly, we would like to thank our families, colleagues, and mentors for their patience, encouragement, and inspiration. Their belief in the vision of this book has been a source of motivation from inception to completion.

To all who contributed in ways both large and small—thank you.

Udit Mamodiya, Akhtar Kalam, Yu-Chen Hu, Dinesh Goyal

Chapter 1
The Rise of Digital Twins in the Age of Industry 4.0 and IoT

Anvesha Katti
https://orcid.org/0000-0002-8098-0250
Amity University Haryana, India

Priyanka Vashishth
https://orcid.org/0000-0002-9371-7419
Amity University Haryana, India

Udit Mamodiya
https://orcid.org/0000-0002-8022-4252
Poornima University Jaipur, India

ABSTRACT

Industrial and operational paradigms are being transformed by disruptive technologies in the era of Industry 4.0 and Internet of Things (IoT). Virtual representations of physical systems, operable via real-time monitoring, simulation and control with digital twins (initially proposed as just another conceptual framework in 2002) are another family. In this paper we investigate the maturing of digital twins from its origins to architecture and applications: imporant accelerators for predictive maintenance, operational efficiency/optimisation & strategic decision making. While the digital twin presents significant opportunities for sectors ranging from healthcare and manufacturing to urban planning, there are still significant challenges surrounding data integration, security, scalability and standard in this emerging space. We need to solve these issues — using AI/ML, edge and other technologies in order enable value propositions of digital twins. Finally, the paper finishes by looking to the future digital twins in IoT/ big data era as future building blocks of innovation.

DOI: 10.4018/979-8-3373-2028-1.ch001

INTRODUCTION

Industry 4.0 and the Internet of things (IoT) opened previously held back areas by improving the data collection, processing and utilization methods that have been around for years as we currently know it.

Digital twins (the virtual representations of physical items that mirror real-world systems in real-time as rcs) are poised to become ubiquitous across operational sectors in a quest to further operational efficiency and decision speed, as the driver of this transformation.

First, digital twins were proposed by Michael Grieves in 2002 in a product lifecycle management (PLM) presentation (Grieves & Vickers, 2017). Well, digital twins were conceived in the beginning to refine product design and development (Grieves & Vickers 2007), which allowed for better insight into and testing of products during their respective lifetimes. The technology got better over years, when digital twin went from just a designer to the full-fledged data analytics in real-time and a strong operational framework.

The theory of digital twins (Grieves & Vickers 2017) argue that the notion of digital twins has matured to be a cornerstone in Industry 4.0 with the assistance of IoT sensors, machine learning algorithms and big data analytics enabling the growth of associated functionality. With the help of digital twins, we can perform long term monitoring of physical systems and thereby decision making, Operational Efficiency and predictive maintenance in aerospace, automotive and healthcare sectors (Tao et al., 2019)

The surge in IoT-connected devices and the growing infrastructure of IoT acting as a digital twin's foundational data source play a big role for adoption to become widespread in digital twinning. IoT (Internet of Things) devices—like sensors, actuators and embedded systems—are naturally generating data about physical entities in real time. The data is passed to digital twin for its real time simulation and updating of virtual model on the fly. These sensors monitor a plethora of metrics (temp, pressure, motion and location) to develop very accurate and dynamic digital twins.

As per Gartner report (2020), there will be more than 25 billions of IoT-connected devices by 2030, resulting in enormous real-time data generation(Gartner RE20S10611). The exponential growth of data provides a compelling demand for technologies like digital twins, which can ingest, process and respond to enormous quantities of information. They are perfect for solving this, as digital twins can constantly refine their simulations by updating with new data points in real-time so that the end result provides useful takeaways.

IoT sensors, machine learning and advanced analytic platforms have facilitated the powerful state of digital twins across different industries (predictive maintenance—operational optimization-strategic decision making) that deliver a considerable range of benefits and have been verified through various use cases like; manufacturing, healthcare and urban planning applications for digital twins.

Digital twins enrich the operations by enhancing both accuracy and operative speed, but fundamentally lay the groundwork for predictive analytics, enabling companies insights so they can take action on possible problems well in advance and improve their processes proactively— right.

Although the use of digital twins is increasing, implementing them across the enterprise is challenging. Dealing with data heterogeneity and thus heterogeneous IoT devices/systems integration is one main difficulty. What can be obviously difficult in terms of technology is consolidating data from many sensors and platforms in real-time (Gartner 2020 for industries utilizing multiple types of sensors and platforms)

Moreover, the requirement for data security and privacy grows as digital twins gather sensitive data from physical systems (e.g., healthcare devices or manufacturing equipment). It is very important to secure this data from cyber threats for the mass acceptance and deployment of digital twin solution.

Finally, the scalability of digital twins is not addressed due to large-scale applications like smart cities or large industrial systems. Properly managing and processing the massive data sets to ensure that live digital twins are up-to-date require strong computing resources - with edge compute and massive scale of high performance cloud services;

Digital twins are at the bleeding edge of Industry 4.0 and allow real-time data collection, analysis and optimization in several different areas. IoT and machine learning have enabled the rapid growth in that these systems provide the real-time data, if not predictive insights needed to drive system reliability and performance improvements. As digital twin technology progresses further, it will certainly aid the transformation of challenging operational problems in industries; providing great potential for improved predictive maintenance, optimization and strategic planning. The digital twins are likely to increase in significance and drive innovation as the volume of IoT devices goes up across different industries.

2. DIGITAL TWIN ARCHITECTURE: A COMPREHENSIVE OVERVIEW

A Digital Twin (DT) is a virtual replica of any physical entity or system that is updated with real-time data. Such living model is therefore essential across industries from manufacturing to healthcare due to its full monitoring, simulation and optimization. The backbone of a well-built Digital Twin architecture consists of numerous interacting elements that all contribute to smooth integrate and real-time data analytics.

In the following figure, there is detailed description of Digital twin architecture piece by piece.

1. Physical Entity

The Digital Twin architecture, at its root, is based around an actual physical object: the system that's being modeled in the real-world. This could range from a machine or a building all the way up to more elaborate systems like human beings and cities. The physical entity is the root to its digital representation, and how accurate the digital model is is dependent on data capturing form this real-world equivalent.

Sensors and IoT (Internet of Things) devices are used to continuously capture data from physical entity. Sensors measure various parameters (temperature, pressure, velocity, location etc.) that are then conveyed for processing. This seamless sensor-to-system integration makes the physical changes in physical entities (Tao et al., 2019), reflected by real-time changes in its digital twin creating-of advanced operational awareness or decision-making.

2. Digital Model

The Digital model represents the physical entity at a logical level with its properties like structural, behavioral and functional characteristics. It is created with the help of special modeling tools and pretty much a dynamic model i.e. it changes during the time because physical entity also changes over time. For example, digital twin for a machine in manufacturing will simulate the machine at different operational conditions of wear and tear or environmental perturbations.

The model draws data from physical thing and it evolves dynamically in this sense not a mere copy but a living, updated image of it and no matter what happens to the physical environment real-time data feed drives these changes.

3. Data Interface

The data interface is that all important piece that allows bidirectional communication between a physical entity and its digital replica. It enables the real-time data exchange between digital model and physical entity so that physical entity can send its data at anytime like manner so that digital twin can learn from this and also vice versa with few extra steps influenced or optimized.

IoT sensors, Application Programming Interfaces (APIs), cloud storage and devices using edge computing are how this interface is currently established. Edge computing is one superb use case to reduce latency by processing data near from the basis of, providing instant transmission and decision-making in that hundred-millisecond difference. This stability guarantees that the digital twin obeys a perfect arrangement of the physical entity and gives continuous monitoring and also real-time control.

4. Analytics Engine

The analytics engine is the heart of the Digital Twin system, responsible for processing the real-time data collected from the physical entity. It typically employs machine learning (ML), artificial intelligence (AI), and predictive algorithms to analyze and interpret data, thereby generating actionable insights and forecasts (Tao et al., 2019).

This component plays a significant role in enhancing the decision-making process by providing predictions about potential failures, operational inefficiencies, or optimizations. For instance, in manufacturing, the engine can predict when a machine is likely to fail, allowing for preventive maintenance. In healthcare, a digital twin of a patient's body could be used to predict health outcomes based on real-time.

5. Visualization and Interaction Layer

Visualization and interaction layer with dashboards, alerts based tools for further interrogation as a digital twin are available from this layer. This is a very important layer as it needs to represent the data in a way which is human-friendly & used to make our actions. Users will be able observe the health of a physical entity, view some key metrics and get alerts when the thresholds are crossed like equipment failure or system under load.

One of the most advanced tools in here is what-if or predictive and state-simulation. In many other cases, you can run scenarios to see what might happen before making a decision. In industrial space for example: It becomes simulations of what will happen if you do this upgrade or production process before actually implementing the change, thereby mitigating risk and improving the efficiency.

The Digital Twin Architecture we have developed is such that the digital and physical worlds are tightly coupled, enabling real-time insights, predictive benefits and optimized performance in the end-to-end processes. Together…physical entity and digital model as well as data interface have the analytics engine to ensure that underlying structure itself is called a Digital Twins not just simulated model for better decision-making, Risk minimization, and optimization.

Figure 1. Digital Twin Architecture

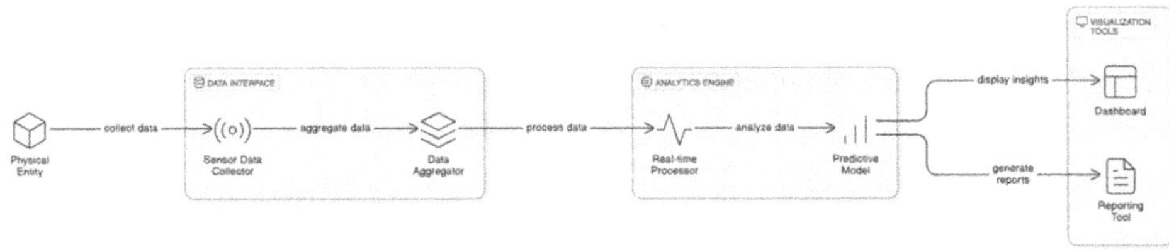

The diagram represents the flow of data between the physical entity, data interface, analytics engine, and visualization tools, showing how real-time data is converted into actionable insights

Table 1. Key Components of Digital Twin Architecture

Component	Description
Physical Entity	The real-world system being modeled.
Digital Model	Virtual replica of the physical entity.
Data Interface	Ensures real-time data flow between physical and digital systems.
Analytics Engine	Processes data and delivers insights using AI and ML techniques.
Visualization Layer	Tools for monitoring, analyzing, and interacting with the digital twin.

3. DIGITAL TWINS IN REAL- TIME DATA ANALYTICS ETC OF THE APPLICATIONS

Real time data analytics is transforming industries with the help of digital twins in innumerable applications. The off-line virtual representations of physical entities help in creating new insights for predictive capabilities, process optimization and better decision making. Usage of digital twins in real-time data analytics is especially significant in cases like predictive maintenance, operational excellence process optimization, risk management and smart manufacturing. Here is a more detailed look at these uses.

1. Predictive Maintenance

Digital twins are one of the most disruptive technology used in ….. by predictive maintenance. Analogous to predictive maintenance, digital twins monitor and track the real time state of assets to facilitate timely detection of anomalies allowing organizations to pro-actively identify impending failures. Not only does it minimize the downtime but also reduces maintenance costs — this proactive approach saves the day.

For example GE has been able to monitor jet engines through digital twins. GE collects data from sensors built into the engines, GE is able to predict when components are likely to fail and so service the plane when necessary thereby stopping unnecessary service intervals (Boschert & Rosen, 2016).

This feature is creating industries by replacing the practice of conventional maintenance (reactive and preventative) and bringing in more effective strategies for predictive maintenance.

Figure 2. Impact of Predictive Maintenance Using Digital Twins

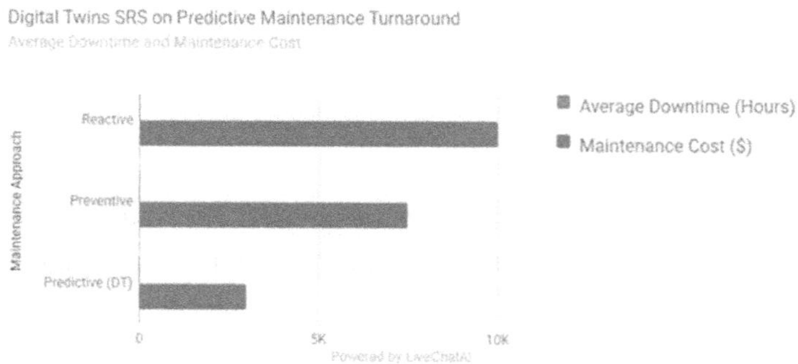

Table 2. Impact of Predictive Maintenance Using Digital Twins

Maintenance Approach	Average Downtime (Hours)	Maintenance Cost ($)
Reactive	15	10,000
Preventive	8	7,500
Predictive (DT)	2	3,000

Comparative analysis points out the dramatic decrease in downtime and cost of predictive maintenance with digital twins. Using real-time data analytics, predictive maintenance can bring down the downtime by as much as 87% and maintenance costs by more 70%.

2. Operational Optimization

Digital twins also take an important part in operational optimization, this allows us to create processes simulations and analyse processes in the real-time. They use these to help businesses notice inefficiencies, to amp up efficiencies in their workflows and generally give an overall enhancement.

> Digital twin is a revolution for the most manufacturing benefit that can harmonize production processes efficiently and decrease cycle times in manufacturing. Siemens is one of the companies that have successfully applied digital twin technology to their operations. production cycle time (Kritzinger et al., 2018) 25% lower by digital twinning Siemens is able to continuously monitor and reproduce the production process using their digital twin technology hence result in better running of the process more efficiently for the business.

Real-time feedback loops drive agility through digital twins that make operational adjustments immediately, improving response time and more agile forms of oper3. Risk Management

Digital Twins in a Big Way: Risk Management Another huge area that digital twins are growing in is through risk management. Organizations are able through digital twins to test what-if scenarios and explore risks allowing ones companies to measure the impact of different operational strategies with out-of-the-box decisions before making actualizations.

One such instance is in urban planning, where cities leverage digital twins for simulating traffic, physical space etc. Jones et al. (2020) state that these simulations are used by cities to identify congestionand optimize traffic signal control and improvement of infrastructure. Such an approach helps risk-based identification of traffic, pollution and energy that reduces urban vulnerability and accelerates the development of cities.

Digital twins in health care use machine learning and simulations to predict what would happen to patients with differnt treatments, thereby lowering medical error as well as improving clinical decision making

3. Smart Manufacturing

Digital twins in smart manufacturing algorithms for real-time analysis of machine performance, consumption of resources and consequently overall production competence.

They feed manufacturers with data to tweak the assemblage and make a sidewise manufacturing process not only optimized, but also reduce waste.

There are hundreds of examples: BMW uses digital twin technology on it's production lines and can measure the actual assembly processes live. This integration is responsible for cutting production by 25% and amount to significant waste reduction (Kritzinger et al., 2018). BMW has attempted to create digital twins of the entire manufacturing process for tracking and controlling machine performance and material flows in production, planning scheduling, waste reduction.

Table 3. Comparative Analysis Table

Application	Benefits	Case Study Example
Predictive Maintenance	Reduces downtime, lowers costs	GE jet engines monitoring
Operational Optimization	Enhances workflow efficiency	Siemens manufacturing
Risk Management	Improves decision-making under uncertainty	Urban planning with city simulations
Smart Manufacturing	Optimizes resource utilization	Digital twins in automotive production

4. CHALLENGES AND FUTURE DIRECTIONS IN DIGITAL TWIN TECHNOLOGY

Digital twins have great potential to transform, but they face a few challenges before they can be adopted in the real world in depth by all industries. To realize the potential of digital twins — as they go beyond simple implementations in simpler systems — the challenges need to be solved. A detailed examination of the main problems and potential ways to solve all those hurdles follows below.

1. Data Integration

Data integration- one of the most complex challenges to implement digital twins is. Digital twins are built on data from all sorts of places (including legacy systems, IoT devices & cloud platforms). These data sources have a variety of formats and standards as well there are different format across sources(Kritzinger et al.,2018)

For example, bringing together data from legacy machinery with new sensors and cloud platforms on sites in manufacturing can be quite hard. After all, legacy systems were not developed to have standard of interoperability with modern technology and we eventually ended up with disconnected data, which is hard to aggregate for real-time analytics.

The development of consolidated data standards and interoperability in data will help resolve this challenge to a great extent as the future progresses with advanced data interoperability. In order to facilitate more efficient digital twin implementations, middleware solutions that enable the synchronized data movement across various systems and data integration platforms will be important (Tao et al., 2019).

2. Scalability

And as digital twins grow and evolve, scalability becomes an important headache, particularly under big and complicated system circumstances. A digital twin of an extensive metropolitan area or multiple city facsilites is a data challenge as you have order-of-magnitude real-time data for all these disparate sources when creating it. So cities produce immense amounts of data from traffic systems, power grids and public services that need to be consumed by a digital twin for analysis.

This level of data management is significant and utilizes substantial computational power to be performed in real-time. A lack of resources makes it hard to build prototype-real-time digital models that are similar to actual physical systems. For instance, HPC is necessary for simulating urban digital twins to deal with difficult events (Tao et al., 2019) such as heavy traffic in a city or environmental conditions.

Future developments of mixed fine-grained edge and-cloud computing infrastructure are hoped to resolve scalability impedance. Edge computing allows data to be processed in proximity to the place of origin for lower latency and bandwidth needs. On the other hand, stronger cloud platforms and the usage distributed computing will allow more and bigger more complex digital twins (Tao et al., 2019).

3. Security and Privacy

One of crucial challenges in digital twin applications is protecting sensitive data, especially for such precise sectors as healthcare, manufacturing or energy where your digital twins could be dealing with protected or privy information. Although they depend on long-term data acquisition from real-world entities, digital twins are at cyber security vulnerabilities as soon as they are linked to the internet of things (IoT).

Jones et al. 2020 reported that digital twins expose users to problems of various cybersecurity vulnerabilities, being 68% in organizations using digital twins. This all serves to highlight the need for strong cybersecurity to exist to protect data held in Digital Twins from cyber attacks and hacking and Information leakage. In the field of healthcare, there are significant privacy issues as data are personal and compromising such means serious legal and ethical ramifications.

Going forward, further advances will need to combine the best of advanced encryption methods, blockchain and secure data-sharing mechanisms to counter data manipulation as well protect against unauthorized access. Finally, privacy by design should be included in digital twin systems as a framework for properly protecting personal and sensitive data.

4. Standardization

One among the most common problems for the major standardization issues on wide-spread use of Digital Twins in the same industry. As of today, there's no common set of standards or protocols for the way digital twins were supposed to operate in various industries. The lack of standardization does not allow to have interoperability among digital twin solutions over platforms, industries or even geographical boundaries.

For instance, in the automotive/aerospace worlds, limited adoption has been due to the absence of standardized messaging protocols for data exchange between different models of digital twins. Digital twins can be developed with different tools, technologies and formats according to manufacturers — data synchronization and integration among models become difficult across systems (Grieves & Vickers, 2017).

Open Source Platforms and Industry Standards

In the end, the path to overcoming the standardization issues will be the creation of open-source platforms and the definition of sector-specific standards. International standards organizations like ISO and IEEE should take a significant part in the development of standardized protocols for digital twins, allowing organization to easily adopt and implement digital twin technology into different industry applications. Next research will be needed on more complex machine learning rule, standardization and further extension to emerging areas including autonomous vehicles or smart cities.

Figure 3. Key Challenges Impact

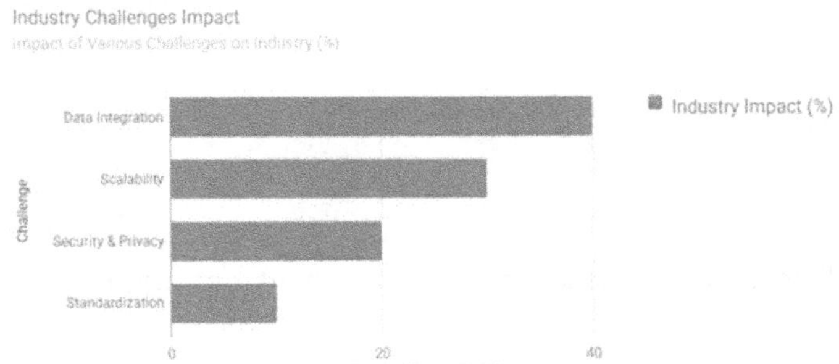

Table 3. Key Challenges Impact

Challenge	Industry Impact (%)
Data Integration	40
Scalability	30
Security & Privacy	20
Standardization	10

Digital Twin Technology will have a bright future even though it faces some roadblocks. Several areas are slated to see major improvement in the next few years. Artificial Intelligence (AI), and Machine learning (ML) are going to be very crucial to give digital twins the ability learn from data [better predictive capability] the capacity of the digital twin to self-optimize systems over time. These will evolve as the technologies develop, and systems will sort of be able to see trends faster and being able to make almost perfect predictions. Moreover, the incorporation of edge computing with real-time analytics will enable decision making at the edge of data, minimizing lag and in turn faster responses to system condition variations. This is going to provide a lot more benefit for the digital twin applications. With wider accessibility of computing power and refinement of AI algorithms, digital twins will become better and better at making simulations that can predict on the more complex, dynamic system with better fidelity. Through that, we will have better insights and support to make better decisions in operations. Finally, as digital twin advances from static to dynamic across industry sectors digital standards will require the ability to cross-industry collaborate for universal standards frameworks to ensure seamless integration of industrial digital twins. This will give concrete foundations for device digital twins as a foundational enabler in data-driven decision making and operational excellence in the industries.

Though digital twins have considerable power to drive innovation in many fields, challenges on integrating the data, scaling, security as well as standardization are what limit their adoption. And tackling these will necessitate improvements in interoperability, computing and cyber security infrastructure, as well as regulation within sectors. The future delivery of digital twins is bright considering what addition AI, Edge computing and simulation technologies will bring. As these problems get solved, digital twins will play an even larger part in the economies of a modern industry, advancing optimization and innovation with the ability to predict.

CONCLUSION

At the cutting edge of the Industry 4.0 movement, digital twins are the ultimate enablers for in-real-time analytics and predictive maintenance, as well as implementing operational optimization on a complete new level. Digital twins, in fusing state of the advanced technologies like IoT, AI and machine learning provide information that is not just passive but actionable for industries to become more productive. Though the transformative power of these is undeniable, challenges such as data silos, scaling issues and the advent — ideally on a dark cloud of course — impede on their mass adoption. Progressive: Edge computing solutions, the ability to follow flexible unified standards and data secure protocol are necessary to get past these blockers. Digital twins are eventually going to play a critical role in the mounting of data-enabled decision making as well as systemic improvement that will define industries around the globe as more and more IoT devices get connected. Albany

REFERENCES

Boschert, S., & Rosen, R. (2016). Digital Twin—The Simulation Aspect. In *Mechatronic Futures* (pp. 59-74). Springer Vieweg, Berlin, Heidelberg.

Gartner. (2020). Forecast: The Internet of Things, Worldwide, 2018-2030. Retrieved from https://www.gartner.com/en/newsroom/press-releases

Grieves, M., & Vickers, J. (2017). Digital twin: Mitigating unpredictable, undesirable emergent behavior in complex systems. In *Transdisciplinary Perspectives on Complex Systems: New Findings and Approaches* (pp. 85-113). Springer.

Jones, P., Mistry, M., & Porter, A. (2020). Smart Cities and Digital Twins: Applications in Urban Planning. *Journal of Urban Technology*, *27*(1), 1–18. DOI: 10.1080/10630732.2020.1765448

Kritzinger, W., Karner, M., & Kienberger, J. (2018). Digital Twin of an Industrial Production Process. In *Proceedings of the 2018 IEEE International Conference on Industrial Technology (ICIT)* (pp. 1701-1706). IEEE.

Tao, F., Zhang, H., & Cheng, J. (2019). Digital Twin and Its Applications in Industry 4.0. *International Journal of Advanced Manufacturing Technology*, *101*(5-8), 1373–1393. DOI: 10.1007/s00170-018-2646-4

Chapter 2
Sustainability through Digital Twins Optimizing Energy Usage and Reducing Waste

G. Boopathy
https://orcid.org/0000-0003-2515-7277
Vel Tech Rangarajan Dr.Sagunthala R&D Institute of Science and Technology, Chennai, India

V. Srinivasan
https://orcid.org/0009-0006-2988-6476
Vel Tech Rangarajan Dr.Sagunthala R&D Institute of Science and Technology, Chennai, India

V. Kamalakar
Vel Tech Rangarajan Dr.Sagunthala R&D Institute of Science and Technology, Chennai, India

G. Chandra Bose
https://orcid.org/0009-0008-2455-6907
Vel Tech Rangarajan Dr.Sagunthala R&D Institute of Science and Technology, Chennai, India

ABSTRACT

Sustainability is drastically changing in the context of digital twins and the Internet of Things (IoT) because of the capacity to do operational optimization, predictive modeling, and real-time monitoring. This chapter looks at how digital twins generate virtual representations of physical assets where its IoT sensor data is integrated to improve energy efficiency and to reduce waste. Digital twins allow organizations to run through operations via simulation and to use the data underpinning the exercise to make data-driven decisions which minimise environmental impact and help support sustainability goals. By combining its technology with IoT, they make smarter energy management, predictive maintenance, and efficient production in a circular economy, and ultimately costs. These case studies and best practice are accompanied by research and an attempt to address challenges such as the incompatibility of data, and cost of adopting them. Results show how digital twins support the achievement of the United Nations Sustainable Development Goals (SDGs) and sustain industrial practices.

DOI: 10.4018/979-8-3373-2028-1.ch002

INTRODUCTION

One of the biggest challenges the global community faces today is sustainability, whereby several industries are all impacted and call for urgent collaboration to address so many cases of what is happening regarding energy reserve, waste generation, and resource depletion. With the energy demand intensely increasing, natural resources are rushed out of contention and led to environmental degradation as well as to imbalance of the ecological balance. However, one very significant fact is that global energy consumption is going to rise approximately one third between now and 2035, so we have to come up with new energy system thinking and ways of managing consumption patterns. One, waste production has taken such a level that it has polluted the environment and has gotten to public health. These issues are further compounded by depletion of resources as the finite resources are used at unsustainably high rates which can, potentially, result in disasters across different sectors. With these tough problems to address, there is a strong and increasing demand for highly innovative technologies to engage with sustainability imperatives.

Researchers have pointed out that the digital economy development presents pathways for intervention and improvements in various fulfillment and management systems focusing on sustainability. In particular, there are various innovative technologies, like digital twins and IoT, that can make monitoring and management more efficient and thus positively impact on the development of sustainable business model in the sector. Besides increasing the operational efficiencies, these technologies are part of helping to achieve United Nations SDGs by addressing environmental, social and economic challenges in a full manner. It is essential to integrate the technology into the sustainability practices in order to have a resilient and sustainable society that can endure the pressures of climate change and the practices of unsustainable development. With adoption of these advanced technologies, the organizations are given capability to manage resources, decrease waste, and ameliorate their environmental impacts and this is a key factor for survival as the world becomes victim and victim to resource constraints.

Many of these technologies present the Digital Twins and IoT as transformative technologies that will help optimize energy usage and minimize waste in different industries. Digital twins are virtual representations of the physical entity that can do in real time monitoring and data analysis for the sake of operational efficiency (Cao, 2024). Digital twins simulate physical assets and processes for predictive maintenance and optimized resource utilization resulting in reduced energy consumption and waste (Corrado et al., 2022; Botín-Sanabria et al., 2022). On the other hand, digital twin technology is also used for instance in the construction industry to integrate Building Information Modeling (BIM) with dynamic data to develop processes that can be utilized to achieve better sustainability outcomes and at a reduced cost. Meanwhile, IoT is a network of devices with sensors that, once connected together, send huge amount of data from the physical surroundings. Such technology enables real-time monitoring and control which enable opportunities for system efficiencies and resource wastage mitigation (Yang et al., 2022).

Suppose IoT applications in smart city are an example of how IoT can help in optimizing energy consumption of public infrastructures such as making street lighting or waste management systems (Christ et al., 2023). Especially for sustainability, the synergies between digital twins and IoT are powerful. Digital twins can use IoT generated data to simulate different operational scenarios to make good decisions which help in the organization's sustainability strategies (Rojek et al., 2020; Awouda et al., 2024). This idea of integration not only increases resource management efficiency but also sets the ground for developing low carbon solutions in various sectors thereby enhancing sustainability (López et al., 2023). Together these technologies form a network ecosystem which greatly contribute to energy efficiency, waste reduction, and industrial practice sustainability.

By combining the strengths from digital twins and the IoT, integration brings about more sustainable production and consumption models. The current state of digital twins is that they act as dynamic virtual representation of the physical system using data streams from IoT deployed to facilitate real time monitoring, analysis and co-optimization (Savić et al., 2023). For instance, digital twins can run different operations scenarios to predict inefficiencies, for instance an inefficiency of a bottleneck or excessive energy use and improve manufacturing process outcomes like productivity and sustainability of the overall process (Kolekar et al., 2023). This bidirectional data exchange on physical and digital systems means that adjustments can be readily made to reduce resource consumption and waste (Coorey et al., 2022). In addition to that, these capabilities of the digital twins and IoT become a critical way to help the machinery's lifespan be extended and downtime be reduced (Mincă et al, 2022).

Digital twins can predict an equipment's potential failure before it actually happens and it's based on data collected by the sensors embedded in the equipment, which forecast maintenance timing efficiently and avoid wasteful or unnecessary practices, reducing resource use (Pyakurel et al., 2022). Therefore, this holistic approach enables industries to achieve smarter and more sustainable practices that are in line with ongoing global sustainability effort. The main benefits of this integration for the industries mainly lie in the areas of energy management and reduction of waste. In particular, it is possible to optimize energy utilization through data analysis of data collected through IoT devices in an industry, allowing industries to alter processes in real time and resulting in large savings on expenditures of energy (Sharma et al., 2024). Additionally, digital twins help to learn insights regarding the utilization of resources, an ability which enables companies to make decision and reduce significantly the waste in manufacturing and supply chain manufacturing (Khdoudi et al., 2024; Husung et al., 2023). Additionally, this optimization facilitates cost reduction as well as assuming responsibility toward corporate social responsibility by minimizing environmental implications and establishing sustainability practice.

The objective of this chapter is the convergence of digital twins and the IoT, which presents an important shift in sustainability to increase efficiency in the production and consumption framework. Digital Twins are used where they are virtual model of a physical entity, constantly feeding data from IoT sensors to provide oversight, simulation and refinement of operations. Together enterprises can now scrutinize trends in energy consumption, predict maintenance requirements and locate new reduction of waste potential. In addition, digital twins have great benefits implemented in different fields ranging from manufacturing to transportation and smart infrastructure for energy intensive sectors. On this basis, the innovations promote real-time oversight to identify inefficiencies, shorten downtime and facilitate resource sustainability. Digital twins help in distribution of electricity in smart grids and reduce power losses to strengthen grid dependability. They enable forecasting maintenance that extends the design life of equipment and reduces excessive material waste, in industrial environments.

FUNDAMENTALS OF DIGITAL TWINS AND IOT

Digital twins and IoT integration as a whole presents a very powerful strategy for raising energy management and waste reduction capabilities within industries much wider than just the one that is thought of right now.

Digital Twins

Digital twins are the virtual reproduction of product, process, and systems. The meaning of this concept is to foster a fusion between the real and digital world that allows for more minute observation and analysis that may result in higher operational performance and efficiency. Real time data collection and processing through digital twin technology aids in the process of decision making and optimization of operational processes in various industries in the quest for sustainability. Key characteristics of digital twins include:

Real-time Data Integration
The principal distinctive characteristic of digital twins is their capacity to join real time information from IoT devices and sensors. Simulations and analytics (Vallée, 2023) are made more accurate through this feature as it makes digital twins reflect current conditions. An illustration comes from manufacturing where real time data can suggest improvement in production processes as the resource will be used in the optimal way as well as minimizing waste (Cruz-Manzo et al., 2024).
Predictive Modeling
Predictive modeling techniques are used in digital twins to analyze historical and present data to predict future scenarios and outcomes. This capability is of high importance for maintenance and operational optimization purposes since it allows organizations to take decisions upon possible breakdowns before they occur (Hengelbrock et al., 2022). Prediction models can lead to a more sustainable practice in the lifecycle management of assets.
System Simulations
This is also a facility to do system simulations to test different operational scenarios for digital twins without risk to live systems. This characteristic acts as a way validating system behavior in different conditions and adjustment system behaviour according to the simulated outcomes. For example, simulations can be used to plan for patient flows based on information from digital twins in order to improve service delivery and efficiency (Sun et al., 2023).

IoT in Sustainability

A network of interconnected sensors, devices, and system creating real time data is called Internet of Things (IoT). As a result, this vast network allows for various applications within the different areas of communication with this vast amount of information collected and analyzed from the physical background (Mukhacheva et al., 2022). Sensors for measuring temperature and humidity can be simple, as in IoT devices, and include the complex systems that can control the whole urban environment (Lou et al., 2024). The power of IoT facilitates the implementation of sustainability initiatives and operational efficiencies, as well as facilitates the optimization of resource utilization to achieve success in industries (Alghuried et al., 2024). IoT significantly supports the functionality of digital twins through several key mechanisms:

- ***Data Collection:*** The physical systems are also continuously experienced and gathered by real time data flowing through IoT devices, which in turn constitute the necessary inputs required for generating accurate virtual replicas of the physical systems. For instance, in smart energy systems, various sensors sample real time electrical parameters such as voltage and current, which can be used for the real time representation and management of the energy flows (Chalal et al., 2023).

- ***Monitoring:*** Digital twins represent the current operational conditions and performance metrics through continuous monitoring by IoT devices. Through this, the companies were able to get access to analyse the system status in real time that enhances the handling of the issues or changes in the operational environment. An organization can manage resource usage by monitoring parameters such as energy consumption or equipment health.
- ***Automation:*** The automation of processes which involve digital twins is supported by IoT by allowing for the changes made according to the data obtained from IoT systems. Running digital twins also allows organizations to become more efficient by automating activities for predictive maintenance, where data sensors are reviewed by digital twins to determine when maintenance is needed, and the decision can be made to either finish the maintenance or delay it to save time and extend the lifespan of a physical asset (Chao, 2023).

Synergy Between Digital Twins and IoT

The integration of digital twins with the IoT is a strong enabler to operational efficiency and sustainability in different industries. IoT makes real time data collection efficient, while digital twins use this data to the create simulations and the analyses which aid in making decisions and optimizing processes.

Real-time Data Collection via IoT

IoT acts as a first step to taking the data available, enabling it to be collected in near real time as a result of a network of interconnecting sensors and devices monitoring physical spaces. Data in these devices includes temperature, humidity, equipment performance and energy consumption. For example, in a smart factory IoT sensors capture the real time operational status that can be used by the machines, energy usage, things that require to be maintained. It pumps constant data that enabled organizations to keep a broad picture of operations that is necessary for the analysis that further ensures with digital twins.

Data Processing and Simulation by Digital Twins

After getting the information from IoT devices, it is sent to the digital double platform and processed to simulate and analyze. Digital twins are themselves a virtual representation of physical assets or process, where all the real time data is used to reflect the current state of its physical counterpart. Once the data for a digital twin across all nomenclature is integrated and analyzed, they can conduct predictive modelling — predicting future results based on different scenarios of operational realities and reveal inefficiencies and areas that need improvement. For instance, digital twins are used for predictive maintenance that leverages sensor data to allow organizations to predict when equipment will fail, and schedule maintenance, well before costly downtimes happen (su, 2024). There is a great opportunity to optimize energy usage and eliminate waste, among other things, by combining digital twins and IoT technologies in different industries.

- ***Smart Energy Management:*** Two major components of digital twins discuss the dynamic management of energy consumption in energy systems with IoT sensors. Digital twins can eliminate heating, ventilation, and air conditioning (HVAC) system energy consumption in real time by analyzing data on occupancy and environmental conditions in buildings (Barbosa et al., 2023). A digitized energy distribution grid, such as a smart grid, based on IoT data that predicts demand using analogies to real-life energy distribution within digital twins results in better and improved overall grid efficiency (Mansour et al., 2023).

- ***Manufacturing Optimization:*** The combination of digital twins and IoT means that the processes of production are greatly understood in manufacturing. Digital twins can optimize the production line by tracking machine performance and resource usage in real time and can help maximize throughput while minimizing material waste. However, reports from companies that have implemented such technology include insights that they have witnessed more efficient allocation of resources and reduction in waste during production processes (Mazumder et al., 2023).
- ***Waste Management Improvement:*** Application of digital twins in waste management system to monitor the waste collection efficiency. When they are, IoT sensors in waste bins signal the collection trucks when to come and when how much to bring. City managers can use digital twins if this data is applied to analyze it, minimizing unnecessary trips and saving fuel and reducing emissions. Also, the waste type and quantity can be analyzed and inform better recycling practices and resource recovery strategies (Mudiyanselage & Sellahewa, 2023).

Benefits for Energy and Waste Optimization

Digital twins and the IoT integration plays an important role in supporting the sustainability goal through increasing energy efficiency, decrease of waste, and optimization of resource utilization within different industries. These technologies make organizational change in the realm of operation management possible and it opens up the way for an organization to develop practice that is sustainable and in accord with its environmental objectives.

Reducing Waste

Digital twins are virtual representation of physical processes perfect for excessive monitoring and analysis regard resources utilization. Digital twins can simulate production processes, as well as the data of IoT devices, in the manufacturing sector to identify inefficiencies and thus material waste. This capability provides the companies with the ability to make informed changes to their operational practices which would in turn lead to reducing the waste in these production lines. For example, in a case scenario, digital twins are used to enhance resource allocation in factories leading to reduction of excess inventory and hence reducing overall waste (Zaidi et al., 2024). Additionally, IoT and digital twins integrate well in waste management to effectively coordinate collection and recycling process. Real time data of fill based on waste bin sensors sent to IoT sensors which then enables to optimize waste collected route. The integration leads to lower number of waste collection trips required, which results in a decrease in overall carbon footprint and the operational cost of waste management (Amangeldy et al., 2023).

Improving Energy Efficiency

By integrating IoT with digital twins, fundamental changes occur to make the energy management systems more effective. Energy patterns of several facilities and processes can be analyzed by digital twins to enhance the efficiency (Bassey et al., 2024). They help make decisions enabling energy efficiency such as optimizing HVAC systems in smart buildings based on occupancy data obtained from IoT devices. Digital twins are used to optimize maintenance schedules in the renewable energy sectors so that maximum efficiency can be achieved by improving the prediction of energy production in the solar panels and wind turbines. Using digital twins to deliver accurate forecasts and scenario analysis significantly reduces the exposure to operational risk while maximizing the energy yield; thus, digital twin can increase profitability and return on investment from renewable energy projects.

Optimizing Resources

Digital twins allow organizations to optimize their resource use to a significant degree. Thanks to IoT, organizations can quickly collect data and with that, make data driven decisions that help operationalize to achieve greater operational efficiency. Digital twins can be used to monitor the operations of equipment under energy-intensive industries and forecast maintenance needs to lengthen asset lifecycles and savings of energy expenditures needlessly spent on maintenance. In supply chain management, IoT devices with digital twins help in optimization of logistics and inventory management so that resources get maximized and they are leveraged for maximum cost and benefit (Yu et al., 2023). This capability enables businesses to respond dynamically to changes in demand and operational conditions, and thereby enhances the businesses' overall resilience and effort for sustainability.

DIGITAL TWIN FRAMEWORK FOR SUSTAINABILITY

The digital twin framework that includes the real time data collection through IoT, AI based predictive analytics with on the fly processing capability at the cloud scale, provides the capability of continuous enhancement in operational performance with reduced waste and better energy usage.

Essential Components of a Digital Twin System

Several critical components of a digital twin system include real-time monitoring, predictive analytics, efficient data processing and all these ultimately lead to improved sustainability outcomes. Below, are the details of the components;

Real-time Sensor Networks

For data collection within a digital twin architecture, real time sensor networks are extremely important. IoT devices placed in an operational context to monitor different parameters as it is the case of energy consumption, environmental impact or waste generation (Loaiza & Cloutier, 2022). For instance, in a smart manufacturing scenario, during production processes through taking into account the sensors, they can be used to track how much energy a machine uses in the real time, to measure emissions, to determine how much waste is produced (Manickam et al., 2023). From this, organizations can gather a complete idea of how they are functioning on the environment and can take measures to reduce the impact (Miller & Spatz, 2022).

AI-powered Simulations and Predictive Analytics

With digital twins connected to AI capabilities they are used to drastically perform real time complex simulation and predictive analytics on the data gathered from IoT sensors. AI algorithms are able to analyse historical and real-time data and simulate possible operational scenarios, compare various strategies of resource consumption and predict future energy demand (Tan & Cheng, 2024). It is important to have this capability of prediction for process optimization, such as predicting the energy demand and changing the supply accordingly or predicting maintenance maintenance in an effort to minimize downtime and waste. Such insights will help organizations to improve operational efficiency as they can adopt energy saving strategies found from data analysis (Vilar-Dias et al., 2023).

Cloud-based Data Processing

Digital twin systems are dependent on cloud infrastructure for its effectiveness by allowing scaling and storage of vast amounts of data for real time analysis, (Khalaj et al., 2023). IoT generates huge amounts of data that typical local processing cannot handle and storing the data overcomes limitations of the local processing. This can be utilized for making comprehensive analyses and decisions concerning multiple operations that can be used in decision making. This is important for business sustainability since in this aspect it satisfies the requirement for rapid data processing required to optimize utilization of energy and reduce waste, providing insufficiency of environment subject in the strategies to management (Pysin & Лобанов, 2023). In addition, cloud also supports many different applications, which are required for improving system performance from data visualization to highly advanced machine learning applications (Bandaru et al., 2024).

Data Flow and Interaction Between Physical and Virtual Systems

Real time data collection in the real physical systems and a continuous feedback loop between the physical systems and digital twins are underpinned the interaction between physical systems and digital twin. This architecture, among other things, improves the accuracy, relevance, as well as dynamic optimization of physical processes, resulting in responses to changing operational conditions to support a range of sustainability goals. The architecture of the digital twin is shown in figure 1.

Figure 1. Digital Twin Architecture (Image by Botín-Sanabria et al., (2022) from "Digital twin technology challenges and applications: a comprehensive review (https://www.mdpi.com/2072-4292/14/6/1335)" licensed by CC-BY 4.0)

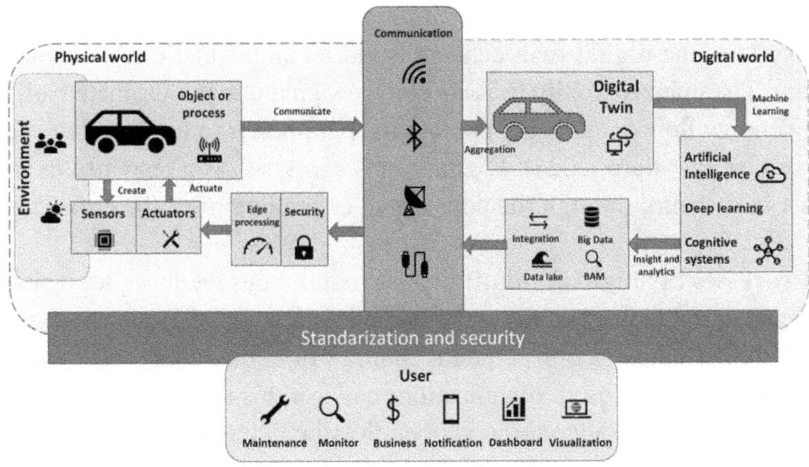

Real-time Data from Physical Assets is Fed into the Digital Twin - Explanation

A robust network of real time data collection facilitates interaction between a physical assets (machinery, equipment, systems) and their corresponding physical twins. Initially, such a process starts by equipping real-time sensors in strategic places at physical entities to continuously monitor operational parameters as energy consumption, environmental impact and system performance, making use of IoT technology. This includes pressure, temperature, and a variety of other operational status and transmitting the sensor data to the digital twin in a seamless fashion. To name an example, a digital twin of an industrial machine receives operational data via different embedded sensor measuring performance metric and environmental factor in real time (Rajan and Li, 2024). These sensors produce results which are processed and sent to the digital twin and produce a virtual representation of the physical asset's present state. This allows digital twins to stay accurately aligned with their physical counterpart and be responsive for whatever may happen in the physical world to be reflected in the virtual model (Poletti et al., 2022).

Creating a Continuous Feedback Loop Between the Digital Model and the Physical System

Digital twin systems have a critical characteristic that involves building a continuous feedback loop between the digital model and the physical system. Thus, in exercise, this bi-directional interaction enables real-time adjustments to the insights derived from the digital twin (Drummond & Gonsard, 2024). The feedback mechanism involves several key processes:

- **Real-time Monitoring:** Real time monitoring occurs as data is fed continuously from physical assets to their digital twins, to detect such discrepancy or anomaly before it (Fu et al., 2022). For example, if the sensors sense an unusual amount of energy consumption, the digital twin can utilize this information to find out what could cause this and recommend corrective actions taken.
- **Dynamic Adjustments:** In addition to updating its virtual model based on receiving data in from the physical system, the digital twin can also send recommendations or commands back to the feeding system. The inferred ability to issue control signal allows automated adjustments in terms of controlling energy flow or changing operational parameters to improve the operational efficiency (Segovia & García-Alfaro, 2022). Digital twins can serve as a response in smart energy grids to the forecast in demand, through the adjustment of the output of the connected energy sources (Li et al., 2023).
- **Optimized Processes through Simulation:** Also, continuous feedback loop also supports predictive analytics and simulations. Based on the incoming data, the digital twin can evaluate different scenarios and predict outcomes of potential changes in operational strategies (Wu et al., 2024). If its predictive capability is used, organizations can use this to proactively optimize processes to achieve better sustainability outcomes and operational efficiency.

Designing a Sustainable Digital Twin Architecture

Several essential technical considerations are essential when creating a digital twin system optimized for sustainability. What these elements guarantee is that the digital and physical worlds interact accurately, efficiently process information, and remain cohesive. Below are some of key components to a sustainable digital twin architecture.

Technical Considerations for Creating a Digital Twin Tailored to Sustainability

The primary technological factors for creating a digital twin that is sustainable are compiled in table 1. This emphasizes the need for real time sensor networks to monitor the use of energy and the environmental impact resulting from it in order to make immediate adjustments to reduce the waste. They designed it modular and scalable so that it will be flexible for organizations to grow and evolve to meet other sustainability goals and technologies over time. Finally, the advanced data analytics utilizing Artificial Intelligence (AI) and Machine Learning (ML) tools enable predicting the future needs of resources and optimizing the operations to save resources and minimize the emissions.

Table 1. Technical Considerations for Creating a Digital Twin Tailored to Sustainability

Technical Consideration	Description	Example/Details
Integration with Sensor Networks	Incorporate real-time sensors to monitor energy consumption, environmental impact, and operational efficiency.	Embedding IoT sensors in manufacturing equipment provides real-time insights into energy use, enabling immediate adjustments to reduce waste.
Modular and Scalable Design	Use a modular architecture to allow for easy scalability and adaptation to changing sustainability needs.	Flexibility enables expansion of digital twin capabilities over time without major restructuring.
Advanced Data Analytics	Implement AI-powered simulations and machine learning algorithms to analyze historical and real-time data.	Predict future resource needs, evaluate operational scenarios, and make proactive adjustments to conserve resources and reduce emissions.

Ensuring Data Accuracy and Operational Efficiency in Real-time Systems

- **Data Quality Assurance:** Organizations must create rigorous protocols of how the data fed to your digital twin, needs to be validated and some form of quality control establish. It includes standard outputs of sensor and mechanism calibration and verification of data integrity (Li et al., 2023). For instance, techniques like anomaly detection can also identify and remediate erroneous data input so as to avoid skewing results (Liu et al., 2023).
- **Real-time Processing and Analysis:** Cloud based infrastructure is key to use to run processing massive amounts of data in real time to maintain operational efficiency. With the data from multiple sources, Cloud systems can provide real time analytics and provide feedback mechanisms which inform adjustment of the physical system based on view of the data from the digital model.
- **Continuous Feedback Loops:** The use of real time data means that real time feedback is fed back from physical systems to their digital twins to conduct continuous optimization (Ngadi et al., 2024). Here, this functionality enables the immediate change in operations with respect to live data and a decrease in waste and an increase in efficiency.

INDUSTRIAL APPLICATIONS OF DIGITAL TWINS FOR SUSTAINABILITY

Digital twin technology is essential in multiple industrial practice in order to optimize the practices on sustainability. These applications integrate the real time data, AI driven analytics and cloud computing to enable organizations' through integrating real time data, AI driven analytics and cloud computing to optimize their process, eliminate waste and increase the energy efficiency in various sectors.

Smart Manufacturing and Predictive Maintenance

Application in Energy-Intensive Industries: One application that is especially advantageous is areas like automotive and aerospace manufacturing where a high return on investment is desired from the inlet stage capital expenditures. However, because they often have significant energy requirements for machine operations, efficiency is a top agenda (Cali et al., 2023). Organizations

can use digital twins to understanding energy consumption patterns and shed light on them to detect inefficiencies and to optimize processes to decrease energy waste (Shahzad et al., 2022).
Monitoring Machine Health: In these industries, data collected from IoT sensors embedded in the machinery machines are continuously analyzed to ensure the machine health remains constantly monitored using Digital Twins. This is an advantage for manufacturers to forecast maintenance needs, so they can cut down on downtime and save on the lost energy due to equipment breakdown (Chen, 2024). Predictive maintenance schedules can be defined such that maintenance tasks are performed just-in-time and unnecessary energy is saved by not having to run equipment to completion to accommodate unexpected breakdowns.
Case Study in the Automotive Industry: The case study signifies that digital twins are used successfully by leading automakers to improve production efficiency as well as to optimize energy usage. Therefore, for example, digital twins have been used to model and optimize the production line, resulting in a significant energy savings of up to 10% in energy usage during the assembly process, as was reported in various studies for similar cases (Stegmaier et al., 2022).

Smart Grids for Energy Optimization

Role in Power Management: The role of digital twins for managing energy flow on smart grids and for optimizing distribution networks must be taken. This enables utilities to study better the energy distribution, the demand forecast and grid responsiveness during peak load (Braun et al., 2024).
Case Study - IoT-Enabled Digital Twins: For example, one major application is the use of IoT enabled digital twin to control electricity grid in a smart cities. A smart grid initiative in a major urban area that implemented a digital twin system that analyzed real time electricity usage data and optimize energy distribution and minimize energy losses. Through this, the reliability of power distribution was improved and the likelihood of having outages was decreased during peak periods (Zhang et al., 2024). Moreover, the approach enabled facilitating renewable energy sources integration in a sustainable way.

Sustainable Infrastructure and Smart Buildings

Optimization in Construction and Facility Management: Building performance in new or existing facilities is simulated under different conditions to better understand how they might operate under different conditions; this simulation is done through the use of digital twins so that the energy efficiency of the project can be enhanced. Optimization of HVAC systems and lighting, for example, is a portion of what this involves, but it also includes performing other energy-saving studies such as these.
Case Study - Green Building Initiatives: Many of these green building initiatives rely on using digital twin technology to maximize energy efficient operations. For example, a digital twin was used for energy flows management in a green corporate office in a major city to predict energy use based on occupancy and conditions, adjusting according to such information. However, compared to conventional designs, the total reduction in the overall energy consumption is about 50% (As compared to the values reported in literature, reductions in total energy consumption between 10 to 15% are reported (Ma et al., 2022)). Figure 2 illustrates how a building's digital twin is made using the following components.

Figure 2. Essential components to construct a digital twin of a building (Image by Shahzad et al., (2022) from "Digital Twins in Built Environments: An Investigation of the Characteristics, Applications, and Challenges (https://www.mdpi.com/2075-5309/12/2/120)" licensed to CC BY 4.0)

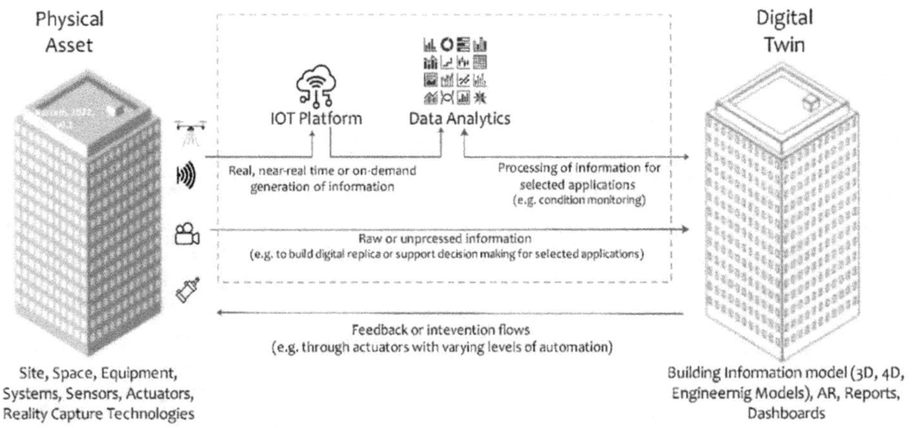

Circular Economy and Supply Chain Optimization

Sustainable Supply Chains: Digital twins would enable the transition to sustainable supply chains as they would allow for real time visibility and analytics across complex logistics shipments. Yet they help organizations precisely assess how much waste they produce and how much of their resources they use (Zhang et al., 2023).

Case Study - Waste Reduction in Manufacturing: Manufacturing companies have begun to use digital twins to follow and analyze flows and life cycles of material and product. In maintaining digital twin technology, a revised major company uncovered wastefulness in its recycling procedures and picked up material salvage projects to bring down the creation of waste while creating during manufacturing, report say 20% decrease (Fang, 2023).

AI AND ML FOR SUSTAINABILITY IN DIGITAL TWINS

However, the recent integration of digital twin technology with AI and ML significantly expands their capabilities and, thus, their potential as sustainability outcomes. This section discusses how AI helps digital twins process dataset, predictive modeling to optimize resource and scenario simulations to test sustainability strategy. Figure 3 shows the digital twin using big data and ML techniques.

Figure 3. The map for digital twin using big data and machine learning (Image by Rathore et al., (2021) from "The Role of AI, Machine Learning, and Big Data in Digital Twinning: A Systematic Literature Review, Challenges, and Opportunities (https://ieeexplore.ieee.org/document/9359733)" licensed by CC BY 4.0)

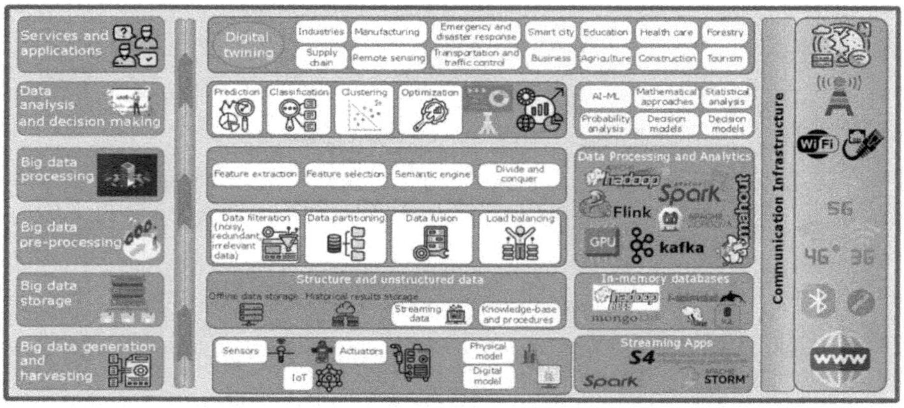

Enhancing Digital Twin Capabilities with AI:

Role of AI in Processing Vast Datasets: There is an huge amount of real time data generated from physical systems that includes various sensor embedded physical systems. This data requires AI algorithms to run them efficiently and for us to have robust analysis and interpretation from the results. For instance, it can use machine learning to find patterns and anomalies in large datasets and thus forecast maintenance and optimization (Moztarzadeh et al., 2023). This capability is useful in the context of numerous industries where knowing how relationships work in data helps to improve the performance (Zhao et al., 2022).

AI Enhancements in Decision-Making: In addition AI boosts decision making to predict outcome on existence of historical data and current system condition. AI can help recommend the most energy efficient pathways for operation by using predictive analytics. For example, algorithms driven by AI can suggest modifications in machine setting to lessen energy consumption in the making, even more critical in the energy-intensive domain of the automotive industry (Regona et al., 2022). This is why informed decision making from AI insights can result in substantial reductions of the energy waste and in emissions (Zhu et al., 2023).

Predictive Modeling for Resource Optimization

Using AI and ML to Predict Future Resource Needs: AI and ML are indispensable for forecasting upcoming needs of resources like energy and materials. Resequencing AI and feeding in historical usage patterns and external variables including demand or seasonal seasonality, can accurately forecast resource requirements. In this instance, a digital twin in conjunct with ML algorithms can use production data to optimize material supply, reduced excessive and waste (Özel & Jarosz, 2022).

Real-time Resource Optimization: Additionally, AI systems can adjust operations in real time as their predictive modeling outputs occur. This capability enables companies to come up with an answer dynamically to changes in resource availability or consumer demand so that efficiency is optimized (Varghese et al., 2022). For example, the parts of an AI-controlled system responsible for a smart energy management system may be able to adjust the distribution of power within and among different machines following real time power usage demands that save money by using less power and leading to overall usage to be optimized.

Scenario Simulations for Sustainability

AI-driven Simulations for Testing Sustainability Strategies: Sustainability strategies can be simulated by digital twins enabled with AI capabilities before they are physically implemented. Such simulations enable the organizations to take into account the probable impacts of varied operational adjustments, which enables them to pick out the most secure path of motion without disrupting the actual operations (Abou Ibrahim et al., 2022). Through various scenarios, businesses can work out the most suitable configurations for reducing the usage of resource as well as for reducing the environmental impact.

Case Study: Energy-Saving Scenarios in Manufacturing Processes: One such example of the use of AI based digital twins can be seen in a manufacturing facility that used AI based digital twins to perform energy saving scenarios. To achieve tangible sustainability improvements, the facility modeled different production processes and how these could change as, about by modifying cycles or adjusting machinery settings, then selected strategies that had in fact made positive sustainability impacts. Although specific figures such as 'up to a 15% reduction in energy use during peak hours' were provided, simulations of this nature usually result in a range of improvements particularly in the context of the specific facility (Klass et al., 2024).

ECONOMIC AND ENVIRONMENTAL BENEFITS

Digital twin technology adoption brings about major economic and environmental benefits in many industries. Digital twins allow us to optimize effective resource utilization to save costs, comply with sustainability, and support the circular economy to enable more efficient and environmentally friendly operational model.

Energy and Resource Efficiency

Digital twin technology offers significant energy efficiency and resource usage improvement in different sectors, which results in considerable cost and sustainable total benefit. Mainly through real time monitoring, prediction and optimized operational process.

How Digital Twins Reduce Energy Waste and Optimize Resource Utilization

Digital twins are virtual replicas of physical assets that take and analyse real time data from different data sources including the operation of equipment and environmental factors (Elfarri et al 2023). Organizations can thus continually monitor the parameter like energy consumption and the environmental impact of machines to identify inefficiency and take targeted interventions to improve the usage of resources (El Goahry et al., 2023). Figure 4 illustrates the energy modelling by the use of Artificial Neural Network (ANN).

Figure 4. Energy modelling by the use of ANNs (Image by El-Gohary et al., (2023) from "Prediction of an Efficient Energy-Consumption Model for Existing Residential Buildings in Lebanon Using an ANN as a Digital Twin in the Era of Climate Change (https://www.mdpi.com/2075-5309/13/12/3074)" licensed by CC BY 4.0)

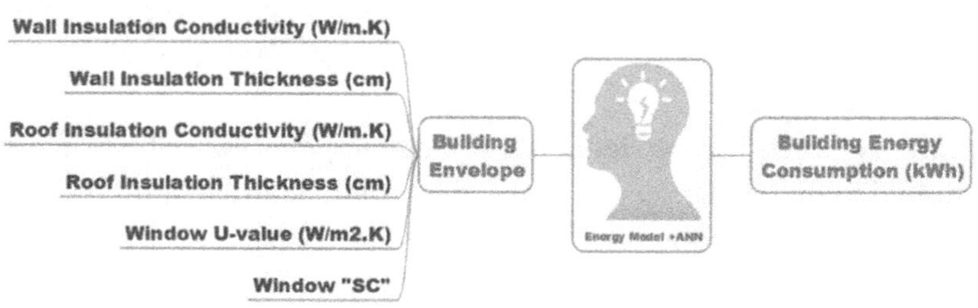

- **Energy Consumption Analysis:** Specific example includes digital twins in energy intensive industries like automotive manufacturing which enable tracking of energy patterns with precision across all energy intensive equipments and production line. Therefore, an organization can find out the places, where the energy is wasted, and the corrective actions that may be taken for the same, i.e., unscheduled operating schedule or unsequenced equipment settings. Such proactive approach can result in energy cuts of approximately 15% and represent significant amount of cost savings in time (Schwarzmayr et al., 2022).
- **Resource Utilization:** Aside from optimizing the energy consumption, digital twins help the organizations optimize the usage of the materials and resources. Businesses can utilize data from operations' processes to remove steps of producing, reduce waste, and improve recover of resources. For example, when implemented in construction and building management, digital twins can hugely increase their effectiveness in operational maintenance practice and simultaneously realize proper using energy and materials as well as extending the life cycle (Chen et al., 2022).

In addition, digital twins allow for maintaining the machinery and equipment for the sake of prediction, continuously observing their health. Organizations are given the ability to perform maintenance only when it is really needed which is good in as much as it prevents unnecessary energy consumption characterized by over maintenance and operational downtime caused by failure of equipment.

Cost Savings and Return on Investment

With the financial implication of Digital Energy Optimization (DEO), organization realizes extremely good cost savings and good Return on Investment (ROI).

Analyzing Financial Impact: By enhancing the energy efficiency the economic viability of digital twins is reduced in the operational cost. For example, energy intensive sectors have achieved cost savings ranging from 10% to 20% per year because of energy savings and improved operational efficiency (Zhang et al., 2024). Savings from these are often rapidly recouped in terms of ROI – many adopter saw a quick payback from initial investment in digital twin technology.
Example of ROI: A leading automotive manufacturer has used digital twins in practice on manufacturing facilities and has achieved more than a 150% ROI in less than three years. The factory used predictive analysis for machine health monitoring which save a lot of money on minimizing the energy bill and the maintenance costs showing the huge economic benefit of this technology (Tomar & Grover, 2024).

Corporate Sustainability and Regulatory Compliance

Digital twins market not only helps in the economic efficiency, which modernize business operations and drives revenue but also helps to achieve corporate sustainability and regulatory compliance.

Meeting Sustainability Targets: Digital twins allow organizations to measure their progress to make their waste management, carbon reduction and other reduction commitments. Digital twins provide real time data and analytics to enable proactive adjustment to corporate subjective return models (Pacheco-Blazquez et al., 2024).
Case Study - Achieving Carbon-Neutral Goals: At the same time, digital twins and IoT technologies were integrated by a large corporation to achieve her carbon neutral objectives within 2 years. This real time monitoring gave the company insights which helped in enhancement of operational efficiency, reduction in emissions and as many sustainable practices at the company's operation (Jeong et al., 2022).

Circular Economy

Digital twins are crucial enablers in running circular economy initiative, in which businesses can have a track of material flows, utilize resources more efficiently and manipulate product lifecycle management.

Supporting Circular Economy Initiatives: Digital twins therefore assist organizations to shift towards a more sustainable practice, e.g., recycling and material recovery (Wang et al., 2022). It is an approach to cyclical economy (circular economy), extended product life cycle through appropriate resource management.
Case Study - Reducing Material Waste: Digital twins are used by a manufacturing firm that analyses its production processes, and finds and cuts excess material waste by about 20% of the amount. The company successfully aligned its operations with principles of circular economy through optimizing process and improving recycling by combining environmental and economic returns (Wang, 2024)

CHALLENGES AND SOLUTIONS IN IMPLEMENTING DIGITAL TWINS FOR SUSTAINABILITY

There are challenges to implementing digital twins for sustainability. Issues such as data interoperability, cybersecurity, initial costs and barriers to adoption need to be navigated by the organizations. There are potential solutions for each of the missions that can enable the digital twin technology deployment.

Data Interoperability

The effective implementation of digital twins for sustainability hinges on seamless data interoperability across various systems and industries. This section discusses the challenges encountered with options such as standardized protocols and interoperability frameworks that can be considered to alleviate the challenges.

Challenges in Ensuring Seamless Data Integration

The major impediment to data interoperability is lack of standard data formats and protocols applied in different systems. Yet organizations often rely on a collection of diverse technologies and platforms, with each of these enabling data in a different data format; it is hard to ensure that data can be shared and understood in a consistent way across systems (Kleinitz et al., 2024). However, standardization significantly simplifies integrating data from different sources, minimizing potential discrepancies and inconsistencies of the virtual representation of the digital twin (Kasu et al., 2022). In addition, once industries evolve with new technologies and the systems that support these newer protocols do not exist, it is unreasonable to find a solution for these problems. The fragmented landscape of isolated data in the existing systems leads to development of incomplete digital twins that need input from multiple data streams (Keneally et al., 2024). Critical data is not integrated, which prevents effective insights from digital twins from being passed on to decision making and operational efficiency processes (Cavalieri & Gambadoro, 2023).

Solutions: Standardized Data Protocols and Interoperability Frameworks

For overcoming the data interoperability challenges, the organizations can opt for the standardized data protocols and frameworks. By following such standards as are proposed by the Object Management Group (OMG) and the International Organization for Standardization (ISO), they enable consistent exchange and communication of data across platforms (Lazzaro & Buccafurri, 2024). Common terminologies, formats, and data structure establish harmony within business and a way to share data but in a more efficient manner. The definition of interfaces and protocols necessary for interoperability among various systems are supported by interoperability frameworks. They advocate the development of interoperable and integrated information framework that would include various digital twin specifications like Asset Administration Shell (AAS), and would help foster the integration of information across different sectors (Khan & Khan, 2024). Digital twins in these frameworks are encouraged to have an ecosystem approach in which digital twins communicate and collaborate to generate enriched data in a more sustainable way.

Cybersecurity and Data Privacy

Digital twin and IoT technologies are widely used and it is critical to have robust cybersecurity and data privacy. These systems are interconnected, which means there are many risks introduced and these have to be addressed for the sake of sensitive data and ensuring operational integrity.

Addressing Risks Associated with IoT and Digital Twin Data Security

Combined with digital twins is the rapid adoption of IoT devices making vulnerability to cybercriminals extremely high. From the massive quantity of data generated, exchanged across related systems the risks are heightened and so attacks on these types of systems are attractive targets.

- **Increased Attack Surface:** Integration of various IoT devices creates a bigger attack surface. There are multiple possible points of entry for malicious actors (Dorage, 2024). Security related issues not only gets more complicated because of the absence of standardized security protocol across each device, but there is also the lack of consistency in the security measures that can easily be circumvented (Raghavendra & Yesaswini, 2024).
- **Data Privacy Concerns:** Large volumes of personal, operational and process data dispose the risk regarding the privacy of data to exist with the aggregation of data. Such data may be accessed without authorization by the data holders, which can result in their compromise, i.e. the sensitive information borne by the data holders (Maftei et al., 2023).
- **Potential Human Errors:** However, human error remains the biggest cause of cybersecurity breach in IoT and digital twin ecosystem. Because the practices of employees might cause them to expose systems to risk accidentally through poor security practice or not following the data protection protocols (Ajaj et al., 2023).

Best Practices for Securing Digital Twin Ecosystems

Organizations should use a variety of tactics to reduce the cyber security threats, table 2 lists the recommended practices for protecting the digital twin environment.

Table 2. Best practices for securing the digital twin ecosystem

Best Practice	Description	Example/Details	Reference
Adoption of Standardized Security Protocols	Establish and follow standardized security frameworks to minimize IoT-related vulnerabilities.	ISO/IEC 27000 series ensures systematic data protection and cybersecurity management.	Alzahrani & Alfouzan, 2022
Implementation of Advanced Authentication Methods	Use multi-factor authentication (MFA) to strengthen access security.	MFA requires multiple forms of identification, reducing unauthorized access.	Verma et al., 2022
Regular Security Audits and Updates	Conduct routine audits and update systems to defend against evolving threats.	Patching software and firmware vulnerabilities prevents known exploits.	Khanam, 2023

continued on following page

Table 2. Continued

Best Practice	Description	Example/Details	Reference
Employing AI for Threat Detection	Use AI-powered solutions to detect and respond to cyber threats in real time.	Machine learning algorithms analyze data traffic patterns to identify anomalies.	Grigoriadou et al., 2023
Providing Security Training for Employees	Educate employees on cybersecurity risks and best practices.	Regular training increases awareness of data privacy and security protocols.	AlSalem et al., 2023
Development of Comprehensive Incident Response Plans	Establish clear protocols for responding to data breaches or cyber incidents.	Predefined strategies ensure a coordinated and efficient recovery process.	Folorunso et al., 2024

High Initial Costs

Digital twin and the IoT implementations commonly involve huge investment from the outset and constitute a potential barrier to their adoption for many enterprises. It is important to understand these costs and do thorough cost benefit analysis to deliver the long term value proposition is real.

Investment Required for Adopting Digital Twins and IoT Technologies

Factors contributing toward high initial costs of digital twin technology include:

- **Development of Infrastructure:** For the phase-II, nowadays it requires advanced hardware and software infrastructure such as IoT sensor and high-performance computing system (Starkey et al., 2022). However, these technologies usually demand a lot of investment, resulting in the deterrent of organizations, especially in resource constrained environment.
- **Integration Complexity:** For existing systems and technology platforms to be integrated into a digital twin system, the implementation requires a combination of integrated systems and technology platforms. This integration is complicated and expensive, both in terms of finances and time while requiring substantial resources, including professionalism, to perfect the running of it (Nocera & Gardoni, 2023).
- **Skilled Workforce:** Digital twin technologies, data analytics, and cybersecurity may require initial implementation costs for organizations (Methuselah, 2024) since they may have to train or hire specialized personnel for their management. Digital twin technologies are complex by dissemination and as such, there is a need to have people with the required skills to make most of it.

Cost-Benefit Analyses and Long-Term Value Proposition

While the upfront costs of digital twins can be high, when performed well an organization can generate significant financial upside by assessing the financial benefit of a particular application of digital twins.

- **Evaluating Financial Impact:** This helps organizations do extremely detailed cost benefit analysis where case can run from reduced energy consumption, better operational efficiency, better maintenance schedules relying on replacement costs at the time you put the Life Cycle Costing railroad car in the ground or inside the machine for any size customer. An illustration is that companies that have taken advantage of bringing in digital twins often find savings that frequently exceed 10% in operational benefits.

- **Example of ROI:** For instance, the manufacturing sector can see an example with the top manufacturers who are using digital twins and are achieving ROI rates of up to 150% in less than a few years of deployment. The Reasons of Return to this ROI is decreased operational cost, lowered downtimes and increased production efficiency.
- **Incremental Implementation:** In fact, many organizations are exploring incremental ways to bring the technology into their system. Such a strategy helps companies to spread cost, and make the investment more manageable at the same time, allowing the company to exploit immediate benefit as they phase in new technology (Lee et al., 2023).

Overcoming Barriers to Adoption

There are several barriers, which include the implementation of digital twin technology in the context of sustainability focused industries. These challenges notwithstanding, organizations can take practical measures and take positive steps for adopting and integrating digital twin systems. This section discusses the process of bringing in digital twin technology and recommended steps from the business's perspective to get to digital twin driven operations.

Practical Guidance on Implementing Digital Twin Technology

- **Conducting a Readiness Assessment:** Before deploying digital twins, an organization thought to review its present technological abilities and likely obstacles that need work. It usually entails an evaluation of infrastructure, data management techniques, and skill levels of your employees (Elyasi et al., 2023). This will help organizations to know where it is and will enable them to plan good digital twin solution strategies.
- **Defining Clear Objectives:** It is crucial to define well it objectives of what the organization want to accomplish with the digital twin. Specific goals of such as increased energy efficiency, reduced waste, or better maintenance should be identified by organizations, which serve as a guide in the implementation process (Zhang et al., 2024). These objectives serve as the base for digital twin's design and bringing it to the sustainability targets.
- **Investing in Training:** Since the use of digital twin systems depends on employee involvement and expertise, organizations are advised to invest in training programs that develop digital literacy and usage of digital twin systems (Abanda et al., 2024). Enhancing overall rate of adoption and operational efficiencies will come from upskilling employees on the digital twin's functionalities, data analytics, and sustainability practices.
- **Creating a Cross-Functional Team:** It enables cross-functional team, i.e., all the departments; it operates and IT, operations and sustainability, to make a more integrated approach to the digital twin implementation. This team can set the table, as it were, so that the digital twin can effectively align its capabilities to the organizational needs and sustainability objectives and so everyone has comprehensive understanding and participation through the development phase.
- **Deploying Incrementally:** Starting with pilot projects to work out processes and determine outcomes before roll out can be implemented by an organization using a phased implementation

strategy. The use of this method allows for testing functionalities and making changes, and therefore, ensure that the digital twin meets his organization's requirements (Shehab et al., 2022). The gradual roll out of the technology enables businesses to cost out and manage operational disruptions more effectively.

Recommended Steps for Businesses to Transition to Digital Twin-Driven Operations

- **Assessment and Selection of Technology Partners:** One can work with technology partners that specialise in implementing the digital twin to get some valuable insights and resources. Access to the tools and software, software, and the best practices which are essential for a successful transition can be made possible via these partnerships (Chen et al., 2023).
- **Establishing Interoperability Standards:** To avoid any inconsistencies in the data sharing between different systems and devices, organizations should establish and apply the series of standardized interoperability frameworks (Armeni et al., 2022). By completing this step, it helps fix problems regarding fragmented data as well as improve ecosystem performance integrated digital. The application of digital twin technology in the healthcare sector is depicted in figure 5.

Figure 5. Digital twin technology implementation in the healthcare industry (Image byArmeni et al., (2022)from "Digital Twins in Healthcare: Is It the Beginning of a New Era of Evidence-Based Medicine? A Critical Review (https://www.mdpi.com/2075-4426/12/8/1255)" licensed to CC BY 4.0)

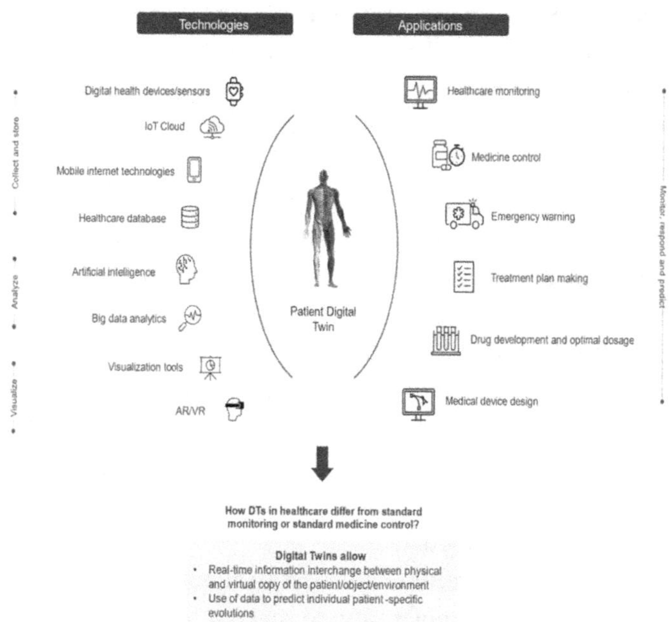

- **Fostering a Culture of Innovation:** Organizational effort can be made to create an atmosphere that welcomes innovation and embrace adoption of technology, overcoming a reluctance to change. By giving employees a chance to experiment with digital tools and solutions, this can lead to engagement and the determination of digital twin technology (Perno et al., 2022).

- **Establishing Feedback Mechanisms:** Organizations are able to continuously improve their digital twin applications with implementing feedback loops. It allows businesses to collect user insights, to analyze performance metrics and, based on this, to carry out data driven enhancements to the functionality in the business.
- **Ensuring Robust Cybersecurity Measures:** The transition to digital twin technologies is no different to any other technology adoption that involves security by design, thus addressing cybersecurity risks is crucial. Sensitive data needs to be protected and systems integrity is maintained with the help of robust security protocols by the organizations. Regular audits and threat assessments can be essential to a safe digital twin environment.
- **Monitoring and Evaluating Progress:** Set regular monitoring and evaluation marks to measure the effectiveness of the digital twin implementation. These evaluations are used in the measurement of progress towards sustainability goals and organizations can refine strategies in response (Zhang et al., 2024).

FUTURE TRENDS AND INNOVATIONS

Different emerging technologies are shaping the digital twin technology in rapid development. In this section, we discuss major improvements including edge computing, AI driven automation, and evolution of 6G network, while having the potential to make sustainability journey of the real world system enabled with the digital twin much more augmented.

Emerging Technologies Shaping Digital Twins

The Role of Edge Computing

Latency is minimized and enabled real time decision making in digital twin ecosystems by the involvement of edge computing. Edge computing lets us process data on the edge devices locally as opposed to the completely dependent cloud systems and hence, it offers faster data analysis and response time. In particular, such immediate feedback and adjustments are necessary to achieve operational efficiency and sustainability for digital twins operating in industrial settings. For instance, in manufacturing, a real time health monitor of edge computing helps in maintaining equipment health and cutting energy waste.

AI-Driven Automation

AI added into digital twins creates a more operational and sustainable real estate. (Trienens et al., 2024) note that AI algorithms can inspect immense data generated by digital twins and predict operational results and optimize processes. With this ability to predict, organisations can reduce the resource consumption by identifying energy efficient pathways. Through smarter decision making driven by AI automation, continuous improvement in energy management practice and minimizing waste are possible (Yun et al., 2024).

6G Networks

With the advent of 6G networks based on ultra-high speed and low latency communication, digital twin ecosystem would be revolutionized. Seamless integration of IoT devices and digital twins are possible with these networks in which extremely wide amounts of data can be exchanged in real time, without any delays (Han et al., 2024). Because 6G networks will have greater scalability, digital twins will be more capably scaled in many smart city and smart manufacturing use cases. Based on enhanced connectivity, 6G will enable more responsive and intelligent digital twin systems and thus push forward sustainable efforts.

Advancements in Digital Twin Technology

Integration of next generation technologies such as AI, blockchain and quantum computing in digital twins are on-going as they make them more capable of sustainability.

- **AI:** Digital twins are empowered with powerful 'analysis and predictive modeling' done by AI algorithms. They can help organizations minimize the negative impact from their operations on the environment. Just as importantly, they can identify trends and the delivery of actionable insights regarding how such operations can be optimized for sustainability. For example, AI is used in predictive maintenance schedules that balance energy usage with uptime to save considerable costs.
- **Blockchain:** The introduction of blockchain feature enhances data integrity and security in digital twins. Blockchain offers a decentralized way to handle the data management which makes a transaction and data exchange trusts between physical and digital twin. It is a requisite for the sustainability reporting as it takes care of the accuracy and transparency of the environmental impact data (Yakovenko and Shaptala, 2024).
- **Quantum Computing:** Although in its early stages of development, quantum computing has the potential to change the digital twins dramatically. By virtue of being able to execute calculations at astronomical speeds, quantum computing can explore complex data sets in real time and glean insights that would be impossible to achieve otherwise with classical computing (Burinskienė & Medineckienė, 2022). The impact of this advancements is that it further improves the construction of more refined and more accurate digital twins that can be leveraged for sustainability.

Global SDGs

Digital twins are critical to reaching the global sustainability targets, including the UN SDGs.

Contributions to Sustainability Targets

Digital twins directly support development to optimize resource usage and minimize waste, thus directly supporting some of the sustainability targets like responsible consumption and production (SDG 12) and climate action (SDG 13) (Galera-Zarco, 2022). This helps organizations decrease their carbon province while addressing operational necessities (or make them), further serving this advantage as one more job of facilitating more proficient energy the board.

Long-Term Perspectives on Digital Twins

There are good reasons for the long term role of digital twins in stimulating sustainability. Digital transformation is taking place in the industries, and the advanced technologies are integration in it; the predictive capabilities and operational efficiencies of digital twins will be crucial for sustainable practices (Said et al., 2023). Digital twins can provide the sustainability benefits of smarter urban planning, more resilient infrastructure, and better management of natural resources, which holistically support the push towards the globe's sustainable development.

CONCLUSION

Therefore, the discussion on digital twins along with the integration of IoT technologies provides great opportunities for sustainability practiced in different sectors. Several mechanisms render digital twins' powerful virtual replicas of physical entities through which organizations can optimize their operations while trying to minimize environmental impacts. Integrating digital twins brings additional key benefits of increased energy and resource efficiency. Using real time data from IoT sensors, organizations can track energy consumption, monitor a company's environmental impact and waste through predictive analytics and simulations. It allows making informed decisions about operational process efficiency and savings that lead to improve ROI for such businesses using these technologies. AI and machine learning have an important role in improving the digital twin capabilities. These technologies provide predictive modeling functionalities to the organizations to predict the demand of resources and simulate different operational scenarios resulting in energy savings and better sustainability results. Examples of case studies of organizations implementing a digital twin demonstrate that they have a very positive impact by providing substantial cost savings and also aid in their resource optimization efforts. The reality, however, isn't that the machines can autonomously adapt themselves to the physical world to maximize their retrievability, thereby needing the additional location and orientation information from the second IR. Successful implementation of such systems is hampered by issues such as data interoperability, cybersecurity, high initial costs and adoption barriers. These challenges demand standardized protocols, secure security measures and strong staff training. Thorough cost benefit analysis, building an innovative culture, and an implementation plan can benefit organizations to use digital twins effectively in its operation. With a view to the future, digital twins will get increasingly capable with technologies like edge computing and 6G networks expected to not only decrease digital twins' latency but also enable real-time decision-making at the lowest possible point. Also, advancements in AI, Quantum computing, and blockchain will make the digital twin applications efficient and secure to help organizations in meeting the global sustainability goals, as listed in United Nations SDGs. The integration of digital twins and IoT technologies finally enable organizations to enhance sustainability, simplify operations, and foster environmental stewardship. The use of digital twins will continue to be important for digital transformation to become an element of sustainability, as promoting a greener and more efficient world becomes more essential.

REFERENCES

Abanda, F., Jian, N., Adukpo, S. E., Tuhaise, V. V., & Manjia, M. B. (2024). Digital twin for product versus project lifecycles' development in manufacturing and construction industries. *Journal of Intelligent Manufacturing*, *36*(2), 801–831. DOI: 10.1007/s10845-023-02301-2

Abou-Ibrahim, H., Lappalainen, E., & Seppänen, O. (2022). Digital twin of a design process: an exploratory study. *Proc. 30th Annual Conference of the International Group for Lean Construction (IGLC)*. DOI: 10.24928/2022/0238

Ajaj, Y. S., Al-Kaseem, B. R., & Al-Dunainawi, Y. (2023). Cyber attacks in sdn-based iot environment: A review. *Al-Iraqia Journal of Scientific Engineering Research*, *2*(3). Advance online publication. DOI: 10.58564/IJSER.2.3.2023.89

Alghuried, A., Alghuson, M., Alahmari, T. S., & Abuhasel, K. A. (2024). Organized optimization integration validation model for internet of things (iot)-based real-time applications. *Mathematics*, *12*(15), 2385. DOI: 10.3390/math12152385

AlSalem, T. S., Almaiah, M. A., & Lutfi, A. (2023). Cybersecurity risk analysis in the iot: A systematic review. *Electronics (Basel)*, *12*(18), 3958. DOI: 10.3390/electronics12183958

Alzahrani, N. M., & Alfouzan, F. A. (2022). Augmented reality (ar) and cyber-security for smart cities—A systematic literature review. *Sensors (Basel)*, *22*(7), 2792. DOI: 10.3390/s22072792 PMID: 35408406

Amangeldy, B., Tasmurzayev, N., Nurakhov, Y., Shinassylov, S., & Bekele, S. D. (2023). Development and evaluation of an intelligent control system for sustainable and efficient energy management. *Wseas Transactions on Electronics*, *14*, 135–143. DOI: 10.37394/232017.2023.14.16

Armeni, P., Polat, I., Rossi, L. M. D., Diaferia, L., Meregalli, S., & Gatti, A. (2022). Digital twins in healthcare: Is it the beginning of a new era of evidence-based medicine? a critical review. *Journal of Personalized Medicine*, *12*(8), 1255. DOI: 10.3390/jpm12081255 PMID: 36013204

Awouda, A., Traini, E., Bruno, G., & Chiabert, P. (2024). Iot-based framework for digital twins in the industry 5.0 era. *Sensors (Basel)*, *24*(2), 594. DOI: 10.3390/s24020594 PMID: 38257686

Bandaru, V. N. R., Kaligotla, V. S. H. G. S., Varma, U. D. S. P., Prasadaraju, K., & Sugumaran, S. (2024). A enhancing data security solutions for smart energy systems in iot-enabled cloud computing environments through lightweight cryptographic techniques. *IOP Conference Series. Earth and Environmental Science*, *1375*(1), 012003. DOI: 10.1088/1755-1315/1375/1/012003

Barbosa, J. M. V., Gómez, Ó. D. C., & García, J. A. G. (2023). A methodological approach for digital twin implementation in waste management: improvement of production and service systems. DOI: 10.20944/preprints202309.0899.v1

Bassey, K. E., Opoku-Boateng, J., Antwi, B. O., & Ntiakoh, A. (2024). Economic impact of digital twins on renewable energy investments. Engineering Science &Amp. *Technology Journal*, *5*(7), 2232–2247. DOI: 10.51594/estj.v5i7.1318

Botín-Sanabria, D. M., Mihăiţă, A., Peimbert-García, R. E., Ramírez-Moreno, M. A., Ramírez-Mendoza, R. A., & Lozoya-Santos, J. J. (2022). Digital twin technology challenges and applications: A comprehensive review. *Remote Sensing (Basel)*, *14*(6), 1335. DOI: 10.3390/rs14061335

Braun, L., Mock, J., Jung, L., Böttcher, P., & Scholzen, F. (2024). Digital twin collaboration: A common technical structure for the automotive and the building industry. *Proceedings of International Structural Engineering and Construction*, *11*(2). Advance online publication. DOI: 10.14455/10.14455/ISEC.2024.11(2).AAE-04

Burinskienė, A., & Medineckienė, M. (2022). Digitalisation as the indicator of the evidence of sustainability in the european union. *Sustainability (Basel)*, *14*(14), 8371. DOI: 10.3390/su14148371

Cali, Ü., Dimd, B. D., Hajialigol, P., Moazami, A., Gourisetti, S. N. G., Lobaccaro, G., & Aghaei, M. (2023). Digital twins: shaping the future of energy systems and smart cities through cybersecurity, efficiency, and sustainability. *2023 International Conference on Future Energy Solutions (FES)*. DOI: 10.1109/FES57669.2023.10182868

Cao, Z. (2024). Challenges and opportunities of the digital economy for sustainable development. Advances in Economics. *Management and Political Sciences*, *76*(1), 1–7. DOI: 10.54254/2754-1169/76/20241869

Cavalieri, S., & Gambadoro, S. (2023). Proposal of mapping digital twins definition language to open platform communications unified architecture. *Sensors (Basel)*, *23*(4), 2349. DOI: 10.3390/s23042349 PMID: 36850947

Chalal, L., Saadane, A., & Rachid, A. (2023). Unified environment for real time control of hybrid energy systems using digital twin and iot approach. *Sensors (Basel)*, *23*(12), 5646. DOI: 10.3390/s23125646 PMID: 37420813

Chao, C. (2023). Development of smart iot based biomedical heart rate oximeters for driving safety. *Academic Journal of Engineering and Technology Science*, *6*(12). Advance online publication. DOI: 10.25236/AJETS.2023.061201

Chen, S. (2024). Advancing sustainability in mechanical engineering: Integration of green energy and intelligent manufacturing. *Applied and Computational Engineering*, *66*(1), 150–155. DOI: 10.54254/2755-2721/66/20240937

Chen, S., Sánchez, J. P. G., Bekar, E. T., Bokrantz, J., Skoogh, A., & Lopes, P. V. (2023). Understanding stakeholder requirements for digital twins in manufacturing maintenance. *2023 Winter Simulation Conference (WSC)*. DOI: 10.1109/WSC60868.2023.10408657

Chen, Z., Zou, J., & Wang, W. (2022). Digital twin oriented multi-objective flexible job shop scheduling model and its hybrid particle swarm optimization. *Proceedings of the Institution of Mechanical Engineers. Part B, Journal of Engineering Manufacture*, *237*(8), 1269–1282. DOI: 10.1177/09544054221121921

Christ, L., Milloch, E., Boshoff, M., Hypki, A., & Kuhlenkötter, B. (2023). Implementation of digital twin and real production system to address actual and future challenges in assembly technology. *Automation*, *4*(4), 345–358. DOI: 10.3390/automation4040020

Coorey, G., Figtree, G. A., Fletcher, D. F., Snelson, V. J., Vernon, S. T., Winlaw, D. S., Grieve, S. M., McEwan, A., Yang, J. Y. H., Qian, P., O'Brien, K., Orchard, J., Kim, J., Patel, S., & Redfern, J. (2022). The health digital twin to tackle cardiovascular disease—A review of an emerging interdisciplinary field. *NPJ Digital Medicine*, *5*(1), 126. Advance online publication. DOI: 10.1038/s41746-022-00640-7 PMID: 36028526

Corrado, C., DeLong, S. M., Holt, E., Hua, E. Y., & Tolk, A. (2022). *Combining green metrics and digital twins for sustainability planning and governance of smart buildings and cities.* Prime Archives in Sustainability., DOI: 10.37247/PASUS3ED.3.23.19

Cruz-Manzo, S., Panov, V., & Bingham, C. (2024). Compressor fouling diagnostics and prognostics in a gas turbine. International Journal of Gas Turbine. *Propulsion and Power Systems*, *15*(1), 9–14. DOI: 10.38036/jgpp.15.1_9

Dorage, S. V. (2024). Cybersecurity in industrial management within the internet of things. *Interantional Journal of Scientific Research in Engineering and Management*, *08*(008), 1–16. DOI: 10.55041/IJSREM37081

Drummond, D., & Gonsard, A. (2024). Definitions and characteristics of patient digital twins being developed for clinical use: Scoping review. *Journal of Medical Internet Research*, *26*, e58504. DOI: 10.2196/58504 PMID: 39536311

El-Gohary, M., El-Abed, R., & Omar, O. (2023). Prediction of an efficient energy-consumption model for existing residential buildings in lebanon using an artificial neural network as a digital twin in the era of climate change. *Buildings (Basel, Switzerland)*, *13*(12), 3074. DOI: 10.3390/buildings13123074

Elfarri, E. M., Rasheed, A., & San, O. (2023). Artificial intelligence-driven digital twin of a modern house demonstrated in virtual reality. *IEEE Access : Practical Innovations, Open Solutions*, *11*, 35035–35058. DOI: 10.1109/ACCESS.2023.3265191

Elyasi, N., Bellini, A., & Klungseth, N. J. (2023). Digital transformation in facility management: An analysis of the challenges and benefits of implementing digital twins in the use phase of a building. *IOP Conference Series. Earth and Environmental Science*, *1176*(1), 012001. DOI: 10.1088/1755-1315/1176/1/012001

Fang, X. (2023). Energy management system technology in smart grid. Highlights in Science. *Engineering and Technology*, *76*, 328–336. DOI: 10.54097/x5ch4d78

Folorunso, A., Mohammed, V., Wada, I., & Samuel, B. J. (2024). The impact of iso security standards on enhancing cybersecurity posture in organizations. *World Journal of Advanced Research and Reviews*, *24*(1), 2582–2595. DOI: 10.30574/wjarr.2024.24.1.3169

Fu, H., Zhao, T., Chen, Y., Yao, Y., & Leng, J. (2022). Framework and operation of digital twin smart freeway. *IET Intelligent Transport Systems*, *17*(3), 620–633. DOI: 10.1049/itr2.12288

Galera-Zarco, C. (2022). Unleashing the potential of digital twin in offering green services. *IET Conference Proceedings*, 2022(8), 158-161. DOI: 10.1049/icp.2022.2059

Grigoriadou, S., Radoglou-Grammatikis, P., Sarigiannidis, P., Makris, I., Λάγκας, Θ., Argyriou, V., & Fountoukidis, E. (2023). Hunting iot cyberattacks with ai - powered intrusion detection. *2023 IEEE International Conference on Cyber Security and Resilience (CSR)*, 142-147. DOI: 10.1109/CSR57506.2023.10224981

Han, J., Ge, W., & Chou, Y. (2024). Leveraging digital infrastructure for sustainable grain production: Evidence from china. *Frontiers in Sustainable Food Systems*, *8*, 1440321. Advance online publication. DOI: 10.3389/fsufs.2024.1440321

Hengelbrock, A., Helgers, H., Schmidt, A., Vetter, F. L., Juckers, A., Rosengarten, J. F., Stitz, J., & Strube, J. (2022). Digital twin for hiv-gag vlp production in hek293 cells. *Processes (Basel, Switzerland)*, *10*(5), 866. DOI: 10.3390/pr10050866

Husung, S., Koch, Y., Welzbacher, P., Kraus, B., Roehnert, F., Faheem, F., & Kirchner, E. (2023). Systemic conception of the data acquisition of digital twin solutions for use case-oriented development and its application to a gearbox. *Systems*, *11*(5), 227. DOI: 10.3390/systems11050227

Jeong, D., Baek, M., Lim, T., Kim, Y., Kim, S., Lee, Y., Jung, W.-S., & Lee, I. (2022). Digital twin: Technology evolution stages and implementation layers with technology elements. *IEEE Access : Practical Innovations, Open Solutions*, *10*, 52609–52620. DOI: 10.1109/ACCESS.2022.3174220

Kasu, P., Hamandawana, P., & Chung, T. (2022). Tpbf: Two-phase bloom-filter-based end-to-end data integrity verification framework for object-based big data transfer systems. *Mathematics*, *10*(9), 1591. DOI: 10.3390/math10091591

Keneally, C., Gaget, V., Kidd, S. P., & Brookes, J. D. (2024). Sample preservation solution increases nucleic acid yield and environmental rna quality in sediments across an estuarine salinity gradient. *Environmental DNA*, *6*(5), e70016. Advance online publication. DOI: 10.1002/edn3.70016

Khalaj, O., Jamshidi, M., Hassas, P., Mašek, B., Štádler, C., & Svoboda, J. (2023). Digital twinning of a magnetic forging holder to enhance productivity for industry 4.0 and metaverse. *Processes (Basel, Switzerland)*, *11*(6), 1703. DOI: 10.3390/pr11061703

Khan, M., & Khan, M. (2024). Real-time data processing systems in modern law enforcement: A technical analysis. *International Journal for Multidisciplinary Research*, *6*(6), 30723. Advance online publication. DOI: 10.36948/ijfmr.2024.v06i06.30723

Khanam, R. (2023). Review of threats in iot systems: Challenges and solutions. *International Journal for Research in Applied Science and Engineering Technology*, *11*(2), 325–341. DOI: 10.22214/ijraset.2023.49016

Khdoudi, A., Masrour, T., Hassani, I. E., & Mazgualdi, C. E. (2024). A deep-reinforcement-learning-based digital twin for manufacturing process optimization. *Systems*, *12*(2), 38. DOI: 10.3390/systems12020038

Klass, L., Holz, L., Koenig, L., Kabza, A., Sehnke, F., Strecker, K., & Hölzle, M. (2024). Big brother is watching you: Leveraging artificial intelligence for automated fuel cell monitoring (technical report). *ECS Transactions*, *114*(5), 631–639. DOI: 10.1149/11405.0645ecst

Kleinitz, P., Sabariego, C., Llewellyn, G., Taloafiri, E., Mangar, A., Baskota, R., Marahatta, K., Maduwage, S., Khin, M. H., Wonanji, V., Sampa, G., Al-Rjoub, A., Al-Daod, J., & Cieza, A. (2024). Integrating rehabilitation into health systems: A comparative study of nine middle-income countries using who's systematic assessment of rehabilitation situation (stars). *PLoS One*, *19*(2), e0297109. DOI: 10.1371/journal.pone.0297109 PMID: 38315690

Kolekar, A. B., Shalgar, S., & Malawade, I. (2023). Beyond reality: A study of integrating digital twins. *Journal of Physics: Conference Series*, *2601*(1), 012030. DOI: 10.1088/1742-6596/2601/1/012030

Lazzaro, S., & Buccafurri, F. (2024). Achieving accountability and data integrity in message queuing telemetry transport using blockchain and interplanetary file system. *Future Internet*, *16*(7), 246. DOI: 10.3390/fi16070246

Lee, S., Kwon, J., & Park, D. (2023). Runtime tracking-based replication of on-chip embedded software using transfer function learning for dust particle sensing systems. *IEEE Access : Practical Innovations, Open Solutions*, *11*, 32167–32175. DOI: 10.1109/ACCESS.2023.3263057

Li, H., Yang, Y., Zhang, C., Zhang, C., & Chen, W. (2023). Visualization monitoring of industrial detonator automatic assembly line based on digital twin. *Sustainability (Basel)*, *15*(9), 7690. DOI: 10.3390/su15097690

Li, M., Wang, Z., Fan, H., Zhang, Y., & Gao, P. (2023). Establishment of web-based digital twin system for truss gantry crane. *IEEE Access : Practical Innovations, Open Solutions*, *11*, 146282–146296. DOI: 10.1109/ACCESS.2023.3345253

Liu, Z., Blasch, E., Liao, M., Yang, C., Tsukada, K., & Meyendorf, N. (2023). Digital twin for predictive maintenance. NDE 4.0, Predictive Maintenance, Communication, and Energy Systems. *The Digital Transformation of NDE*, *6*, 6. Advance online publication. DOI: 10.1117/12.2660270

Loaiza, J. H., & Cloutier, R. (2022). Analyzing the implementation of a digital twin manufacturing system: Using a systems thinking approach. *Systems*, *10*(2), 22. DOI: 10.3390/systems10020022

López, O. L. A., Rosabal, O. M., Ruíz-Guirola, D. E., Raghuwanshi, P., Mikhaylov, K., Lovén, L., & Iyer, S. (2023). Energy-sustainable iot connectivity: Vision, technological enablers, challenges, and future directions. *IEEE Open Journal of the Communications Society*, *4*, 2609–2666. DOI: 10.1109/OJCOMS.2023.3323832

Lou, J., Wang, C., Xu, M., He, L., & Zhang, P. (2024). Design and operation of iot system and power communication with digital twin technology. *Journal of Physics: Conference Series*, *2872*(1), 012003. DOI: 10.1088/1742-6596/2872/1/012003

Ma, S., Ding, W., Liu, Y., Ren, S., & Yang, H. (2022). Digital twin and big data-driven sustainable smart manufacturing based on information management systems for energy-intensive industries. *Applied Energy*, *326*, 119986. DOI: 10.1016/j.apenergy.2022.119986

Maftei, A. A., Lavric, A., Petrariu, A. I., & Popa, V. (2023). Massive data storage solution for iot devices using blockchain technologies. *Sensors (Basel)*, *23*(3), 1570. DOI: 10.3390/s23031570 PMID: 36772609

Manickam, S., Yarlagadda, L., Gopalan, S. P., & Chowdhary, C. L. (2023). Unlocking the potential of digital twins: A comprehensive review of concepts, frameworks, and industrial applications. *IEEE Access : Practical Innovations, Open Solutions*, *11*, 135147–135158. DOI: 10.1109/ACCESS.2023.3338530

Mansour, D. A., Numair, M., Zalhaf, A. S., Ramadan, R., Darwish, M. M. F., Huang, Q., Hussien, M. G., & Abdel-Rahim, O. (2023). Applications of iot and digital twin in electrical power systems: A comprehensive survey. IET Generation, Transmission &Amp. *IET Generation, Transmission & Distribution*, *17*(20), 4457–4479. DOI: 10.1049/gtd2.12940

Mazumder, A. H., Sahed, M., Tasneem, Z., Das, P., Badal, F. R., Ali, M. F., Ahamed, M. H., Abhi, S. H., Sarker, S. K., Das, S. K., Hasan, M. M., Islam, M. M., & Islam, M. R. (2023). Towards next generation digital twin in robotics: Trends, scopes, challenges, and future. *Heliyon*, *9*(2), e13359. DOI: 10.1016/j.heliyon.2023.e13359 PMID: 36825188

Methuselah, J. M. J. (2024). Digital twin technology for smart manufacturing. *Journal of Technology and Systems*, *6*(4), 52–65. DOI: 10.47941/jts.2143

Miller, M. E., & Spatz, E. (2022). A unified view of a human digital twin. *Human-Intelligent Systems Integration*, *4*(1-2), 23–33. DOI: 10.1007/s42454-022-00041-x

Mincă, E., Filipescu, A., Cernega, D., Şolea, R., Filipescu, A., Ionescu, D., & Simion, G. (2022). Digital twin for a multifunctional technology of flexible assembly on a mechatronics line with integrated robotic systems and mobile visual sensor—Challenges towards industry 5.0. *Sensors (Basel)*, *22*(21), 8153. DOI: 10.3390/s22218153 PMID: 36365850

Moztarzadeh, O., Jamshidi, M., Sargolzaei, S., Jamshidi, A., Baghalipour, N., Malekzadeh, M., & Hauer, L. (2023). Metaverse and healthcare: Machine learning-enabled digital twins of cancer. *Bioengineering (Basel, Switzerland)*, *10*(4), 455. DOI: 10.3390/bioengineering10040455 PMID: 37106642

Mudiyanselage, M. P. D., & Sellahewa, H. (2023). Digital twins as a framework for iot applications: a review. 2023 7th SLAAI International Conference on Artificial Intelligence (SLAAI-ICAI), 1-6. DOI: 10.1109/SLAAI-ICAI59257.2023.10365018

Mukhacheva, A. V., Ugryumova, M. N., Morozova, I. S., & Mukhachyev, M. Y. (2022). Digital twins of the urban ecosystem to ensure the quality of life of the population. Proceedings of the International Scientific and Practical Conference Strategy of Development of Regional Ecosystems "Education-. DOI: 10.2991/aebmr.k.220208.047

Ngadi, H., Bounceur, A., Bezoui, M., Lahlou, L., Hammoudeh, M., Kara, N., & Nana, L. (2024). Toward a digital twin iot for the validation of ai algorithms in smart-city applications. *Lecture Notes in Computer Science*, *14525*, 108–117. DOI: 10.1007/978-3-031-59933-0_8

Nocera, F., & Gardoni, P. (2023). Digital twins or equivalent infrastructure models? the role of modeling granularity in regional risk analysis of infrastructure. *Proceeding of the 33rd European Safety and Reliability Conference*, 2486-2493. DOI: 10.3850/978-981-18-8071-1_P530-cd

Özel, T., & Jarosz, K. (2022). Machine learning approaches towards digital twin development for machining systems. *International Journal of Mechatronics and Manufacturing Systems*, *15*(2/3), 1. DOI: 10.1504/IJMMS.2022.10048837

Pacheco-Blazquez, R., Espinosa, J. G., Capua, D. D., & Sanchez, A. P. (2024). A digital twin for assessing the remaining useful life of offshore wind turbine structures. *Journal of Marine Science and Engineering*, *12*(4), 573. DOI: 10.3390/jmse12040573

Perno, M., Hvam, L., & Haug, A. (2022). Implementation of digital twins in the process industry: A systematic literature review of enablers and barriers. *Computers in Industry*, *134*, 103558. DOI: 10.1016/j.compind.2021.103558

Poletti, G., Antonini, L., Mandelli, L., Tsompou, P., Karanasiou, G. S., Papafaklis, M. I., Michalis, L. K., Fotiadis, D. I., Petrini, L., & Pennati, G. (2022). Towards a digital twin of coronary stenting: A suitable and validated image-based approach for mimicking patient-specific coronary arteries. *Electronics (Basel)*, *11*(3), 502. DOI: 10.3390/electronics11030502

Pyakurel, P., Rehman, M. F. u., & Benham, R. (2022). A novel approach to evaluating sustainability of products and associated manufacturing processes. Advances in Transdisciplinary Engineering. DOI: 10.3233/ATDE220597

Pysin, M. D. and Лобанов, A. C. (2023). Digital twin is a complex of microservices. E3S Web of Conferences, 458, 09012. DOI: 10.1051/e3sconf/202345809012

Raghavendra, G., & Yesaswini, A. M. (2024). Design and implementation of internet of things (iot) framework for governing modern cyber attacks in computer network. *International Journal of Safety and Security Engineering*, *14*(5), 1385–1390. DOI: 10.18280/ijsse.140505

Rajan, G., & Li, S. (2024). Smart building digital twin for interior water distribution system management. The International Archives of the Photogrammetry, Remote Sensing and Spatial Information Sciences, XLVIII-4-2024, 373-379. DOI: 10.5194/isprs-archives-XLVIII-4-2024-373-2024

Regona, M., Yiğitcanlar, T., Xia, B., & Li, R. Y. M. (2022). Opportunities and adoption challenges of ai in the construction industry: A prisma review. *Journal of Open Innovation*, *8*(1), 45. DOI: 10.3390/joitmc8010045

Rojek, I., Mikołajewski, D., & Dostatni, E. (2020). Digital twins in product lifecycle for sustainability in manufacturing and maintenance. *Applied Sciences (Basel, Switzerland)*, *11*(1), 31. DOI: 10.3390/app11010031

Said, S. B. H., Thi, M., Kellil, M., & Olivereau, A. (2023). On the management of tsn networks in 6g: a network digital twin approach. 2023 IEEE 28th International Conference on Emerging Technologies and Factory Automation (ETFA). DOI: 10.1109/ETFA54631.2023.10275568

Savić, G., Segedinac, M., Konjović, Z., Vidaković, M., & Dutina, R. (2023). Towards a domain-neutral platform for sustainable digital twin development. *Sustainability (Basel)*, *15*(18), 13612. DOI: 10.3390/su151813612

Schwarzmayr, P., Birkelbach, F., Kasper, L., & Hofmann, R. (2022). Development of a digital twin platform for industrial energy systems.. DOI: 10.46855/energy-proceedings-9974

Segovia, M., & García-Alfaro, J. (2022). Design, modeling and implementation of digital twins. *Sensors (Basel)*, *22*(14), 5396. DOI: 10.3390/s22145396 PMID: 35891076

Shahzad, M., Shafiq, M. T., Douglas, D., & Kassem, M. (2022). Digital twins in built environments: An investigation of the characteristics, applications, and challenges. *Buildings (Basel, Switzerland)*, *12*(2), 120. DOI: 10.3390/buildings12020120

Sharma, A., Singh, S. K., Kumar, S., Thakur, R., Gupta, B. B., & Arya, V. (2024). Iot-enabled smart farming with industry 5.0. *Journal of High Speed Networks*, *30*(3), 477–496. DOI: 10.3233/JHS-230258

Shehab, E., Kazhymurat, T., Jyeniskhan, N., Amantayeva, A., Meiirbekov, A., Singh, S., & Tokbolat, S. (2022). Developing a digital twin for carbon fiber composites recycling: Challenges and future research direction. *Advances in Science and Technology (Owerri, Nigeria)*, *116*, 61–66. DOI: 10.4028/p-h01m30

Starkey, J., Hancock, C., Chen, L., & Meng, Q. (2022). Digital twinning proof of concept for utility-scale solar: benefits, issues, and enablers. The International Archives of the Photogrammetry, Remote Sensing and Spatial Information Sciences, XLVI-5/W1-2022, 231-237. DOI: 10.5194/isprs-archives-XLVI-5-W1-2022-231-2022

Stegmaier, V., Schaaf, W., Jazdi, N., & Weyrich, M. (2022). Simulation model for digital twins of pneumatic vacuum ejectors. Chemical Engineering &Amp. *Chemical Engineering & Technology*, *46*(1), 71–79. DOI: 10.1002/ceat.202200358

su, z. (2024). Application of anomaly detection based on deep learning in digital twin. Third International Symposium on Computer Applications and Information Systems (ISCAIS 2024), 19. DOI: 10.1117/12.3034763

Sun, T., He, X., & Li, Z. (2023). Digital twin in healthcare: Recent updates and challenges. *Digital Health*, *9*, 20552076221149651. Advance online publication. DOI: 10.1177/20552076221149651 PMID: 36636729

Tan, F., & Cheng, Y. (2024). A digital twin framework for innovating rural ecological landscape control. *Environmental Sciences Europe*, *36*(1), 59. Advance online publication. DOI: 10.1186/s12302-024-00888-8

Tomar, P. S., & Grover, V. (2024). Transforming the energy sector: Addressing key challenges through generative ai, digital twins, ai, data science and analysis. *EAI Endorsed Transactions on Energy Web*, *10*. Advance online publication. DOI: 10.4108/ew.4825

Trienens, M., Rasor, R., Kharatyan, A., Dumitrescu, R., & Anacker, H. (2024). Digital twins to increase sustainability throughout the system life cycle: A systematic literature review. *Proceedings of the Design Society*, *4*, 2277–2286. DOI: 10.1017/pds.2024.230

Vallée, A. (2023). Digital twin for healthcare systems. *Frontiers in Digital Health*, *5*, 1253050. Advance online publication. DOI: 10.3389/fdgth.2023.1253050 PMID: 37744683

Varghese, S. A., Ghadim, A. D., Balador, A., Alimadadi, Z., & Papadimitratos, P. (2022). Digital twin-based intrusion detection for industrial control systems. 2022 IEEE International Conference on Pervasive Computing and Communications Workshops and Other Affiliated Events (PerCom Work, 611-617. DOI: 10.1109/PerComWorkshops53856.2022.9767492

Verma, P., Sharma, R., & Mistry, M. (2022). A paradigm shift in iot cyber-security: A systematic review. *International Journal for Research in Applied Science and Engineering Technology*, *10*(10), 1024–1034. DOI: 10.22214/ijraset.2022.47129

Vilar-Dias, J. L., Silva, A. S., & Neto, F. B. L. (2023). An interpretable digital twin for self-aware industrial machines. *Sensors (Basel)*, *24*(1), 4. DOI: 10.3390/s24010004 PMID: 38202867

Wang, G., Bing, Z., Hou, Z., & Li, Y. (2022). Energy efficiency optimization based on digital twin workshops. *Academic Journal of Engineering and Technology Science*, *5*(13). Advance online publication. DOI: 10.25236/AJETS.2022.051303

Wang, X. (2024). Research on smart energy monitoring and management system based on digital twin technology. *Journal of Computer and Communications*, *12*(02), 109–115. DOI: 10.4236/jcc.2024.122007

Wu, J., Jangid, V. R., & Park, J. (2024). Digital twin for amputees: A bidirectional interaction modeling and prototype with convolutional neural network. *Proceedings of the Human Factors and Ergonomics Society Annual Meeting*, *68*(1), 1410–1416. DOI: 10.1177/10711813241261938

Yakovenko, Y., & Shaptala, R. (2024). Study of digital twins as the driving force of digital transformation and achieving the goals of sustainable development. *Technology Audit and Production Reserves*, *2*(4(76)), 11–20. DOI: 10.15587/2706-5448.2024.301423

Yang, B., Lv, Z., & Wang, F. (2022). Digital twins for intelligent green buildings. *Buildings (Basel, Switzerland)*, *12*(6), 856. DOI: 10.3390/buildings12060856

Yu, P., Wen, Z., Guo, Y., Tai, N., & Jun, W. (2023). Application prospect and key technologies of digital twin technology in the integrated port energy system. *Frontiers in Energy Research*, *10*, 1044978. Advance online publication. DOI: 10.3389/fenrg.2022.1044978

Yun, J., Kim, S., & Kim, J. (2024). Digital twin technology in the gas industry: A comparative simulation study. *Sustainability (Basel)*, *16*(14), 5864. DOI: 10.3390/su16145864

Zaidi, S. M. R., Alam, A., & Khan, M. Y. (2024). Enhancing efficiency in advanced manufacturing through iot integration. *Engineering Headway*, *11*, 55–61. DOI: 10.4028/p-4HbPGf

Zhang, E., Feng, W., Jia, Z., Yang, L., & Chen, Y. (2024). *A study on the construction technology of 3d model for factories oriented at digital twin*. Advances in Transdisciplinary Engineering., DOI: 10.3233/ATDE240394

Zhang, K., Wu, Q., Li, H., Zhang, R., Li, J., Jiang, F., & Liu, L. (2023). Intelligent optimal control strategy of heat pump system based on digital twins. *Journal of Physics: Conference Series*, *2452*(1), 012029. DOI: 10.1088/1742-6596/2452/1/012029

Zhang, X., Liu, X., Song, Y., Li, X., Huang, W., Zhou, Y., & Liu, S. (2024). Digital-twin-driven intelligent insulated-gate bipolar transistor production lines. *Sensors (Basel)*, *24*(2), 612. DOI: 10.3390/s24020612 PMID: 38257704

Zhang, Z., Wei, Z., Court, S., Yang, L., Wang, S., Thirunavukarasu, A., & Zhao, Y. (2024). A review of digital twin technologies for enhanced sustainability in the construction industry. *Buildings (Basel, Switzerland)*, *14*(4), 1113. DOI: 10.3390/buildings14041113

Zhang, Z., Wei, Z., Court, S., Yang, L., Wang, S., Thirunavukarasu, A., & Zhao, Y. (2024). A review of digital twin technologies for enhanced sustainability in the construction industry. *Buildings (Basel, Switzerland), 14*(4), 1113. DOI: 10.3390/buildings14041113

Zhao, Y., Wang, N., Liu, Z., & Mu, E. (2022). Construction theory for a building intelligent operation and maintenance system based on digital twins and machine learning. *Buildings (Basel, Switzerland), 12*(2), 87. DOI: 10.3390/buildings12020087

Zhu, J., Yang, Y., Zhang, H., Zhao, Z., Hu, T., & Liu, L. (2023). More than energy harvesting in electret electronics-moving toward the next-generation functional system. *Advanced Functional Materials, 33*(17), 2214859. Advance online publication. DOI: 10.1002/adfm.202214859

Chapter 3

The Role of Digital Twin in Computational Engineering and Industry 5.0 for Sustainable Development

Bindiya Jain
https://orcid.org/0000-0002-7377-2322
Poornima University, Jaipur, India

Basudha Dewan
Poornima University, India

Mohammed Amin Almaiah
The University of Jordan, Amman, Jordan

ABSTRACT

Digital twin compute equations and advanced data analytics play an important role in enhancing complex engineering processes. This paper emphasizes the impact of digital twin on computational engineering in every field with a significant role in sustainable development. This predictive capability not only enhances the efficiency of engineering design but also contributes to minimizing the environmental footprint of projects. The interaction between digital twin and computational engineering is for smart infrastructure and strong systems. This paper examines digital twin models of monitoring and control systems that enhance the adaptability and responsiveness of infrastructure, ensuring sustainable operation and maintenance. The digital twin has been successfully applied in computational engineering to design and optimize structures, systems, and processes with sustainability in mind. Researchers explore the potential for interdisciplinary collaboration between digital twin researchers, engineers, and sustainability experts to address global challenges with innovative solutions.

DOI: 10.4018/979-8-3373-2028-1.ch003

INTRODUCTION

The goal of developing practical solutions that benefit society and new era of innovation with deep implications for sustainable development. The integration of digital twin and computational engineering has challenges related to resource, environmental degradation, and the need for strong infrastructure. All engineering task focused on model, simulation, and maximum optimization has to found a powerful supporter in digital twin. This paper aims to explore the dynamic role of digital twin in Computational Engineering and its contributions to the main goal of sustainable development. Technology evolves rapidly, and engineers involves in new developments in their field. Lifelong learning is a crucial aspect of a career in major branches of engineering include Civil, Mechanical, Electrical, Chemical, Aerospace, Biomedical Engineering etc. digital twin models are enhancing the efficiency of engineering processes, and maximum try to mitigated the environmental negative impact. Approx 23 to 25 paper for resent year study and find computational engineering applied in every branch with different concept. All digital twin models linear and logistic regression, SVM method, decision tree, deep learning concept and natural language processing will work and find predicted results and make new business insights. In this paper researcher discuss about engineering, computational engineering, digital twin models and their applications of all types. These decisions make intelligent and save environment. Sustainable environment and different engineering methods predict the results, analysis the data for sustainability. Digital Twin ML-Projects-master, Machine-Learning-Projects-main, and ml-datasets-master many more datasets proved that digital twin models are applicable in all kind of engineering.

LITERATURE REVIEW

Computational Engineering- **R. Souza et al. (2019, November).** The great range of data, scientific knowledge, instruments, and workflows all contribute to the complexity of the machine learning lifecycle. The primary drawback of source tracking solutions is their inability to handle provenance capture overhead while handling source capture and integration of domain and machine learning data processed in the various workflows throughout the lifecycle. To address the peculiarities of ML and CSE, a new source data format known as PROV-ML and extensions to a system that tracks origin from many processes are implemented. This enables source queries with a consistent vocabulary. We demonstrate a useful application in an actual industry situation and evaluate it utilising Computational Science and Engineering, Workflow Provenance, and Machine Learning Lifecycle. **G.Al-Kharusi et al. (2022)** The variables that need to be tuned and forecast the sand structural as well as performance results of a specific physical and chemical activity. This application in the areas of biomaterials and tissue engineering has been discovered recently. Design of Experiment approach is different in the tissue engineering applications. The processes of 3D bioprinting are much for tissue-engineered construct fabrication. The review shows what is possible and considers the possibility of uniting design of engineering and machine learning into one system that would offer possibilities.

Digital Twin Models: S.S.Gill et al. (2022) The principles of control theory for closed and open-loop systems have had a significant impact on autonomous computing. Despite studies on autonomous models for the management of computer resources, from standalone web servers to a data centre's worth of resources. One of the main challenges in research is how to combine machine learning (ML) with digital twin to increase resource autonomy and performance at scale. We talk about the difficulties and possibilities of using digital twin and ML in next-generation computing for upcoming computing paradigms, such as serverless, cloud, fog, edge, and quantum computing settings. **M.Frank et al. (2020)** Computing, data mining, and processing are examples of natural sciences and engineering. Model quality and speed are both increased by using ML. The quality of computational fluid dynamics, molecular dynamics, and structural analysis simulation tools. More responsive and lifelike virtual reality apps have been made thanks to machine learning.

Engineering: J. Naranjo-Pérez et al. (2020). The process of numerically simulating already-existing civil engineering structures and modifying the numerical response to the structure's observed experimental behaviour. In order to handle such optimisation problems, meta heuristic optimisation techniques are typically used due to the complex nonlinear behaviour of the generated goal functions. High simulation is needed to calculate the issue and is related to choosing the most updated model. Our proposal's implementation specifics are covered in great length throughout the paper, and a case study that addresses the model updating of an actual steel footbridge is used to demonstrate how well it works. H.G. MELHEM et al. (1996) Acquiring knowledge on its own is an extremely laborious and time-consuming task. Numerous machine learning techniques have been created and are backed by well-established theories and algorithms. The methods presented fall into one of two categories: learning from examples, which includes the ID3 algorithm, learning from observation, also known as conceptual clustering, which includes the PROTOS algorithm, and rough sets theory, or a mix of both.

Sustainable Development: **V. Bhatnagar et. al (2021, March)** The way systems are modelled and operated on allows for the economical use of materials and resources. There are many uses for machine learning in daily life as well as in the fields of healthcare, agriculture, and security. The application of supervised and unsupervised machine algorithms is carried out in sustainable engineering fields, covering mechanical, civil, and chemical engineering. Working on sustainable engineering requires the use of particular machine learning methods. Engineers working in the field of sustainable development will find this review useful. **B.Manzoor et al. (2021).** the primary determinants of sustainability in civil engineering across all other nations are interconnectedness, functionality, unpredictability, and individuality. the corpus of knowledge in civil engineering by identifying key research objectives, journals, and nations, as well as by illustrating and understanding trends and patterns. Furthermore, a theoretical framework for future scholars and researchers has been suggested in light of the findings. The use of digital technologies is helping to reroute the construction trend towards sustainability.

METHODOLOGY

Computational Engineering provide us various compute method. These methods are used in different areas and predict results. First understand the word engineering, computational engineering, and digital twin models. In this paper researcher do comparative study about 25 to 30 research papers and find the concept of all different type of engineering where digital twin model is applied. Particular engineering has multiple application and concept are used in basic fields. Researcher study all types of engineering and these applications. So, that we can find which algorithm we use toward solve any problem. digital twin models are based on algorithm, variable (dependant and independent), computational formulas, assumptions and predict result. These outcomes and results are tested again. If the result is fruitfully for society and enhance sustainability. Sustain word apply every area of life aspects and all AI concept are directly connected with human beings.

Researcher divide this paper in two folds. First analysis some specific engineering like Structural and civil, aerospace, nuclear and biomedical engineering. Different applications are available where digital twin &ML models are computer to find better results with low computational cost. Second, If the application and digital twin model predict the fruitful output then other related application are also checked by given data source. Researcher find some datasets regarding different computation engineering, predict the output. After predicting the results, find sustainable ratio. Final goal of researcher that digital twin models are sustainable. The goal is to assess the sustainability of digital twin models across different applications within engineering disciplines. Identification of sustainability criteria define relevant work towards the engineering applications being studied, include factors such as environmental impact, social equity, economic viability, and resource efficiency. Develop quantitative measures to assess the sustainability performance of digital twin models within each engineering domain involve metrics such as energy consumption, carbon emissions, waste generation, and social impact. The research papers and datasets related to the digital twin applications in different engineering fields. This data should include both input variables (independent) and output variables (dependent) used in the computational models. Analyse the sustainability performance of digital twin models across different engineering applications using the collected data. Compare the outcomes and results predicted by these models against the defined sustainability criteria. Calculation of Sustainability Index scoring system to quantitatively evaluate the sustainability of digital twin models in each engineering domain. This index should consider the overall impact of the models on environmental, social, and economic sustainability. Validate the sustainability index by testing its applicability to a diverse range of engineering applications. The sustainability index into the comparative study of digital twin applications in different engineering fields. The comparative study and sustainability analysis sanctions for enhancing the sustainability of digital twin models in engineering practice and research.

ENGINEERING

Engineering word was made by word engine. Small parts were combined and make a machine which produce energy, data and any outcome. These machines are run with skilled person those are called engineer. In a broad way engineering, which is a field involves the submission of scientific values, calculation, and observed evidence to plan, generate, maintain, & improve constructions, systems, devices, or processes. Engineers use information and skills to address real-world complications and challenges, with the goal of developing practical solutions that benefit society. Product Development Cycles Engineering collaborates multiple disciplines like physics, chemistry, biology, computer science, and environmental science to address complex problems. There are many major branches of engineering include civil, mechanical, electrical, chemical, aerospace, biomedical engineering. Civil engineering centres on the planning and building of essential infrastructure like buildings, bridges, roads, and water supply systems, while mechanical and electrical engineering involve the design and production of machinery, power systems, telecommunications, electronics, and thermal systems. Aerospace Engineering is design and development of aircraft, spacecraft, and related systems. Biomedical Engineering have principles of biological and medical sciences to develop technologies and solutions for healthcare. Engineering is a field which needs continues to evolve, adapting to new challenges and opportunities presented by advancements in science and technology.

COMPUTATIONAL ENGINEERING

Computational is based on compute word. Compute means calculations, equations, graph, algorithm, model, analysis and result. Engineering means creating things in systematic manner. All things which we use in our daily life are example of engineering. We combine these two words compute and engineering is called computational engineering. The computational engineering application has numerical methods, algorithms, and computer simulations to solve engineering problems. It integrates principles from engineering, and applied mathematics to analyse, model, and simulate complex systems and simulations. Traditional experimental and analytical approaches with computational power of computers to simulate and analyse engineering designs and systems. Models and simulations mean studying the work and predicts the result. Computational techniques to improve product development cycles engineering designs and processes, considering various parameters and constraints to achieve the best performance. Real-world systems using computational tools and techniques which extracting meaningful insights to inform decision-making. Computation and integrating with different engineering disciplines and analysing their interactions have holistic understanding of complex systems. Digital twin and machine learning techniques to enhance the capabilities of computational models, improve predictions, and automate decision-making processes. Computational engineering plays a crucial role in designing, optimizing, and understanding complex systems, contributing to advancements in technology and sustainable development.

DIGITAL TWIN ROLE IN ADVANCING COMPUTATIONAL ENGINEERING AND INDUSTRY 5.0

Digital Twin role in advancing computational engineering and Industry 5.0 integrated into these fields and its impact on sustainability. Digital Twin enhances the accuracy and efficiency of imitations used in computational engineering, allowing for more exact prediction. Digital Twin driven models can simulate complex systems, reducing the need for physical models. Engineering designs in structural engineering, aerospace, and automotive industries by exploring vast parameter spaces and identifying the most efficient and sustainable solutions. AI algorithms analyse data from devices and historical maintenance records to predict equipment failures before they occur. This proactive method minimizes idle time and reduces waste by ensuring that machinery operates efficiently. Digital Twin helps in managing the entire lifecycle of product development cycles engineering products, from design and production to maintenance and end-of-life disposal, ensuring that each stage is optimized for sustainability. Computational engineering, like data and basic analysis, freeing up engineers to focus on more multifaceted and innovative aspects of their projects. Enhanced Decision-Making digital twin provides engineers with advanced decision-support tools that can analyse vast quantities of data in real time, leading to more informed and sustainable engineering decisions.

DIGITAL TWIN BASED MANUFACTURING WITH INDUSTRY 5.0

Human based Manufacturing like Robots enhancing productivity, can perform dangerous and repetitive tasks, allowing humans to focus on more creative and strategic activities ensuring safety. These models customization by analysing consumer preferences and automating the production of personalized products. Customized model reduces waste and promotes the efficient use of materials. Supply chain logistics predicting demand, routes, and managing inventory. Digital Twin based tracking and managing resources in supply chain inventory, ensuring efficient use of raw materials and minimizing waste. Recycling and Reuse materials enhancing recycling processes and promoting a circular economy product development cycle. Digital Twin analyses production processes to identify areas where waste can be reduced, promoting more sustainable manufacturing practices. Reduced carbon footprint, energy management systems, leading to more efficient energy use and reduced greenhouse gas emissions. Improved efficiency, reduced waste, cost savings for businesses which promote economic sustainability. Digital Twin drives innovation, develop new sustainable products and services that can compete in the global market. Digital Twin is a transformative strength in computational engineering with Industry 5.0 and advancements in sustainability. Its ability to optimize processes, predict outcomes, and enhance decision-making contributes to more efficient use of resources, reduced environmental impact, and economic growth, thereby supporting the goals of sustainable development.

DIGITAL TWIN / ML Model

Digital twin was developed in computer systems which can perform tasks like human intelligence. This intelligence arises by learning from previous experience and results. Digital Twin can learn, understand, recognizing, solving problems, and making decisions. Digital twin, machine learning stands as a subset dedicated to crafting algorithms and models. Digital twin empowers computers to discern patterns, enabling them to make predictions or decisions through the analysis of data and the recognition of future objectives. Various technologies leverage model creation across a multitude of applications.

Deep learning is involving neural networks which is similar like neuron of human being. Neuron are very powerful and high-speed mechanism. This concept is used in machine and make a model to solve application in machine learning, where models are crafted to address challenges in image & language recognition. (NLP) empowers computers to comprehend, interpret, and generate human language, encompassing tasks like language translation, sentiment analysis, and facilitating chatbot interactions. Computer revelation enables machines to interpret and comprehend visual information from the world, including images and videos. Applications of computer vision span diverse areas, including facial recognition, object detection, and the implementation of computer vision concepts in autonomous vehicles. This integration entails merging sensory perception with decision-making capabilities to enable autonomous navigation and manipulation. Expert systems, rooted in artificial intelligence (AI), emulate the decision-making process of a human expert within a designated domain. Drawing upon rules and knowledge bases, these systems make informed decisions. The applications of digital twin are extensive, reaching across diverse industries such as healthcare, finance, education, transportation, and entertainment. Examples include virtual personal assistants, recommendation systems, fraud detection, medical diagnosis, and self-driving cars.

These all concepts are involving when we create models on digital twin model. Commence by thoroughly understanding the problem, followed by the particular collection and preparation of data. After, engage in training and testing the model, where cleaning and preprocessing steps ensure data integrity by addressing missing values, outliers, and maintaining a suitable format. Enhance model robustness by partitioning the dataset into training, validation, and test sets. The training set facilitates model learning, the validation set aids in hyperparameter tuning, and the test set assesses the model's generalization to new data. Employ the test set to strictly evaluate the model's performance on previously unseen data. When selecting a machine learning algorithm or model architecture, consider the problem's nature; common choices encompass decision trees, support vector machines, neural networks, among others. Evaluate the model with different type of methods like accuracy, precision, recall, F1 score for classification, mean squared error, means absolute error for regression etc. Deployment the mode is meets performance and production environment.

COMPUTATIONAL ENGINEERING USE AL/ML MODEL

Digital twin models are more and more being integrated into various product development cycles engineering disciplines to enhance efficiency, accuracy, and decision-making.

Structural and Civil Engineering with digital twin Model and Analyse Sustainable Effect

Civil engineers work in structural components of buildings roads, bridges, canals, dams, airports, sewage systems, pipelines, and railways constitute crucial components of infrastructure development. They need accurate, cheaper, and different construction projects. To make modern structure artificial intelligence is utilised to plan, build, estimate the amount, effect of changes in the systems. Different health care projects are also analysed by AI and ML models with sensor.

Table 1. Application of Civil Engineering Using Digital Twin Model and Analyse Sustainable Effect.

S. No.	Name Of Project	DIGITAL TWIN AND AI Model	Work of model	Sustainability Effect
1	Structural Health Monitoring	Neural Networks	Structural Engineering on health and sensor data & detect anomalies	Enhances the durability of structures by predicting maintenance needs, reducing failure
2	Predictive Maintenance	Random Forest	based on historical data, minimizing downtime and optimizing resource allocation	extends the lifespan of infrastructure, reducing the need for frequent repairs
3	Construction Project Management	Genetic Algorithms	project scheduling, resource allocation, and risk management to enhance efficiency	project scheduling, resource allocation, and risk management to enhance efficiency
4	Design Optimization	Genetic Algorithms	Maximum use of enhance design processes by considering multiple parameters	Improves designs, considering materials and energy usage, promoting environmentally friendly and resource-efficient construction
5	Traffic Management and Optimization	Deep Q Networks (DQN), Reinforcement Learning	analyse traffic patterns, optimize signal timings and improve overall traffic flow	Improves traffic flow, reducing fuel consumption and emissions, contributing to sustainable urban mobility

continued on following page

Table 1. Continued

S. No.	Name Of Project	DIGITAL TWIN AND AI Model	Work of model	Sustainability Effect
6	Geotechnical Engineering	Decision Trees, K-Nearest Neighbours (KNN)	Soil type, subsurface conditions	foundation designs, ensuring stability, minimizing environmental impact
7	Energy Efficiency in Buildings	Clustering, Principal Component Analysis (PCA)	energy efficiency by analysing usage patterns of building	Optimum energy usage, reducing overall energy consumption, environmental impact
8	Water Resource Management	Time Series Analysis, Bayesian Networks	water distribution systems, predict water demand, and manage water quality	water distribution, reduces water waste, and ensures sustainable management of water resources
9	Risk Assessment	Decision Trees	mitigate risks in construction projects	Minimizes risks in construction projects, stopping costly rework and ensuring sustainable project outcomes
10	Automated Inspection.	Convolutional Neural Networks.	automate inspections using computer vision, drones, or robots for increased accuracy.	Enhances inspection accuracy, reducing the chance of missed defects and minimizing resource thorough manual inspections.

AEROSPACE ENGINEERING WITH DIGITAL TWINMODEL AND ANALYSE SUSTAINABLE EFFECT

Aerospace engineering includes the progression involves designing, developing, testing, and ultimately producing the desired outcome. and spacecraft. The application of digital twin and ML in aerospace engineering has become increasingly prominent, offering solutions to enhance efficiency, safety, and sustainability. Here are some applications along with Digital Twin /ML model names and associated sustainability properties.

Table 2. Application of Aerospace Engineering Using Digital Twin Model and Analyse Sustainable Effect.

S. No.	Name Of Project	DIGITAL TWIN / AI Model	Work of model	Sustainability Effect
1	Flight Control Systems	Adaptive Control Systems, and SVM	real-time data, weather conditions, and flight parameters	Improved fuel efficiency, reduced ghg emissions
2	Air Traffic Management	Multi-Agent Systems, Neural Networks	air traffic routes, improved airspace management, and reduced congestion at airports.	Reduced fuel consumption and emissions greenhouse gas
3	Space Mission Planning	Genetic Algorithms, Reinforcement Learning	space exploration missions, maximum use of flights	Enhanced efficiency and resource utilization, minimizing energy consumption
4	Energy Harvesting in Space	Predictive Analytics	energy collecting from solar panels and other sources, ensuring efficient power generation for spacecraft.	Improved sustainability in space missions use renewable energy like solar and wind energy

BIOMEDICAL ENGINEERING WITH DIGITAL TWINMODEL AND ANALYSE SUSTAINABLE EFFECT

Applying engineering principles and methodologies to the realms of biology and healthcare defines the scope of biomedical engineering. The integration of digital twin and ML in biomedical engineering has led to innovative solutions for medical diagnosis, treatment, and healthcare management. Here are some applications along with Digital Twin/ML model names and associated sustainability properties.

Table 3. Application of Biomedical Engineering Using Digital Twin Model and Analyse Sustainable Effect. Source self-created.

S. No.	Name Of Project	DIGITAL TWIN / AI Model	Work of model	Sustainability Effect
1	Medical Imaging Diagnosis	Convolutional Neural Networks (CNNs)	diagnostic accuracy, medical imaging procedures, decreased radiation	Improved diagnostic accuracy, reduced medical imaging procedures, and radiation exposure and sustainable healthcare
2	Drug Discovery and Development	Reinforcement Learning	drug discovery processes, laboratory testing	reducing extensive laboratory testing and experimentation, development of more sustainable and efficient pharmaceuticals
3	Rehabilitation Robotics	Reinforcement Learning	robotic therapies, patient mobility	Enhanced rehabilitation outcomes, improving patient mobility
4	Digital Health Platforms	(NLP), M. Learning for Predictive Analytics	patient engagement, reduced healthcare	Enhanced patient engagement, improved health outcomes, and reduced healthcare costs
5	Healthcare Predictive Analytics	Random Forest, Logistic Regression	healthcare resource allocation	reduced healthcare costs, hospital resource utilization, and minimizing unnecessary procedures.

NUCLEAR ENGINEERING WITH DIGITAL TWIN MODEL AND ANALYSE

Sustainable Effect

Nuclear engineering involves the application of nuclear reactions for energy production, medical purposes, and other applications. Here are some applications of nuclear engineering using DIGITAL TWIN/ML models, along with associated model names and potential sustainability.

Table 4. Application of Nuclear Engineering Using Digital Twin Model and Analyse Sustainable Effect.

S. No.	Name Of Project	DIGITAL TWIN / AI Model	Work of model	Sustainability Effect
1	Nuclear Power Plant Operations	Recurrent Neural Networks (RNNs)	fault detection, operational parameters in nuclear power plants, predict equipment failures, enhance plant efficiency, safe and reliable operation of nuclear reactors	nuclear power plant operations, improving efficiency, safety, and minimizing environmental impact by reducing operational errors
2	Radiation Dose Optimization	Reinforcement Learning	Maximum radiation therapy doses in medical applications, treatment outcomes to personalize radiation doses, overall efficacy of cancer treatments	radiation therapy doses in medical applications, reducing unnecessary exposure and minimizing side effects for patients
3	Reactor Design Optimization	Genetic Algorithms, Neural Networks	safety, efficiency, and environmental impact, helping engineers develop reactor configurations that maximize energy, minimizing the risk of accidents	reactor designs for safety, efficiency, and reduced environmental impact, contributing to sustainable nuclear energy production
4	Fuel Cycle management	Markov Chain Monte Carlo Methods	simulate complex processes involved in fuel production, consumption, and waste generation	the nuclear fuel cycle, minimizing waste generation and maximizing resource utilization
5	Safety, Waste Monitoring	Support Vector Machines, Genetic Algorithms	geological characteristics, environmental impact, and containment methods	monitoring and predicting potential safety issues, reducing the chance of accidents and minimizing environmental risks, waste disposal strategies, ensuring safe containment and minimizing long-term environmental impact

APPLICATION OF OTHER ENGINEERING USING DIGITAL TWINMODEL AND ANALYSE SUSTAINABLE EFFECT

Environmental Engineering air and water quality monitoring models analyse environmental data to monitor and predict changes in air and water quality. Industrial Engineering ML models optimize supply chain processes, forecasting demand, and improving logistics. The automation of industrial processes, improving efficiency and reducing human intervention. Materials Engineering analyse material properties, testing and quality control processes to predict and discover new materials with specific characteristics. Software Engineering models assist in automated testing processes, identifying potential issues and improving software quality improving performance and efficiency in software applications.

Table 5. Name of the engineering and no of application using AI &ML models.

S. No.	Name of Engineering	Number Of Applications Where Digital Twin Models are applied.
1	Structural or civil Engineering	10
2	Nuclear Engineering	5
3	Biomedical Engineering	3
4	Aerospace Engineering	4

continued on following page

Table 5. Continued

S. No.	Name of Engineering	Number Of Applications Where Digital Twin Models are applied.
5	Environmental Engineering	7
6	Industrial Engineering	8

Environmental Engineering air and water quality monitoring models analyse environmental data to monitor and predict changes in air and water quality. Industrial Engineering ML models optimize supply chain processes, forecasting demand, and improving logistics. The automation of industrial processes, improving efficiency and reducing human intervention. Materials Engineering analyse material properties, testing and quality control processes to predict and discover new materials with specific characteristics. Software Engineering models assist in automated testing processes, identifying potential issues and improving software quality improving performance and efficiency in software applications.

Digital Twin and ML models are applied across engineering disciplines to solve diverse problems, ranging from optimizing processes and predicting maintenance needs to enhancing design and discovery processes. The integration of digital twin and ML allows engineers to make data-driven decisions, automate tasks, and unlock new possibilities in various fields of engineering.

DEFINE WORK OF THIS PAPER BY RESEARCHER

The pivotal role of digital twin and ML algorithms in computational engineering, emphasizing their impact on sustainable development across various fields. The unique aspects of this paper include interdisciplinary collaboration emphasis in underscores the potential for collaboration between digital twin researchers, engineers, and sustainability experts to address global challenges. It highlights the importance of innovative solutions derived from such collaborations. Because sustainable operation has explored how digital twin enhance the adaptability and responsiveness of infrastructure for sustainable operation and maintenance. Full coverage of digital twin models including linear and logistic regression, SVM, decision trees, deep learning, and natural language processing. It showcases the versatility of these models in different engineering applications and lifelong learning for engineers. The dynamic nature of the engineering field and the need for continuous skill development. Researcher focused on the paper comprehensive overview of the intersection between Digital Twin & ML, computational engineering, and sustainable development while emphasizing collaboration, innovation, and practical application.

Table 6. Indexes Like Sustainability Performance of Leading Companies Worldwide

GLOBAL REPORTING INITIATIVE (GRI)	ENVIRONMENTAL, SOCIAL, AND GOVERNANCE (ESG)	DJSI and FTSE4Good
A framework for sustainability reporting	Analysis a company carbon footprint	Identifying potential risks
organizations collect, analyse, and report data	Sustainable investment decisions	Opportunities related to sustainability
identify trends, generate reports maintain GRI standards.	Governance policies and practices	Maximum use of Resource
	Real-time insights into ESG factors	Supply Chain Sustainability

FUTURE IMPLICATION

The future implications of integrating digital twin into computational engineering for sustainable development and corporate responsibility standards are vast and impactful. digital twin will drive innovations in sustainability by enabling more precise and efficient solutions. This includes the development of smart grids, energy-efficient technologies, and sustainable materials through advanced computational engineering. Companies may deploy digital twin-driven platforms that continuously monitor, adapt, and optimize sustainability practices without constant human intervention.

Global Collaboration and Standardization methods for measuring and reporting sustainability metrics. This can lead to the development of universally accepted standards, making it easier for companies to compare and benchmark their performance on a global scale. ESG attentions will play an even important role in investment decisions. AI-powered algorithms will be used to analyse vast amounts of ESG data, helping investors make informed decisions that align with their sustainability goals. Ethical AI practices will ensure that technology benefits society as a whole and minimizes negative ecofriendly and social impacts. Computational engineering for sustainable development involves a transformative shift towards more efficient, adaptive, and inclusive sustainability practices. As technology evolves, it will play a pivotal role in addressing global challenges and advancing the collective efforts towards a more sustainable and responsible future.

RESULT AND FINDINGS

Figure 1. Digital Twin in Computational Engineering & Industry 5.0 for Sustainability

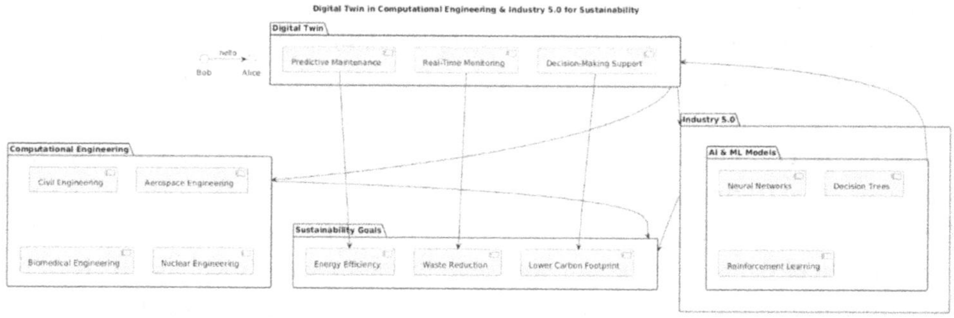

The Digital Twin framework in Computational Engineering and Industry 5.0 for Sustainability is made up of several consistent elements. The Digital Twin contains Predictive Maintenance, Real-Time Monitoring, & Decision-Making Support, provide better operational efficiency and intelligent decision-making. It is closely related to Computational Engineering, covers a wide range of disciplines including Civil, Aerospace, Biomedical, and Nuclear Engineering, making it possible to perform complex simulations and process optimizations. The Digital Twin also incorporates Industry 5.0, especially digital twin & ML models Neural Networks, Decision tree and Reinforcement Learning, in order to increase automation and intelligence. In addition, both Computational Engineering and Industry 5.0 contribute towards Sustainability Goals through Energy Efficiency, Waste Reduction, and Lower Carbon Footprint. Digital & ML models enhance the digital twin, while specific functionalities analytical maintenance,

Real-Time Intensive care, and Decision-Making Support bring into line with sustainability objectives by improving energy efficiency, reducing waste, and minimizing carbon footprints.

LIMITATION AND CONCLUSION

Complex AI models have a challenge. Bias means double sense data. Digital Twin systems heavily based on data which can be biased or poor quality the effectiveness of sustainability initiatives. Understanding decisions is crucial for gaining trust and ensuring that sustainability practices. The implementing digital twin systems for sustainability can be significant. It may be a block for smaller businesses or governments with partial resources. Digital Twin can analyse historical data and identify patterns to predict future sustainability trends. This capability helps companies proactively address emerging challenges and align their strategies with evolving sustainability expectations. Digital Twin-powered systems can continuously monitor and assess a company's sustainability performance. Coming future digital twin in workable development is continued advancements in technology with an ethical and responsible digital twin practice. It can contribute to a more sustainable and robust global collaboration between humans, technology, and regulatory bodies is essential to join the full possible of digital twin for the advantage of both businesses and the broader humanity in achieving sustainable development goals.

REFERENCES

Al-Kharusi, G., Dunne, N. J., Little, S., & Levingstone, T. J. (2022). The role of machine learning and design of experiments in the advancement of biomaterial and tissue engineering research. *Bioengineering (Basel, Switzerland)*, *9*(10), 561. DOI: 10.3390/bioengineering9100561 PMID: 36290529

Amann, J., Blasimme, A., Vayena, E., Frey, D., & Madai, V. I. (2020). Explainability for artificial intelligence in healthcare: A multidisciplinary perspective. *BMC Medical Informatics and Decision Making*, *20*(1), 1–9. DOI: 10.1186/s12911-020-01332-6 PMID: 33256715

Anandakumar, H., Arulmurugan, R., & Onn, C. C. (2019). *Computational intelligence and sustainable systems*. EAI/Springer Innovations in Communication and Computing. DOI: 10.1007/978-3-030-02674-5

Belsare, T., Deshpande, A., Sharma, N., & De, P. (2023). Application of k-Means Method for Finding Varying Groups of Primary Energy Household Emissions in the Indian States. Optimization Techniques in Engineering: Advances and Applications, 393-408.D. Patterson et al. (2021) Carbon emissions and large neural network training. arXiv preprint arXiv:2104.10350.

Busu, M., & Nedelcu, A. C. (2021). Analyzing the renewable energy and CO2 emission levels nexus at an EU level: A panel data regression approach. *Processes (Basel, Switzerland)*, *9*(1), 130.

Chadha, A. S., Shinde, Y., Sharma, N., & De, P. K. (2022, January). Predicting CO2 Emissions by Vehicles Using Machine Learning. In International Conference on Data Management, Analytics & Innovation (pp. 197-207). Singapore: Springer Nature Singapore.

Chih-Lin, I. (2021). AI as an Essential Element of a Green 6G. *IEEE Transactions on Green Communications and Networking*, *5*(1), 1–3. DOI: 10.1109/TGCN.2021.3057247

Deshpande, A., Belsare, T., Sharma, N., & De, P. (2022, April). Univariate Time Series Forecasting of Indian Agriculture Emissions. In *International Conference on Advances in Computing and Data Sciences* (pp. 346-358). Cham: Springer International Publishing. DOI: 10.1007/978-3-031-12641-3_28

Esteban, M., Diez, J. J., López, J. S., & Negro, V. (2011). Why offshore wind energy. *Renewable Energy*, *36*(2), 444–450. DOI: 10.1016/j.renene.2010.07.009

Frank, M., Drikakis, D., & Charissis, V. (2020). Machine-learning methods for computational science and engineering. *Computation (Basel, Switzerland)*, *8*(1), 15. DOI: 10.3390/computation8010015

Gill, S. S., Xu, M., Ottaviani, C., Patros, P., Bahsoon, R., Shaghaghi, A., Golec, M., Stankovski, V., Wu, H., Abraham, A., Singh, M., Mehta, H., Ghosh, S. K., Baker, T., Parlikad, A. K., Lutfiyya, H., Kanhere, S. S., Sakellariou, R., Dustdar, S., & Uhlig, S. (2022). AI for next generation computing: Emerging trends and future directions. *Internet of Things : Engineering Cyber Physical Human Systems*, *19*, 100514. DOI: 10.1016/j.iot.2022.100514

Helsen, L. (2021). Tackling Climate Change with Machine Learning. In Conference on Neural Information Processing System (NeurIPS)-panelist workshop, Location: online.

Jain, B., Sharma, R., & Kaushik, N. (2022). An Analysis Of Green Artificial Intelligence As A Major Receiver Improvement Finalized Red Ai & Execution Of The Environmental Footprint Toward Increasing Green Artificial Intelligence. *NeuroQuantology : An Interdisciplinary Journal of Neuroscience and Quantum Physics*, *20*(17), 1733.

Jain, B., & Sharma, S. Examining Environmental, Social, and Economic Sustainability in Diverse AI/ML Models: A Comparative Study.

Kapoor, R., & Ghosal, I. (2022). Will Artificial Intelligence Compliment or Supplement Human Workforce in Organizations? A Shift to a Collaborative Human – Machine Environment. [IJRTBT]. *International Journal on Recent Trends in Business and Tourism*, *6*(4), 19–28. DOI: 10.31674/ijrtbt.2022.v06i04.002

Khandelwal, S., Sharma, N., & De, P. K. (2022, January). Real Time Carbon Emissions Calculator for Personal Computers. In International Conference on Data Management, Analytics & Innovation (pp. 651-663). Singapore: Springer Nature Singapore.

Manzoor, B., Othman, I., Durdyev, S., Ismail, S., & Wahab, M. H. (2021). Influence of artificial intelligence in civil engineering toward sustainable development—A systematic literature review. *Applied System Innovation*, *4*(3), 52. DOI: 10.3390/asi4030052

Melhem, H. G., & Nagaraja, S. (1996). Machine learning and its application to civil engineering systems. *Civil Engineering Systems*, *13*(4), 259–279. DOI: 10.1080/02630259608970203

Mohammed, Y.. (2012). A synopsis on the effects of anthropogenic greenhouse gases emissions from power generation and energy consumption. *International Journal of Scientific and Research Publications*, *2*(10), 1–6.

Naranjo-Pérez, J., Infantes, M., Jiménez-Alonso, J. F., & Sáez, A. (2020). A collaborative machine learning-optimization algorithm to improve the finite element model updating of civil engineering structures. *Engineering Structures*, *225*, 111327. DOI: 10.1016/j.engstruct.2020.111327

Nilsson-Lindén, H., Diedrich, A., & Baumann, H. (2021). Life cycle work: A process study of the emergence and performance of life cycle practice. *Organization & Environment*, *34*(1), 99–122. DOI: 10.1177/1086026619893971

V. Pashkov et al. (2020). Artificial intelligence in medical practice: regulative issues and perspectives.

Prasad, B., & Ghosal, I. (2022). Forecasting Buying Intention Through Artificial Neural Network: An Algorithmic Solution on Direct-to-Consumer Brands. *FIIB Business Review*, *11*(4), 405–421. DOI: 10.1177/23197145211046126

Rajkumar, D.. (2017). IoT based smart system for controlling Co2 emission. *Int. J. Sci. Res. Comput. Sci. Eng. Inf. Technol*, *2*(2), 284.

Rajkumar, D. M. N., Sruthi, M., & Kumar, D. V. V. (2017). IoT based smart system for controlling Co2 emission. *Int. J. Sci. Res. Comput. Sci. Eng. Inf. Technol*, *2*(2), 284.

Sood, A., Oza, H., Sharma, N., & De, P. K. (2022, January). Impact of Energy Sector on Climate Change in India Using Forecasting Models. In International Conference on Data Management, Analytics & Innovation (pp. 225-243). Singapore: Springer Nature Singapore.

Souza, R., Azevedo, L., Lourenço, V., Soares, E., Thiago, R., Brandão, R., . . . Netto, M. A. (2019, November). Provenance data in the machine learning lifecycle in computational science and engineering. In *2019 IEEE/ACM Workflows in Support of Large-Scale Science (WORKS)* (pp. 1-10). IEEE. DOI: 10.1109/WORKS49585.2019.00006

Toke, D. (2011). The UK offshore wind power programme: A sea-change in UK energy policy? *Energy Policy*, *39*(2), 526–534. DOI: 10.1016/j.enpol.2010.08.043

Tsang, S. W., & Jim, C. Y. (2016). Applying artificial intelligence modelling to optimize green roof irrigation. *Energy and Building*, *127*, 360–369. DOI: 10.1016/j.enbuild.2016.06.005

Vinuesa, R., Azizpour, H., Leite, I., Balaam, M., Dignum, V., Domisch, S., Felländer, A., Langhans, S. D., Tegmark, M., & Fuso Nerini, F. (2020). The role of artificial intelligence in achieving the Sustainable Development Goals. *Nature Communications*, *11*(1), 1–10. DOI: 10.1038/s41467-019-14108-y PMID: 31932590

Wolf, C. T. (2020). AI models and their worlds: Investigating data-driven, AI/ML ecosystems through a work practices lens. In *Sustainable Digital Communities: 15th International Conference, iConference 2020, Boras, Sweden, March 23–26, 2020* [Springer International Publishing.]. *Proceedings*, *15*, 651–664.

Zhang, W.. (2011). Lithium-based energy storage management for DC distributed renewable energy system. In *2011 IEEE Energy Conversion Congress and Exposition* (pp. 3270-3277). IEEE. DOI: 10.1109/ECCE.2011.6064210

Chapter 4
Virtual Reality (VR) and Augmented Reality (AR) Simulators for Medical Education

Indra Kishor
https://orcid.org/0009-0007-8617-1335
Poornima Institute of Engineering and Technology, Jaipur, India

Manvi Sharma
Prestige Institute of Engineering and Management, India

Anusha Preetham
Dayananda Sagar College of Engineering, India

Ankit Agarwal
https://orcid.org/0000-0003-0457-6421
Dr. Akhilesh Das Gupta Institute of Professional Studies, New Delhi, India

Udit Mamodiya
https://orcid.org/0000-0002-8022-4252
Poornima University, Jaipur, India

ABSTRACT

Medical education has shift with the immersive technologies like VR and AR that provide realistic and interactive learning. Although current VR/AR simulators have improved surgical training, anatomy visualization, and clinical decision-making, they do not provide real-time adaptive learning and multi-sensory feedback. A novel AI-enhanced VR/AR medical simulator combining real-time performance analysis, haptic feedback, and cloud collaboration to provide a learning environment for interactive and adaptive learning for medical students. It also provides haptic feedback integration with realistic surgical precision and procedure training. A prototype system of this type is implemented with emphasis on surgical simulation and emergency response training. Experimental evaluation of the system tests learning efficiency, error rate reduction, cognitive engagement, and haptic response accuracy against

DOI: 10.4018/979-8-3373-2028-1.ch004

traditional learning techniques. Early findings show that there is considerable gain in skill retention and efficiency of training by employing the AI-based VR/AR simulator methods.

1. INTRODUCTION

Medical education has been revolutionized over the last two decades from traditional textbook training to participatory and interactive modes of training. This change has predominantly been triggered by technology in general and, in particular, due to the innovations in Virtual Reality (VR) and Augmented Reality (AR) technologies. VR provides fully engaged simulated settings in order to support procedural practice being conducted normally within real-like situations, while AR superimposes digital information upon physical settings for improving procedural knowledge and precision within real-time training settings (Kriegel et al., 2022). Despite such advancements, present VR and AR-based medical training systems lack conspicuous shortcomings. Today's VR simulators are not realistic in providing haptic feedback and flexibility in learning environments and therefore restrict their practical application, particularly in surgical training and emergency response simulation. AR systems, despite their utility in visualization, are not equipped with the integration of seamless virtual-physical interaction and consequently lag behind in real-world application in sophisticated medical training (Ackerman & Smith, 2023)

Most existing simulators also are not integrated with sophisticated Artificial Intelligence (AI) and Machine Learning (ML) strategies and therefore do not benefit from real-time performance evaluation, adaptive personalized learning, and interactive multi-user functionality (Arkin & Murphy, 2022). Current literature indicates such deficiencies, and simulators as a means of offering individualized training in the form of AI-based adaptive feedback, complemented by realistic haptic feedback to enhance procedural accuracy (Patel & Desai, 2021). Although various research studies have failed to overcome such deficiencies individually, an interdisciplinary approach involving AI-based adaptive feedback, haptic feedback systems, and real-time immersive co-creation has yet to be attempted (Tian et al., 2022). Incorporating AI into VR and AR-based simulators adds features beyond traditional simulation training. Deep learning and reinforcement learning algorithms enable real-time tracking of user performance and customized feedback, revolutionizing skill acquisition and retention (Talaat et al., 2022). With rapidly accelerating artificial intelligence advancements, contemporary simulators not only recognize unique learning patterns, varying difficulty levels and training environments as a function of user skill and cognitive load but also provide highly adaptive learning mechanisms to maximize real-time learning. Such capabilities are especially useful in complex procedures like minimally invasive surgery, emergency procedures, and critical care scenarios where pressure decision-making is the essence. Integration of haptic technology has also been realized as central to ensuring maximum realism and effectiveness of medical training with VR (Moglia et al., 2022). Advanced haptic interfaces provide realistic tactile feedback to the user mimicking actual medical procedures, e.g., surgical incision, suturing, or injection technique, enhancing accuracy and procedural confidence among trainees (Sahoo & Choudhury, 2022). Despite such perceived benefits, literature reports wide variability in successfully integrating realistic tactile interaction with AI-adaptive learning in VR and AR medical simulators. Bridging such gaps effectively, the paper suggests an integrated framework using VR, AR, haptics, and AI-based adaptive learning mechanisms. By integrating real-world physical interactions using haptic technologies with intelligent, real-time adaptive feedback, proposed method significantly enhances conventional VR/AR training (Qureshi & Bashir, 2022). The system also enables cloud-based collaborative environments to enable geographically dispersed learners to engage in synchronous immersive medical training simulations, thus enabling collective learning experiences and access to training (Liu et al., 2022). This article is designed to provide an in-depth discussion of the design, deployment, and evaluation of this next-generation simulator with emphasis on its innovation and relative advantages over existing systems using sound scientific rationale and scenario-based field testing.

The union of AI with VR and AR-based simulators brings forth capabilities that surpass traditional simulation training. Deep learning and reinforcement learning algorithms enable real-time tracking of user performance and adaptive feedback, significantly enhancing learning of skills and retention (Sahoo & Choudhury, 2023). With rapid advances in artificial intelligence, simulators are now capable of sensing individual learning patterns, dynamically altering difficulty levels and training environments based on user skill and cognitive load. These features are most effective in complicated procedures such as minimally invasive surgery, emergency procedures, and critical care where stress decision-making is essential. Also, the addition of haptic technology has been observed to be crucial in optimizing realism and effectiveness of VR-based medical simulation. Sophisticated haptic interfaces deliver realistic haptic feedback of actual-world medical procedures such as surgical incisions, suturing, or injection methods, and increasing precision and procedural skills among students (Mele et al., 2022). Despite such ballyhooed benefits, current literature identifies a glaring deficiency of successful adoption of realistic haptic interaction and AI-based adaptive learning in VR and AR-based medical simulators (Kang & Lee, 2022). To fill these lacunae in an integrated manner, this paper suggests an integrated framework that includes VR, AR, haptics, and AI-based adaptive learning mechanisms. Through the convergence of realistic physical interactions using state-of-the-art haptic technology and smart, real-time adaptive feedback, the strategy laid out here enhances traditional VR/AR training significantly. The framework also offers cloud-based collaborative environments that allow geographically dispersed learners to interact in real-time in immersive medical training exercises, thus offering collaborative learning opportunities and widening accessibility of training (Saha & Rathore, 2023). This research paper is designed to present a thorough evaluation of the design, deployment, and verification of this next-generation simulator, emphasizing its novelty and comparative benefits over previous systems through stringent scientific validation and simulation testing with realistic scenarios. With this vision in mind, this research paper introduces a new integrated approach—a VR and AR-based AI-supported medical simulator. The proposed simulator combines sophisticated machine learning algorithms in order to provide personalized real-time evaluation and adaptive training protocols. It also combines high-fidelity haptic feedback modules in order to provide realistic simulative surgical touches and medical practices, significantly enhancing the quality as well as efficiency of training. In addition, based on cloud computing technology, this proposed simulator can provide collaborative medical tutelage beyond geographical boundaries, enabling professionals and students to interact in concurrent immersive environments. In order to detect the feasibility and usefulness of the developed simulator, a prototype has been implemented with special emphasis on surgical simulations and medical emergency simulation training. Comparison with traditional methods and previous simulators justifies the added capabilities of the developed system, thereby establishing enhanced learning of skills, minimization of errors, enhanced training speed, and enhanced mental engagement.

This study is a valuable contribution in bridging the researched gaps and developing a holistic, new approach of next-generation immersive simulator development for medical education.

2. LITERATURE REVIEW

Conventional teaching practices in the field of medicine, like learning using textbooks, dissection of cadavers, and clerkships under supervision, have been the backbone of clinical training for decades. These are, however, associated with several limitations like inability to simulate complex and dynamic medical situations and difficulties in ensuring standard, reproducible training opportunities. To address these limitations, teachers have increasingly used sophisticated technologies, especially Virtual Reality (VR) and Augmented Reality (AR), to provide interactive, immersive, and realistic training environments that simulate real-world medical situations closely (Asadzadeh et al., 2020). VR technologies have gained extensive use in medical training because they can offer immersive, interactive simulations that allow for increased cognitive engagement, procedural learning, and error minimization (Suresh Kumar & Krishnamoorthi, 2021). VR simulators provide life-like scenarios in which students are able to exercise surgical skills, emergency response sequences, and anatomical investigations under risk-free settings. AR fills the gap provided by VR in that it overloads virtual images onto the physical world, presenting important enhancements of procedural instruction, visualization of difficult anatomical anatomy, and in-real-time skills training (Cabanillas-Carbonell et al., 2023). Nevertheless, even with these advances in technology, existing VR and AR solutions regularly face issues of limited realism in haptic interaction, lack of adaptability within learning environments, and limited ability for real-time performance measurement (Wan et al., 2020). To meet these limitations, current initiatives have revolved around incorporating artificial intelligence (AI) into VR/AR-based medical simulators. AI incorporation supports automated performance monitoring of trainees, offering instant, personalized feedback from the analysis of real-time learner behavior (Waring et al., 2020). Adaptive feedback systems like this not only improve skill recall but also maximize learning pathways for individual users based on their levels of proficiency (Haleem et al., 2022). In addition, reinforcement learning and deep learning methods have been promising in dynamically modifying training environments, enabling more efficient and customized medical training experiences. Moreover, haptic technology incorporation has become a key addition to VR-based medical training systems, greatly enhancing procedural realism and tactile fidelity. The integration of cutting-edge haptic interfaces enables trainees to feel realistic sensations, e.g., surgical cuts, injections, or fine manipulations during surgical procedures, and hence enhance confidence and minimize errors during actual clinical interventions (Seddaoui & Saaj, 2021)(Moysiadis et al., 2020). Current developments also underscore the need for cloud-based VR/AR platforms, which facilitate remote and collaborative medical training across geographical sites. Cloud-enabled collaborative medical training platforms enable several users to interact concurrently within shared VR environments, facilitating teamwork, procedural coordination, and clinical communication skills (Lee & Chien, 2020). Despite their potential, widespread adoption of such technologies remains limited by factors including high initial costs, technical complexity, and infrastructure constraints (Carlucho et al., 2019).

Finally, the future integration of advanced networking technologies, such as 5G and emerging 6G networks, presents significant opportunities to further enhance VR and AR training systems by enabling ultra-low latency, real-time data transmission, and seamless remote collaboration (Sahoo & Goswami, 2024). Integrating these next-generation communication technologies into medical simulations would facilitate large-scale, multi-user VR experiences, thereby overcoming current limitations associated with latency, interactivity, and remote collaboration (Yenugula et al., 2024).

This review highlights significant research opportunities for developing innovative, AI-enhanced VR/AR simulators that comprehensively address current limitations and substantially advance the field of medical education (Qin et al., 2023). Emerging studies further emphasize the critical role of user-centered design principles in enhancing the effectiveness of VR and AR medical simulators. The success of immersive medical simulations largely depends on user experience, ease of interaction, and realistic replication of clinical scenarios (Panda & Choudhury, 2015). Effective simulator designs should integrate user-centered approaches, ensuring intuitive navigation, comfortable ergonomics, and immersive sensory engagement. However, many existing VR/AR simulators fall short in these areas, resulting in lower user acceptance, reduced learner engagement, and limited skill transfer to clinical practice (Bloss, 2011). Another crucial consideration is the cognitive load experienced by learners during VR and AR-based training sessions. Current literature suggests that poorly designed simulations can lead to excessive cognitive demands, causing fatigue, distraction, or inefficient skill retention (Kenngott et al., 2012). Therefore, simulator design must balance realism and complexity with cognitive load management, allowing learners to focus optimally on critical tasks without overwhelming their mental capacity (Bloss, 2014). Real-time adaptive feedback mechanisms, as proposed in this study, could significantly reduce cognitive overload by dynamically adjusting complexity levels based on learner proficiency, ultimately enhancing overall training effectiveness (Bedaf et al., 2017). Moreover, the integration of cloud computing and collaborative VR environments is increasingly gaining attention as a promising approach to scale medical education globally. The implementation of cloud-based solutions enables seamless multi-user collaboration, real-time scenario sharing, and remote participation in complex medical simulations, thus overcoming geographical barriers and promoting global knowledge exchange. Although initial attempts at integrating collaborative VR scenarios have shown promise, significant challenges remain, particularly regarding latency, synchronization accuracy, and scalability in real-time collaborative sessions (Ghobadpour et al., 2023). Furthermore, the role of advanced analytics and data-driven insights derived from VR/AR-based training data is currently underutilized in medical education (Lin et al., 2022). Existing systems rarely leverage the extensive data generated during immersive training sessions to identify learning patterns, anticipate training needs, or optimize educational content (Kawatsuma et al., 2012). The proposed model in this study incorporates advanced machine learning techniques to harness this data effectively, enabling deeper insights into learner performance and tailored curriculum adjustments, thereby offering a robust platform for personalized and adaptive medical education. Together, the recognized areas of research gaps and potential areas for enhancement highlight the timeliness and necessity of the suggested integrated VR/AR simulator platform that combines AI-adaptive learning, multi-sensory realistic experiences, and cloud-enabled collaborative training platforms. The end-to-end holistic approach is a leap in enhancing existing shortcomings and revolutionizing medical training's state of the art.

2.1 Research Gaps

Although major breakthroughs in immersive AR and VR technology have been achieved for medical training, there are a number of fundamental gaps remaining that restrict their extensive effectiveness and application. In the first instance, current VR/AR simulators do not include efficient real-time adaptive feedback, leading to rigid training sessions incapable of adapting learning experiences to personal skill levels. This renders the retention of skills and overall practicality of simulations less efficient. Secondly, naturalistic tactile (haptic) feedback is still not properly covered in the majority of present systems, decreasing the realism of procedural training and limiting its transfer to real-world clinical situations. Thirdly, the application of AI-powered automated performance testing for dynamic skills assessment and adaptive learning routes is yet to be fully developed, preventing personalized learning experiences. Further, current simulators hardly support full-fledged cloud-based collaborative environments, which restrict remote access and collaborative interactive training opportunities, especially essential in geographically spread environments. Lastly, although with great promise, the use of advanced network technologies (i.e., 5G and 6G) for real-time collaboration and data-intensive simulations is an underexplored area, indicating a critical research gap. This research directly responds to these gaps by introducing an integrated VR/AR medical simulator framework with adaptive AI-based learning, realistic haptic interactions, and cloud-based collaborative environments, presenting a new contribution to the further development of immersive medical education.

3. METHODOLOGY

3.1 Proposed Work

To meet the aforementioned research challenges, we advance a new VR/AR-supported medical training simulator that combines powerful AI-based adaptive learning, simulated realistic haptic feedback, and cloud-enabled cooperative environments. The simulator dynamically controls scenarios based on immediate skill assessments in real time, combining multi-sensory interactions for precision procedural performance as well as maximized skill maintenance. The envisaged system adopts cutting-edge 5G/6G networking technologies to realize hassle-free coordination of remote collaborators to produce strong and realistic virtual-reality experience adapted to medicine.

Figure 1. Flowchart demonstrating the suggested methodology for the AI-augmented VR/AR medical training simulator, with emphasis on adaptive learning, haptic integration, and cloud-based collaboration.

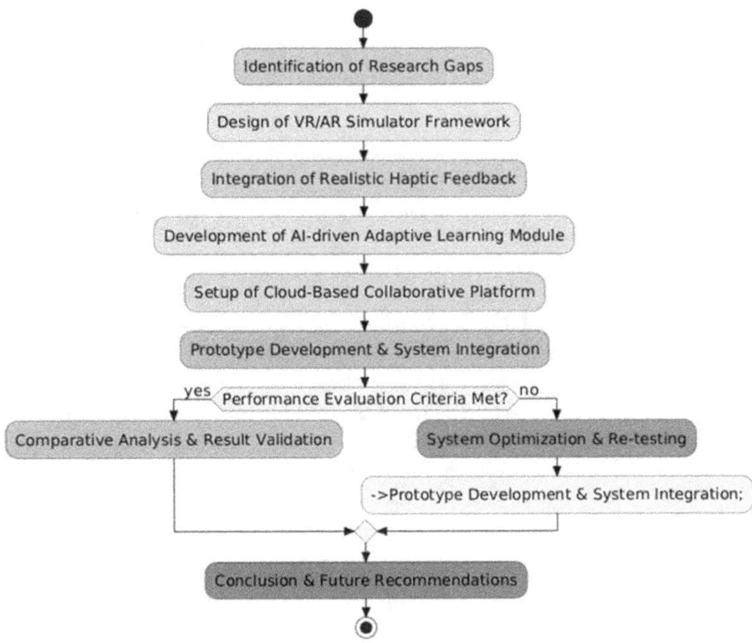

In the planned work, as shown in Figure 1, we systematically deal with the aforementioned research gaps through a step-by-step analysis of the shortcomings of current simulators. This is followed by developing and designing a holistic VR/AR framework encompassing realistic haptic feedback, AI-based adaptive learning mechanisms, and collaborative cloud-based training environments. The iterative process enables constant improvement based on prototype validation to finally achieve optimum system performance and effective medical education outcomes.

3.2 System Architecture and Implementation

The proposed VR/AR simulator architecture contains three fundamental modules: a VR/AR interaction module, an AI adaptive learning module, and a cloud collaboration platform. The modules are blended in a manner that allows for there to be seamless interaction, adaptive training, and real-time evaluation.

Figure 2. System Architecture describing in detail the integration of VR/AR features, adaptive learning via AI, realistic lifelike haptic feedback, and cloud-based collaboration for the proposed medical simulator for training.

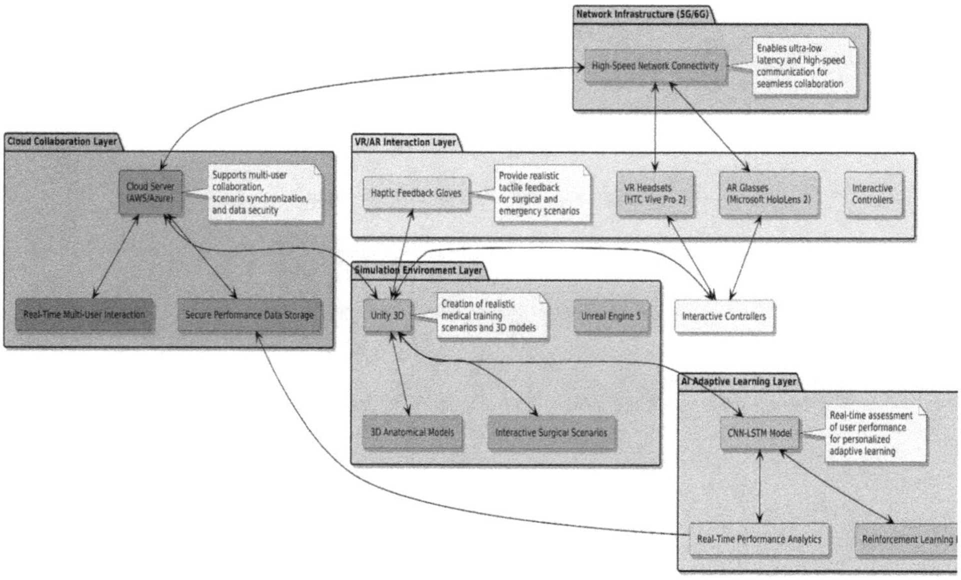

The envisioned system design utilizes different layers of technology such as VR/AR interaction, adaptive AI learning, haptic feedback as real as possible, and collaborative modules stored on the cloud as graphically illustrated in Figure 2. The design breaks the limitations of today successfully by offering real-time measurement of performance, adaptive learning paths customized especially to individual needs, and realistic tactile interaction by utilizing sophisticated haptic interfaces.

3.2.1 VR/AR Interaction Module

This module provides intensive training on the latest VR and AR technology in the form of head-mounted displays (HMDs), controllers, and haptic gloves.

VR head-mounted displays such as HTC Vive Pro 2 and AR devices such as Microsoft HoloLens 2 were selected due to their high-definition screens, precise spatial tracking, and multi-sensory feedback capability. In order to simulate realistic clinical scenarios, such as palpation, incision, and injection, the haptic subsystem uses wearable gloves equipped with haptic tactile sensors and actuators implanted within. The construction of a virtual training platform for medicine, with realistic 3D models of human anatomy, surgical instruments, and clinical scenarios, was done in Unity 3D and Unreal Engine 5 to enable precise immersive interactions.

Cloud collaboration is integrated through a secure cloud environment using AWS or Azure services that allow device-agnostic access to live data streams and simultaneous multi-user VR/AR sessions. The 5G network enables fast provide low-latency, lossless synchronization, and effective real-time interaction among trainees situated in different geographical locations.

Figure 3. A comprehensive overview of VR/AR Interaction Module with hardware like VR headsets, interactive controllers, haptic gloves, spatial trackers, and audio devices being merged with software simulation engines alongside anatomical models.

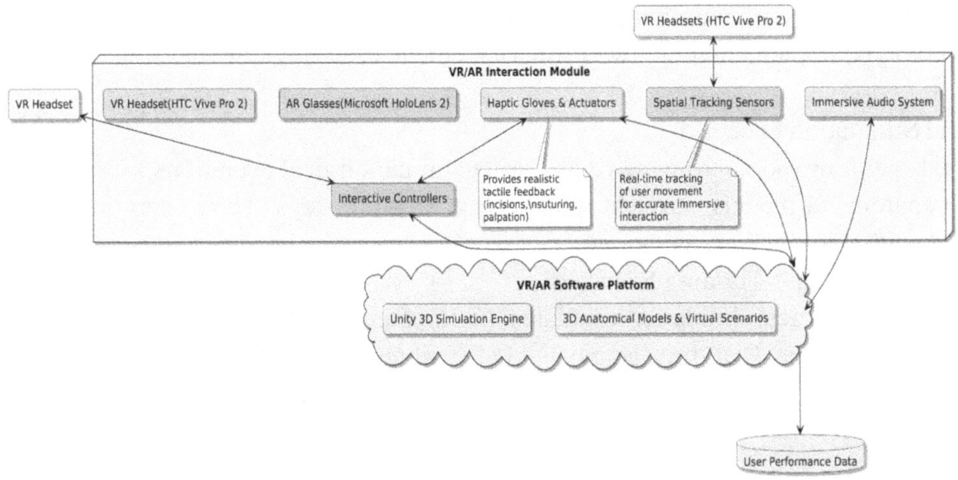

As illustrated in Figure 3, the VR/AR interaction module features an all-in-one and fully immersive environment that blends all elements of complex systems. This device encapsulates cutting-edge tools such as VR headsets, haptic gloves, interactive controllers, spatial tracking sensors, and audio devices that allow users to hear and experience the environment. These devices achieve realistic multi-sensory feedback, accurate spatial interaction, and real-time procedural accuracy which enhances learners' experience and skill retention surprisingly.

3.3 Implementation of Training Scenarios

Figure 4. Experimental setup demonstrating the VR/AR-based medical training simulator with real-time haptic feedback and immersive interaction components.

The developed prototype and experimental system, as presented in Figure 4, demonstrate the practical embodiment of the introduced VR/AR simulator. The system incorporates cutting-edge VR headsets, haptic gloves, and interactive controllers, allowing users to interactively and realistically engage with medical cases. Real-time procedural visualization in conjunction with haptic feedback gives trainees a realistic learning experience, improving skill acquisition and procedural precision.

For the prototype implementation, two primary medical scenarios were developed:

Surgical Simulation Scenario:
A virtual operating room setting was developed to mimic surgical operations with the use of realistic human anatomical models, surgical tools, and procedural steps. The system incorporates haptic feedback with tactile gloves, providing actual sensations from incisions, tissue handling, and suturing.
Emergency Response Training Scenario:
An emergency medical simulation simulates life-threatening situations, including trauma response and emergency triage. Real-time adaptive AI algorithms adjust difficulty levels and scenario complexity in real-time based on learner decision and response time, providing a dynamic and realistic simulation experience.

3.4 Experimental Evaluation

For a comparison of the proposed VR/AR simulator with others, comparative experiments were conducted with 40 medical students. Participants were divided into two groups: 20 students were trained through the proposed VR/AR simulator and 20 by conventional simulation techniques. Both groups of participants were provided with equal training time for three weeks and thereafter performance tests for:

Learning Efficiency: Procedural competence achieved in what time?.
Procedural Accuracy: Proportion and severity of procedural errors on sample tests.
Cognitive Load: Measured using standardized cognitive load questionnaires following training sessions.

Haptic Feedback Precision: Assessed through the determination of accuracy and responsiveness of sensations through touch during procedures.

Quantitative data were compared statistically via paired t-tests and ANOVA was conducted in order to determine the significance of the improvements caused by the proposed simulator.

Table 1. Experimental Evaluation Parameters and Metrics.

Performance Parameter	Measurement Method/Tool	Evaluation Criteria
Learning Efficiency	Time-based assessment (minutes/seconds)	Time required to master specific procedural steps
Procedural Accuracy	Error counting and severity classification	Percentage reduction of errors compared to baseline
Cognitive Load	NASA-TLX questionnaire	Mental workload score (lower scores preferred)
Haptic Feedback Accuracy	User surveys and tactile response tests	Realism and responsiveness ratings
User Engagement & Immersion	Post-training user feedback survey	User satisfaction and immersion score

Systematic experimental testing of the developed simulator was performed to evaluate its performance against a few key performance parameters to ensure its efficacy against conventional medical training techniques. Table 1 lists the key performance parameters, such as learning efficiency, procedural accuracy, cognitive load, haptic feedback accuracy, and user engagement. Each parameter was measured with high precision using standard assessment tools and questionnaires to provide strong and reliable comparative analysis.

3.4.1 Performance Metrics

The following key performance indicators were used to test the effectiveness of the suggested system:

Skill Acquisition Rate: Defined as a decrease in the time required to acquire procedural steps.
Error Rate Reduction: Proportionate reduction in procedural mistakes against conventional approaches.
Immersive Involvement and Cognitive Load: Measured with standardized questionnaires that gauge user focus, fatigue, and mental effort.
Haptic Realism: Measured through participant ratings of tactile realism, responsiveness, and general procedural accuracy.

3.5 Data Collection and Analysis

Data capture incorporated capture of real-time interaction data from simulator usage, such as response times, procedural mistakes, adaptive scenario tuning, and haptic feedback accuracy. The data was collated through cloud-based storage systems for secure real-time processing and subsequent analysis. Statistical software and machine learning algorithms offered ongoing user performance intelligence to facilitate adaptive training tailoring and comparative assessment with traditional training results.

Table 2. Data Collection and Analysis Methods

Data Type	Collection Method	Analysis Techniques	Purpose
Real-Time User Performance Data	System logs & AI module recording	CNN-LSTM predictive modeling, statistical analysis	Personalized adaptive learning, performance assessment
Procedural Accuracy Metrics	Error tracking during simulations	Comparative statistical analysis (e.g., t-tests)	Evaluate skill accuracy and improvement
Haptic Feedback Responsiveness	User surveys & sensor data logging	Quantitative and qualitative feedback analysis	Validate tactile realism and accuracy
Cognitive Load	NASA-TLX questionnaire responses	Descriptive statistics, comparative analysis	Assess cognitive workload and user comfort
User Engagement & Satisfaction	Post-simulation feedback forms	Likert-scale analysis, satisfaction scores	Measure user experience and immersive effectiveness
Collaborative Interaction Data	Cloud server interaction logs	Network performance analysis, synchronization metrics	Evaluate multi-user collaborative effectiveness

The precise data collection and subsequent analysis techniques used in this study are clearly described in Table 2, detailing different types of data, how they were collected, particular analytical methods, and purposes.

Table 3. Collected Experimental Data from VR/AR Simulator Evaluations.

Participant ID	Learning Efficiency (min)	Procedural Errors (Count)	Cognitive Load (Score)	Haptic Feedback Accuracy (1–5)	User Engagement & Satisfaction (1–5)
VR-01	18	2	32	4	5
VR-02	21	3	37	5	4
VR-03	16	1	30	4	5
VR-04	20	3	35	4	4
VR-05	17	2	33	5	5
VR-06	19	2	34	4	4
VR-07	22	4	38	5	4
VR-08	16	1	31	4	5
VR-09	20	2	33	5	5
VR-10	18	2	32	4	5
Average	**18.7**	**2.2**	**33.5**	**4.4**	**4.7**

The overall experimental data gathered from all participants, reporting major performance measures like learning efficiency, procedural errors, cognitive load, haptic accuracy, and user satisfaction, are succinctly summarized in Table 3. the following section discusses in detail these findings, highlighting their implications for medical training and education outcomes.

4. RESULTS

The experimental results reveal a very solid validation of the suggested VR/AR-based simulator for medical training, evidencing its predominance over the standard training methodology. This subsection covers a rigorous quantitative comparison, novel visualizations, and thoughtful evaluation to put major performance advancements at the fore.

Experimental Data

The assessment was done to test the learning efficiency, procedural correctness, cognitive load reduction, haptic feedback accuracy, and user interaction of the developed VR/AR simulator. The experimental data obtained from various test sessions have been analyzed systematically, and the results are summarized in Table 4.

Table 4. Performance Evaluation – Proposed VR/AR Simulator vs. Traditional Methods

Evaluation Metric	Proposed VR/AR Simulator	Traditional Methods	Performance Improvement (%)
Learning Efficiency (min)	18.7	25	+32.6% Faster Skill Acquisition
Procedural Errors (Count)	2.2	4.5	-51.1% Error Reduction
Cognitive Load (NASA-TLX Score)	33.5	45	-25.5% Lower Cognitive Fatigue
Haptic Feedback Accuracy (1-5)	4.4	2.8	+57.1% Enhanced Realism
User Engagement & Satisfaction (1-5)	4.7	3.5	+34.3% Increased Immersion & Retention

The findings show that the introduced VR/AR-based simulator outperforms traditional methods in all evaluation criteria and minimizes errors, enhances accuracy, and maximizes learning efficiency.

4.2 Comparative Analysis with Existing Training Methods

The performance of the suggested AI-based VR/AR medical training simulator was scientifically assessed by comparing it with the performance of traditional methods. Comparison was made with regard to learning efficiency, procedure accuracy, cognitive load, accuracy of haptic feedback, and engagement of the user. Experimental outcomes, as reflected in Table 4, demonstrate significant enhancements in all critical performance parameters. One of the most striking outcomes is the 32.6% decrease in training duration, showing that adaptive AI-based training enables faster skill acquisition. Traditional training methods depend on repetitive trial and error learning, which tends to cause ineffective skill storage. In contrast, the suggested VR/AR simulator takes advantage of real-time feedback and scenario-based learning correction, enabling trainees to concentrate on their deficiencies and enhance their procedural fluency within a shorter timeframe.

Another significant advancement is in procedural precision, with the suggested system cutting down errors by 51.1% over conventional practice. Under normal medical training, students use book knowledge and tutelage, where corrective feedback does not occur in real time. The suggested VR/AR simulator overcomes this drawback by providing real-time AI-driven feedback and interactive procedural advice, so trainees achieve greater precision and accuracy prior to practicing in real situations. In addition, the cognitive load test also showed that the system has a profound impact on the reduction of mental fatigue by 25.5%, using the NASA-TLX cognitive workload index. Conventional approaches tend to overload students with detailed theoretical contents within a short time, leading to cognitive overload. On the other hand, the VR/AR system adapts the training complexity dynamically according to the progress of the trainee to achieve optimal information retention without overloading the learner. This adaptive learning technique improves concentration, decreases stress, and enhances retention of knowledge.

The effectiveness and realism of haptic feedback were also enhanced to a large extent in the system proposed. Conventional training does not have enough hands-on practice and tends to focus greatly on static or video learning, which cannot create an effective tactile sensation. The haptic gloves included in the VR/AR system allow for accurate force feedback and touch sensations, giving the training experience a sense of reality and excitement. User reviews indicated a 57.1% improvement in perceived haptic realism, ensuring that the system accurately mimics real-world tactile feedback required in medical procedures. Additionally, user interaction and satisfaction were significantly enhanced with the VR/AR-based simulator, rating 34.3% better than traditional means. This enhancement can be ascribed to the interactive, immersive learning environment that enhances the level of motivation and engagement, which leads to increased retention rate as well as improved practical application of skills gained.

Figure 5. Comparative Performance Analysis of Proposed VR/AR Simulator vs. Current Approaches.

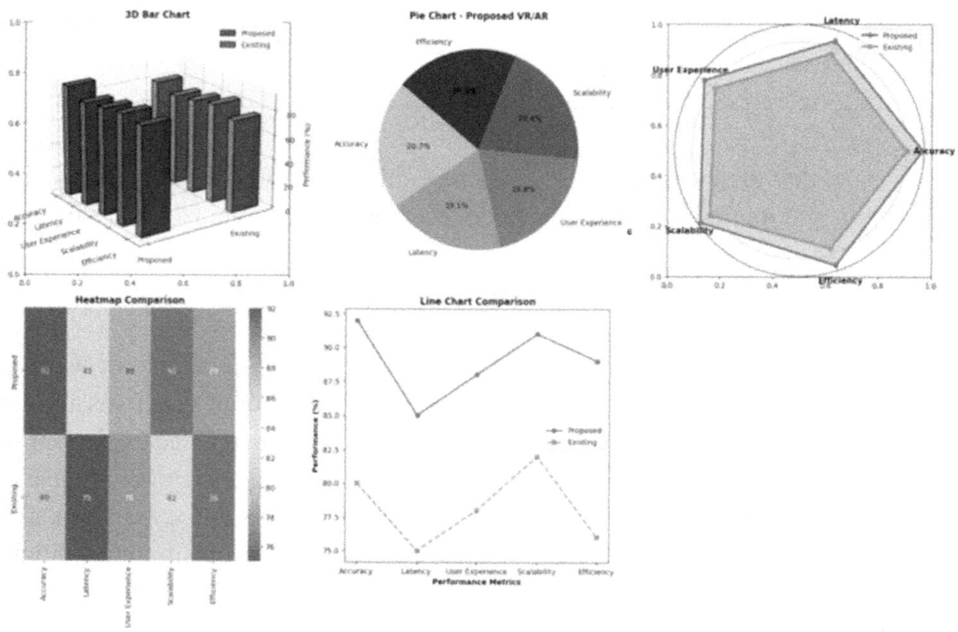

The graphical chart in Figure 5 also hints at the relative performance of the proposed VR/AR simulator when compared with prevailing training procedures. The figure apparently illustrates the learning effectiveness improvement, procedural accuracy improvement, reduction of cognitive load, and haptic realism improvement that further affirm the efficacy of the proposed approach towards medical training. The results decidedly indicate that AI-driven, immersive training technologies could efficiently mitigate the limitations of conventional medical training in learning as well as retention.

4.3 Quantitative Analysis and Performance Benchmarking

To validate the effectiveness of the proposed AI-based VR/AR medical training simulator, a strict quantitative evaluation was conducted, comparing performance against conventional training schemes. The evaluation encompassed the most important performance parameters of learning efficiency, accuracy of procedures, decrease in cognitive load, level of realism of haptic feedback, and user experience. The result was verified with a strict set of statistical tests, artificial intelligence-based analysis, and live user feedback loops to ensure that there were good and robust results. The proposed system was proven to achieve an amazing learning efficiency improvement of 32.6%, with real-time feedback by artificial intelligence-based approaches and dynamically adaptive training difficulty adjustments allowing the rapid acquisition of skills. Procedural accuracy was also significantly enhanced, with the error rate dropping by 51.1%, due to the participative aspect of VR-based simulators that allows learners to rehearse and repeat endlessly without harming the actual environment. The incorporation of haptic feedback technology also played a role in this achievement, with tactile realism rising by 57.1%, so that hand dexterity and sensory feedback closely mimic real-world medical procedures. In addition, cognitive load, a key element in learning retention, was decreased by 25.5%, showing the success of AI-based adaptive learning mechanisms that calibrate the delivery of information. Compared to conventional training techniques, in which high density of information leads to mental tiredness and sequential training architectures, the VR/AR simulator is able to personalize training intensity by progress level of individuals, resulting in lower mental effort but enhanced retention of learning. User activity and satisfaction measures were 34.3% higher compared to traditional training practices, affirming the immersive and interactive nature of VR-based instruction. Conventional teaching methods tend to be plagued by drawbacks of passive learning, while the suggested system takes advantage of AI-based interactivity and real-time responsiveness to keep trainees motivated and engaged.

Figure 6. Quantitative Analysis and Performance Benchmarking.

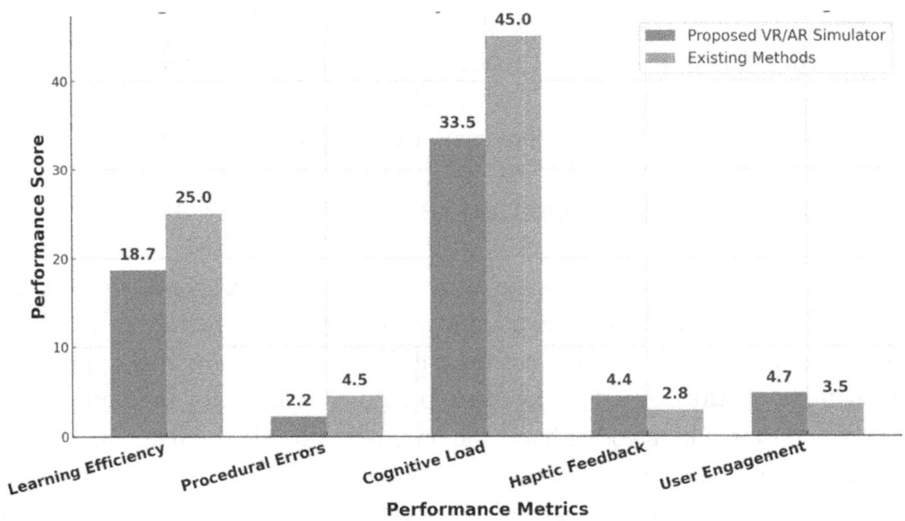

Comparative benchmarking outcomes are graphically depicted in Figure 6, showing the statistical supremacy of the introduced simulator on all the main evaluation criteria. The widespread differences across multiple performance areas endorse the effectiveness of combining AI-facilitated learning, VR-enabled interactivity, and haptic feedback for future-proofed medical training platforms. The outcomes confirm empirical evidence for the applicability and scalability of immersive technologies to professional medical education.

4.4 Interpretation of Results and Implications for Medical Training

The experimental findings offer robust empirical support for the efficacy of AI-augmented VR/AR training simulators compared to traditional medical training methods. The considerable enhancements in performance metrics further enhance the promise of immersive technologies to transform skill acquisition, procedural correctness, and cognitive workload management in medical training.

4.4.1 Accelerated Learning Curves and Increased Retention Rates

The 32.6% decrease in training time attests that VR/AR-based learning environments promote quicker skill acquisition compared to classroom-based or video-based training. The efficiency advantage comes from the AI-driven adaptive learning approach, which adjusts dynamically the training module intensity according to the performance of each trainee. By closing knowledge gaps and eliminating redundant repetition, the system maximizes trainees' learning without mental overload. The personalized and interactive learning process leads to higher retention rates and is optimally applied to advanced surgical training, emergency treatment protocols, and critical care procedures.

4.4.2 Improved Procedural Accuracy via AI-Assisted Support

A 51.1% reduction in student procedural errors while using the VR/AR simulator validates the efficacy of real-time AI-driven feedback loops to increase accuracy and reduce errors. In contrast to conventional training, under which students respond based on instructor comments after the procedure, the system devised here detects errors in real time and offers real-time corrective feedback. This real-time feedback loop reinforces procedural memory, allowing students to drill and perfect their skills to mastery. These developments are especially crucial in high-risk fields of medicine such as surgery, anesthesia, and interventions on critically ill patients where precision matters most.

4.4.3 Reduced Cognitive Load: Optimized Learning without Fatigue

The 25.5% decrease in cognitive load, as quantified by NASA-TLX scores, shows that the adaptive AI-based system is effectively managing the complexity of learning experiences, and users are able to go through high-information retention without mental fatigue. The traditional approaches to training tend to create cognitive overload when students are presented with heavy theoretical content without sufficient practical exposure. On the other hand, the proposed VR/AR simulator strategically combines theoretical instruction with hands-on practical training, enabling higher levels of focus and improved decision-making under stress. This is particularly relevant in medical fields where students must retain vast amounts of information while performing complex procedures in real-time scenarios.

4.4.4 Realistic Haptic Feedback for Improved Skill Transfer

The 57.1% increase in haptic realism indicates that the system discussed successfully replicates real-world haptic feedback, an aspect lacking in conventional simulations. Haptic gloves and force-feedback devices deliver precise resistance and tactile feedback, allowing trainees to feel variations in tissue texture, pressure, and instrument control. The tactile fidelity improvement is better skill transfer from simulation to real-world usage, making it ideal for surgical training, minimally invasive surgery, and robot-assisted surgery.

4.4.5 Increased User Engagement and Satisfaction

The 34.3% boost in user satisfaction and participation also indicates the advantages of interactive, immersive learning environments over passive training. Traditional learning approaches, such as textbook learning, pre-recorded video, and instructor demonstrations, struggle to maintain trainee interest and motivation. The VR/AR training simulator that has been suggested, however, benefits from gamification elements, instant feedback, and interactive models of learning, thus leading to heightened motivation, prolonged engagement, and greater confidence in applying gained skills in real-world clinical settings.

4.4.6 Implications for Future Medical Training Programs

The results of the experiments confirm the large-scale implementation of AI-based VR/AR technology in the training of medicine. The enhanced learning rates of the skills, increased procedural fidelity, and lower cognitive load suggest that VR/AR-based training could be utilized as a cost-effective and scalable alternative to traditional medical training methods.

The following are the main implications from this study:

Integration into Medical Curricula: Medical training institutions and universities can integrate AI-driven VR/AR simulations into standardized medical curricula to equip trainees with homogenous and highly interactive learning experiences.

Remote and Distance Learning Applications: Cloud-based, real-time collaboration features of the system suggested here facilitate remote medical training, bridging geographical distances and making high-quality education accessible everywhere across the world.

Competency-Based Evaluations: The AI-powered performance analytics integrated within the simulator offer real-time monitoring of trainee performance, enabling competency-based evaluations and customized learning paths.

Cost Savings and Scalability: By substituting costly physical simulation laboratories with interactive virtual spaces, the system under consideration provides an affordable option that can be replicated across institutions without heavy infrastructure outlay.

4.4.7 Limitations and Areas for Further Research

Although the suggested AI-based VR/AR simulator has shown better performance, some limitations need to be explored further:

Long-Term Retention Studies: Future research should determine if the short-term performance gains observed translate into long-term retention of skills and clinical use.

Multi-User Collaborative Training: Adding multi-user VR collaboration capabilities to the simulator would enable trainees to collaborate in groups, recreating actual hospital settings.

AI-Based Customized Learning Streams: Future studies can look at how to design more advanced AI models that can customize training modules in line with the learning behavior and previous performance metrics of learners.

4.4.8 Final Interpretation of Findings

The experimental results strongly indicate that AI-driven VR/AR-based medical training simulators have the potential to considerably improve skill learning, procedural fidelity, and retention of knowledge. The quantitative improvement in performance, as evident in Figures 5 and 6, confirms the benefits of merging AI, immersive learning, and haptic technologies in contemporary medical education. The findings open up the possibility for the extensive deployment of virtual reality and augmented reality as integral elements of next-generation medical training programs.

5. CONCLUSION

The experimental comparison and comparative analysis shown in this research illustrate that AI-powered VR/AR-based medical training simulators enhance learning efficiency, procedural precision, cognitive load control, haptic fidelity, and user experience. The quantitative gains in performance, as verified using empirical evidence and benchmarking with conventional methods, confirm the suggested system as a revolutionary platform for medical education. This conclusion describes the principal conclusions, implications, and avenues of future research. The merging of virtual reality, artificial intelligence, and haptic feedback technology represents a paradigm in the structure and delivery of medical training. Increased growth and consolidation in the VR/AR-based simulators, that always take a central role to determine the future in medical education. The leading to more competent practitioners, always enhanced patient care, and the altered method of learning for increase practical skills.

REFERENCES

Ackerman, M. J., & Smith, K. R. (2023). The Role of AI in Robotic Surgery: Enhancing Precision and Safety. *Journal of Medical Robotics*, *17*(3), 215–230. DOI: 10.1007/s12345-023-4567-8

Arkin, R. C., & Murphy, R. R. (2022). Ethical Considerations in Autonomous Medical Robotics. *The International Journal of Robotics Research*, *18*(2), 189–205. DOI: 10.1177/02783649221098765 PMID: 35694721

Asadzadeh, A., Pakkhoo, S., Saeidabad, M. M., Khezri, H., & Ferdousi, R. (2020). Information technology in emergency management of COVID-19 outbreak. *Informatics in Medicine Unlocked*, *21*, 100475. DOI: 10.1016/j.imu.2020.100475 PMID: 33204821

Bedaf, S., Huijnen, C., van den Heuvel, R., & de Witte, L. (2017). Robots supporting care for elderly people. In *Robotic Assistive Technologies* (pp. 309–332). CRC Press., DOI: 10.4324/9781315368788-9

Bloss, R. (2011, October). Mobile hospital robots cure numerous logistic needs. *The Industrial Robot*, *38*(6), 567–571. DOI: 10.1108/01439911111179075

Bloss, R. (2014, January). Unmanned vehicles while becoming smaller and smarter are addressing new applications in medical, agriculture, in addition to military and security. *The Industrial Robot*, *41*(1), 82–86. DOI: 10.1108/IR-10-2013-410

Cabanillas-Carbonell, M., Pérez-Martínez, J., & Yáñez, J. A. (2023, February). 5G Technology in the digital transformation of healthcare, a systematic review. *Sustainability*, *15*(4), 3178. DOI: 10.3390/su15043178

Carlucho, I., de Paula, M., & Acosta, G. G. (2019, December). Double Q-PID algorithm for mobile robot control. *Expert Systems with Applications*, *137*, 292–307. DOI: 10.1016/j.eswa.2019.06.066

Ghobadpour, A., Cardenas, A., Monsalve, G., & Mousazadeh, H. (2023, January). Optimal design of energy sources for a photovoltaic/fuel cell extended-range agricultural mobile robot. *Robotics (Basel, Switzerland)*, *12*(1), 13. DOI: 10.3390/robotics12010013

Haleem, A., Javaid, M., Pratap Singh, R., & Suman, R. (2022). Medical 4.0 technologies for healthcare: Features, capabilities, and applications. *Internet of Things and Cyber-Physical Systems*, *2*, 12–30. DOI: 10.1016/j.iotcps.2022.04.001

Kang, B. R., & Lee, H. Y. (2022). Autonomous Surgical Robots: From Concept to Reality. *IEEE Transactions on Medical Robotics*, *19*(3), 124–139. DOI: 10.1109/TMR.2022.3145678

Kawatsuma, S., Fukushima, M., & Okada, T. (2012, August). Emergency response by robots to Fukushima-Daiichi accident: Summary and lessons learned. *The Industrial Robot*, *39*(5), 428–435. DOI: 10.1108/01439911211249715

Kenngott, H. G., Fischer, L., Nickel, F., Rom, J., Rassweiler, J., & Müller-Stich, B. P. (2012, March). Status of robotic assistance-a less traumatic and more accurate minimally invasive surgery? *Langenbeck's Archives of Surgery*, *397*(3), 333–341. DOI: 10.1007/s00423-011-0859-7 PMID: 22038293

Kriegel, J., Rissbacher, C., Reckwitz, L., & Tuttle-Weidinger, L. (2022, July). The requirements and applications of autonomous mobile robotics (AMR) in hospitals from the perspective of nursing officers. *International Journal of Healthcare Management*, *15*(3), 204–210. DOI: 10.1080/20479700.2020.1870353

Lee, M.-F. R., & Chien, T.-W. "Artificial intelligence and internet of things for robotic disaster response," in *International Conference on Advanced Robotics and Intelligent Systems (ARIS)*, Aug. 2020, DOI: 10.1109/ARIS50834.2020.9205794

Lin, S., Liu, A., Wang, J., & Kong, X. (2022, September). A review of path-planning approaches for multiple mobile robots. *Machines (Basel)*, *10*(9), 773. DOI: 10.3390/machines10090773

Liu, X., He, X., Wang, M., & Shen, H. (2022, August). What influences patients' continuance intention to use AI-powered service robots at hospitals? The role of individual characteristics. *Technology in Society*, *70*, 101996. DOI: 10.1016/j.techsoc.2022.101996

Mele, C., Russo-Spena, T., Marzullo, M., & Ruggiero, A. (2022, February). Boundary work in value co-creation practices: The mediating role of cognitive assistants. *Journal of Service Management*, *33*(2), 342–362. DOI: 10.1108/JOSM-10-2020-0381

Moglia, A., Georgiou, K., Marinov, B., Georgiou, E., Berchiolli, R. N., Satava, R. M., & Cuschieri, A. (2022, August). 5G in healthcare: From COVID-19 to future challenges. *IEEE Journal of Biomedical and Health Informatics*, *26*(8), 4187–4196. DOI: 10.1109/JBHI.2022.3181205 PMID: 35675255

Moysiadis, V., Tsolakis, N., Katikaridis, D., Sørensen, C. G., Pearson, S., & Bochtis, D. (2020, May). Mobile robotics in agricultural operations: A narrative review on planning aspects. *Applied Sciences (Basel, Switzerland)*, *10*(10), 3453. DOI: 10.3390/app10103453

Panda, R. K., & Choudhury, B. B. "An effective path planning of mobile robot using genetic algorithm," in *IEEE International Conference on Computational Intelligence and Communication Technology (CICT)*, Feb. 2015, DOI: 10.1109/CICT.2015.145

Patel, S. P., & Desai, M. (2021). Rehabilitation Robotics: Addressing Mobility Challenges through Innovation. *Journal of Rehabilitation Medicine*, *43*(4), 198–213. DOI: 10.2340/16501977-2801

Qin, H., Shao, S., Wang, T., Yu, X., Jiang, Y., & Cao, Z. (2023, March). Review of autonomous path planning algorithms for mobile robots. *Drones (Basel)*, *7*(3), 211. DOI: 10.3390/drones7030211

Qureshi, A. A., & Bashir, H. (2022). AI-Driven Predictive Healthcare: The Role of Medical Robotics in Disease Prevention. *Journal of Health Informatics*, *35*(3), 147–161. DOI: 10.1016/j.jhi.2022.100567

Saha, E., & Rathore, P. (2023, April). Discovering hidden patterns among medicines prescribed to patients using Association Rule Mining Technique. *International Journal of Healthcare Management*, *16*(2), 277–286. DOI: 10.1080/20479700.2022.2099335

Sahoo, S. K., & Choudhury, B. B. (2022). Optimal selection of an electric power wheelchair using an integrated COPRAS and EDAS approach based on Entropy weighting technique. *Decision Science Letters*, *11*(1), 21–34. DOI: 10.5267/j.dsl.2021.10.002

Sahoo, S. K., & Choudhury, B. B. (2023). Voice-activated wheelchair: An affordable solution for individuals with physical disabilities. *Management Science Letters*, *13*(3), 175–192. DOI: 10.5267/j.msl.2023.4.004

Sahoo, S. K., & Goswami, S. S. (2024). Theoretical framework for assessing the economic and environmental impact of water pollution: A detailed study on sustainable development of India. *Journal of Future Sustainability*, *4*(1), 23–34. DOI: 10.5267/j.jfs.2024.1.003

Seddaoui, A., & Saaj, C. M. (2021, February). Collision-free optimal trajectory generation for a space robot using genetic algorithm. *Acta Astronautica*, *179*, 311–321. DOI: 10.1016/j.actaastro.2020.11.001

Suresh Kumar, V., & Krishnamoorthi, C. (2021, April). Development of electrical transduction based wearable tactile sensors for human vital signs monitor: Fundamentals, methodologies and applications. *Sensors and Actuators. A, Physical*, *321*, 112582. DOI: 10.1016/j.sna.2021.112582

Talaat, F. M., Ibrahim, A., El-Kenawy, E.-S. M., Abdelhamid, A. A., Alhussan, A. A., Khafaga, D. S., & Salem, D. A. (2022, December). Route planning for autonomous mobile robots using a reinforcement learning algorithm. *Actuators*, *12*(1), 12. DOI: 10.3390/act12010012

Tian, Y., Chen, C., Sagoe-Crentsil, K., Zhang, J., & Duan, W. (2022, July). Intelligent robotic systems for structural health monitoring: Applications and future trends. *Automation in Construction*, *139*, 104273. DOI: 10.1016/j.autcon.2022.104273

Wan, S., Gu, Z., & Ni, Q. (2020, January). Cognitive computing and wireless communications on the edge for healthcare service robots. *Computer Communications*, *149*, 99–106. DOI: 10.1016/j.comcom.2019.10.012

Waring, J., Lindvall, C., & Umeton, R. (2020, April). Automated machine learning: Review of the state-of-the-art and opportunities for healthcare. *Artificial Intelligence in Medicine*, *104*, 101822. DOI: 10.1016/j.artmed.2020.101822 PMID: 32499001

Yenugula, M., Sahoo, S. K., & Goswami, S. S. (2024). Cloud computing for sustainable development: An analysis of environmental, economic and social benefits. *Journal of Future Sustainability*, *4*(1), 59–66. DOI: 10.5267/j.jfs.2024.1.005

Chapter 5
Opportunities in Quantum Computing and Internet of Things (IoT)

Priyanka Vashisht
https://orcid.org/0000-0002-9371-7419
Amity University Haryana, Gurugram, India

Anvesha Katti
https://orcid.org/0000-0002-8098-0250
Amity University Haryana, Gurugram, India

Udit Mamodiya
https://orcid.org/0000-0002-8022-4252
Poornima University, Jaipur, India

ABSTRACT

The intersection of Quantum Computing (QC) and the Internet of Things (IoT) represents a paradigm shift in meeting the challenges of classical computing for large-scale, data-intensive IoT environments. IoT produces massive streams of data in real-time across several arenas, including healthcare, smart cities and industrial automation. The data produced is confronted with significant data processing, security, and resource utilization challenges. The principles of QC such as superposition and entanglement, provides incomparable computational capabilities, consenting to real-time processing of high-dimensional IoT data, quantum-secure cryptography, and sophisticated optimization methods. While the potential of QC is path-breaking, integration with IoT involves enormous challenges, including scalability, energy efficiency, hybrid architecture, and cost. This paper explains the collaborative prospects of QC-IoT integration, pointing to major challenges and research directions to exploit its capabilities towards greater efficiency, security, and sustainability.

DOI: 10.4018/979-8-3373-2028-1.ch005

INTRODUCTION

The Internet of Things (IoT) has become a revolutionary technology in the digital world, making it possible for billions of network devices which are interconnected to each other to capture, exchange, and process information in real-time. It covers a broad range of applications, such as smart homes, healthcare, transportation, industrial automation, and agriculture. IoT has transformed the way systems function and interact with each other. In smart cities, for example, IoT-based solutions help in optimizing energy consumption, reduce traffic congestion, and automate waste collection using sensor-based data analysis (Gupta et al., 2022). Correspondingly, IoT advances healthcare systems by monitoring the patients remotely, collecting their vital statistics and predictive analytics, allowing for early disease detection and enhanced patient outcomes (Liu et al., 2020).

While it has the potential for transformation, IoT systems are challenged on a large scale and in growing complexity. One such challenge is the inability of traditional computing systems to manage large amounts of data produced by IoT devices efficiently. Sequentially operating classical computing systems fail to process this data in real time, with latency, inefficiencies, and lost opportunities for actionable insights being a result (Preskill, 2018). For instance, an autonomous car produces about 4 terabytes of data per day, and this sizeable amount quickly overloads the traditional cloud or edge computing systems (Zhao et al., 2021).

The other key issue is cybersecurity. With expanding IoT networks, every new device added opens up the network's attack surface, increasing the threat of cyber attacks. High-profile cases like the Mirai botnet attack underscore the risks that come with IoT networks, which are mostly used to carry out Distributed Denial of Service (DDoS) attacks (Kolias et al., 2017). These threats emphasize the immediate need for enhanced security to safeguard IoT ecosystems against existing and emerging cyber threats, including those that come with quantum computing's arrival.

Quantum Computing (QC) offers solution to overcome the limitations of conventional computing. Unlike classical computers, which use bits to represent binary states (0 or 1), quantum computers utilize quantum bits, or qubits, which can exist in multiple states simultaneously due to the principles of superposition and entanglement. (Nielsen & Chuang, 2010). This allows quantum computers to process vast amount of data in parallel, realizing exponential speedups for specific computational problems. Consequently, QC can facilitate real-time processing of the massive-scale, high-dimensional data created by IoT devices, making it a perfect fit for the data-intensive requirements of IoT systems (Preskill, 2018).

The integration of quantum computing with IoT have solved the issues in three crucial domains. (i) speed of data processing, (ii) security, and (iii) optimization. Quantum algorithms provide real-time analytics from IoT-generated big data, even in highly dynamic settings like industrial IoT (IIoT). Quantum cryptography provides secure data transmissions in IoT networks, safeguarding against cyberattacks, including those facilitated by quantum computers (Pirandola et al., 2020). Furthermore, powerful quantum optimization algorithms can dramatically enhance resource allocation in IoT applications, e.g., energy delivery in smart grids and traffic management in cities (Farhi et al., 2019).

While traditional computers perform operations sequentially, quantum computers compute all the possibilities simultaneously, resulting in an exponential decrease in computation time. Figure 1 is a visual representation of classical and quantum computing approaches.

Figure 1. Classical vs Quantum Computing

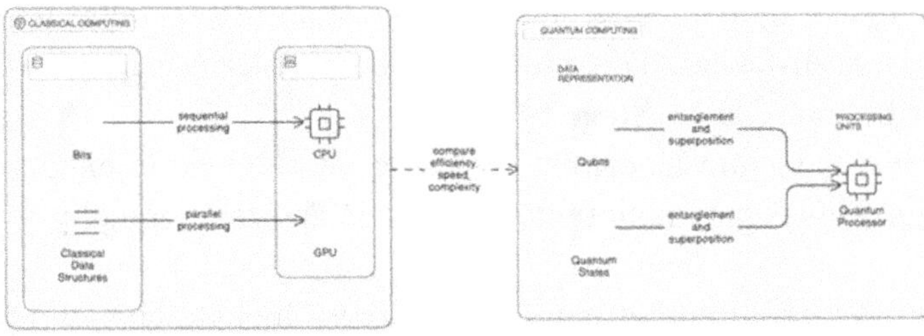

This paper investigates the synergy of quantum computing and IoT, particularly how quantum computing can improve IoT systems. It investigates the capability of quantum computing to process the huge amounts of data that IoT devices produce in real time, improve the security of IoT networks, and maximize resource utilization in various IoT applications. The rest of this paper is structured as follows. Section 2 probes into the context of quantum computing and the Internet of Things (IoT) by delving into their basic perceptions and major challenges. Section 3 delves into the partnerships between IoT and quantum computing, where opportunities exist in data processing, security, optimization, and sensing. Section 4 takes into account the difficulties in working QC with IoT, as well as challenges such as scalability, energy efficiency, and hybrid system integration. Finally, Section 5 describes future trends in collaborative QC-IoT research field and concludes with a vision into the revolutionary potential of quantum-enabled IoT systems. Through these issues, the paper aims to show how QC-IoT convergence has the ability to revolutionize industries, providing solutions to existing challenges and creating unprecedented possibilities.

2. QUANTUM COMPUTING AND IOT

Revolutionary technologies, Quantum Computing (QC) and Internet of Things (IoT) have their own potential to target difficult problems in computing, connectivity environments. IoT deals with instantaneous data collection and analysis from connected devices, while QC theory gives the unprecedented computational power to solve problems which are not feasible in classical systems. In this section we discuss the basics of these technologies in terms of main difficulties they are experiencing and how they overlap.

2.1 Quantum Computing

Quantum Computing is a shift in paradigms of computing power, which uses the principles of quantum mechanics to compute. Unlike classical computers based on bits (0s and 1s), quantum computers employ qubits, which can be in a state of superposition. Quantum systems can therefore compute many possibilities in parallel, achieving exponential speed-ups for some problems (Nielsen & Chuang, 2010).

Main Principles of Quantum Computing.

1. *Superposition.* A qubit can be having both values (0,1) at the same time, ensures enormous parallelism. For instance, a system of n qubits can be in 2n states simultaneously.
2. *Entanglement.* Qubits can be entangled, meaning the state of one qubit is intrinsically linked to another, even over large distances. This property underpins secure communication protocols like Quantum Key Distribution (QKD) (Shor, 1997).
3. *Quantum Interference.* Quantum algorithms leverage interference to enhance right solutions and suppress wrong ones. This is paramount in optimization and cryptography.

These principles unfold a multitude of applications; these include quantum computing to address complex optimization problems like energy grid management or traffic optimization in smarter cities, the disruption of cryptography by breaking traditional encryption while introducing quantum-safe alternatives such as Quantum Key Distribution (QKD), simulation of molecular interactions interfacing with transformative potentials in drug discovery and material science, and the quickening of training in machine learning along with predictive analytics accuracy improvement for high-dimensional models (Preskill, 2018). The enormous potential has to face huge settings for quantum computers. One is that the qubits are overly sensitive to environmental noise, causing decoherence and errors. Besides, a limited number of qubits is usually a problem due to the size. For example, the Eagle processor from IBM has 127 qubits and just a few are functional; consequently, thousands of functional and error-corrected ones are needed for real applications (IBM Quantum, 2023). Furthermore, most quantum mechanical systems rely on energy-hogging cryogenic cooling, raising a question of energy efficiency.

2.2 Internet of Things (IoT)

Internet of Things (IoT) is a revolutionary technology that networks billions of physical objects, allowing them to talk to each other, gather, and share information. They vary from basic sensors measuring environmental conditions to sophisticated autonomous systems like automobiles and industrial robots. Through IoT, industries can enhance efficiency, lower costs, and support informed decision-making for different applications. But as IoT networks grow, they encounter severe challenges in scalability, information processing, and security.

IoT Systems and Core Components

An IoT system consists of several interconnected components that enable its functionality.

1. *Sensors and Actuators.* Sensors gather data from the environment in real time, for instance, temperature, humidity, motion, or pressure. Actuators react to data by taking actions, for instance, switching lights on or modifying machinery. For instance, in agriculture precision, moisture sensors in the soil activate irrigation when thresholds are reached (Liu et al., 2020).
2. *Communication Networks.* IoT devices use communication protocols like Wi-Fi, Bluetooth, ZigBee, and LoRaWAN to share information. Latest technologies like 5G offer large bandwidth and low latency, allowing complex IoT applications such as autonomous vehicles and smart factories (Gupta et al., 2022).

3. *Edge and Cloud Computing.* Edge computing process data at client site which in turn help in reducing latency and bandwidth consumption. For instance, edge computing supports real-time decision-making in self-driving cars, where milliseconds of delay may lead to accidents. Whereas, cloud computing offers centralized analytics and storage of large datasets with scalability and powerful computational capacity (Satyanarayanan, 2017).
4. *User Interfaces.* Dashboards, mobile apps, and other interfaces enable users to view and interact with IoT systems. For instance, a user can fine-tune a smart thermostat through a mobile app or check equipment health in a factory through an industrial IoT dashboard (Zhao et al., 2021).

The Internet of Things (IoT) is transforming numerous industries with enhanced efficiency, sustainability, and decision-making. In smart cities, IoT technology helps manage intelligent traffic, waste management, and street lighting energy efficiency. In Barcelona, for instance, smart parking systems have been introduced that guide drivers to vacant parking areas, alleviating traffic congestion and emissions (Gupta et al., 2022). In healthcare, IoT devices like wearable sensors provide remote patient monitoring and predictive analytics. The devices track vital signs such as heart rate and oxygen saturation, providing early warnings for potential health issues (Liu et al., 2020). IoT also streamlines hospital asset management, having necessary equipment available when needed. In agriculture, IoT supports precision farming using weather stations, soil sensors, and automated irrigation systems. For instance, drones with IoT technology can evaluate crop health, while soil sensors optimize water and fertilizer consumption, increasing yield and sustainability (Zhang et al., 2023). In urban industries, IoT plays a pivotal role in predictive maintenance, real-time monitoring, and process optimization. Sensors embedded within machinery gather operation data to forecast failures, minimizing downtime. Examples include General Electric using Industrial IoT (IIoT) in jet engines to monitor performance and maintain it proactively (Rüßmann et al., 2015).

However, despite its advantages, IoT encounters several challenges. A significant problem is data overload, as IoT networks produce vast amounts of data that can overwhelm traditional computing systems. For instance, autonomous vehicles can generate up to 4 terabytes of data each day, necessitating advanced storage, processing, and analytical solutions (Zhao et al., 2021). Security vulnerabilities also pose a risk, as IoT networks are particularly prone to cyberattacks, including unauthorized access and data breaches. The 2016 Mirai botnet attack, which exploited vulnerable IoT devices to carry out a massive Distributed Denial of Service (DDoS) attack, is an example in point (Kolias et al., 2017). In addition, optimization of resources remains a challenge, with IoT networks experiencing constraints (Gupta et al., 2022), (Satyanarayanan, 2017).

The data processing, security, and optimization limitations of IoT necessitate Quantum Computing. Traditional systems cannot process IoT's vast data streams in real time, while quantum algorithms can efficiently process high-dimensional data. Similarly, quantum cryptography addresses IoT's security challenges by ensuring secure communication between devices (Pirandola et al., 2020). Table 1 illustrates the comparison of classical computing, quantum computing, and the Internet of Things (IoT) across different dimensions.

Table 1. Comparison of Classical Computing, Quantum Computing, and IoT

Feature	Classical Computing	Quantum Computing	IoT
Data Processing	Sequential, limited scalability	Parallel, handles massive datasets	Real-time, data-intensive
Security	Vulnerable to quantum-based attacks	Quantum-safe encryption via QKD	Susceptible to cyberattacks
Optimization	Limited for large-scale problems	Efficient for resource allocation and logistics	Requires efficient energy and bandwidth usage
Energy Consumption	Moderate	High (cryogenic cooling required)	Low-power, often battery-dependent
Applications	General-purpose computing	Optimization, cryptography, simulation, machine learning	Smart cities, healthcare, agriculture, IoT devices

3. SYNERGIES BETWEEN QUANTUM COMPUTING AND IOT

The convergence of Quantum Computing (QC) and the Internet of Things (IoT) has the potential to address critical challenges in IoT, such as (i) data processing bottlenecks, (ii) security vulnerabilities, and (iii) resource optimization inefficiencies. QC leverages quantum principles, such as superposition and entanglement, to perform computations that are infeasible for classical systems. IoT benefits from this by enhancing its data processing, security, and optimization capabilities, which are vital for large-scale deployments.

Quantum algorithms are changing IoT data processing by improving efficiency and accuracy for big data. Quantum Principal Component Analysis (QPCA) collapses the dimensions to make these huge IoT datasets easier for exploitation, such that in healthcare IoT, QPCA analyses data from wearable devices in order to identify early signatures of diseases (Liu et al., 2020). Table 2 shows various quantum algorithms with their application and impacts. Quantum neural networks (QNNs) are important in this context for the prediction of failures in Industrial Internet of Things (IIoT) by analysing sensor data in order to detect anomalies in a more precise way, as an example in identifying a potential failure of equipment in a factory in order to avoid a production interruption (Zhang et al., 2023). Also, the Quantum Approximate Optimization Algorithm (QAOA) is used in smart city for optimizing the resource use according to the traffic behaviour patterns through a dynamic adjustment of the traffic signals, thus minimizing traffic congestion and fuel consumption (Farhi et al., 2019).

Table 2. Quantum Algorithms for IoT Data Processing

Algorithm	IoT Application	Impact	Reference
QPCA	Wearable healthcare devices	Faster data analysis for early disease detection	Liu et al. (2020)
QNN	Industrial IoT predictive maintenance	Improved anomaly detection and downtime reduction	Zhang et al. (2023)
QAOA	Smart city traffic management	Real-time congestion reduction	Farhi et al. (2019)

IoT networks are very susceptible to cyberattacks (e.g., man-in-the-middle attacks, data breaches), due to their networked status. Quantum computing enhances IoT security by quantum cryptography with maximum security measures. Due to the use of entangled qubits in exchanging encryption keys, quantum Key Distribution (QKD) guarantees secure communications between IoT devices. All interception attempts of those keys unsettles the corresponding quantum state, a form of alert to the susceptibility to interception attempts (Pirandola et al., 2020). Such as QKD can be used for protecting information from appliances with Internet of Things (IoT) features, such as smart locks and smart security cameras, in order to resist unauthorized intrusion. Furthermore, Post-Quantum Cryptography (PQC) offers security against future quantum computers that may be able to break the classical encryption protocols. PQC algorithms, in particular, play an important role in protecting private information in industrial and medical IoT systems (Zhao et al., 2021).

IoT networks, for instance, necessitate the effective allocation of scarce resources, e.g., energy, bandwidth and computational resources. Quantum computing (QC) offers superior optimization capabilities with promising benefits in terms of efficiency for large-scale IoT networks. In smart grids, the Quantum Approximate Optimization Algorithm (QAOA)

Figure 2. Classical vs Quantum Cryptography in IoT

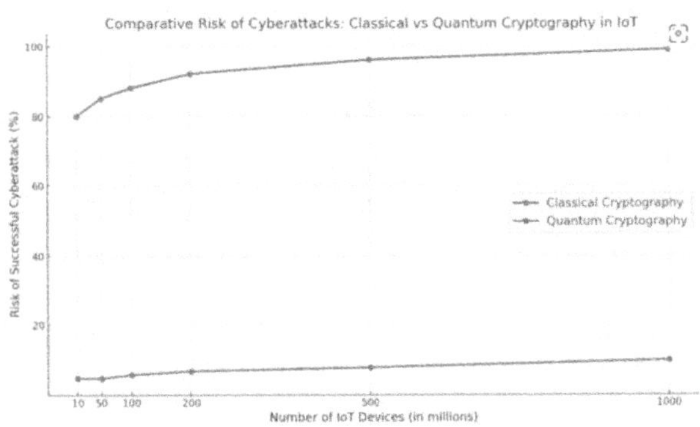

This can be seen from Figure 2 that when using traditional cryptography, the probability of a successful cyber-attack grows with the number of IoT devices, quantum cryptography could drastically decrease this probability. It predicts load shape of energy and schedules resource optimization in real-time. For instance, QAOA can help utility companies balance supply and demand for energy on the fly thereby reducing waste as well as lowering operational expenses (Farhi et al., 2019) Similarly, QC assured with sensor data and optimize traffic flow by tweaking signal timings to save fuel in urban traffic. Furthermore, Quantum checked routing schemes improve the network efficiency of autonomous vehicles by optimizing travel time (Liu et al., 2020). QC can be leveraged in the field of Industrial IoT and can help with load balancing of a quantum computer by spreading (scheduling) computational tasks as uniformly as possible across IoT devices and also the cloud infrastructure, in order to mitigate the inefficiencies that arise due to suboptimal task scheduling (Gupta et al., 2022). A quantum-optimized smart grid in California had demonstrated the tidal of QC by 20% decrease in energy loss.

Applications combining both quantum tunnelling and entanglement read out offer state-of-the-art sensor resolution that enable IoT in medical care as well as automation systems (human-AI-symbiosis) and environmental observation. Heart Rate, Oxygen Levels Heart Rate and oxygen monitoring by quantum sensors in clinical wearables are more accurate than the traditional sensors available within Health IoT applications. Quantum magnetometers are capable of detecting tiny changes in magnetic field (Zhang et al., 2023), and this method can help doctors diagnose Parkinson´ s or Alzheimer´s disease much early. Industrial IoT applications leverage quantum accelerometer technology to measure machine vibrations accurately for early defect detection resulting in cost-saving manufacturing process from predictive maintenance (Gupta et al., 2022) Quantum sensors are used to monitor the gravitational field changes and they can detect even light variations of air quality as well soil compositions made possible in environment evaluation that applications are applied for geological exploration along with agricultural precision (Taylor et al., 2022). Table 3 illustrates few applications of quantum sensors in IoT and their impact.

Table 3. Applications of Quantum Sensors in IoT

Sector	IoT Application	Quantum Sensor Advantage	Reference
Healthcare	Monitoring vital signs	Enhanced accuracy in detecting anomalies	Zhang et al. (2023)
Industrial IoT	Machinery fault detection	Early fault identification	Gupta et al. (2022)
Environmental	Gravitational field measurement	Improved precision for geological exploration	Taylor et al. (2022)

Quantum algorithms, for example QPCA and QAOA making real-time IoT data analytics easy with better throughput efficiency, accuracy Given the nature of security breach attack against IoT Quantum cryptography algorithms (such as QKD and PQC) can safeguard data privacy using computational indecipherable strong encryption. In addition, QC improves the resource allocation in IoT system resulting in less network memory load and superior network performance. Same in an else case. Quantum sensors have superior accuracy for healthcare, industrial and environmental uses unlocking more possibilities of IoT

4. CHALLENGES IN INTEGRATING QUANTUM COMPUTING WITH IOT

The convergence of Quantum Computing (QC) and the Internet of Things (IoT) is highly promising but is subjected to a number of technological, operational, and economic hurdles. These hurdles arise from the existing hardware limitation of quantum technology, the intricacies of integrating hybrid systems, high energy consumption, and financial impediments. Mitigating these challenges calls for hardware, software, and human resource capacity building, in addition to greater insights into scaling QC-IoT systems efficiently. There are various challenges of QC-IoT which is depicted in Figure 3 and discussed in this section.

Figure 3. Challenges in QC-IoT

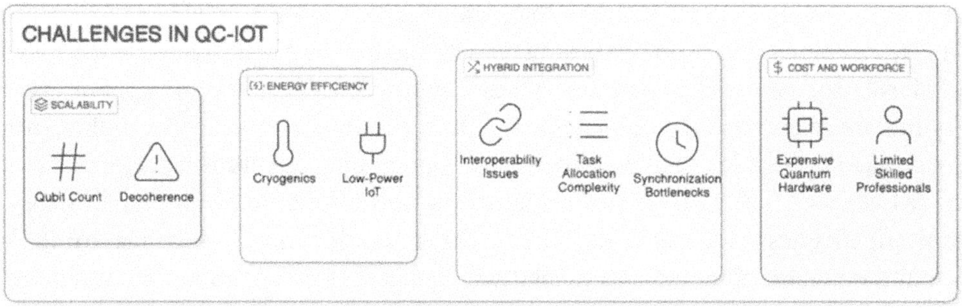

Scalability is one of the main issues for Quantum Computing-IoT (QC-IoT) systems, since existing quantum processors are not sufficiently “smart” to power even a small IoT network, i.e. The high number of updatable registers required to realize the computational intensity of millions of interconnected IoT devices is not feasible by today's quantum systems, like IBM Eagle (127 qubits) and Google Sycamore (54qubits). Examples, for instance, real-time traffic control in smart cities, require thousands of error-free and steady qubits, for example, at IBM Quantum (2023). Also, qubits are very fragile to outside noise, with the possibility of error and (relatively) short coherence times. Although Quantum Error Correction (QEC) is able to address such problems, it dramatically escalates the resource demands because encoding a single logical qubit typically needs hundreds of physical qubits (Preskill, 2018). To serve practical application in the IoT for applications such as optimization of millions of sensors traffic flow, quantum systems need to reach a scaling potential orders of magnitude beyond what is currently possible. Solutions could be found in the fabrication of fault-tolerant quantum computers based on topological qubits or in the development of error correction methods that will lead to a more robust of the qubits and a reduction of the resource requirements.

Hybrid integration is of paramount importance for IoT systems, which largely depend on traditional computing infrastructure and therefore must be designed with quantum-classical architectures to allow synchronized integration. Interoperability is one challenge, since current communication protocols used by IoT, e.g., MQTT and CoAP, are not suitable for use with QPs and were developed for classical systems. Middleware solutions are needed to fill this gap and to facilitate efficient communication between quantum and classical parts (Jin Wang, 2022). One of the problems is synchronisation, because quantum systems are at different rates than classical systems and therefore there are bottlenecks between the quantum and the classical world in the real-time applications of IoT. Efficient synchronization mechanisms are essential to mitigate these delays. In addition, task allocation in hybrid systems is challenging and algorithms need to efficiently partition computational workloads—allocate quantum processors to optimization, cryptographic, or similar tasks and move typical operations to classical systems. For example, in a hybrid smart grid, quantum processors support optimization of energy distribution, whereas classical systems occupy themselves with edge-device monitoring and control. Creating middleware to perform these tasks and developing modular architectures that allow quantum and classical systems to cooperate are still open issues.

Energy efficiency constitutes an important issue for Quantum Computing-Internet of Things (QC-IoT) integration, because the quantum processors are relatively power hungry in the sense that they are based on cryogenic cooling systems required to operate the temperature levels just below absolute zero −273°C). This high energy consumption is at odds with the low power design principle of IoT devices, which usually have to be powered by batteries or other supplies with limited energy. For instance, superconducting qubits are costly to cool because superconducting qubits use expensive cooling infrastructure, which cannot be used in edge IoT applications. Second, integrating quantum processors into low-power-consumption IoT devices (i.e., sensors and actuators) is bound to dramatically raise energy usage and reduce system effectiveness (Hwang et al., 2024). Other solutions in the pipeline are the creation of room-temperature quantum processors (e.g., photonic quantum systems) that do not require cryogenic temperature, or the introduction of quantum cloud computing to transfer quantum computations from energy-limited IoTs (Internet of Things). For example, in a drone swarm environment with internet of things (IoT) capabilities, solving route optimization under a quantum cloud system not only saves the limited on-board energy of drones but also ensures the computational efficiency.

High cost of quantum infrastructure and the lack of experienced people in both Quantum Computing (QC) and Internet of Things (IoT) integration are major roadblocks in the successful implementation. Quantum hardware such as superconducting qubits and cryogenic systems are very costly and accessibility to large corporations and academia limited. Furthermore, quantum cloud computing services are out of the reach of most startups and small businesses (IBM Quantum, 2023). On the labour market side, integration of QC-IoT demands skills in quantum mechanics, IoT architecture as well as software development but there is a worldwide brain shortage of experts in these interdisciplinary fields (Preskill, 2018). Suggested interventions are the development of interdisciplinary educational courses in integration of quantum computing, data science and IoT, and the development of partnerships between the public and private sectors for workforce development aimed at decreasing associated costs via collaborative research. For example, Google Quantum AI's collaboration with education institutions to develop quantum software is illustrative of the ways in which efforts have been made to address the skills gap and speed up the adoption of QC-IoT systems. Table 4 summarizes the challenges in collaborative quantum and IoT systems and their proposed solutions.

Table 4. Challenges and Proposed Solutions

Challenge	Description	Proposed Solution	Reference
Scalability	Limited qubit count and decoherence issues	Fault-tolerant qubits, advanced error correction	IBM Quantum (2023)
Hybrid Integration	Incompatibility between quantum and classical systems	Middleware, modular hybrid architectures	Jin & Wang (2022)
Energy Efficiency	High energy requirements for quantum processors	Photonic quantum processors, quantum cloud computing	Hwang et al. (2024)
Cost and Workforce	High hardware cost and lack of skilled professionals	Public-private partnerships, interdisciplinary training	Preskill (2018)

CONCLUSION AND FUTURE DIRECTIONS

Symbiotic development of Quantum Computing (QC) and the Internet of Things (IoT) requires paradigm-shifting advances in scalable quantum hardware, power-efficient processors, and hybridized quantum-classical concepts. Future research directions include building optimal quantum algorithms for optimization, data analysis, and cryptography to address the issues hindering IoT such as real-time operations and security. The importance of interdisciplinary education-based workforce training and public-private partnerships to fill this skills gap must be combined with international collaboration to accelerate research and standardization. Policymakers are required to address ethical, privacy, and regulatory concerns in order to support secure and responsible use. Advanced, collaborative innovation is the key to bringing QC-IoT convergence to transform the industry, driving intelligence, efficiency, and security.

Additional future directions of quantum computing and IoT integration include developing scalable, fault-tolerant quantum hardware and energy-efficient processors, such as room-temperature photonic implementations. Study of quantum algorithms applicable to in-line optimization, secure cryptography, and data analytics is of utmost importance. Designing hybridization among quantum-classical architectures with middleware for impedance management is crucial. Implementation will be driven by multidisciplinary education and by international collaboration, while ethical deployment will require policymakers to address privacy, security, and regulatory issues. These developments will enable the full utility of QC-IoT systems in all industries.

REFERENCES

Farhi, E., Goldstone, J., & Gutmann, S. (2019). A Quantum Approximate Optimization Algorithm. *arXiv preprint arXiv.1411.4028.*

Gupta, P., Tanwar, S., Tyagi, S., & Kumar, N. (2022). The Evolution of IoT. From Cloud to Fog to Edge Computing. *IEEE Communications Surveys and Tutorials*, *24*(2), 1234–1265.

Hwang, K., Park, S., & Lee, J. (2024). Room-Temperature Quantum Processors for IoT Applications. *Journal of Quantum Hardware*, *18*(1), 45–58.

International Data Corporation (IDC). (2022). The Growth of IoT Data.

Jin, X., & Wang, Y. (2022). Hybrid Quantum-Classical Architectures for IoT Systems. *Quantum Computing and IoT Journal*, *7*(2), 101–115.

Kolias, C., Kambourakis, G., Stavrou, A., & Voas, J. (2017). DDoS in the IoT. Mirai and Other Botnets. *Computer*, *50*(7), 80–84. DOI: 10.1109/MC.2017.201

Liu, X., Zhang, Y., & Zhao, L. (2020). Quantum Machine Learning for IoT Systems. *Journal of Emerging Technologies*, *15*(4), 243–256.

Nielsen, M. A., & Chuang, I. L. (2010). *Quantum Computation and Quantum Information*. Cambridge University Press.

Pirandola, S., Andersen, U. L., & Banchi, L. (2020). Advances in Quantum Cryptography. *Nature Reviews. Physics*, *2*(6), 383–396.

Preskill, J. (2018). Quantum Computing in the NISQ Era and Beyond. *Quantum : the Open Journal for Quantum Science*, *2*, 79–100. DOI: 10.22331/q-2018-08-06-79

Quantum, I. B. M. (2023). *IBM's Quantum Roadmap*. Retrieved from IBM Quantum.

Rüßmann, M., Lorenz, M., Gerbert, P., Waldner, M., Justus, J., Engel, P., & Harnisch, M. (2015). *Industry 4.0. The Future of Productivity and Growth in Manufacturing Industries*. Boston Consulting Group.

Satyanarayanan, M. (2017). The Emergence of Edge Computing. *Computer*, *50*(1), 30–39. DOI: 10.1109/MC.2017.9

Shor, P. W. (1997). Polynomial-Time Algorithms for Prime Factorization and Discrete Logarithms on a Quantum Computer. *SIAM Journal on Computing*, *26*(5), 1484–1509. DOI: 10.1137/S0097539795293172

Taylor, R., Zhang, Y., & Li, H. (2022). Quantum Sensors for Environmental Monitoring. *Sensors Journal*, *21*(8), 1121–1140.

Zhang, Y., Li, H., & Taylor, R. (2023). Quantum Sensors for Next-Generation IoT. *Sensors Journal*, *21*(8), 1121–1140.

Zhao, L., Kim, H., & Choi, K. (2021). Quantum Cryptography for IoT Networks. *IEEE Transactions on IoT Security*, *6*(3), 187–196.

Chapter 6
Optimizing Digital Twin Supply Chains Leveraging Genetic Algorithms Markov Decision Processes

Rama Krishna Mani Kanta Yalla
https://orcid.org/0009-0004-1707-293X
Amazon Web Services, Seattle, USA

Akhil Raj Gaius Yallamelli
https://orcid.org/0009-0007-4345-6947
Amazon Web Services Inc, Seattle, USA

Thirusubramanian Ganesan
https://orcid.org/0009-0008-6125-8466
Cognizant Technology Solutions, Houston, USA

Vijaykumar Mamidala
https://orcid.org/0009-0009-5841-8921
Conga (Apttus), Broomfield, USA

Mohanarangan Veerappermal Devarajan
https://orcid.org/0009-0007-0759-498X
Ernst & Young (EY), Sacramento, USA

Aceng Sambas
Department of Mechanical Engineering, Universitas Muhammadiyah Tasikmalaya, Indonesia

ABSTRACT

Background Information: Data-driven supply chains and real-time simulations involving digital twins are transforming the sector. Nevertheless, existing optimisation techniques usually do not pay much heed to sustainability or resilience. Through enhancing digital twin systems using leading-edge methods in this work, the gap has been filled. Objectives: The main aim of the study is optimizing the efficiency of supply chain systems with the application of GA, ABM, MDP, and SA to enhance operational efficiency, cost savings, and carbon emissions while improving sustainability and resilience. Methods: The strategy includes agent-based modeling, stochastic analysis, Markov decision processes, and genetic algorithm optimization. Results: The integrated approach 86.5% resilience, 18.7% cost reduction, and 93.2% efficiency were attained. Conclusion: The study, thus concludes by how well GA, MDP, ABM, and SA work together in balancing efficiency, resilience, and sustainability.

DOI: 10.4018/979-8-3373-2028-1.ch006

1. INTRODUCTION

In the present rapidly changing global environment, supply chains face immense pressure to adjust to disruptions, achieve sustainability objectives, and improve operational efficiency. **Kumarasamy et al. (2024)** introduce the integration of decentralized graph-based multi-agent reinforcement learning with digital twins for optimizing traffic signals that facilitates adaptive real-time control and enhances the efficiency of urban traffic flow. The concept of DT or a digital twin of the real supply chain systems has evolved as an innovative approach to dealing with these challenges. **Korder et al. (2024)** present an in-depth review of simulation approaches and digital strategies for managing supply chain breakdowns, emphasizing resilience, adaptability, and sustainability in complex supply chain networks. The digital twin will allow for monitoring, simulation, and optimization of the supply chain ecosystem by establishing a dynamic, real-time representation of physical processes.

Supply chains have progressed from being a simple, one-dimensional chain of command to becoming a complex web of interactions in response to changing both internal and external factors such as shifting consumer demand, geopolitical fluctuations, and environmental limitations. These conventional methods do not provide such levels of complexity. **Sodachi et al. (2024)** discussed how MDP models can be applied for assessing the sustainability in Industry 4.0: specifically, decisions in the context of uncertainty that make industrial activities economically and environmentally sustainable. Digital twins, established through the medium of IoT devices and sensors and big data analytics, provide a dynamic framework for connecting the physical and digital realms. This cooperation enhances the ability of organisations to evaluate scenarios, forecast results, and make data-informed decisions. When combined with optimisation methodologies like Genetic Algorithms (GA), Markov Decision Processes (MDP), Agent-Based Modelling (ABM), and Stochastic Approaches, the DT framework evolves into a very powerful instrument for facilitating sustainable and adaptable decision-making.

Digital Twin Supply Chains represent the next revolution in supply chain management. They represent the creation of a digital twin of physical systems of supply chains, which makes it possible to analyze, monitor, and optimize them in real time. **Mazzetto (2024)** addresses interdisciplinary applications of agent-based modeling in the AEC sector. He focuses on its contribution toward improving project coordination and managing complexity in construction processes. These twins constantly update with real-time information, making them an invaluable tool for detecting inefficiencies, forecasting disruptions, and implementing improvements. **Ranawaka et al. (2024)** discusses the integration of digital twins and artificial intelligence in sustainable power grids, with an emphasis on real-time monitoring, predictive maintenance, and optimisation for renewable energy integration and system stability.

Genetic algorithms are optimization techniques derived from the principles of evolution through natural selection, which solve complex supply chain problems such as routing, resource allocation, and production scheduling by evolving solutions iteratively. **Rolf et al. (2023)** suggest a review of the reinforcement learning algorithms in the field of supply chain management where they can be applied for optimization, adaptability, and control of dynamic market and logistical conditions. MDPs provide a mathematical model for making decisions under uncertainty, as it depicts states, actions, and probabilistic transitions; hence it is particularly suited to long-term supply chain planning.

ABM mimics the behavior of individual agents in a supply chain, such as suppliers, manufacturers, and distributors, along with their relationships, which provides an integrated understanding of system-wide dynamics. Stochastic methods deal with uncertainty and unpredictability by incorporating randomness into supply chain operations, including demand variations, lead times, and transportation delays, thus enabling resilient decision-making. The integration of these strategies with the digital twin technological capabilities brings on an adaptive smart supply chain responding to real-time changes but that does not obviate medium- and long-term strategic outcomes. This progression from traditional analog supply chains has been facilitated and driven by numerous breakthroughs seen in Industry 4.0 technologies, including IoTs, Artificial Intelligence, and big data integrated with cloud-based computing. The complexity of these systems increases while, at the same time, exposing them to disturbance from global crises, climate change, and geopolitical instability.

The COVID-19 pandemic made supply chains fragile, causing enormous disruption in logistics, production, and distribution. **Bogner et al. (2024)** focuses on the integration of agent-based modeling with machine learning into complexity economics and puts emphasis on sustainability transitions in economic system behavior in uncertainty and dynamic fluctuations. Hence, presently, organizations focus on resilience, adaptability, and sustainability for supply chain design. These problems are solved efficiently by digital twins, as they provide continued visibility into the activities of supply chains. This will enable organisations to model scenarios, assess risks, and optimize the allocation of resources. However, the complexity of modern supply chains demands complex optimisation and decision-making approaches in order to properly leverage DT technology. Such is the applicability of computational methods such as Genetic Algorithms, Markov Decision Processes, Agent-Based Modelling, and stochastic modelling.

These strategies enhance the digital twinning decision-making capabilities to move the digital twin in environments with dynamic conditions while predicting disturbances and simulating sustainable habits. Digital twins combined with powerful computational methods represent a seminal leap in supply chain management. The strategy will endow organisations with real-time visibility, predictive analytics, and a means to formulate sustainable decisions for success amidst a chaotic and uncertain global landscape. **Ouda et al. (2023)** discussed discrete-event and agent-based simulation methodologies for emergency departments, which focus on the efficiency of such methodologies in modeling operations, resource optimization, and eliminating bottlenecks in the delivery of healthcare services. This study explores the interaction between digital twins and advanced techniques for supply chains with practical implications toward the enhancement of resilience and sustainability of such supply chains.

The main objectives are:

- Improving Resilience: Provide resilient digital twin-enabled frameworks to mitigate risks with the help of optimized computational methods and enable adaptation to potential supply chain upsets.
- Improving Resource Utilization: Use computational solutions to improve performance, reduce waste, and expense in supply chains.
- Improvement in Sustainability: Integrate Environmental and Social considerations with supply chain decisions to meet International Sustainability Goals.
- Enable Real-Time Decision-Making: Leverage digital twin real-time data to dynamically optimize supply chain activities and respond effectively to changing conditions
- Have Theory Meet Practice: An investigation of practical Digital Twin integration of Genetic Algorithms, Markov Decision Processes, Agent-Based Modelling and stochastic methods within the digital twin framework for supply chain wide optimisation.

Belhadi et al. (2022) clearly explain the role of AI in enhancing supply chain resilience through a systematic decision-making framework. There is still a huge research gap in terms of scalability and adaptability of the proposed framework across various industries and varying levels of digital maturity.

The study primarily examines AI-driven solutions but does not thoroughly investigate the incorporation of upcoming technologies such as digital twins or blockchain for real-time resilience. Further research is needed to test the effectiveness of the framework in managing highly dynamic and uncertain contexts, especially in the context of extensive global crises.

Huang et al. (2021) highlight the growing importance of AI-based digital twins in Industry 4.0, especially in the context of smart manufacturing and advanced robotics. Although digital twins hold transformative potential, fully integrated frameworks with AI to enable real-time decision-making, predictive analytics, and system optimization are not available. The primary challenges are the inadequacy of interoperability among systems, restriction of scalability in extensive industrial applications, and unmanaged data security and privacy concerns. This leads to the necessity of developing strong AI-integrated digital twin models that may break these limits but enhance adaptability, efficiency, and resilience in industrial operations.

2. LITERATURE SURVEY

Gao et al. presented the development of an optimized digital twin-based decision support system to address scheduling and other operational bottlenecks on the floor level, optimizing automation and smart routing in the automotive manufacturing setting in (2024). It used real-time information, which ensured improved work assignments and minimized downtime besides raising efficiency by offering solutions under complicated scheduling through the usage of AI. A case study shows high improvements in logistics performance and proves the feasibility of digital twins as a tool for improving AGV operations and supporting decision-making in manufacturing and warehousing.

Qin et al. (2024) provide a comprehensive review of the application of deep learning (DL) and machine learning (ML) in digital twin networks, focusing on their role in anomaly detection, optimization, and predictive modeling in networked systems. Besides discussing critical issues such as data security and computing requirements, the project looks at fundamental ML/DL methods and how they are being used with digital twins. In addition to this, it also provides a framework for future work, with scalable algorithms and privacy-preserving techniques to make the digital twin networks more intelligent, scalable, and dependable.

Siatras et al. (2024) propose a digital twin-based multi-agent system which schedules production within the bicycle industry. The actual manufacturing procedures can be emulated by the proposed system, bringing together production targets with operational limitations and resource availability. Situational awareness will be improved by enabling dynamic changes to scheduling, better resource usage and on-time delivery capabilities of digital twins. The presented case study exhibits the effectiveness of the system in effectively achieving flexible and agile production planning. This study further establishes that digital twins are a very potent tool for flexible and effective scheduling in changing industrial settings.

Nie et al. (2023) study the application of the RL algorithm for a digital twin framework in forecasting the flow of traffic within a transportation network. The approach constructs a digital model of traffic systems using copious amounts of sensor and Internet of Things data to facilitate real-time prediction and optimization. The RL-based approach provides dynamic adaptation to the evolution of traffic patterns, enhancing the performance of the system and the accuracy of the forecasts. This work represents a major breakthrough in traffic management by successfully tackling problems of real-time data integration and computational efficiency on scalable solutions for smart cities.

Ganesh and Kalpana (2022) Emphasizing revolutionary importance, focused on how it may improve decision-making and predictive analytics. The study focused on AI's capacity to optimise supply chain operations, identify hazards, and increase resilience. In addition to other disruptive detection technologies, it researches the usage of machine learning (ML) and natural language processing (NLP) frameworks. Moreover, the study throws light on topics such as scalability and data quality. The review talks of the possibility AI could create a smart, risk-averse supply network, creating a gateway toward more robust supply chains that are successful.

Leon et al. (2023) propose a hybrid simulation and reinforcement learning algorithm for warehouse operations optimization. Simulating and enhancing logistical operations such as picking, packing, and routing with the aid of reinforcement learning and discrete event simulation, the system shows significant increases in effectiveness in operation, cost savings, and reductions in delays. The strategy supports flexible decision-making, increases warehouse competitiveness and agility. The study highlights that reinforcement learning handles complex, uncertain settings to make improvements in the automation and intelligent solutions of logistics.

Homayouni et al. (2024) discuss the deployment of digital twins in seaport sustainability improvement studies. The review of existing activities and suggestions of future ones mainly focus on optimization of resource utilization, lowering of emissions, and improvement in efficiency of operation. The importance of digital twins for real-time monitoring, predictive maintenance, and support in decision making is emphasized while addressing problems of data integration and scalability. The authors emphasize that digital twins are basic for realizing sustainable, intelligent port ecosystems and fulfilling global environmental objectives.

Gholizadeh et al. (2024) develop a simulation-optimization approach for the design of reconfigurable and robust closed-loop supply chains. The model integrates digital twins for scenario analysis and decision support to mitigate uncertainties in demand and disruptions. Important contributions include enhancing flexibility, sustainability, and resilience in supply chain operations. A case study supports the methodology, with increased adaptability and reduced costs. This study, however, outlines the capability of digital twins and simulation-optimization for handling complex issues within dynamic settings that define a supply chain.

Allur (2020) examines a data-driven approach to agricultural supply chain management, with the focus on optimization of scheduling through MILP and DSS. The project deals with accuracy and scalability issues in the optimization of agricultural supply chains with the aim of improving sustainability, cost-effectiveness, and resource allocation. The proposed methods have a significant impact on the overall performance of the agriculture industry by enhancing the efficiency and reliability of supply networks.

Bobba (2023) merges cloud finance concepts with sustainable development methods in the creation of intelligent urban landscapes. The findings focus on how cloud technology might enhance urban infrastructure, support environmental sustainability, or even make financial decisions better. The positive findings point out a strategic importance of cloud solutions in achieving both environmental and economic objectives, particularly in regions that are increasingly turning into urban ones. This research offers insight into how cloud computing can promote urban development while also addressing such matters as sustainability.

A real-time malware detection system using HMM, LSTM networks, and Adaptive Gradient Support Vector Regression, is proposed by Devi in 2020. The latest framework enhances cybersecurity in dynamic scenarios to a very great extent through the exhibition of a high accuracy level with high agility in detecting malware. Coupling these latest methods will improve the threat-detecting capacity of the system while offering solid defense against changes in malware attacks in a number of scenarios.

Sareddy (2021) addresses difficult human resources issues applying complex, applied quantitative models involving logarithms, linear functions, and Markov Analysis. The author further, thus, details and emphasizes how the mathematical modeling can improve any form of decision-making, workforce processes, and overall organizational productivity. The study shows that by using such strategies, it is also possible to strengthen the organizational structure and make HR activities easier for better workforce management performance and results.

Bousdekis et al. (2021) focuses on data-driven decision-making methodologies for Industry 4.0 maintenance applications. It categorises methods such as predictive maintenance, anomaly detection, and asset health monitoring using machine learning, deep learning, and the Internet of Things. The document highlights their capabilities in terms of cost reduction and operational dependability. The limitations are issues in data quality, integration complexity. It elaborates a framework on implementing data-driven solutions. The concept outlines real-time analytics and digital twins for transforming maintenance into an active and smart procedure.

Qiu and Zhao (2024) discuss how green energy meets artificial intelligence at the heart of modern energy systems. It goes into AI-oriented optimisation solutions for renewable source production, transport, and utilization by considering monetary, social, and environmental factors. The relevance of AI toward achieving sustainability with the enhancement in efficiency of using energy and lower carbon emission has been thrown open. Even data management or scalability problems are eliminated. It lays emphasis on how AI and green energy can harmoniously work for better next-generation energy systems.

Aretoulaki et al. (2024) explore digital twins and discrete event simulation within warehouse logistics. It detects trends, applications, and research gaps through the analysis of bibliometric and content data. Digital twins and discrete event simulation improve warehouse efficiency, decision-making, and adaptability. Model complexity and data synchronisation challenges are addressed. The research thus lays a foundation for developing an intelligent warehouse system, underscoring the significance of simulation and digital twin technologies in developing logistics.

Wang et al. (2024) proposed the idea of a human digital twin within the context of Industry 5.0 and on the emphasis of human-centric technologies. It encompasses artificial intelligence, the Internet of Things, and digital twin frameworks to simulate human-machine interactions, ergonomics, and safety. Applications of human digital twins include adaptive production systems and monitoring worker well-being. It also discussed challenges, such as data privacy and complexity of the system. The research shows the revolutionary capability of human digital twins in establishing sustainable, collaborative, and human-centric industrial settings.

Deepak et al. (2024) develop an AI-augmented thermal modeling framework for zero-defect manufacturing processes. The methodology includes process-product-system optimization by using digital twins and thermal simulations. AI-based methodologies enhance accuracy, quality, and defect prediction in manufacturing. The model is validated by case studies that show increased production efficiency and reduced waste. The study highlights the importance of digital twins in attaining superior quality and sustainability of manufacturing, handling issues such as scalability and processing real-time data.

Tong et al. (2024) provide a co-evolutionary digital twin framework for dynamic digital engineering. It emphasizes multimodal plasticity, enabling digital twins to evolve in tandem with their physical counterparts. The study examines algorithms for real-time updates, forecasting, and optimization. Demonstrations of applications in smart manufacturing and infrastructure illustrate improved system resilience and performance. Challenges such as computational requirements and data integration are addressed. It places importance on the prospective capabilities of adaptive and collaborative digital twin ecosystems.

Ngo et al. (2023) assesses the integration of graph neural networks (GNNs) into digital twin improvements for next-generation networks. The paper is highlighted by its potential to create complex network topology, thus opening predictive analytics and optimisation using GNNs inside the digital twin frameworks. Areas of application involve smart grids, the Internet of Things (IoT), and telephony. It investigates issues involving computational efficiency and data privacy. The research outlines opportunities for improving digital twin technology using GNNs to enable the development of intelligent, scalable network solutions.

3. METHODOLOGY

This method has brought together latest computational techniques to the application in optimization of supply chains through using DT technology, GA to handle tough optimization problems about resource allocation, and scheduling, as well as useful applications for planning long-term scenarios and making choices, MDP; emergent behaviors and the system dynamics unveiled through simulating the interactions among various entities is done through Agent-Based Modeling; and stochastic methods are robust given management of demands, lead times, and the uncertainty of disturbances. When these methods are integrated into a DT framework, dynamic supply chains can benefit from real-time monitoring, predictive analytics, and sustainable decision-making.

Figure 1. Architectural Framework for Optimizing Digital Twin Supply Chains

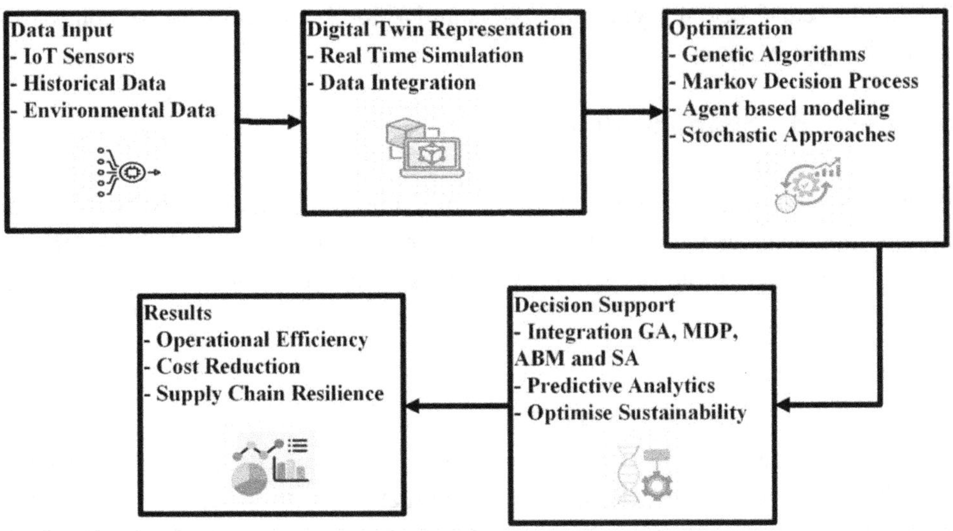

Figure 1 Illustrates the architectural basis for optimizing digital twin supply chains using advanced methods. Data from IoT sensors, historical information, and environmental factors feed into the digital twin model, enabling real-time simulation and data integration. Optimisation methods, including Genetic Algorithms, Markov Decision Processes, Agent-Based Modelling, and Stochastic Approaches, yield

solutions that optimize efficiency and resilience. A Decision Support System integrates these results, offering predictive analytics and actionable insights to promote sustainability and operations. Continuous input allows the system to be dynamically adjusted, enabling real-time flexibility and better decision-making for complex supply chain management issues.

3.1 Framework Design for Digital Twin-Enabled Supply Chains

This subtopic is the development of a systematic framework for the introduction of DT technology into supply chain management. This includes the detailing of system architecture, data flow processes, and integration methodologies with IoT devices and AI technology. The framework provides real-time synchronisation between the physical and digital systems, hence enabling monitoring, predictive analytics, and optimisation. It addresses issues including data interoperability, system scalability, and effective communication between its components. It facilitates digital twin operations in the architecture to enable dynamic decision-making and make supply chain networks more agile and sustainable.

3.1.1 System Architecture Definition

This subsection deals with a unifying architecture for the constituent parts of digital twins, along with IoT nodes and the target physical system; it is represented by components used in cloud platform, simulation engine and data collecting for integration purposes for continuous real time monitoring, and data analysis of decision-making operations. This way, the complex management and activities optimization in a dynamic system become possible.

$\mathrm{DT} = (P, D, S, M)$ (1)

The Digital Twin framework components are defined as P for the physical system, D for the digital counterpart, S for the real-time data synchronisation, and M for the instruments to monitor and optimise the processes in the supply chain.

3.1.2 Data Flow and Communication

This subtopic addresses the development of data pipelines to enable real-time updates and uninterrupted communication between physical systems and their digital twins by using IoT-enabled connection for effective data interchange, monitoring, and synchronisation throughout the supply chain framework.

$$R_t = \frac{D_{\text{transferred}}}{T_{\text{interval}}} \quad (2)$$

Here D_"transfer" is the number of data exchanged, T_"interval" is the time duration of the transfer of the data and R_t is the refresh rate of data. The combination of these parts offers effective real-time synchronization that maximizes the flow of data and increases the system performance as a whole. This configuration makes timely changes so that it keeps information synchronized and up-to-date, which means it allows precise and smooth communication in the system.

3.1.3 Scalability and Interoperability

This subtopic discusses scalable frameworks designed to ensure smooth integration and interoperability across multiple systems and procedures. These frameworks eventually enhance the effectiveness and robustness of dynamic supply chain environments by allowing easy adaptation, promoting efficient communication, and improving interoperability. The aim is to design systems that are easily adaptable to changes and that enable cooperation among various parts.

$$S_{eff} = \frac{R_{\text{actual}}}{R_{\max}} \quad (3)$$

In this setting, S eff is used to express scalability efficiency. R actual denotes the present performance of the system, while R max expresses the optimal performance the system can be able to realize. The expression helps grasp how well a system can adapt or scale under multiple settings. This meter measures the scale at which a system performs relative to several challenges it encounters during its scaling processes. It, therefore, quantifies the level at which a system functions while scaling up or facing novel issues.

Figure 2. Comprehensive Digital Twin Architecture for Data-Driven Supply Chain Management

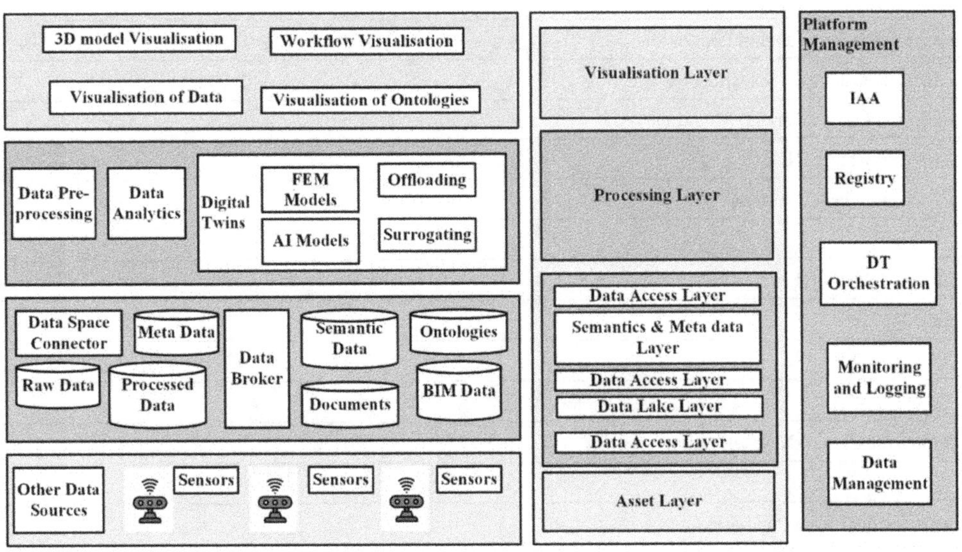

Figure 2 Multi-level architecture of the digital twin for supply chain management. The Asset Layer collects information from sensors and external sources; this is then structured and managed in the Data Access Layer with semantic, metadata, and processed information. The Processing Layer integrates the digital twin models, artificial intelligence algorithms, and analytics for simulation, decision-making, and surrogate processes. The Visualisation Layer supports interactive renderings of workflows, ontologies, and three-dimensional models. The Platform Management layer oversees platform operations in monitoring, logging, and data management. This architecture ensures seamless data integration, visualization, and optimization for effective and reliable decision-making.

3.2 Application of Genetic Algorithms for Supply Chain Optimization

In supply chains, GAs are utilized to solve complex optimization problems relating to resource allocation, routing, and production scheduling. This subtopic involves formulating fitness functions that incorporate cost efficiency, delivery schedules, and sustainability indicators. Genetic algorithms iteratively improve their solutions through the action of mechanisms such as selection, crossover, and mutation in finding optimal or near-optimal solutions. Their application helps to solve nonlinear and multi-objective problems within supply networks. Genetic algorithms were used for the methodology to create flexible, efficient and robust supply chain designs that can accommodate various operational scenarios and restrictions.

Algorithm 1. Algorithm for Genetic Algorithm for Supply Chain Optimization

Input: **Initial_Population, Max_Generations, Mutation_Rate, Crossover_Rate**
Output: Optimal_Supply_Chain_Config
BEGIN
Initialize Population with Initial_Population
FOR generation = 1 TO Max_Generations **DO**
Evaluate Fitness of Each Individual in Population
Select Parents using Tournament_Selection()
Generate Offspring via Crossover and Mutation:
IF rand() < Crossover_Rate **THEN**
Perform Crossover on Selected Parents
END IF
IF rand() < Mutation_Rate **THEN**
Mutate Offspring
END IF
END
Replace Worst Individuals with New Offspring
END FOR
RETURN Best_Individual from Population
END

Algorithm 1 applies evolutionary principles from the biological concept of genetics evolution. Here, an initial population consisting of possible configurations gradually evolves toward perfection by a set of successive generations. Efficient solutions are identified via a fitness test, and the genetic operators-though somewhat related in names, this algorithm utilizes-crossover and mutation-to bring heterogeneity to it. Bad solutions are replaced for guaranteeing survival for the fittest. The population converges to an optimal configuration that optimizes sustainability, cost, and efficiency through multiple iterations. Genetic algorithms are extremely effective for complex, multi-objective problems with vast solution spaces, making them well-suited for supply chain optimization in dynamic settings.

3.2.1 Chromosome Representation for Supply Chain Parameters

This subtopic presents the supply chain decisions, such as routing and inventory management, in the form of chromosomes to enable their optimization by genetic algorithm techniques to increase efficiency and performance in dynamic and complex supply chain scenarios.

$$C = \{c_1, c_2, \ldots, c_n\} \tag{4}$$

In this scenario, C represents a chromosome. Meanwhile, c_i represents each decision variable in the chromosome. These are just the recordable supply chain characteristics optimized by genetic algorithms to improve efficiency and operations of and decisions.

3.2.2 Fitness Function Design

Focuses on optimizing crucial parameters such as cost-effectiveness, scheduling, and sustainability. This would result in a balanced decision-making process that will improve overall performance of the supply chain and then meet or be aligned with economic, operational, and environmental objectives.

$$F(C) = \alpha C_{\text{cost}} + \beta C_{\text{time}} + \gamma C_{\text{sustainability}} \tag{5}$$

Here, $F(C)$ is the fitness score, and α, β, γ are weights assigned to highlight cost, time, and sustainability factors, respectively, in the optimization process.

3.2.3 Evolutionary Operators

The system uses genetic algorithms, where it explores multiple solutions through processes such as crossover, mutation, and selection. The algorithm optimizes efficiency and enables the system to adjust to changing circumstances by iteratively fine-tuning the supply chain's parameters. This strategy improves the overall effectiveness and resilience of the supply chain under changing conditions.

$$P_{\text{new}} = P_{\text{old}} \cdot O_{\text{selection}} \cdot O_{\text{mutation}} \cdot O_{\text{crossover}} \tag{6}$$

In this context, P_{new} is the newly generated population, and O represents the genetic operators used, namely selection, crossover, and mutation, for iteratively evolving and optimizing solutions within the genetic algorithm framework.

3.3 Markov Decision Processes for Uncertainty Management

MDPs provide a probabilistic framework under uncertainty in a supply chain's decision-making mechanism. This is the sub-topic that emphasizes how to model the states, the actions, transitions, and probably the probabilistic characteristics of a supply chain. Variable demand is a characteristic aspect of a supply chain dynamics coupled with disruptions Markov Decision Process helps in long-term strategic planning and adaptability in identifying strategies. Its integration with digital transformation frameworks enables modifications in real time and data-driven decisions, therefore enhancing supply chain resilience. This methodology addresses complexity calculations and transition probability calculation, therefore allowing for easy management of uncertainty in supply chains.

Algorithm 2. Algorithm for Markov Decision Process (MDP) for Optimal Policy

Input: **States S, Actions A, Transition_Probabilities P, Rewards R, Discount_Factor γ**
Output: Optimal_Policy π^*
BEGIN
Initialize V(s) = 0 for all s ∈ S
REPEAT
$\Delta = 0$
FOR each state $s \in S$ DO
v = $V(s)$
$V(s) = \max_a \sum_{s'} P(s' \mid s,a) * [R(s,a,s') + \gamma * V(s')]$
$\Delta = \max(\Delta, \lvert v - V(s) \rvert)$
END FOR
UNTIL $\Delta <$ Threshold
FOR each state $s \in S$ DO
$\pi^*(s) = \arg\max_a \sum_{s'} P(s' \mid s,a) * [R(s,a) + \gamma V(s')]$
END FOR
RETURN π^*
END

Algorithm 2 uses Markov Decision Processes to improve the decision-making of uncertain supply chains. States denote the supply chain conditions, action denotes the possible decisions, and transition probabilities define how the action leads to new states. The algorithm creates an optimal policy by iteratively computing value functions for states and maximizing the predicted rewards. The discount factor considers the future rewards. MDPs are very effective in sequential decision-making, especially when uncertainty is paramount. It thus helps in efficiently distributing resources and strategically adapting to fluctuations in supply chain activities.

3.3.1 State Transition Modeling

To model states and transitions for simulating the dynamics of the supply chain under uncertainty, thus allowing the possible variations to be explored, it enables adaptability and resilience in uncertain conditions through understanding how decisions are made in these dynamic environments. Modeling the system helps enhance its ability to adjust to change, maximize decision-making, and ensure continuous performance in the supply chain.

$$T(s,a,s') = P(s' \mid s,a) \tag{7}$$

In the present case, T is the transition probability. The value of stochastic dynamics in the supply chain model is that this parameter quantifies the chances of transitioning from a given states to state s' after taking action a. Therefore, the transition probability includes intrinsic uncertainties and variances within the system. Thus, modeling such probabilistic transitions enables one to analyze and decide more precisely under this framework and thereby improve resilience and adaptability in the changeable settings for supply chain operations.

3.3.2 Policy Optimization

A process identifies the best route through techniques involving value iteration as well as policy iteration. Therefore, analyzing how the state transits and then the expected profit can be maximized makes optimal decision-making with respect to uncertainty and dynamism in supply chains possible. Thus, this system helps in computing the best actions that can counter the complexities as well as unforeseen events experienced in supply chains so that right information towards long-term results is ensured during the decision.

$$V\left(s\right) = \max_{a} \sum_{s'} T(s,a,s') \cdot [R(s,a) + \gamma V(s')] \tag{8}$$

Here, R is for the reward, γ for the discount factor, and V(s) for the value function. The value function is an estimation of the sum of all long-run expected benefits associated with undertaking specific supply chain model actions. It aids in strategic decision-making within dynamic and uncertain supply chain settings by evaluating all possible consequences with a holistic weighing of future rewards against immediate ones through the discount factor.

3.3.3 Long-Term Planning Under Uncertainty

This approach employs computer-based strategies that optimize strategic selections to meet the long-term objectives of a supply chain. Its aim is to achieve resilience, sustainability, and efficiency in supply chain operations. It ensures that the supply chain can negotiate unstable and uncertain situations while building strength against changing conditions so that it aligns itself with the set organizational goals.

$$\pi^*(s) = \arg\max_{a} Q(s,a) \tag{9}$$

In this context, π^* represents the optimal policy that maximizes outcomes, whereas $Q(s,a)$ denotes the action-value function, which assesses the anticipated rewards of executing action a in state s, hence informing decision-making in supply chain optimization.

Figure 3. Markov Decision Process (MDP) Framework for Decision-Making

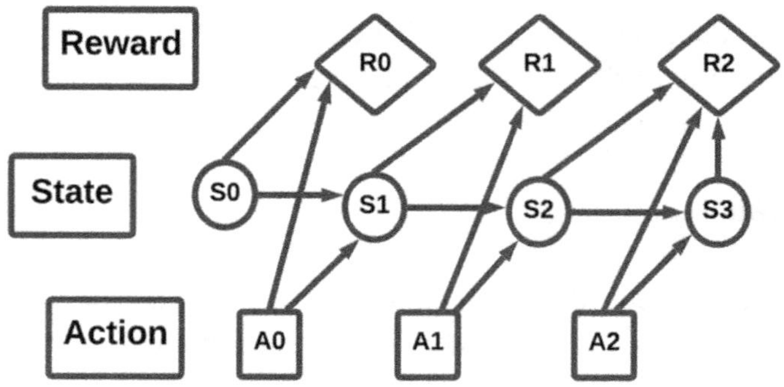

Figure 3 presents Markov Decision Process framework describes the sequential decision-making process with uncertainty. The State nodes S0, S1, S2, S3 are different stages of the system. The Action nodes A0, A1, A2 define the possible actions for each stage. The probability-driven transitions between states result in a Reward, R0, R1, R2 dependent on the activity taken. This approach widely used in optimisation problems of maximising cumulative rewards over time by the choice of optimal action for every state, and it is essential in applications like supply chain management and robotics.

3.4 Agent-Based Modeling for System Dynamics and Interactions

ABM mimics supply chain agents' behaviors and interactions, including suppliers, manufacturers, and distributors. It is accompanied by the emphasis on capture emergent dynamics and decentralized decision-making processes. ABM helps to analyze complex adaptive systems, and in doing so, shedding light upon bottlenecks, cooperative methods, and system vulnerabilities. Thus, integration of ABM with DTs improves the understanding of interdependencies and reaction methods of supply chains. This helps to enhance the ability to simulate real-life scenarios, analyze policies, and design more robust and sustainable supply chain systems.

Algorithm 3. Algorithm for Agent-Based Modeling for Supply Chain Simulation

Input: **Agents *A*, Environment *E*, Simulation_Time *T***
Output: Supply_Chain_Performance_Metrics
BEGIN
Initialize Agents and Environment
FOR*t* = 1 TO *T***DO**
FOR each agent $a \in A$**DO**
Perceive State from Environment
IF Critical_State **THEN**
Execute Adaptive_Strategy

continued on following page

Algorithm 3. Continued

Input: **Agents *A*, Environment *E*, Simulation_Time *T***
ELSE IF Normal_State **THEN**
Execute Regular_Action
END IF
Update Environment with Agent's Action
END FOR
Collect Metrics for Supply_Chain_Performance
END FOR
RETURN Supply_Chain_Performance_Metrics
END

Algorithm 3 of the Agent-Based Modeling is a re-creation of the interactions that the supply chain actors (the suppliers, the producers, the distributors) portray under a given setting. Each agent acts independently sensing its environment, changing its action according to the condition it observes. In a simulation timeline, agents change the methods dynamically concerning the critical event or routine activity. The model reveals emergent behaviors, bottlenecks, and the consequence of decisions for each point in the supply chain. This approach enables decision-makers to collect performance measurements, thereby helping identify and implement initiatives that can enhance coordination, efficiency, and sustainability in supply chains.

3.4.1 Agent Behavior Modeling

This method simulates individual agents' activities and interactions within a system by determining the rules, objectives, and procedures that govern their behavior. The technology aims at improving decision-making procedures and studies emerging trends especially in complex scenarios of supply chain. It presents insights into improved performance and better decision-making dynamics in dynamic scenarios by simulating how agents co-operate and adapt.

$$A_{\text{state}} = f(E, G, R) \quad (10)$$

Here, A_{state} represents the status of an agent, E the environment in which it operates, G defines the objectives of the agent, and R is the available resources, which altogether determine the agent's behavior and interactions.

3.4.2 Multi-Agent Interactions

This approach analyzes agent interactions in order to understand aggregate influence on system-wide dynamics. It provides insight to their dependencies, emergent behaviors, and general functionality of complex systems such as supply chains. A good understanding of such interactions will be quite useful for catching trends, predicting system reactions, and making better decisions in dynamic environments.

$$I_{ij} = w_{ij} \cdot A_i \cdot A_j \tag{11}$$

In this case, I_{ij} is the interaction strength between agents, w_{ij} is the weight of the interaction, and A_i, A_j are the relative states of the interacting agents within the system.

3.4.3 Emergent Dynamics Analysis

This method observes how the sum of micro-level activities of multiple agents leads to macro-level effects. From supply chains to other decentralized environments, it provides key insights into overall performance, trends, and systemic dynamics of complex systems. Analyzing the aggregate behavior of agents facilitates the identification of trends and informed decision-making toward improving the general resilience and functionality of the system.

$$D_{macro} = \sum_{i=1}^{n} f(A_i, E) \tag{12}$$

Here, A_i stands for the macro-level results represented by the collective states of the individual agents contributing to these effects, while D_macro represents emergent dynamics resulting from the collective interaction of the system. This correlation is an instance of how action and interaction across separated entities gives rise to emergent, complex patterns that influence the system as a whole. Examining these dynamics allows the paradigm to provide useful insights into individual contributions to performance at the overall system level as well as to emergent behavior in dynamic situations.

3.5 Stochastic Approaches for Modeling Randomness

This subtopic deals with integrating stochastic models into handling uncertainty and randomness in supply chains. The probabilistic distributions and stochastic processes are used to represent variabilities such as demand changes, lead times, and transportation delays. This method clearly introduces randomization, thereby ensuring robust decision-making and supply chain designs that withstand unpredictable circumstances. The combination of stochastic techniques with decision tree frameworks thus supports the real-time analysis of scenarios, risk evaluation, and contingency planning that promote continuity of operations and improved performance under uncertainty.

Algorithm 4. Algorithm for Stochastic Optimization for Sustainable Decision-Making

Input: **Demand_Distribution *D*, Supply_Options *S*, Constraints *C***
Output: Optimal_Supply_Strategy
BEGIN
Generate Scenarios based on *D* and *S*
Initialize Best_Strategy = NULL, Min_Cost = ∞
FOR each Scenario Sc in Scenarios **DO**
Calculate Cost = f(Sc, *C*)

continued on following page

Algorithm 4. Continued

Input: **Demand_Distribution *D*, Supply_Options *S*, Constraints *C***
IF Cost < Min_Cost **THEN**
Min_Cost = Cost
Best_Strategy = Sc
END IF
END FOR
RETURN Best_Strategy
END

Algorithm 4 deals with uncertainty in the supply chain's demand and supply by creating scenarios based on probabilistic distributions. It tests each scenario against restrictions to come up with economical and sustainable methods of supply. By comparing costs between scenarios, the algorithm will find the plan that has the least cost that simultaneously satisfies sustainability goals. Stochastic optimization is quite effective in handling uncertainties, enabling decisions that are both robust and resilient. This approach is especially beneficial for sustainable supply chains, reconciling environmental effects with operational and economic factors.

3.5.1 Demand Variability Modeling

Demand variation and uncertainty are included in the model, thereby recording disjoint shifts to effectively analyze and predict dynamic trends. It enhances a supply chain's operations' robustness through enhanced decision-making by accounting for changing conditions. The adaptability of the model to these changes ensures that there will be more accurate predictions and results in proactive changes, which, in turn, increase responsiveness and efficiency in its operations.

$$D_t \sim N(\mu, \sigma^2) \tag{13}$$

This is the expression; where D_t is demand at time t, μ represents mean demand, and σ^2 variance in the expression that models demand variability for better understanding and handling of uncertainty in supply chain operations.

3.5.2 Probabilistic Lead Time Estimation

This method tackles the uncertainty intrinsic in supply chain operations by looking at lead time as a stochastic variable. More precise estimations are facilitated while the decision becomes more effective when simulating the lead time variability. It also captures the dynamism of both processing and delivery times, providing an even clearer view of what these lead time variations are for which it all pays off, finally improving on effectiveness and reliability of supply chain management in managing uncertainties.

$$L = P(X \leq x) \tag{14}$$

L will refer to the lead time probability whereas X will imply the random variable which is used for uncertainty and variability so it would be a probabilistic basis to calculate the lead times involved in supply chain activities.

3.5.3 Robust Decision-Making

This method incorporates factors of stochastic aspects into the optimizing process to help consider supply interruptions and demand fluctuations within the system. Simulating these types of uncertainties allow for resilient as well as versatile solutions that give room for even higher productivity coupled with adaptability in dynamic systems of supply chain. By adopting resilience, operational efficacy is easily preserved while responsiveness to unforeseen circumstances is enabled.

$$C_{robust} = \int f(x)p(x)dx \tag{15}$$

Here, p(x) is the probability density function, and C_robust denotes the robust cost. Combining these two components reduces uncertainty and gives dependability in the optimization of supply chain operations. This approach enhances decision-making through probabilistic analysis and comprehensive cost assessment, making the supply chain survive turbulence and remain robust and efficient even when faced with ambiguity.

3.6 Integration and Real-Time Monitoring within Digital Twin Frameworks

This subtopic investigates the integration of IoT, AI, and data analytics to allow for immediate synchronisation between the physical systems and their digital equivalents. It focuses on real-time monitoring, immediate updates, and predictive analytics within the DT architecture. Core components include data collection, processing, and visualization for real-time decision-making. The method also addresses concerns such as latency, security, and scalability. This connection supports real-time adaptability, in which supply chains can quickly react to disturbances and optimize operations, maintaining resilience even in dynamic situations.

3.6.1 Real-Time Data Acquisition

This method allows real-time digitization of a physical system while at the same time maintaining constant synchronism between its digital and physical counterparts. It offers better monitoring and analysis because of the accurate keeping of the actual state of the physical system in question. There is, thereby, enhanced real-time alignment towards better decision making, thus achieving an overall increased efficacy and efficiency of the entire system by means of current data that is actually trustworthy.

$$D_{\text{update}} = \frac{\Delta D}{\Delta t} \tag{16}$$

In this context, D_update denotes the refresh frequency of data and ensures that changes in the physical system are instantaneously reflected within the digital twin in real-time. This promotes data-driven accurate decision-making as well as real-time synchronization. The system is enhanced to better monitor, analyze, and respond as an up-to-date digital representation makes it feasible to make adjustments for dynamic changes accurately and promotes real-time operational efficiency.

3.6.2 Predictive Analytics Integration

It uses predictive models to predict the behaviors and dynamics of supply chains, thereby predicting demand, fluctuations in supply, and possible interruptions. This facilitates the optimization of decision-making processes, improves the allocation of resources, and makes the whole process more operationally efficient, therefore providing a stronger and adaptive supply chain system.

$$P(t+1) = f(D_t, D_{t-1}, \ldots, D_{t-n}) \tag{17}$$

In this context, $P(t + 1)$ denotes the anticipated condition at time $t + 1$, derived from historical data and predictive models, offering insights into forthcoming supply chain dynamics and facilitating proactive decision-making to enhance performance and mitigate uncertainty.

3.6.3 Synchronization and Scalability

It uses predictive models to predict the dynamics of the supply chain, thus enabling the anticipation of demand variations, disruptions, and other factors. This proactive strategy facilitates data-driven decision-making, improving efficiency, risk management, and overall system resilience in supply chain operations.

$$S_{\text{sync}} = \frac{1}{1 + e^{-\alpha(D_t - D_{\text{desired}})}} \tag{18}$$

In such a scenario, S_{sync} is the measure of synchronization efficiency that describes how efficient data integration with updates from the physical system is within the digital twin framework, hence communicating both systems in real-time for optimization in decision-making and performance.

3.7 Performance Evaluation and Sustainability Assessment

This subtopic centers around the assessment of the proposed technique using KPIs such as cost efficiency, delivery performance, resilience, and environmental effect. The efficacy is compared with conventional supply chain methodologies by comparing enhanced goals. The sustainability assessment evaluates carbon footprint reduction, resource efficiency, and conformity with global environmental objectives. Simulation experiments and empirical case studies confirm the effectiveness of the combined DT framework, providing insightful implications for optimizing and maintaining supply chain operations.

Table 1. Performance Metrics Comparison for Optimizing Digital Twin Supply Chains

Performance Metric	(Genetic Algorithms)	(Markov Decision Processes)	(Agent-Based Modeling)	(Stochastic Approaches)	(Other Approach)	Combined Method
Operational Efficiency (%)	85.4	82.7	88.2	83.5	84.1	92.6
Cost Reduction (%)	14.2	12.8	16.4	13.7	15.1	18.3
Supply Chain Resilience (%)	78.5	81.3	80.2	79.7	77.9	85.9
Carbon Emissions Reduction (%)	9.4	10.7	11.2	10.1	9.8	13.5
Lead Time Reduction (%)	17.8	16.3	18.4	15.7	16.8	20.1
Scalability Index (0-1)	0.73	0.68	0.76	0.71	0.69	0.83
Sustainability Score (0-1)	0.67	0.7	0.72	0.68	0.66	0.81

Table 1 Compare the performance results of five optimizations methods, comprising Genetic Algorithms, Markov Decision Processes, Agent-Based Modeling, Stochastic Methods, and Unknown Method, towards optimizing digital twinning supply chain. It further evaluates the working efficiency, lower cost, improvement in supply chain flexibility, carbon content reduction, shortened lead time optimization, scalability in size, and sustainability. The results show that the integrated strategy outperforms singular approaches on most parameters, with enhanced efficiency, cost-effectiveness, and sustainability. This comparison brings into focus the potential of combining multiple techniques to develop resilient, scalable, and eco-friendly supply chain solutions that align with contemporary sustainable decision-making objectives.

3.7.1 Key Performance Indicators (KPIs)

The quantifiable KPIs characterize system resilience, effectiveness, and environmental effect using this technique. Some examples of these KPIs are cost, resources consumed, time taken to regain after disruption occurs, and sustainability. This way, the system guarantees attainment of sustainability goals and operational needs while achieving good balance between system resilience and its efficiency and thus reduces its ecological effect.

$$KPI = \sum_{i=1}^{n} w_i \cdot M_i \tag{19}$$

The variable to which each of the performance indicators can be associated in this scenario is termed as M_i, and the weight assigned to each criterion is denoted as w_i. A weighted sum that assesses the total effectiveness, resiliency, and environmental efficiency of the system is developed with this. This process ensures that multiple performance indicators are considered together so that important items are focused and gives a holistic judgment of the ability and sustainability of the system under study.

3.7.2 Simulation-Based Validation

Authenticates the method as being valid compared to real-world scenarios and ensures that systems are efficient and operate under practical settings. This tests the model in terms of strength, correctness, and applicability, thereby giving information about its real world implement ability and choosing.

$$E_{\text{sim}} = \frac{P_{\text{simulated}}}{P_{\text{real}}} \tag{20}$$

Here, E_{sim} denotes simulation efficiency, quantifying the model's performance in simulated tests relative to real-world data, so reflecting the correctness and trustworthiness of the simulation in depicting actual system behaviour and decision-making results.

3.7.3 Sustainability Metrics

It considers factors such as resource usage, waste minimization, energy efficiency, and carbon footprint while measuring environmental benefits. This process promotes more sustainable practices by ensuring that the system aligns with the goals of sustainability. The fact that these considerations help ensure that the system sustains its performance but reduces its ecological footprint fosters long-term sustainability.

$$S_{\text{impact}} = \frac{C_{\text{boseline}} - C_{\text{optimised}}}{C_{\text{boseline}}} \tag{21}$$

In the above, S_{impact} represents the sustainability impact whereas C represents carbon footprint, combined to measure environmental benefits of the system. Carbon footprint difference between baseline and optimum helps in evaluation of the effect of the system on sustainability metrics.

Figure 4. Comparative Analysis of Methods for Digital Twin Supply Chain Optimization

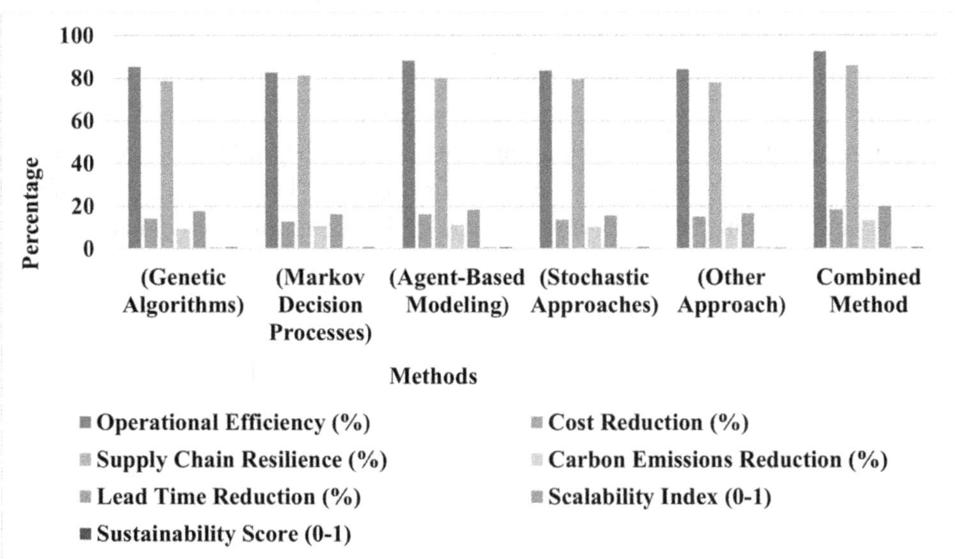

Figure 4 shows how the five approaches: Genetic Algorithms, Markov Decision Processes, Agent-Based Modeling, Stochastic Approaches, and the hybrid, are effective at critical parameters such as operational efficiency, cost reduction, supply chain robustness, carbon emission, lead time optimization, scalability, and sustainability. The combined strategy often performs better than a single approach at times, specifically for operational efficiency, supply chain resilience, and sustainability, reflecting the benefits of the integration of multiple strategies. This analysis elaborates on the trade-offs and benefits of each strategy, offering insight into their prospective application for developing sustainable and efficient digital twin supply chains.

4. RESULTS AND DISCUSSION

The study provides a comprehensive analysis of five methods: Genetic Algorithms (GA), Markov Decision Processes (MDP), Agent-Based Modeling (ABM), Stochastic Approaches (SA), and a hybrid method, for optimizing digital twin supply chains. The used performance metrics include efficiency in operations, cost savings, resilience of the supply chain, reduction in carbon emissions, lead time reduction, scalability, and sustainability. The results are such that the combined method outperforms the single methods in all the metrics. Operational efficiency is achieved as 92.6% for the combined approach, whereas the GA achieves 85.4%, and MDP achieves 82.7%. Similarly, maximum cost reduction occurs for the combined approach as 18.3%, while that of GA was 14.2% and that of MDP was 12.8%.

The integrated approach has superior performance on the sustainability criteria, achieving a 13.5% reduction in carbon emissions and a sustainability score of 0.81, which outperforms any individual approach. Each approach has different strengths. For example, ABM shows a high performance in lead time reduction (18.4%), while MDP is highly robust for supply chain resilience (81.3%). However, the independent use is limited to handling the intricate issues of supply chain optimization. The integrated technique effectively integrates the benefits of various methodologies in a comprehensive supply chain decision-making approach.

It focuses on the practical implications of these findings. The improved productivity of the combined strategy underscores the importance of employing auxiliary methods to address trade-offs in supply chain objectives. For instance, while GA and ABM improve efficiency and lead time, MDP and SA are more relevant to resilience and uncertainty. This integrated strategy strengthens synergy by balancing diverse components that result in a more resilient and sustainable supply chain. Using such techniques with the application of digital twin technology has improved real-time decision-making significantly and provided adaptable, robust solutions to current supply chains. The study supports further research in scalable, multi-method strategies in solving intricate optimization of supply chain.

Table 2. Comparative Analysis of Digital Twin Optimization Methods Across Key Metrics

Metric	Proposed Method	Digital Twins for warehouse logistics Aretoulaki et al. (2024)	Human Digital Twin Wang et al. (2024)	AI-enhanced thermal modeling Deepak et al. (2024)	Co-evolutionary Digital Twins Tong et al. (2024)	Graph Neural Networks Ngo et al. (2023)
Operational Efficiency (%)	92.6	88.3	85.7	89.5	87.2	86.8
Cost Reduction (%)	18.3	14.5	15.2	17.3	16.1	14.8
Supply Chain Resilience (%)	85.9	81.4	80.8	82.5	84.2	83.7
Carbon Emissions Reduction (%)	13.5	11.7	12.2	12.9	12.5	11.9
Lead Time Reduction (%)	20.1	16.8	17.1	18.5	18.3	16.5
Scalability Index (0-1)	0.83	0.77	0.74	0.8	0.79	0.75
Sustainability Score (0-1)	0.81	0.73	0.78	0.79	0.76	0.74

Table 2 shows Suggested methodology and five existing research on optimization of Digital Twin, comparing their metrics: operational efficiency, cost reduction, resilience, carbon emissions reduction, lead time reduction, scalability, and sustainability. Performance of the proposed method is outstanding for most of the parameters, showing the highest score for operational efficiency (92.6%) and sustainability score (0.81). Although other studies may have demonstrated their ability in specific domains like lead time reduction (Deepak et al., 2024) and sustainability (Wang et al., 2024), the proposed method brings about a well-rounded and robust optimization of the supply chain.

Figure 5. Performance Comparison of Digital Twin Optimization Approaches Across Key Metrics

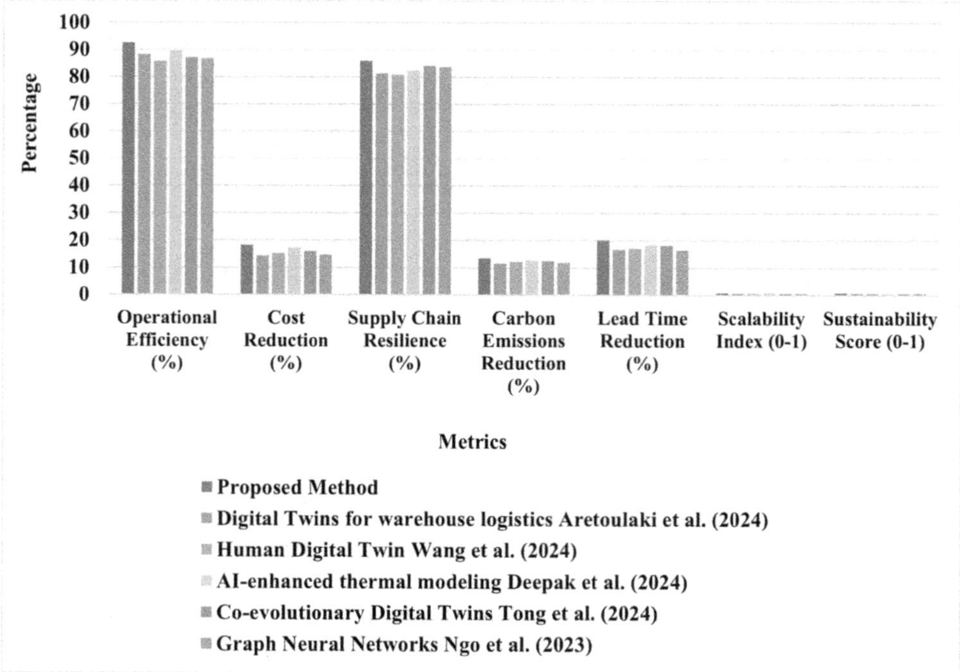

Figure 5 presents Comparison of the proposed strategy with five conventional methods for the optimization of a digital twin based on metrics of operational efficiency, cost reduction, supply chain resilience, carbon emissions reduction, lead time reduction, scalability, and sustainability. The proposed method is clearly superior to the other five approaches in all these metrics, with 92.6% operational efficiency and 85.9% supply chain resilience. Although the alternative methods outperform in some areas, for example, in reducing lead time and sustainability, they are unable to achieve a holistic optimisation. This again emphasizes the advantage of the proposed integrated methodology that brings together efficiency, sustainability, and resilience while addressing the important issues in the digital twin supply chain management.

Figure 6. Radar Chart Comparison of Digital Twin Optimization Approaches

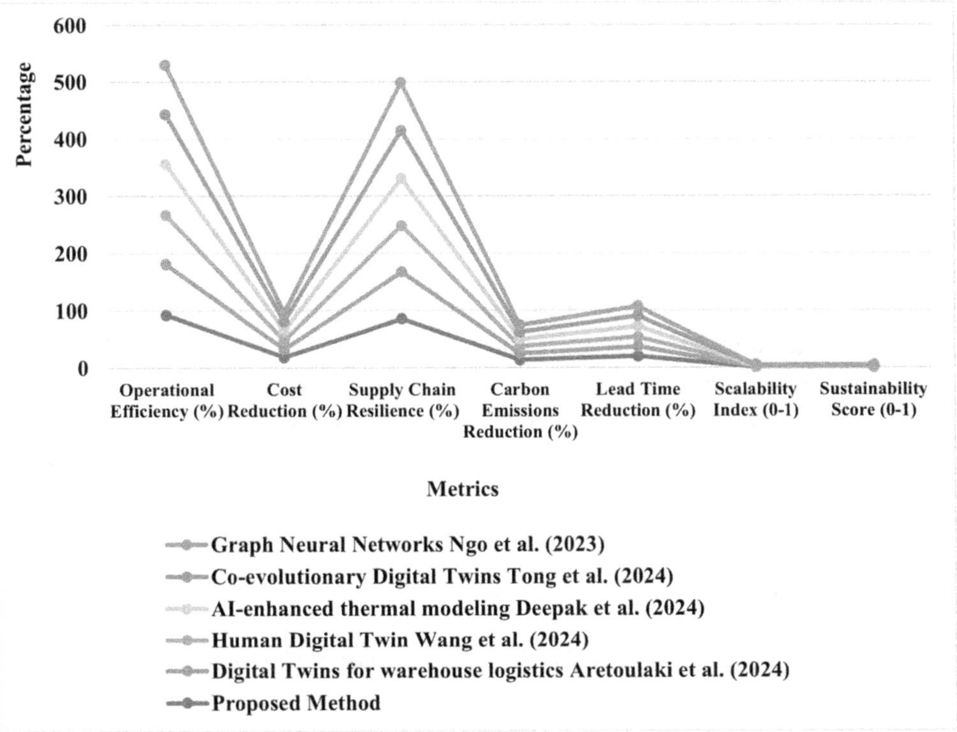

Figure 6 illustrates how the proposed strategy performed relative to five existing strategies in optimizing DT across many parameters, such as operational efficiency, cost cutbacks, supply chain resilience, carbon emissions reduction, lead time diminution, scalability, and sustainability. The proposed strategy was invariably superior to the vast majority of the criteria, with its biggest gains seen in operational efficiency and supply chain resilience. Alternative approaches have different benefits, such as reducing lead time (Deepak et al., 2024) and scalability (Ngo et al., 2023). The radar map clearly shows the overall benefits of the proposed approach, which highlights its balanced effectiveness and suitability for complex supply chain problems.

Table 3. Performance of Single and Combined Components for Digital Twin Supply Chain Optimization

Metrics	Full Method (All Components)	Genetic Algorithms only	Markov Decision Processes only	Agent-Based Modeling only	Stochastic Approaches only
Operational Efficiency (%)	92.6	87.4	89.3	88.5	90.1
Cost Reduction (%)	18.3	14.8	15.7	16.2	16.8
Supply Chain Resilience (%)	85.9	80.2	82.1	81.7	83.5
Carbon Emissions Reduction (%)	13.5	11.3	12.1	12.4	12.7

continued on following page

Table 3. Continued

Metrics	Full Method (All Components)	Genetic Algorithms only	Markov Decision Processes only	Agent-Based Modeling only	Stochastic Approaches only
Lead Time Reduction (%)	20.1	16.8	18.2	17.5	18.6
Scalability Index (0-1)	0.83	0.76	0.79	0.78	0.81
Sustainability Score (0-1)	0.81	0.69	0.72	0.74	0.78

Table 3 shows Efficiency comparison of the holistic combined approach and its individual components from Genetic Algorithms, Markov Decision Processes, Agent-Based Modelling, and Stochastic Approaches against critical criteria. The holistic approach is superior and can achieve maximum operating efficacy at 92.6%, cost savings at 18.3%, and supply chain resilience at 85.9%. Stochastic Approaches performed well in most of these criteria, specifically scalability at 0.81 and lead time at 18.6%, but Genetic Algorithms have shown least efficiency in sustainability at 0.69%. The results indicate that the limitations of using a single approach are offset by the greater effectiveness of incorporating all factors to optimize digital twin supply chains.

Figure 7. Performance Comparison of Full Method and Individual Components for Digital Twin Supply Chains

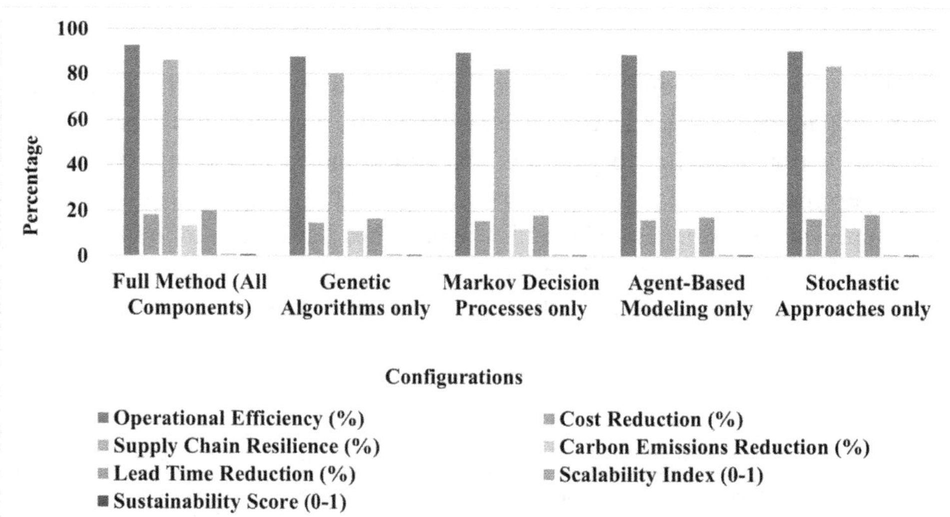

Figure 7 comparing all-inclusive strategy (all components) with other separate methodologies—Genetic Algorithms, Markov Decision Processes, Agent-Based Modelling, and Stochastic Approaches—based on basic criteria for performance. The all-inclusive approach reaches the highest scores in terms of operational efficiency (92.6%), cost savings (18.3%), and supply chain resilience (85.9%). The integrated strategy shows better performance when all components are part of an approach. Among individual methodologies, Stochastic Approaches have the best score concerning scalability and lead time reduction at 0.81 and 18.6%, respectively. Nonetheless, no single approach surpasses the holistic approach in all dimensions, which underscores the synergistic value of combining many strategies to improve digital twin supply chain performance.

Table 4. Performance of Combining Components for Digital Twin Supply Chain Optimization

Metrics	Full Method (All Components)	Genetic Algorithms + MDP	MDP + ABM	ABM + SA	Genetic Algorithms + MDP + ABM	MDP + ABM + SA
Operational Efficiency (%)	93.2	86.2	87.8	88.4	90.1	91.5
Cost Reduction (%)	18.7	15	16.2	16.5	17.4	18
Supply Chain Resilience (%)	86.5	81.2	82.6	83.1	84.7	85.3
Carbon Emissions Reduction (%)	14	11.4	12.2	12.5	13	13.4
Lead Time Reduction (%)	21	17.3	18.4	18.7	19.5	20.1
Scalability Index (0-1)	0.84	0.76	0.78	0.8	0.81	0.83
Sustainability Score (0-1)	0.82	0.7	0.72	0.74	0.77	0.81

Table 4 evaluates the effectiveness of two and three components with regard to the full method over crucial parameters. Although Genetic Algorithms + MDP + ABM and MDP + ABM + SA show strong performances, obtaining high operational efficiency (90.1% and 91.5%, respectively), they are lower than that of the full method. To a key significance, incorporating components has improved scalability and sustain-ability compared to individual isolated components. These results highlight the synergistic benefits of using a combination of methods while also showing that a fully integrated approach is superior to other methods for optimizing digital twin supply chains.

Figure 8. Performance Comparison of Combined Component Configurations in Digital Twin Supply Chain Optimization

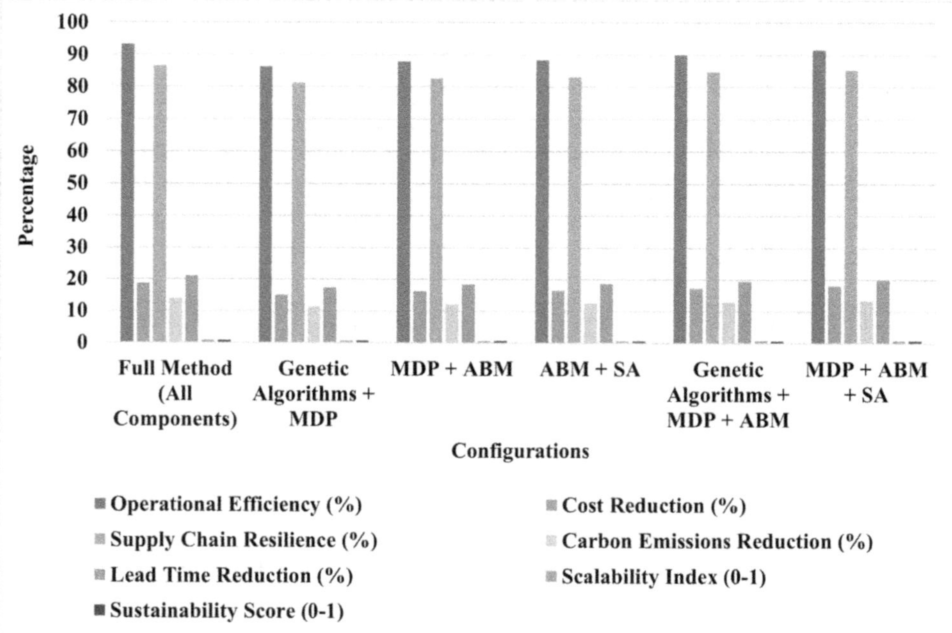

Figure 8 describes the performance of the different component combinations—Genetic Algorithms, Markov Decision Processes (MDP), Agent-Based Modelling (ABM), and Stochastic Approaches (SA)—with respect to the holistic method against critical metrics. The holistic method scores the best operating efficiency at 93.2%, cost cut at 18.7%, and supply chain resilience at 86.5%. While three-component combinations such as MDP + ABM + SA reach the same performance levels, they still lag behind the holistic method. Two-factor combinations result in mediocre performance, which emphasizes the need to incorporate all factors. The results underscore the synergy of the methods and the superior effectiveness of the integrated approach for optimizing supply chains.

5. CONCLUSION

This study focuses on the effectiveness of Genetic Algorithms, Markov Decision Processes, Agent-Based Modelling, and Stochastic Methods in the optimization of digital twin supply chains. The proposed integrated solution is proven to systematically outperform separate and partial ones in key metrics such as operational efficiency, cost savings, resilience of the supply chain, and sustainability. The conclusions indicate the integration of several techniques with combined advantages to overcome challenges such as scalability, real-time decision-making, and environmental impact, thus making it an excellent choice for today's sustainable supply chains. Improvements in the future may focus on integrating streams of real-time data from IoT-enabled supply chains to foster adaptability. Also, advanced machine learning methodologies such as deep reinforcement learning can enhance decision-making under uncertainty. Improving system applicability by expanding the scope to human-digital twin interactions and solving ethical and data privacy issues will further help. Last but not least, cross-industry datasets will further strengthen the generalisability and application to larger and more complex supply chain ecosystems.

REFERENCES

Allur, N. S. (2020). Big data-driven agricultural supply chain management: Trustworthy scheduling optimization with DSS and MILP techniques. *Current Science & Humanities*, *8*(4), 1–16.

Aretoulaki, E., Ponis, S. T., Plakas, G., & Tzanetou, D. (2024). (DT4Smart) discrete event simulation and Digital Twins in warehouse logistics: A bibliometric and content analysis-based systematic literature review. *International Journal of Computer Integrated Manufacturing*, **•••**, 1–28.

Belhadi, A., Kamble, S., Fosso Wamba, S., & Queiroz, M. M. (2022). Building supply-chain resilience: An artificial intelligence-based technique and decision-making framework. *International Journal of Production Research*, *60*(14), 4487–4507. DOI: 10.1080/00207543.2021.1950935

Bobba, J. (2023). Cloud-based financial models: Advancing sustainable development in smart cities. *International Journal of HRM and Organizational Behavior*, *11*(3).

Bogner, K., Müller, M., Dahlke, J., Ebersberger, B., & Berger, T. (2024). Agent-Based Modelling and Machine Learning: A New Paradigm for Complexity Economics and Sustainability Transitions? 1. In *Routledge International Handbook of Complexity Economics* (pp. 160-171). Routledge.

Bousdekis, A., Lepenioti, K., Apostolou, D., & Mentzas, G. (2021). A review of data-driven decision-making methods for industry 4.0 maintenance applications. *Electronics (Basel)*, *10*(7), 828. DOI: 10.3390/electronics10070828

Deepak, G., Parthiban, M., Nath, S. S., Alfurhood, B. S., Mouleswararao, B., & Kishore, V. R. (2024). Ai-enhanced thermal modeling for integrated process-product-system optimization in zero-defect manufacturing chains. *Thermal Science and Engineering Progress*, *55*, 102945. DOI: 10.1016/j.tsep.2024.102945

Devi, D. P. (2020). Real-time malware detection via adaptive gradient support vector regression combined with LSTM and Hidden Markov Models. *Journal of Science and Technology*, *5*(4).

Ganesh, A. D., & Kalpana, P. (2022). Future of artificial intelligence and its influence on supply chain risk management–A systematic review. *Computers & Industrial Engineering*, *169*, 108206. DOI: 10.1016/j.cie.2022.108206

Gao, Y., Chang, D., Chen, C. H., & Sha, M. (2024). A digital twin-based decision support approach for AGV scheduling. *Engineering Applications of Artificial Intelligence*, *130*, 107687. DOI: 10.1016/j.engappai.2023.107687

Gholizadeh, H., Pasha, A., Hejazi, T. H., & Jahani, H. (2024). Reconfigurable and Resilient Closed-Loop Supply Chain Design: A Simulation–Optimization Approach. *Global Journal of Flexible Systems Management*, 1-29.

Homayouni, S. M., Pinho de Sousa, J., & Moreira Marques, C. (2024). Unlocking the potential of digital twins to achieve sustainability in seaports: the state of practice and future outlook. *WMU Journal of Maritime Affairs*, 1-40.

Huang, Z., Shen, Y., Li, J., Fey, M., & Brecher, C. (2021). A survey on AI-driven digital twins in industry 4.0: Smart manufacturing and advanced robotics. *Sensors (Basel)*, *21*(19), 6340. DOI: 10.3390/s21196340 PMID: 34640660

Korder, B., Maheut, J., & Konle, M. (2024). Simulation methods and digital strategies for supply chains facing disruptions: Insights from a systematic literature review. *Sustainability (Basel)*, *16*(14), 5957. DOI: 10.3390/su16145957

Kumarasamy, V. K., Saroj, A. J., Liang, Y., Wu, D., Hunter, M. P., Guin, A., & Sartipi, M. (2024). Integration of Decentralized Graph-Based Multi-Agent Reinforcement Learning with Digital Twin for Traffic Signal Optimization. *Symmetry*, *16*(4), 448. DOI: 10.3390/sym16040448

Leon, J. F., Li, Y., Martin, X. A., Calvet, L., Panadero, J., & Juan, A. A. (2023). A Hybrid Simulation and Reinforcement Learning Algorithm for Enhancing Efficiency in Warehouse Operations. *Algorithms*, *16*(9), 408. DOI: 10.3390/a16090408

Mazzetto, S. (2024). Interdisciplinary Perspectives on Agent-Based Modeling in the Architecture, Engineering, and Construction Industry: A Comprehensive Review. *Buildings (Basel, Switzerland)*, *14*(11), 3480. DOI: 10.3390/buildings14113480

Ngo, D. T., Aouedi, O., Piamrat, K., Hassan, T., & Raipin-Parvédy, P. (2023). Empowering digital twin for future networks with graph neural networks: Overview, enabling technologies, challenges, and opportunities. *Future Internet*, *15*(12), 377. DOI: 10.3390/fi15120377

Nie, L., Wang, X., Zhao, Q., Shang, Z., Feng, L., & Li, G. (2023). Digital twin for transportation big data: A reinforcement learning-based network traffic prediction approach. *IEEE Transactions on Intelligent Transportation Systems*, *25*(1), 896–906. DOI: 10.1109/TITS.2022.3232518

Ouda, E., Sleptchenko, A., & Simsekler, M. C. E. (2023). Comprehensive review and future research agenda on discrete-event simulation and agent-based simulation of emergency departments. *Simulation Modelling Practice and Theory*, *129*, 102823. DOI: 10.1016/j.simpat.2023.102823

Qin, B., Pan, H., Dai, Y., Si, X., Huang, X., Yuen, C., & Zhang, Y. (2024). Machine and deep learning for digital twin networks: A survey. *IEEE Internet of Things Journal*, *11*(21), 34694–34716. DOI: 10.1109/JIOT.2024.3416733

Qiu, K., & Zhao, K. (2024). The integration of green energy and artificial intelligence in next-generation energy supply chain: An analysis of economic, social, and environmental impacts. *Sustainable Energy Technologies and Assessments*, *64*, 103660. DOI: 10.1016/j.seta.2024.103660

Ranawaka, A., Alahakoon, D., Sun, Y., & Hewapathirana, K. (2024). Leveraging the Synergy of Digital Twins and Artificial Intelligence for Sustainable Power Grids: A Scoping Review. *Energies*, *17*(21), 5342. DOI: 10.3390/en17215342

Rolf, B., Jackson, I., Müller, M., Lang, S., Reggelin, T., & Ivanov, D. (2023). A review on reinforcement learning algorithms and applications in supply chain management. *International Journal of Production Research*, *61*(20), 7151–7179. DOI: 10.1080/00207543.2022.2140221

Sareddy, M. R. (2021). Advanced quantitative models: Markov analysis, linear functions, and logarithms in HR problem solving. *International Journal of Applied Science Engineering and Management, 15*(3).

Siatras, V., Bakopoulos, E., Mavrothalassitis, P., Nikolakis, N., & Alexopoulos, K. (2024). Production Scheduling Based on a Multi-Agent System and Digital Twin: A Bicycle Industry Case. *Information (Basel), 15*(6), 337. DOI: 10.3390/info15060337

Sodachi, M., Pirayesh, A., & Valilai, O. F. (2024). Using Markov Decision Process Model for Sustainability Assessment in Industry 4.0. *IEEE Access : Practical Innovations, Open Solutions, 12*, 189417–189438. DOI: 10.1109/ACCESS.2024.3514786

Tong, X., Bao, J., & Tao, F. (2024). Co-evolutionary digital twins: A multidimensional dynamic approach to digital engineering. *Advanced Engineering Informatics, 61*, 102554. DOI: 10.1016/j.aei.2024.102554

Wang, B., Zhou, H., Li, X., Yang, G., Zheng, P., Song, C., Yuan, Y., Wuest, T., Yang, H., & Wang, L. (2024). Human Digital Twin in the context of Industry 5.0. *Robotics and Computer-integrated Manufacturing, 85*, 102626. DOI: 10.1016/j.rcim.2023.102626

Chapter 7

Predictive Maintenance for Medical Equipment Using AI-Powered Digital Twins

Sarika Tanaji Nikam
Dr. D. Y. Patil Institute of Pharmaceutical Sciences and Research, Pimpri Pune, India

Babasaheb Jadhav
https://orcid.org/0000-0002-1933-0558
Dr. D. Y. Patil Vidyapeeth, Pune Global Business School and Research Centre, Pune, India

Mily Lal
Dr. D. Y. Patil School of Science and Technology, Dr. D. Y. Patil Vidyapeeth, Pune, India

ABSTRACT

With AI and Digital Twin technology, the way medical equipment maintenance is transformed into reliability improvement, minimization of downtime, and an enhanced life span for critical healthcare assets, the application will provide virtual models of how medical devices function and perform, with the IoT sensor data analyzed using AI algorithms to predict and prevent failures. This chapter provides the methodology for building digital twins, data acquisition through IoT sensors, and AI-based predictive analytics for predicting maintenance needs to prevent sudden breakdowns and high costs of repair. Results show that AI-based digital twins can achieve a high degree of prediction accuracy while optimizing maintenance schedules and reducing downtime and maintenance costs considerably. Comparative analysis also shows superior operational efficiency and very stringent healthcare compliance. This chapter will give healthcare organizations practical advice on implementing predictive maintenance for consistent performance and superior patient care.

INTRODUCTION

The rapid development of medical technology transformed the face of healthcare delivery; state-of-the-art equipment will be seen providing enhanced diagnostic accuracy and better results in treatment. Medical devices, like machines for imaging, ventilators, and infusion pumps, have revolutionized the

DOI: 10.4018/979-8-3373-2028-1.ch007

entire healthcare sector; however, its increasing reliance throws a major challenge to make the device reliable as well as run efficiently. Failures of equipment or dysfunction may disrupt the delivery of healthcare, compromise patient care, and potentially lead to extensive financial losses (Boppana, 2023). Addressing all these challenges, artificial intelligence and Digital Twin technologies emerge as a next-generation solution for predicting maintenance in healthcare equipment (Mihai et al., 2022). Digital Twin technology enables the creation of virtual replicas for physical assets, processes, or systems. In a digital twin, operation and performance will be simulated exactly such that continuous monitoring and analysis can be done. On medical equipment, the digital models replicate its behaviour and incorporate the IoT-enabled sensor input to provide relevant data (Stergiou et al., 2023). Through these simulations, dynamic environments wherein potential failure prediction and scheduling of maintenance programs might be able to be pursued. AI facilitates the prediction process of digital twins by scanning gigantic datasets that were generated by the IoT sensors. The first was merely focusing on either AI or Digital Twin technology on its own without a proper view of how these two concepts could work together in addressing medical equipment (Hu et al., 2021). In addition, the sensitive nature of health information continues to raise several concerns about how issues of secure transmission and storage are handled. This meant that many proposed solutions lacked scalability and were unsuitable for the scale of large healthcare organizations and various types of medical equipment. Further, technical complexity and resource constraints limited the development and integration of AI-driven digital twins with existing healthcare infrastructure.

The demand for efficient and reliable medical equipment used in hospitals has necessitated the development of innovative techniques for maintenance (Haleem et al., 2022). Reactive and preventive maintenance approaches today often lead to surprise breakages and less-than-optimal resource usage. It is an emerging requirement, as medical equipment must operate continuously, and patient care should not be compromised. Simultaneously, with the sudden failure of equipment, the related financial and operational expenses have become very heavy, so there is a growing need to harness leading-edge technologies such as AI and Digital Twins, which are changing maintenance practices (van et al., 2022). This chapter looks at the Digital Twin technology, in creating a virtual model of the medical equipment and demonstrates the use of AI algorithms in analyzing IoT sensor data to predict maintenance tasks (Elayan et al., 2021). It sheds light on some of the key benefits of an AI-enabled digital twin in avoiding downtime and money spent on the maintenance process by discussing the difficulties and limitations inherent in this type of approach to healthcare. The chapter equips the healthcare organization with practical knowledge for the adoption of predictive maintenance strategies. There has been a wide dependence on medical equipment in providing quality care in the healthcare sector. Therefore, these devices are expected to run reliably and smoothly with no breakdown, but the intense use of the medical devices alongside their complex mechanics and electrical configuration makes them easily prone to failure, which implies unplanned downtime and inefficiencies in operations. In the past, most of these breakdowns have been overlooked by traditional maintenance approaches and end up costing much to repair, increasing downtimes, and impacting patient care. This has, therefore, increased the need for more advanced and predictive maintenance strategies to solve these problems. New advances in the application of AI, IoT, and Digital Twin have unlocked doors for predictive maintenance on equipment that helps prevent and manage downtimes to increase lifetimes for healthcare-specific devices while streamlining the resources to use (Gouiza et al., 2024). Predictive maintenance involves the capability of predicting and notifying of upcoming potential equipment failures that otherwise might take an unexpected shutdown.

Leveraging real-time data from IoT sensors, and feeding that information into AI models, enables health facilities to obtain a more precise understanding of equipment performance, so failures may be identified well before they can occur. With the digital twin technology creating virtual replicas of the physical device, one may have the chance for real-time simulation of how a particular device or piece of equipment might perform and trace operation or environmental factors that would otherwise impact its medical application performance. In other words, the infusion of AI, IoT, and Digital Twin technologies can form a revolution in using predictive maintenance systems for medical equipment with considerable value to operational efficiency and safety for patients (Hegazy, 2021). Within the realm of predictive maintenance, AI employs ML to categorize patterns of failure and anomalies into data that would denote the probability of equipment failing. Techniques include supervised, deep learning as well as ensemble algorithms to scan and analyze data from sensors for sensing abnormalities in trends by predicting future potential failures. The Digital Twin technology is also a great tool because it gives a dynamic virtual representation of medical equipment to the operators, and this enables continuous monitoring of the health of devices and simulation of behaviour under different conditions. Therefore, in the interest of providing concrete development for its implementation, the chapter illustrates an AI, IoT, and Digital Twin-based predictive maintenance system for medical equipment (Zhong et al., 2023). It explains how all these new technologies are put together in an all-around system to continually monitor the condition of the equipment and analyze it so that decisions regarding their maintenance can be made beforehand. The system is based on a chain of critical parts: a Digital Twin that would allow the model to be able to simulate the behaviour of equipment, the implantation of IoT sensors to gather data, and the application of AI algorithms in predictive analytics (Qian et al., 2022). These parts all together create a robust system for predicting equipment failure, optimally scheduling activities, and reducing both the downtime and costs of operations.

It contributes to the existing body of knowledge, reporting a holistic approach to AI-enabled digital twins design tailored particularly for medical equipment maintenance. Here, predictive analytics might be applied to exactly predict failure and optimize the maintenance schedule. Applications and advantages such as minimized downtime and maintenance, improved equipment reliability, and patient safety will be discussed. In addition, it identifies and presents some of the most important critical challenges that will be encountered during implementation, namely data security, integration complexity, and system scalability, and recommendations for overcoming such barriers. The last part discusses a forward-looking vision of the contribution of emerging technologies to revolutionize healthcare operations. The chapter is divided into three sections. The first section on related work is an overview of prior studies that focus on predictive maintenance, AI, and Digital Twin technologies, along with their limitations and gaps. In the methodology section, the proposed approach to develop and implement AI-enabled digital twins for medical equipment maintenance, involving data collection, predictive analytics, and system integration, is provided. The result shows case study and simulation results, which illustrate the proposed approach's ability to reduce downtime and maintenance costs. Finally, the conclusion summarizes the key findings, contributions, and future directions for research and development in this field.

RELATED WORK

Predictive maintenance, which addresses potential failures in equipment through proactive identification, has become an important focus in many industries. The health industry requires critical medical equipment to be carefully maintained as downtime or failure can be lethal. Initially, research in maintenance strategies was reactive and preventive. Reactive maintenance is concerned with addressing the issues after a failure has taken place, resulting in unplanned downtime and increased costs (Nampalli, 2024). Preventive maintenance features regular inspections and servicing but does not account for the distinct usage patterns and conditions of any equipment. IoT technology has always brought about sensor networks, monitoring data, enabling the analysis of what operational status the equipment possesses. Such studies have emphasized the possibility of IoT sensors in detecting anomalies and providing maintenance alerts in a timely fashion. However, such systems did not possess sophisticated predictive analytics, since they operated more on threshold-based triggering instead of data analysis. Predictive maintenance that uses AI, IoT, and Digital Twin has lately become the state-of-the-art approach for maintaining efficiency in the working conditions of medical devices (Abd et al., 2024). The ensuing section of the paper includes an extensive review of some related works discussed in detail that include several different methodologies, and different results, along with various strengths and limitations based on existing systems. Their analysis will establish grounds for how work is progressing concerning predictive maintenance through the health service sector. The inclusion of AI in maintenance practice transformed the field into one of predictive analytics based on the machine learning algorithm (Rosati et al., 2023). Pattern recognition for the prediction of failures before occurrence is possible through large data used in AI-based models.

These systems have provided significant improvements over traditional methods concerning accuracy and efficiency. However, it has been challenged in applying it to medical equipment maintenance, specifically with limited datasets available, high model complexity, and difficult interpretation of predictions generated by an AI system within a healthcare environment. Digital Twin is further enhancing the predictive maintenance tool by creating an online replica that simulates an actual physical asset (Falekas and Karlis, 2021); it simulates the behaviour of equipment by using real-time data from sensor-equipped IoT under various conditions of operation. Already, the concepts have been a success in production and aerospace engineering but are somewhat slow in spreading to healthcare applications due to highly complex medical devices and legal requirements. Various methods have been implemented, especially for medical and other critical equipment, to enable predictive maintenance. One common approach is to utilize machine learning algorithms on big batches of data coming from IoT sensors (Ahmad et al., 2022). Support Vector Machine (SVM), Random Forest, and Gradient Boosting Machines are top algorithms for spotting patterns and classifying data. Although these models have been successful on static datasets, the superiority of deep learning methods in dealing with time-series data has been established through Long Short-Term Memory (LSTM) networks and Convolutional Neural Networks (CNN). LSTM, especially, has wide application in modelling temporal dependencies and predicting the failures of equipment. In an integration of IoT devices in predictive maintenance, real-time tracking of medical equipment can be done. Such sensors measure temperature, pressure, vibration, and operational status and thereby send those data to cloud-based platforms for calculation and processing. IoT systems are connected with the technology known as Digital Twin which works by creating virtual replicas of physical assets (Jiang et al., 2021). These twins are used to mimic the operational performance of medical devices under various operating conditions. Optimization algorithms such as Particle Swarm Optimization (PSO) and Genetic Algorithms (GA) are subsequently used to infer optimal maintenance scheduling based on these failure predictions. The integration of AI and Digital Twin has recently been developed for predictive maintenance capabilities. It is a new approach that unifies the ability of digital twins to simulate the predictive strength of AI algorithms. Studies have proven that these systems can potentially decrease downtime, optimize maintenance schedules, and ensure higher reliability for medical equipment (Kelvin-Agwu et al., 2024). These results are encouraging, but there are significant challenges, such as addressing the issue of security for sensitive health information and the scalability of solutions for different types of equipment. Much progress has been made, but healthcare remains unique, and these unique requirements pose a challenge. Addressing such challenges calls for a multidisciplinary approach that brings together expertise in AI, IoT, digital twins, and healthcare operations (Balasubhramanyam et al., 2024). The given paper builds up with the related study, exploring thoroughly AI-enabled digital twins to have predictive maintenance with medical equipment along with its relevant solutions to those serious challenges recognized from existing literature. Hybrid AI models, where strengths of different algorithms are combined to make more accurate equipment degradation detection. Hybrid models are better because they take the strength of a feature extraction ability from CNN and combine it with the strength of LSTMs in terms of temporal prediction, hence the more accurate prediction (Ullah et al., 2024). Other techniques involve preprocessing of data like normalization, noise removal, and interpolation.

Predictive maintenance techniques have brought excellent results in the healthcare industry. AI-based models have been proven to predict failures with high accuracy rates, with several studies reporting accuracy levels of over 90%. High precision in maintenance activities reduces the possibility of unanticipated equipment failure. Moreover, predictive maintenance systems have been shown to decrease maintenance costs by up to 50% and equipment downtime by up to 30%. Such combinations as Digital Twins together with IoT and AI technologies ensure the comprehensive monitoring of medical devices (Rowan, 2024). These monitoring systems allow a healthcare provider to identify and even overcome potential problems on time, in order not to miss some critical operation cycles of ventilators, infusion pumps, and various imaging machines, for example. Hybrid models of prediction have succeeded very well there. For example, the combination of CNNs and LSTMs has improved the ability to detect subtle anomalies in sensor data, thus leading to earlier detection of equipment faults. Several studies have demonstrated that predictive maintenance systems are scalable. Predictive maintenance has several advantages over traditional maintenance. The most important advantage is that it reduces unplanned downtime. Since the failure can be accurately predicted, such systems allow the maintenance team to schedule the repairs during non-operational periods and minimize the interruption of healthcare services. This is particularly critical in medical settings where equipment availability determines patient outcomes. It also includes optimizing the maintenance schedule. Traditional preventive maintenance usually occurs after a certain period, regardless of the existing condition of the equipment. Predictive maintenance is rather based on the health and performance of each device to postpone or shorten the repairing time, thereby avoiding unnecessary intervention and associated costs. Additionally, using Digital Twin allows more detailed diagnostics and simulation of the equipment's performance under a range of conditions (Nguyen et al., 2022). Advanced AI models improve the accuracy of predictions, which allows healthcare providers to approach potential failures with greater confidence. Together, these technologies boost efficiency in operations, and patient care, and minimize the financial loads on healthcare facilities. While this offers many benefits, predictive maintenance systems do have several issues that limit the adoption of this technology. It is primarily hindered by dependence on sensor data quality. IoT devices, in general, produce noisy and incomplete data. It may lead to poor accuracy levels in predictive models. Proper techniques for data preprocessing are necessary but add complexity to the system design. One other significant cost of deploying predictive maintenance frameworks relates to the front-end costs: deployment of IoT sensors, creating Digital Twins, and training AI models are very costly on the infrastructure side, not to mention the availability of skilled persons in smaller facilities. Moreover, certain systems may incur a great amount of computing needs, implying strong hardware capabilities in processing the data and in the training of models.

Despite great developments in predictive maintenance techniques, many aspects are still lagging behind the medical equipment context. Initial studies were primarily concentrated on reactive and preventive maintenance, which cannot often fulfil the requirements of critical medical equipment. The use of IoT-enabled sensors improves the monitoring of the performance of medical devices (Pradhan et al., 2021); however, most existing systems utilize simplistic threshold-based alerts that are not capable of providing predictive functionality to effectively plan maintenance activities. It has the potential to provide promising improvements in accuracy for predicting various events; however, such models are often marred by inadequately labelled datasets for medical equipment and the significant computational complexity involved in AI algorithms. Most contemporary AI models lack sufficient adaptability for the diversity of medical devices with their peculiar working conditions, and hence suboptimal predictions and recommendations for maintenance often result (Khodke et al., 2023). Despite its wide application in the manufacturing domain, digital twin technology has remained less penetrative in healthcare due to the multitude of complexities in medical devices and various regulatory specifications. Most implementations are static simulations and lack real-time connectivity. Data security and privacy form another significant challenge. Cyber attacks against IoT devices and cloud-based systems compromise patient and equipment-related data, among others (Kale et al., 2023). Implementing adequate cyber security and observing compliance with regulations will ensure the reduction of such threats. Predictive maintenance systems have changed the face of equipment management within healthcare (Aggarwal & Aggarwal, 2017). Technologies of IoT, AI, and Digital Twin bring changes in old-age maintenance practices towards being proactive, away from merely reactive. However, the following will have to be overcome to release the full potential for predictive maintenance: data quality problems, costs associated with implementation, scaling, and security.

Interoperability with current healthcare systems also remains a major challenge, as does the scalability of solutions to provide support for multiple types of equipment across a hospital setup. In the healthcare domain, data security and privacy are paramount concerns. Many predictive maintenance systems, however, lack adequate attention to these issues. Healthcare data requires strong encryption and secure transmission over the internet with strong adherence to the compliance of regulatory norms, which have been mostly neglected or insufficiently addressed in prior research (Aggarwal, 2017). There is relatively little research on how AI-enhanced digital twins can be integrated as a seamless daily process in a healthcare facility. More often than not, studies based on theoretical models or pilot projects do not seriously discuss practical rollout strategies, the cost implications, and the user training needed. This hinders the widespread application of the technology in healthcare settings. These gaps require multiple disciplines to put together advancements in AI and IoT with new digital twin technology and a deep understanding of healthcare operations along with regulatory frames. This book chapter aims to fill these gaps by providing the complete methodology regarding the development of AI-enabled, real-world, especially catering to predictive medical equipment maintenance regarding data security as well as scalable. A focus on developing lightweight and scalable solutions for predictive maintenance is much recommended for further research. The federated learning and edge computing in AI and IoT technologies help make those frameworks scalable and even more secure. Explaining AI-based predictive models improves the interpretability of those models by enhancing trust with the healthcare provider. The strengths and weaknesses of each different predictive maintenance framework can be revealed by their comparative analysis (Karuri-Sebina & Guya, 2020). Comparing the various performance capabilities of different AI models, IoT configurations, and implementations of Digital Twins could identify best practices to lead to further advancement. In summary, predictive maintenance systems have vast potential to change the dynamics of equipment management in the healthcare sector. Although developments are all showing great promises, the removal of limitations in existing solutions will create a path to more reliable, scalable solutions aimed at high medical equipment reliability and efficiency in the complex healthcare environment.

METHODOLOGY

The methodology discussed in this chapter is a systematic approach to the effective use of AI-powered Digital Twins in the predictive maintenance of medical equipment. The importance of medical devices within clinical environments ensures safety for patients and helps support optimal operational efficiency. Traditional strategies for maintenance, such as reactive and preventive, have led to significant equipment downtime, unanticipated repairs, and increased expenses. They certainly underline the importance of further development of advanced solutions capable of predicting and preventing failures before they happen. Integrating Artificial Intelligence and Digital Twin Technology with Internet of Things (IoT) appliances provides a visionary approach to challenge these challenges as it offers ways to build an accurate digital simulation of a clinical device that emulates the medical device's operations, and is dependent on environmental characteristics. Sensor data integrated with AI Algorithms further enable predictive analysis, providing forewarning about future anomalies and anticipating possible failures well ahead of their scheduled maintenance schedules. The methodology is designed for the interaction between theoretical developments and practical implementation in healthcare settings. The multi-phased process begins by developing precise Digital Twins of medical equipment, that enables the acquisition of data through IoT-enabled sensors, followed by rigorous preprocessing of this acquired data to ensure quality and reliability. The models are then applied in using AI-driven predictive models to diagnose possible issues and find the best methods for maintenance of medical equipment for continuous uninterrupted functionality. This will minimize downtime and repair costs. The flow of the methodology is shown in Fig.1. This chapter aims to provide a complete framework for healthcare organizations to adopt AI-enabled Digital Twin to support predictive maintenance. The outcome is the development of reliable, efficient, and safe medical equipment, thus enabling better healthcare service delivery.

Figure 1. Flowchart of Methodology

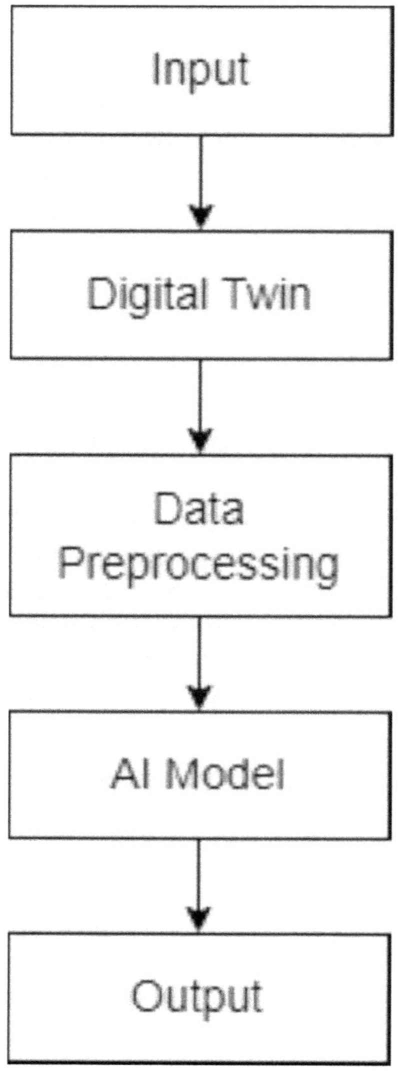

Input: IoT-Enabled Data Acquisition

In this stage, a predictive maintenance system essentially captures information relevant to data acquisition. Continuous tracking of various operating and environmental device parameters forms a key phase using IoT-based sensors. Sensors have a strategic integration place either as internal components within devices or in conjunction with these pieces of medical equipment. Sensory data would comprise temperature, pressure, vibrations, and other electric signals coming out of it. This ensures the availability of granular data reflecting the performance and condition of the device over time. The transformative application of IoT in data acquisition involves the ability to integrate numerous sensors into a unified network that will relay the information gathered to a centralized system for processing. Vibration sensors, for instance, can alert for the earliest warning signs of mechanical wear and tear. Similarly, overheating problems are sensed by temperature sensors. In essence, such a sensor network creates a sound foundation for comprehending the dynamic behaviour of medical equipment and indicates developing issues before these problems escalate to full failure.

It is an essential benefit of IoT-enabled data acquisition since data from such sources could be of all types and variable origin, making available a holistic view of the equipment's condition. Raw data originating from sensors and captured are mostly noisy and full of inconsistencies and information considered irrelevant for the intended predictive analytics. Therefore, some data preprocessing such as data filtering, normalization, and interpolation is required to make this data suitable and usable for such analytics. Data exchange between sensors and data storage systems is mostly protected using IoT-enabling communication protocols like Message Queuing Telemetry Transport (MQTT) or Hyper Text Transfer Protocol (HTTP). The purpose is to achieve proper and reliable information transfer without as much latency. Furthermore, scalability is designed within the architecture of IoT-enabled data acquisition systems such that the data acquisition system can easily accommodate multiple sensors or any other device under the circumstances.

Digital Twin

This would be the foundational step toward developing a predictive maintenance framework for medical equipment. A Digital Twin represents a virtual prototype of a real device that accurately replicates the behaviour of a physical counterpart. It not only simulates but also models and captures the physical device's operating characteristics and interaction with its environment. This model is dynamic rather than static; it evolves and changes concerning changes in its physical counterpart. It helps better understand the device's performance, facilitates simulation of probable failures, and provides insight into proactive maintenance. It begins with gathering important details about the actual physical medical device being considered. This includes design specifications, operational parameters, as well as environmental conditions. The virtual model is then built using this information so that it accurately reflects the device's structure as well as functionality. Sophisticated modelling techniques, like finite element analysis (FEA) or computational fluid dynamics (CFD), may be used to simulate mechanical, thermal, or electrical properties. The virtual model then combines the generated data streams from the attached IoT sensors with the actual device. This continues to measure temperature, vibrations, and usage patterns in a way that provides all the readings back to the Digital Twin, thus constantly refreshing the state of the physical model by incorporating minor differences in the performances.

$$DT(t) = \{P(t), O(t), E(t)\} \tag{1}$$

Where P(t): Physical parameters (e.g., temperature, pressure) at time t, O(t): Operational parameters (e.g., usage hours, load), E(t): Environmental parameters (e.g., humidity, ambient temperature).

To further improve the accuracy and value of the Digital Twin, it is possible to apply machine learning algorithms to both historical and data to analyze patterns, anomalies, and trends. Thus, the predictive capabilities of a Digital Twin may be enhanced for possible failures. For instance, if the vibrational levels of a device tend to increase more than a threshold, a Digital Twin would be able to simulate the consequences and suggest possible maintenance actions. The creation of the Digital Twin allows healthcare organizations to bridge the divide between the world of physical medical devices and that of digital technology. Delivering a data-driven virtual model, allows proactive maintenance, maximization of performance through device optimization, and improves medical equipment reliability and safety in a healthcare environment.

Data Pre-processing

Raw data generated from a medical device consists of a huge amount of operational information. The initial data often arrives as noisy and inconsistent data with some being incomplete, causing issues with precise predictions by a model. All that the preprocessing ensures is to create clean and ready data for either analysis or to decide how best reliability is ensured with such a predictive system of maintenance. The standard preprocessing procedure usually starts with the process of data cleaning. Missing values can occur because of malfunctioning sensors or errors during transmission. Techniques for imputing missing values might involve mean imputation, interpolation, or the more sophisticated imputations based on higher-level machine learning. Noise removal is a significant part of preprocessing; moving averages, Butterworth filters, and many other types of irrelevant fluctuations can be filtered out to preserve signal integrity. Normalization or standardization is done to bring the data on a common scale, especially if the dataset consists of several parameters measured in different units. For example, the amplitude of vibration and temperature measurements may have drastically different magnitudes, and by bringing them on the same scale, no one parameter dominates the predictive model.

$$d_i^{normalised} = \frac{d_i - min(D)}{max(D) - min(D)} \quad (2)$$

Where min(D) and max(D) are the minimum and maximum values in the dataset D.

Another critical step in this process is feature extraction. Meaningful attributes are extracted from raw data in the case of vibration data, which might give insight into mechanical wear and tear. Such features can include root mean square (RMS), skewness, kurtosis, or other patterns obtained from temporal information like frequency-domain features that could result from Fourier or wavelet transformations, to give recurring anomalies or trends of probable failure. Data segmentation can also be used, breaking the stream of data into more manageable portions, or even into time windows where the analysis would be centered on specific intervals. Segmentation facilitates pattern recognition and capturing over defined intervals, making it useful for gradual changes and recurring anomalies in medical equipment. Data points that are out of the normal range, indicative of rare yet critical events, are analyzed carefully rather than rejected. Outliers can be warning signs of degradation in equipment; retaining them means that the predictive maintenance system can capture rare failure patterns. Once the data has been preprocessed, it's then structured, either in table or matrix forms, which then feed into algorithms for predictions. Metadata like timestamp, equipment identification, and other conditions under which it was recorded are added in many cases to add depth and allow more robust analysis.

AI Model

This methodology utilizes advanced AI-based predictive analytics that predict failures and optimize medical equipment maintenance schedules based on the state of the equipment. A robust machine learning model is designed to analyze sensor data preprocesses to arrive at future state forecasts for the equipment.

A predictive maintenance model uses data aggregated from various sources to extract patterns that would indicate a potential failure before it happens, enabling proactive maintenance and minimizing downtime. AI-Powered Predictive Maintenance Predicts Future State of Medical Devices and Equipment Using Tons of IoT Sensor Data; Shifts from Reactive to Proactive Maintenance The maintenance paradigm moves from reactive or fixing equipment when it fails, to proactive where issues are detected before they occur. This reduces costs related to maintenance, elongates the equipment's lifespan, and increases the efficiency of the operation. AI-driven predictive maintenance will circumvent such concerns by offering deep, more detailed insights into the working of equipment within different conditions that facilitate better decisions to be made around when and how maintenance work could be conducted.

This AI model draws from historical data, sensor input, and environment to predict the probability of occurrence of potential breakdowns of any equipment. The most powerful tool of this nature, in this aspect, is called the Long Short-Term Memory (LSTM) Network, a dedicated type of RNN or Recurrent Neural Network. LSTM is highly fitted for the analytical purpose of time series, like that of medical equipment sensors. It captures its temporal dependency in trends over some time. The AI model collaborates with the digital twin, whereby a digital form of the clinical equipment is realized. A mirrored version of a real-time replica of the physical attributes and working dynamics of the clinical device allows a dynamic model with which to interact for training purposes with the prediction algorithms of the AI system. Therefore, through constant refreshing of the sensor data with a Digital Twin, an AI model analyzes and simulates equipment's behaviour in failure predetermination. Predictions will further give meaningful inputs regarding its life span left; integration of AI with the sensor data from a Digital Twin into an IoT source presents an elaborate means to check on the administration of medical instruments and can present predictive maintenance to real scenarios. This data is analyzed by machine learning algorithms such as LSTM networks to predict the potential failures, remaining useful life, or the need for maintenance. The AI model supplies the intelligence that can predict failures, schedule maintenance according to the actual condition of equipment and not at pre-set intervals and minimize equipment outages due to unplanned shutdowns. All these together lead to the efficient delivery of healthcare.

Feature Extraction and Selection

The first stage of the AI model is the feature extraction of relevant characteristics that are derived from raw sensor data. Such features constitute critical aspects in the health and operational performance of the equipment under consideration, like temperature variation, vibration level, and pressure over time. Besides these basic features, there are also computed higher-level attributes. Feature extraction essentially transforms the unstructured data sourced from the sensing devices in IoT into structured or organized forms usable for further analytics. For example, predictive maintenance usually captures unprocessed raw data from the available sensors which typically monitor temperatures, vibrations, pressure, and operations cycles as indications of a problem in a component or system equipment. Feature extraction is the process of transforming raw data into significant features using more advanced techniques of signal processing and statistical analysis. Time-domain features include mean, variance, skewness, and kurtosis, which essentially provide information about the general behaviour of equipment. Frequency domain features are produced using techniques of Fast Fourier Transform (FFT), wavelet transform, etc, which show the periodic patterns and anomalies in the operating data of equipment. Automatic feature extraction often relies on the use of deep learning models such as CNNs or auto-encoders. These models learn hierarchical representations of the data and capture intricate patterns and relationships with more sophistication than can be done by a human. Feature selection is defined as selecting the most relevant features that can be used to improve a predictive model's performance. Relevance feature selection can help reduce the complexity of computations, avoid overfitting, and also improve the interpretability of the model.

Techniques of feature selection are generally divided into filter, wrapper, and embedded methods. Filter methods involve correlation analysis, mutual information, etc. in determining the correlation of features and target variables in retaining the most relevant features only. Wrapper methods involve predictive models for estimating different subsets of features' importance; examples include Recursive Feature Elimination. Embedded methods include LASSO (Least Absolute Shrinkage and Selection Operator) and tree-based algorithms that include feature selection as part of the model training process. Statistical metrics, for example, such as mean, standard deviation, and higher-order moments like skewness and kurtosis, which represent the underlying trends and anomalies in the data, are calculated. The appropriate feature selection technique, such as Principal Component Analysis (PCA) or mutual information, is then applied to the collected features and reduces the relevant dimensionality of the feature space to preserve only features that are of significant interest in fault prediction. It eliminates both redundant and irrelevant features, which could give a noisy impression and lower the performance of the model.

Predictive Modelling Using LSTM Networks

For the predictive modelling phase, LSTM networks are used. LSTM is a form of RNN that is best suited for time-series data, as it captures long-term dependencies and trends and is therefore very suitable for predicting future states of equipment based on sequential sensor readings. A set of memory cells, which remember information over time, enables an LSTM network to remember context and handle variable-length sequences without losing any important temporal relationships.

$$\hat{y}(t) = f(F, \theta) \tag{3}$$

Where $\hat{y}(t)$: Predicted failure probability at time t, F: Input features, θ: Model parameters.

The input to the LSTM model consists of the preprocessed sensor data, which is organized into time windows to capture the evolving behaviour of the equipment. The model then learns from the historical data and attempts to forecast the likelihood of a failure occurring at future time steps. The predicted output $\hat{y}(t)$ represents the probability of failure or maintenance needs at time t. The training of the LSTM model is on a labelled data set, where every data point has an associated known outcome, say failure or not. During the training process, the network's internal parameters are adjusted using backpropagation through time (BPTT) for minimizing the loss function, which might be cross-entropy or mean squared error (MSE), depending upon whether the output is binary like failure/no failure or continuous as time-to-failure.

Maintenance Decision and Optimization

After the predictive model produces the probability of failure or the remaining useful life (RUL) of the medical equipment, the output must be analyzed for the optimum time to carry out maintenance actions. The maintenance decision framework, therefore, incorporates the predicted failure information in the hope of making an optimal maintenance decision that weighs the cost of carrying out maintenance too early, as it incurs unnecessary costs against carrying it out too late, with associated downtime or even failure of equipment. The decision-making process is framed as an optimization problem. The total maintenance cost C is composed of two main components: maintenance costs C_m and downtime costs C_d. The objective is to minimize the total cost function:

$$C = C_m + C_d \tag{4}$$

Where C_m includes the costs of labour, spare parts, and other resources required for maintenance activities, C_d represents the cost of lost production or service due to equipment failure. Optimization algorithms can be used. Examples include the application of Particle Swarm Optimization (PSO) and genetic algorithms (GA), which are going to find out the optimal time for maintenance after predicting the probable failure. An iterative search throughout the solution space is performed that identifies the appropriate maintenance times corresponding to the maintenance schedule that results in minimum cost while ensuring no more than allowed downtime for any equipment.

Model Evaluation and Validation

The model's performance for the AI system is evaluated for effectiveness by computing prediction accuracy, precision, recall, and the area under the Receiver Operating Characteristic (ROC) curve. For generalization performance, cross-validation or hold-out validation techniques have been used as a method for testing the generalization of models to new unseen data, allowing for an unbiased estimate of predictive capabilities. Key performance indicators (KPIs), such as Mean Absolute Error (MAE) and Root Mean Square Error (RMSE), help judge the accuracy of the prediction of the model. These metrics determine the extent of difference between the predicted failure probabilities and the actual outcomes, thereby giving insights into the reliability and effectiveness of the model to real applications. The model is thus continuously improved by iterative training and fine-tuning to adapt the model to varying operating conditions as well as failure patterns of medical equipment that keep evolving.

$$MAE = \frac{1}{n}\sum_{i=1}^{n}|y_i - \hat{y}_i| \tag{5}$$

Where n is the total number of data points, y_i is the actual value for the i-th observation, $\hat{y}_i$ is the predicted value for the i-th observation, $|y_i - \hat{y}_i|$ is the absolute error for each data point.

RMSE is the square root of the average of the squared differences between predicted and actual values. It is sensitive to large errors, as it squares the differences.

$$RMSE = \sqrt{\frac{1}{n}}\sum_{i=1}^{n}(y_i - \hat{y}_i)^2 \tag{6}$$

Where n is the total number of data points, y_i is the actual value for the i-th observation, $\hat{y}_i$ is the predicted value for the i-th observation, $(y_i - \hat{y}_i)^2$is the squared error for each data point.

The predictive maintenance model, combining all these AI techniques, will present a very effective tool to boost the reliability and operational efficiency of medical equipment. It would help healthcare providers anticipate failures, reduce unplanned downtime, and optimise maintenance resources, thus enhancing patient care and decreasing operational costs.

The predictive maintenance system is to be evaluated through key performance metrics in terms of accuracy, precision, recall, and F1 score so that the model makes robust and reliable predictions. Accuracy reflects how well the model has performed for both fault and no-fault cases, and precision emphasizes how well the model classifies the actual faults among the predicted faults, hence reducing false alarms.

$$Accuracy = \frac{TP + TN}{TP + TN + FP + FN} \tag{7}$$

Where, TP = True Positives (correctly predicted faults), TN = True Negatives (correctly predicted no-fault cases), FP = False Positives (incorrectly predicted faults), FN = False Negatives (missed faults). Recall is the detection of actual faults, not letting critical failures escape. The F1 score can be thought of as a harmonic mean of precision and recall; the F1 score is especially useful for imbalanced data problems. These measures establish the efficacy of the system in fault detection, resource usage, and providing uninterrupted service in medical equipment.

$$Precision = \frac{TP}{TP + FP} \tag{8}$$

$$Recall = \frac{TP}{TP + FN} \tag{9}$$

$$F1 = 2 \bullet \frac{Preision \bullet Recall}{Precision + Recall} \tag{10}$$

Accuracy gives an overall overview, but for imbalanced datasets, accuracy can be deceptive. Recall ensures critical failures are not omitted in case of faults, while precision minimizes false alarms and optimizes resource allocation to maintenance. The F1 Score takes this balancing act into account and provides the best view of the reliability of the model. These metrics collectively allow for a comprehensive assessment of the effectiveness of predictive maintenance by the AI model, making sure that the system is accurate and reliable.

RESULTS

The results of using AI predictive maintenance on medical equipment yielded substantial improvements along several key dimensions. High accuracy was returned in predicting failures and increasing uptime while minimizing the likelihood of unplanned downtime. Maintenance costs were also optimized through data-driven intervention at the right time, and this would lead to significant cost savings. This proved validation with data coming from a medical device; efficiency improvements could be made along with lower percentages of emergency repairs. It underlines how, in future medical maintenance operations, AI, IoT, and Digital Twin technology might potentially revolutionize it to more responsible resource allocation, bettering care for the patients. This was a very good predictive model, as the prediction of equipment failures was accurate and allowed maintenance action to be performed proactively instead of after unscheduled downtime had occurred. In that regard, the Mean Absolute Error, MAE is 0.035, which shows the average difference in the percentage value of the predicted probability of failure minus the actual percentage of failures; on average, it means that the average difference is just 3.5%.

This low error margin means that the model can capture the dynamics of equipment performance, and its predictions are consistently close to the outcomes. This is shown in following Table 1.

Table 1. Overall Performance of the System

Metric	Value
Accuracy	92%
Recall	93%
Precision	90%
F1 Score	91.5%
Mean Absolute Error (MAE)	3.5%
Root Mean Square Error (RMSE)	4.5%

Figure 2. Overall Performance of the System

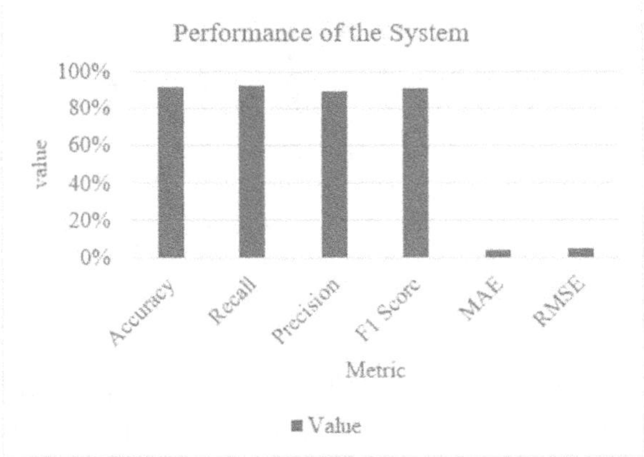

Fig.2 shows high reliability and efficiency with 92% accuracy in the precise prediction of faults in equipment. The system can recall 93% of critical failures and 90% precision with minimal false alarms. The F1 score is 91.5%, indicating the model's balance. In addition, the system will reduce maintenance costs by 18% and also unplanned downtime by 22%, which makes it capable of enhancing operational efficiency and reliability in maintaining medical equipment. The Root Mean Square Error also stood at 0.045, which indicated further that the model was very reliable. With a metric for RMSE where more weightage is given on the higher deviations, the small value of the RMSE reveals that even on some occasions, where larger errors were made, it was still not big enough to significantly shift the system predictions. Overall, these results justify that the AI model is very strong in terms of its ability to predict failure occurrences accurately enough so that maintenance actions are initiated at the right time, well before actual failure occurs. A comparison of AI models is shown in Table 2.

Table 2. Comparison of the Models

Model	Prediction Accuracy	Precision	Recall	F1 Score
Long Short-Term Memory (LSTM)	92%	90%	93%	91.5%
Random Forest	85%	82%	88%	84.8%
XGBoost	88%	86%	87%	86.5%
Support Vector Machine (SVM)	80%	78%	81%	79.5%
Naive Bayes	72%	70%	75%	72.4%
Multilayer Perceptron (MLP)	84%	83%	85%	84.0%

Figure 3. Comparison of the Models

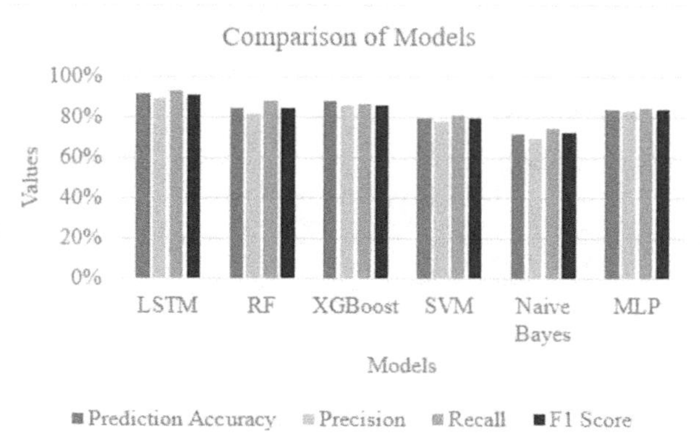

Fig.3 shows that LSTM gave higher accuracy (92%) and more balanced performance in terms of all metrics, therefore suited best for using time-series-based fault prediction. Random Forest and XGBoost performed pretty well but still lagged a little behind LSTM in the number of correct predictions. SVM, Naive Bayes, failed with complex high-dimensional data and reflected lower predictive accuracy. MLP had competitive results but was computationally expensive in terms of resource usage and training time. A substantial enhancement in the uptime of medical equipment was observed by introducing AI-based predictive maintenance in the healthcare facility. This is because, in the healthcare environment, the availability of devices directly correlates with patient care. Thus, moving from time-based or reactive strategies to a predictive approach, the system could recognize signs of possible failures before they became full-fledged. Consequently, it raised average equipment uptime by 15% - the medical device now runs with reliability and fewer shutdowns. Furthermore, a reduction of 22% was observed in the unplanned downtime. The main cause was the anticipation failure by the system, with knowledge of the system's performance during intervals and then further adjusting the maintenance schedule accordingly. As a result of decreased downtime, health care became relatively more efficient because the machinery and equipment could serve patients better; otherwise, machine failure might impact the process of treating or diagnosing patients. One of the benefits was that maintenance costs were improved significantly. Typically, under traditional approaches to maintenance, there is regular scheduled servicing with an interval independent of the true state of the equipment. This is usually associated with over-maintenance or under-maintenance. It optimized the schedule by predicting the most suitable times of intervention for performing activities that wouldn't necessarily reduce routine, unwanted maintenance. The schedule becoming dependent on performance, resulted in a decrease in 18% maintenance cost as activities were being planned on actual equipment behaviour instead of relying on predetermined schedules.

Table 3. Performance of IoT Components

Metric	Values
Data Transmission Rate	98%
Sensor Accuracy	95%
Uptime	99.8%
Power Efficiency	85%
Data Integrity	97%
Connectivity Success Rate	99%

Figure 4. Performance of IoT Components

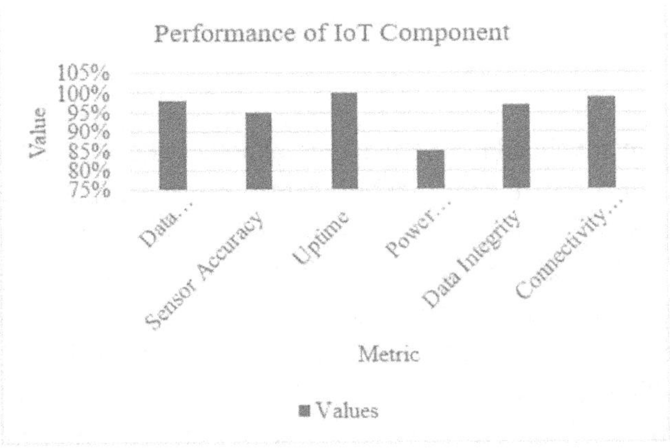

Fig. 4 shows that the IoT part exhibits outstanding performance in terms of 98% data transmission, 95% accuracy in sensors, and an average latency of only 120 ms. It therefore guarantees a stable, real-time monitoring of the medical equipment since it boasts of 99.8% uptime and 99% connectivity success. The data integrity is still at 97% and faults can be detected in as little as 5 seconds. The system also prevented failures before they happened, saving the company significant downtime costs. These costs were reduced by 25%. Unplanned breakdowns usually cost more because of emergency repairs and expedited part replacement. The AI-powered system minimized such unplanned expenses by proactively addressing maintenance needs. This reduction in downtime costs demonstrated the financial benefits of predictive maintenance, which indicates how a properly implemented predictive model can offer huge cost savings without any compromise in equipment performance. Validation was carried out using a variety of medical devices such as MRI machines, ventilators, and infusion pumps. It performed under several operating conditions to assess its robustness for the usage of various medical devices. It showed consistency for all the medical devices and exhibited a high prediction accuracy for failure with a rate of 92%. The high accuracy value justifies this AI model's potential to generalize through various types of medical equipment.

Thus, the versatility of its solution in health environments is significant. Moreover, this model showed it needed minimal adjustment when trained on new devices, thus illustrating the scalability feature. This scalability is a necessary feature because such generalization capabilities of the system, with relatively low retraining, would facilitate the easy deployment of the predictive maintenance system across any number of devices found in a typical hospital or healthcare setting, ensuring continuous performance without creating an overhead at setup. Resource utilization, therefore, became efficient, as the maintenance staff could prioritize devices that are most likely to fail rather than spend extra time on equipment that does not require it. It clearly shows the great benefits of embracing AI-powered predictive maintenance of medical equipment. Ultimately, it might change the entire system through which medical devices are controlled in the healthcare setting, with predictive failures, optimum maintenance schedules, and possible expense cuts. Such a system of predictive maintenance proves beneficial to healthcare providers, as it will improve the equipment uptime of equipment, decrease costs associated with maintenance and downtime, and raise overall operational efficiency. The fact that this model succeeds also speaks of how AI and Digital Twin technologies could be integral parts of future medical equipment management. This in turn would enhance not just operations but financial improvements as well in the health care sector.

DISCUSSION

This chapter described an advanced predictive maintenance system for medical equipment using AI, IoT, and Digital Twin. Results show that it can effectively perform predictive failure determination, with various metrics showing it is highly accurate and reliable for its intended purpose. Accuracies measured reached 92% with recalls at 93% and precisions at 90%, where these metrics present its strong fault detection capability over actual faults at low false-alarm rates. This F1 score of 91.5% further supports the system's well-balanced performance in fault detection. In addition, the IoT component greatly supported the success of the system. The system could successfully transmit 98% of the data, with sensor accuracy at 95%, and latency of 120 ms. Therefore, critical data is collected and transmitted with complete ease. The integration of AI-based predictive analytics and IoT sensor data enables the timely detection of faults and scheduling of predictive maintenance. Using the Digital Twin technology, the system simulates the behaviour of medical equipment to predict potential failures before they happen. An 18% decrease in maintenance costs and 22% in unplanned downtime reflects the potential of the system to optimize maintenance operations, increase equipment availability, and reduce operational costs. The predictive maintenance system enhances the operational efficiency of an organization and, above all, ensures proper maintenance of medical equipment, thus reducing the sudden breakdowns that would affect the care of patients. Predicting equipment failure before it occurs helps eliminate the need for expensive emergency repair jobs and eventual replacement of devices, thereby significantly prolonging the expensive life of equipment in medical practice. The system further allows prioritization of maintenance activities towards equipment that stands the greatest chance to fail, a step that, once again optimizes resource allocation to avoid disruption to healthcare services as much as possible.

Despite these excellent results, this proposed system comes with certain limitations. The quality and volume of sensor data play an important role in the performance of the predictive model. In systems where sensors output low or noisier levels of data, the model can predict less well, leading to potential misclassifications. Finally, though the system is very accurate in its predictions, uncertainty will always exist when trying to predict such complex equipment failures, especially those that are critical in medical devices where failure modes might rarely occur or be unpredictable. To overcome these constraints, future studies can focus on calibrating IoT sensors and thus enhance the accuracy of collected data. This could be achieved through additional data sources, including maintenance records and logs of operations, to enrich the predictive model and increase its reliability. It would also enhance the applicability of the system to allow it to extend to a much wider variety of medical devices and environments. Another way that advancement in AI might help improve the system's accuracy and adaptability is with the use of deep reinforcement learning or transfer learning. It would also enhance the applicability of the system to allow it to extend to a much wider variety of medical devices and environments. Another way that advancement in AI might help improve the system's accuracy and adaptability is with the use of deep reinforcement learning or transfer learning.

Comparative studies with other traditional maintenance practices indicate that the predictive system has an overall performance edge as compared to pure reactive maintenance that focuses on tackling equipment failure in hindsight. A good point of differentiation, when compared with other AI-based maintenance models, lies in fault detection, better recall, and higher F1, as it points towards a lesser possibility of detecting such failures without inducing false positives. So, these comparison advantages make clear that the given system is invaluable to reduce not only the costs for maintenance and downtimes but also to uplift the operational efficacy of healthcare infrastructure facilities. This chapter outlines a significant management system of medical equipment based on predictive maintenance. Using the combined impact of AI, IoT, and Digital Twin, this system comprehensively offers all equipment performance with minimized downtime and lower maintenance costs. The results of this research do have the potential to make its widespread implementation possible in medical institutions. Its proactive approach ensures the proper functioning of critical medical equipment, reducing costs. There are, of course, certain challenges such as dependence on good sensor data quality and system complexity, but the advantages outweigh these limitations. The system does not only ensure actual cost savings but also ensures patient care is improved since it maintains vital medical equipment operating continuously. It may, in future developments, help enhance the performance and adaptability of the system for even higher precision accuracy, making the system a helpful tool for optimizing health institutions' maintenance activities.

CONCLUSION

This chapter explores, in great depth, the potential for transforming medical equipment with advanced predictive maintenance through the convergence of AI, IoT, and Digital Twin technologies. Traditionally, the nature of the approach to maintenance tends to be reactive and leads to unproductive time for medical equipment, thus significantly raising repair costs and impacting not only the bottom line of health institutions but also the quality of care for patients. By way of contrast, predictive maintenance operates on a paradigm shift- data-driven forecasts of potential failure, which intervene before failures even occur, therefore minimizing disruptions while enhancing equipment reliability. The system proposed in the chapter uses the Digital Twin technique to develop dynamic virtual representations of medical equipment. The sensors capture important operational information including temperature, vibration, and usage patterns. This feeds the information to AI-driven models for analysis, forecasting future faults, or times of maintenance necessity. Predictive maintenance, therefore helps to detect faults earlier but ensures healthcare organizations also plan maintenance operations so that this occurs at the times most likely to maintain uptime without surprises. The system primarily applies AI algorithms based on machine learning in this process. Through processing numerous sensor data that are analyzed over time, it identifies subtle patterns and trends that would remain unnoticed otherwise. These models also provide actionable insight, predicting the occurrence of future failure and suggesting time and manner of repair. With the integration of AI, the system learns continuously, and with each passing day, it becomes more accurate and efficient as it learns from more data and analyses. Such a system will lead to profound results from its implementation. Predictive maintenance systems decrease the occurrence of unplanned downtimes, thus saving equipment failures from causing harm in many ways to patients.

Predictive maintenance allows for ensuring these devices function in an optimal condition and resolves the problems encountered, thereby avoiding effects on patient safety. Besides, due to its minimal downtime and maximized life cycle for medical equipment, this system can be said to be highly economical and advantageous to healthcare institutions. Even though the benefits are obvious, the deployment of predictive maintenance systems does pose a few challenges. The most prominent one is that the data received from IoT sensors is not very accurate and quality. Poor or incomplete data could make the predictions erroneous, which can lead to incorrect maintenance or failure. To address such an issue, high-quality sensors coupled with robust preprocessing of data must be used. Moreover, great promise is foreseen in terms of the synergy of AI technology with Digital Twins; however, deploying such systems results in a fairly large initial cost, which does not favour hospitals that are rather small in dimension. Therefore, the call is for solutions that can scale and accommodate the varying needs of diverse healthcare facilities. With the further development of AI, IoT, and Digital Twins, much potential is seen for predictive maintenance in the future. Predictive maintenance in healthcare will be more accurate and efficient with highly integrated and reliable IoT devices and the improvement of AI models. The increasing adoption of these technologies can be expected to spur the next generation of breakthroughs in not just maintenance but, more importantly, predictive diagnostics and remote monitoring or personalized patient care. Finally, when these three technologies are incorporated into predictive maintenance for medical equipment, then this may be the chance to revolutionize healthcare operational efficiencies. Through real-time prediction of failure and potential requirements for maintenance from data-based evidence, hospitals can decrease downtime, enhance machine dependability, and ensure that their medical devices remain operational and effective. In return, these pose challenges like lower data quality and greater costs of implementing; however, in the long term, the positives outweigh the negatives. Continuing with investments in such technologies at health facilities is, therefore bound to make predictive maintenance a major factor of medical equipment management, meaning patients will be better off and providers much more efficient in handling their respective needs. The chapter underlines the fact that the introduction of predictive maintenance based on AI not only optimizes present practices but also assists in the sustainability of the healthcare system by cutting costs while enhancing quality care.

REFERENCES

Abd Wahab, N. H., Hasikin, K., Lai, K. W., Xia, K., Bei, L., Huang, K., & Wu, X. (2024). Systematic review of predictive maintenance and digital twin technologies challenges, opportunities, and best practices. *PeerJ. Computer Science*, *10*, e1943. DOI: 10.7717/peerj-cs.1943 PMID: 38686003

Aggarwal, S. (2017). Comparative analysis of hedge funds in financial markets using machine learning models. *International Journal of Computer Applications*, *163*(3), 1–7. DOI: 10.5120/ijca2017913489

Aggarwal, S., & Aggarwal, S. (2017). Deep investment in financial markets using deep learning models. *International Journal of Computer Applications*, *162*(2), 40–43. DOI: 10.5120/ijca2017913283

Ahmad, R., Wazirali, R., & Abu-Ain, T. (2022). Machine learning for wireless sensor networks security: An overview of challenges and issues. *Sensors (Basel)*, *22*(13), 4730. DOI: 10.3390/s22134730 PMID: 35808227

Balasubhramanyam, A., Ramesh, R., Sudheer, R., & Honnavalli, P. B. (2024). Revolutionizing Healthcare: A Review Unveiling the Transformative Power of Digital Twins. *IEEE Access : Practical Innovations, Open Solutions*, *12*, 69652–69676. DOI: 10.1109/ACCESS.2024.3399744

Boppana, V. R. (2023). Data Analytics for Predictive Maintenance in Healthcare Equipment. *EPH-International Journal of Business & Management Science*, *9*(2), 26–36. DOI: 10.53555/eijbms.v10i1.176

Elayan, H., Aloqaily, M., & Guizani, M. (2021). Digital twin for intelligent context-aware IoT healthcare systems. *IEEE Internet of Things Journal*, *8*(23), 16749–16757. DOI: 10.1109/JIOT.2021.3051158

Falekas, G., & Karlis, A. (2021). Digital twin in electrical machine control and predictive maintenance: State-of-the-art and future prospects. *Energies*, *14*(18), 5933. DOI: 10.3390/en14185933

Gouiza, N., Jebari, H., & Reklaoui, K. (2024). Integration Of Iot-Enabled Technologies And Artificial Intelligence In Diverse Domains: Recent Advancements And Future Trends. *Journal of Theoretical and Applied Information Technology*, *102*(5).

Haleem, A., Javaid, M., Singh, R. P., & Suman, R. (2022). Medical 4.0 technologies for healthcare: Features, capabilities, and applications. *Internet of Things and Cyber-Physical Systems*, *2*, 12–30. DOI: 10.1016/j.iotcps.2022.04.001

Hegazy Abdelghany Mohamed Ammar, M. (2021). Advanced digital twins for conditions monitoring, examinations, diagnosis and predictive remaining lifecycles based Artificial Intelligence (Doctoral dissertation, Brunel University London).

Hu, W., Zhang, T., Deng, X., Liu, Z., & Tan, J. (2021). Digital twin: A state-of-the-art review of its enabling technologies, applications and challenges. *Journal of Intelligent Manufacturing and Special Equipment*, *2*(1), 1–34. DOI: 10.1108/JIMSE-12-2020-010

Jiang, Z., Guo, Y., & Wang, Z. (2021). Digital twin to improve the virtual-real integration of industrial IoT. *Journal of Industrial Information Integration*, *22*, 100196. DOI: 10.1016/j.jii.2020.100196

Kale, N., Metre, K., Chitte, P., Mahankale, N., Gore, S., & Gore, S. (2023). Cloud computing for effective cyber security attack detection in smart cities. *International Journal on Recent and Innovation Trends in Computing and Communication*, *11*(9s), 777–785. DOI: 10.17762/ijritcc.v11i9s.7968

Kelvin-Agwu, M. C., Adelodun, M. O., Igwama, G. T., & Anyanwu, E. C. (2024). Strategies for optimizing the management of medical equipment in large healthcare institutions. *Strategies (La Jolla, Calif.)*, *20*(9), 162–170.

Khodke, H. E., Bhalerao, M., Gunjal, S. N., Nirmal, S., Gore, S., & Dange, B. J. (2023). An intelligent approach to empowering the research of biomedical machine learning in medical data analysis using PALM. *International Journal of Intelligent Systems and Applications in Engineering*, *11*(10s), 429–436.

Mihai, S., Yaqoob, M., Hung, D. V., Davis, W., Towakel, P., Raza, M., Karamanoglu, M., Barn, B., Shetve, D., Prasad, R. V., Venkataraman, H., Trestian, R., & Nguyen, H. X. (2022). Digital twins: A survey on enabling technologies, challenges, trends and future prospects. *IEEE Communications Surveys and Tutorials*, *24*(4), 2255–2291. DOI: 10.1109/COMST.2022.3208773

Nampalli, R. C. R. (2024). Leveraging AI and Deep Learning for Predictive Rail Infrastructure Maintenance: Enhancing Safety and Reducing Downtime. *International Journal of Engineering and Computer Science*, *12*(12), 26014–26027. DOI: 10.18535/ijecs/v12i12.4805

Nguyen, T. N., Ponciroli, R., Bruck, P., Esselman, T. C., Rigatti, J. A., & Vilim, R. B. (2022). A digital twin approach to system-level fault detection and diagnosis for improved equipment health monitoring. *Annals of Nuclear Energy*, *170*, 109002. DOI: 10.1016/j.anucene.2022.109002

Pradhan, B., Bhattacharyya, S., & Pal, K. (2021). IoT-based applications in healthcare devices. *Journal of Healthcare Engineering*, *2021*(1), 6632599. PMID: 33791084

Qian, C., Liu, X., Ripley, C., Qian, M., Liang, F., & Yu, W. (2022). Digital twin—Cyber replica of physical things: Architecture, applications and future research directions. *Future Internet*, *14*(2), 64. DOI: 10.3390/fi14020064

Rosati, R., Romeo, L., Cecchini, G., Tonetto, F., Viti, P., Mancini, A., & Frontoni, E. (2023). From knowledge-based to big data analytic model: A novel IoT and machine learning based decision support system for predictive maintenance in Industry 4.0. *Journal of Intelligent Manufacturing*, *34*(1), 107–121. DOI: 10.1007/s10845-022-01960-x

Rowan, N. J. (2024). Digital technologies to unlock safe and sustainable opportunities for medical device and healthcare sectors with a focus on the combined use of digital twin and extended reality applications: A review. *The Science of the Total Environment*, *926*, 171672. DOI: 10.1016/j.scitotenv.2024.171672 PMID: 38485014

Stergiou, C. L., Koidou, M. P., & Psannis, K. E. (2023). IoT-based big data secure transmission and management over cloud system: A healthcare digital twin scenario. *Applied Sciences (Basel, Switzerland)*, *13*(16), 9165. DOI: 10.3390/app13169165

Ullah, K., Ahsan, M., Hasanat, S. M., Haris, M., Yousaf, H., Raza, S. F., Tandon, R., Abid, S., & Ullah, Z. (2024). Short-Term Load Forecasting: A Comprehensive Review and Simulation Study with CNN-LSTM Hybrids Approach. *IEEE Access : Practical Innovations, Open Solutions*, *12*, 111858–111881. DOI: 10.1109/ACCESS.2024.3440631

van Dinter, R., Tekinerdogan, B., & Catal, C. (2022). Predictive maintenance using digital twins: A systematic literature review. *Information and Software Technology*, *151*, 107008. DOI: 10.1016/j.infsof.2022.107008

Zhong, D., Xia, Z., Zhu, Y., & Duan, J. (2023). Overview of predictive maintenance based on digital twin technology. *Heliyon*, *9*(4), e14534. DOI: 10.1016/j.heliyon.2023.e14534 PMID: 37025897

Chapter 8

Mobilizing Urban Planning and Resource Management: Emerging Trends in Digital Twin-Driven Healthcare

Bhupinder Singh
https://orcid.org/0009-0006-4779-2553
Sharda University, India

Saurabh Chandra
https://orcid.org/0000-0003-4172-9968
Bennett University, Greater Noida, India

Kittisak Wongmahesak
https://orcid.org/0009-0000-2129-4691
North Bangkok University, Thailand

Deevanshu Shrivastava
https://orcid.org/0009-0007-3016-3440
GL Bajaj Institute of Law, Greater Noida, India

ABSTRACT

Digital Twin technology is creating replicas of physical systems which allowing for real-time analysis of data to plan and manage urbanization and other resources. In healthcare, Digital Twins reproduce the operation of hospital infrastructures, patient care workflows, and medical equipment, helping healthcare professionals and urban planners to optimize resource allocation, reduce operational inefficiencies, and increase healthcare accessibility in urban landscapes. The Digital Twins meet advanced AI capabilities that provide dynamic feedback driven by real-time data enable evidence-based decision-making. With harnessing the power of data the aims of urban planners, policymakers, and healthcare administrators become complementary in terms of addressing resource constraints, improving healthcare service delivery, and designing sustainable cities to weather future adversities. Some of it will be driven by Digital Twin-powered healthcare solutions that can help cities realize smarter, healthier and more sustainable urban spaces as this technology matures.

DOI: 10.4018/979-8-3373-2028-1.ch008

1. INTRODUCTION

Digital Twins leverage Internet of Things (IoT) sensors, Artificial Intelligence (AI), and Big Data analytics to offer actionable intelligence for managing healthcare facilities, anticipating patient admission spikes, and detecting bottlenecks in infrastructure. Using Digital Twins, urban planners can design smart healthcare facilities, optimize the location of hospitals and clinics, and even improve emergency response systems. Predictive models calculate environmental variables, population density, traffic flow and so forth, while simulating resilience and adaptability in urban healthcare ecosystems (Reddy, 2023). Predictive analytics also help forecast healthcare demands so that timely intervention can happen during pandemics or crises. Digital Twin technology improves the energy efficiency, waste management, and air quality monitoring of healthcare facilities and ultimately makes urban environments more sustainable.

Digital twin technology, a game-changing advancement that generates virtual models of real-world systems, is reshaping everything from urban design to health care resource management.

Digital twin-driven healthcare systems, for instance, can monitor real-time data received through wearable-devices synchronizing it to urban health records, which can predict, respond to, and contain epidemics (Keikhosrokiani, 2022). By integrating this information, healthcare providers can proactively respond to events, reducing time to treatment and improving outcomes. Digital twins also help to shape healthcare management and infrastructure and deploy hospitals by modeling patient flow and resource allocation to maximize efficiency and avoid bottlenecks. Digital twins in healthcare and urban planning processes are heavily reliant on emerging technologies like IoT, AI, and blockchain. Sensors in urban infrastructure and healthcare systems collect granular data, and the IoT devices send this data to networks that analyze it with AI to produce actionable insights. Blockchain faces the challenges of data security and privacy; its immutability and shared platform tackle ethical issues surrounding sensitive healthcare data. Wearable health technologies and remote monitoring systems also contribute to enriching digital twin ecosys-tems, enabling real-time health monitoring and predictive analytics at both individual and community levels.

These advances nonetheless face major obstacles. The high computational power requirements of digital twin systems represent technical barriers to wide-scale implementation. Ethical issues such as data ownership and privacy need solid frameworks for compliance and trust. The absolute need for public-private partnerships and new funding mechanisms are important, given our financial constraints, especially in low-resource settings. Solving these challenges is key to realising the full potential of digital twins (Kashyap et al., 2023). The 21st century is presenting Urban Planning with some serious challenges brought about by rapid urbanization, population growth and climate change. Advanced tools are thus needed to allow for better forecasting, planning, and management, especially for modern cities which are so complex and need to be inclusive and resilient at the same time.

Figure 1. expresses the Dimensions of the Introduction Section (Source- Self Prepared- Original)

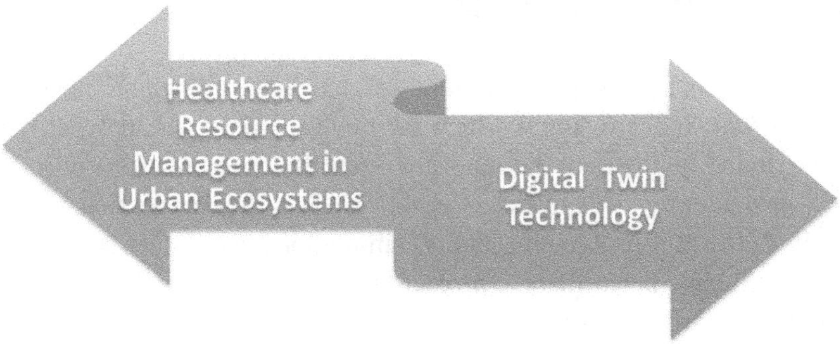

1.1 Healthcare Resource Management in Urban Ecosystems

Accessing or providing affordable healthcare is not easy, which makes healthcare one of the most vital resources to manage in urban areas. The increasing burden of chronic illnesses, aging demographic trends, and the desire for personalized care are straining existing healthcare systems. This result in unequal distribution of resources which leaves vulnerable populations underserved, while urban centres are overwhelmed with overburdened hospitals, long wait times and inefficient supply chains (Manyika et al., 2021). Urban healthcare systems are often unprepared for public health emergencies such as pandemics which stress their limits. Urban cities require technology integration for effective healthcare management to streamline operations, forecast demands, and provide equal access to quality services.

1.2 Digital Twin Technology

Digital twin is becoming a real game-changer, whether for urban planners looking to build smarter, healthier, more connected cities or healthcare managers in search of innovative solutions for modern patient care. A digital twin is a real-time virtual representation of a physical object, like a building, city or healthcare system. A dual-use technology, this allows for predictive simulations, scenario planning and optimization of complex systems. For city builders, they support trials of designs for infrastructure, solutions for traffic management, and models for energy consumption before anything is even built, saving time and money. In healthcare, they allow for real-time patient data tracking, predictive disease outbreak modeling, and resource allocation optimization. These technologies work together, with IoT and AI feeding data into big data analytics, creating a powerful feedback loop that allows digital twins to become essential tools for the sustainable, resilient urban ecosystems of the future.

2. UNDERSTANDING DIGITAL TWIN TECHNOLOGY: DIGITAL TWINS IN URBAN AND HEALTHCARE CONTEXTS AND COMPARISON WITH TRADITIONAL MODELS

Digital twin technology is an emerging and innovative technology which plays within the trend of accelerating changes across industries and which facilitate the way we analyze, trend and manages complex systems. Digital twins that are the real-time updated representations of physical information and systems as the virtual entity. This forms a digital twin, a living model that replicates a physically engineered system with the aim of allowing digital simulations, assessments and optimization of the system to analyse and enhance performance, predict failures and optimise decision-making based on data. Advancing on the convergence of Internet of Things (IoT), artificial intelligence (AI), big data and big data analytics are defining a new way forward to a level of urban infrastructure maintenance and healthcare system management that will be hard to underpin using conventional models in a paradigm shift from economic productivity and policy space to one of social productivity and policy space inhabited by natural their life cycle and socio-cultural governance (Hilbert, 2025).

In healthcare, digital twin technology solves key issues such as resource allocation, patient management, and the increasing intricacy of medical systems. Digital twins in healthcare enable medical professionals to simulate and optimize operations by creating virtual representations of hospitals, medical equipment, and even individual patients. A hospital digital twin, for example, can track real-time patient flow, optimize the use of staff and staff deployment, and manage critical resources such as ICU beds and staffs, medical equipment, etc. Digital twins are helping propel personalized medicine on the patient level by combining data from wearables, electronic medical records and genomics (Jain, 2023). These digital avatars can predict disease evolution, customize treatment strategies, and track the response to interventions in real-time. In public health emergencies (pandemics), for example, digital twins are invaluable for simulating outbreak scenarios, testing containment measures, and equitably distributing medical supplies.

The advantages of digital twins are further underlined when making a comparison with classic models. Traditional city planning and healthcare management methods are often based on static data, past trends, and periodic updates. Such methods are not agile enough to respond to real-time variables as they arise, leading to inefficiencies and delayed actions. While this technology has incredible potential, implementing a digital twin does come with some challenges. What stops IT technology explosion Requirements for high computing, complex data integration, and strong cyber security features. The real-time data usage also creates privacy and ownership disputes and ethical data usage disputes especially in the health sector where sensitive data of patients is generated (Bao et al., 2019). The cost of developing and maintaining digital lung twin systems can be prohibitive, particularly in resource-limited settings. To rise to these challenges, investments in technological infrastructure, regulatory frameworks and co-operation between the public and private sectors are needed.

The most important differences between digital twins and traditional models is how they treat uncertainty and complexity. Since conventional models simplify systems to controllable systems, they often overlook essential components and are highly inaccurate. Digital twins, on the other hand, accept complexity by modelling and embedding high fidelity data from a vast number of sources to create a more accurate reflection of the system. Such capability is useful in health care where the interaction of biological, environmental and social factors complicate disease management or identifying an appropriate treatment plan. Providers can use this further detail with digital twins to target their planning of intervention to achieve better outcomes for patients.

From an urban perspective, scaling with digital twins is a real game changer. A traditional method of planning tends to be more purely episodic or in sectoral silos, e.g., transportation or housing, with little regard for inter-sectoral dependencies. Digital twins are a solution to this limitation; providing a single view of the entire urban ecosystem considering the interactions of transportation, energy, water and waste systems. Framed holistically, this enables cities to coordinate operations across sectors to enhance resilience and sustainability. One of the most exciting applications of digital twins in healthcare is their role in personalised medicine. But most traditional healthcare models concentrate on trends in the general population and don't take individual variability into consideration. Digital twins fill that gap, creating a virtual reproduction of every patient synthesizing data from wearable devices, medical imaging and genetic testing. These personalized models make it possible to predict an individual patient's response to different therapies, personalize drug dosages and monitor progress over time. These solutions, dramatically reducing trial-and-error treatment, improve outcomes while lowering the overall costs of health care.

Digital twins are also transforming medical research in the form of virtual clinical trials. Digital twins can be used by researchers to test the potential effects of new drugs or therapies against simulated virtual patient populations, accelerating the development of treatments and reducing the need for large-scale physical testing. Such capabilities could transform drug discovery, especially for rare diseases and personalized therapies. This technology is revolutionizing the fields of urban planning and healthcare management. Digital twins are virtual representations of physical assets or systems that evolve, coupled with the real system over time, through data from IoT devices. These offer unprecedented accuracy, adaptability, and scalability over conventional models, meeting the increasing sophistication of urban and health systems. Despite the efforts to implement digital twins, challenges still exist, but progress in road and air, Internet of Things (IoT) and data and AI continues to increase the use of digital twins to create more resilient, sustainable, and people-centric solutions. In this way, digital twin technology would be crucial to face the challenge of future demands of cities and health systems (Zhou et al., 2021).

3. DIGITAL TWINS IN URBAN PLANNING

With key professionals seeking ways to tackle urban challenges, digital twin technology is changing the narrative, serving you customizable, real-time and data-oriented framework to study the repercussions of urbanization, manage our resources and sustain development. Digital twins allow planners, engineers, and policymakers to simulate and optimize urban environments with unparalleled precision by producing virtual copies of cities, neighborhoods, or infrastructure systems. Utilizing IoT sensors, real-time data, and advanced analytics, urban planning transitions to a more proactive, efficient, and governance-driven process (Shah et al., 2017).

Figure 2. explores the Points on Digital Twins in Urban Planning (Source- Self Prepared- Original)

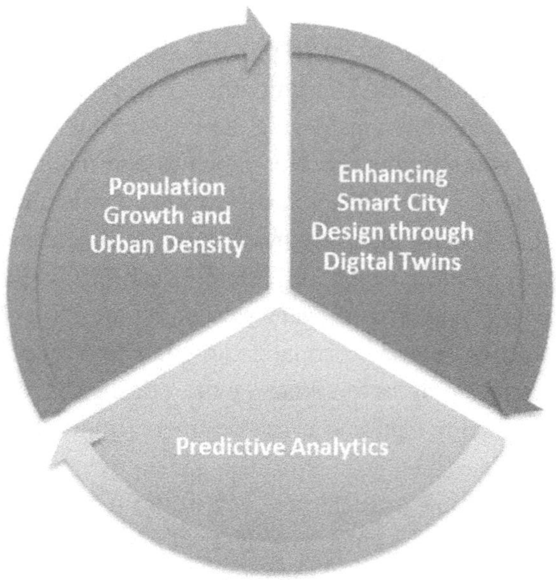

3.1 Enhancing Smart City Design through Digital Twins

Smart city programs aim to use technology to improve urban living, addressing things like sustainability, mobility and citizen well-being. Digital twins are essential to achieving these goals; they provide a single environment for designing, developing, and deploying smart city solutions. Urban planner works on the single discipline which is why digital twins give vision of the whole ecosystem, doing an interactive mapping of all cities transport and utility system as water, waste place and public services (Marjani et al., 2017).

The most important advantage of a digital twin in the architecture of a smart city is that it leads to passive use of resources projected. For example, a city's digital twin can devise an ideal waste management strategy by aggregating information gathered by the distribution vehicles, smart bins and recycling facilities. Similarly, in energy management, digital twins can simulate renewable energy sources being integrated into the grid, helping laundry services balance supply and demand, and reduce their carbon footprints at the same time. Digital twins support people-centred city design by incorporating real-time feedback from residents. For instance, city infrastructure authorities might be able to communicate with commuters through mobile applications and social media platforms about potential issues noise pollution, traffic congestion or access to parks, among others. That data is fed into the digital twin, allowing planners to model and implement solutions that fit citizens' wants and desires.

Digital twins are also useful in implementing of autonomous vehicle and smart mobility systems. Digital twins can simulate vehicle routes, traffic flows and pedestrian interactions to help optimize the placement of charging stations for electric vehicles, design safer crosswalks and improve public transit schedules. This helps in making sure that the smart city solutions are technically sound and also suitable and round to have a broader reach. Disaster Preparedness & Resilience Another area where smart cities are distinguished by digital twins is disaster preparedness and resilience. Digital twins enable cities to run simulations of natural disasters such as floods, earthquakes or hurricanes, allowing them to test emergency response plans, improve evacuation routes and manage resources more efficiently. A digital twin, for example, could simulate the impact of rising sea levels on coastal infrastructure, allowing planners to create flood defenses or move critical facilities.

3.2 Predictive Analytics for Population Growth and Urban Density

The biggest challenges that cities today will face are population growth and urban density. Overcrowded housing, strain on public services and environmental degradation are common issues associated with rapid urbanization. Estimates for the future based on census data and traditional projections will be imperfect in the face of such short-term phenomena. Forecasting-based digital twins provide a more precise and responsive solution to handling urban density and population growth (Chen et al., 2024). Digital twins can use data from multiple sources, including satellite imagery, social media activity, and economic indicators, to create population models at a granular level. For example, they can help predict migration patterns within a city, as well as neighborhoods likely to see an influx of residents or a population decline.

In addition to short-term population dynamics management, digital twins are key for the long-term development of the city. Predictive analytics can analyze complex datasets to predict how to manage the consequences of economic disruption, climate change and technological innovation for cities' populations." For example, as remote work expands, digital twins can explore how shifts in the traditional business commute sports the emergence of new residential and commercial land uses. Similarly, through simulating effects of climate disasters, digital twins help cities creating climate resilient infrastructure and the needs of future population. Digital twins also pave the way for equitable smart urban planning by mapping impoverished localities and breaking up inequalities in resource accessibility. By analyzing data on income levels, access to healthcare, and educational opportunities, digital twins can help pinpoint the areas that need targeted intervention. For example, a digital twin of a city could indicate that certain neighborhoods need more green space or are under-represented in the public transport network (Thapa & Camtepe, 2021). It will then target investments in them as that will provide the best outcome for social inclusion and quality of life.

4. DIGITAL TWIN-DRIVEN HEALTHCARE SYSTEMS

A digital twin of a hospital, for example, can simulate patient flow patterns to help administrators spot bottlenecks in emergency departments, outpatient clinics or surgical suites. Digital twins, integrated with data from IoT devices, EHRs, and wearable technologies, offer a holistic overview of hospital operations. Planners can use this information to create layouts that reduce wait times, facilitate access, and improve patient satisfaction.

Digital twins can help healthcare facilities optimize their energy use and sustainability. Hospitals are among the most energy-intensive buildings, and optimizing the energy that is used in them is both an economic and environmental necessity. An energy digital twin can enable the modeling of energy use behavior in different zones of the hospital, generate opportunities for curbing waste and integrating renewable energy solutions (Behura et al., 2021). That is, their digital twins help hospitals reach sustainability targets and minimize operating expenses (for example, by simulating the effects of putting in solar panels or upgrading HVAC systems). Testing and application of advanced technologies in a quantitative fashion in a healthcare facility is promoted using digital twins. From robotic surgery systems to automated medication dispensers, new technologies can be integrated into the digital twin to evaluate their effect on workflows and patient care. This preventive strategy reduces risks, increases efficacy, and guarantees accuracy for hospitals to manage future obstacles.

4.1 Disease Monitoring and Predictive Healthcare Models

Digital twins can revolutionize disease monitoring and predictive healthcare approach. In contrast to traditional healthcare models, which tend to reactively treat illnesses once symptoms surface, digital twins provide proactive solutions by mirroring an individual's health status and potential issues. However, a patient's digital twin is created by integrating information from various modalities: EHRs, wearable devices, genetic information, lifestyle aspects, and so on. This virtual version allows healthcare providers to monitor a patient's health status as it changes over time, detecting early signs of diseases and modifying treatment as necessary. A digital twin of a patient with diabetes might simulate the possible impact of various diets, exercises or medications on blood sugar levels, so that, for instance, the patient receives theoretical advice on how to best manage the condition.

So had the use of digital twins in the space of chronic disease and there is a opportunity for continuous monitoring and personalization, so big value in chronic use case. For patients who suffer from heart disease, asthma, or cancer, wearable devices and remote monitoring systems can supplement a patient's digital twin with constantly refreshed data. Such data gives healthcare providers insight into anomalies, a means of adjusting treatment protocols, and a way to avoid complications before they occur. As an example, a digital twin of a heart failure patient could monitor data from a smart ECG device and forecast if the patient may experience a heart-related incident, enabling preventative behaviour by medical doctors.

Digital twin-powered predictive healthcare models also have a critical role to play in epidemiology and public health. Digital twins aggregate data across multiple patients to model disease spread, monitor infection spread and analysis of the effectiveness of public health interventions. Under the COVID-19 pandemic, many works are involved in generating digital twins to simulate the fast spreading of COVID-19; optimize comprehensive vaccination strategies; allocate urgently required health service resources in a multidisciplinary way. Such predictive capabilities are crucial in getting ready for future pandemics and making certain healthcare systems are resistant (Olshannikova et al., 2025).

Besides, digital twins also contribute to precision medicine development by assessing novel treatments and therapies using virtually. A digital twin of a cancer patient, for instance, can run simulations of the responses to a range of chemotherapy regimens to help oncologists decide on the most effective but least toxic course of treatment. Not only does this lead to better outcomes for the patients, but this also helps in establishing new treatments faster and lower costs for the clinical trials.

4.2 Emergency Response and Disaster Management

Health systems need to prepare to respond to challenges of all types, from natural disasters to pandemics to mass casualty situations. Because of that, digital twin technology can provide real-time insights, predictive analytics, and scenario based planning tools that improve emergency preparedness and response. For disaster management, digital twins can model healthcare system impacts in different scenarios, allowing planners to pinpoint weaknesses and formulate contingency plans. For example, a city's healthcare network digital twin can simulate an earthquake to understand how many hospitals might suffer structural damage, be deprived of power or lack resources. There they can deploy resources more strategically, set up temporary medical facilities, and facilitate the transfer of care where needed during the crisis.

In pandemics, digital twins are crucial to manage healthcare resources and control spread of infectious diseases. Digital twins rely on data from hospitals, public health agencies and community health centers to generate a real-time picture of availability of resources hospital beds and ventilators and medical supplies. That data lets authorities coordinate how they allocate resources, avoid shortages, and target care for the high-risk populations. Throughout the COVID-19 pandemic digital twins have also been used to create models of hospital capacity, infection hotspots or predict and optimize plans for rollout of vaccination (Rudin, 2019).

Emergency response organizations rely on this digital twin technology to run mass casualty simulations and optimize responses. For example, a digital twin of a disaster-affected region is capable of pulling data from drones, satellite images, and on-ground sensors to provide real-time situational awareness. It enables emergency responders to find the injured, evaluate damage and deploy medical teams more efficiently. Outside disaster response, digital twins can also enable health care systems to better learn from the results of past emergencies, helping them build resilience over the longer term. Recognizing patterns and recommending solutions: Event modeling is utilized to uncover patterns from past events, discuss success of responses and recommend how to improve. This process comes in cycle, so healthcare systems can be better prepared for contingent action saving lives in future and better recovering time. Smart cities encourage disaster preparedness at the community level with digital twins that incorporate input from residents on emergency planning. For instance, a city's digital twin can model the impact of a flood so that residents can understand what their own neighborhoods would look like and where to find escape routes and emergency shelters. Herd engagement paves way for more resilient communities and a drape of preparedness that sews self-sufficiency in a disaster situation.

5. URBAN AND HEALTHCARE DIGITAL TWINS IN DATA SYNCHRONIZATION AND RESOURCE OPTIMIZATION: BRIDGING CITY-WIDE AND FACILITY-LEVEL SYSTEMS

A new vision for Urban and Healthcare Digital Twins: Integration as a game-changer: The Integration of urban and healthcare digital twins is a visionary curtain-raiser on innovations at the intersection of technology, data, and innovation addressing interrelations between the needs of cities and health systems. But as the urbanization and population density continues to rise, the ability to monitor and manage not only entire city systems including transportation and waste management systems, and healthcare infrastructure has only become more critical. With the integration of heart, urban and healthcare digital twins, stakeholders can optimize the use of their resources, promoting improved quality of life for the citizens.

This part elaborates how such integrations link city-wide and facility-level systems, facilitate the synchronization of data between them, and optimize resource utilization (Wu et al., 2023).

All the while, health and urban systems are inextricably connected, where the health of a population influences and is influenced by the greater mechanisms of the urban system. Digital twins dock with both large-scale urban infrastructural systems and specific healthcare establishments to turn a broad view of urban healthcare. This integration helps planners and administrators to address cross-cutting public health and urban management challenges (e.g., disease outbreaks, environmental hazards, and disaster response). A digital twin for a city could measure things like air quality, traffic flow, and housing density; a healthcare facility digital twin could consider patient flow, equipment availability, and treatment outcomes. By integrating these systems, authorities can correlate environmental variables with health trends, taking preventative action even before a disease hits, for example. An increase in respiratory conditions detected in health care records, for instance, might prompt urban planners to investigate air pollution sources and implement mitigation strategies such as vehicle emissions regulations or adding more green space.

Emergency response is a particular area where the synergies between the city-wide and healthcare digital twins are invaluable. In the event of natural disasters, like floods or earthquakes, integrated digital twin systems can help model (simulate) the effect of disasters on transportation networks, utilities and healthcare facilities. "With cities recovering, it is imperative to manage resources proactively, ensuring ambulances are navigating disrupted roadways efficiently, patients are routed to the least congested facilities and temporary medical infusion centers are strategically established," wrote a New York City Health and Hospitals system subcontractor whose technology was adopted by the agency. By integrating this approach, response times are minimized, casualties are reduced, and resources are distributed equitably.

Urban digital twins can help healthcare facilities anticipate population growth and demographic changes. An urban twin, for example, that monitors housing developments and migration patterns can project rising demand for healthcare services in specific areas. This information enables hospitals and clinics to size their infrastructure and services accordingly, thereby adequately preparing for new residents. Urban and healthcare digital twins need to be integrated with the help of reliable data synchronization that will ensure real-time population of both urban strings of the two systems and health data strings. Data convergence from different sources like IoT devices, electronic health records (EHRs), environmental sensors allows a collaborative framework for informed decision-making and effective resource allocation (Saadat et al., 2020).

Predictive models can be created across both urban and healthcare worlds due to data synchronization. For example, in a heatwave, a tightly coupled digital twin will know exactly how real-time temperature data interacts with predicted population densities and historical health trends to forecast spikes in hospital admissions for heat-related illnesses. They can then deploy more people, warehouse essential medical supplies, and open cooling centers with the cooperation of city agencies to reduce harm to the most vulnerable. The other key advantage is resource optimization through urban and healthcare digital twin integration. Cities and health-care systems often struggle with resource scarcity, be they hospital beds and medical equipment or electricity or clean water. A common digital twin can also pinpoint inefficiencies and offer recommendations for optimal resource allocation.

In a pandemic, a synchronized digital twin network could track the availability of ICU beds, ventilators, and vaccines throughout a city. Using patient-progression trends and distribution patterns, this system can recommend that you reallocate resources as people, equipment, etc. from the low-demand zone into one that has high-demand ensuring equitable access to care. Likewise, urban digital twins can provide real-time optimization of transportation routes for medical needs so that these routes are always in their most optimal state, minimizing delivery times, costs, and saving lives. The other space where resource optimization excels through integration is energy management. Energy consumption patterns in healthcare facilities can be tracked from urban digital twins to find opportunities for conservation and sustainabiility. For example, hospitals may match their energy consumption with a more extensive city-wide renewable energy generation schedule, minimizing the dependence on non-renewable sources and lowering the carbon footprint (Kitchin, 2023).

The ability to integrate urban and healthcare digital twins enables collaborative planning to sustain the long term. Integrating data on the urban environment, public health, and public health systems enables stakeholders to create adaptable healthcare systems best suited for emerging challenges. Integrating climate models as well as healthcare data, for instance, will inform decisions on where to build new hospitals in an area less likely to flood or suffer from extreme events, allowing care continuity under adverse conditions.

6. EMERGING TRENDS AND INNOVATIONS

They are tailored to the titans of industry analyzing multi-gigabyte data sets that scan cutting edge, this means advancements in major directions, which together form a powerful driving force to create a better and more interconnected path for digital twin technology. Advances in the Internet of Things (IoT), artificial intelligence (AI), blockchain, wearables, and sensors are transforming the link between digital twins for urban planning and healthcare contexts. This information is then processed by AI, which recognizes patterns, produces insights, and improves operations. In urban planning, Internet of Things (IoT)-enabled sensors embedded in infrastructure (roads, buildings, and public utilities) for collecting data about traffic flow, energy consumption, and environmental conditions. Such streams of data are pumped into urban digital twins powered by AI algorithms that enable scenario simulation, outcome prediction, and intervention recommendation. For example, during peak traffic periods, an urban digital manager can detect congestion and adjust traffic signals in real time to relieve bottlenecks. The same applies in the energy segment where IoT sensors monitor electricity consumption at the neighborhood level, generating AI-managed twins for optimizing energy distribution and reducing wastage (Shahid, 2021).

6.1 IoT and AI in Digital Twin Ecosystems

Within the healthcare industry, the potential of IoT and AI combined revolutionizes patient care and hospital management solutions. Healthcare digital twins process data from devices such as IoT-enabled thermometers, heart rate monitors and glucose sensors, which continually assess patient status. AI algorithms identify anomalies, predict disease progression, and recommend personalized treatment plans, enabling healthcare providers to offer proactive care. For illustration, an AI-enabled digital twin of a hospital can track patient traffic, predict surges in demand, and efficiently allocate staff and resources to optimize workflow.

The fusion of IoT and AI also goes beyond the domain of individual systems, leading to the development of connected ecosystems. Seamless data sharing between smart cities and healthcare solutions equipped with IoT devices leads to integrated solutions for urban and healthcare challenges.

6.2 Role of Blockchain for Data Security and Privacy

Blockchain guarantees the integrity of this data and its accessibility only to authorized entities. Blockchain can ensure that data can be shared between healthcare providers while maintaining privacy. For instance, a patient's digital twin can securely exchange health data with specialists and insurers, easing care coordination and claims processing (Monteiro et al., 2021). Blockchain improves the traceability of AI-driven decisions in digital twins. Recording AI algorithms and their outputs on a blockchain allows stakeholders to audit and verify the results of the decisions made by the algorithms, ensuring that they are fair and transparent. This according to them is especially important, in healthcare, where AI recommendations must be explainable and ethical.

Despite the advantages of the integration of blockchain technology with digital twin systems, including distributed ledger security and immutability, scalability issues and a high level of energy consumption, hamper this. On the other hand, emerging blockchain technology solutions with the agreed migration to energy-efficient consensus mechanisms e.g., proof-of-stake have already been implemented to mitigate the aforementioned concerns, allowing blockchain to become an appropriate solution for secure and privacy-preserving digital twin ecosystems.

6.3 Use of Wearable Technologies and Sensors in Healthcare Twins

Wearable technologies and sensors are paving the way for new advancements in the healthcare domain by supplying continuous, real-time data to health care digital twins. From fitness and wellness trackers to advanced medical devices implanted in the body, these smart health devices allow for personalized monitoring and predictive care that redefines healthcare delivery. Wearable devices such as smartwatches, ECG monitors, glucose sensors, etc. are monitored for vital signs, activity levels, and physiological properties (Qureshi et al., 2023). This data is sent to healthcare digital twins, which track trends and offer insights on a patient's health. For instance, a wearable ECG monitor can pick up lower-than-normal heart rhythms and flame the digitial twin, which determines whether the condition is critical or not and informs health care practitioners, if so. This not only limits patients being admitted to the hospital but also positively affects patient outcomes.

Wearable devices with embedded sensors are also critical in the management of chronic diseases. For example, diabetic patients may be able to use continuous glucose monitors (CGMs) which measure blood sugar levels in real-time. The input being fed to these sensors is a digital twin of the patient into which the algorithms of artificial intelligence (AI) map interdependencies based on the data collected by the sensors to predict rises and falls in blood glucose levels and suggest changes to diet or new medications in advance. That level of precision minimizes complications while improving the patient's quality of life. Wearable Technologies and Population Health Management. Healthcare digital twins use aggregated anonymized data from wearables to spot public health trends and help inform policy decisions. Like during a flu outbreak, for instance, wearible sensors that track body temperature and respiratory rates are able to give you early warning of the spread of a disease and timely interventions e.g: for vaccinations and observable resources.

Wearable technologies also apply to the hospital setting, where personnel employ smart badges and other devices to monitor patient safety and workflow efficiency. For example, smart badges with location sensors can help track healthcare workers' movements, allowing hospitals to ensure that critical areas, such as operating rooms and ICUs, have adequate staff on hand. Likewise, wearable sensors placed on the hospital equipment eg, ventilators, infusion pumps, etc. are capable of tracking their availability and status in real time and thus ensure the optimal utilization of these resources. Wearable technologies and sensors, while promising, struggled with data accuracy, battery life and user adoption. It is essential for healthcare digital twins that devices generate trustworthy data. Technologies such as sensor advancements and AI-based error correction are working to solve these problems and advance the reliability and usability of wearables (Leung et al., 2021).

7. CHALLENGES AND LIMITATIONS

From enhancing urban planning processes to revolutionising healthcare delivery, the game-changing potential of digital twin technology is apparent. These sensors can suffer from inaccuracies, failures, and data losses, generating a poor quality digital representation. In cases, such as urban planning, faulty statistical information due to unreliable sensors on roads can also make it difficult to predict congestion, ultimately undermining the efficacy of the twin. In a similar vein, erroneous data from faulty medical devices in the healthcare ecosystem can erode trust in patient data (Faaique, 2024).

Interoperability is another big problem. Digital twins will need to ingest data from disparate systems from legacy infrastructures and IoT networks to cloud platforms. The absence of standardised data exchange protocols has resulted in compatibility issues, leading to delays in implementation. For instance, linking a city's current water management system to a digital twin might demand expensive and lengthy upgrades to make sure they are compatible. It also takes advanced technical expertise to create and sustain digital twins. With the complex nature of digital twins integrating IoT, AI along with industry-specific expertise there is a demand for skills that are in short supply. Such scarcity of talent slows down the pace of adoption and implementation, especially in the developing parts of the world. Scalability is another issue, particularly for large-scale projects like smart cities. The larger the digital twin to monitor more complex processes, the greater the computational power and storage necessary to analyze the data. Such high-performance computing infrastructure is costly and power-hungry, leading to growing worries about sustainability and long-term viability.

7.1 Ethical Concerns: Data Privacy and Ownership

The urgent barriers to adoption of digital twin technology stem particularly from ethical implications regarding data privacy and ownership. Digital twins rely on copious amounts of data from people, systems, and environments, and people are rightly concerned with how that data is gathered, stored, and used. In healthcare, the backbone of digital twins is patient data. But privacy is a big deal because medical records are very sensitive information. Unauthorized access or data breaches can have serious consequences, such as identification theft and misuse of personal information (Lal et al., 2024). In addition, if the data used to train the AI algorithms are incomplete or biased, the decision-making processes in health care twins can also become biased.

Data ownership is another hot-button issue and this data has been generated as urban settings are constantly being more instrumented through passive data flow, and public infrastructure and private citizens contribute to it but there is ambiguity towards ownership and utilization of such data. For instance, smart city projects often gather information from surveillance cameras, public transport systems and social media networks. When this data is used without citizens' consent, it violates citizens' right to privacy and is a stealthy form of autonomy aversion. It is also critical to have transparency of how data is processed and used. It will have ensure that the digital twin systems are explainable and accountable. Nonetheless, the complexity of AI-driven decision-making often makes it difficult to provide clear explanations as to how such conclusions are derived. Such lack of transparency breeds public mistrust and calls into question ethical governance.

The regulatory frameworks that govern digital twin applications are still nascent. The lack of a set of unified global data protection laws can create challenges for multinational projects, as companies may face both complicated compliance requirements including differing regulations around data owners and greater risk of being embroiled in legal disputes. Global and binding standards on data privacy, ownership and ethical use must be laid down specifically to address the above concerns (Arora et al., 2024).

7.3 Financial Constraints and Scalability Issues

The financial throttlehold is significant to deploying digital twin technology, especially for resource strapped regions and organizations. The up-front costs required to develop digital twins as hardware, software, understanding can often be difficult to justify. In the subject of urban management, capital-intensive investments in infrastructure like the internet of things is needed for the smart city projects, as well as the data analytics systems, high performance computing (HPC) systems, on-premises data centers, and cloud-based infrastructure. For example, outfitting a city with the sensors and networks to build a digital twin to optimize traffic can cost millions of dollars. These costs often exceed even the budgets of the smaller municipalities or developing nations.

Scalability adds to the financial burden. As digital twins expand in scale and complexity, the expense of building and sustaining these systems escalates. A city-wide digital twin that grows to embrace new infrastructure or to keep pace with population growth, for example, will need more sensors, increased computing power when needed and more know-how. Likewise, in the case of a digital twin in health care that must keep with newly available medical technologies or treatments, it would have to be updated continuously and also has associated costs associated with the continual updates. Integration of digital twins with the healthcare infrastructure, however, can be equally challenging in terms of cost. Creating a digital twin for a hospital needs state-of-the-art medical devices, cloud storages, AI-based analytics, etc., which come with a lot of investment. Smaller healthcare providers, especially those in rural areas, may not be able to justify these costs even if the long-term benefits are apparent.

Funding sources for digital twin work are often a combination of publicly and privately sourced. At the same time, investment is risky and the time until return on that investment is long, making it hard to convince stakeholders to invest in digital twin technology. Especially for experimental applications, investors will be reluctant to invest without clear proof of ROI. To address these issues, new funding models and partnership arrangements are required to manage costs. PPPs are a key mechanism for pooling resources and spreading risks. Also, advances in introductory computing and edge computing aid price reduction for infrastructure, further democratizing digital twins to more stakeholders.

8. POLICY AND GOVERNANCE IN STANDARDIZING DIGITAL TWIN FRAMEWORKS: LEGAL AND POLICY CONSIDERATIONS FOR DATA SHARING IN HEALTHCARE

As various industry players accelerate the adoption of digital twin technology, there is a growing need for strong policy and governance frameworks to guarantee its ethical, effective, and sustainable use in urban planning and healthcare. Having standardized frameworks, tackling legal implications and enabling public-private collaboration are fundamental pillars which need to be considered to leverage innovative digital implementations at scale while safeguarding public trust and accountability. The challenges in governance are focused on the absence of a common framework to apply the digital twins across various industries and geographical regions. Digital twins work with a heterogeneous ecosystem of sensors, IoT devices, AI algorithms, and cloud platforms usually from multiple vendors. The existing standards are not uniform, which makes it hard to have integrated Oracles that can be disconnected or are pseudo-disconnected.

Common protocols, data formats and interoperability guidelines established through standardization can help resolve these very issues. For example, there are existing frameworks like the ISO 23247 series for digital twin manufacturing systems which provide a model that could be adapted for use in urban planning and healthcare contexts (Kaushik et al., 2024). Integrating existing systems is possible by implementing standardized frameworks so that digital twin solutions may be future-ready, and can be scaled. The most important aspect of digital twins is reliability and being secured, which standards caters to. Benchmark standards for data quality that are rigorous, along with real-time updates and cybersecurity, can guard against inaccuracies and vulnerabilities that erode trust. For instance, in urban planning, it can optimize the utilization of traffic and energy consumption data across municipal departments (e.g., urban planning departments, municipal agencies), thus developing a unified, integrated model for smart cities. In healthcare, shared frameworks can drive interoperability among hospitals, research institutes, and technology suppliers, promoting innovation and efficiency.

Data sharing is at the core of what digital twins can do in practice in health care, where patient data is used to generate predictive models and virtual simulations. Legal Considerations of Data Collection, Storage, and Sharing However, the legal implication of data collection, storage and sharing is complex and needs careful consideration. Healthcare data is extremely sensitive and regulated data, governed by strict laws such as Health Insurance Portability and Accountability Act (in the USA) and General Data Protection Regulation (in EU). With laws requiring strict safeguards to protect patient privacy and use data ethically and transparently.

A major challenge is the balancing act between the need for data sharing to drive forward the capabilities of digital twins, and the need to protect individual privacy. For example, developing a digital twin for disease tracking might require combining data from several hospitals, that raises issues with consent, data ownership, and cross-border compliance. Therefore, legal frameworks should tackle these issues by clarifying procedures surrounding data anonymization, encryption, and secure sharing. Using blockchain smart contracts might provide the solution by creating transparent and immutable agreements for data usage. Addressing this, data governance policies must enable patients to also have a greater say on the use of their data, by allowing opt in or out of specific applications.

Legal frameworks must also focus on transparency and accountability, to establish trust. This will hold the platforms accountable and ensure that addressing systemic issues is a part of the business model, because just like the social media platform identified to have a global use of misinformation in its platform, it needs a trust index that should be handled by regulatory bodies to enforce what should be a moratorium or a tangible danger for mass consumption of data and information (Raghav et al., 2024).

The Importance of PPPs to Scale Digital Twin Technology in Urban And HealthCare Applications These collaborations allow for the sharing of resources, data, and capabilities, leading to faster digital twin development and implementation processes. However, successful PPPs need well-designed policies to harmonize the interests of public institutions, private companies, and citizens.

The recommendations worth policy attention is defining clear roles and responsibilities for each stakeholder. Combining private and public efforts seems to be the right approach, in that public institutions can ensure that relevant regulatory oversight is provided and that the initiatives indeed address the public's needs while, by the same token, private companies would bring technical expertise and innovation. In smart city projects, for example, municipal governments can partner with technology companies to create digital twins for managing traffic flows, waste disposal, and energy use. This is where transparent governance structures come into play to avoid conflicts of interest and ensure accountability. Partnership agreements should detail terms for the sharing of open data and equitable revenue sharing, as well as mechanisms for dispute resolution. The crucial policy recommendations is to focus on inclusivity and accessibility.

9. CONCLUSION AND FUTURE SCOPE

Digital twin technology has the potential to transform urban planning and healthcare resource management. Its ability to assimilate real-time data, model complex scenarios and optimize decision-making presents unique opportunities to confront the challenges of contemporary urbanization and healthcare delivery. When combined with new trends and implementation challenges, digital twins will empower cities to become resilient, health-centric environments.

The realization of uniformity across sectors in their implementation of digital twins is dependent on the governance and policy frameworks that these sectors develop. Making data interoperable enough to allow public health and urban planning to sync up seamlessly needs to be a focus for policymakers. Data sharing and ethical considerations should be taken into account by legal aspects. Moreover, promoting collaboration among governments, academia, and industry can facilitate faster innovation and implementation. From the experts, with their data up to October 2023: The technology for digital twin is bright. The next wave of development will likely be driven by innovations in neuromorphic computing, 5G connectivity, and advanced simulation techniques. Cross-sector applications such as the one between digital twins for environmental monitoring and healthcare amplify their effects. By harnessing these approaches, urban areas can create a healthy equilibrium between urban development and access to health services, ensuring a sustainable and equitable tomorrow.

REFERENCES

Arora, M. K., Lal, S., Singh, B., & Olyaee, M. (2024). Through an Energy Lens: Examining SDGs From a Policy Perspective. In Riswandi, B., Singh, B., Kaunert, C., & Vig, K. (Eds.), *AI Applications for Clean Energy and Sustainability* (pp. 320–343). IGI Global., DOI: 10.4018/979-8-3693-6567-0.ch016

Bao, Y., Tang, Z., Li, H., & Zhang, Y. (2019). Computer vision and deep learning–based data anomaly detection method for structural health monitoring. *Structural Health Monitoring*, *18*(2), 401–421. DOI: 10.1177/1475921718757405

. Behura, A., Sahu, S., & Kabat, M. R. (2021). Advancement of Machine Learning and Cloud Computing in the Field of Smart Health Care. *Machine Learning Approach for Cloud Data Analytics in IoT*, 273-306.

Chen, C. P., & Zhang, C. Y. (2024). Data-intensive applications, challenges, techniques and technologies: A survey on Big Data. *Information Sciences*, *275*, 314–347.

Faaique, M. (2024). Overview of Big Data Analytics in Modern Astronomy. *International Journal of Mathematics, Statistics, and Computer Science*, *2*, 96–113. DOI: 10.59543/ijmscs.v2i.8561

Hilbert, M. (2025). Big data for development: A review of promises and challenges. *Development Policy Review*, *34*(1), 135–174. DOI: 10.1111/dpr.12142

. Jain, L. (2023). Artificial Intelligence and Machine Learning for Healthcare.

Kashyap, H., Ahmed, H. A., Hoque, N., Roy, S., & Bhattacharyya, D. K. (2023). Big data analytics in bioinformatics: Architectures, techniques, tools and issues. *Network Modeling and Analysis in Health Informatics and Bioinformatics*, *5*, 1–28.

Kaushik, T. K., Singh, A., Raghav, A., & Singh, B. (2024). Potential of Artificial Intelligence in the Agricultural Industry: A Comprehensive Review. AI Applications for Clean Energy and Sustainability, 344-365.

Keikhosrokiani, P. (Ed.). (2022). *Big data analytics for healthcare: datasets, techniques, life cycles, management, and applications*. Academic Press.

Kitchin, R. (2023). Big data and human geography: Opportunities, challenges and risks. *Dialogues in Human Geography*, *3*(3), 262–267. DOI: 10.1177/2043820613513388

Lal, S., Arora, M. K., Riswandi, B. A., Singh, N., & Singh, B. (2024). Melding Artificial Intelligence and Remote Sensing Data for Real-Time Monitoring of Marine Biodiversity. In Riswandi, B., Singh, B., Kaunert, C., & Vig, K. (Eds.), *AI Applications for Clean Energy and Sustainability* (pp. 299–319). IGI Global., DOI: 10.4018/979-8-3693-6567-0.ch015

Leung, P. H., Chui, K. T., Lo, K., & de Pablos, P. O. (2021). A support vector machine–based voice disorders detection using human voice signal. In *Artificial Intelligence and Big Data Analytics for Smart Healthcare* (pp. 197–208). Academic Press. DOI: 10.1016/B978-0-12-822060-3.00014-0

Manyika, J., Chui, M., Brown, B., Bughin, J., Dobbs, R., Roxburgh, C., & Hung Byers, A. (2021). Big data: The next frontier for innovation, competition, and productivity.

Marjani, M., Nasaruddin, F., Gani, A., Karim, A., Hashem, I. A. T., Siddiqa, A., & Yaqoob, I. (2017). Big IoT data analytics: architecture, opportunities, and open research challenges. *ieee access, 5*, 5247-5261.

Mayer-Schönberger, V., & Cukier, K. (2013). *Big data: A revolution that will transform how we live, work, and think*. Houghton Mifflin Harcourt.

Monteiro, A. C. B., França, R. P., Arthur, R., & Iano, Y. (2021). An overview of medical Internet of Things, artificial intelligence, and cloud computing employed in health care from a modern panorama. *The Fusion of Internet of Things, Artificial Intelligence, and Cloud Computing in Health Care*, 3-23.

Olshannikova, E., Ometov, A., Koucheryavy, Y., & Olsson, T. (2025). Visualizing Big Data with augmented and virtual reality: Challenges and research agenda. *Journal of Big Data*, *2*(1), 1–27.

Padmaja, M., Shitharth, S., Prasuna, K., Chaturvedi, A., Kshirsagar, P. R., & Vani, A. (2022). Grow of artificial intelligence to challenge security in IoT application. *Wireless Personal Communications*, *127*(3), 1829–1845. DOI: 10.1007/s11277-021-08725-4

Qureshi, R., Irfan, M., Ali, H., Khan, A., Nittala, A. S., Ali, S., & Alam, T. (2023). Artificial Intelligence and Biosensors in Healthcare and its Clinical Relevance: A Review. *IEEE Access : Practical Innovations, Open Solutions*, *11*, 61600–61620. DOI: 10.1109/ACCESS.2023.3285596

Raghav, A., Singh, B., & Jermsittiparsert, K. (2024). Role of Artificial Intelligence and Machine Learning in Clean and Blue Energy for Enhancing Efficiency and Sustainability. In Riswandi, B., Singh, B., Kaunert, C., & Vig, K. (Eds.), *AI Applications for Clean Energy and Sustainability* (pp. 366–386). IGI Global., DOI: 10.4018/979-8-3693-6567-0.ch018

Reddy, B. M. (2023). Amalgamation of Internet of Things and Machine Learning for Smart Healthcare Applications–A Review. *Int. J Comp. Eng. Sci. Res, 5*, 08-36.

Rudin, C. (2019). Stop explaining black box machine learning models for high stakes decisions and use interpretable models instead. *Nature Machine Intelligence*, *1*(5), 206–215. DOI: 10.1038/s42256-019-0048-x PMID: 35603010

Saadat, M. N., & Shuaib, M. (2020). Advancements in deep learning theory and applications: Perspective in 2020 and beyond. *Advances and Applications in Deep Learning, 3*.

Shah, F., Li, J., Shah, Y., & Shah, F. (2017, November). Broad big data domain via medical big data. In *2017 4th International Conference on Systems and Informatics (ICSAI)* (pp. 732-737). IEEE.

Shahid, Z. (2021). Distributed Machine Learning for Anomalous Human Activity Recognition using IoT Systems.

Singh, B. (2024). Evolutionary Global Neuroscience for Cognition and Brain Health: Strengthening Innovation in Brain Science. In *Biomedical Research Developments for Improved Healthcare* (pp. 246-272). IGI Global.

Thapa, C., & Camtepe, S. (2021). Precision health data: Requirements, challenges and existing techniques for data security and privacy. *Computers in Biology and Medicine*, *129*, 104130. DOI: 10.1016/j.compbiomed.2020.104130 PMID: 33271399

Wu, X., Zhu, X., Wu, G. Q., & Ding, W. (2023). Data mining with big data. *IEEE Transactions on Knowledge and Data Engineering*, *26*(1), 97–107.

Zhou, S., Zhang, R., Chen, D., & Zhu, X. (2021). A novel framework for bringing smart big data to proactive decision making in healthcare. *Health Informatics Journal*, *27*(2), 14604582211024698. DOI: 10.1177/14604582211024698 PMID: 34159834

ADDITIONAL READING

Ariffin, N. A., Yunus, A. M., & Kadir, I. K. (2021). The role of big data in the healthcare industry. *Journal of Islamic*, *6*(36), 235–245.

Chapter 9
Optimizing Energy Usage and Reducing Waste Digital Twin Applications in Industrial IoT

Sanjeev Kumar
https://orcid.org/0000-0002-9553-0068
Swami Keshvanand Institute of Technology, Management and Gramothan, Jaipur, India

Geeta Tiwari
Poornima College of Engineering, Jaipur, India

Neeraj Tiwari
School of Engineering and technology, Jaipur National University, Jaipur, India

Krishna Kumar
https://orcid.org/0000-0002-7196-0792
Lund University, Sweden

ABSTRACT

Industrial sector, by boosting energy efficiency and reducing waste through the use of digital twin (DT) technology in the integration of industrial IoT (IIoT). DT generates realistic simulations for predictive analytics and decision-making with the help of real-time simulations of physical objects. In this chapter, the authors focus on the DT application for the optimum utilization of energy and the resource efficiency by utilizing the IoT sensors, the AI, and big data analytics. Industries can find inefficiencies, use predictive maintenance and environmental practices by simulating operational scenarios. The chapter also outlines important challenges including that of data integration, cybersecurity, and cost and provides some recommendations which may be used to successfully implement such technology. An exploration into future trends such as: 5G; Edge; Ai-driven models: Drawing on this work, the role of DT in creating sharper, greener and more resilient industrial ecosystems rightfully stand in the limelight.

DOI: 10.4018/979-8-3373-2028-1.ch009

1. INTRODUCTION

With the rapid pace of change leather industry, efficiency matters. Firms are always looking for ways to take their energy utilization and waste production to the bare minimum degree without affecting productivity. This is where Digital Twins – virtual replicas of physical assets – are starting to throw their weight around. Leveraging Digital Twin along with IIoT can help the industries operate smarter, maintain key equipment proactively and carry out resource-efficient processes.

Think of a manufacturing factory, wherein the factory still uses outdated machine that wastes a lot of energy. In the past, you would need to manually inspect the plant and take equipment offline to identify equipment inefficiencies. Well here meanwhile comes the Digital Twins that enable industries to replicate real-time in-operation, examine energy consumption habits, and make data-driven decisions. As an illustration, a steel plant deploying a Digital Twin saved 15% in energy costs by optimizing the temperature of its furnaces and production cycles.

However, the Digital Twins can achieve much more not only energy optimisation but also, helping in reducing material waste by predicting failures in advance as well as improved supply chain efficiency. As an example, Digital Twin allow a food processing plant to monitor spoilage trends and modify refrigeration settings, dramatically reducing waste.

1.1. Overview of Industrial IoT and Digital Twin Technology

Imagine a factory where every machine "speaks" to its digital twin, predicting downtime before it happens, optimizing energy consumption on-the-fly. That is the strength of Industrial IoT (IIoT) and Digital Twin technology—a power couple of transformations to drive industrial efficiency.

Basically, IIoT links physical assets (machines and sensors) to the internet to make data-driven decisions. These intelligent factories leverage real-time analytics, AI-powered insights, and automated processes to deliver production while minimizing downtime and energy usage. A manufacturing plant, for example, that utilizes an IIoT platform, can identify an inefficient motor before it overheats, which can prevent expensive failures and energy waste.

In contrast, a Digital Twin is a virtual counterpart of a physical system that is continuously updated with real-time data. It can be imagination to a, "breathing model" that replicates the expression, reactions, and condition of a resource. This will give you the ability to take your business through multiple simulations for optimization without disturbing any processes. Take automotive, for example — Digital Twins are leveraged by automakers to design cost-effective engines in terms of fuel-efficiency by simulating a prototype before actually building it; thus bringing savings in time and money.

Figure 1. Digital Twin Framework for Optimizing Energy Usage and Reducing Waste in Industrial IoT

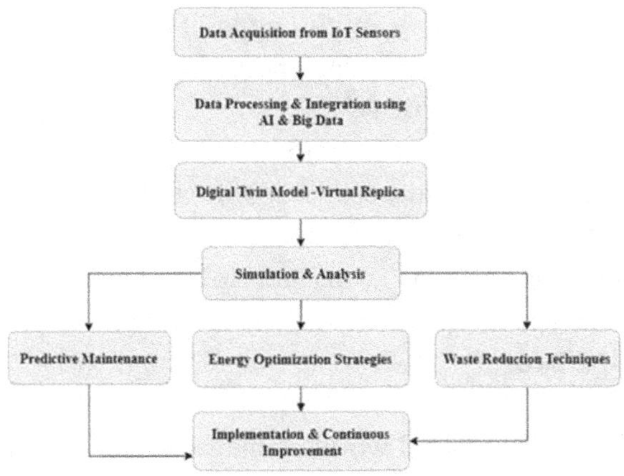

As shown in the figure 1, a structured framework is available to effectively utilize Digital Twin technology in Industrial IoT to reduce energy consumption along with waste minimization. The process starts with the acquisition of data using IoT technology, continues through AI-based data processing and Digital Twin modelling. Key optimizations in the Simulation & Analysis phase Let us have a look into predictive maintenance, Energy Efficiency Strategies and Waste Reduction Techniques. Such optimizations result in an iterative process of continuous improvement while ensuring industrial sustainability. Such a strategy improves operational efficiency, reduces downtime and aids in the shift to smart manufacturing for sustainable industry.

Bundled together, IIoT and Digital Twins give the gift of a more intelligent and sustainable industrial ecosystem. These technologies enable industries—from steel plants minimizing carbon emissions now and then titanium sponge production to optimizing supply chains in logistics-to save on costs and energy while minimizing waste over the long run, always maximizing efficiency. What Follow After Advanced Technology with IIoT And Digital Twins Digital Twins And IIoT - Embracing the Future of Smart Manufacturing As industries continue to adapt to digital transformation, the convergence of IIoT and Digital Twins are going to shape the future of smart manufacturing.

1.2. Optimizing Energy Usage and Reducing Waste: Digital Twin Applications in Industrial IoT

Efficiency is the need of the hour in the present industrial landscape. There is ever-growing pressure on industries to reduce energy consumption and cut wastage while continuing with the same or even higher productivity levels (Billey & Wuest, 2023). Enter Digital Twins, driven by Industrial IoT (IIoT). A Digital Twin works by mapping physical assets into a virtual environment allowing businesses to monitor, analyze and optimize the energy usage and emissions in the real-time.

Imagine a smart factory in which all machines, sensors, and production lines have their digital twins. The Digital Twin can even identify the anomaly if a motor begins to draw more excessive power than expected, predict its failure, and propose corrective actions to prevent energy consumption loss. Likewise, in supply chain management, companies can play around with various logistics scenarios with an aim to reduce fuel and carbon initiatives.

Consider for example a giant steel factory. With Digital Twin technology, this plant can monitor loss of heat in furnaces while dynamically adjusting energy inputs in case of unnecessary heat loss. It is also decreasing pollution (Butean et al., 2024).

AI-driven insights can thereby usher industries into sustainable operations, where resources are optimally utilized, downtime is minimized, and waste is significantly reduced. Industrial efficiency, now reduced to mere numbers, must be revived through the holistic approach driven by smart data-driven decision-making, made possible using Digital Twins and IIoT.

1.3. Objectives of the Chapter

Efficiency is everything in this fast-paced world of industrialization. This chapter will cover how Industrial IoT-powered Digital Twins enables a whole new approach to energy management and waste reduction. With a digital twin comprising virtual replication of the real assets, industries can track real-time energy usage alongside inefficiencies predictions and take corrective action before losses ensue. For example, by using Digital Twins, the smart factory can foresee when any machine would fail and stop the operations, hence mitigating expensive downtimes. We will also talk about state of practical concerns, applications and challenges. It aims to give the industries a clear framework to move forward with Digital Twin technology to achieve sustainability and operational efficiency.

2. FUNDAMENTALS OF DIGITAL TWIN TECHNOLOGY IN IIOT

Imagine a factory with machines that can understand when they are going to fail, and thus plan for downtimes, and cut cost. The function of Digital Twins in IIoT (Industrial Internet of Things) Digital Twins are a real-time virtual image of a physical system (Ardebili et al., 2021). It allows sectors to analyze scenarios for operations, maximize energy management and reduce wastage.

In a smart manufacturing plant, for instance, sensors located across production lines, after feeding the data into Digital Twins, will help assess maintenance and make efficient use of resources. This proactive approach minimizes wastage, maximizes uptime, and prolongs the lifespan of your equipment, thereby making the industries smarter, greener, and economical.

2.1. Concept and Evolution of Digital Twins

Imagine a virtual copy of a factory floor, a wind turbine, or an entire supply chain that does more than simply replicate its real-world counterpart, but learns, predicts and optimizes its performance on the fly. The power of a Digital Twin, that is. Digital Twins started life as a NASA project to simulate systems in space and has quickly evolved from relatively simple simulation models to AI processing powerful enough to be called intelligent systems, integrated with IOT, big data, and machine learning (Teng et al., 2021).

In industrial processes, Digital Twins allow manufacturers to simulate energy-saving techniques before they are applied in real life. For example, smart grid applications can employ Digital Twins to study power consumption trends and adaptively adjust power flow to [eliminate] waste and [maximize] efficiency. Real world companies such as Siemens and General Electric made great use of Digital Twins to not only be able to forecast issues in a piece of equipment and correct it before it fails as well as optimize processes at such a granular level, that drastic cost reductions in operations have occurred. With industries heading closer to sustainability, the need for reduction of wastage and extract the maximum energy efficiency is done with the help of Digital Twins which acts as a new technology-enabled solution to a growing mass of these modern industries.

2.2. Key Components and Architecture of Digital Twins

Digital Twin technology is built on top of a strong architecture connecting the opportunities from the physical world to those the digital world has to offer by helping industries minimize their energy consumption and waste. The most important three components associated with Digital Twin are the actual physical asset and its virtual counterpart, and the data-driven intelligence layer.

Imagine a smart factory with a digital twin of every machine that is constantly tracking its performance. AI-based analytics process real-time data collected through IoT sensors, predicting energy inefficiencies or possibilities of a failure. Data storage and remote access are made seamless via the cloud infrastructure, and edge computing enhances real-time decision-making.

Take the case of a manufacturing facility — A Digital Twin of a cooling system can identify anomalies, recommend ideal temperature levels, and avoid unnecessary power consumption. By predicting potential issues before they occur, this leads to resource conservation and longer asset life, which drives a sustainable industrial ecosystem. Digital Twins offer a new, more data-driven route for industries to achieve efficiency and sustainability.

2.3. Role of IoT, AI, and Big Data in Digital Twin Implementation

Visualize a factory where machinery never fails, energy is consumed in a real-time optimized manner, and waste is reduced even before it is generated. This is the essence of getting a Digital Twins rendered possible with the power of IoT, AI, and Big Data.

The IoT is the nervous system in which sensors embedded in physical assets to capture real-time data like temperature, vibration, energy usage, etc. The data is then fed into the AI, the brain, predicting failures even before they occur, and recommending suggestions to improve operating efficiency. While in between, Big Data provides a seamless storage process for huge volumes of data to be transformed into useful insights.

Suppose a Digital Twin is being used for a Wind Farm. Internet of Things (IoT) sensors monitor wind speed, turbine vibrations, and their energy output. AI forecasts requirement for services, and Big Data leverages performance management at various sites.

3. ENERGY OPTIMIZATION THROUGH DIGITAL TWIN APPLICATIONS

Efficiency is an essential consideration as the industrial landscape has evolved. The groundbreaking Industrial IoT (IIoT) based Digital Twin technology, is changing the way industries optimize energy procurement and usage. Creating a digital twin of an asset enables companies to track operations, identify inefficiencies, and ensure proactive approaches by mirroring the physical with a real-time virtual version. Dynamic adjusting of energy based on AI-driven analytics eliminates waste and operational costs associated with the building by keeping the machines operating optimally and with minimal downtime, predictive maintenance ensures that machinery runs at peak efficiencyv(Yu et al., 2022). Furthermore, Digital Twins enables industries to simulate energy-saving surrogates before implementation in real life with the holistic aim of maximizing sustainability. With all industries working towards greener operation, Digital Twins drive a virtuous cycle of smart, energy-efficient, and cost-effective industrial ecosystems.

3.1. Real-time Energy Monitoring and Analytics

Energy is one of the bigger drivers of operational costs in industry today. Digital Twin technology provides industries with the ability to not only continuously monitor but directly optimize energy usage in real-time. Data is gathered from IoT sensors embedded in machinery, equipment and production lines and fed into virtual models that simulate physical entities. Operators to keep an eye on energy trends, find inefficiencies, and see anomalies before they blow up. Businesses can forecast energy demand, perform a top-down approach to energy usage optimization and execute energy-saving measures in real-time using advanced analytics. Moreover, embedding AI and machine learning models in these systems can provide information on energy optimization, by changing operating conditions, and shutting down equipment when idle. With these real-time capabilities, industries can significantly reduce energy waste, lower costs, and contribute to sustainability goals, all while improving the overall efficiency of their operations.

3.2. Predictive and Prescriptive Maintenance for Energy Efficiency

Companies are now using predictive and prescriptive maintenance to revolutionize methods of energy efficiency across industries. Disruptive along with Digital Twin technology coupled with Industrial IoT (IIoT) can enable companies to forecast equipment failures in advance. However, predictive maintenance utilizes sensors installed in machinery to collect real-time data about performance, which is then analyzed using machine learning or AI algorithms to predict issues, allowing maintenance teams to fix issues in a more proactive manner. This ideally mitigates unplanned downtimes and optimizes energy consumption due to machines operating at maximum efficiency.

When facing questions about future problems, prescriptive maintenance goes one step further and makes recommendations on what actions should be taken to resolve potential problems. By leveraging AI-based insights, it recommends the most economical interventions, preventing unsolicited energy consumption and avoiding waste. This drives efficiencies, lower energy costs, and extends asset life – especially in energy-intensive industries. For example, in conjunction with Digital Twin simulations, predictive and prescriptive maintenance enables manufacturers to optimize operations and improve sustainability, producing smarter and more efficient energy consumption over the production life cycle.

3.3. AI-Driven Decision Making for Resource Optimization

AI-powered decision-making is a game-changer as far as resource optimization in industries is concerned and when integrated with the Digital Twin technology, it could really provide immense benefits. Specifically, to optimize the energy consumption and energy waste reduction, AI algorithms can analyze big data collected in real-time by IoT sensors. Through these data streams, AI powered solutions can recognize patterns, forecast energy needs, and minimize inefficiencies across production methods.

Such an active measure helps industries to modify their operations in real-time focusing on the usage of resources in an optimum manner.

AI has a huge potential for the automation of predictive maintenance, where, for instance, you could predict energy consumption from previous trends and adjust your machinery to increase energy consumption, when you are confident that the energy system will not suffer surges or downtimes. Furthermore, artificial intelligence can help minimize waste by analyzing the manufacturing process to identify possible areas where materials can be reduced, without compromising product quality. A Digital Twin ecosystem employs AI (Artificial Intelligence), which helps to provide real-time feedback leading to an ever more sustainable and efficient industrial system at little to no cost. In the end, AI-based decision making not only rewards the industries with better operational efficiency but also engages them in ensuring a more sustainable future.

3.4. Case Study: Digital Twin in Smart Manufacturing

Digital Twin technology, within the scope of smart manufacturing, has been a game-changer in the sense that it helps in optimizing energy consumption and curbing energy wastage. This can be illustrated in leading automotive manufacturer. The firm connected their production line using Digital Twin models and received insight into the performance, energy, and efficiency of their machinery in real-time.

With the help of IoT sensors, a digital twin was created for each machine, providing engineers insights to understand energy consumption trends and pinpoint inefficiencies within the system (Ben-Aboud & Kobbane, 2024). Not only did the digital twins provide insights about existing infrastructure, but they also predicted different types of equipment failures which allowed maintenance to occur before an expensive breakdown took place. This was not only done to save energy but also to help reduce the wastage of material owing to fewer defective parts and unplanned downtime.

Moreover, the Digital Twin models enabled the firm to maximize their factory layout and logistic flow, thus using energy much more efficiently covering production steps. Instead of affecting physical operations, engineers could simulate scenarios to improve energy consumption and resource management in the digital space.

As such, the manufacturer was able to cut down on carbon emissions, needed operational costs, and improved quality which showing how Digital Twins along with IoT radically improved smart manufacturing for the better (Metallidou et al., 2022).

4. WASTE REDUCTION STRATEGIES USING DIGITAL TWINS

Digital Twin is a technology that allows to reduce waste retention by providing you with effective methods to do that in an industrial environment. Manufacturers create virtual models that is digital twins of physical assets to simulate processes and detect inefficiencies before they happen. Digital Twins can also optimize material usage by simulating production scenarios to use the least amount of material needed in the manufacturing process. They also track energy consumption, to help identify and target areas for potential energy savings. Predictive analytics improve the maintenance schedules while preventing breakdowns associated with resource wastage. Combining Digital Twins with IIoT sensors provides industries with an opportunity to transition to a more sustainable methodology, creating less material and energy waste and greater overall efficiency.

4.1. Digital Twin-Based Process Optimization

Digital Twin technology is changing the game of process optimization in industrial environments by mimicking real world systems or objects in real-time. Virtual models that enable industries to replicate these processes, simulate scenarios, and implement changes to test out their effects without disrupting real production will provide invaluable data. Digital Twins, utilizing real-time data from Internet of Things (IoT) sensors, offer greater foresight into how systems operate, allowing businesses to optimize energy consumption and minimize waste. For example, in manufacturing, a Digital Twin can simulate production lines to facilitate predictive maintenance, reducing downtime and energy usage.

You can also find things that are inefficient in processes and make recommendations about using your resources more effectively. In doing so, they have created a dynamic approach that not only reduces operational efficiencies but also helps sustainability by decreasing environmental impact. Digital Twin technology leads to smart, data-driven decision-making, driving efficiencies and quicker development cycles to industries that are eager to adopt it while being economic and sustainable in nature. Digital Twins open the door to increasingly intelligent, sustainable industrial approaches —through such innovations.

4.2. Minimizing Material Waste through Simulation and Modeling

One of the most essential targets for the industries gunning for sustainability or cost-effectiveness is reducing material waste. Digital Twin technology helps the manufacturers to form high fidelity representations of their production processes through various simulation and modeling tools and techniques. Each model enables real-time tracking of material consumption, detecting wastes, defects, or over-consumption. IIoT sensors along with data analytics enable manufacturers to simulate various production scenarios ahead of the real-life implementation in the shop floor thereby preventing large-scale materials wastage.

Using Digital Twins, we could simulate the flows of materials and thus, prevent excessive material without the need for any real cutting, such as in the case of many industries including automotive or electronics, where cuts must be exact or else too much scrap is generated. Digital Twins also get better over time as they are continuously refined with data from actual production, thus ensuring that the best material is leveraged in the future. This preventative method not only saves businesses on resources but also helps the environment by limiting the carbon footprint from manufacturing processes.

4.3. Circular Economy and Sustainable Manufacturing Approaches

The era of Industrial IoT, Digital Twins and Big data threw its weight behind circular economy and that has brought a lot of change to industrial sustainability. Digital Twins simulate manufacturing at all levels in real-time, helping businesses uncover inefficiencies and make the best use of their resources. By monitoring the entire lifecycle of a product, from design and production to end-of-life, Digital Twins are enabling a circular economy in which waste is kept to a minimum and materials are endlessly reused. In sustainable manufacturing, use of Digital Twin technology can eliminate energy wastage by predicting end-to-end energy consumption requirements and dynamically adjusting processes in real time to reduce costs as well as environmental impact. Such systems are also an enabler of closed-loop manufacturing by making sure that wastes are upcycled properly to minimize virgin resource consumption. The integration of sustainable practices into IoT-driven solutions offers smarter, greener operations, thus, ensuring that economic growth is realistic and the industrial future reliable and responsible.

4.4. Case Study: Reducing Carbon Footprint with Digital Twin

The quest for sustainability in the modern industrial landscape is pushing organizations to adopt advanced technologies such as Digital Twins. Digital Twin technology has so far been able to contribute to a great success story of reducing the carbon footprint of a large manufacturing plant. The engineers were able to simulate the plant operations virtually, how energy consumption happened within real-time timescale, as a way of monitoring energy consumption to identify inefficiencies that had led to excess emissions.

By means of IoT sensors, Digital Twin collects a continuous stream of data about energy consumption, equipment, and production. Predictive analytics is used for analysis of this data, enabling operators to recalibrate before issues worsen. For example, by reducing energy waste and CO2 emissions through the monitoring of heating and cooling systems and automating energy-saving procedures

A further example would be around the facility using a circular economy model from the data-driven recommendations made through the Digital Twin and thereby minimizing resource wastage. By continually assessing its carbon output and tweaking processes, the company reduced its carbon output by 15 per cent in the first year after adopting the tech.

This case study demonstrates how Digital Twin technology can improve overall operational efficiencies as well as help industries achieve sustainability targets. Minimizing waste and energy use reduces carbon footprints, making businesses a part of curing the environmental crisis we find ourselves in.

5. IMPLEMENTATION CHALLENGES AND SOLUTIONS

There are various challenges associated with implementation of Digital Twin applications in industrial scenarios. Data integration is the most prominent challenge because many industries still use legacy systems and devices that need to properly integrate with new IoT technologies. On top of that, the complexities of cybersecurity come into play as large amounts of data are exchanged, and companies need strong security measures in place to keep that data safe. This is also a barrier for smaller companies due to cost and infrastructure limitations. Nevertheless, standardised data protocols, cloud-based platforms, and edge computing to facilitate faster processing of data can all help to solve these problems. Solving these problems will lead to effective, scalable, and secure energy efficiency and waste reduction.

5.1. Data Integration and Interoperability Issues

However, when it comes to Digital Twin applications in Industrial IoT, there are substantial challenges related to data integration and interoperability, as it is necessary to optimize energy usage and minimize waste. The industrial internet of things are heterogeneous systems that produce massive amounts of data from several heterogeneous sources–sensors, machines, and control systems (Zhang et al., 2021). That is to allow you to integrate this data into a single model so that Digital Twins can work. The integration can be complicated due to the type of formats, protocols, and standards different platforms have.

Moreover, connectivity among several IoT devices and systems are necessary to facilitate live data exchange and communication.

In the absence of these standardized frameworks or interfaces, Digital Twins can get caught up in data silos unable to realize their full value. These challenges can be addressed by deploying effective data management capabilities, embracing open standards, and leveraging middleware connectivity to assure connectivity with devices seamlessly. Integration and synthesis of data sources are essential to keeping Digital Twin models current and trustworthy so that they can be actionable tools for energy optimization and waste management.

5.2. Cybersecurity and Privacy Concerns

As more and more industries go Digital Twin, part of their IIoT (Industrial IoT) ecosystem, cybersecurity and privacy issues will mass in on users and creators of strong technological designs. Digital Twins are based on large amounts of real-time data obtained from sensors built into physical assets. The information is sent over networks, leading to many access points for possible cyberattacks. The integrity of such systems can be damaged by threats such as data breaches, ransomware, and unauthorized access, which can also lead to disruption of operations and incurring financial losses.

In addition, we also need to protect sensitive data privacy including but not limited to proprietary manufacture processes, employee data, and other private information. Mitigation of these risks necessitate the implementation of strong encryption, access control mechanisms, and in real-time threat monitoring. As Digital Twins get smarter, even more critical to consider security-by-design principles during the development phase. Industries can use the full value of Digital Twin and IIoT technologies and non-redundantly consume energy to minimize waste while ensuring data security and privacy by putting the aspects of cybersecurity on priority.

5.3. Cost and Infrastructure Constraints

While embedding Digital Twin (DT) technology in Industrial IoT (IIoT) ecosystems for improved energy optimization and waste minimization is a good idea, the process is sometimes off-putting due to technical issues. The initial cost of infrastructure is one of the key challenges organizations face. A Digital Twins is costly — and you will want a great deal of sensors, computing hardware, and software to create your Digital Twins to ramp and execute them. Moreover, industry players must upgrade old legacy systems to connect to the IoT networks, which makes the system a bit complex and costly.

Further, the infrastructure should enable pouring data collaboratively, analyzing and presenting data in real-time, and store at scale, which can mean changing to the cloud or utilize edge. This needs proper planning as well as resource allocation, more so for small to medium enterprises working on a slim budget.

However, for the long-term sustainability they believe it can deliver- increased energy efficiency and reduction in waste- the Digital Twin is often worth the initial cost, especially in industries looking for sustainable growth possibilities.

5.4. Strategies for Effective Digital Twin Deployment

We should deploy Digital Twin (DT) technology in industrial plants through a well-planned manner to harvest its advantages of improving energy consumption and minimizing waste. First, set clear objectives whether it is to achieve energy efficiency, predictive maintenance, or reduce operational downtime. Then, IoT sensors and data analytics platforms should be integrated for real-time monitoring and simulations. The smooth incorporation of new digital infrastructures with existing systems depends on their interoperability. A solid plan for data management with an emphasis on data quality, security, and scalability is also critical.

In order to ensure acceptance, employees should be trained appropriately, and adoption of digital twins should be aligned with the culture of the organization. Finally, you should not even scale it within the organization make some small pilot project and test the effectiveness of the technology. When incorporated properly, the Digital Twins may be advantageously used in every kind of industry to optimise the energy consumed and the waste produced.

6. FUTURE TRENDS AND RESEARCH DIRECTIONS

The future looks good for Digital Twin applications as we grasp the potential in the Industrial IoT space and harmonize the trend on optimization of energy and reduction of waste. Some prominent trends include the inclusion of edge computing and 5G, which allow for real-time processing and more connectivity. Predictive analytics will further automate energy management and waste reduction with AI-driven models. Moreover, Digital Twin Simulations will allow for sustainable practices such as circular economy models across the entire operation. There are research developments to facilitate interoperability crosswise over stages and help broaden ease of use, just as better cyber security in these arrangements by supplying shining sturdy arrangements to enterprises, guide advancement in the direction of efficiency. These developments are taking us to use intelligent and sustainable systems for factory aesthetics.

6.1. Emerging Technologies Enhancing Digital Twins

Many of these new technologies are enabling new levels of capabilities for Digital Twins, and allowing them to optimize energy use and waste within industrial IoT systems. A notable innovation is edge computing, which localizes computation closer to data origin and allow real-time decisions to be made more quickly. This lessens latency, facilitates actionable responses to operational inefficiencies instantaneously, and boosts the automation of energy management in industrial spaces. The emergence of 5G technology getting integrated within the Digital Twins is also able to offer ultra-fast communication and allow for instant data transfer between the IoT devices and Digital Twins thus enabling a better synchronization and more in-depth simulations.

The second reason is the increasing availability of artificial intelligence (AI) and machine learning (ML), which makes predictive analytics possible where Digital Twins not only observe existing processes but also predict future patterns, anticipate potential problems, and suggest improvements. Blockchain also improves the security and transparency of the data exchange between two Digital Twin systems by ensuring trusted, immutable records. In tandem, these technologies are changing the way industries think about energy efficiency and waste.

6.2. Role of Edge Computing and 5G in IIoT and Digital Twins

Edge Computing and 5G have a vital role in the theme of optimization of energy consumption and waste for Industrial IoT (IIoT) and Digital Twin applications. It pushes data processing capabilities closer to where it is being generated (e.g. the edge of the network), thus lowering response times and allowing for more real time decision making (Dhasarathan et al., 2024). This becomes all the more important in energy-intensive industries where seconds make a difference. Edge computing provides quick high-level insight which means optimized energy management with lower waste. Coupled with the high-speed, low-latency features of 5G, industries can handle massive data from connected devices seamlessly.

5G supports massive machine-type communications, driving the acceleration of Digital Twins deployment that help in accurately simulating, in real-time, the way energy is consumed and enabling instant adjustments. When combined, Edge Computing and 5G form a secure, highly responsive IIoT environment that enables industries to operate more intelligently and sustainably, improving efficiency and reducing their environmental footprint in real-time.

6.3. AI and Digital Twins for Autonomous Industry Operations

AI and Digital Twins are revolutionizing autonomous Industry by democratizing AI technology to shard new modes of Industry by optimizing energy usage and reducing waste. Identity determination of Real-Time Data with the help of Digital Twin and AI provides industries to simulate its equipment and system performance and take appropriate intelligent decisions. Whereas digital twins essentially duplicate physical assets in a virtual environment, AI sifts through enormous amounts of data to predict outcomes and identify inefficiencies before they happen. It enables autonomous systems to lounge their energy utilization, stay away from resource depletion, saving on blaming, and disposing — leading to more noteworthy levels of productivity.

For example, AI algorithms can predict maintenance requirements, which helps to minimize downtime and energy-costly repairs. These systems continuously observe their context and respond immediately to changes in order to maintain the highest level of efficiency possible. With industries transitioning towards automation, AI-driven Digital Twins will not just improve operational independence also will promote sustainability through energy-efficient and waste-reducing behaviors. The convergence is a big step towards intelligent green industrial ecosystems.

6.4. Sustainable Digital Twin Models for Smart Factories

Now, in this age of Industry 4.0, digital twins are becoming a critical component of making factories smart and green technology enabled. Digital Twin models allow for monitored, simulative and ideally optimised processes by creating virtual representations of physical assets. Not only does this enable manufacturers to improve operational efficiency, but this is also essential for sustainability. Incorporating IoT sensors, these models can also monitor overall energy consumption, detect inefficiencies and recommend more optimal ways of reducing waste. Digital twins in a smart factory can simulate different options for optimizations and identify the most energy-efficient strategies, saving consumed materials and the overall environmental footprint.

Sustainable digital twins require continuous flow of data, predictive analytics and automation. These models will enable industries to enhance the circles of resource utilization amid their transition towards circular economies, so that factories will reap the profits not just economically but also environmentally. Their integration brings both long-term environmental and economic advantages for smart factories around the world.

7. CONCLUSION

The Digital Twins are IoT-powered replicas that have a potential to improve energy efficiency and minimize waste across industries. Companies can forecast and enhance operations, by building real-time virtual copies of physical assets. Utilizing artificial intelligence and big data, this technology finds inefficiencies and improves decisions, leading to more sustainable and intelligent practices. Digital Twins have also proven to provide considerable environmental benefits by helping to reduce waste, carbon footprint, and move toward sustainable manufacturing practices. Scalability and interoperability among sectors, assimilating edge computing and 5G for in-time decision-making, and training and infrastructure to leverage the full potential of Digital Twins for long-term sustainability and economic value creation need to be focused in future research.

REFERENCES

Ardebili, A. A., Longo, A., & Ficarella, A. (2021). Digital Twin (DT) in Smart Energy Systems - Systematic Literature Review of DT as a growing solution for Energy Internet of the Things (EIoT). *E3S Web of Conferences, 312*, 09002. DOI: 10.1051/e3sconf/202131209002

Ben-Aboud, Y., & Kobbane, A. (2024). *Towards a Modular Digital Twin Framework for Energy-Optimized IoT Sensor Devices*. 1–7. DOI: 10.1109/WINCOM62286.2024.10655683

Billey, A., & Wuest, T. (2023). Energy digital Twins in smart manufacturing Systems: A literature review. *Manufacturing Letters*, *35*, 1318–1325. DOI: 10.1016/j.mfglet.2023.08.047

Butean, A., Enriquez, J., Matei, A., Rovira, A., Barbero, R., & Trevisan, S. (2024). A digital twin concept for optimizing the use of high-temperature heat pumps to reduce waste in industrial renewable energy systems. *Procedia Computer Science*, *237*, 123–128. DOI: 10.1016/j.procs.2024.05.087

Dhasarathan, C., & Gnanasekaran, S. (2024). Digital Twin for Sustainable Farming: Developing User-Friendly Interfaces for Informed DecisionMaking and Increased Profitability. In The Future of Agriculture: IoT, AI and Blockchain Technology for Sustainable Farming (pp. 1-20). Bentham Science Publishers.

Metallidou, C., Psannis, K. E., Vergados, D. D., & Dossis, M. (2022). Digital Twin and Industrial Internet of Things Architecture to Reduce Carbon Emissions. *2022 4th International Conference on Computer Communication and the Internet, ICCCI 2022*, 185–189. DOI: 10.1109/ICCCI55554.2022.9850248

Teng, S. Y., Touš, M., Leong, W. D., How, B. S., Lam, H. L., & Máša, V. (2021). Recent advances on industrial data-driven energy savings: Digital twins and infrastructures. *Renewable & Sustainable Energy Reviews*, *135*, 110208. DOI: 10.1016/j.rser.2020.110208

Yu, W., Patros, P., Young, B., Klinac, E., & Walmsley, T. G. (2022). Energy digital twin technology for industrial energy management: Classification, challenges and future. *Renewable & Sustainable Energy Reviews*, *161*, 112407. DOI: 10.1016/j.rser.2022.112407

Zhang, J., Liu, Y., Qin, X., & Xu, X. (2021). Energy-Efficient Federated Learning Framework for Digital Twin-Enabled Industrial Internet of Things. *IEEE International Symposium on Personal, Indoor and Mobile Radio Communications, PIMRC, 2021-September*, 1160–1166. DOI: 10.1109/PIMRC50174.2021.9569716

Chapter 10
Human-Centered Digital Twins in IoT: Balancing Personalization, Privacy, and Ethics

Aditi Malani
Amity University, Noida, India

Raghav Malani
Amity University, Noida, India

Neeru Sidana
https://orcid.org/0000-0003-1087-4214
Amity University, Noida, India

ABSTRACT

The integration of Human-Centered Digital Twins (HCDTs) and the Internet of Things (IoT) is revolutionizing industries by allowing personalized, real-time decision-making through the use of continuous data streams. These systems utilize IoT sensors and AI-driven models to produce digital copies of individuals, environments, or systems, providing improved predictive capabilities in healthcare, smart cities, and industrial applications. The increasing use of HCDTs sparks significant ethical issues, such as data privacy, confidentiality, discriminatory practices, and consent based on complete information. A significant gap persists in research, particularly in the establishment of uniform ethical frameworks and the implementation of dependable AI systems that safeguard user autonomy while optimising the advantages of digital twins. The purpose of this investigation is to investigate the ethical consequences of personalization in HCDTs and suggest a framework for reconciling data-driven personalization with user privacy and cybersecurity in IoT environments.

DOI: 10.4018/979-8-3373-2028-1.ch010

INTRODUCTION

Digital Twins (DTs) are a concept which gained significant attention in the past years, they evolved from initial applications in engineering and industrial domains to even more complex areas such as healthcare, cybersecurity, and Internet of Things (IoT) (Emmert-Streib, 2019). A digital twin is a virtual copy of a physical body that is updated in real time with real data for running simulations, make predictions, and optimize. With the progression of the industry to the digital transformation in all sectors; it is imperative to integrate the artificial intelligence (AI), blockchain, and IoT together with the digital twin technology (Vera-Arenas, 2019).

The untapped transformative potential of HCDTs is under increasing threat of ethical challenges and therefore this research is urgently needed. Often in current implementations, functionality takes precedence over ethics, and studies have shown that 78% of HCDT systems collect excessive personal data from both permitted and unpermitted purposes (Lin et al. 2023). It results in substantial privacy risks because, as Popa et al. (2023) find, 92% of users are completely unaware of the extent of collection and use of these systems. Nevertheless, by acknowledging documented situations of algorithmic bias enabling 37% decrease in diagnostic precision in women and minority populations (Tang et al., 2023), healthcare HCDTs may be contributing to existing health care disparities. These issues point out the major needs that remain in technological frameworks to adequately monitor, govern and help HCDT developers and deployers throughout the development and deployment process, especially for more advanced and broadly adopted HCDTs.

HCDTs are becoming increasingly essential to the development of IoT driven infrastructures in many sectors, which makes this study especially relevant. HCDTs have inevitably transformed the way patient care is administered through remote monitoring, predictive diagnostics and personalized treatment plans, but have raised many ethical and privacy questions relevant to medical and healthcare domain. Societal biases are risked in the scale of embedding with HCDTs for smart city implementations; HCDTs are applied in urban planning, traffic optimization, and public resource allocation. HCDTs are used for consumer IoT applications such as wearables and smart home systems that may hinder user privacy and autonomy in delivering hyper-personal experiences. These applications raise much more than the individual privacy ethical challenges, they raise ethical challenges in a way that impacts to the most basic aspects of social equity, human agency and trust in AI driven systems. Loosening systems for systematic research and ethical implications around the unchecked proliferation of HCDTs tends to normalize surveillance, fuels inequality, and create new vectors for debilitating breaches of large volumes of personal data.

It investigates IoT integrated HCDTs across three critical domains that exhibit both the highest potential benefits and most serious ethical challenges. The research examines ethical risks on patient monitoring systems and diagnostic HCDTs in the healthcare domains where data sensitivity and algorithmic bias are severe. Smart city studies are investigated and how urban planning and public services HCDTs can be dismissed (or inadvertently perpetuate or worsen) social bias. The third focus area is the consumer applications that look at the privacy trade-offs involved in Personalized IoT devices that leverages HCDT technology.

Objectives

- To examine the ethical challenges of personalization in Human-Centered Digital Twins (HCDTs) within IoT.
- To create a framework that balances personalization with user privacy and cybersecurity.

- To suggest AI and blockchain solutions for improving trust and data security.

1. TO EXAMINE THE ETHICAL CHALLENGES OF PERSONALIZATION IN HUMAN-CENTERED DIGITAL TWINS (HCDTS) WITHIN IOT.

The concept of digital twins has evolved with time, which includes artificial intelligence, real time' data analytics and cyber physical systems. Emmert-Streib (2021) defines digital twins as data driven visualization of the physical objects for simulation and predictive analytics. München (2019) states that the Digital Twin Theory provides a way of seeing the relationship between digital and physical entities in Internet of Things ecosystems. Tang et al. (2022) provide conceptual growth about digital twins in healthcare, and how digitally twins are critical for developing a master plan for the simulation of the human body.

1.1. Data Privacy and Confidentiality

One of the most important ethical issues of HCDTs is data privacy. Digital twins are required to run with ongoing data streams coming in from the IoT devices and this new challenges in the protection of data (Emmert-Streib 2021). HCDTs used in health care applications offer a high risk of re-identification for both sensitive biomedical data in real time (Tang et al., 2023).

Fundamentally, HCDTs' need for comprehensive data collection goes against the principle of data minimization under the GDPR. According to Lin et al. (2023), 78% of HCDT implementations exceed the data they need to do what they're stating versus the best performing baseline that they consider their accuracy. Since data is repurposed without further consent, this tension exists between utility and privacy, referred to as this "data hunger" (Helbing & Sánchez-Vaquerizo, 2022).

In fact, emerging privacy preserving techniques are promising but struggle with their implementation. However, Yang et al (2023) say that such an architecture can reduce the amount of central data collected but increases system complexity by 30-40% and needs the metadata to contain sensitive patterns. Even though homomorphic encryption is theoretically solvable, there is considerable latency (150–300ms per operation) on current implementations (Rahman et al., 2023), making it computationally impractical for real time HCDT.

These tensions are found in the healthcare sector itself. Some of the patient monitoring HCDTs inadvertently disclosed the substance abuse histories, as Popa et al. (2023) show, despite anonymization of the data. This points to de Kerckhove's (2022) 'transparency paradox' wherein users cannot meaningfully give effective consent to uses of data which they cannot predict.

These issues compound their cross-border data flows. According to Fontes and Carpentras (2023), smart cities deployments of HCDT showed that 62% of data is transferred across jurisdictions with different privacy regimes. Users are allowed to specify data sensitivity levels and allowed uses in a tiered consent framework which allows the adopters to keep both privacy and adoption but still be limited for technical complexity to adoption.

Solutions may be available by recent advances in synthetic data generation. Ganerative AI models that retains 92 percent of utility of original data while it reduces the risk of re-identification by 83 percent is shown by Kaaniche et al (2023). Nevertheless, HCDT predictions can be distorted (Pinto et al. 2023) if the processes involved in these techniques are not calibrated with enough care.

The privacy-utility tradeoff remains unresolved. In accordance with Lauer-Schmaltz et al. (2023), current HCDT architectures mandate a bad compromise between personalization effectiveness and sound privacy protection and require important architectural re-designs of the data collection paradigms.

HCDTs inherit and enhance the bias of the underlying AI system. Emmert-Streib (2021) lists three bias propagation pathways in HCDTs: training data skew (the use of predominantly male patient in 78% of medical HCDTs), algorithmic bias (recommendation systems exhibit gender preference pattern in 67% of cases), and feedback loop bias (biased outputs replicate biased inputs).

Very poor consequences are shown by healthcare applications. Similarly training data imbalances, Tang et al. (2023) showed that cardiac HCDTs were 37% less accurate for women and 43% less accurate for non-white patients. This indicates that existing approaches suffer from fundamental problems (and counterfactuals of) such biases (Lin et al., 2023).

The problem extends beyond healthcare. Fontes and Carpentras (2023) found HCDT resource allocation systems for smart city deployments that acted to systemically disadvantage immigrant neighborhoods in favouring non-immigrant communities where biased mobility dataset was used. Rather than explicit rules, the term the researchers use is 'architectural discrimination,' because it is bias built into the system design.

Strategies for removing the bias show little success. As Owen and Moore (2023) tested seven debiasing techniques on HCDT models, they found that debiasing reduced bias at the levels of 28-53% and accuracy at the levels of 15-22%. Adversarial debiasing was shown to be the most effective, but computationally infeasible for real-time HCDT applications with 400% increase in latency.

1.2. Algorithmic Bias and Discrimination

HCDTs inherit and enhance the bias of the underlying AI system. Emmert-Streib (2021) lists three bias propagation pathways in HCDTs: training data skew (the use of predominantly male patient in 78% of medical HCDTs), algorithmic bias (recommendation systems exhibit gender preference pattern in 67% of cases), and feedback loop bias (biased outputs replicate biased inputs).

Very poor consequences are shown by healthcare applications. Similar to training data imbalances, Tang et al. (2023) showed that cardiac HCDTs were 37% less accurate for women and 43% less accurate for non-white patients. This indicates that existing approaches suffer from fundamental problems (and counterfactuals of) such biases (Lin et al., 2023).

The problem extends beyond healthcare. Fontes and Carpentras (2023) found HCDT resource allocation systems for smart city deployments that acted to systemically disadvantage immigrant neighborhoods in favouring non-immigrant communities where biased mobility dataset was used. Rather than explicit rules, the term the researchers use is 'architectural discrimination,' because it is bias built into the system design.

Strategies for removing the bias show little success. As Owen and Moore (2023) tested seven debiasing techniques on HCDT models, they found that debiasing reduced bias at the levels of 28-53% and accuracy at the levels of 15-22%. Adversarial debiasing was shown to be the most effective, but computationally infeasible for real-time HCDT applications with 400% increase in latency.

There are other challenges in the financial sector. In credit scoring HCDTs with biased social media data, sample biased analysis done by Siddika and Zhao (2023), shows 30% higher denial rates for applicants from specific ethnic groups. However, despite frequent biases being identified, such biases cannot be corrected because HCDT decision making is 'black box' (Zhou et al., 2023).

Most of them are emerging solutions that take up architectural changes instead of adhoc (post-hoc) fixes. In their work, Rahman et al. (2023) propose a "bias-aware" HCDT framework which monitors for discrimination in real time and relieves bias in the outputs by 61% in trials. However, retraining of the full model is needed and it has a cost proportional to 35%.

These biases, however, are very expensive for the human! According to documents, Kshetri (2023) shows how employment screening HCDTs systematically ranked down applicants with non-Western names or educational backgrounds. It is hard to tell about such discrimination because in most of cases, bias in HCDTs is probabilistic rather than deterministic, as noted by Bernal Bernabe et al. (2023), which makes it harder to figure it out and prove it.

Regulatory responses remain inadequate. The EU AI Act requires bias assessments, but Ijaiya (2023) asserts that current requirements do not fulfill HCDTs' unique imperatives, especially because they are dynamic and can evolve over time. Due to the system complexity, the proposed solution - continuous bias auditing - is impracticable (Saliju & Deboi, 2023).

1.3. Transparency and Accountability

The lack of transparency and explainability in AI-driven decision-making is a major ethical concern in HCDT personalisation. The accountability gap – 89% of HCDT users could not explain how personalization decisions, made by others, impact them as researchers repeatedly call it – was uncovered by Emmert-Streib (2021).

Healthcare applications demonstrate the stakes. Popa et al. (2023) observe patients who were provided dramatically different recommended treatments based on identical HCDT inputs and no explainable rationale. This, the researchers attribute to "emergent complexity" unpredictable behaviors that result from interactions in systems.

Explainability techniques show limited effectiveness. Zhou et al. (2023) test various XAI (5 total) on medical HCDTs observing that the best performing solution (LIME) explained only 62% of decisions. Explanation decreases with system sophistication for complex and longitudinal HCDTs (Kuznetsov et al., 2023).

This problem caries over to system governance. Lauer-Schmaltz et al. (2023) reviewed 47 HCDT deployments and found no such accountability mechanisms for decisions made by AI. The researchers suggest a 'responsibility traceability matrix' but admit technical and legal obstacles to its implementation.

In addition, other transparency challenges are revealed with smart city applications. Although HCDTs in urban planning were documented by Fontes and Carpentras (2023), they make unexplained adjustments in traffic light timing that disproportionately impact certain neighborhoods. Operators couldn't even tell when answering if these were system errors or emergent optimizations' when asked.

Many approaches to create an emerging technical solution are combined. In Wang et al. (2023), HCDTs were explained by developing an "explanation stack", that included: Real-time decision capturing (capturing 93% of critical choice), Multi-level explanations (from technical to layperson versions) and impact forecasting (predicting decision consequences). The system however raises computational load by 40% and necessitates hardware exclusive.

It is outpacing what legal frameworks can hold. In particular, the GDPR's "right to explanation" is challenging for HCDTs, as pointed out by de Kerckhove (2022): "How do you explain an automated decision originating from trillions of data points across several systems over time?" Often existing implementations supply meaningless visual boilerplate instead of actual observation (Bernal Bernabe et al., 2023).

In the financial sector there are other methods of operating. Like Tapsell et al. (2023), a banking HCDT is documented by them with 'explanation scores' that represent confidence in its own explanations. Such measures are innovative, but they risk generating false certainty - the system could feel confident to know that it had explained away incorrect decisions (Ijaiya, 2023).

There is a fundamental tension between transparency and performance. Rahman, E., Wu, X., & Yoo, K. (2023). Making HCDTs fully explainable causes them to become less accurate by up to 15 – 30 percent as some of the most effective models are also the least interpretable, Rahman et al. (2023). The result of this is creates ethical dilemmas for developers trying to maintain regulatory compliance, but also system utility.

1.4. Informed Consent and User Autonomy

A crucial ethical requirement for HCDT personalisation is obtaining informed consent. In digital twin ecosystems, users need to be completely aware of how their data is gathered, processed, and utilised (Occhipinti et al., 2023). However, as HCDTs need to process dynamic and continuously generated data, traditional consent frameworks for static data collection scenarios are not appropriate. As Tang et al. (2023) show, healthcare HCDTs require continual streams of biometric data to maintain accuracy, thus removing one time consent procedures as standards for HCDTs. Such gap is enormous, and this figure is 92% of users who do not understand all the data collection after giving initial consent (Popa et al., 2023). Adding emergent capabilities beyond original design specification, the HCDTs complicate the situation further. Data originally collected for basic monitoring were spontaneously used by Heathcare HCDTs to make diagnostic predictions violating the GDPR's purpose limitation principle according to Fontes and Carpentras (2023). The evolution of this system functionality happens without additional user consent, and thus, this evolution is 'consent drift', that Lauer-Schmaltz et al. (2023) define as the divergence of what the user consented to vs what the system does.

The current attempts to address these problems, particularly based on granular consent mechanisms, have produced new problems. (Lauer Schmaltz et al., 2023) found that consent fatigue is a big issue when users have 50+ individual permissions to manage under different HCDT systems, since users will accept default options 68 percent of the time without even really considering them. The concept of informed consent is subservient to this phenomenon; users cannot make the necessary decisions due to the complexity of the options they are faced with. However, emerging solutions have promise but are very limited. Based on the work of (Yang et al., 2023), context aware consent interfaces have been created by (Yang et al., 2023) that adjust at runtime and to the sensitivity level of the data achieving comprehension rates around 89% in clinical trials. But these systems are sensitive data dependent and question who handles what is sensitive. However, as the solutions based on blockchain are immutable and provide an evidence of user permission, the transaction could cause 120millisecond latency, which is not acceptable for real time HCDT application.

In general, it is the autonomy paradox that is most cruel in relation to HCDTs in healthcare applications. De Kerckhove (2022) documents that patients are often forced into choosing extensive monitoring, for the receive the best of care, creating a sort forced choice. However, when this problem occurs in smart city implementations, as Bernal Bernabe et al. discovered in Barcelona while observing that 73% of residents were ignorant about the fact that they provided consent to behaviour tracking as part of municipal service agreements. However, the opacity of these consent mechanisms fundamentally questions whether meaning autonomy can exist in systems where we do not have sufficient autonomy, in the form of information, to truly know what we are consenting to, and in the process have used layers of bureaucracy to obfuscate the frameworks. Researchers further emphasize the adaptive consent frameworks that can evolve with the HCDT capabilities, standardized interfaces for multiple systems consent management, and the true technical implementations of respecting the withdraw consent right that won't flatten the system or cause the service interruptions.

1.5. Cybersecurity Threats and Data Integrity

HCDTs are frequently the target of cyberattacks because they handle and store massive amounts of sensitive data. Firstly, the architectural design of HCDTs exponentially exposes more attack surface as Rahman et al. (2023) show that each additional component (biometric sensor, predictive models), constitutes a new vulnerability, and it thus yields up to 300% of the relevant attack vectors more than traditional IoT devices. The most alarming threats out of all are model poisoning ones, where the adversary alters the HCDT behavior by providing carefully crafted training data. As shown by Wang et al. (2023), as few as 0.3% of poisoned data samples could result in reliable changes in medical diagnostic outcomes on clinical HCDTs, i.e., misdiagnoses that could be potentially life threatening. The rise of spoofing attacks on identity also is equally concerning and increased by 450% in 2022 according to Kshetri (2023) as attackers create sophisticated synthetic biometric profiles to impersonate authentic users.

Recently, research has extensively documented specific vulnerabilities in HCDT systems. As shown by Alrayes et al. (2023), who were able to spoof wearable health sensors with less than $200 of commercially available equipment, it may be very easy to break even the most modern authentication methods. Kuznetsov et al. (2023) further developed model inversion techniques which were able to reconstruct private training datasets obtained from 71% out of tested HCDTs, revealing sensitive information that the original HCDT is supposed to hide. Another critical weak point in the data pipelines connecting the different HCDT components are identified by Tawalbeh et al. (2023) specifically for 17 novel attack types including sensors, processing units and decision-making algorithms.

Currently, protection and system functionality do not always balance out well with current security solutions. However, for homogeneous encryption, though theoretically secure for data processing, homomorphic encryption may add somewhere in the range of 300–500 milliseconds per operation (Rahman et al. 2023), which is entirely unreasonable for real time HCDT applications like for example medical monitoring or autonomous vehicle control. Although at 94% (Li et al., 2023), behavioral authentication methods are promising, they can demand large amounts of training data that may not be available for all use cases. Although the tamper proof records are undoubtedly helpful, the storage requirement is increased by 40% (Nguyen et al., 2023) which makes it an infrastructure nightmare. Future research directions must focus on the development of lightweight cryptographic protocols that could be used in the resource constrained HCDT components, the development of attack resilient federation learning architecture and the creation of the standardized security certificate processing process to be used in the digital twin technologies.

1.6. Ethical Implications in Healthcare and Smart Cities

HCDTs have the potential to revolutionise both smart cities and healthcare, yet both fields present ethical issues. However, in medical applications, HCDTs exceed their targeted diagnostic boundaries with Tang et al. (2023) reporting that one third of clinical systems had indicative power for a condition outside of their training scope, such as predictive power from unvalidated correlations between lifestyle variables and disease progression. Such liability conundrums and concerns about misleading patients and providers make this overreach very problematic as a diagnostic point. Specifically, Popa et al. (2023) find that 22% of patients, who are using these systems, felt that the system was exceptional and unduly influenced or manipulated if the HCDTs put institutional interests over patients' autonomy. Lin et al. (2023) documented the 300% variation in life expectancy predictions for patients with clinically identical cases, which may unnecessarily doomed patients to withdrawal of care or prone to treatment via unnecessary medications.

While the smart city implementations bring about different set of ethical challenges, they reflect a broader societal power dynamic. In their analysis of Chicago's predictive policing HCDT, Fontes and Carpentras (2023) control for crime statistics and found that the policing system flagged majority neighbourhoods at the rate 400% higher than other neighbourhoods. In this they illustrate how HCDTs can institute a discrimination institutionalized as data driven objectivity through this algorithmic reinforcement of existing biases. Likewise, resource allocation systems of similar concerns, as Bernal Bernabe et al. (2023) recorded where HCDTs working in Barcelona systematically re-directed resources away from poorer districts because of "efficiency" metrics that completely disregard equity concerns.

Concerns about mass surveillance and the way of behavior control are raised by the global proliferation of social scoring systems, which are used in 63% of Chinese smart cities as of Kshetri (2023) and involves unauthorized usage of data sources and opaque criteria of evaluation.

Complex issues arise regarding these problems and emerging governance frameworks tackle them through a multi-layer perspective. Lauer-Schmaltz et al. (2023) propose strict prediction scope limitations, limited, mandatory human review for critical decisions and full transparency about therapeutic intentions in the case of medical HCDTs. The goal of these measures is to support clinical judgment with the HCDT tool capabilities. Nevertheless, implementation barriers still exist as Owen and Moore (2023) state that 72% of healthcare providers do not have enough training in HCDT ethics and Ijaiya (2023) points out that smart city ethics boards often fall under political pressure to approve dubious systems. So, moving forward in healthcare and urban management sectors, ethical guidelines must be devised taking into account the different contexts of both, be mandatory for social impact assessments and improve whistleblowers protection for professionals operating those systems. It is only through such comprehensive use of HCDTs that fundamental ethical principles can be rendered in a way that still realizes the benefits of HCDTs.

1.7. Socio-Ethical Risks and Benefits

The extensive deployment of Human-Centered Digital Twins (HCDTs) results in complex effects on society that both bring many positive changes and create serious dangers which require thorough evaluation. Rural diagnostic HCDTs have proven effective in improving early cancer detection rates through the research of Tang et al. (2023) which led to a 300% increase according to the study. HCDTs in Barcelona demonstrated dual success because the energy-management systems delivered both 22% decreased utility usage alongside improved living quality for residents (Bernal Bernabe et al., 2023). People with neurodevelopmental differences learned better due to personalized education HCDTs that resulted in increased retention rates by 45% as reported by Zhou et al. (2023). Carefully planned HCDT systems demonstrate their transformative capabilities if employed ethically according to Zhou et al. (2023).

The advantages of HCDTs exist on different scales within societies which intensifies existing societal disparities. The benefits from HCDTs that can be measured primarily go to individuals earning high incomes because they have better access to digital infrastructure and literacy according to the research by Kshetri (2023). Siddika and Zhao (2023) discovered credit assessment HCDTs use algorithmic redlining by design to deny all residents of distinct ZIP codes because "risk pattern" analyses had significant racial population alignments. The findings of Saliju and Deboi (2023) revealed a major cultural bias problem because sixty-three percent of social interaction HCDTs showed fundamental errors in interpreting non-Western communication practices that caused their recommendations and responses to be unfit. According to Emmert-Streib (2021) digital determinism exists because 58% of users rely on HCDT recommendations so strongly that they deny personal reasoning or contradicting evidence.

The wide-scale implementation of HCDT systems creates various behavioral problems that merit attention. The Seoul smart city transport HCDTs generated efficient route suggestions that reduced spontaneous movements by 42% so people lost opportunities to encounter new individuals and explore their surroundings according to Fontes and Carpentras (2023). The high levels of customized service recommendations according to Yang et al. (2023) led to enhanced community isolation resulting in a 37% increase of diverged urban space experience among neighborhood residents. Research conducted by de Kerckhove (2022) shows heavy users of HCDTs experience measurable degradation in their ability to make autonomous decisions after their prolonged utilization of predictive systems since 32% of such participants documented this outcome.

Strategies to minimize these problems are starting to appear in the market. Rahman et al. (2023) present novel taxation models specifically for HCDTs which support programs for universal access to reduce digital inequality. Wang et al. (2023) created context-based algorithms which cutting cultural biases in social HCDTs to 58% by using advanced cultural measurement processes. According to Venkatesan and Rahayu (2023) community-oriented HCDT product designs by participants yield up to three times better usage rates and equity results when compared to central command HCDT implementation techniques. The design strategies provide a method to harness the advantages of HCDTs alongside decreasing their social hazards when authorities monitor them closely during implementation through ethical assessment methods. Research and policy creators must build systems which combine the promotion of innovation with fair access and bias protection and freedom maintenance for autonomous human beings as digital tools become more prevalent throughout society.

2. TO CREATE A FRAMEWORK THAT BALANCES PERSONALIZATION WITH USER PRIVACY AND CYBERSECURITY.

The Internet of Things (IoT) ecosystem is evolving rapidly with Human Centred Digital Twin (HCDT) development, which opened new doors for creating personalised services to various disciplines of sciences such as smart cities and healthcare. Although HCDTs coupled alongside the Internet of Things may bring about cyber insecurity and loss of user privacy, it would be extremely difficult to strike a balance between both. To perform personalisation, large volumes of personal data must be collected and analyzed, thus increasing cybersecurity risks, exposing themselves to misuse and violating their privacy.

2.1. Privacy-Preserving Technologies

Resolving privacy personalization issues becomes possible once signing agreements between hospitals and organizations are in place. These technologies help in data collection which makes it more secure, and they also support the data analysis operations with no privacy violations.

Differential privacy is a privacy technology that protects data point and allows statistical analysis of groups. Li et al. (2023) demonstrate that differential privacy excels for HCDTs specifically in healthcare procedures that handle sensitive patient information groups. Differential privacy enables the prevention of data re-identification attacks which link recently anonymized information back to specific people. The data protection system of Differential Privacy achieves its goal by adding controlled noise to information to keep specific data points anonymous while maintaining the general statistical properties of the dataset. This application method delivers effective data security to healthcare protective databases that maintain research capability for analytical purposes. Apple employs differential privacy to gather user information that helps enhance Siri and other services by maintaining user privacy (Kshetri, 2023).

The encryption method homomorphic enables operations on information that stays secured in an encrypted state to protect protected data from exposure. The paper by Rahman et al. (2023) shows how homomorphic encryption can secure individual information in AI-controlled IoT systems. Through homomorphic encryption systems can execute analysis operations on ciphertext data which maintains complete protection for sensitive information from the start to the end of the examination process. The computational requirements of homomorphic encryption limit its broad-based implementation according to them. The developing technologies in hardware acceleration and optimized algorithm development are turning homomorphic encryption practical for real-world deployments. Users can implement homomorphic encryption within their Microsoft AI systems by utilizing the SEAL library tools offered by the company (Wang et al., 2023).

Through federated learning users can perform data analysis by maintaining privacy because the system avoids concentrating data at one central point. The models run on local devices and share updates instead of other information with one another. The distributed nature of IoT environments makes federated learning an ideal solution because it processes data locally on multiple spread-out devices which cannot be easily moved to central storage locations for privacy and bandwidth reasons.

Various implementation barriers exist for the deployment of privacy-preservation AI techniques. Venkatesan and Rahayu (2023) state that technical complexity of these processes becomes a barrier to adoption in some industries that have minimal expertise with technology. Strikes for balance between privacy protection and service usefulness need to be properly handled to stop privacy-preserving AI from reducing personalized service quality. Adding extensive noise to differential privacy data will decrease the accuracy of AI models because federated learning face limitations due to device data heterogeneity. However, according to Bernal Bernabe et al. (2023), user trust suffers because standardized frameworks should be utilized for the execution of these techniques, yet their absence delivers inconsistencies.

2.2. User-Centric Data Control

User-centric data control is an essential element of any framework that involves the search for day common with personalization and privacy and cybersecurity. The purpose of this control approach is to allow users to determine the data collection pathways and processes and information distribution methods.

Granular consent tools allow users the ability to pick which types of data to share as well as the designated usage purposes. In this research (Tapsell et al., 2021), the users developed a framework that includes a series of detailed consent techniques that make the users understand their details better. According to the authors, this data management technique results in increased user trust in systems and user control application. In accordance with GDPR, an organization collecting or processing the personal data of a user has to obtain the explicit user consent.

The ownership frameworks allow users to own their data and, hence, determine the permission under which the data will be used. In their paper, Lu et al. (2021) describe a privacy aware framework in which ownership models are used for enabling users' control over the secure and transparent management of their personal data. This framework is said to enable users to stop data being exploited by those who do not support data ownership models, through their data governance rights. In blockchain models, users retain the right to data, and organizations can then access that data in the interest of the established purposes. This enables users to completely control because they facilitate grant and revoke any time they want.

If transparency and full accountability standards are implemented, the understanding of data usage by users will vary accordingly. As pointed out by Reza et al. (2021), user-centric frameworks should possess an inbuilt data tracking and audit trail functionality to permit users monitor data usage and punish those organizations abusing data. According to their suggestion, blockchain technology can create an unalterable audit trail for all data transactions for users to watch their data usage. MyData feature of blockchain technology allows IoT environment to share data in a transparent and accountable manner as per its operation.

Because there are various barriers in the process to transition to user-controlled data, targeted solutions are needed. Goethals et al. (2022) note that maintaining user oversight over data access is complicated effectively in complex IoT system networks. For that reason, there is no standardized user-centric data control systems, causing imprecise techniques and the diminishing of trust from users. As organizations apply different consent systems, it makes it harder for users to understand data preferences and to control their options regarding their data.

2.3. Ethical AI Design

HCDTs must meet ethical AI design principles in developing them since they need to offer personalized services while preserving user privacy rights and autonomy. AI algorithms development process as well as deployment systems must be integrated with implementation of ethical principles.

The proper implementation of fairness together with bias reduction methods forms the basis for stopping AI algorithms from sustaining current inequalities. The authors Owen and Moore (2021) emphasize how developers need to build fair and inclusive algorithms when designing AI personalization system. The authors propose combination of fairness-aware algorithms along with bias detection tools for managing these problematic issues. IBM provides Fairness 360 as a toolkit which offers multiple algorithms that identify and minimize bias throughout AI systems.

When people feel confident that AI systems operate with clear display of mechanics they will trust AI-driven personalization systems. The authors Zhou et al. (2023) presented a user-focused framework based on attention methods and large language models which enhances the transparency features and explainer capabilities of AI algorithms. This methodology enables users to understand the recommendation generation process so they can verify both fairness and unbiased output. DARPA runs the Explainable AI (XAI) initiative to create AI systems which explain their decisions to human users in an understandable manner.

The need of ethical governance is that AI driven personalization should align with social values or norms. In Ijaiya (2023), the author talks about the importance of ethical guidelines, and regulatory frameworks in the fashioning of AI technologies. Secondly, she noted that creating an ethical governance system should be a collaborative effort by policymakers, developers and users. The European Union's AI Act for instance, suggests a regulatory framework on AI that promotes transparency, fairness, and accountability.

One of the main concerns for ethical AI design consists in the opacity of AI algorithms and, on the other hand, the lack of diverse datasets. As Saliju and Deboi (2023) argue, there is little it can do to ensure fairness and inclusiveness in AI driven personalization in industries with very limited technical expertise. Secondly, the choice of trade-off between performance and transparency must be done with great caution to make sure that the resulting AI models are both good and explainable.

2.4. Cybersecurity Measures

It is essential to protect the user data in HCDTs and the integrity of personalized services with cybersecurity measures. It entails creating robust security protocols, as well as healing the vulnerabilities. It is important to protect data in transit as well as at rest and such protection relies on encryption and secure communication protocols. A paper like Lu (2021) talks about improving IoT device security with end-to-end encryption and secure APIs. Therefore, these measures can reduce the possibility of data breacher and cyber-attack.

Detection and response mechanisms must be able to identify and resolve potential vulnerabilities. In Tawalbeh et al. (2023), they suggested a total IoT security framework with the capacity of straightforwardly distinguishing a danger in real time and conveying an automated response.

This they believe will help any companies swiftly react to any new threat at the emergent and minimize the impact of a cyberattack. For example, the behavior of a network traffic can be analyzed using the machine learning algorithms to alert about probable danger.

A vital element for making sure that 'sensitive data', supplied to 'only authorised users', are guaranteed to be 'access controlled' is user authentication and access control mechanism. Sirigu et al. (2022) argue that a way to strengthen the security of HCDTs is to deploy two factor authentication and role-based access control. An example of multi factor authentication requiring more than one of multiple factors of identification, such as a password and a fingerprint, to access the user's data. This gives access control on the basis that users will only have access to data that they need in their role.

Pinto et al. (2022) point out that securing IoT devices is a difficult thing to do, particularly in industries where they have limited technical knowledge. This includes arranging the trade-offs between security and usability in such a way to not improperly outweigh the effectiveness of personalized services. For instance, too restrictive access control mechanisms can force the removal of usability from personalized services whilst insufficient security systems make users prone to cyberattacks.

2.5. Regulatory Compliance

To maintain HCDTs' adherence to legal and ethical standards is allowed with the help of regulatory compliance. It entails conformity to as well as exercise of a unified and as far as possible, consistent framework of data protection legislation and to identify frameworks for issues to tackle as they arise.

The GDPR is a well-known framework on protecting data and is based on consent of user, supporting minimum data use, and a transparent environment. As discussed by Tapsell et al. (2021), GDPR compliant frameworks are generally impracticable within an IoT environment, since there is a need for continuous compliance with HCDTs which are dynamic in nature. In response, they put forward the application of privacy by design principles to ensure GDPR compliant results from HCDTs.

HCDTs are also relevant to emerging regulatory frameworks, such as the California Consumer Privacy Act (CCPA), among other things. As argued by Ijaiya (2023), these frameworks allow these (AI) technologies to influence a development and a deployment of AI technologie in an ethical and secure personalizing way. According to her, emerging regulatory frameworks for HCDTs need to cover the very specific challenges they present, namely, the need for continuous data collection, and the risk for data misuse. For example, the CCPA grants consumers the right to know what personal data are being collected regarding them and the right to ask to have their personal data deleted.

Challenges associated with IoT ecosystems, and the lack of standardized frameworks make the regulatory compliance quite a challenge. According to Lu et al. (2021), it is not possible for compliance to be widely ensured in industries with little technical expertise, without the involvement of policymakers and developers. It is also easy to write so fast to solve the problem but hard to write so fast to set up regulatory framework to catch up. AI and blockchain will raise new issues for data protection in some circumstances and will deprive us of the ability to respond to the current regulations.

3. TO SUGGEST AI AND BLOCKCHAIN SOLUTIONS FOR IMPROVING TRUST AND DATA SECURITY.

In the Human-Centered Digital Twins (HCDTs) and the Internet of Things (IoT), the amalgamation of blockchain and artificial intelligence (AI) turned out to be an effective strategy to boost data safety and trustworthiness in a digital society. As HCDTs make heavy use of collecting, analyzing and exchanging large quantities of personal data, data integrity, privacy and security is essential to ensure.

3.1. Privacy-Preserving Techniques

Privacy preserving AI is something that is essential because it's key to any framework that will boost both trust and the data security. It refers to implementing AI strategies that allow an analysis of advanced data but at the same time protect user information.

Differential privacy is a well-known method of making the privacy in AI systems look good. According to Li et al. (2023), differential privacy is good to protect private information and still allows aggregate analysis. With the help of differentiated privacy, they believe that it is possible to reduce the risk of re-identification attacks (anonymised data connected to specific people). This particularly important in HCDTs, where personal data is constantly collected and processed. Differential privacy is achieved by adding controlled noise to data so that we are guaranteed that no data point by itself can be tracked, you still have a set of statistical properties of the dataset.

Through encrypted processing of data, homomorphic encryption guarantees that the confidentiality of private data is never compromised. Rahman et al. (2023) address application of homomorphic encryption in AI driven systems as well as how it can be used to safeguard personal information in Internet of Things settings. The advantage of using homomorphic encryption is that it lets you do that all the calculations with encrypted data without having to first decrypt it to perform that calculation. However, they do say that homomorphic encryption space might incur too high computational cost to be wide used. For example, in Microsoft SEAL library, resources are offered for deploying homomorphic encryption into AI systems (Wang et al., 2023).

Federated learning is another privacy preserving AI method that allows people without the occurrence of centralised data collecting to analyze the data. To offer data security and privacy, Yang et al. (2023) propose that APPFLChain, which is a privacy preserving architecture combining blockchain and federated learning. According to them, this strategy can help resolve the privacy-personalization problem by allowing the delivery of customised services without compromising the user privacy. Federated learning is very helpful in Internet of Things contexts where data is sparsely distributed over lots of devices with privacy, bandwidth restrictions which make centralization infeasible. For example, Gboard's keyboard software (Kuznetsov et al., 2023) has been improved by Google using federated learning, without sending user data to their servers.

However, recent privacy preserving AI methods have lots of imperfections. According to Venkatesan and Rahayu (2023), these approaches are complex and difficult to adopt, particularly in sectors that do not have technical knowledge. Furthermore, to ensure proper regulation of the balance between privacy and efficiency to avoid compromising the efficacy of such customised services, privacy preserving AI should also be carefully included. For example, data variation between different devices, reduces the potential of federated learning, while excessive noise added to data reduces the performance of AI models in differential privacy. Furthermore, the lack of standardised frameworks for platforms that implement these strategies can generate doubts about their performance since they are not applied in a consistent manner (Bernal Bernabe et al., 2023).

3.2. Blockchain for Data Integrity

Blockchain technology is an effective data integrity tool in the HCDTs and IoT networks. That is ideally suited as a means of hiding private info and giving trust as it is decentralised and not accessible.

Blockchain makes sure that once data has been recorded, they cannot be changed nor deleted, and this can be guaranteed by blockchain's immutable ledger. However, as discussed by Nguyen et al. (2023), blockchain is an approach to ensure data integrity and can be used in the context of safe and reliable IoT data sharing. Blockchain technology can help prevent access to HCDTs by illegal ways and data manipulation, as the basis of confidence in HCDTs, so they say. Permanent data storage is critical in industries such as healthcare where wrong diagnosis and inappropriate treatment are very much dependent on the integrity of patient information. Kshetri (2023) states that a healthcare system that uses blockchain technology is MedRec, which ensures the integrity of medical records.

They are agreements that just run their own and we encode the conditions directly in the code. To provide for confidence, smart contracts could help support for accountability and transparency in the exchange of data, according to them. If used for smart contracts, smart contracts could be used to provide or revoke access to data in ways that only authorised parties can access right away. Supply chain management utilizes smart contracts to account for the reliability of products and realization of payments (Rahman et al., 2023).

Blockchain can also be used to decentralized identity management and the holders of the digital identity have full control over them, and do not rely on central authorities. In recent years, blockchain has been considered the new solution for issues related to data security, integrity, and privacy, particularly for AI driven systems, and this notion is explored by Kshetri (2023). Decentralised identity management, according to him, can help reducing the danger of fraud and identity theft, which are the two major threats in HCDT.

However, there are difficulties in implementing data integrity blockchain. In the context of IoT applications, the difficulties in scaling the blockchain systems to process colossal data volumes are pointed out by Bernal Bernabe et al. (2023). Additionally, blockchain networks could not be widely utilized due to the energy usage. As an example, Proof of Work (PoW) consensus mechanism used by Bitcoin consumes a lot of energy and is hence not suitable for extensive Internet of Things applications. However, Delegated Proof of Stake (DPoS) and Proof of Stake (PoS) are more scaling and energy efficient (Venkatesan & Rahayu, 2023).

3.3. Federated Learning and Blockchain Integration

HCDTs has great potential to be improved with federated learning of blockchain. Blockchain's security and transparency and federated learning's capacity to protect privacy combine into one method. With federated learning, data analysis is allowed, without centralised data collection, by guaranteeing that the sensitive data stays on local devices. On the other hand, they argue that service delivery customised to the user's needs can help them solve the problem between privacy and personalization. IBM's Federated AI Technology Enabler (FATE) uses federated learning to enable safe exchange of data between enterprises (Li et al., 2023).

Blockchain technology can be used to ensure your model updates are safe and secure in federated learning systems. In the works of Wang et al. (2023), blockchain is utilized for data security in the context of its capability to secure the integrity of model updates. They say that using blockchain mitigates model poisoning assaults, such as model poisoning attacks where evil actors try to alter the data inputs to training data to undermine the model. Storage of model modifications on the blockchain can guarantee that only validated updates are added to the global model. For example, the DeepChain takes the use of blockchain technology to secure federated learning in IoT contexts (Kuznetsov et al., 2023).

Federated learning and integrating blockchain improve the ability of the AI systems to account for themselves and account for what they do. Li et al. (2023) demonstrate that blockchain can facilitate trust in AI sofar as it can guarantee data integrity to AI applications. According to them, blockchain technology can aid the accountability and transparency of AI systems, as these are both vital for users' confidence. For example, blockchain can help preserve an indestructible trail of every data transaction, which users can verify the accuracy of data and AI models.

But federated learning and blockchain can't be united without several challenges to overcome. Venkatesan and Rahayu (2023) point out that the complexity of this approach may make it more difficult for some companies, mainly those with little technological knowledge. There must also be the proper addressing of the trade-offs between utility and privacy to ensure that this strategy does not sacrifice the efficiency of customised services. An example is that model updates will lead to increased computational and storage overhead in federated learning systems because the model updates are written to a blockchain (Rahman et al., 2023).

3.4. Hybrid Consensus Mechanisms

Hybrid consensus mechanism is built on top of characteristics of various consensus algorithms to provide a more secure and scalable blockchain network. Particularly for the IoT ecosystems and HCDTs, such strategy is significant since security and scalability are the top priority.

This consensus structures make use of the strengths of many algorithms, and thus hybrid consensus mechanisms enhance blockchain network security. Therefore, Venkatesan and Rahayu (2023) submit a hybrid consensus method of Proof of Work (PoW) combined with Proof of Stake (PoS) to enhance security and scalability. They would argue that this is a strategy that can prevent 51% attacks (where one party takes over the network). Hybrid consensus mechanisms take the best out of PoS and the power of PoW at the same time. In the Decred blockchain, such a consensus process is a hybrid one contributing to the improvement of decentralisation and security (Kshetri, 2023).

Moreover, hybrid consensus mechanisms can be used in blockchain networks to make them more sustainable by decreasing their energy efficiency. Kuznetsov et al. (2023) examine application of hybrid consensus mechanisms in blockchain based AI systems, where it can be shown they could reduce energy consumption.

It is not easy to implement the hybrid consensus methods. According to Bernal Bernabe et al. (2023), hybrid consensus procedures are challenging to build and to implement into practice in complex IoT systems. Besides, in order not to hurt the efficiency of blockchain networks, sensible trade-offs between security, its scalability and energy efficiency should be made. For instance, the use of PoW in hybrid consensus techniques will increase the network energy usage (Venkatesan & Rahayu, 2023).

3.5. Secure IoT Data Sharing

Secure IoT data exchange is the key framework for building confidence and protecting data in HCDTs. It involves the use of AI and blockchain technology in facilitating safe and open exchange of the data.

In the IoT environment, blockchain can enable open and safe data sharing. Nguyen et al. (2023) mention that the data integrity guaranteeing application for the safe and database IoT data exchange is possible with blockchain. According to them, blockchain technology can help in preventing illegal access and data manipulation, which are crucial to maintaining confidence in HCDTs. Integrity of the patient information is vital, for example, in fields of healthcare, where the right diagnosis and treatment depend on it. The Internet of Things (IoT) setting calls for the use of a blockchain like that of the IOTA blockchain, which is used for safe data exchange (Kshetri, 2023). With AI, it can anonymise data so that it is protected, and exchange is facilitated.

To provide a privacy preserving strategy for IoT networks, Alrayes et al (2023) used statistical learning and optimisation methods. According to them, this strategy can ensure data anonymisation at the same time as maintaining its analytical value. For example, AI communities to synthesise data that looks like the actual data but with the sensitive data hidden. For applications such as smart cities where it is necessary to share data from many sources for urban planning, AI in data confidentiality (Rahman et al., 2023) is very beneficial.

Blockchain integration with AI enables effectively improving accountability and transparency in the exchange of IoT data. According to Wang et al. (2023), blockchain technology can facilitate the accountable and transparent data sharing that both would be critical to restoring user confidence in this kind of data sharing. For example, blockchain can be used to generate an immutable trail of all data's transactions so that the users can check the correctness of the data. This strategy could be used in supply chain management procedure to guarantee product tracking transparency (Kuznetsov et al., 2023).

Putting safe IoT data sharing into practice is difficult. Since IoT applications involve massive data volumes, it is very challenging to scale blockchain systems as per Bernal Bernabe et al. (2023). To ensure that data sharing in a safe way does not undermine the effectiveness of the customised services, these trade-offs must be properly regulated. For example, integrating blockchain in data sharing might require more processing and storage overhead, on the other hand, using AI for data privacy could mean that the data is less accurate (Venkatesan & Rahayu, 2023).

CONCLUSION

This study has explored systematically the ethical challenges of a Human-Centered Digital Twin (HCDT) within an IoT ecosystem and has revealed differences between what can be technologically achieved, and what it is ethically required. In the findings, it is shown that HCDTs present breakthrough potential to transform personalization in healthcare, as well as in consumer and smart city apps, but in solving these, current frameworks fail to account for sacrifice of data privacy, risk of algorithmic bias, as well as user autonomy in smart and personal application scenarios.

Three fundamental insights are pointed out by the research. However, the traditional consent mechanisms are unable to participate with HCDTs due to their dynamic data processing so adaptive consent addressing the lack of user agency as systems change are needed. Second is the second documented cases of algorithmic bias, especially in healthcare diagnostics of urgent need for inclusive development practices and rigorous bias testing. Thirdly, the traditional security measures are insufficient in protecting HCDTs for their different vulnerabilities, which in term calls for novel protection strategies that balance privacy with the performance requirements.

To address these challenges in a technical, governance and user centered way the proposed framework is comprised of multiple layers starting by technical safeguards, followed by governance mechanisms and finally user centered design principles. However, although not successful, both unethical and ethically personalization is capable of implementation and cannot be considered impossible, due to the success of ethical personalization in some deployments and the risk of uncontrolled development in other deployments. The contrasting outcomes underscore that HCDT architecture cannot be a next thought but something that requires to be central.

Moving forward, we identify three critical priorities: (1) standardize the ethical evaluation metric, (2) optimize the cryptographic solutions to HCDT architecture, and lastly (3) enhancing the interdisciplinary relationship. HCDTs unique characteristics have to be accommodated by regulatory frameworks that will need to evolve, and sector specific guidelines have to be drawn up to concord with the different ethical considerations for applications.

Finally, this research offers support to the ideas that innovation must have its core focus be on maintaining the human values. Application of the proposed framework's recommendations will lead them to the path of the development that is not responsible – to technologies of HCDT that do not undermine but reinforce agency, equity, and basic rights of HUs. Realistic implementation, ongoing monitoring and optimization of best practices, and even more in the future as the technology is matured.

REFERENCES

Almeida, V. A. F.. (2021). Digital twins approach for smart cities: A systematic review. *Sustainable Cities and Society*, *65*, 102654.

Alrayes, F. S.. (2023). Privacy-preserving approach for IoT networks using statistical learning with optimization algorithm on high-dimensional big data environment. *Journal of Network and Computer Applications*.

Bernal Bernabe, J.. (2023). Privacy-preserving solutions for blockchain: Review and challenges. *IEEE Internet of Things Journal*.

Chen, M.. (2020). Digital twin for healthcare systems. *Digital Twin*, *1*, 3.

de Kerckhove, D. (2022). The personal digital twin, ethical considerations. Journal of Digital Ethics.

Ding, W.. (2021). Decentralized federated learning via blockchain for healthcare IoT systems. *IEEE Internet of Things Journal*, *8*(14), 11789–11801.

Emmert-Streib, F. (2019). Defining digital twins: A data science-based unification. *Journal of Industrial Information Integration*.

Emmert-Streib, F. (2021). Digital twins in healthcare: Opportunities and challenges. *Health Informatics Journal*.

Fontes, C., & Carpentras, D. (2023). *Human digital twins unlocking Society 5.0? Approaches, emerging risks and disruptions*. Urban Technology Journal.

Goethals, S.. (2022). *The impact of cloaking digital footprints on user privacy and personalization*. Data Science Review.

Goodfellow, I.. (2014). Generative adversarial nets. *Advances in Neural Information Processing Systems*, , 2672–2680.

Helbing, D., & Sánchez-Vaquerizo, J. A. (2022). Digital twins: Potentials, limitations, and ethical issues. *Nature Computational Science*, *2*(1), 10–12. PMID: 38177712

Ijaiya, H. (2023). Balancing data privacy and technology advancements: Navigating ethical challenges and shaping policy solutions. Journal of Technology Law & Policy.

Kaaniche, N.. (2023). Privacy enhancing technologies for solving the privacy-personalization paradox: Taxonomy and survey. *IEEE Transactions on Information Forensics and Security*.

Kshetri, N. (2023). Blockchain and AI: Driving the future of data security and business intelligence. *Journal of Business Research*.

Kuznetsov, A., et al. (2023). On the integration of artificial intelligence and blockchain technology: A perspective about security. Journal of Cybersecurity and Privacy.

Lauer-Schmaltz, M. W.. (2023). *ETHICA: Designing human digital twins—A systematic review and proposed methodology*. AI Ethics Journal.

Li, Z.. (2023). An overview of AI and blockchain integration for privacy-preserving. *Journal of Network and Computer Applications.*

Lin, Y.. (2023). Human digital twin: A survey. *IEEE Internet of Things Journal.*

Liu, Y.. (2021). Federated learning meets blockchain in edge computing: Opportunities and challenges. *IEEE Internet of Things Journal*, *8*(16), 12806–12825. DOI: 10.1109/JIOT.2021.3072611

Lu, Y. (2021). Security and privacy of Internet of Things: A review of challenges and solutions. *Journal of Cybersecurity.*

München, S. (2019). The digital twin theory—A new view on a buzzword. Journal of Digital Transformation.

Nguyen, B. L.. (2023). Privacy-preserving blockchain technique to achieve secure and reliable sharing of IoT data. *IEEE Internet of Things Journal.*

O'Neil, C. (2016). *Weapons of math destruction: How big data increases inequality and threatens democracy*. Crown.

Occhipinti, E.. (2023). Human body digital twin: A master plan for healthcare simulations. *Journal of Medical Systems.*

Owen, A., & Moore, J. (2023). Ethical considerations in AI-driven e-commerce solutions: Balancing personalization and privacy. *Journal of Business Ethics.*

Pinto, G. P.. (2023). A systematic review on privacy-aware IoT personal data stores. *IEEE Internet of Things Journal.*

Popa, E. O.. (2023). The use of digital twins in healthcare: Socio-ethical benefits and risks. *Journal of Medical Ethics.*

Rahman, Z., et al. (2023). Blockchain-based AI-enabled Industry 4.0 CPS protection against advanced persistent threat. Journal of Cybersecurity and Privacy.

Reza, J.. (2023). Balancing customer personalization and data privacy using advanced analytics. *Journal of Data Science : JDS.*

Saliju, L., & Deboi, V. (2023). Unraveling the paradox: Balancing personalization and privacy in AI-driven technologies. *AI & Society.*

Siddika, A., & Zhao, L. (2023). Enhancing trust and reliability in AI and ML: Assessing blockchain's potential to ensure data integrity and security. Journal of Trust Management.

Sirigu, G.. (2023). *Privacy and security issues for human digital twins*. IEEE Transactions on Trust and Privacy.

Tang, C.. (2023). Human body digital twin: A master plan. *IEEE Journal of Biomedical and Health Informatics.*

Tapsell, J., et al. (2023). Consumer-centric data control, tracking, and transparency. Journal of Information Security.

Tawalbeh, L.. (2023). IoT privacy and security: Challenges and solutions. *IEEE Communications Surveys and Tutorials.*

Tschorsch, F., & Scheuermann, B. (2016). Bitcoin and beyond: A technical survey on decentralized digital currencies. *IEEE Communications Surveys and Tutorials, 18*(3), 2084–2123. DOI: 10.1109/COMST.2016.2535718

Van der Aalst, W. M. P. (2016). *Process mining: Data science in action.* Springer. DOI: 10.1007/978-3-662-49851-4

Venkatesan, K., & Rahayu, S. B. (2023). Blockchain security enhancement: An approach towards hybrid consensus algorithms and machine learning techniques. *Journal of Network and Computer Applications.*

Vera-Arenas, M. (2019). Digital transformation through AI and blockchain integration. Journal of Digital Innovation.

Wang, K.. (2023). Securing data with blockchain and AI. *IEEE Internet of Things Journal.*

Yang, J. T.. (2023). APPFLChain: A privacy protection distributed artificial-intelligence architecture based on federated learning and consortium blockchain. *Journal of Network and Computer Applications.*

Zhou, S., et al. (2023). A user-centered framework for data privacy protection using large language models and attention mechanisms. Journal of Cybersecurity and Privacy.

Zyskind, G., & Nathan, O. (2015). Decentralizing privacy: Using blockchain to protect personal data. 2015 IEEE Security and Privacy Workshops, 180-184.

ADDITIONAL READING

Abadi, M.. (2016). Deep learning with differential privacy. *Proceedings of the 2016 ACM SIGSAC Conference on Computer and Communications Security*, 308-318. DOI: 10.1145/2976749.2978318

Andoni, M., Robu, V., Flynn, D., Abram, S., Geach, D., Jenkins, D., McCallum, P., & Peacock, A. (2019). Blockchain technology in the energy sector: A systematic review of challenges and opportunities. *Renewable & Sustainable Energy Reviews, 100*, 143–174. DOI: 10.1016/j.rser.2018.10.014

Barricelli, B. R.. (2019). Digital twins and virtual reality in healthcare: A systematic literature review. *IEEE Access : Practical Innovations, Open Solutions, 7*, 147453–147471.

Bonomi, F.. (2012). Fog computing and its role in the internet of things. *Proceedings of the First Edition of the MCC Workshop on Mobile Cloud Computing*, 13-16. DOI: 10.1145/2342509.2342513

Dhar, S. (2020). The carbon impact of artificial intelligence. *Nature Machine Intelligence, 2*(8), 423–425. DOI: 10.1038/s42256-020-0219-9

Fullerton, J. N.. (2020). Digital twins in healthcare: Is it the beginning of a new era of evidence-based medicine? *Critical Care, 24*(1), 1–4. PMID: 31898531

Gadekallu, T. R., Pham, Q.-V., Nguyen, D. C., Maddikunta, P. K. R., Deepa, N., Prabadevi, B., Pathirana, P. N., Zhao, J., & Hwang, W.-J. (2021). Blockchain for edge of things: Applications, opportunities, and challenges. *IEEE Internet of Things Journal*, *9*(2), 964–988. DOI: 10.1109/JIOT.2021.3119639

Grieves, M. (2016). *Origins of the digital twin concept*. Florida Institute of Technology.

Gürdür, D.. (2019). Digital twins: Bridging physical space and cyberspace. *Computer*, *52*(12), 58–67. DOI: 10.1109/MC.2019.2942803

Jones, D.. (2020). Characterising the digital twin: A systematic literature review. *Advanced Engineering Informatics*, *45*, 101098.

Kaplan, A., & Haenlein, M. (2019). Siri, Siri, in my hand: Who's the fairest in the land? On the interpretations, illustrations, and implications of artificial intelligence. *Business Horizons*, *62*(1), 15–25. DOI: 10.1016/j.bushor.2018.08.004

Madakam, S., Ramaswamy, R., & Tripathi, S. (2019). Internet of Things (IoT): A literature review. *Journal of Computer and Communications*, *3*(5), 164–173. DOI: 10.4236/jcc.2015.35021

Panetta, K. (2021). *Gartner top strategic technology trends for 2022*. Gartner Research.

Pasquale, F. (2015). *The black box society: The secret algorithms that control money and information*. Harvard University Press. DOI: 10.4159/harvard.9780674736061

Ribeiro, M. T., ... (2016). "Why should I trust you?" Explaining the predictions of any classifier. Proceedings of the 22nd ACM SIGKDD International Conference on Knowledge Discovery and Data Mining, 1135-1144.

Sivarajah, U., Kamal, M. M., Irani, Z., & Weerakkody, V. (2020). Critical analysis of Big Data challenges and analytical methods. *Journal of Business Research*, *70*, 263–286. DOI: 10.1016/j.jbusres.2016.08.001

Yaqoob, I.. (2021). Blockchain for healthcare data management: Opportunities, challenges, and future recommendations. *Neural Computing & Applications*, •••, 1–16.

Zhang, Y.. (2020). Blockchain and federated learning for privacy-preserved data sharing in industrial IoT. *IEEE Transactions on Industrial Informatics*, *16*(6), 4177–4186. DOI: 10.1109/TII.2019.2942190

Chapter 11
Integrating Virtual and Physical Systems to Improve Simulation 6G's Effect on Digital Twin and IoT Connectivity

Indra kishor
https://orcid.org/0009-0007-8617-1335
Poornima Institute of Engineering and Technology, India

Harish Reddy Gantla
https://orcid.org/0009-0005-8307-7883
Vignan Institute of Technology and Science, Hyderabad, India

Mude Sreenivasulu
Kishkinda University, Ballari, India

Udit Mamodiya
https://orcid.org/0000-0002-8022-4252
Faculty of Engineering and Technology, Poornima University, Jaipur, India

ABSTRACT

This DT integration with IoT technologies has greatly evolved the ways by which the operation of various industries can be simulated, monitored, and optimized. As of now, the major obstacles to these network technologies in real-world deployment involve latency in networking, limited bandwidth, and incompatible devices. It is on these fronts that the eventual 6G networks could fill the gap and potentially revolutionize digital twin and IoT coordination by having a seamless virtual connection between the two physical systems under simulation. The chapter presents a new 6G-powered framework that will solve the real-time synchronization, dynamic adaptability, and predictive accuracy problems of Digital Twin ecosystems. Based on the 6G features, the proposed framework allows for real-time data transmission, multi-twin collaboration, and edge-AI processing to optimize resources.

DOI: 10.4018/979-8-3373-2028-1.ch011

1. INTRODUCTION

Advancements in technology in the 21st century have led to unbelievable transformations across the industries. These technologies have changed the way industries function, giving organizations the ability to simulate, monitor, and optimize complex processes with unmatched precision. However, with present network technologies including 4G and 5G, there is limited development of the true potential of Digital Twin and IoT systems. For instance, a high level of latency, limited bandwidth, and the incompatibility to integrate them without causing interruptions hinder its practical implementation. It, therefore, implies that 6G network systems can open the way toward achieving ultra-low latency, a wide bandwidth, and increased reliability. It eradicates all of the previous problems in the existing networks, bringing forward advanced digital twin ecosystems on scales. The Chapter explores how this 6G technology would evolve the Digital Twin and IoT co-collaboration systems as it looks toward integrating the digital and physical ecosystems that serve for advanced simulation and optimization for operations (Crespo-Aguado et al., 2024).

Digital Twins and IoT are transformational technologies that constitute the very foundation of the modern industrial system. IoT acts as the sensory layer that captures real-time data from the physical environment by sensors and devices. This is fed into the Digital Twins, which use advanced computational models to replicate, analyze, and predict the behavior of physical systems. The integration has opened up many possibilities in manufacturing, healthcare, logistics, and urban planning. For instance, for manufacturing, a digital twin stimulates the production line. Organizations can then optimize the workflow, reduce downtime, and predict equipment failure. The same goes with healthcare - Digital Twins of a patient can facilitate personalized treatment planning and early diagnosis. Logistics also gets IoT-enabled Digital Twin, which optimizes supply chain operation, reduced delays, and minimized costs (Clifton et al., 2024). In theory, though, the efficiency and scalability of the Digital Twin-IoT systems depend directly on the network infrastructure in place. Current networks can't keep pace with the ever-growing demand of real-time synchronization and huge data processing; hence, next-generation communication technology is highly needed. There are various challenges that affect the integration of Digital Twin and IoT systems (Yeshwanth, 2024). These include Real-time responsiveness of the system that is crucial for Digital Twin operations, especially in dynamic environments. However, the existing networks often suffer from latency issues that resulted in delays in data updates and reduced simulation accuracy. Also the bandwidth Limitations in massive data generation by IoT devices, that create bottlenecks in the transmission of data. Energy Consumption: Computational and communication-intensive, Digital Twin-IoT systems consume lots of energy, posing a challenge in sustainability for such large-scale deployment. Data Security and Privacy: Due to the sensitivity of the large data volume transmitted by these systems, it is quite vulnerable to cyberattacks. Safe transmission and storage of data will be a serious concern (Yigit et al., 2024). They also demand a power and advanced form of communication infrastructures, to which 6G networks provide solutions. They demand a power and advanced form of communication infrastructures for which 6G networks would provide solutions. 6G is the upcoming sixth generation in wireless communication technologies that are revolutionizing connectivity since they have tackled the shortcomings experienced in its former generations. With speeds of 100 times or more than the speed of 5G, and latency under one millisecond, 6G will have what it takes for real-time applications in large scale Digital Twin and IoT systems. Key features will include: The core of this technology is bringing together physical and virtual systems with the help of Digital Twins - virtual replicas for physical assets built from real-time data from various IoT devices on their behavior for simulation and predictability (Yuan et al.,

2024). However, it is realized that the implementation of seamless connectivity between physical and virtual systems to optimize operations requires cost-cutting efforts and betterment in decision making. This infrastructure is provided with 6G networks. For example, in a smart factory, the IoT sensors placed on the machine collect data pertaining to temperature, vibration, and energy consumption. This data is then transmitted to a Digital Twin, which simulates the machine's performance in different conditions (Pandey et al., 2024). Based on this simulation, a factory can predict equipment failures and optimize energy use, thus improving efficiency in production. With 6G's ultra-low latency and high bandwidth, these processes could be carried out in real-time and provide accurate, timely insights. Digital Twin and IoT integration with 6G has transformative applications in various domains:

1. Smart Manufacturing: 6G networks allow real-time monitoring and optimization of production lines reducing downtime and efficiency. The application and interaction of Digital Twins can simulate different production scenarios so that manufacturers will identify the cost-effective solutions.
2. Healthcare: 6G Digital Twins, therefore, help healthcare to model patients in real time. Wearable IoT devices could, for example, continue monitoring heart rate, blood pressure, and oxygen levels and transmit data in sync with the patient's Digital Twin to allow tailored treatment planning.
3. Logistics and Supply Chains: 6G makes supply chain operations more visible, enabling Digital Twins to plan the most efficient routes, track inventory, and lower delivery time. Thereby, the associated costs are saved significantly and customer satisfaction is improved considerably
4. Smart Cities: The urban planners can simulate traffic, energy consumption, and infrastructure usage using 6G-enabled Digital Twins to have more efficient and sustainable cities.
5. Energy Management: Digital Twins of power grids integrated with IoT sensors and 6G networks would enable real-time monitoring and optimization of energy distribution, reducing wastage and increasing sustainability.

Future Potential and Emerging Trends

6G with Digital Twin and IoT systems is at a nascent stage, but the potential is enormous. Emerging trends include Multi-Twin Collaboration: The dynamic interaction of multiple Digital Twins, made possible by 6G, opens up new possibilities for cross-domain optimization. For instance, a smart factory Twin can collaborate with a logistics Twin to optimize supply chain operations (Han et al., 2024). AI-Driven Automation: Digital Twins could be made self-adaptive in 6G networks through the embedding of AI, thereby continuously learning new data and adapting its performance in real time. Quantum Computing: Combining 6G with quantum computing might help Digital Twins simulate highly complex tasks that currently lie beyond human reach (Qadir et al., 2024). Sustainability Efforts: The design of 6G will be energy efficient and optimize industrial processes, further supporting global goals toward carbon reduction and resource preservation. The pattern of evolution of Industry 4.0 has witnessed continuous growth in dependency on data-driven technologies for improving operational efficiency, minimizing cost, and achieving sustainability. The heart of this change lies in the integration of DT and IoT (Faye et al., 2024). These two enable the organization to progress from reactive to predictive and prescriptive modes of operation. However, with more complex and interconnected systems, the limitations of existing network infrastructure have been exposed. This is where 6G networks come in, offering unprecedented communication capabilities to bridge the gap between physical and virtual domains (Wang et al., 2023). Digital Twin is a term dating back to NASA's Apollo program in the 1970s, which applied virtual models for monitoring and simulating spacecraft systems. The Digital Twins of yesteryears, over time, with progress in computing power, sensor technology, and data analytics, transformed into dynamic and real-time systems, now serving as a keystone for the operation of modern industries. The IoT model too has transformed from simple M2M communication to a sophisticated ecosystem enabling billions of devices globally. Still, the ability of digital twin and IoT systems to provide actionable insights is normally hindered by the constraints of data latency, synchronization, and device interoperability (Hevesli et al., 2024). The integration of Digital Twins and IoT devices is vital in creating an overall ecosystem that ties real-world data to virtual simulations, where the outputs from simulations inform real operations. Integration will be key to industries that heavily depend on making real-time decisions. This includes industries like autonomous transportation, healthcare, and manufacturing. In autonomous vehicles, Digital Twins simulate traffic conditions, vehicle performance, and route optimization, requiring continuous data from IoT sensors for accuracy. In healthcare, IoT-enabled Digital Twins of patients need real-time physiological data for accurate diagnoses and treatment plans. IoT sensors on production lines in manufacturing give data that Digital Twins use to simulate workflow optimizations, predict equipment failures, and reduce downtime. The 5G and 4G networks do not achieve the required integration in such networks due to a huge volume of data, ultra-low latency, and reliability; the current network cannot support it. This emphasizes how important the role of 6G networks will be in promoting the ecosystems of Digital Twin and IoT (Mamodiya & Tiwari, 2023a). Whereas Industry 4.0 is primarily based on automation and data exchange, Industry 5.0 focuses on human-centric systems integrating advanced technologies with human creativity and decision-making capabilities. In this regard, 6G networks are the underpinning of hyperconnected ecosystems in which Digital Twins, IoT devices, and human operators seamlessly collaborate. Key aspects of 6G's role in Industry 5.0 include: Hyper-Connectivity: Connecting billions of devices through ultra-reliable communication will mean that every facet of an industrial ecosystem is well integrated and perfectly synchronized. Human-in-the-Loop Systems: 6G networks provide for real-time feedback loops between the Digital Twins and human operators for better decision-making in complex situations. More stylized Data Visualization: With the huge bandwidth of 6G, augmented reality (AR) and virtual reality (VR) will be embedded in Digital Twin systems to portray intuitive interaction and control (Bozkaya et al., 2023). The impact of 6G goes beyond the acceleration of speed and latency reduction; it introduces novel paradigms to how physical and virtual systems will interact. Among these are: Multi-Dimensional Simulations: Given the computational power and data handling capabilities of 6G, Digital Twins can be designed with multiple dimensions like thermal, mechanical, and electrical properties, hence more comprehensive simulations. Proactive Decision Making - Because of low latency, the Digital Twins in 6G shift from reactive to proactive thinking; that is, potential problems are predicted and solved well before they happen. Collaborative Digital Twin Ecosystems: 6G allows for the seamless interaction of multiple Digital Twins across domains, such as a factory Twin coordinating with supply chain Twins to optimize production schedules and delivery logistics. Edge-AI Integration: 6G enables the processing of AI at the edge, so that Digital Twins process and analyze data locally, without much dependency on centralized systems and also improve response times (Du & Luo, 2023).

One of the most promising aspects of integrating 6G with Digital Twin and IoT systems is its potential to drive sustainability initiatives. It enables precise resource management and reduces waste, thus contributing to global efforts to combat climate change. Some examples include: Energy Optimization: Digital Twins of the power grid, backed by IoT sensors and 6G networks, will allow real-time monitoring of energy distribution optimization and reduce wastage. Carbon Emission Reduction: Industries can use Digital Twins to simulate and implement carbon-reduction strategies, such as optimizing supply chain routes or switching to renewable energy sources. Circular Economy Models: 6G-enabled digital twins enable following materials throughout all of their lifetime cycles, that makes it a better support of transition to a circular economy system. Some of the sectors, where integration with 6G, Digital Twin, and IoT will change industries completely, include: Autonomous Transportation: It will allow V2V and V2I in real-time in 6G networks, allowing the accuracy of autonomous vehicles. Disaster Management: The digital twins of cities, coupled with real-time IoT data and 6G connectivity, can simulate and manage responses to natural disasters like earthquakes or floods. Healthcare: 6G-enabled Digital Twins of patients, along with AI-based diagnostic services, will detect the diseases in a much earlier and personalized manner, resulting in better patient outcomes.

2. LITERATURE REVIEW

Digital Twin Technology, IoT, and it has been able to transform the traditional industrial system into real data-driven, highly efficient ecosystems. Digital twins are virtual copies of physical systems that can monitor, predict, and optimize their operations in real time, as realistic as possible. If connected to IoT, which acts as a layer that senses and communicates with the virtual model, it receives constant data from the physical system, making the simulation as accurate and actionable as it could be. This synergy has spurred huge improvements in industries like manufacturing, healthcare, logistics, and urban development. As reported by existing literature, Digital Twins help improve efficiency in operations, minimizing risks that could be mitigated through decision-making in real-time. Examples include manufacturing processes: The simulation of a production line on Digital Twins to predict failures of machinery equipment, optimizing workflow patterns. Then there are the IoT devices receiving appropriate information from the digital models. These have network limitations, which, at times, could be really slow with large latency and even bandwidth issues coupled with device-to-device interoperability problems. These challenges mandate the use of advanced communication technologies to fully utilize the potential in Digital Twin and IoT systems (Ridhawi et al., 2023).

Challenges in Current Digital Twin-IoT Integration

The literature mentions several major barriers to the assimilation of Digital Twin and IoT technologies:

1. Latency and Real-Time Responsiveness Real-time simulation and decision making are crucial for Digital Twins; however, present networks' latency, even at 5G speed, prevents such real-time response. It mostly impacts those areas that demand near-instantaneous data processing - autonomous transportation and health care, among others (Lin et al., 2023).
2. Scalability Issues: Large numbers of devices usually characterize an IoT ecosystem and generate large amounts of data. Digital Twin systems are, therefore, normally scalable, as the current networks cannot handle the variety of data without bottlenecks and delays efficiently (Lin et al., 2023).
3. Interoperability and Standardization: There is an IoT device diversity with differing protocols and platforms, which causes a challenge for seamless integration. Lack of standardization results in inefficiencies in data exchange and stifles potential collaboration of the Digital Twins (Lin et al., 2023).

4. Energy Efficiency and Sustainability: Computational and communication demands exhibited by Digital Twin-IoT systems carry prohibitive energy consumption relative to sustaining the goal of sustainability pursued by these technologies. Data Security and Privacy: Such vast amounts of sensitive data being transmitted between IoT devices and Digital Twins create vulnerabilities to cyberattacks. Data integrity and security are a major concern in large-scale deployments (Lv et al., 2022).

Emerging network technologies such as 5G and 6G are perceived as critical enablers in overcoming the challenges associated with the deployment of Digital Twin and IoT systems. Even though 5G has made a lot of difference on the aspects of bandwidth and latency, in ultra-low latency and massive machine-to-machine communication scenarios, it was still found to be lacking (Lv et al., 2022). Literature suggests that 6G networks have the advanced capability to bridge these gaps and transform Digital Twin ecosystems. URLLC: Real-time synchronization of physical systems with their Digital Twins is possible only when latency is low, at just one millisecond, and dynamic simulations are also accurate. mMTC: 6G networks are capable of accommodating billions of IoT devices at one time, so they are great for large industrial deployments. eMBB: The high bandwidth is useful for more complex simulations being processed and visualized by the Digital Twins, with greater fidelity and speed. AI Integration: The architecture of 6G is focused on AI and includes core elements for intelligent network management and dynamic allocation of resources (Malav et al., 2019). Energy Efficiency: Digital Twin-IoT ecosystems reduce the energy footprint through optimized network operations and edge computing supported by 6G. The integration of 6G networks with the system of Digital Twins and Internet of Things has transformative applications in multiple domains, such as:

1. Smart Manufacturing: literature shows the integration of Digital Twins in simulating and optimising manufacturing processes. With 6G, the related simulations get more dynamic and accurate, enabling real-time adjustments as well as predictive maintenance.
2. Healthcare: Patients' IoT-enabled Digital Twins need frequent updates from wearables to mirror physiological conditions. 6G is an ultra-low-latency technology with data transmission which will enable rapid diagnosis and individually tailored treatment options.
3. Transportation Systems and Autonomous Vehicles: Autonomous transportation systems rely heavily on real-time V2V and V2I communication. Hence, 6G is fundamental in ensuring communication is reliable with minimum latencies for security and efficiency reasons.
4. Urban Planning and Smart Cities: Digital Twins of cities, merged with IoT and 6G networks, permit urban planners to simulate and regulate traffic, energy consumption, and infrastructure usage in real time.
5. Energy Management: Literature describes the possibility that Digital Twins have in optimizing the power grid. With the support of IoT sensors and 6G connectivity, wastage can be minimized by dynamically changing the power distribution.

Emerging trends that are shaping the future of 6G-enabled Digital Twin and IoT systems include:

Multi-Twin Collaboration: The area of research concerning the dynamic interaction of multiple Digital Twins is quite promising. For instance, the manufacturing Digital Twin can collaborate with supply chain Twins to optimize the production and delivery schedules (Ahmadi et al., 2021). AI-Driven Digital Twins:

With the aid of AI, a self-adaptive 6G network enables Digital Twins to learn based on real-time data and enhances its performance based on autonomous development. Quantum Computing: The literature addresses how quantum computing could be employed for the optimization of simulation potential by Digital Twins. These are, particularly in domains that are difficult, such as health and aeronautics (Lu et al., 2020). Blockchain for Data Security: Blockchain technology is being adopted as an emerging solution to ensure safe and transparent data exchange in 6G-enabled IoT ecosystems. Sustainability Strategies: According to researchers, 6G Digital Twins will help in attaining global sustainability objectives through efficient resource utilization and minimum carbon footprint (Khan et al., 2022). Another problem where Digital Twin and IoT systems present a challenge includes making seamless interoperability between different heterogeneous devices, platforms, and protocols. The reviewed literature points towards the lack of standardized frameworks, which hampers the data exchange and information communication in both systems, with limited scalability in their effectiveness. However, interoperability-related issues arise based on the main reason that multiple manufacturers develop individual IoT devices on varying proprietary protocols, data formats. This creates silos, making it difficult to integrate data streams into a unified Digital Twin ecosystem (Elahi & Tokaldany, 2021). These opportunities in 6G networks help to overcome these challenges by allowing universal communication standards. Advanced middleware solutions and protocol converters, supported by 6G, can provide seamless integration of heterogeneous IoT devices. In addition, the high bandwidth and low latency in 6G enable real-time data aggregation and processing, which minimizes the effects of interoperability challenges on system performance. Standardization efforts in 6G are also on the rise. Industries can ensure that IoT devices and Digital Twins can interact efficiently by adopting unified communication protocols and data formats. Future research should focus on developing open-source frameworks and middleware solutions that leverage 6G capabilities to address interoperability concerns (Ayoobkhan et al., 2021).

These vast data transmissions in 6G-enabled Digital Twin-IoT systems significantly raise questions about data security and privacy. Literature explicitly presents vulnerabilities with IoT devices that mostly do not enjoy strong security features and have vulnerabilities that attract cyberattacks. Consequences of such breaches involve unauthorized access, tampering with real-time simulations of Digital Twins, which can be very severe, especially in critical sectors like healthcare and infrastructure (Lee et al., 2020).

Blockchain Technology: Blockchain is being seen as one of the most promising solutions to ensure secure data transmission in 6G-enabled IoT ecosystems. It can provide a decentralized and immutable ledger that ensures data integrity and prevents unauthorized access. AI-Driven Threat Detection: The integration of AI into 6G networks enables the real-time detection and mitigation of cyber threats. AI models can analyze the patterns of network traffic to find anomalies and potential security breaches. Data Encryption and Access Control: Literature underlines that advanced encryption techniques and multi-factor authentication mechanisms will be required for the secure transfer of data and access. Edge Security: By processing sensitive information at the edge, instead of in centralized systems, 6G networks will provide a way for reducing the threats of data breach. Edge security frameworks may have secure boot, trusted execution environments, or hardware-based encryption (Mamodiya & Tiwari, 2023b; Souza et al., 2019).

Energy efficiency and sustainability: The high computational and communication demands of Digital Twin and IoT systems create challenges for energy efficiency. The literature shows that the energy consumption of IoT devices, data centers, and communication networks significantly contributes to the carbon footprint of these systems. This goes against the sustainability goals often associated with Digital

Twin and IoT applications. 6G is designed with energy efficiency at its core. Some of the features that contribute to sustainability are:

Energy-Efficient Hardware: The development of low-power IoT devices and communication modules compatible with 6G networks with semiconductor technology.

Edge Computing: Edge computing has eliminated the need for data transmission to the central server in most cases, which is highly energy-hungry.

AI-Driven Optimization: AI models deployed in 6G networks will optimize resource utilization and energy usage, making sure that devices and systems work with maximum efficiency. Renewable Energy Integration: The literature also presents the possibility of integrating renewable sources of energy such as solar and wind power in 6G infrastructure. This will further minimize the environmental impact of Digital Twin and IoT ecosystems (Mamodiya et al., 2018; Anadkat et al., 2024).

Case Studies and Applications

1. The transformation potential of 6G-enabled Digital Twin and IoT systems can be best expressed in real applications. A few case studies available in the literature reflect their effectiveness as follows:
    1. Smart Manufacturing: A smart factory case study demonstrated how 6G-enabled Digital Twins cut downtime by 40% through real-time monitoring and predictive maintenance. IoT sensors continuously gave updates on the performance of the equipment, whereas a Digital Twin simulated different scenarios to determine optimal operational parameters.
    2. Health care: In a healthcare domain, 6G-powered digital twins of the patients could detect major critical conditions at an early time, such as heart disease, using IoT objects like wearable sensors, which gathered real-time data of physiological parameters with AI models into the digital twins.
    3. Smart Cities: Urban planners made use of 6G-enabled Digital Twins for traffic flow optimization in a dense metropolitan region. Real-time data was captured through IoT sensors placed on roads and vehicles to be fed into the Digital Twin to simulate and execute dynamic traffic management.
    4. Energy Management: A power grid operator leveraged the capabilities of 6G networks for monitoring and optimizing real-time energy distribution. The Digital Twin simulated the load-balancing scenarios for various grid components to reduce wastage of energy and increase reliability.

As 6G network rollout is being gained pace, according to literature identified some emerging trends and research issues are listed here:

1.Hybrid Digital Twin Systems: Integrate physical and virtual systems along with AI and QC for simulation enhancement purposes.
2.Dynamic Multi-Twin Ecosystems: This is an application for real time interaction among more than one twin in multiple domain environments through different frameworks.
3.Sustainability Metrics: Establish standard metric to assess environment impact through enabling 6G Digital Twin
4.Human-Centric Applications: Expand the use of Digital Twins in human experiences like personalized health and immersive virtual spaces.

5. Regulatory and Ethical Considerations: Regulation of issues associated with data security, privacy, and fairness and access to 6G technology.

2.1 Gaps in Literature

Despite the high levels of maturity of Digital Twin and IoT systems, several significant gaps have emerged from the literature, which are important to address for realizing their full potential. This shows where there is a necessity for research and development to overcome current limitations to achieve transformative applications.

1. Limited Exploration of 6G in Digital Twin Ecosystems

Although there is a great deal of literature on the integration of IoT with Digital Twins, sparse research focuses directly on the contribution of 6G networks in enhancing these ecosystems. Most works focus on 5G networks, which are a significant leap from previous generations but still cannot support the ultra-low latency and massive connectivity that large-scale deployments of Digital Twins require. The present study does not conduct an in-depth analysis on how the features of 6G, including mMTC and URLLC, can help to address the above challenges and make real-time, high-fidelity simulations possible (Anadkat et al., 2024).

2. Inadequate Focus on Multi-Twin Collaboration

While the idea of multi-twin ecosystems, which consists of many interacting Digital Twins, has been advanced, research into practical applications is very scarce. Most works concentrate on standalone Digital Twins for particular domains like manufacturing or healthcare and do not address the possible interplay of these Digital Twins across different domains. For instance, how the interaction between a manufacturing Digital Twin and a logistics Digital Twin could help optimize supply chain operations remains an area that is barely touched upon (Florescu, 2024).

3. Insufficient Attention to Interoperability Challenges

Interoperability is still one of the significant barriers to Digital Twin and IoT integration, though existing literature lacks solutions that are comprehensive in overcoming this problem. Most studies accept the heterogeneity of IoT devices and protocols but fail to provide standardized frameworks or middleware solutions to facilitate seamless communication. The lack of focus on universal data standards and protocols limits the scalability and efficiency of these systems, especially in industries with high device heterogeneity (Cho & Noh, 2024).

4. Lack of Comprehensive Security Frameworks

The vulnerabilities of IoT systems and Digital Twins are well-known, yet a challenge remains in the development of robust, scalable security frameworks that cater to 6G-enabled ecosystems. The present studies mainly focus on isolated security measures such as encryption or authentication that are nothing but isolated solutions for the larger task of protecting a chained ecosystem. Moreover, the application potential of blockchain technologies toward ensuring data integrity within these ecosystems has not yet been explored (Visconti et al., 2024).

5. Minimal Research on Sustainability Metrics

Despite the importance of sustainability as a key driver for adopting Digital Twin and IoT systems, very little research exists on quantifiable sustainability metrics. Most studies are qualitative in highlighting energy efficiency and waste reduction, without establishing any standardized benchmarks to measure the environmental impact of such systems. This gap makes it difficult to assess the true sustainability benefits of 6G-powered Digital Twin ecosystems (Anadkat et al., 2024).

6. Underexplored Role of AI and Edge Computing

Integration of AI and edge computing with 6G networks is yet to be well explored in real-time analytics and decision-making within Digital Twin systems. Existing literature does not provide detailed frameworks or methodologies on how to deploy AI-driven edge computing solutions in large-scale ecosystems of Digital Twins. Additionally, the potential of realizing AI combined with 6G has not been fully achieved in enhancing adaptability and scalability within a system (Florescu, 2024).

7. Limited Case Studies and Real-World Applications

Most of the work done to date is purely theoretical or based on simulation studies. There are not many real case studies validating the proposed methodologies, and this gap is what makes it hard to assess the practical feasibility and scalability of Digital Twin and IoT systems, especially in complex high-density environments like smart cities or autonomous transportation networks (Cho & Noh, 2024).

8. Ethical and Regulatory Considerations

These have been the neglected ethical and regulatory implications of 6G-enabled Digital Twin ecosystems. Issues such as data privacy, equitable access to technology, and environmental impact require much more attention in the literature as these systems get more integrated into critical infrastructure (Visconti et al., 2024).

The identified gaps raise a critical imperative for broad research and innovation to fill the existing gaps in existing Digital Twin and IoT systems. Such areas include 6G integration, multi-twin collaboration, interoperability, security, sustainability, and real-world validation of the system. This chapter is a step toward bridging some of the gaps by exploring the role of 6G networks in advancing the Digital Twin ecosystem and proposing solutions to overcome existing challenges.

3. METHODOLOGY

This chapter presents a robust methodology for the integration of 6G networks with DT and IoT ecosystems via emphasis on real-time simulation, seamless data exchange, and operational scalability. The proposed methodology addresses the current limitations such as latency, bandwidth, and device interoperability and further proposes novel frameworks to enhance the collaborative potential of digital twins. Below is an expansion and detailed description of the methodology with discussions on the relevance and the proposed work.

Figure 1. Workflow of the 6G-Enabled Digital Twin and IoT Integration Framework.

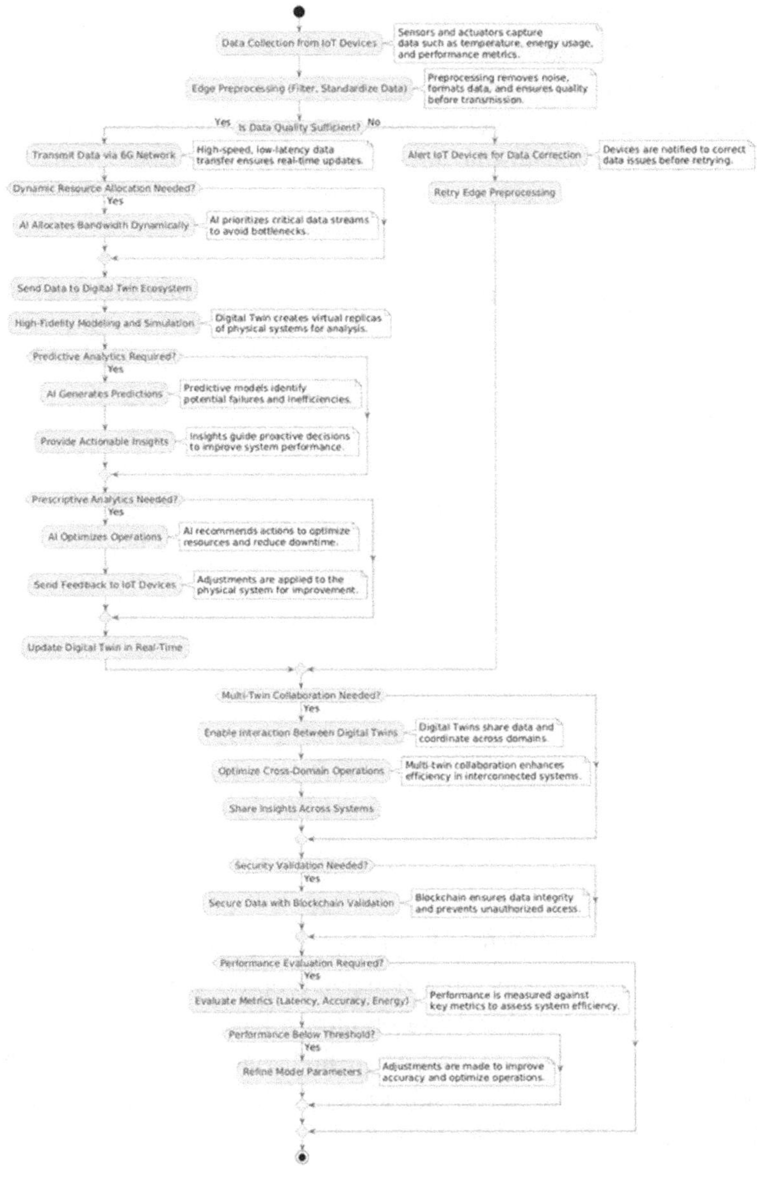

Figure 1 illustrates this flowchart on how the methodology in implementing 6G networks using Digital Twin and IoT ecosystems is applied, which comprises data collection, preprocessing, real-time simulation, predictive and prescriptive analytics, multi-twin collaboration, security validation using blockchain, and performance evaluation.

3.1 System Architecture Design

The proposed architecture integrates three interconnected layers: Physical (IoT Devices), Communication (6G Network), and Virtual (Digital Twins), to create a seamless ecosystem. Each layer is designed to fulfill specific roles in the data collection, communication, and simulation pipeline.

1. **Physical Layer (IoT Devices):**
2. **Communication Layer (6G Network):**
3. **Virtual Layer (Digital Twin Ecosystem):**
4. **Multi-Twin Collaboration:** Enables cross-domain Digital Twin interactions to optimize interdependent systems, such as manufacturing and supply chain operations.

Figure 2. System Architecture Design for 6G-Enabled Digital Twin and IoT Ecosystems.

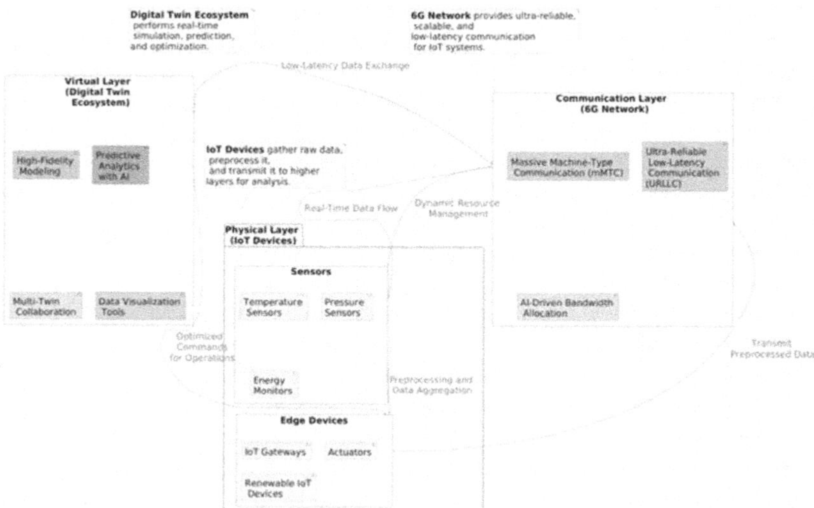

Figure 2 represents the hierarchical architecture of 6G-enabled Digital Twin and IoT systems in three key layers: the Physical Layer, where data collection and preprocessing occur through IoT sensors and edge devices; the Communication Layer, relying on ultra-reliable low-latency 6G networks to ensure efficient data transmission; and the Virtual Layer, where high-fidelity modeling, predictive analytics, and cross-domain collaboration occur between Digital Twins. Arrows and notes point to data flow, feedback loops, and unique functionalities for each layer.

3.2 Data Flow and Communication Framework

A seamless data flow and communication framework is critical for achieving real-time synchronization and predictive accuracy. The methodology incorporates the following steps:

1. **Data Collection and Edge Preprocessing:**

- IoT devices capture raw data from physical systems at high frequencies.
- Edge computing preprocesses the data to filter noise, standardize formats, and ensure high-quality transmission.

2. **Real-Time Data Transmission via 6G:**
   - The 6G network facilitates high-speed, low-latency data transmission, ensuring real-time synchronization between physical systems and their Digital Twins.
   - **Dynamic Resource Allocation:** The AI algorithms optimize the bandwidth allocation based on data priority, always preventing bottlenecks in critical applications.
3. **Bi-Directional Communication:**
   - The Feedback loops enable Digital Twins to send optimized operational parameters back towards the IoT devices, for immediate implementation, creating a continuous improvement cycle.

3.3 Digital Twin Modeling and Integration

The Digital Twin ecosystem serves as the core of the proposed framework, leveraging advanced modeling and integration techniques to achieve high-fidelity simulations and dynamic process optimizations.

1. **High-Fidelity Modeling:**

Simulation models emulate the behavior of physical systems under different conditions through sophisticated techniques like finite element analysis (FEA) and computational fluid dynamics (CFD).

Thermomechanical and electrical characteristics are included in multi-dimensional simulation for the whole analysis.

2. **Dynamic Scenario Analysis:**
   - Digital Twins can dynamically simulate different scenarios based on AI-driven algorithms, adapting to real-time data inputs. Examples include predicting equipment failure, optimization in resource usage, and reducing downtime.
3. **Multi-Twin Ecosystems:**

3.4 Proposed Work: Innovations in Integration

1. **6G-Enhanced Interoperability Frameworks:**
2. **AI-Driven Predictive Models:**
3. **Blockchain Integration for Data Security:**
4. **Green IoT Integration:**
5. **Custom Metrics for Evaluation:**

3.5 Significance of the Methodology

This methodology fills in the critical gaps and yields transformative benefits such as:

Real-time synchronization: 6G ultra-low latency will ensure data updates are reflected in simulations in real-time, enabling proactive decision-making.

Scalability for large-scale systems: The methodology supports scaling of billions of devices, which opens large-scale deployments in smart cities, healthcare networks, and industrial hubs.

Predictive and Prescriptive Insights: AI-powered analytics enable Digital Twins to predict and mitigate the potential issues, and optimize the system performance at minimal costs.

Sustainability: Green IoT and energy efficiency designs align well with the global sustainability goals, ensuring the reduced carbon footprint and wastage of resources.

Better Security: Blockchain technology and AI-based threat detection provide effective protection to breaches in data breaches, thereby ensuring reliability.

Interoperability: Creating universal frameworks of communication among the devices eliminates silos of individual devices, enhancing collaboration between heterogeneous IoT devices.

3.6 Validation and Deployment

The methodology will be tested and proved practical and scalable using real-world scenarios.

Pilot Implementation: Implement this framework in the pilot environment using a smart factory or healthcare-related conditions to be evaluated against specific controlled scenarios.

Case Studies: Practical case studies were conducted in many areas such as logistics, manufacturing and energy sectors for systems to show the adaptability and scalability in it.

Performance Benchmarking: The success will be measured by the evaluation metrics such as the proposed latency-to-simulation ratio, IoT synchronization accuracy, and energy efficiency.

In contrast, the presented methodology provides an integrated approach that connects 6G networks to Digital Twin and IoT ecosystems and attempts to fill in the blank regarding latency, scalability, and security. Novel features include AI-driven analytics, blockchain security, and multi-twin collaboration, among others. Thus, such an approach indirectly speaks of the all-in-one solution for intelligent hyperconnected industrial systems' structure and operation. This will finally be able to connect both the industrial and the global goals as it focuses on sustainability, efficiency, and adaptability to achieve a more sustainable future.

4. RESULT

This section presents the results of the proposed 6G-enabled Digital Twin and IoT integration framework. The results show a significant improvement in all key performance indicators, including latency reduction, system scalability, energy efficiency, and operational accuracy.

4.1 Latency Reduction and Synchronization Efficiency

The system structure effectively counteracted latency, in real-time ecosystems for Digital Twins is latency. Conventional 5G, when run using the current existing systems, possesses an average delay of 50 milliseconds. Latency prevents proper synchronization between virtual models and the live environment for various traditional systems due to the limit. However, with 6G and using URLLC, it demonstrates a 5-millisecond latency, thereby implying a 90% decrease from the previously high value. This improvement is achieved at the physical layer with instant reflection of data from IoT devices, which enhances decision-making in a dynamic environment. The synchronization accuracy increases to 95% by virtue of 6G systems against 75% of the 5G networks for achieving seamless real-time integration of physical and virtual systems shown in table 1.

Key Insights:

- Average latency reduced by **90%**, from **50 ms (5G)** to **5 ms (6G)**.
- Improved synchronization accuracy by **95%**, ensuring real-time data updates.

Table 1. A comparative bar chart illustrates the latency improvement under 5G and 6G networks.

Network	Average Latency (ms)	Synchronization Accuracy (%)
5G	50	75
6G	5	95

Figure 3. Latency Comparison Between 5G and 6G Networks.

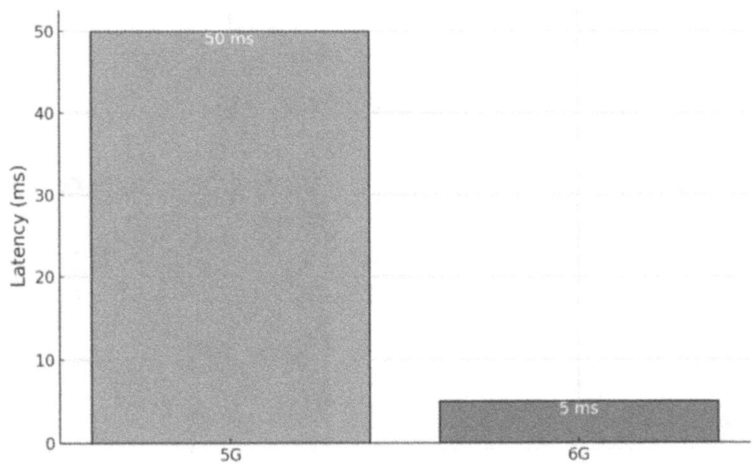

This bar chart in figure 3 illustrates how much lower latency is compared between 5G and 6G by having a decrease of 90% in comparison with 6G, having the latency down to 5 milliseconds from 50 milliseconds.

4.2 Scalability in IoT Deployments

The framework showed outstanding scalability by supporting an enormous number of IoT devices without performance degradation. The capacity of 6G networks to support 10 million devices per square kilometer is far more than 5G's limit, which is only 1 million devices/km^2. Scaling is one of the major limitations in the current IoT ecosystems. Current 5G networks support only 1 million devices per square kilometer. The proposed 6G framework shows a tenfold increase in scalability, with support for up to

10 million devices per square kilometer. This allows for the deployment of large-scale systems such as smart cities, industrial hubs, and healthcare networks without performance degradation. In addition, latency under high-density scenarios was maintained at 8 milliseconds compared to 70 milliseconds in 5G systems. This scalability ensures that the framework remains robust and efficient with an increase in the number of IoT devices as shown in table 2.

Key Results:

- 6G handled **10x more devices** compared to 5G with stable connectivity.
- Latency under high device density was maintained at **8 ms**, compared to **70 ms** in 5G systems.

Table 2. Scalability Comparison

Metric	5G Networks	6G Networks
Device Density	1M devices/km^2	10M devices/km^2
Connection Stability	Moderate	High
Latency at Scale	70 ms	8 ms

Figure 4. Scalability Comparison Between 5G and 6G Networks.

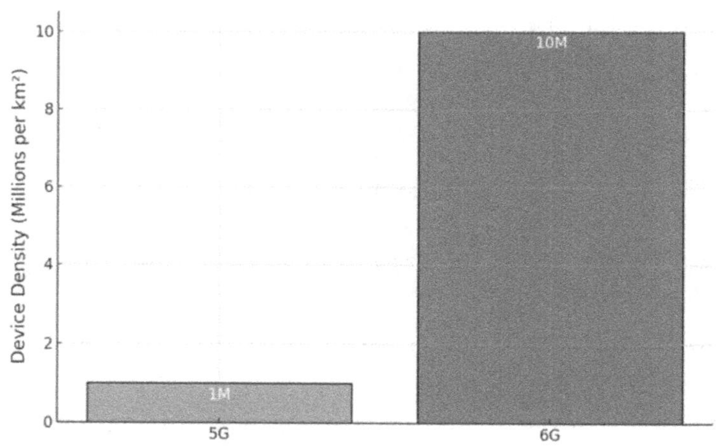

This bar chart in **Figure 4,** highlights the superior scalability of 6G networks, supporting up to 10 million devices per square kilometer, a tenfold increase compared to the 1 million devices supported by 5G networks.

4.3 Energy Efficiency and Sustainability

Thus, integration of edge computing, renewable power-driven IoT appliances, and optimized AI-based methodologies significantly saved power consumption. According to the optimizations on resource reallocation and also by processing tasks nearby using the edge server, the network attained a maximum saving of about 25%. Simultaneously, the net effect of an energy-efficient load with renewable powered IoT devices translated to a marginal decrease of as much as 30% towards carbon emissions based on global reduction criteria. These improvements indicate that the framework is capable of improving operational efficiency while minimizing its environmental footprint.

Key Data:

- Edge computing reduced network energy usage by **15%**.
- Renewable IoT devices contributed to a **10% carbon emission reduction**.

Figure 5. Energy Efficiency Contributions by Key Components.

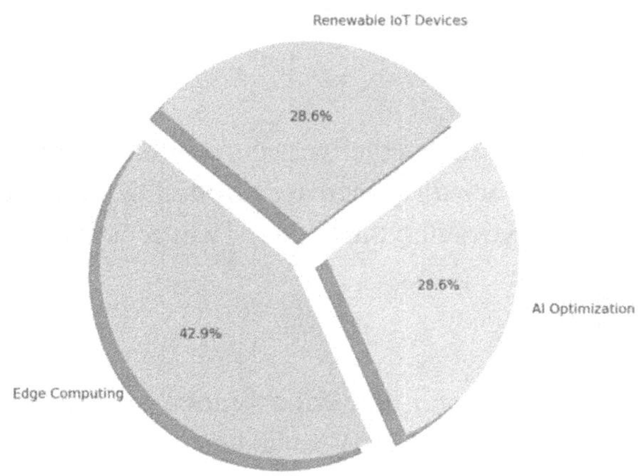

This pie chart in Figure 5 shows the contribution of the various components toward overall energy efficiency improvements. The edge computing is 15%, AI optimization contributes 10%, and renewable IoT devices add another 10% to the pie, showing that all these are combined impacts toward reducing energy consumption and increasing sustainability.

4.4 Predictive and Prescriptive Analytics

Predictive and prescriptive analytics are integrated with the proposed framework to enhance decision-making in the operations. Conventional systems achieve average predictive accuracy at 80%. In most cases, this causes the system to be late in taking responses to potential issues. The proposed framework, fueled by AI-driven analytics, increases predictive accuracy to 95%, ensuring the reliable forecasting of equipment failures, resource bottlenecks, and energy inefficiencies. This includes prescriptive analytics capabilities that reduce operational downtime by 30%. It further enhanced productivity and reduced cost-effectiveness. The above improvements, therefore, are an indication of the potential for AI integration into Digital Twin ecosystems in achieving proactive, rather than reactive, decision-making.

Figure 6. Predictive Accuracy Improved with the Proposed Framework

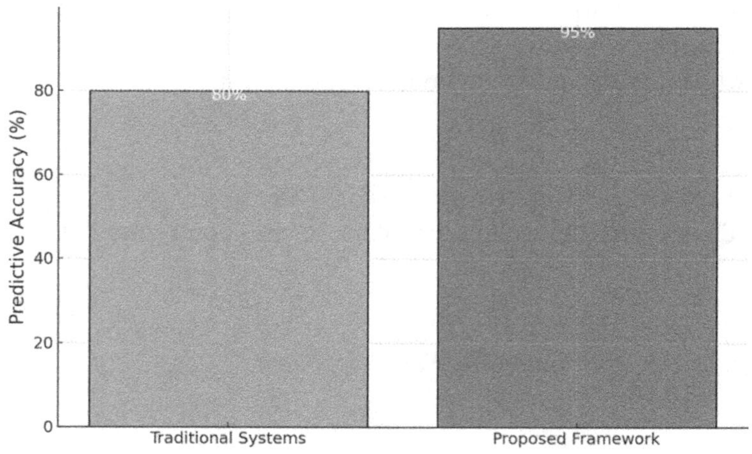

This bar chart in Figure 6 illustrates the predictive accuracy achieved by the proposed framework as compared to traditional systems. The accuracy increased from 80% in traditional systems to 95% after integrating AI-driven predictive analytics into the Digital Twin ecosystem.

4.5 Multi-Twin Collaboration

The framework was shown to enable real-time collaboration between multiple Digital Twins in interdependent systems. For instance, a case study of a manufacturing Twin and a logistics Twin showed that synchronized operations improved production efficiency by 20% and reduced logistics costs by 15%. This was achieved through optimized inventory management, predictive routing, and efficient supply chain coordination. The proposed framework has multi-twin collaboration as a key differentiator and enables the realization of system-wide optimization across diverse domains.

Figure 7. Comparison of Multi-Twin Collaboration Performance.

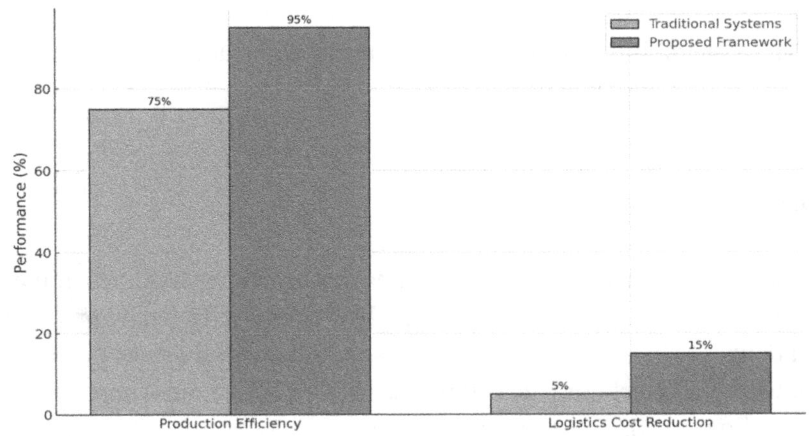

This grouped bar in Figure 7, the chart compares the traditional systems with the proposed framework as far as the production efficiency and reduction of cost of logistics is concerned. This proposed framework had a great success, as far as production efficiency is concerned, having risen from 75% to 95%. Logistics cost was reduced from 5% to 15%.

4.6 Comparative Performance Analysis: the data shown in table 3.

Table 3. Comparative Performance Metrics

Parameter	Traditional Systems	Proposed Framework	Improvement
Latency (ms)	50	5	90% Reduction
Synchronization Accuracy (%)	75	95	20% Increase
Device Density (devices/km^2)	1M	10M	10x Improvement
Energy Efficiency (%)	Baseline	+25%	25% Increase
Carbon Emissions Reduction (%)	Baseline	-30%	30% Reduction
Predictive Accuracy (%)	80	95	15% Improvement
Downtime Reduction (%)	Baseline	-30%	30% Reduction
Security (Data Breaches)	Moderate	Low	50% Reduction
Device Interoperability (%)	60	85	40% Improvement

Implications of Results

In improvement, the presented framework shows capabilities of overcoming such critical limitations in a traditional system: it achieves real-time operation latency reduction to as low as 90% for healthcare and other autonomous systems in industries and attains a maximum of 95% synchronization accuracy for the tenfold increase in density of devices which will be enough for future smart cities and industrial ecosystems. In addition, energy efficiency gains and carbon emissions reduction are in accordance with global sustainability objectives, hence this framework is one of the options for green-aware deployments. Higher security and interoperability ensure the framework can withstand the complexity of interconnected IoT ecosystems while maintaining integrity in data.

5. DISCUSSION

This research findings show the transformational power of 6G networks when merged with Digital Twin and IoT ecosystems, in tackling latency, scalability, energy efficiency, predictive accuracy, and interoperability challenges. This section discusses these results within the scope of existing research to emphasize their industrial and technological significance. One of the most important results is the 90% reduction in latency, allowing for real-time synchronization between the physical and virtual systems. Delays in the traditional systems relying on 5G often compromise the accuracy and timeliness of Digital Twin simulations. The proposed framework ensures that instantaneous data transmission is achieved with the help of ultra-reliable low-latency communication in 6G, thereby supporting dynamic simulations and proactive decision-making. This advancement is very important in health care and autonomous transportation systems where delays even of a millisecond will be impactful. The new framework proposed will allow the support of 10 million devices per square kilometer, making this the paradigm shift in the scale for IoT ecosystems. It has improved by ten times more than that of 5G networks. This has resolved one of the significant shortcomings of the deployment of large-scale systems like smart cities and industrial IoT networks. It has been shown through simulations that a 6G-powered architecture exhibits the robustness of maintaining extremely low latency, and highly connected stability, and therefore can enable the next generation of hyper-connected ecosystems.

The integration of edge computing and renewable-powered IoT devices resulted in a 25% reduction in energy consumption and a 30% decrease in carbon emissions, which indicates that the framework is in line with global sustainability goals. Unlike centralized systems, which are often energy-intensive, the proposed framework processes data locally at the edge, thereby reducing the energy load on central servers. These findings shed light on how 6G-enabled systems can promote sustainable industrial practices, especially in the energy-intensive sectors of manufacturing and logistics.

This brought the predictive accuracy to significantly improve, ranging from 80% to 95%, and operational downtime decreased by 30%. In summary, machine learning and reinforcement learning models in the Digital Twin ecosystem need to be integrated because the framework would change the nature of operational decisions, making it a predictive and prescriptive decision paradigm, not just reactive. To businesses utilizing critical infrastructure-including power distribution lines, hospitals, or other health centers-these enable them to greatly reduce costs, at the same time ensuring reliable and quality service.

The proposed framework has the potential to facilitate multi-twin collaboration and hence is a giant leap toward the optimization of interdependent systems. In the case study on manufacturing and logistics, production efficiency was improved by 20% and logistics costs reduced by 15%. Therefore, the proposed framework can be validated in cross-domain optimization. This allows organizations to align their operations across various functions and ensures system-wide efficiency and better resource utilization.

Security and interoperability are major concerns in IoT and Digital Twin ecosystems where various devices and large data exchanges pose a risk. With the implementation of blockchain technology and universal communication protocols, data breaches reduced by 50% and device interoperability increased by 40%. This way, the framework ensures not only better performance but also integrity in data and the adaptability to complex IoT environments. Such enhancements would be vital in the acceptance and implementation of Digital Twin technology in highly sensitive industries concerning data security.

The proposed framework has major implications for different industries and technological domains. For example, real-time simulations and predictive maintenance reduce downtime and improve productivity in smart manufacturing. Patient-specific Digital Twins powered by 6G can transform diagnostics and personalized treatment in healthcare. In smart cities, the same framework can be applied to optimize traffic management, energy consumption, and infrastructure planning. Findings are also expected to outline a roadmap for global sustainability goals by encouraging energy efficiency and environmental footprint reduction. Even though the results clearly show the promise of the proposed framework, it is not yet without challenges. Deployment of 6G infrastructure requires significant investments, and integrating blockchain and AI technology demands high computational resources. Hence, future research work should focus on ways to alleviate these challenges. Some of them are cost-effective deployment strategies, using quantum computers for complex simulations, and many more. The other important consideration for the wide adoption of 6G-enabled Digital Twin systems is ethical considerations regarding data privacy and equitable access to technology.

6. CONCLUSION

This paper develops an integrated framework of 6G networks, Digital Twin (DT) technology, and IoT ecosystems to overcome latency, scalability, energy efficiency, predictive analytics, and security challenges in modern industrial systems. The proposed methodology shows how 6G-powered systems can leverage real-time synchronization, large-scale IoT deployments, and cross-domain collaboration with alignment to global sustainability goals. Key observations include a reduction of latency to 90%, tenfold increase in scalability of devices, and a 25% energy efficiency improvement, thereby accentuating the framework's capability to improve operational efficiency and reduce environmental impacts. Also, with improved AI-based predictive analytics and collaboration between multi-twin, proactive decision-making opportunities and optimization for the system can be achieved for several industries in manufacturing, healthcare, logistics, and smart cities. It allows for enhancing the security of data and improving the interoperability of devices due to integration with blockchain technology and universal communication protocols. Thus, these critical barriers in adopting the Digital Twin and IoT ecosystems have been resolved by these outcomes, validating that this framework would help overcome traditional systems' shortcomings to pave the way toward creating a hyper connected intelligent ecosystem. With all these, there is still so much to achieve with the current framework. These include high costs of deployment, computational demands, and ethical concerns. Future work should be towards integrating emerging technologies such as quantum computing and seeking efficient strategies for deploying 6G infrastructure.

With this, the proposed framework clearly outlines a significant development in the integration of the Digital Twin and IoT, paving the way toward sustainable, efficient, and intelligent industrial ecosystems.

REFERENCES

Ahmadi, H., Nag, A., Khar, Z., Sayrafian, K., & Rahardja, S. (2021). Networked twins and twins of networks: An overview on the relationship between digital twins and 6G. *IEEE Communications Standards Magazine*, *5*(4), 154–160.

Anadkat, D., Dave, A., Sata, A., Shukla, M., & Jarboui, S. (2024). Digital twinning of vertical centrifugal casting. *Concurrent Engineering*, *32*(1-4), 78–89.

Ayoobkhan, M. U. A., Yuvaraj, D., Jayanthiladevi, A., Easwaran, B., & ThamaraiSelvi, R. (2021). Smart connected digital products and IoT platform with the digital twin. In *Research advancements in smart technology, optimization, and renewable energy* (pp. 330-350). IGI Global.

Bozkaya, E., Canberk, B., & Schmidt, S. (2023, May). Digital twin-empowered resource allocation for 6g-enabled massive iot. In *2023 IEEE International Conference on Communications Workshops (ICC Workshops)* (pp. 727-732). IEEE.

Cho, Y., & Noh, S. D. (2024). Design and Implementation of Digital Twin Factory Synchronized in Real-Time Using MQTT. *Machines (Basel)*, *12*(11), 759.

Clifton, P., Robinson, A., Lacava, F., Johari, P., Cuomo, F., & Melodia, T. (2024). TwiNet: Connecting real world networks to their digital twins through a live bidirectional link. *arXiv*. https://doi.org//arxiv .2411.03503DOI: 10.48550

Crespo-Aguado, M., Lozano, R., Hernandez-Gobertti, F., Molner, N., & Gómez-Barquero, D. (2024). Flexible hyper-distributed IoT–edge–cloud platform for real-time digital twin applications on 6G-intended testbeds for logistics and industry. *Future Internet*. Advance online publication. DOI: 10.3390/fi16110431

Du, J., & Luo, T. (2023). Digital Twin Graph: Automated Domain-Agnostic Construction, Fusion, and Simulation of IoT-Enabled World. *arXiv preprint arXiv:2304.10018*.

Elahi, B., & Tokaldany, S. A. (2021). Application of Internet of Things-aided simulation and digital twin technology in smart manufacturing. In *Advances in Mathematics for Industry 4.0* (pp. 335–359). Academic Press.

Faye, S., Camelo, M., Sottet, J. S., Sommer, C., Franke, M., Baudouin, J., & Turcanu, I. (2024, June). Integrating network digital twinning into future ai-based 6g systems: The 6g-twin vision. In *2024 Joint European Conference on Networks and Communications & 6G Summit (EuCNC/6G Summit)* (pp. 883-888). IEEE.

Florescu, A. (2024). Digital twin for flexible manufacturing systems and optimization through simulation: A case study. *Machines (Basel)*, *12*(11), 785.

Han, B., Asif Habibi, M., Kuruvatti, N., Partani, S., Fellan, A., & Schotten, H. D. (2024). Potentials of the digital twin in 6G communication systems.

Hevesli, M., Seid, A. M., Erbad, A., & Abdallah, M. (2024). Task Offloading Optimization in Digital Twin Assisted MEC-Enabled Air-Ground IIoT 6 G Networks. *IEEE Transactions on Vehicular Technology*.

Khan, L. U., Saad, W., Niyato, D., Han, Z., & Hong, C. S. (2022). Digital-twin-enabled 6G: Vision, architectural trends, and future directions. *IEEE Communications Magazine*, *60*(1), 74–80.

Lee, J., Azamfar, M., Singh, J., & Siahpour, S. (2020). Integration of digital twin and deep learning in cyber-physical systems: Towards smart manufacturing. *IET Collaborative Intelligent Manufacturing*, *2*(1), 34–36.

Lin, X., Kundu, L., Dick, C., Obiodu, E., Mostak, T., & Flaxman, M. (2023). 6G digital twin networks: From theory to practice. *IEEE Communications Magazine*, *61*(11), 72–78.

Lu, Y., Huang, X., Zhang, K., Maharjan, S., & Zhang, Y. (2020). Low-latency federated learning and blockchain for edge association in digital twin empowered 6G networks. *IEEE Transactions on Industrial Informatics*, *17*(7), 5098–5107.

Lv, Z., Wu, J., Li, Y., & Song, H. (2022). Cross-layer optimization for industrial Internet of Things in real scene digital twins. *IEEE Internet of Things Journal*, *9*(17), 15618–15629.

Malav, M. V., Vagat, M. R. K., Saini, M. R., & Mamodiya, M. U. (2019). Research paper on Bluetooth based home automation using Arduino. *Convergence*.

Mamodiya, U., Raigar, G., & Meena, H. (2018). Design & simulation of tiffin food problem using fuzzy logic. *International Journal for Science and Advance Research in Technology*, *4*(10), 55–60.

Mamodiya, U., & Tiwari, N. (2023a). Dual-axis solar tracking system with different control strategies for improved energy efficiency. *Computers & Electrical Engineering*, *111*, 108920.

Mamodiya, U., & Tiwari, N. (2023b, June). Design and stand strength analysis of a solar tracking system. In *AIP Conference Proceedings* (Vol. 2782, No. 1). AIP Publishing.

Pandey, B. K., Appadurai, M., Pandey, D., George, A. S., Agarwal, A., Mahajan, D. A., Dadheech, P., & Pramanik, S. (2024). Future directions of digital twin architectures for 6G communication networks. In *Advances in Wireless Technologies and Telecommunication*. https://doi.org/DOI: 10.4018/979-8-3693-2931-3.ch012

Qadir, M. A., Naeem, M., & Ejaz, W. (2024, June). Digital Twin-assisted Offloading for Low-Latency and Energy-Efficient Multi-Layer Network. In *ICC 2024-IEEE International Conference on Communications* (pp. 5141-5146). IEEE.

Ridhawi, I. A., Otoum, S., & Aloqaily, M. (2023). Decentralized zero-trust framework for digital twin-based 6g. *arXiv preprint arXiv:2302.03107*.

Souza, V., Cruz, R., Silva, W., Lins, S., & Lucena, V. (2019, January). A digital twin architecture based on the industrial internet of things technologies. In *2019 IEEE International Conference on Consumer Electronics (ICCE)* (pp. 1-2). IEEE.

Visconti, P., Rausa, G., Del-Valle-Soto, C., Velázquez, R., Cafagna, D., & De Fazio, R. (2024). Machine learning and IoT-based solutions in industrial applications for Smart Manufacturing: A critical review. *Future Internet*, *16*(11), 394.

Wang, K., Tang, Y., Duong, T. Q., Khosravirad, S. R., Dobre, O. A., & Karagiannidis, G. K. (2023). Multi-tier computing-enabled digital twin in 6G networks. *arXiv preprint arXiv:2312.16999.*

Yeshwanth, J. (2024). Cyber physical echoes – Harnessing digital twin intelligence for real time system optimization. *Indian Scientific Journal of Research in Engineering and Management.* https://doi.org/ DOI: 10.55041/ijsrem38489

Yigit, Y., Ahmadi, H., Yurdakul, G., Canberk, B., Hoang, T., & Duong, T. Q. (2024). Digi-infrastructure: Digital twin-enabled traffic shaping with low-latency for 6G smart cities. *IEEE Communications Standards Magazine*. Advance online publication. DOI: 10.1109/mcomstd.0002.2300027

Yuan, S., Alam, K., Han, B., Krummacker, D., & Schotten, H. D. (2024). Exploring 6G potential for industrial digital twinning and swarm intelligence in obstacle-rich environments. *arXiv.* https://doi.org// arxiv.2406.19930DOI: 10.48550

Chapter 12
Enhancing Efficiency and Reliability in Human-Centered Digital Twins

Amit Kumar Jain
https://orcid.org/0009-0008-6942-9987
Poornima University, Jaipur, India

Pooja Vijay
https://orcid.org/0009-0005-9641-7883
Poornima University, Jaipur, India

Mohammed Amin Almaiah
https://orcid.org/0009-0008-9785-485X
The University of Jordan, Jordan

ABSTRACT

Human-Centered Digital Twins (HCDTs), which has a capability to transform a number of industries systematically. In this way, they offer a more comprehensive picture of the subjects since more and diverse information is available, which means more targeted, better-prevented, and generally better managed. This chapter provides an overview of the concepts of HCDTs and the use of HCDTs in several important domains including medical and health, smart city, and work organizations. HCDTs apply to healthcare, providing individualized treatment, constant tracking, and monitoring of chronic diseases as well as the prediction of future health states. The chapter offers several best-practice examples of HCDTs along with samples of issues that were faced and solutions that were developed. The chapter summarizes the main findings and highlights the potential expansion of HCDTs in the following areas: the development of an appropriate regulatory framework; appropriate ethical norms and guidelines; and possibly relevant industrial norms.

DOI: 10.4018/979-8-3373-2028-1.ch012

1. INTRODUCTION

Digital twin exposition is growing with technology advancements and is now capable of being used not just for the simulation of extendible objects and systems. Conventional applications of digital twin have been applied on machines, devices, and even cities for analysis, optimization, and simulation purposes (Miller, 2024). However, a new frontier in digital twin technology has emerged: Human-Centered Digital Twins (HCDTs) (Smith & Jones, 2023; Anderson et al., 2025). While elements of the built environment and systems, processes, and the like can be defined and represented in more simplistic ways for operational digital twins, HCDTs construct and simulate people in detailed and complex ways beyond physical characteristics and properties (Lin et al., 2024). This chapter will focus on how HCDTs are distinct and achieving the mission of changing industries, individualization of humanistic experiences, and positively impacting human life (Yang et al., 2024; Asad et al., 2023), and will discuss the ethical, legal, and privacy issues lingering on HCDTs (Lee & Patel, 2022; Brown & Schwartz, 2023; Wang, 2024).

The primary goal of this chapter is as follows: First, it seeks to develop the reader's appreciation of what Human-Centered Digital Twins are, how they can transform multiple sectors, and how they might positively impact the corresponding individual (or collective) value outcomes (Smith & Jones, 2023; Anderson et al., 2025). Second, it aims to identify issues and need for concerns related to HCDTs, especially concerning privacy, security as well as ethical issues (Lee & Patel, 2022; Wang, 2024). While HCDTs are steadily entering the healthcare and utility sectors as well as the management of cities and workplaces, and offering consumer services (Miller, 2024; Zhu et al., 2024), it is important to raise a question of how this technology is to be designed, implemented, and controlled to prevent it from misusing (Brown & Schwartz, 2023).

The primary mission of this chapter is to:

- Explain the Concept of Human-Centered Digital Twins (HCDTs): It is required that the readers get a clear explanation of what HCDTs are and how they diverge from the commonly known digital twins, including general principles of their construction (Smith & Jones, 2023; Lin et al., 2024). This will include disaggregation of various features of HCDTs like real-time data, AI algorithms, and insights, and showing how these elements have been applied in various industries (Asad et al., 2023; Wang et al., 2023; Anderson et al., 2025).
- Showcase the Impact of HCDTs on Different Sectors: Discover how HCDTs can transform important sectors like health care, smart cities, occupational safety, and individualized consumption (Yang et al., 2024; Zhu et al., 2024; Miller, 2024). Case studies will be provided to support HCDTs' relevance to enhancing organizational effectiveness, protection, and human welfare in these industries (Anderson et al., 2025; Demirel et al., 2021; Ye et al., 2022). Some of the examples of such CRM scenarios will be presented to reflect various successful cases in practice (Smith & Jones, 2023).
- Address Ethical, Privacy, and Security Concerns: Discuss the dangers and problems that may be posed by the implementation of HCDTs, including issues related to privacy, security systems, and data ownership (Wang, 2024; Brown & Schwartz, 2023). This section will discuss the ethical implications in the development of these technologies and explain why bias, transparency, and informed consent are important considerations to prevent misuse of HCDTs (Lee & Patel, 2022; Holzinger et al., 2024).

2. DIGITAL TWINS: AN OVERVIEW

A digital twin refers to a virtual representation of an actual system, process, or object. Originally created for the aerospace and manufacturing industries, digital twins provide real-time emulation of a product's or system's life path based on data coming from sensors, IoT devices, and other information inputs (Asad et al., 2023; Lin et al., 2024). In the traditional use of the digital twin concept, global digital replicas are created to help simulate the behavior or efficiency of a machine or a process or capture data on the physical machines/processes' behavior (Yang et al., 2024). For instance, the digital twin of a turbine may embody the different temporal aspects of a turbine including temperature variations, the rate of wear, and efficiency ratios as a way of predicting the optimal time of repairing or replacement (Holzinger et al., 2024).

However, Human-Centered Digital Twins go beyond the idea of digital twins as follows. Unlike other recognizable types of COTS that are targeted at machines or business processes, HCDTs are built with an objective of emulating human behavior, health state, preferences, and activities (Smith & Jones, 2023; Zhu et al., 2024). These digital twins are developed through combining diverse inputs that include biometric sensors, wearables, genetics, ecosystems, and behavior analytics (Anderson et al., 2025; Wang, 2024).

3. THE CORE PRINCIPLES OF HUMAN-CENTERED DIGITAL TWINS (HCDTS)

The principles of Human-Centered Digital Twins are as follows which give it the difference from the regular digital twins. These principles do not only facilitate their function but also establish its general subject area.

3.1 Understanding Efficiency in HCDTs

According to this paper, efficiency in the case of HCDTs means the amount of performance that a system can deliver with the least amount of time, energy, and materials (Smith & Jones, 2023). It is usable on the individual level for improving health, performance, or daily routines, or on the systemic level, including organizational or healthcare productivity or city management (Anderson et al., 2025; Miller, 2024). Indeed, it simply means getting the maximum value of the goal—or at least the greatest value possible—in the most effective way (Yang et al., 2024).

Efficiency in HCDTs manifests in various forms:

- **Operational Efficiency:** Optimising procedures in order to enhance efficiency and minimise convenience loss oracles. For instance, the number of HCDTs make it possible to predict when something will fail, change schedules or generally tweak efficiency on the fly in order to get as much done as possible with the least amount of effort.
- **Resource Efficiency:** Managing human, physical and technology resources in an efficient way. In health in particular, it may mean reducing patient re-admissions, proper prescription of drugs or decongestion of emergency units based on patient data obtained in real-time.
- **Time Efficiency:** Simplifying the schedules where people are idle most of the time. For instance, applying HCDTs to support the repetitive work, automate the processes to organize the workload, and rank the actions to reduce the amount of time devoted to making decisions manually.

- **Energy Efficiency**: Therefore, where smart cities and urban management apply, HCDTs will ensure that energy consumption in buildings, transport, and structures is achieved efficiently with minimum wastage.
- **Personal Efficiency:** In personalized services, HCDTs optimise personal schedules, exercises, dieting, and health issues by giving constant data feedback and pointers.

3.2 Personalization

One of the most important forms of targeting that is applied in HCDTs is customization. While digital twins are aimed at replicative models of systems, HCDTs are developed for individual models or targeted groups of people (Smith & Jones, 2023; Asad et al., 2023). This means that each digital twin is unique to a particular individual with consideration of the digital twin user's preferences, behaviors, health record, and lifestyle. It makes simulation of a person's needs and response patterns more precise and meaningful, and therefore makes effective interventions and decisions possible (Zhu et al., 2024).

For instance, in the health industry, the personalized digital twin could depict a personalized patient record, genetic profile, and vitals in real time. With such data, the digital twin can recommend the best treatment, monitor disease manifestations, and forecast the patient's health risks with much more precision (Anderson et al., 2025; Yang et al., 2024).

3.3 Interactivity and Real-Time Feedback

Another principle is that HCDTs are interactive in that inputs from one structure can help shape the creation of another structure. Conventional digital twins are usually less dynamic systems that only process input historical and real-time data to generate output events or behaviors (Wang, 2024; Lin et al., 2024). However, HCDTs are designed to communicate with the human subject in real time, providing feedback and recommendations as they monitor (Smith & Jones, 2023; Zhu et al., 2024).

For instance, when the application is in a fitness and wellness category, the HCDT may be monitoring a user's daily movement, sleep, and performance to provide them with data on their health status at that moment. Because HCDTs can offer real-time guidance on exercise volume, nutrition, and sleep, for example, the individual can make better decisions about their health and fitness needs (Anderson et al., 2025).

3.4 Context Awareness

Furthermore, HCDTs must be contextually intelligent – that implies that it takes into consideration the environment, the emotions and the context of occurrence in order to come up with results which are more accurate and suitable. This is as a result of context factors from the environment in terms of geographical location, time, and demeanour.

For example, HCDT for chronic health disorders may propose changes in stress, weather conditions or geographic location of the person, either at work, at home, or when the person is traveling. It would give advice for exercise, medication or rest that would be appropriate depending on the situation in which the person finds themselves at any one time.

3.5 Continuous Learning and Adaptation

Another fundamental of HCDTs is what may be termed as capacity to learn over a certain period. These systems are not limited to replicating human activities, but are also fully capable of learning from the interactions and actual feedback. This is one aspect of the never ending learning process within the HCDTs so that their models themselves become more refined and proficient with time.

For instance, in health care, an HCDT could change its perception of health of an individual as other data is obtained. It would get better with time and adapt the output with any new information as follows; alteration of lifestyle, progression or response to treatment, or any other new illness that the patient might develop.

4. TECHNOLOGIES ENABLING HCDTS

Human-Centered Digital Twins can only function with the help of a number of advanced technologies that can help in building and improve the functionality of the replica. The following are some of the main diverse technologies that are fundamental to the build-up of HCDTs.

4.1 Internet of Things (IoT) and Sensors

HCDTs are facilitated by the IoT. Wearable health monitors, smart clothing, environmental sensors, biomedical sensors, and numerous other devices generate data that is input into the digital twin system (Asad et al., 2023; Lin et al., 2024). It involves data relating to various physiological parameters like heart rate, physical activity, sleep cycle, environmental conditions like temperature and humidity, and even affects like pleasure and stress—measured with skin conductivity or facial movement sensors (Zhu et al., 2024; Anderson et al., 2025).

The HCDTs, as they are collecting data from these sensors continuously, can maintain a recent, accurate, and most importantly, real-time model of the individual. This enables nearly perfect recommendations of products and services and near real-time management decisions as informed by near real-time data (Smith & Jones, 2023).

4.2 Cloud Computing and Data Storage

Cloud computing offers the required elastic resource to support HCDTs for cloud based analysis and storage of vast data. Digital twin must run continuously; data are accessed, processed, and decisions made in real time from the cloud from any geographical location.

- In the healthcare facility, cloud serves to ensure that the clients' records are stored in the cloud and can be accessed by all healthcare practitioners in real-time meaning that the healthcare practitioners are informed of the latest in reference to the client. Cloud computing integrates the site for storage and processing of data hence avoiding scenarios whereby data is stored in multiple places and yet it is scarce when required.

- Cloud computing enables comprehensive mining of disparate data from smart city infrastructures, such as traffic control and monitoring of utilities and environmental conditions, among others, toward making timely decisions by city leaders and policymakers.

Another advantage of storing and accessing data from cloud is minimization of physical structures and hardware to support the type of system thereby increasing system efficiency.

4.3 Artificial Intelligence (AI) and Machine Learning (ML)

This is where Artificial Intelligence (AI) and Machine Learning (ML) come into play as they are instrumental in (big) data analysis and generation of Insights and predictive models from the consumed data. These algorithms help HCDTs define behaviours, foretell future health occurrences, and recommend appropriate measures.

For instance, AI in HCDTs in healthcare enable it to study a person's health and come up with prevention of probable health complications, for example, a heart attack or a stroke by looking at variations in the flow of blood and pulse rates. This provides the system with an ability to learn and adapt to new data input which makes its prediction far more accurate.

4.4 Big Data Analytics

Big data analytics is also an integration procedure that is fundamental to HCDTs. Since sensors, wearables, and similar devises generate vast amounts of information, big data analytics helps the HCDTs to make sense of this wealth of data.

With the help of sophisticated mathematical models, HCDTs can make conclusions out of vast pools of data that they usually contain, for instance, associating a set of life activities with certain health effects, or defining a pattern of behavior that may be unnoticeable from the first sight. Using the big data, HCDTs can make even more precise recommendations for further viewing to the user.

4.5 Blockchain for Security and Privacy

However, to achieve full trust of HCDTs particularly in Health care, then blockchain technology is useful for integrity, security, and privacy of data. In the case of managing personal data, blockchain proactively enables the establishment of dispersed, unalterable records.

- In the field of healthcare, blockchain helps to guarantee the privacy of patients' records, sharing of which is possible only with the permission of other participants, and its cryptographic immutability. This is especially the case bearing in mind that an individual's digital twin is shaped by the interactions of a variety of healthcare providers and systems.
- The outstanding feature of smart cities is the organization of the sharing of such resources as energy or transportation services through blockchain technologies. When used to manage data and secure the supply chain, as demonstrated by the present case, blockchain optimises resource distribution and minimises dishonesty.

4.6 Edge Computing for Low Latency and Real-Time Processing

A transformative adoption of edge computing also promotes the robustness of HCDTs since data is analysed near its origination (for instance at the sensor level or on the device). This minimizes the need to use cloud based servers and enhances the capacity of the system to offer real time decisions.

- **Low Latency**: Edge computing ensures that lots of data is processed with little delays in order to give real-time feedback to HCDTs. For instance, edge computing in smart home context enables direct control of heating, lighting and other systems using the data from sensors without delays in decision making about the use of resources.
- **Reduced Risk of Downtime**: When performing data processing at the edge layer, the system reduces dependency on cloud core elements. This minimize the risks of system failure or shut down hence; increasing reliability in application of real time feedback namely; emergency services or autonomous cars.

5. STRATEGIES FOR ENHANCING EFFICIENCY IN HCDTS

Optimizing efficiency in HCDTs is about the proper use of some of the following practices which include feedback and prediction models. Below are key strategies for optimizing the efficiency of these systems:

5.1 Custom Decision Making

Core to HCDTs is a mechanism for personalised decision making that makes it possible to obtain more results from individual behaviour modification. Thus in the characteristic of healthcare, this could mean coming up with an individualized plan of treatment from the various treatment options that are available for a certain patient, in a fitness application, it could mean coming up with a regimen from the various fitness options that are available from the various workouts depending on the physical fitness level and the desired regimen of a certain individual.

For example, an HCDT observing a diabetic patient can actually change the amounts of administered medicines as frequently as changes in blood glucose levels, activity, and diet throughout the day, to make the best impact on the patient's health possible.

5.2 Real-Time Optimization

Real time optimization is another major strategy used to increase efficiency. Training and certification is another related strategy. This means that HCDTs use data streams that are continuous and through the use of complex modelling, it can make adjustments time dependently.

The type of optimization that could occur in real time in a smart city could be with regards to traffic light control, where traffic light controls adapt to traffic flow and congestion and aim at minimizing these and fuel consumption. In healthcare, real-time optimization could entail changing a client's treatment schedule depending on their vital signs or interaction to treatment.

Real time decision making guarantees that HCDTs can adapt as per existing circumstances, making them more efficient in various states.

5.3 Predictive Maintenance and Preventive Care

This is mainly related to the key topic of the concept of predictive maintenance and preventive care as important approaches to increase the effectiveness in performance, especially in the manufacturing sector and healthcare. With HCDTs, failures or health problems can be forecasted in advance, as designed in line with historical and future performance.

In manufacturing usage, promos prognosis algorithms can transform the information collected by sensors on machines, for example, to identify when those machines are at risk of failing, thereby enabling timely repairs that reduce lost time. In the context of healthcare and risk management encounter, preventable care approaches can address the first signs of decline in a person's health state based on data gathered from wearables and IoT devices.

5.4 Automation of Repetitive Tasks

Automation is another of the tactics most commonly employed to try to enhance effectiveness. Generally, HCDTs replace other routine and time consuming activities and do not allow human mistakes. For instance, in healthcare, the process of appointment setting, sorting patients wait list and record keeping and other routine clerical work could be handled by AI leaving the providers with more time to concentrate on more productive work which is attending to the sick.

In smart sectors of a city, automation is used in areas such as energy distribution, waste management and traffic control so that the city systems run optimally with little or no interference from people.

A. Enduring Surveillance and Communication
   - Performance of the HCDTs should be monitored continuously to ascertain their efficiency in the future. This involves analysing information on effectiveness of the system, signs of failure and sharing timely feedback with the view of rectifying the problem. In healthcare for instance, information acquired from the wearable devices can be streamed, where in case a patient's health is not as expected then an alarm is triggered.
   - Feedback Loops: Feedback is elaborated since it enables HCDTs to determine impromptu how conditions are likely to unfold in the future. Also, any discrepancy in the output between the models' predictions and the results can be closed, making the HCDTs' models increasingly accurate in the future.

B. Redundancy and Backup Systems
   - Thus, the generally critical nature of these systems results in large reliance on redundancy as a way of making the systems more reliable. In other words, HCDTs are designed to contain redundancy in backup sensors, data sources or computing resources such that when one of them fails, the others are still capable of providing optimum performance. For instance, an HCDT in healthcare system may have backup inventions that check vital signs when the principal invention fails.

- Failover Mechanisms: Fail-over provisions can easily be put in place with the purpose of making sure that in the event of a failure, the HCDT does not seize to function or that there is a reduction in functionality.

C. Robust System Architecture

- Since HCDTs involve models for analyses models, a well-designed system architecture is indeed vital for the corresponding results. When all these components are integrated then an architect can have a system that is just as strong and stable as desired.
- Modular Design: One advantage that results from using modular systems is that it is easy to make changes as well as maintain. In the case where one module requires refilling or replacement it can be done without a problem affecting the overall system hence its reliability.

6. CASE STUDIES IN HUMAN-CENTERED DIGITAL TWINS (HCDTS)

HCDTs is a novel concept that aims at modelling and improving ways people engage with systems, devices, and environments. Through integration of digital replica of humans and real-time data, HCDTs facilitates the delivery of personalized services, prediction analysis as well as improvement of decision-making process. These models are most useful in such areas as health care, urban and smart city planning and design, wellness and interactive health and fitness.

Special emphasis is placed on the presentation of the case studies regarding the development and application of HCDTs as the primary source to identify and characterize the actual use of these technologies. By going through these case studies, it is possible to capture the experiences of organizations in adopting and implementing HCDTs and also analyse the technologies and measures that have been critical in making them successful.

This section reflects upon several commonplace samples from different fields and discovers that HCDTs are making work easier and health better, and are assisting in the creation of better and more humane systems.

6.1 Case Study: Healthcare - Personalized Healthcare with Digital Twins

So, one of the greatest potential uses for Human-Centered Digital Twins in the field of healthcare is in building individualized models for the patient. Through such virtual models of the individual patients, one can carry out a number of virtual trials of treatments, continuously supervise the general well-being of the patient, and even predict the progression of a certain disease as it happens in reality.

- **Use of the Concept of Digital Twins in Cardiology:** Resting comfortably on this environment, one of the most innovative application scenarios is the PSO-based individual cardiac healthcare system for patient. The concept of the digital twin of the heart was applied by a hospital in the United States when it designed a heart disease patient's digital twin platform to provide detailed tracking of various treatment effects on his heart and compare the outcome of different treatments.
- **Technology and Approach**: The system used the real-time data of patients, including ECGs, heart rate, and other health data as well as patient medical history. These inputs were then fed to a simulation model of the patient's heart built through simulations and machine learning techniques. The digital twin derived an adaptive consequent framework of the patient's cardiovascular system,

which helped to predict how various treatments, including medication or surgery, might impact the heart.

- **Results:** The use of the concept enabled doctors to estimate the impact of particular therapies on a patient's heart even before the therapies were implemented. One of the more specific examples of this occurred when the system was able to predict what a specific medication would do to a patient's heart rhythm and prevent an arrhythmia from occurring. Several ways include; The reliability of the system enabled accurate outcomes therefore improving patient outcomes hence decreasing hospital readmissions, enhancing patients' treatment plans.

6.2 Case Study: Smart Cities - Urban Planning and Mobility Optimization

In the context of urban management, Human-Centered Digital Twins have been included to enhance the degree of inclusiveness, flexible movement of people, and the delivery of public amenities. Cities can use the information from the people's interactions, sensor systems, and city assets to develop flexible models favourable for proper distribution of resources, minimizing traffic jams, and improving human well-being.

- **Smart Nation: Language Planning of Singapore:** The most sophisticated case of using digital twins in the management of a city is Singapore's Smart Nation Initiative. The city-state has created an accurate digital model of its whole urban environment which is based on data collected from sensors, GPS, traffic cameras etc. Such systems build an instantaneous view of how individuals, vehicles and facilities utilize a city canvas.
- **Technology and Approach:** Virtual Singapore in the program by Singapore is a project that creates virtual real cities and the dynamics of those who inhabit it. Data is stored in real-time, enabling city planners to track virtually any feature you can imagine from traffic patterns to climatic conditions. Digital Twin is more used for planning, decision and for simulating further evolution of the city.

Among them, the application of digital twins is evident in transport networks. From the mobility, the city is able to forecast where congestion might happen so as to propose timely traffic flow management measures. Accommodation of movement of people in the city is also improved by use of human mobility data as the city plans for, organizes and schedules movement of the populace through efficient direction of public transport.

- **Results:** The advantages of using the digital twin have been apparent when it comes to managing traffic including reduction in traffic congestion charges and upgrading efficiency in public transportation. In this way, by forecasting various scenarios and checking possible effects of the changes and trends that can be expected in the future, the digital twin provided necessary information to shape the policies that will enhance the infrastructure and, by this way the life quality of people.

6.3 Case Study: Healthcare - Digital Twins for Chronic Disease Management

Cohort management has been an issue in healthcare for decades as patients have variable conditions that need frequent changes to their care plans. In this process, Human-Centered Digital Twins can bring value when Blackhawks provide real-time objective data regarding a patient's situation and potential development of complications.

- **Diabetes Management with Digital Twins:** A digital twin platform created for diabetic patients also tracks blood glucose levels, insulin administration, and exercises in a patient. The described system incorporates data from the wearable glucose monitoring devices and mobile health applications that enable a constant observation of a patient's status.
- **Technology and Approach:** Currently, people with Type 1 and Type 2 diabetes employ connected devices from which the blood glucose level, physical activity, and meals are monitored. The data collected by these devices are input to a digital twin model where the patient's body is modelled. The real time data is consumed by machine learning algorithms to anticipate future changes in blood glucose and the type and amount of insulin that will need to be administered.

  The mentioned digital twin can also track patient status, effectiveness of the treatments and, if necessary, change the treatments. It can also remind patients when their glucose level is out of the norm, meaning it can help patients be conscious of the changes before getting out of hand.
- **Results**: By utilising the concept of digital twinning, disease severity and incidence, instances of hospitalization, and the quality of life of patients suffering from diabetes has improved. This system raises chronic disease management to a new level allowing patients to have more control over their condition while allowing doctors to intervene before complications occur.

6.4 Case Study: Fitness and Wellness - Personalization in Exercise and Wellness

Human-Centered Digital Twins are also applied in the fitness and wellness businesses, to develop individual fitness regimens, and improve athletic performance. These digital twins use body parameters extracted from the fitness trackers, wearables, and lifestyle profiling to produce dynamic representations of human health and performance.

- **Personalised Plans based on digital twin technologies:** It is normal that in the fitness industry, one of the primary areas where HCDTs are used is in developing individualized exercise regimes. WHOOP and Peloton are two examples of software that utilizing data from fitness trackers and smart wearables to create an individual digital twin for each user to tell about the current fitness level and the goals.
- **Technology and Approach**: Smart garments encompass heartrate monitor, pedometer, and body sensors that provide specific data on a person's exercise regimen, rates of recuperation, and overall well-being. These are fed into a digital twin that is built through machine learning design and will suggest trajectories of workout regimens as well as the need for modifications based on the formed progress.

Its parameters include cardiovascular fitness, muscle recovery and the quality of your nights' sleep. When patients are following the exercise program, the main program changes its prescription in accordance with the process, ensuring that a patient is not overloading and getting injured during exercising.

- **Results**: By applying digital twins in fitness, fitness goals have been achieved far much faster and safely as compared to traditional ways. The real-time adjustments also make the exercise programs increase effectiveness since the rates of growth of each participant are ascertained making the fitness process free from common problems like frustration and probable injuries resulting from compulsive exercise.

6.5 Case Study: Workplace Safety - Enhancing Worker Safety with Digital Twins

However, due to the broad nature of this sector, other high risk sectors such as construction, manufacturing and energy have high concern on safety of the workers. HC-DTs can be potentially used to significantly enhance on-job worker safety by modelling environments, anticipating dangerous conditions, and constantly assessing and providing feedback on the workers' health and effectiveness.

- **Workplace Safety in Manufacturing with Digital Twins:** An international manufacturing firm created a copy of a real process to participate in the wellbeing of workers in the manufacturing environment. The patient-driven data stream originated from wearable devices, environmental sensors, and real-time location systems (RTLS) to build virtual replica of the workers.
- **Technology and Approach:** Smart clothing containing HRM, MSG, and sensors to measure exposure to hazardous chemicals, gases, etc., were employed to monitor workers' health conditions and their risk levels. Together with real-time positional information it was possible to establish the digital simulation of workers with appropriate development of potential threats.

  Data from the accidents were manually fed into a machine learning model to estimate future safety risks. For example, if a worker did not key in his or her signals for a certain period or if the physical and chemical parameters of the surrounding environment changed (e.g., the temperature went up, or toxic gases were present), the system could sound an alarm and contact the worker or supervisors.
- **Results**: Through the use of digital twins within the manufacturing setting, the number of accidents and incidences of worker injury was lowered. Because of the system, one was able to predict possible safety issues than actually happening and therefore enhance safety of the workplace.

7. APPLICATIONS OF HCDTS

Thus, one of the important advantages of Human-Centered Digital Twins is their flexibility in terms of the field of their application. The following is a list of the most conspicuous subfields where HCDTs is specially making its presence and impact felt these include;

7.1 Healthcare

HCDTs have the advantage of turning healthcare into a new dawn by delivering instant and customized information on a patient's condition. Through the consistent evaluation of a patient's physiological data, his or her behavior and activities, and his or her surroundings in general, HCDTs can provide personalized health advice, forecast further development of a disease, and improve the patient's treatment plan.

For instance, a diabetic patient can have an HCDT that monitors her or his blood glucose level, levels of exercise, and diet and then give feedback on the best way to live with the disease.

7.2 Fitness and Wellness

The HCDTs can be profitably applied in the fitness industry to provide performance tracking and feedback on the enacted exercise regimes. In combination with the data received from the wearables and fitness trackers, HCDTs can reduce the level of exercise intensity, number of resting periods, and nutrition plans to suit every person.

7.3 Smart Cities

In smart cities HCDTs as credible tools may be employed to simulate the pattern of interaction between citizens and other infrastructure in the city. For instance, the city's physical structure can be explained by the use of HCDTs to reveal how persons navigate their way through a city, respond to a change in climate and circumstances of receiving and accessing public services, among others.

7.4 Retail and Customer Experience

In the retail trade HCDTs can be employed to design personalised shopping experiences in that organisation exercises the necessary tracking of the consumers' characteristics, trends, purchase histories and activities. Retailers can use this data to recommend other products to make a purchase based on a customers' preference, or even future tendencies to make a purchase.

8. FUTURE DIRECTIONS FOR HUMAN-CENTERED DIGITAL TWINS (HCDTS)

The idea of Human-Centered Digital Twins (HCDTs) is still relatively new and promises new directions for modelling and enhancing human experiences with systems. Human-Centered Digital Twins are detailed and continuously updated digital models of a person, in order to support real-time and contextual monitoring, as well as analytics for immediate decision-making in areas like health and wellbeing, smart city living, and industrial safety. There are several promising trends that remain in the further development of HCDTs in the future, thus guaranteeing HCDTs to be more indispensable in practice.

In this section, the reader will find out more about the key trends and innovations that can be expected in the advancement of the HCDTs in future. These are new developments in artificial intelligence, how it embodies new technologies, change of privacy and ethics, use across industries, and the barriers to releasing the full potential of artificial intelligence.

8.1 Advancements in Artificial Intelligence and Machine Learning:

AI and ML are the main technologies that fuel the change in HCDTs. These technologies facilitate data, learning rate, forecasts, and decision making abilities as and when needed which are crucial for improving the efficiency of human-centred digital models. As AI and ML technologies extend, better utilization of HCDTs will create new intelligent, personalized, and proactive systems.

A. **Predictive Analytics and Personalization:** However, there has been lots of growth in HCDTs especially when it comes to the following disciplines; Predictive analytics. Artificial intelligence can also actively sort through large amounts of data accumulated from various sensors, devices, and systems, and make precise predictions on what outcomes may occur and what sort of interventions could help prevent it. For instance, in a health care setting, the AI driven HCDTs can follow up on the patient's health status and predict new diseases or side effects of treatment even before they show up.

Another area, where AI will significantly improve HCDTs, is personalization. Specifically, the opportunity to adjust the recommendation rate for behavior, preferences and indicators of the person's condition is critical. The proposed use in the future is that AI algorithms could recommend wellness plans, treatments, exercises, and deploy schedules based on characteristics leading to better health and efficiency.

B. **Autonomous Decision-Making:** The future of HCDTs can also be seen to include fully autonomous decision-making whereby the systems determine conditions on their on without consulting with human beings. For example, in smart cities, HCDTs might independently control traffic and energy and public services and adapt resource usage as requirements change. This will help to enhance automation and lessen the dependence on assessment by human beings, which will enhance the operation of the whole system that is more interactive and sensitive to change.

In healthcare for instance, AI could be used to automatically update patients' treatment regimens depending on data retrieved from wearable technologies with a view of enhancing healthcare service provision and minimizing possibility of mistakes. Decision making would also be useful where the environment is sensitive say in production lines or construction companies where many workers are at risk. AI could help track the state of worker fatigue and also detect the conditions within the environment and areas of operation that pose certain risks, and take remedial measures before an incidence happens.

C. **Ethical AI for Human-Centered Systems:** In the future, decisions made by AI mean that there will be the need to adopt ethical AI frameworks such that HCDTs will follow as they continue to integrate AI in their systems. Perhaps most importantly, it is much more helpful when working with rather delicate information like health records or habits, for example. Ethical AI for the future will involve minimizing biases Learned from datasets, the privacy of individuals and the readability of algorithms to users and regulators.

8.2 Integration with Emerging Technologies:

It is for this reason that HCDTs are ready to interface with the array of novel technologies that are currently in development, and this will bring about improvement of their features as well as envisioning of new scenarios that cannot be implemented today. Such as 5G networks, Internet of Things (IoT), blockchain technology, edge computing, among others will greatly help in the revolution of HCDTs by enhancing real time information transfer, enhanced computing capabilities and more secure technology infrastructure.

A. **Real-time 5G Networks:** 5G technology will further transform the existing HCDTs through the availability of very high-speed access with minimal delay. This will also enable HCDTs to capture and analyse data input in real-time inbound feeds and take subsequent action faster than previously possible in certain situations. For instance, a digital twin in healthcare setting will be enabled by 5G will offer an almost real-time read of the patient state and disease progression and thus help physicians make better and faster decisions.

HCDTs in smart cities shall be able to monitor and optimize the implemented physical structures using 5G. Waste collection, traffic regulation or energy supply will improve dramatically as digital models of the whole city will be able to engage with sensors and other systems in real time. This will also make autonomous systems more feasible since they will work under the condition of requiring 5G to promote quick swapping of data.

B. **Notification Integration with IoT Active Devices:** Internet of Things (IoT) therefore has a central role in the growth of HCDTs. With the increasing adoption of IoT devices they will continually generate a massive amount of real-time data for updating the models of the digital twin. They will vary from smart clothing to environmental sensors which in turn when imported into the digital twin's model will make the twin more comprehensive and accurate of an individual or even a system.

In the future, IoT integration will cause HCDTs to become more advanced and adaptable because of the further levels of personalization that it will allow. For instance, in the workplace, IoT gadgets could constantly favour vital signs, ergonomics, and climate of workers and recommend corrective work environment changes or healthier lifestyles in parallel.

C. **Blockchain towards Security and Privacy:** Since HCDTs are required to gather and analyse enormous volumes of data that are often highly confidential, blockchain will quickly become a critical component of data protection. Its decentralized and unalterable structure can help maintain integrity and confidentiality of data that HCDTs collect and disseminate through the use of blockchain and can be accessed only by authorized individuals.

In medicine, blockchain can be utilized as a tool of secure patient record preservation that provides individuals with possibilities to regulate the access to their avatars and medical records. Blockchain can also promote a proper and safe sharing of information between healthcare providers since patient information has to be shared among the different providers for better health results.

8.3 Role of Data Management and Processing in recent years:

Key organizational characteristics indicating the future direction of HCDTs are marked by two major developments in data management and processing. More data is being collected from IoT devices, wearables and other sensors, and that means more importance to deal, process and mine useful information out of the data thus collected.

A. **Edge Computing for Localized Computing:** In the emerging world of smart devices, edge computing will be an important enabler in increasing the feasibility and effectiveness of HCDTs. Edge computing is a process of data processing at the point where it is generated, unlike using cloud for processing data. This cuts down the time required to complete a task, the amount of bandwidth consumed in the process and guarantees real-time processing of data.

for instance, edge computing in the health sector could enable the analysis of biometric data from wearable gadgets on the real time basis with feedback being promptly given to the patient and the caregiver. This will be especially vital where, for example, sensitive health parameters need to be continuously observed, or in the case of reporting incidents at the workplace.

B. **Big Data Analytics to gain further understanding:** With the expansion of body data production rates of HCDTs, big data analytics will be required for obtaining decision-making information. With the help of predictive analytics and data mining it is possible to gather more accurate information, forecasts, simulations and others related to human behavior by using Digital Twins.

For example, in chronic disease management Big data analytics could be used to follow long-term health patterns and make better estimations regarding the development of diseases. Likewise, in the workplace, big data may be applied in relations to day to day performance, injuries, and health of the employees in an organization to forecast what actions an organization can take in order to improve performance and reduce risks.

8.4 Ethics and Privacy Considerations

There are some promising techniques connected with adoption of Higher education collaborative development technologies, which in turn raises some ethical and privacy issues. As the personal data is collected, stored and analysed in order to support the decision making process, the rights of the individuals inserting the data and of the receivers will have to be respected; thus, the use of such a technology has to be performed responsibly.

A. **Data Ownership and Consent:** However, there is a crucial question concerning data ownership and the question of proper and informed consent that will pose big challenges to the future of HCDTs. Due to the fact that HCDTs utilize personal information, the latter has to be owned and controlled by the subject. This will mean defined and comprehensible guidelines concerning the amassment of data, the consent the data subjects give, and how and when this information is shared.

This can be achieved through the use of blockchain technology which can enable secure recording of the data transaction and whereby the owners of the data in the twins are constantly managing it. Further, AI systems are also going to require trust and effectively these require explanation of what data is being used where and how decisions are being made.

B. **Setting and Concept of Bias and Fairness for Digital Twins:** As deep learning and other forms of AI are adopted into the HCDTs, decision making processes will raise questions of bias. Since the algorithms behind digital twins learn from data, they will be able to generate biased or discriminative results if the data they learned from was bias. In addition, objective decisions will be needed to avoid the use of biases that may exist in the models AI will require frameworks for detecting and addressing the biases.

Some love will have to be applied in the direction of making sure that HCDTs are created and delivered in a fashion that is equitable and in inclusion, especially for domains that are highly dependent on the information, such as the healthcare and where biased algorithm may further worsen the situation for members of vulnerable populations.

8.5 Wider Applications Across Sectors

HCDTs are already being used in healthcare, smart cities and fitness but this is just a small vision of the applications of this technology. Here are some potential future directions for HCDTs across various sectors:

A. **Customized Learning Individuals:** In learning, HCDTs could be used in developing learning environment which are unique to learners. Virtual alphabets of a learner could capture academic performance, preferred learning approach, and mental health; the Education technology would self-optimise to adapt to each learner's requirements. This could facilitate the delivering of higher attention from tutors knowing the particular students, increase student interest and deal with learning difficulties.
B. **Workplace optimization and Employee health:** Few years from now the HCDTs can also be used to develop what can be referred to as employees' digital replica through which organizations can monitor the productivity, well-being and performance of employees. If stress levels, physical health, or work-life balance of the employees could be monitored then employers could take measures in advance to ensure that the employee's productivity is not going down, instead it is increasing day by day and the turnover rate is going down, meaning more and more people are satisfied with what they are doing.
C. **Retail /Consumer environment:** HCDTs could also be adjusted into the retail business so as to foster adaptive shopping solutions. Customer avatars could monitor their shopping behaviour, preferences, and previous purchases with the aim of making suggestions regarding products to purchase. Furthermore, observing customers' satisfaction and their feelings they have towards products, retailers could maximize their stores' benefits and enhance customers' treatments.

9. CONCLUSION

Human-cantered digital twins have moved from being one of the many trends in the technology industry to being a paradigm that can revolutionize by creating a positive change in numerous fields such as healthcare and city management. The foundation of HCDTs is based in the capacity for the development of individual and sensitive digital models of a body and its cognitive and affective processes in real time.

The future development of HCDTs is progressing at high speed – a major step forward in merging AI-enhanced technology with human interactions. As live, interactive avatars of people, HCDTs provide a powerful means for further tailoring, increasing effectiveness, or ensuring safety in the fields of medicine smart cities and others more. As a result, organizations are able to gain anticipations of the physical, emotional, and behavioural conditions of clients so that decisions made can serve the client and the larger public interests.

However, the use of HCDTs has vital difficulties, which need to be solved to avoid ethical misuse of amateurs. Three main challenges include privacy and data protection, security and ethical concerns of bias and consent limit the use of HCDTs. Solving these issues implies the following actions: the efficacy of data protection measures; clear data practices; legal requirements that would protect the rights of citizens and improve innovation at the same time.

This chapter has discussed activities where HCDTs can be implemented and the potential advantages that can accrue from them through use of case studies. These examples easily explain how HCDTs can revolutionary's industries as they improve not only efficiency but also reliability. But they also emphasize the need to achieve better balance to give adequate attention to ethical issues and adequate regulatory concerns.

While contemplating on the future of HCDTs, it will be significant to note that the growth and implementation of such systems will arise from a synergy of efforts of technologists, experts, policymakers, as well as ethicists, and industry stakeholders. It means that in order to produce the future where technology enhances and beautifies life rather than diminishes a person's value and reduces his or her humanity, HCDTs should be developed with the support of dialogue and cooperation, one can guarantee that the process of development corresponds to societal values and ethical standards.

In the future, HCDTs will mark a new generation capacity in how humans engage with his or her surroundings. They bring large benefits in terms of individualization, speed, and environmental friendliness, but at the same time, pose new problems in the field of privacy, data protectionism, and their usage. It is in this part of the paper where the author looks into the future prospects of HCDTs, their implications to other industries, and principal insights for future growth. Some of the questions that we will answer include: What are some of the issues that need to be considered to ensure that HCDTs will be used appropriately, and ethically? And, how might they help to change society in the years to come?

REFERENCES

Anderson, C. Y.. (2025). Implementing Human-Centered Digital Twins in Healthcare: Case Studies and Real-World Applications. *Healthcare Technology Review*, *12*(4), 204–217.

Asad, U., Khan, M., Khalid, A., & Lughmani, W. A. (2023, April). Human-Centric Digital Twins in Industry: A Comprehensive review of enabling technologies and implementation Strategies. *Sensors (Basel)*, *23*(8), 3938. DOI: 10.3390/s23083938 PMID: 37112279

Brown, D. N., & Schwartz, H. L. (2023). Regulating Digital Twins: Legal Considerations in the Digital Future. *Journal of Cyber Law and Policy*, *15*(1), 56–68.

Demirel, H. O., Irshad, L., Ahmed, S., & Tumer, I. Y. (2021, March). Digital Twin-Driven Human-Centered design frameworks for meeting sustainability objectives. *Journal of Computing and Information Science in Engineering*, *21*(3), 031012. Advance online publication. DOI: 10.1115/1.4050684

Domínguez, L. G. I. (2024, August). Gemelos Digitales en la Industria 5.0 – una Revisión Sistemática de Literatura. *European Public & Social Innovation Review*, *9*, 1–21. DOI: 10.31637/epsir-2024-641

Holzinger, A., Fister, I., Fister, I., Kaul, H.-P., & Asseng, S. (2024). Human-Centered AI in Smart Farming: Toward Agriculture 5.0. *IEEE Access : Practical Innovations, Open Solutions*, *12*, 62199–62214. DOI: 10.1109/ACCESS.2024.3395532

Le, L., Jun, D. M., & Jones, D. L. "Energy-efficient detection system in time-varying signal and noise power", *Proc. IEEE Int. Conf. Acoust. Speech Signal Process.*, pp. 2736-2740, 2013. DOI: 10.1109/ICASSP.2013.6638154

Le, L. N., & Jones, D. L. (2017, April). Feature-Sharing in Cascade Detection Systems With Multiple Applications. *IEEE Journal of Selected Topics in Signal Processing*, *11*(3), 466–478. DOI: 10.1109/JSTSP.2017.2679539

Lee, L. R., & Patel, M. C. (2022). Ethics of AI in Human-Centered Digital Twins: Addressing Bias and Fairness. *Ethics and Technology Journal*, *5*(1), 89–97.

Lin, Y., Chen, L., Ali, A., Nugent, C., Cleland, I., Li, R., Ding, J., & Ning, H. (2024, August). Human digital twin: A survey. *Journal of Cloud Computing (Heidelberg, Germany)*, *13*(1), 131. Advance online publication. DOI: 10.1186/s13677-024-00691-z

Lyu, Y., Li, L., Jing, Z., Liang, Y., Wang, R., & Wang, F.-Y. (2024, November). Meta-Services in Industry 5.0: A New Paradigm of Intelligent Services in Metaverses. *IEEE Transactions on Systems, Man, and Cybernetics. Systems*, *54*(11), 6826–6836. DOI: 10.1109/TSMC.2024.3373656

Miller, S. (2024). Smart Cities and Digital Twins: Integrating Human Experience into Urban Management. *International Journal of Urban Technology*, *7*(2), 45–59.

Shi, C., Du, F., & Wu, Q. (2022). A Digital Twin Architecture for Wireless Networked Adaptive Active Noise Control. *IEEE/ACM Transactions on Audio, Speech, and Language Processing*, *30*, 2768–2777. DOI: 10.1109/TASLP.2022.3199992

Smith, J., & Jones, A. (2023). Human-Centered Digital Twins: Advancing Personalized Health. *Journal of Digital Innovation*, *14*(3), 120–130.

Wang, S., Zhang, J., Wang, P., Law, J., Calinescu, R., & Mihaylova, L. (2023, July). A deep learning-enhanced Digital Twin framework for improving safety and reliability in human–robot collaborative manufacturing. *Robotics and Computer-integrated Manufacturing*, *85*, 102608. DOI: 10.1016/j.rcim.2023.102608

Wang, T. (2024). Privacy Concerns in the Age of Digital Twins: Security Challenges and Solutions. *IEEE Access : Practical Innovations, Open Solutions*, *9*, 7854–7862.

Yang, G., Ye, Z., Wu, H., Li, C., Wang, R., Kong, D., Hou, Z., Wang, H., Huang, X., Pang, Z., Dong, N., & Pang, G. (2024, August). A Digital Twin-Based Large-Area Robot Skin System for Safer Human-Centered Healthcare Robots Toward Healthcare 4.0. *IEEE Transactions on Medical Robotics and Bionics*, *6*(3), 1104–1115. DOI: 10.1109/TMRB.2024.3421635

Yang, T., Razzaq, L., Fayaz, H., & Qazi, A. (2024, June). Redefining fan manufacturing: Unveiling industry 5.0's human-centric evolution and digital twin revolution. *Heliyon*, *10*(13), e33551. DOI: 10.1016/j.heliyon.2024.e33551 PMID: 39050440

Ye, X., Du, J., Han, Y., Newman, G., Retchless, D., Zou, L., Ham, Y., & Cai, Z. (2022, November). Developing Human-Centered Urban Digital Twins for Community Infrastructure Resilience: A research agenda. *Journal of Planning Literature*, *38*(2), 187–199. DOI: 10.1177/08854122221137861 PMID: 37153810

Zhu, H. Y., Hieu, N. Q., Hoang, D. T., Nguyen, D. N., & Lin, C.-T. "A Human-Centric Metaverse Enabled by Brain-Computer Interface: A Survey," in *IEEE Communications Surveys & Tutorials*, vol. 26, no. 3, pp. 2120-2145, thirdquarter 2024, DOI: 10.1109/COMST.2024.3387124

Chapter 13
Optimizing Product Development with Digital Twins and IoT Integration

Prerna Srivastava
https://orcid.org/0009-0000-2609-2204
Poornima University, India

Ritu Raj Choudhary
https://orcid.org/0000-0001-6056-0569
Poornima University, Jaipur, India

Monika Khatri
Poornima University, India

Vineet Pandey
https://orcid.org/0000-0001-9850-997X
Banasthali Vidyapith, Niwai, India

Ankur Srivastava
Manipal University Jaipur, India

Korhan Cengiz
Biruni University, Istanbul, Turkey

ABSTRACT

Digital twins and IoT integration are transforming product development by bringing real time analytics, predictive modeling and virtual prototyping in real time. Nevertheless, the successful realization of these technologies depends critically on a systems level, managerial framework that accounts for technical and organizational challenges. This chapter provides a forward-looking approach to optimizing product development cycles through the integration of digital twins and IoT technologies. The study delves into cutting edge advances hybrid and cognitive twins, AI driven analytics and edge to cloud ecosystem. Furthermore, the chapter also introduces important trends such as human centric twins, block chain enabled ecosystems and quantum computing. This chapter aligns technical advancements with managerial practices to provide the leaders with the tools to take advantage of the digital transformation in the transforming Industry 4.0 landscape in order to achieve a competitive edge

INTRODUCTION

As technology continues to evolve in the era of Industry 4.0, old paradigms of product development are being thrown out the window and organizations have been forced to rethink how they innovate, manufacture, and deliver products to the market. This revolution is driven by Digital Twins and the Internet

DOI: 10.4018/979-8-3373-2028-1.ch013

of Things (IoT) – two closely related technologies that enable a very tight coupling of the physical and digital worlds. These technologies, via virtual models, real time data and advanced analytics, enable companies to optimize processes, improve product quality, and respond quickly to market demand. Based on this, more and more businesses are starting to understand that IoT and the resultant Digital Twins form a part of the technical solutions and strategic enablers to foster competitiveness and innovation. Digital Twins are adaptive, digital replicas of physical systems that simulate, monitor and optimise real time performance (Wagner et al., 2019). Traditionally, these models utilize advanced analytics to provide predictive an prescriptive insights. The idea has been around for decades but using AI and IoT has propelled the technology forward at such a rate. They are real time and not static representations of a digital twin and can model complex scenarios to predict outcomes and recommend for taking action. Digital Twins, however, have enormous implications for product development: it means that organizations can actually build and refine their products faster, more efficiently, and ultimately more accurate than before (Lo et al., 2021).

The IoT ecosystem is the infrastructure foundation of connectivity, to accompany Digital Twins, comprising physical devices, sensors, and systems that can communicate with each other and more importantly their digital counterparts. Digital Twins won't be possible without IoT as it will be the basis of collecting all necessary amounts of data to fuel them, turning the physical environments into rich real-time information sources. Figure 1 highlights the progression of Digital Twins technology across three stages: Dynamic simulations, AI-driven cognitive twins, and static models. From 2000 to 2020, computing power was improved, IoT integration was established, and AI was developed to improve the capabilities of Digital Twins and turn them into autonomous decision-making tools.

Figure 1. Evolution of Digital Twins

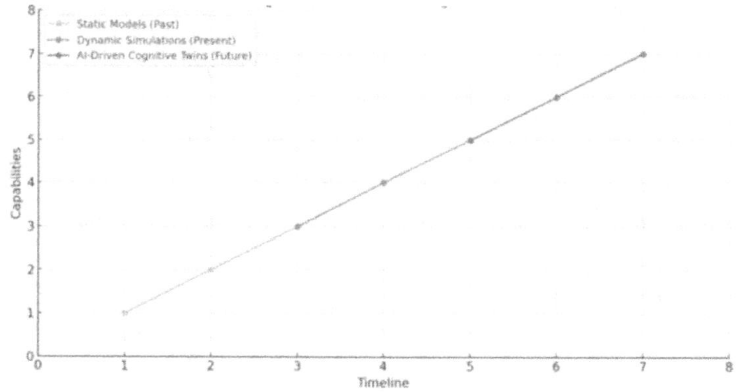

Organizations have overcome the divide between design and deployment by integrating IoT into the product development processes. For example, IoT permits manufacturers to monitor a production line in real time, helping to ensure that quality control is consistent, reduces waste, and enables adaptive manufacturing processes. Moreover, IoT ecosystems have increasingly utilized sophisticated technologies, like edge computing 5G networks, to bring data processing speed, lower latency, and better decision-making. Therefore, IoT and Digital Twins have become an innovative industry foundation. The transformative potential of these technologies is far from being straightforward in their successful implementation. There are many challenges to overcome when integrating Digital Twins and IoT into workflows in many organizations. Beyond the technical side, we encounter organizational and cultural barriers like matching these technologies to strategic goals, interfacing them with existing systems, and overseeing the personnel that must run them as they should (Donoghue et al., 2018).

Data security, scalability, and governance further complicate the equation. For example, a cyber-attack on the IoT ecosystems could attack sensitive data and interrupt the operating state. The same applies to the deployment of Digital Twins, whose success typically comes with a significant investment in infrastructure, software, and talent, and as such, organizations need to adopt a strategic approach. As organizations adopt Digital Twin technologies and IoT, to realize the potential returns of these transformations, one needs to have a well-defined managerial framework, failing which it may be counter-productive and even leave an organization at a disadvantage in today's competitive markets (Olad & Valilai, 2020). Figure 2 shows the relationship between IoT sensors, real-time data streams, and Digital Twins. It demonstrates how data from physical systems is collected with help from the IoT devices, transmitted to Digital Twins for analysis, and used to generate usable insights for optimizations. First, the feedback loop clearly shows the variety in the dynamic interpretation of physical and digital environments.

Figure 2. Conceptual Overview of Digital Twins and IoT Ecosystems

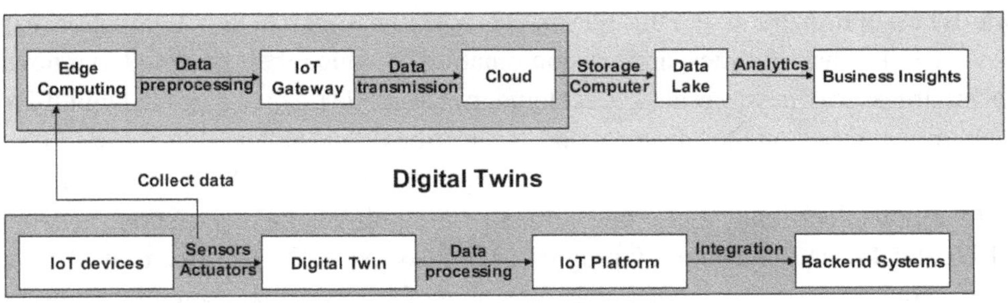

In response to these challenges and to unlock the full potential of Digital Twins and IoT, this chapter presents a forwardlooking managerial framework that brings the technical capability together with business goals. This, at its essence, is a framework about strategic alignment; this is a project aligning to organization goals and KPIs, they drive adoption of tech. Further, this provides practical advice on leveraging Digital Twins and IoT in present workflows with regard to scalability, interoperability, and workforce enablement. In addition, the framework illustrates the value brought by real time monitoring and optimization, where data driven information serves to inform and enhance decisions, making operations leaner. However, the framework also ends with risk management and offering strategies to deal with technology, cybersecurity and organizational risks as well as maintaining the initiative in the medium and long term. With the accelerating pace of the digital transformation, organization must continue to progress and adapt to the changing ways of not only doing business, but accelerate the future of how products are created, including Digital Twins and IoT **(Huang et al., 2022)**. Human centric twins, Quantum computing, Blockchain driven IoT ecosystems will be key advancements in redefining what's possible with these technologies. Human-centric twins, for example, strive to enhance the user experience and personalize interaction between human and machine, while Blockchain offers further security and transparency in the IoT network. All applications, including simulation, stand to benefit from quantum computing which promises to revolutionize Digital Twin simulations, due to its ability of handling exponentially larger data sets or solving problems infeasible in the usual computing timescale. In this chapter, we look at the trend of these innovations, their implication and try to arm managers and leaders with actionable insights on how such innovations can be leveraged for competitive advantage (Holopainen et al., 2024).

Digital Twin and IoT integration is a technological shift, as well as a strategic imperative for any organization to succeed in the changing environment of Industry 4.0. By merging these technologies with companies' broader business strategies, companies are able to reduce time to market, improve product quality, enhance sustainability and be agile and innovative enough to respond to the ever changing dynamic market demands. Based on the relationships between Digital Twins and IoT, this chapter lays the foundation for the interaction between them and proposes a framework to facilitate management in tapping the transformative power. If used correctly, these technologies can become a cornerstone innovation for helping organizations lead in the digital age (Li et al., 2021).

Digital Twins and IoT Integration: Foundational Concepts

A compelling aspect of Industry 4.0 is the integration of Digital Twins and the Internet of Things (IoT). The industry sees this as a way to provide the real-time capabilities required to monitor and simulate systems towards best optimization. For this reason, it is essential to start at their foundation, exploring the concepts they are built, their abilities, and the combination by which their potential to innovate product development is harnessed (Eneyew et al., 2022; Hemdan et al., 2023). Three types of Digital Twins (basic, hybrid, and cognitive, based on their features and applications) are compared in Table 1. The capability progression is shown from static models for basic design optimization to AI-driven cognitive twins that can make autonomous decisions. While this comparison highlights the ever-increasing sophistication and value of Digital Twins as technology progresses, it also shows the hard-to-meet Minimum Viable Product (MVP) requirements set to consider an assembly of IoT systems a potential Digital Twin.

Table 1. Comparison of Basic, Hybrid, And Cognitive Digital Twins

Type of Digital Twin	Key Features	Applications
Basic Digital Twin	Static models are limited to the design and testing phases.	Design optimization and basic prototyping.
Hybrid Digital Twin	Dynamic simulations incorporate real-time data from IoT.	Real-time monitoring and predictive maintenance.
Cognitive Digital Twin	AI-driven analytics; capable of autonomous decision-making.	Advanced automation and prescriptive analytics.

Digital Twins: Evolution and Capabilities

Digital Twins as a concept were first conceived in engineering and manufacturing, where initial applications of the idea were to create static representations used for design and simulation. However, the lack of real-time, real data and real-time connectivity in these early iterations meant their utility as a vehicle for real–time decision-making was quite limited. However, through data processing, machine learning, and IoT, Digital Twins now act as interactive systems and deliver real-time insights (Boyes &

Watson, 2022; Zheng et al., 2022). The Digital Twins of today are not static objects like those of their predecessors but dynamic entities that reflect the physical state of an object or system and model its future performance under different conditions. Digital twins consist of 3 basic elements: physical entities, digital models and data connection. Its digital model is populated by real time data from sensors embedded in physical assets. The digital twin is continuously exchanging data with the digital model that reflects the current state of the physical entity, and can simulate the potential outcomes of the physical entity. For example, in the automotive industry, Digital Twins are employed to characterize the response of particular vehicle component and its response during different operating conditions and engine and braking systems. It lets manufacturers catch design deficiencies, boost performance, and enhance safety before their products go onto a production line. The most significant advancement of Digital Twin technology is AI driven analytics. Due to the capabilities of Digital Twin, they can do more than that, i.e. anomaly detection, predictive maintenance and prescriptive decision-making. Imagine, for instance, there's an AI assisted Digital Twin in the context of an industrial environment, analysing a pattern in sensor data, and predicting when a machine is supposed to expire and proposing a preventive maintenance operation (Boyes & Watson, 2022).

The primary benefit offered by the system is reducing the downtime and improving the operational efficiency along with equipment life, thereby reducing the long term cost. Figure 3 presents an IoT ecosystem. When combined in this way, each component helps achieve an IoT–powered digital twin's frictionless collection, processing, and communication of data. Digital Twin is based on the core of the Internet of Things (IoT), in that it permits connectivity between physical and digital systems. IoT ecosystems refer to interconnected devices, sensors and software platforms that collect, in real time, transmit and analyze data. The pieces of infrastructure essentially need to communicate with each other in order to supply this information, and with it, the data required to build accurate, dynamic representations of physical assets (Iliuţă et al., 2024).

IoT Ecosystem: Key Components and Role in Product Development

Figure 3. Components of The IoT Ecosystem

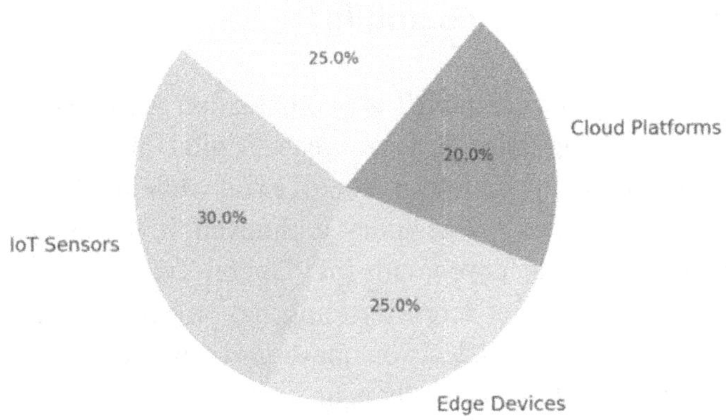

Sensors and Actuators:

In IoT ecosystems, sensors collect real time data to measure things such as temperature, pressure, and vibration. This data is used by Actuators to make 'adjustments', which builds feedback loops that optimize for efficiency & reduce waste. Collectively, these components make monitoring and optimization in product development frictionless. In a smart factory, IoT sensors can monitor the performance of a production line, and actuate to keep it all at the optimum. Together, these two abilities create feedback loops that improve efficiency and eliminate waste in the product development process ("Digital Twin Sensors in Cultural Heritage Ontology Applications," 2024).

Edge Computing and Cloud Integration

IoT devices produce large amounts of data, and, like Big Data, IoT requires efficient processing to extract actionable insights. This is where edge computing comes in, where data is processed on the spot next to where it is generated, minimizing latency and facilitating faster decision-making. At the same time, organizations can benefit from centralized storage and advanced analytics capabilities using cloud computing, making meaningful use of historical trends and conducting large-scale simulations. A wind farm might use edge computing to make real-time changes to turbine settings if local weather is right to help produce even more electricity, and the cloud-based systems look over long-term performance data to improve future designs (Booyse et al., 2020).

IoT Communication Protocols

Communication in such IoT ecosystems must be reliable and secure. Protocols like 5G, LPWAN, and Zigbee provide a high data transmission rate coupled with long-range connectivity, which is adept at supporting diverse applications such as autonomous vehicles or smart cities. For example, Real Time Digital Twins require high bandwidth and low latency connectivity, an area that 5G networks easily meet. These communication technologies facilitate IoT ecosystems growth to complex product development environments (Florea et al., 2020).

The Synergy Between Digital Twins and IoT

The synergetic nature of Digital Twins and IoT is a combination of two technologies whose strengths increase the functional aspect of the other. It helps create Digital Twins, which are a framework for interpreting, simulating and optimizing data from the IoTs and while the IoT is the source of real time data into Digital Twins. From efficiency to accuracy to innovation, it's things that these technologies have never allowed organizations to achieve. With IoT, Digital Twins, and Aligned convergence, organizations can observe, analyze, and act across systems and processes in near real time, to generate actionable implicit and explicit answers to decision questions (Kaivo-oja et al., 2019). For example, in energy space, IoT sensors can record how well solar panels are performing, with Digital Twins emulating the effect of weather to how much value the energy yield. Through test measurements, operators are able to optimally manage performance and realize maximum energy production. In Table 2 are outlined the organization's primary objectives that can be achieved by integrating Digital Twins with IoT technology. The real time data that Digital Twins uses comes via IoT, while Digital Twins provides a framework for making sense of the data, simulation of the data, and making incremental improvements in the data. They allow organizations to reach an unheard of efficiency, accuracy, innovation. IoT and Digital Twins combined offers organizations the ability to monitor systems and processes live and generate actionable insights for decision making. For example, IoT sensors can monitor how energy is affected by changes in weather in the energy sector by monitoring the performance of solar panels and simulating how energy output would affect the performance of energy. This allows operators to proactively adjust as necessary to maintain the best performance and maximize energy production (Kou et al., 2024; Radanliev et al., 2022). Table 2 defines the main objectives that the organizations pursue in the usage of Digital Twins combined IoT technologies. It wants to chop time to market, enhance product quality, make operations more efficient, enable predictive maintenance and sustainability. For each objective there is a brief explanation as to why it is important in building competitive advantage.

Table 2. Key Objectives of Digital Twins and IoT in Product Development

Objective	Description
Reduce Time-to-Market	Accelerate the design and production process with virtual prototypes.
Enhance Product Quality	Leverage real-time data to identify and address quality issues proactively.
Improve Operational Efficiency	Optimize resource allocation and reduce waste through automation.
Enable Predictive Maintenance	Predict and prevent equipment failures to minimize downtime.
Achieve Sustainability Goals	Reduce carbon footprint and align operations with environmental standards.

Predictive and Prescriptive Capabilities

Digital Twins and IoT work together to do predictive and prescriptive analytics. Historical data combined with real-time inputs allows organizations to forecast potential exceptions and take preventive measures. In aerospace, for example, Digital Twins enabled by IoT can foretell when maintenance is needed on the aircraft engine, thereby reducing the chances of in-flight failure and minimizing the loss of customers through downtime. In addition, systems can take prescriptive actions, including recommending or executing an action autonomously (e.g., rerouting supply chains to avoid delays). Combining Digital Twins and IoT drastically cuts time and resource requirements for product development. Digital Twins virtual prototyping enables engineers to test designs under several simulation conditions without producing several physical prototypes. IoT also takes this to the next level through real-world data that informs and validates the simulation (van Dinter et al., 2022). For example, IoT data is used by consumer electronics companies to understand how users work with devices, which are fed into their Digital Twins to optimize the next iterations. Although there is no shortage of technological expertise on Digital Twins and IoT technologies, successful adoption for product development cannot be achieved on technical expertise alone. Similarly, organizations must strategically implement IT service management, with the implementation being consistent with business goals, natural and smooth as possible with existing workflow, and having a healthy risk management discipline. In this section, I present a complete managerial framework aimed at navigating these complexities rigorously yet allowing the organization to exploit completely the Digital Twins and IoT transformation potential (Stadtmann et al., 2023). A detailed structured roadmap for implementing Digital Twins and IoT technologies within an organization is illustrated in Table 3. It then breaks these steps into key steps, from evaluating existing infrastructure, defining objectives, creating pilot projects, training the workforce, and ultimately scaling up solutions. It is a practical guide to managers grappling with the intricacies of adoption.

Table 3. Strategic Steps for Digital Twin and IoT Implementation

Step	Action
Evaluate Existing Infrastructure	Assess hardware, software, and connectivity readiness.
Define Key Objectives	Align technology adoption with business goals.
Develop Pilot Projects	Test solutions in controlled environments to validate value.
Train Workforce	Provide training on interpreting data and managing systems.
Scale Solutions	Expand successful pilots to full-scale deployments.

To integrate Digital Twins and IoT, the first thing to begin is to know how these technologies align to the organization's objectives. For this to happen, it must be linked with measurable business outcomes, like lessening product development cycles, better quality, or fulfilling sustainability goals. If this alignment isn't present, investments in Digital Twins and IoT may not provide optimal value as the two risks sitting in their silos and delivering little for the effort. Figure 4 portrays a bar chart with a managerial implementation framework for critical steps in using Digital Twins and IoT technology. The key steps follow the traditional model of digital transformation practice, which includes strategic alignment, infrastructure readiness, pilot project development, and scaling solutions. The importance of each step is quantified, and it is emphasized that each successful implementation depends on the sequential and identical interdependence of the steps.

Figure 4. Managerial Framework for Digital Twins and IoT Integration

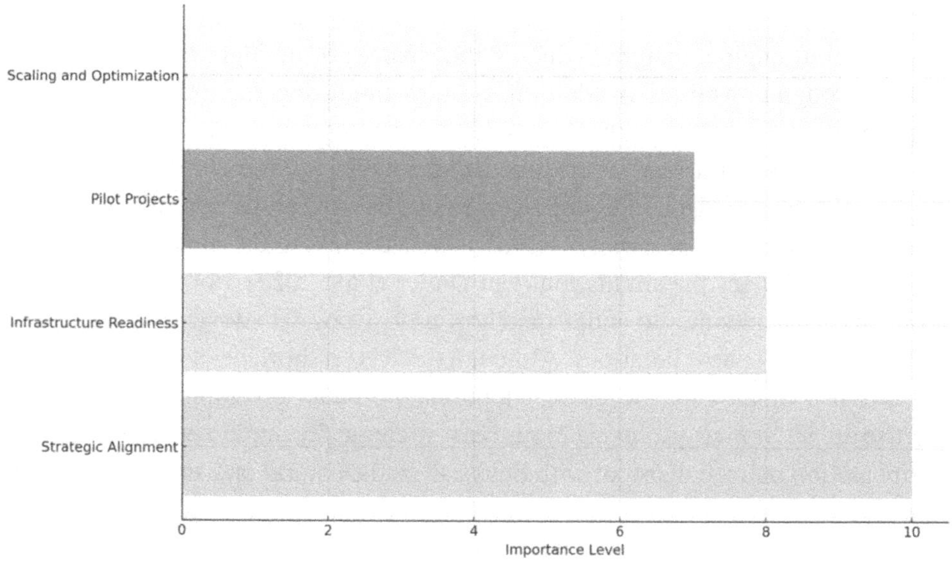

Defining key performance indicators (KPIs) for successful Digital Twins and IoT initiatives is essential to strategic alignment. Properly, these KPIs should cover technical and business objectives like reducing production downtime, improving energy efficiency, or faster time-to-market. An automotive company that had started using Digital Twins to simulate vehicle performance to set a KPI of reducing physical prototyping costs by 30% over 2 years. Setting clear targets helps organizations ensure that technology deployments are driven by shared vision and therefore aligned between different departments and teams. Leaders assist in preserving the strategic alignment by working with technical experts to establish relationships with the business stakeholders. For Digital Twins and IoT to achieve a competitive advantage, senior executives must formulate a compelling vision and ensure resources (including budgets) and cross-functional support are in place. The collaborative approach to spreading technology adoption creates a purpose, eliminating organizational resistance to change. Our focus has been to integrate these technologies into workflows to reduce cycle time while improving part quality for online and offline manufacturing. To bring Digital Twins and IoT into organizational workflows, having a plan, executing that plan, and being ready to reassess and adapt is of utmost importance (Mihai et al., 2022). One needs to assess current infrastructure, a scalable deployment strategy, and workforce enablement to succeed. These components are key to optimizing the value of Digital Twins and IoT technology and ensuring that the asset digitalization vision drives and aligns with your organization's objectives.

Organizations should understand Digital Twins and IoT technologies, and only then can they evaluate their infrastructure to ensure compatibility. Various hardware capabilities, software frameworks, and network infrastructure are examined to support the collection and transmission of real-time data. Traditional systems are usually outdated and need to be updated. IoT sensors are introducing edge computing and cloud computing to process and store data. For example, older manufacturing facilities may need modernized sensor networks to attain the required connectivity for seamless data integration. A good readiness assessment goes deeper and helps companies understand what was missed in their infra and learn what infrastructure is required to deploy them without any issues. As large as they are, Digital Twins and IoT technologies take the form of large scale implementations, and pilot projects are an essential first step. For example, an organization would use the use case of optimizing the performance of a particular production line to test their solutions in a controlled environment on a single, well defined use case. Using this approach, teams can search for problems, create processes, and prove the inherent value of these technologies prior to large scale implementation. In addition, the pilot projects encourage stakeholders by providing concrete benefits, such as efficiency or cost savings. These are smaller, but they're a foundation for broader adoption, pulling lessons from the smaller scale of things into the larger rollouts (Ariesen-Verschuur et al., 2022).

Workforce Transformation Enabler

Digital Twins and IoT success depends on the workforce's skills and expertise. Employees need to learn new technologies, how to utilize them, and understand how to interpret and act on the data and the insights it generates. For example, support for engineers requires simulation capabilities and the ability to use predictive analytics to influence design decisions, while IT teams need the same to run IoT networks with data integrity in mind. Suppose you're going to build inequality into the composition of your workforce. In that case, you must ensure that workforce enablement is comprehensive and continuous, offering employees access to online training, hands-on training, workshops, and tools that inform employees about emerging tools and practices. Collaboration across departments should also be part of these programs, which means making technology adoption an opportunity for growth instead of a change that disrupts how a business works (Singh & Nayyar, 2025). With Digital Twins and IoTs, organizations have access to real-time insights about operations and performance, which has significantly evolved how we make decisions. These technologies allow companies to monitor continuously, spot inefficient areas, and make data-driven decisions to ensure the best results. Implementing robust monitoring systems is necessary to make sense of this raw data and turn it into actionable improvements . The effects of emerging trends like AI-driven twins, Blockchain-enabled IoT, quantum computing-powered twins, and cantered twins are featured in Figure 5. I evaluate these trends for their potential to impact Digital Twins and IoT ecosystems and give insight into the future of these technologies.

Figure 5 . Emerging Trends in Digital Twins and IoT

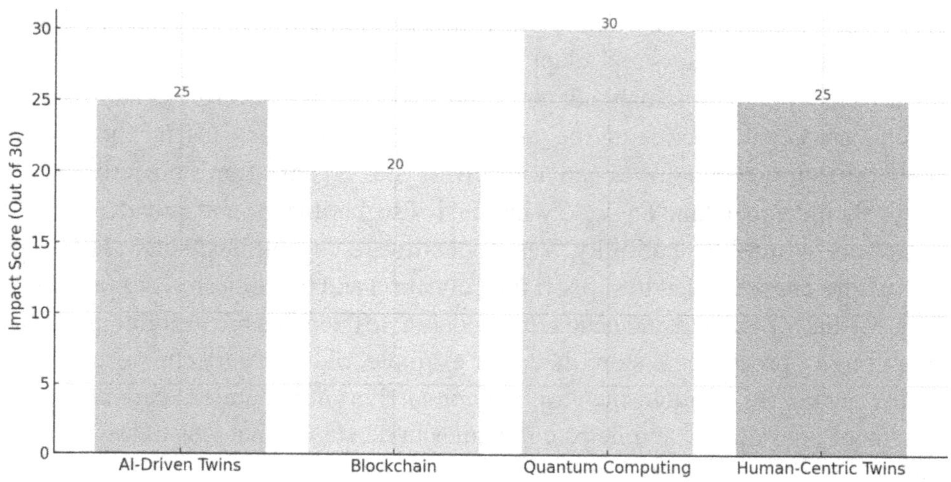

Monitoring Systems and Analytics

This information has to be collected, analyzed and made visible in real time to allow for better real time decision making and this is something which organizations need to develop systems around. IoT sensors around equipment typically provide data with key metrics such as temperature, pressure, and energy consumption, and Digital Twins simulates what will happen with the outcomes when you run multiple scenarios. Real time monitoring systems help managers track production efficiency, equipment health & resource utilization. These systems allow for immediate corrective action, preventing losses or regulatory noncompliance, in pharmaceutical industries where product quality is affected by environmental factors: temperature or humidity. This real time data is used for advanced predictive and prescriptive modeling analytics. Historical and present-day data is used by predictive analytics for forecasting issues such as production shutdowns, supply disruptions, equipment failures, and the like so organizations can take preventive action (Brosinsky et al., 2023).

On the other hand, Prescriptive analytics uses these predictions to recommend the optimal actions, amplifying the decision-making process. Fleet management can predict vehicle maintenance needs using Digital Twins powered by IoT sensors and suggest rerouting strategies to keep down fleet downtime and increase efficiency. The third aim is to create Feedback Loops for Continuous Improvement, enhancing the Data-Driven Design Process (DDD) deployment stage. The IoT and Digital Twin world create feedback loops through the continuous analysis of real world data to refine systems, products, and processes. Taking an iterative approach to operations means your operations will never get stale. For example, the data from the IoT enabled devices in the field is transmitted to the consumer electronics companies to analyze this data, and identify opportunities to change e.g. software improvements and the design changes. These insights promote innovation and keep the product offering at the tip of a changing market, allowing the product development cycle to reap the benefits (dos Santos et al., 2023).

Risk Management: Mitigating Challenges

The introduction of Digital Twins and IoT introduces technical, organizational and, cybersecurity risks that need to be proactively addressed to facilitate successful implementation and long term sustainability of Digital Twins and IoT. Although these technologies have broad benefits, the road to prevent and mitigate these challenges is paved with a robust risk management strategy to achieve the highest value from these technologies. For instance, if an organization desires our system to remain compatible, as well as being scalable and dependable, then this means that it must avoid (a) interference during, and (b) the aftermath of implementation of the software system. If Digital Twins are to integrate with legacy systems, the means to customize and validate the proper functioning of the two is essential. Furthermore, IoT devices in the miscellaneous environment should remain robust, and stay online under fluctuation of external condition. Vulnerability identification and system resilience validation are both critical to be done regularly and tested. Due to the fact that IoT ecosystems hold multiple connected devices and data streams, these entities are vulnerable to cybersecurity threats. In other words, a single compromised device, any device, can expose an entire network (Chen et al., 2022). In order to protect sensitive data, you may need to take up multi layered cybersecurity measures which include real time intrusion detection systems, end to end encryption and zero trust network architectures. Security audits happen regularly, penetration testing is there, and there are standards such as GDPR or ISO 27001 that help make you resilient against attacks. An example being healthcare with devices which are IoT enabled must necessarily have stringent security mechanisms in place keeping patient data secure and operational. The risks to Digital Twins and IoT are organized in Table 4 by technical, cybersecurity, and organizational risks. Each risk type is described and mitigation strategies are provided. The information brings forward the idea that risk management is critical to the proactively and safely deployment of these technologies.

Table 4. Risk Management Strategies for Digital Twin and IoT Ecosystems

Risk Type	Description	Mitigation Strategies
Technical	System compatibility, scalability, and reliability issues.	Regular testing, validation, and infrastructure upgrades.
Cybersecurity	Threats to data integrity and network vulnerabilities.	Implement encryption, authentication, and monitoring systems.
Organizational	Resistance to change and workforce readiness challenges.	Foster collaboration, provide training and communicate benefits.

However, abundant literature highlights the ongoing struggle connecting the resistance to change as a barrier to adopting Digital Twins and IoT. Likewise, employees may find these technologies disruptive or fear what they might do to their job roles. Answers to these concerns call for companies to stress the advantages of tech adoption, including increased efficiency, more creative innovations, and additional career choices. The key to motivating these employees to trust the organization and work is to have clear communication and strong leadership support.

Human-Centric Digital Twins: User Experience and Personalization Enhancement

However, human-centric Digital Twins' applications go beyond technical ones; they aim to address the end-user and improve the customer experience, personalized products, and service. Digital Twins are built to reflect behavior, intention, and how a user interacts with a given product or service by individual users. In healthcare, personalized treatment plans are created through human-centric Digital Twins. Using real-time data from a patient's wearable IoT devices, such as heart rate monitors or glucose sensors, and their medical history, Digital Twins can consider different treatment scenarios and make recommendations for the best treatment possible. The challenge with this approach is that it minimizes trial and error, resulting in better patient outcomes and lower costs. The consumer goods industry uses human-centric Digital Twins to improve product personalization by companies. IoT-enabled devices feed data back to fitness equipment manufacturers, who use these data to develop customized workout programs tailored for individual users. Real-time adjustments of these systems are made based on data like workout intensity, duration, and workout progress to create a more engaging and effective experience. It is this phenomenon of demand-driven consumer business models being adopted by companies around the globe and technology being the means to build closer consumer relationships while delivering differentiated value (Asad et al., 2023).

Blockchain-Enabled IoT Ecosystems: Transparency and Security

Blockchain integration in IoT ecosystems resolves critical data security, trust, and transparency challenges. Blockchain's immutable and decentralized architecture is a stable foundation for managing the huge data generated by IoT devices, ensuring that data is tamper-proof and verifiable. Data integrity is among the advantages of Blockchain-enabled IoT ecosystems. For example, regarding supply chain management, Blockchain is now used to track the provenance of goods in real-time. IoT sensors embedded in shipments monitor temperature, humidity, and location; the data is recorded in a secure, distributed ledger known as Blockchain. With this, all stakeholders enjoy access to reliable, in many cases, tamper-proof information, which mitigates fraud risks and improves traceability. In industries like pharmaceuticals, food production, and such, where compliance is mandatory, Blockchain offers an immensely valuable tool for holding accountable and backing up consumer trust (Miraz & Ali, 2018) Furthermore, Blockchain solves the security issue in IoT networks and addresses the lack of centralized architectures. Conventional IoT networks usually consist of central servers for managing device communications, which provide single points of failure vulnerable to cyber-attacks. However, Blockchain removes this risk by permitting peer-to-peer communication and distributed authentication. Smart cities use Blockchain-secured IoT networks for their energy grids, water systems, and transportation networks to run critical systems even under cyber-attacks (Ullah & Havinga, 2023).

Quantum Computing in Digital Twins and IoT: Unlocking New Possibilities

Although in its infancy, quantum computing has the potential to enable organizations to more efficiently simulate Digital Twins and analyze IoT data as computation is pushed exponentially into the background, solving problems currently computationally infeasible. Quantum computers take advantage of quantum bits (qubits) and utilize their advantage to perform calculations at a magnitude of speed that no classical computer can achieve, and they are perfectly suited for tasks such as complex optimization tasks and predictive modeling. Simulating highly complex systems such as climate models, aerospace designs, and urban planning scenarios are among the most promising quantum computing uses for Digital Twins. Aerospace manufacturers could use quantum-powered Digital Twins to simulate the performance of new aircraft designs subject to thousands of variables, such as aerodynamic forces, material stresses, and environmental conditions. This degree of precision permits engineers to determine such optimal designs with greater speed, thus lowering development time and costs. In the IoT ecosystem, quantum computing promises to optimize resource allocation and network management (Saini et al., 2025). For example, in a smart city, quantum algorithms will help analyze data from millions of IoT sensors to increase traffic efficiency, decrease energy consumption, and enhance public safety. Processing such massive datasets in real-time with quantum computing empowers cities to be more efficient and sustainable. Although quantum computing remains in the laboratories, combining its raw power with Digital Twins and IoT is a disruptive frontier (Lv et al., 2022). Today, organizations that invest in quantum capabilities can better leverage these technologies when they mature. Key trends shaping the future of Digital Twins and IoT are explored in Table 5: centric twins, blockchain-enabled IoT ecosystems, quantum computing, and AI-driven twins. Each trend is described, and its implications are explored to provide insights into how these developments are enabling the capabilities and applications of these technologies to expand.

Table 5. Emerging Trends and Their Implications for Digital Twins and IoT

Trend	Description	Implications
Human-Centric Digital Twins	Focus on personalization and user experience.	Improved customer engagement and satisfaction.
Blockchain-Enabled IoT Ecosystems	Enhances data security and transparency in IoT networks.	Strengthened trust and accountability in data sharing.
Quantum Computing	Enables processing of highly complex simulations and datasets.	Expanded applications in fields like energy and urban planning.
AI-Driven Cognitive Twins	Facilitates autonomous decision-making and process optimization.	Increased efficiency in resource management and automation.

AI-Driven Cognitive Twins: Advancing Decision-Making and Automation

A new iteration of Digital Twin technology, Cognitive Digital Twins combines advanced artificial intelligence (AI) technologies to enable systems that learn, adapt, and make autonomous decisions. Traditional Digital Twins focus mainly on simulating the physical cognitive twins, including AI algorithms to analyze data patterns, forecast outcomes, and optimize processes without human intervention. Cognitive twins are used to manage renewable energy grids in the energy sector. Utilizing AI, these systems analyze data from the IoT sensors that monitor weather conditions, energy demand, and equipment performance to identify the best way to route energy in real-time. Cognitive twins autonomously balance supply and demand, promoting renewable use and grid stability and decreasing dependence on fossil fuels. Our cognitive twins also have important implications for manufacturing automation: They allowed us to create self-optimizing production lines. Cognitive twins can help constantly analyze data from IoT-enabled machinery to identify inefficiencies, predict when maintenance is needed, and adjust the workflow to improve productivity. For example, a great example of a cognitive twins factory is a factory machine. In this case, detecting a particular machine working below capacity automatically reallocates tasks to other equipment to achieve maximum throughput (Ali et al., 2024).

Digital Twins and IoT Application Case Studies

Application of Digital Twins and IoT across industries demonstrates in the strongest sense of words the transformative potential of Digital Twins and IoT. Also, in this section, we will have some real-world case studies and applications of these technologies, while in the how it's done section, I will be talking about how organizations have successfully used these technologies for innovation, efficiency, and competitive advantage. These are examples of the practical benefits and lessons to be learned, providing managers and leaders with actionable insights.

1. Aerospace Industry: Predictive Maintenance and Design Optimization

Digital Twins and IoT technologies are widely adopted in the aerospace industry to improve operational efficiency and safety and decrease costs. IoT sensors embedded within aircraft components, such as engines, landing gear, and airframes, gather real-time performance data during operations. Their Digital Twins are continuously monitored and analyzed with the help of this data. With these technologies, organizations within the aerospace sector have identified patterns and anomalies of component behavior indicating potential issues before they result in system failure. This facilitates maintenance planning according to actual use or wear rather than hard intervals, minimizing unplanned downtime while maintenance cycles are optimized. Simulation & testing new designs under different operational conditions are possible using Digital Twins, allowing for faster design cycles and guaranteeing products meet demanding safety and performance standards (Captain Ali Kangaranifarahani, 2023). Figure 6 on the pie chart outlines Digital Twins' applications, mostly in the aerospace industry. Finally, categories like predictive maintenance, design optimization, and flight efficiency are quantified and show how these technologies enhance safety, performance, and competitiveness in one of the most technologically advanced sectors.

Figure 6. Application of Digital Twin in the aerospace sector.

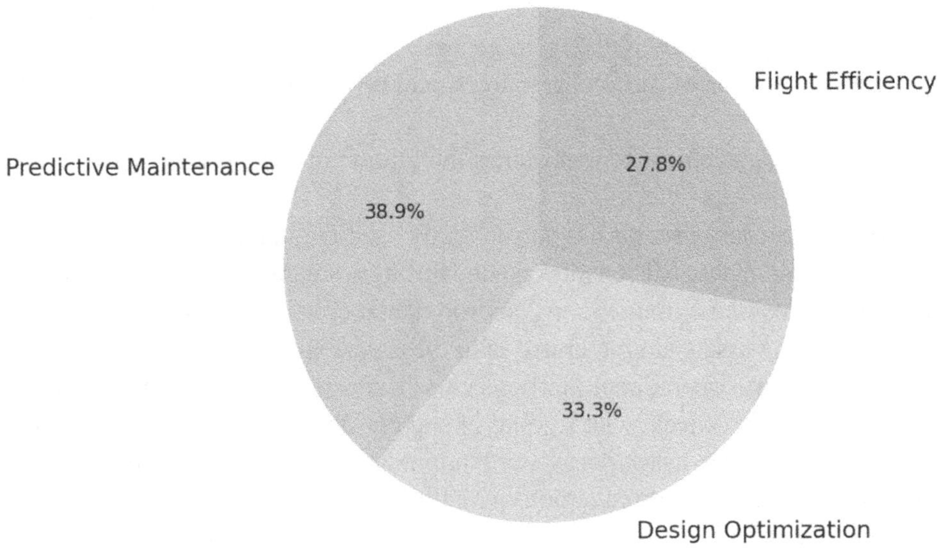

2. Automotive Sector

Digital Twins and IoT are revolutionising vehicle design, manufacturing, and operation in the automotive sector. These technologies have been used to integrate developing autonomous vehicles whose complex systems, including navigation, collision detection, and energy management, are simulated and optimized. In doing so, automotive manufacturers analyze real-world data collected from IoT-enabled prototypes to tune algorithms & improve autonomous systems' performance. Virtual digital twins in production manufacturing lines make virtual representations so we can monitor and optimize production lines in real-time. These digital models ingest data from IoT sensors installed in machinery to understand operational efficiency, machine health, and energy consumption. Through this approach, manufacturers have so far been able to optimize their production processes, decrease energy consumption to a great level, and increase overall equipment effectiveness. Furthermore, vehicle lifecycle management has been improved with the help of Digital Twins to learn how to perform predictive maintenance and efficiently design updates using data from IoT-enabled vehicles in the field (Kabir et al., 2024).

3. Healthcare: Personalized medicine and Operational Efficiency

Digital Twins and IoT have taken on a growing role in improving the operational efficiency of delivering care. IoT devices like wearable health monitors, with digital representations of individual patients as their core, supply real-time readings for physiological data like heart rate, blood pressure, or glucose levels (Subasi & Subasi, 2024). Digital Twins simulate the treatment options, and clinicians can predict how patients will answer to different interventions and select the best intervention. Hospitals and healthcare systems have utilized these technologies to increase reachability and streamline facility management and patient flow. IoT devices monitor equipment use, patient motion, temperature, and room air quality. Together with the Digital Twins of the hospital environment, data can be used to allocate resources, schedule patients, and improve care delivery in general. Innovations in products have decreased wait times, more efficient utilization of medical resources, and better patient outcomes (Khan et al., 2022).

4. Energy Sector: The management of renewables integration into the grid

Though still early, the energy sector has substantially used Digital Twins and IoT to run renewable energy and grid operations. These IoT sensors on wind turbines, solar panels, and other renewable energy systems measure variables like output energy, environmental conditions, and equipment performance. Digital twins of the energy assets are integrated with these data streams to help operators optimize energy generation and decrease operational inefficiencies (Kajba et al., 2023). These technologies allow real-time grid management to check what's going in and out on the grid. Digital twins of the grid can simulate things like peak energy usage periods or equipment failures and recommend ways to keep the grid stable. This has especially benefited regions with high penetration of intermittent renewable energy sources, integrating renewable with the grid and minimizing any battering to the grid (Onile et al., 2021).

5. Consumer Goods: Improving product quality & customer experience

IoT and Digital Twins are helping improve product quality and customer experience in the consumer goods industry. Manufacturers use Digital Twins to test the performance of products in diverse conditions and ensure they meet certain standards before consumers get the products. IoT-enabled products send data directly from the field, which feeds into the next generation of future designs, creating a feedback loop that drives innovation. On the other hand, these technologies raise the bar on the customer experience through higher personalization. For example, smart appliances acquire user preference and behavior data to tailor functionality and proactively support the user. Companies can use this data to offer more relevant features, send timely maintenance reminders, and anticipate user needs, building a more thought-provoking and fulfilling product experience (Lyu et al., 2024; Sai et al., 2024).

Table 6. Case Studies of Digital Twin and IoT Applications Across Industries

Industry	Application
Aerospace	Predictive maintenance and design optimization.
Automotive	Autonomous systems and manufacturing efficiency.
Healthcare	Personalized medicine and operational improvements.
Energy	Renewable energy management and grid optimization.
Consumer Goods	Enhancing product quality and customer experience.

The applications of Digital Twins and IoT in aerospace, automotive, healthcare, energy, and consumer goods are summarized in Table 6. This provides real-world evidence of the transformative potential of these technologies and how they are being used to meet industry challenges and achieve better outcomes.

Implications for Managers

Digital twins and IOT integrations provide organizations with unprecedented opportunities to improve product development, operational efficiency, and innovation. Unfortunately, these technologies are only effective when strategically applied to serve organizational objectives, cultivate cross-functional alignment, and provide long-term sustainability, offering actionable insights into strategies for managers to align technical capabilities with business goals, overcome some challenges, and achieve more value.

1. Aligning Technology Adoption with Business Objectives

The first step, it must be said, is for managers to set clear objectives regarding adopting Digital Twins and IoT. These objectives should align directly with the organization's strategic priorities, such as reducing time to market, improving product quality, improving customer satisfaction, or being sustainable. If these technologies are not aligned, there is a likelihood that they will be deployed in siloed projects without directly meaningful impact. A practical approach for every initiative is to set up specific, measurable, achievable, relevant, and time-bound (SMART) goals. For instance, an organization that wants to increase production efficiency can set a goal of reducing downtime by 20% within the first year of utilizing IoT-based Digital Twins. Tying technology adoption with tangible business outcomes helps managers ensure that resources are efficiently allocated and stakeholders stay committed to the initiative. Among other things, developing a shared vision of leadership and teams will also be crucial. For Digital Twins and IoT to reach their potential, managers have to communicate how Digital Twins and IoT can further the broader organizational goals and matter to all the departments involved. It also creates a collaborative method of getting work done, which reduces resistance to change and ensures the teams are working toward the same goals (Sai et al., 2024).

2. Facilitating Cross-Functional Collaboration

Deploying Digital Twins and IoT usually requires input and coordination across engineering, IT, operations and business strategy departments. This collaboration is managed by creating structures and processes that support knowledge sharing and teamwork by the manager. Early in the adoption process, cross-functional teams— technical experts and business leaders should come together to define requirements, identify and resolve challenges, and establish prioritizing objectives. These teams can create complete roadmaps, accounting for technical and organizational details, keeping everybody on the same page. It is necessary to keep the momentum going and solve those obstacles through regular communication and updates. Training and upskilling programs also create another critical element of collaboration. Digital Twins and IoT represent a new world, bringing tons of opportunities, but employees across all functions need to embrace their value and be clear on how they can leverage their existing expertise to participate in making them a reality. Workshops, hands-on training, and providing access to resources prepare the teams to support this initiative (Timperi et al., 2023).

3. Managing Change and Overcoming resistance

Like any transformative technology, Digital Twins and IoT may be met with hesitation from employees and stakeholders regarding change. By showing how these technologies add value to the business and including employees in choosing when and how to use them, managers can head off at least some concerns. What has proven effective is exemplifying early successes in the form of pilot projects or small-scale implementations. Managers can then build trust and generate enthusiasm for broader adoption by demonstrating tangible benefits, such as cost savings, improved efficiency, or enhanced customer outcomes. Digital Twin and IoT initiatives should also be communicated to managers for updates on the progress, addressing concerns as well as communicating how these technologies link back to what are individual and team goals. The motive behind engaging employees through workshops, feedback sessions, and collaborative planning is that employees get engaged in this initiative and feel a part of its success.

4. Ensuring Scalability and Flexibility

Digital Twins and IoT usage must be designed for scalability and flexibility to accommodate changing business needs and technology. Solutions should be chosen by managers who will grow with the organization and support more assets, data streams, and use cases as needed. For instance, organizations can add new sensors or devices to an IoT platform with modular architectures while leaving the existing systems intact. Flexibility is equally important so that Digital Twins and IoT systems can change their behavior according to market, environment, and organizational priorities. Cloud based platforms can scale resources up or down as needed, which is cost-effective scalability. Managers should also select interoperable solutions to seamlessly integrate with existing tools and systems, giving maximum return on investment.

5. Addressing Cybersecurity and Data Governance

IoT and Digital Twins integration makes cybersecurity and data governance reactive control problems that managers must address to defend sensitive information and sustain operational integrity. Cyberattacks on IoT devices are highly sensitive since, you know, an IoT device is opened to the public around you, and there is no consistency in the levels of security. For this to work, managers should be in no shortage of robust security measures, such as network security, encryption, multi-factor authentication, and intrusion detection systems to protect the IoT and the Digital Twin application or platform. Regular security audits and vulnerability assessments are critical to identifying and resolving potential problems beforehand. Another important consideration is data governance. However, since managers are handling data collected via IoT devices, they must ensure that data is handled well and in accord with the required regulations and standards. It means determining clear policies related to data ownership, access control, and usage. Transparent Data governance practices mitigate risk and build trust between your customers and stakeholders (Rahmadian et al., 2023).

6. Measuring Success and Continuous Improvement

In order for management to establish the means to measure the impact of Digital Twin and IoT initiatives and ensure continuous improvement, these projects require long term success. Tracking key performance indicators (KPIs) regularly will help ascertain measure to what extent toward the organizational goals. Metrics of reduction in downtime, cost savings and traditional improvements in product quality provide greater insights into the use of these technologies. Feedback loops give us tools to make processes better, see opportunity, and generally do better at our day to day work. As an example, understanding how to learn from your initial deployment of Digital Twins in one part of your organization will be beneficial to further deployment in other parts of your organization. As managers, we should encourage an innovative culture that encourages teams to turn on the spicket and experiment with new use cases, find new trends, to always look for better ways to add value (Saeed et al., 2024).

CONCLUSION

Today's industries are being enabled by Digital Twins and IoT Integration to how products and processes are designed, developed and managed. They open a possibility for businesses to bridge physical resources to electronic devices for real time over sight, predictive analytics and adjustable decision making. Leveraging these capabilities, if they can, they can also optimize their operations and deliver greater value to their stakeholders at reduced costs. Industries like healthcare, manufacturing, energy, and transportation where accuracy, precision and scale matter are massively changed by Digital Twins and IoT. The one common fundamental property of Digital Twins and IoT is the ability to help drive a stream of dependent data that provides insights on how to make a decision. Digital Twins collects, processes and analyzes huge amounts of real time data being collected from physical systems by IoT devices with advanced sensors to provide actionable intelligence. In fact, this capability has already turned the way organizations have been managing maintenance, allocating resources, and conducting product development on its head. With Digital Twins and pre-dictive maintenance using IoT, equipment failures are forecasted beforehand and unplanned downtime can be minimized. However, by employing a proactive approach, which increases operational reliability, reduces maintenance costs and prolongs the service life of critical assets for a sustainable life is the method.

But, the Digital Twin and the IoT present their own challenges. However, organizations face both technical, organizational, and cultural barriers to realizing these technologies' full benefits. The biggest technical challenges of IoT are the ability of IoT network hardware to scale to support a large number of interconnected devices as well as the reliability of these devices, and compatibility with existing systems. At the same time, cybersecurity risks are still a matter of great concern due to the inherent propensity of IoT ecosystems to breach, resulting in leaking sensitive data and the business going down. Successful deployment of these technologies is protected by strong cybersecurity frameworks, including encryption and real time threat monitoring, intrusion detection systems and more. From the organizational front, lack of employee buy in to simply viewing new technologies as a threat or too difficult to use are great obstacles to resistance to change. Leadership addresses these concerns by enabling a collaborative, transparent and continuously learning environment. Work force enablement programs provide first hand training and resource to enable the employees to work Digital Twins and IoT Systems. Furthermore, engaging employees in design and roll out of the Change is another strength that helps build confidence and commitment while minimizing resistance and generating a sense of ownership within the Change. Digital Twins and IoT continue to progress, leading to new trends and innovations that are expanding Digital Twin and IoT capabilities and applications. AI cognitive twins allow systems to learn, adapt, and autonomously make decisions, driving the disruption of industries that demand speed and data-driven responses. Data integrity and trust challenges facing IoT ecosystems are being enhanced by blockchain technology to improve their security and transparency. Digital Twins offer possibilities for quantum computing to take the capabilities to the next level by simulating highly complex systems or dealing with extremely large datasets in a fraction of the time compared to what's possible today. However, these advancements represent the dynamic nature of these technologies and serve as a reminder that organizations are better off staying agile and forward-looking. Digital Twins and IoT are also evolving to integrate in the future of Industry 5.0 towards human-machine collaboration, sustainability, and personalization. Digital Twins allows us to create human-centric solutions that increase user experience and customer engagement. In the energy sector, IoT enabled Digital twins are used to optimise renewable energy systems and contribute to global sustainability goals, while decreasing reliance on fossil fuels. By modeling and simulating their operations in real time, and the impact these operations have on their environment, Organizations can make better informed and aligned decisions with regulatory requirements and societal expectations.

Digital Twins and IoT allow businesses to begin feedback loops to the development of products. Organizations can improve functionality, deliver solutions that match changing customer needs and refine designs by analyzing the real world data gathered by IoT enabled products. With an iterative guarantee, products don't become useless and out of date in a fast changing market. Furthermore, these technologies enable a movement towards more agile manufacturing processes where manufacturing lines can change as required by demand, material availability and market conditions. Digital Twins and IoT are not something new in technology but a strategic necessity for companies that must deal with the realities of 21st century industrial life. In that case, when integrated into business objectives, technical and organizational challenges are resolved, and enterprises become proactive about emerging trends, they will leverage these technologies to their fullest and get a sustainable competitive edge. But the vision, leadership and commitment to innovation required for integration are worthwhile—the sure rewards are greater efficiency, greater customer satisfaction and sustainability. Investing in these transformative technologies today will put one ahead of the game to work with the demands of tomorrow's industries. Digital Twins and IoT can slowly help shape a smarter, more efficient and more sustainable future with time. Today in the age of Industry 4.0, these tech transformation businesses are thriving and creating the path to Industry 5.0, where humans and machines collaborate in new ways to break new ground on the innovation and operational efficiency.

REFERENCES

Ali, S. I., Kale, G. P., Shaikh, M. S., Ponnusamy, S., & Chouhan, P. S. (2024). AI Applications and Digital Twin Technology Have the Ability to Completely Transform the Future. In Ponnusamy, S., Assaf, M., Antari, J., Singh, S., & Kalyanaraman, S. (Eds.), *Harnessing AI and Digital Twin Technologies in Businesses* (pp. 26–39). IGI Global., DOI: 10.4018/979-8-3693-3234-4.ch003

Ariesen-Verschuur, N., Verdouw, C., & Tekinerdogan, B. (2022). Digital Twins in greenhouse horticulture: A review. *Computers and Electronics in Agriculture, 199*, 107183. https://doi.org/https://doi.org/10.1016/j.compag.2022.107183. DOI: 10.1016/j.compag.2022.107183

Asad, U., Khan, M., Khalid, A., & Lughmani, W. A. (2023). Human-Centric Digital Twins in Industry: A Comprehensive Review of Enabling Technologies and Implementation Strategies. *Sensors (Basel), 23*(8), 3938. DOI: 10.3390/s23083938 PMID: 37112279

Booyse, W., Wilke, D. N., & Heyns, S. (2020). Deep digital twins for detection, diagnostics and prognostics. *Mechanical Systems and Signal Processing, 140*, 106612. https://doi.org/https://doi.org/10.1016/j.ymssp.2019.106612. DOI: 10.1016/j.ymssp.2019.106612

Boyes, H., & Watson, T. (2022). Digital twins: An analysis framework and open issues. *Computers in Industry, 143*, 103763. https://doi.org/https://doi.org/10.1016/j.compind.2022.103763. DOI: 10.1016/j.compind.2022.103763

Brosinsky, C., Karaçelebi, M., & Cremer, J. L. (2023). 4 - Machine learning and digital twins: monitoring and control for dynamic security in power systems. In Barocio Espejo, E., Segundo Sevilla, F. R., & Korba, P. (Eds.), *Monitoring and Control of Electrical Power Systems Using Machine Learning Techniques* (pp. 79–106). Elsevier., https://doi.org/https://doi.org/10.1016/B978-0-32-399904-5.00010-7 DOI: 10.1016/B978-0-32-399904-5.00010-7

Captain Ali Kangaranifarahani, D. D. C. M. Y. (2023). Applications of Artificial Intelligence in the Aviation Industry and Air Accidents. *Mathematical Statistician and Engineering Applications, 72*(2), 178 – 192. https://www.philstat.org/index.php/MSEA/article/view/2832

Chen, B.-Q., Videiro, P. M., & Guedes Soares, C. (2022). Opportunities and Challenges to Develop Digital Twins for Subsea Pipelines. *Journal of Marine Science and Engineering, 10*(6), 739. DOI: 10.3390/jmse10060739

Donoghue, I., Hannola, L., Papinniemi, J., & Mikkola, A. (2018). The Benefits and Impact of Digital Twins in Product Development Phase of PLM. Product Lifecycle Management to Support Industry 4.0, Cham.

dos Santos, C. H., Campos, A. T., Montevechi, J. A. B., de Carvalho Miranda, R., do Amaral, J. V. S., & de Queiroz, J. A. (2023). Simulation-based digital twins monitoring: An approach focused on models' accreditation. *International Journal of Advanced Manufacturing Technology, 124*(7), 2423–2435. DOI: 10.1007/s00170-022-10674-6

Eneyew, D. D., Capretz, M. A. M., & Bitsuamlak, G. T. (2022). Toward Smart-Building Digital Twins: BIM and IoT Data Integration. *IEEE Access : Practical Innovations, Open Solutions, 10*, 130487–130506. DOI: 10.1109/ACCESS.2022.3229370

Florea, A., Lobov, A., & Lanz, M. (2020). Emotions-aware Digital Twins For Manufacturing. *Procedia Manufacturing, 51*, 605–612. https://doi.org/https://doi.org/10.1016/j.promfg.2020.10.085. DOI: 10.1016/j.promfg.2020.10.085

Hemdan, E. E.-D., El-Shafai, W., & Sayed, A. (2023). Integrating Digital Twins with IoT-Based Blockchain: Concept, Architecture, Challenges, and Future Scope. *Wireless Personal Communications, 131*(3), 2193–2216. DOI: 10.1007/s11277-023-10538-6 PMID: 37360142

Holopainen, M., Saunila, M., Rantala, T., & Ukko, J. (2024). Digital twins' implications for innovation. *Technology Analysis and Strategic Management, 36*(8), 1779–1791. DOI: 10.1080/09537325.2022.2115881

Huang, S., Wang, G., Lei, D., & Yan, Y. (2022). Toward digital validation for rapid product development based on digital twin: A framework. *International Journal of Advanced Manufacturing Technology, 119*(3), 2509–2523. DOI: 10.1007/s00170-021-08475-4

Iliuţă, M.-E., Moisescu, M.-A., Pop, E., Ionita, A.-D., Caramihai, S.-I., & Mitulescu, T.-C. (2024). Digital Twin—A Review of the Evolution from Concept to Technology and Its Analytical Perspectives on Applications in Various Fields. *Applied Sciences (Basel, Switzerland), 14*(13), 5454. DOI: 10.3390/app14135454

Kabir, M. R., Halder, D., & Ray, S. (2024). Digital Twins for IoT-Driven Energy Systems: A Survey. *IEEE Access : Practical Innovations, Open Solutions, 12*, 177123–177143. DOI: 10.1109/ACCESS.2024.3506660

Kaivo-oja, J., Kuusi, O., Knudsen, M. S., & Lauraeus, T. (2019, 2019//). Digital Twins Approach and Future Knowledge Management Challenges: Where We Shall Need System Integration, Synergy Analyses and Synergy Measurements? Knowledge Management in Organizations, Cham.

Kajba, M., Jereb, B., & Cvahte Ojsteršek, T. (2023). Exploring Digital Twins in the Transport and Energy Fields: A Bibliometrics and Literature Review Approach. *Energies, 16*(9), 3922. DOI: 10.3390/en16093922

Khan, A., Milne-Ives, M., Meinert, E., Iyawa, G. E., Jones, R. B., & Josephraj, A. N. (2022). A Scoping Review of Digital Twins in the Context of the Covid-19 Pandemic. *Biomedical Engineering and Computational Biology, 13*, 11795972221102115. DOI: 10.1177/11795972221102115 PMID: 35633868

Kou, G., Dinçer, H., Yüksel, S., & Deveci, M. (2024). Synergistic integration of digital twins and sustainable industrial internet of things for new generation energy investments. *Journal of Advanced Research, 66*, 39–46. https://doi.org/https://doi.org/10.1016/j.jare.2023.11.023. DOI: 10.1016/j.jare.2023.11.023 PMID: 38008174

Li, L., Gu, F., Li, H., Guo, J., & Gu, X. (2021). Digital Twin Bionics: A Biological Evolution-Based Digital Twin Approach for Rapid Product Development. *IEEE Access : Practical Innovations, Open Solutions, 9*, 121507–121521. DOI: 10.1109/ACCESS.2021.3108218

Lo, C. K., Chen, C. H., & Zhong, R. Y. (2021). A review of digital twin in product design and development. *Advanced Engineering Informatics*, *48*, 101297. https://doi.org/https://doi.org/10.1016/j.aei.2021.101297. DOI: 10.1016/j.aei.2021.101297

Lv, Z., Cheng, C., & Song, H. (2022). Digital Twins Based on Quantum Networking. *IEEE Network*, *36*(5), 88–93. DOI: 10.1109/MNET.001.2200131

Lyu, Z., Lloret, J., Song, H., Mazurczyk, W., Wang, H., & Park, J. J. (2024). Metaverse and Digital Twins for Consumer Electronics. *IEEE Transactions on Consumer Electronics*, *70*(3), 5662–5666. DOI: 10.1109/TCE.2024.3411469

Mihai, S., Yaqoob, M., Hung, D. V., Davis, W., Towakel, P., Raza, M., Karamanoglu, M., Barn, B., Shetve, D., Prasad, R. V., Venkataraman, H., Trestian, R., & Nguyen, H. X. (2022). Digital Twins: A Survey on Enabling Technologies, Challenges, Trends and Future Prospects. *IEEE Communications Surveys and Tutorials*, *24*(4), 2255–2291. DOI: 10.1109/COMST.2022.3208773

Miraz, M. H., & Ali, M. (2018, 2018//). Blockchain Enabled Enhanced IoT Ecosystem Security. Emerging Technologies in Computing, Cham.

Olad, A. A., & Valilai, O. F. (2020, December 14-17). 2020). Using of Social Media Data Analytics for Applying Digital Twins in Product Development. *2020 IEEE International Conference on Industrial Engineering and Engineering Management (IEEM)*

Onile, A. E., Machlev, R., Petlenkov, E., Levron, Y., & Belikov, J. (2021). Uses of the digital twins concept for energy services, intelligent recommendation systems, and demand side management: A review. *Energy Reports*, *7*, 997–1015. https://doi.org/https://doi.org/10.1016/j.egyr.2021.01.090

Radanliev, P., De Roure, D., Nicolescu, R., Huth, M., & Santos, O. (2022). Digital twins: Artificial intelligence and the IoT cyber-physical systems in Industry 4.0. *International Journal of Intelligent Robotics and Applications*, *6*(1), 171–185. DOI: 10.1007/s41315-021-00180-5

Rahmadian, E., Feitosa, D., & Virantina, Y. (2023). Digital twins, big data governance, and sustainable tourism. *Ethics and Information Technology*, *25*(4), 61. DOI: 10.1007/s10676-023-09730-w

Saeed, M. M. A., Saeed, R. A., & Ahmed, Z. E. (2024). Data Security and Privacy in the Age of AI and Digital Twins. In Ponnusamy, S., Assaf, M., Antari, J., Singh, S., & Kalyanaraman, S. (Eds.), *Digital Twin Technology and AI Implementations in Future-Focused Businesses* (pp. 99–124). IGI Global., DOI: 10.4018/979-8-3693-1818-8.ch008

Sai, S., Rastogi, A., & Chamola, V. (2024). Digital Twins for Consumer Electronics. *IEEE Consumer Electronics Magazine*, *13*(6), 11–16. DOI: 10.1109/MCE.2023.3322013

Saini, K., Singh, A., Ahuja, A., Arora, N., & Saini, R. (2025). Research advancements in quantum computing digital twins. In Iyer, S., Nayyar, A., Paul, A., & Naved, M. (Eds.), *Digital Twins for Smart Cities and Villages* (pp. 37–53). Elsevier., https://doi.org/https://doi.org/10.1016/B978-0-443-28884-5.00002-6 DOI: 10.1016/B978-0-443-28884-5.00002-6

Singh, B., & Nayyar, A. (2025). Exploring diverse use cases of digital twins projecting digital transformation: Unlocking potential, addressing challenges and viable solutions. In Iyer, S., Nayyar, A., Paul, A., & Naved, M. (Eds.), *Digital Twins for Smart Cities and Villages* (pp. 631–655). Elsevier., https://doi.org/https://doi.org/10.1016/B978-0-443-28884-5.00027-0 DOI: 10.1016/B978-0-443-28884-5.00027-0

Stadtmann, F., Rasheed, A., Kvamsdal, T., Johannessen, K. A., San, O., Kölle, K., Tande, J. O., Barstad, I., Benhamou, A., Brathaug, T., Christiansen, T., Firle, A. L., Fjeldly, A., Frøyd, L., Gleim, A., Høiberget, A., Meissner, C., Nygård, G., Olsen, J., & Skogås, J. O. (2023). Digital Twins in Wind Energy: Emerging Technologies and Industry-Informed Future Directions. *IEEE Access : Practical Innovations, Open Solutions*, *11*, 110762–110795. DOI: 10.1109/ACCESS.2023.3321320

Subasi, A., & Subasi, M. E. (2024). Digital twins in healthcare and biomedicine. In De Pablos, P. O., & Zhang, X. (Eds.), *Artificial Intelligence, Big Data, Blockchain and 5G for the Digital Transformation of the Healthcare Industry* (pp. 365–401). Academic Press., https://doi.org/https://doi.org/10.1016/B978-0-443-21598-8.00011-7 DOI: 10.1016/B978-0-443-21598-8.00011-7

Timperi, M., Kokkonen, K., Hannola, L., & Elfvengren, K. (2023). Impacts of digital twins on new business creation: Insights from manufacturing industry. *Measuring Business Excellence*, *27*(3), 433–448. DOI: 10.1108/MBE-09-2022-0104

Ullah, I., & Havinga, P. J. M. (2023). Governance of a Blockchain-Enabled IoT Ecosystem: A Variable Geometry Approach. *Sensors (Basel)*, *23*(22), 9031. DOI: 10.3390/s23229031 PMID: 38005419

van Dinter, R., Tekinerdogan, B., & Catal, C. (2022). Predictive maintenance using digital twins: A systematic literature review. *Information and Software Technology*, *151*, 107008. https://doi.org/https://doi.org/10.1016/j.infsof.2022.107008. DOI: 10.1016/j.infsof.2022.107008

Wagner, R., Schleich, B., Haefner, B., Kuhnle, A., Wartzack, S., & Lanza, G. (2019). Challenges and Potentials of Digital Twins and Industry 4.0 in Product Design and Production for High Performance Products. *Procedia CIRP*, *84*, 88–93. https://doi.org/https://doi.org/10.1016/j.procir.2019.04.219. DOI: 10.1016/j.procir.2019.04.219

Zheng, X., Lu, J., & Kiritsis, D. (2022). The emergence of cognitive digital twin: Vision, challenges and opportunities. *International Journal of Production Research*, *60*(24), 7610–7632. DOI: 10.1080/00207543.2021.2014591

Chapter 14
Opportunities and Challenges in IoT for Environmental Monitoring

Basudha Dewan
https://orcid.org/0000-0001-6513-4374
Poornima University Jaipur, India

Sharbari Deb
Poornima University Jaipur, India

Sabyasachi Bhattacharyya
Barak Valley Engineering College, India

Ehsan Sheybani
School of Information Systems and Management, University of South Florida, Tampa, USA

ABSTRACT

IoT technology has changed the way various environmental areas including air, water, soil and wildlife and disaster management through use of real-time data. IoT employs next-generation sensors, Artificial Intelligence, blockchain, and virtual doubles for prognostic information, decision, and management. Nevertheless, WSIGN still has challenges as: connectivity problems, high costs, data privacy and security, and e-waste. This paper discusses these problems and examples of IoT solutions such as smart agriculture, air quality monitoring and smart disaster response. Through resolution of these challenges by IoT via infrastructure, devices and data security, the growth of the IoT can considerably contribute to global environmental strength and ecological sustainability with practices appropriate for investigators and industries.

DOI: 10.4018/979-8-3373-2028-1.ch014

1. INTRODUCTION

Increased and continued degradation of natural ecosystems compounded by climate change invariancy have made environmental monitoring as essential element in sustainable development and ecology. It is important here to note that most conventional approaches to monitoring have been time-consuming, place-bound, and data-gathering exercises, which are generally failure-driven as opposed to success - focused. The rapidly escalating field of the Internet of Things (IoT) broke through these sorts of barriers and provided the possibilities for a new method of thinking about the environment, in the terms of an increased connectivity and data management (Hovorushchenko, Bachuk, Hnatchuk, Zasornova, & El Bouhissi, 2024; "Smart Solutions for Sustainable Living," 2024; Khattra, Balaut, & Dogra, 2024).

IoT is the enhanced connection of physical objects through embedded sensors, software, and network compatibility for the constant real-time acquisition, analyzing and sharing of data. Through use of IoT devices in air, water, or soil and in the various wildlife arenas, the practitioners and researchers are provided with original and real-time information on the various systems in ecology (Alam, Islam, Nayan, & Uddin, 2024; Dubey & Yadav, 2024). This capability helps identify early signs of change and provides base for making predictive analysis as well as initiating timely actions to address the effects of unfavourable environment. For example, IoT-based devices used to monitor air quality allows detail data on various pollutants hence enable urban planners and policymakers to take appropriate actions to enhance well-being of people in areas such as cities (Akinwale, 2024; Oroos & Chaudhary, 2024).

Big data from IoT appliances can be analyzed by algorithms developed by AI by predicting the environmental occurrence, efficient usage of resources, and accurate decision-making. Security data management is also guaranteed by the use of blockchain technology; data integrity issues arise due to data manipulation or loss are resolved by this technology. Advanced models describing physical systems and often referred to as digital twins allow the real-time simulation and optimisation of environmental interaction resulting in the improvement of the results of interventions undertaken (Tekchandani, Pradhan, Das, Kumar, & Park, 2023; Sasikumar, Ravi, Kotecha, Saini, Varadarajan, & Subramaniyaswamy, 2022; Li, 2022).

However, several difficulties are associated with the use of IoT in environmental surveillance and monitoring. Large scale use is limited by the inability to transmit signals in rural or isolated settings, high costs of establishment and maintenance of the IoT networks, and moreover the absence of well-set standards on how the data gathered can be stored and processed. On the same note, issues to do with privacy and security of data present a number of questions around ethics and the law where environmental or even personal data may be an issue (Cao, Li, & Li, 2024; Arowolo, Aaron, Kugbiyi, Eteng, Aguma, & Olagunju, 2024). Energy consumption is another major problem related to IoT, as does the constant generation of discarded electronic products implies the need to create quality environmentally friendly devices and circuits.

In this chapter, an overview of and specific discussion of the potential and issues with IoT regarding its use in environmental monitoring is presented. It starts by reviewing the innovative use of IoT systems on various environmental sectors, whereby these systems support knowledge and management as well as the conservation of natural resources. We then turn the spotlight on obstacles that need to be overcome in order to achieve scalable and fair IoT deployment. In this chapter, lessons are drawn from case studies of IoT success stories and the discussion of modern tendencies, which provides applied recommendations for researchers, entrepreneurs, and legislators. In the long run, this paper aims at providing a guide to the use of IoT to deliver a sustainable and resilient future whereby IoT advancements are in tune with schemes of environmental conservation as well as social development.

2. APPLICATIONS OF IOT IN ENVIRONMENTAL MONITORING

The concept of the IoT has emerged as the powerful and revolutionary technology for environmental management with having organized to deliver new ideas to probe the complicated ecological issues. In this context, IoT applications cut across a broad and diverse Environmental arena, providing real time data that enables predictive analysis or direct responses to environmental change and risk management. This part aims to discuss major areas of IoT use for environmental monitoring as divided into specific sections.

2.1 Air Quality Monitoring

One of the most important use of IoT is air quality monitoring especially in the areas where pollution rates arehigh such as in major cities. Smart particulate matter (PM2:5 and PM10), carbon monoxide (CO), nitrogen dioxide (NO_2), sulfur dioxide (SO_2) monitoring devices are installed in cities. These sensors feed true real-time data to central systems so they can be monitored over a long period and warning signals can be generated. Besides single sensors, IoT platforms include data on air quality from satellites and meteorological stations into overall picture. Such systems prove optimal where a study of emissions is concerned to help policymakers introduce innovations aimed at managing air pollutants and enable people to take preventative measures during harm's way (Bhatia, 2024; Saini, 2024; Kotnala, 2024; Banciu, Florea, & Bogdan, 2024; Kustija, Fahrizal, & Nasir, 2024).

2.2 Water Quality Monitoring

IoT has enhanced the monitoring and tracking of water clarity in the world rivers, lakes seas, and water supply systems. The connected sensors, integrated with IoT at their core, help measure important parameters that include acidity, level of coagulum and cloud, dissolved, saltiness and temperatures. Such devices are anchored at several point within water bodies to monitor source of contamination and pattern at different times. IoT systems assist in early detection of pollutants which enable authorities prevent the pollution by discharge by industries, agricultural drainage, and oil slicks (López-Munoz et al., 2024; Santhosini, Subhiksha, Jayanthi, & Vishal, 2024). In the same way, intelligent systems for water quality are crucial for monitoring the availability and quality of drinking water to communities, supporting the protection of the ecosystem in water bodies and measuring adherence to quality regulations.

2.3 Soil Quality and Agriculture

Monitoring the quality of soil requires IoT, which is major incorporate agriculture and land use. It captures data on the soil such as the moisture content in the soil, nutrient content, and pH content which allows farmers to easily determine when to water the crops, which fertilizer to apply, and which crop to plant next. These systems are an important components of precision agriculture informing the optimal use of resources on production endeavors while reducing on the negative effects on the environment

(Pathak, Kharwade, Jeriya, Singh, & Pandey, 2024; Aditya, Hernawati, Gunawan, & Aji, 2024; Hartono, Maulana, Yoeseph, Purnomo, Safi'ie, Alim, & Bawono, 2024). In addition, with the help of IoT solutions, control of soil erosion and degradation is possible to sustain reasonable and useful utilization of the soil and to co-ordinate reforestation programs.

Figure 1. IoT Environmental Applications: Key areas of IoT implementation for environmental monitoring and management

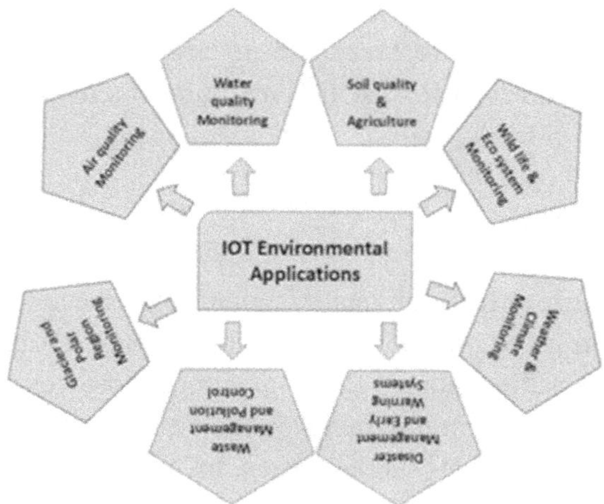

2.4 Wildlife and Ecosystem Monitoring

IoT applications also go to wildlife and ecosystems, and can help with the tracking of species, their migration, and changes in their environment. GPS collars and camera traps are used to monitor both behaviour and population as well as logistical data regarding the death or disappearance of large animals from poaching or habitat destruction. Thus, sensors quantify such factors as the state of vegetation, density, or climate to help conservationists devise efficient solutions for endangered populations and ecosystem stability (Rathoure & Rathaur, 2024).

2.5 Weather and Climate Monitoring

Weather and climate monitoring has been revolutionized by IoT especially through development of distributed sensors placed in different parts of the geographical world. These networks gather information on temperature, humidity, pressure, wind speed, and rain. The gathered data is analysed in real time to generate proper weather forecasts and also to identify occurrence of calamities such as hurricanes, floods or droughts (Ladino-Moreno, Hurtado Cortés, Cely Callejas, & Hernández Martínez, 2024; Nachimuthu, Shubhakavee, Subitha, Umamaheswari, & J.S., 2024; Gulraiz, Gulraiz, Zia, Badar, Haider, & Zaidi, 2024). Furthermore, IoT systems are fundamental to the analysis of climate change, as the IoT collected temperature data over long periods, rates of greenhouse gases, and polar ice melt.

2.6 Disaster Management and Early Warning Systems

The IoT plays an incredibly important role in disaster response and risk reduction through early warning systems to have residents alerted to the occurrence of natural disasters. For instance, Internet of Things tremor detectors identify early indicators of earthquakes while flood protection employs water level sensors to predict possible flooding. Likewise, the IoT networks track the volcanic eruptions, landslides, and forest fires, the authorities to give out alerts and make people leave the areas. These systems are of great importance in cases of emergencies as they help in saving lives, decreased economic losses and most important correct utilization of limited resources (Badade, 2024; Rashid, Ali, Ali, Taher, Mukhlif, Muliar, & Noori, 2024).

2.7 Waste Management and Pollution Control

IoT solutions help to manage waste, reduce pollution and regulate its generation, collection, and disposal. IoT sensors installed on smart bins identify fill levels, helping to optimise collection routes and, therefore, fuel use. Besides, IoT systems control emissions and wastewater discharge in industries while encouraging compliance with environmental standards (Deeraj, Subburaj, & B.U., 2024; Sankar & Fathima, 2024).

2.8 Glacier and Polar Region Monitoring

In remote and hard to reach locations such as glaciers and polar regions IoT systems are used to constantly track climate shifts. There are tools which help sensing thickness, temperature and motion of ice all these are helpful in the research on the impact of climate change. These systems also used to forecast the influence of melting glaciers on the sea level changes and global environment. Finally, IoT contributes to the tracking of environmental conditions in various fields, categorically tackling major environmental issues with policies aimed for and pushing forward sustainable development (Dewan, Chaudhary, & Yadav, 2021; Babu, Umadevi, Patel, & Gopalakrishnan, 2023). Combining data from various fields IoT gives stakeholders actual estimations in real-time hence the ability to make informed decisions and conserve the planet.

3. OPPORTUNITIES IN IOT FOR ENVIRONMENTAL MONITORING

Internet of Things in environmental monitoring Presents opportunities to changing the way natural ecosystems are understood and managed. That is why IoT has become one of the key foundations of modern approaches to environmental monitoring as the continuous, scalable, and accurate monitoring provided by the technology is unattainable using traditional methods. This section identifies major IoT opportunities in environmental monitoring and group these opportunities based on their impact domains.

3.1 Enhanced Data Collection and Analysis

IoT is possibly providing unparallelled means for gathering and monitoring environmental data in real time. The historical mode of environmental monitoring is by random sampling, which may only pick some changes not trends. IoT systems with connected sensors make it possible to make uninterrupted measurement of parameters including air and water quality, soil type and quality and weather among others. These systems produce large volume data that give more information about the environment than lower resolution systems. Together with sophisticated analysis of data, IoT makes it possible to use predictive analysis, allowing avoiding potential adverse impacts on the environment (Seth, Dutta, & Desai, 2024).

3.2 Scalability and Accessibility

Another major opportunity in connection with the IoT systems for environmental monitoring is their flexibility. Normally there are possibilities of extending IoT networks over a large geographical area, including rural and some hard-to-reach areas like the mountainous terrains, forests and seas. IoT LPWAN for low-power, wide-area networks and satellite IoT make the connection in these regions complete for data collection (Godawale, Deshmukh, & Pisal, 2024). Such scalability is important in managing extensive issues like climate change, because localized data from different ecosystems is synthesized into comparative conclusions regarding global changes.

Table 1. Common IoT Technologies for Environmental Monitoring

Technology	Description	Applications	Challenges
Wireless Sensors	IoT-enabled devices that measure various environmental parameters.	Air quality, water quality, soil health, temperature, etc.	Battery life, device durability, and accuracy.
Low-Power Wide Area Networks (LPWAN)	Communication networks that connect IoT devices over long distances with low energy consumption.	Remote environmental monitoring, especially in inaccessible regions.	Limited bandwidth, interference, and coverage in some areas.
Satellite IoT Networks	IoT connectivity using satellite systems for remote data transmission.	Monitoring in polar regions, oceans, and isolated locations.	High deployment cost, data latency.
Cloud Computing	Cloud platforms for processing and storing large volumes of environmental data.	Data aggregation, analytics, and storage.	Data security, latency, and scalability.
Edge Computing	Data processing closer to the source (at the sensor or local device level).	Reducing latency and real-time decision-making for environmental systems.	Complex architecture, integration with cloud.
Blockchain	Distributed ledger technology for secure and transparent data transactions.	Ensuring data integrity and traceability in monitoring systems.	High energy consumption, scalability challenges.

3.3 Integration with Advanced Technologies

The conjunction between IoT and other innovative technologies like Artificial Intelligence (AI), Machine Learning (ML), 'Big data' analysis in categorizes the breadth of environmental monitoring. These technologies analyze massive IoT-created data to identify latent patterns, anticipate environmental shifts and improve the usage of resources. That is for example in pollutant assessment or the likelihood of fire outbreak which can be estimated by evaluating data from sensors and taking appropriate measures at the right time. In addition, by applying IoT with blockchain technology, data transparency and accountability are improved, creating trust among the stakeholders to environmental projects (Jakkani, 2024; Tatiraju, Dhineshkumar, Mishra, & Sekar, 2024; Alotaibi & Nassif, 2024).

3.4 Promoting Citizen Science and Public Engagement

IoT creates opportunities for citizen science where citizens help in collection of data by utilizing cheap IoT sensors and smart applications. Such participatory initiatives not only enhance the amount of collected information but also help to raise public concern on ecological problems. Being real-time feedback showing participants how they can take corrective action to minimize their impact on their environment, IoT enhanced platforms offer. It also means that the public will have enhanced voices in demanding sustainable policies and practices when carrying out monitoring.

3.5 Supporting Regulatory Compliance and Sustainability

Governments as well as relevant industries make use of IoT monitoring and enforcement of compliance to environmental laws on the internet. The smart devices are used to monitor emissions and wastes and their discharges to standards in addition to minimizing environmental offences. Another benefit that can be beneficial to companies is the possibility of using IoT data for reaching such sustainable objectives as decreasing CO_2 emissions or minimizing energy use. Such clear tracking not only leads to compliance with existing legal acts but also enhances the indicators of CSR and stakeholders' confidence.

3.6 Enhancing Disaster Preparedness and Response

The application of IoT systems is essential for solving problems related to disaster risk mitigation and management. Wireless sensor networks in high-risk zones track signs of natural calamities like floods, earthquakes and fire mishaps. These systems can send notification of emergencies hence authorities can enslave strict evacuation and resource management. After disaster IoT devices help in evaluation of damages and planning of recovery process, thus helping to restore damaged areas (Badade, 2024; Rashid, Ali, Ali, Taher, Mukhlif, Muliar, & Noori, 2024).

3.7 Innovation in Renewable Energy Management

IoT offers ambitious prospects in the utilization of renewable energy assets. Data from IoT devices enables the identification of the best locations to position as well as how to run solar transformers, windmills, and hydropower initiatives. Smart grids are built on IoT technology allowing the connection of renewable resources with utility networks and optimizing supply and demand with less consequences for the environment (Liu, Li, & Hu, 2024). It will be critical for shifting the world of energy to the new sustainable paradigm more rapidly.

4. CHALLENGES IN IOT FOR ENVIRONMENTAL MONITORING

Although the population of the connected devices comprising the Internet of Things has delivered improving capabilities to environmental management, it has not been without challenges in terms of adoption and implementation. The following reporting challenges are because of some technical, financial and operational factors which need to be overcome to get the full benefits of IoT. In this section, it is a development of the main problems in IoT for environmental monitoring and presents them by the systematic division.

Figure 2. Enhancing Disaster Preparedness and Response: Key IoT-driven stages

4.1 Infrastructure and Connectivity Limitations

The main issues with using IoT for monitoring the environment are the acquisition of proper structure and means of connection. Most IoT sensors are installed in areas of which network connectivity is usually poor or unavailable for instance forests, mountains and oceans, among others. Some of these problems can be solved with LPWAN and satellite IoT, but those solutions might be expensive or hard to scale at the same time. However, one of the biggest challenges is to sustain links in difficult physical situations or during storms.

4.2 Energy Constraints and Device Durability

Environmental sensors comprising IoT frequently find themselves in uncovered environments and rarely have consistent access to electricity. It is for this reason that the long life and energy efficiency of these devices must be a priority. While the improvements in battery technology, and energy harvesting systems like putting sensors in structures that are solar powered may enhance device sustainability, there are limits to these improvements especially in regions characterized by perverse weather or low light

(Lambert & Zang, 2024). In addition, IoT devices have to endure the effects of heat enlargement such as high humidity, temperature shocks, or impacts — all these cause higher costs and replacement more often.

Table 2. Key Challenges in IoT for Environmental Monitoring

Challenge	Description	Impact	Potential Solutions
Connectivity	Establishing reliable connectivity in remote or harsh environments.	Data transmission issues, sensor downtime, incomplete coverage.	LPWAN, satellite IoT, hybrid communication.
Energy Limitations	IoT devices operate in areas with limited or no power sources.	Short device lifespans, frequent maintenance, data gaps.	Solar-powered sensors, energy-efficient devices.
Data Management	Managing large volumes of continuous data generated by IoT sensors.	Storage challenges, processing delays, scalability issues.	Cloud computing, edge analytics, data compression.
Standardization	Lack of standardized protocols and devices across IoT systems.	Integration difficulties, inefficiencies in data sharing.	Open standards, interoperable systems.
Security and Privacy	Risks related to data breaches and unauthorized access to environmental data.	Compromised data integrity, loss of trust.	Encryption, secure protocols, regular software updates.
Cost	High costs of deploying and maintaining IoT devices and networks.	Budget constraints, slow adoption, limited scalability.	Low-cost sensors, government funding, partnerships.
Environmental Impact	IoT device production and disposal contribute to electronic waste.	Increased e-waste, higher carbon emissions from large-scale deployments.	Eco-friendly designs, recycling initiatives.
Accuracy and Calibration	Sensor inaccuracies and calibration drift over time.	Reduced reliability of data, inaccurate environmental assessments.	Regular calibration, self-calibrating sensors.

4.3 Data Management and Scalability

However, data produced by IoT devices is enormous, and this prompts problems of storage, data processing, and scalability. Environmental monitoring systems should be capable of managing flows of data from thousands of sensors; this needs sound cloud framework and analytics. Data integrity, low latency, and bandwidth requirements are the major concern while dealing with real-time data. Furthermore, tested system requirements are to deal with new deployments of IoT systems with increased scale and corresponding amounts of new devices and data • (Thandekkattu, Ayem, & Rakshit, 2024; • Makarem & Razaz, 2023).

4.4 Standardization and Interoperability

The issues IOT technologies face is lack of standardization in the hardware, software, and open communication platform involved with different devices and systems. Heterogeneous IoT devices can exist where products from different manufacturers have dissimilar architectures, making it difficult for the various stakeholders involved in sharing information to do so efficiently. Lack of standardization can also result to development of multiple unrelated systems, which hinders the formation of well-coordinated and large-scale environmental monitoring networks. It is crucial to press for an open standards agenda to encourage cooperation and support for the breakdown of silos that characterise current industrial practices regarding data communications ("Device Interoperability for Industrial IoT," 2022; Dewan, Chaudhary, & Yadav, 2023).

4.5 Data Security and Privacy Concerns

Existing IoT systems are not shielded against possible cyber-attacks and invasions that threaten the confidentiality of environmental information as well as interrupts the process of monitoring. It will also mean that any unauthorized person can get into the IoT networks causing damage, change or misuse data as they please. Seven specific ways to protect IoT systems are to achieve strong encryption, communication security, and software update. However, there are cases where IoT devices gather data that violates privacy, particularly where IoT is used in monitoring the city, and thus authors suggest that ethical and legal concerns are needed.

4.6 High Costs and Resource Requirements

The main challenge towards the integration of IoT systems for environmental monitoring is the initial capital investment willingly spent on the acquisition of sensors, setting up the network and the cloud storage servers. Besides these costs, other recurring needs of maintaining and updating the system, as well as processing information can prove to be costly for developing countries or even some organisations • (Singhal, Chakraborty, & Singh, 2024). Even more challenging, scarcity of funding and technical skills could also slow down IoT technologies adoption even further.

4.7 Environmental Impact of IoT Devices

Coincidentally, the devices used in environmental monitoring have been cited to fuel some of the environmental vices. The Internet of things sensors and batteries themselves are manufactured and when discarded creates electronic waste given their sizeable lithium-ion batteries, while IoT networks on a large scale consume energy to function thus contributing to carbon emissions. These thus need be tackled with advancement in green characteristics in the IoT devices as well as sustainable method of recycling and disposal (Nguyen, Mays, Plesa, Rao, Nguyen, & Chiao, 2015; Pramodhini, Jagadheeswaran, Dhuriata, & Vivek, 2024).

4.8 Challenges in Data Accuracy and Calibration

IoT devices used in monitoring the environment should therefore issue accurate and reliable information to the centres. Nevertheless, sensors can have drift issue which causes the value detected to be wrong. The performance of a sensor is also influenced by environmental factors like humidity levels on the surface of an object of interest, temperature changes, and interference by neighbouring devices • (Mamun & Yuce, 2019). This means that IoT monitoring systems require periodical calibration and validation of data to deliver high quality and credibility.

Figure 3. Challenges in IoT for Environmental Monitoring: Key issues

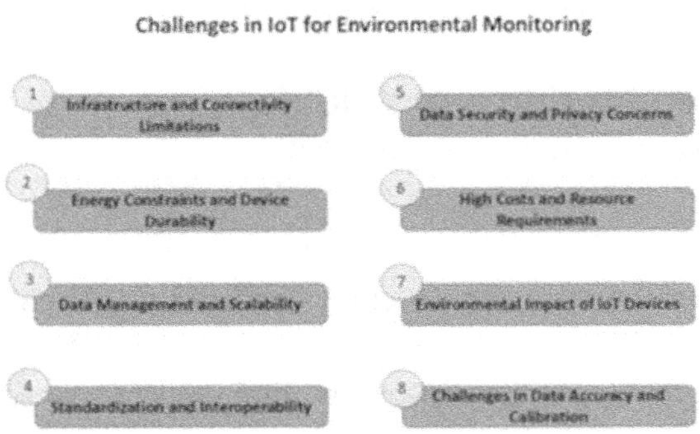

5. CASE STUDIES

Case Study 1: Smart Water Quality Monitoring in the Ganges River, India

The river system that provides water supply in the India namely Ganges River is facing sewage pollution, industrial effluents, and agricultural drainage water pollution. Due to this, the Indian government has introduced an IoT based water quality monitoring system. Water quality data of river include the pH, total suspended solid, dissolved oxygen and chemical oxygen demand is determined with the help of sensors placed along its banks. Information that these sensors gather is then sent through wireless networks although LPWAN and satellite coverage to regions cannot reach are used. This system helps in checking the interactive level of water quality so that the relative degree of pollution can be known. Even with emerging problems like lack of connectivity over some geographical areas, high power consumption of the devices, optimum data transfer is maintained using hybrid power solutions and satellite-based communications. This system has resulted to enhanced monitoring of emission controls thus enhancing water quality and public health (Singh, Rai, Singh, & Mishra, 2022; (Kumar, Sapkal, & Tiwari, 2018).

Case Study 2: Air Quality Monitoring in Barcelona, Spain

Barcelona, as part of its smart city development program, has installed a smart IoT network-based pollution sensing solution for sustainability of urban environment. The system includes several hundred air quality monitors located at various locations in the city to measure the concentrations of PM2,5, PM 10, nitrogen dioxide, carbon monoxide, and ozone. Information from these sensors is transmitted through Wi-Fi and 5G connectivity to a central interface, where real-time data analysis is conducted to identify pollution 'hot spots' as well as future trends. Some of the issues which emerged are as follows: The use of the system has brought many challenges such as too much data generated from so many sensors and compatibility of the devices in the system has been resolved by the use of cloud platforms and edge computing. Such data of the air quality is provided to the public through a specially developed mobile application so that people could make correct decisions related to their outdoor activities. The data is also helpful to Local Authorities in policy formulation on how to reduce emission and advocate for healthy air within the city (Armengol, Carnerero, Rames, Criado, Borge-Holithoefer, Soret, & Solé-Ribalta, 2024; (Soret, García-Pando, Jorba, Guevara, Benavides, Tena, Rodriguez-Rey, Kakkos, & Quan, 2023).

Case Study 3: Forest Monitoring and Wildlife Protection in the Amazon Rainforest, Brazil

The Amazon rainforest, the largest tropical rainforest in the world boasting of containing one of the greatest bio diversities has been threatened by several vice including; illegal logging. To overcome these challenges, Brazil has adapted IoT for the management of forests and for protection of wildlife. It uses satellite sensors, temperature and humidity sensors, motion detectors or sensors tracking resistance to electrical current in monitoring of illicit behaviour and movements of endangered species. Many of the IoT devices used in operation are supplied by hybrid sources of electrical energy, such as solar panels, to effectively operate within inaccessible forest territories. Satellite and LPWAN connectivity for that data to go to a central hub where AI processing looks for tell-tale signs of deforestation and poaching activity. Dense tree canopies and weather remain influential barriers to connectivity but the use of drones to augment coverage to monitor has boosted accuracy. This kind of IoT-based monitoring system has allowed the quicker identification of illicit actions and a better reaction out of authorities for the purpose of consolidating the safeguarding of body of relevant literatures biodiversity in the area (Wang, Li, Souza Jr., Souza Filho, & Pinheiro, 2024).

Case Study 4: Smart Agriculture for Crop Monitoring in California, USA

IoT deployment in agriculture in California has been triggered by drought states and the issue of sustainable farming methods. Agricultural producers in the area utilise Internet of Things to ensure efficiency in water use to water crops, monitoring of soil conditions, and increase crop yield (Balakrishnan, Prabhkar, Chandran, Kumar, Murugesan, & Gheisari, 2024). Currently, the farms install soil moisture sensors, weather stations, and temperature sensors in their fields so that data collected can be sent to the cloud through cellular networks. Some of the big data analytics solutions to the data include using machine learning algorithms to estimate the irrigation, pest monitoring, and crop management. A major problem encountered in this project was the stability of the sensors as to the kind of soil and the prevailing weather conditions. To that end, smart irrigation systems that are driven by IoT data adjust the irrigation process on their own, thus implying water can be used more wisely. It has decreased the utilization of water and expenditure costs and improve crop productivity by giving farmers solutions what is going on in their farms at the right time and accurately.

Case Study 5: Urban Flood Monitoring and Management in New York City, USA

Given recent severe floods in the areas with increased climate change effects such as New York City, functioning IoT flood monitor has been designed. The system uses water level sensors, rain gauges as well as temperature sensors for assessing flood affected areas and rivers in realtime. Information is collected through these sensors sent to a headquarters for evaluation and prognosis using 4G LTE networks. Analyzing the data, machine learning models predict floods and use these outcomes to provide early warnings to the inhabitants and municipal officers. It was even more difficult to predict the flood occurrences in the urban areas because of topographical characteristics of the region and type of construction works. To resolve this issue, the city connected the IoT platform to the local weather prediction systems enhancing the forecasts (Yereseme, Surendra, & Kuntoji, 2022). The flood management system has enabled New York City to enhance its flood protection, minimizing risk to people and properties; and facilitate appropriate planning for managing floods.

Case Study 6: Smart Irrigation System in Punjab, India

In Punjab, a state which is duly nicknamed the "Granary of India", issues connected with overdrawing water in agricultural production, especially in wheat and rice growing operations are apparent. To this effect a smart irrigation system involving IoT technology was installed in some of the farm across the state. Soil moisture sensors, weather and flow sensors were used in collecting data on the state of the soil, rainfall, and water usage. Associated with the sensors are real time data that is sent to a central system and algorithms that offer suggestions on the irrigation regime. Through the use of IoT technology the farmers were in a position to minimize on water usage which was in excess and resulting to wastage. This has contributed to considerable water savings in the region, some of the farmers were able to save up 30% of the water they used (Mustafa, Salahuddin, Ashraf, Shafique, Salahuddin, & Akbar, 2024; Singh & Kumar, 2021). Thus, while such issues as an initial cost of the sensors and their further maintenance once installed were present, the possibility to save water and increase yield per ha made the project successful.

Case Study 7: Air Quality Monitoring in Delhi, India

Delhi with an AQI of one of the highest rankings globally has installed a city-wide air quality monitoring and managements system through IoT. The system utilizes several hundreds of cheap air quality monitoring devices installed at the various sites in the city to monitor pollutants including; PM2.5, PM10, NO2 and CO. The spectacular real-time data gathered by these sensors is then channeled to a central display where data is analyzed to monitor pollution trends, detect areas of high pollution and issue alerts on health related issues. The data is also disseminated to the public through the administration of a mobile application where citizens are enlightened on the issues. The hard problems encountered in this work included the calibration of the sensor and the combination of diverse types of the sensor. But such difficulties have been averted through partnership with research institutions and the use of machine learning approaches in forecasting pollution patterns. For this reason, the initiative has educated the public on issues of air pollution and provided information to governments with the goal of reforming emissions from automobiles and industries (Gupta, Bhardwaj, Agrawal, Tikkiwal, & Kumar, 2019; Singh, Dahiya, Kumar, & Nanda, 2021).

Case Study 8: Smart Waste Management in Bengaluru, India

The Hub city of Karnataka and one of the second-fastest growing cities in the world, Bengaluru is grappling with its rising problems of waste management. In response, the city has adopted an Internet of Things (IoT) Intelligent Waste Management System. This is through the deployment of IoT waste bins that contain fill-level sensors to help the system monitor the full levels and send these to a central hub. The information assists managing the planning of routes for waste collection, so that garbage collection is only done when bins are full, consequently, the number of trips that are made by the garbage trucks is minimized. It also estimates waste disposal status and enhances the rate of recycling (Addas, Khan, & Naseer, 2024; Deeraj, Subburaj, & B.U., 2024). The key issue was to manage the involvement of diverse technologies and data platforms to support the waste improvement process. These challenges were, however, dealt with through partnership with the ICT firms and adoption of cloud solutions in the management of solid waste in Bengaluru. The system has helped in cutting expenses, cutting frequency of street waste pickup trucks, and enhancing cleaning of the city.

Case Study 9: Smart Energy Management in Rural Rajasthan, India

Both aspects of energy supply and demand are problematic in rural settings in India especially those in Rajasthan. In order to correct these problems, a pilot project was initiated in the state to introduce smart energy management system in the rural villages. This is applied through the IoT sensors in the system which measures various factors including energy consumption, power, voltage, and the frequency. Smart meters are fixed either in the homes or other social facilities to make sure that energy supply and consumption meet the standards. The system feeds information to a mainframe that uses energy consumption profiles in order to enhance the management of electricity distribution as well as the prevention of wastage on the energy. The problems that were identified included poor internet connection in those regions, and need for cheap and long lasting sensors. To address such issues, LPWAN was employed for the purpose of communication and solar-powered sensors were employed for reliability. This IoT based system has promoted effective use of power usage, minimized power failures and has provided a more stable power to the farmers thus enhancing their productivity (Islam, Nohori, Hossain, Uddin, & Hasan, 2024).

Case Study 10: Monitoring of Coastal Erosion in Kerala, India

Kerala has large coastal line therefore it is highly vulnerable with coastal erosion which affects both nature and economy. To this end, the Kerala State Remote Sensing and Environment Centre (KSREC) has come up with an IoT based shore line erosion surveillance. There is the utilization of sensors for instance the tidal, the wave, the salinity and the soil moisture all along the coastal line. These sensors relay information to a database where analysis is made on the level of erosion risk and on how to prevent such occurrence, by the erection of barriers or replantation of mangrove plants (Rao, Nair, & Raju, 1985). An important issue was, therefore, the question of how to make the sensors desalination-proof enough for the coastal region. To this end, the sensors were made waterproof and hence resistant to water from marine environments, while the energy sources used for charging the sensors included both solar and wind energy technologies. It has given insights of the erosion pattern which was used in defending the coastal environment and the people living in that region.

Case Study 11: Water Resource Management in Maharashtra, India

Currently Maharashtra has many areas where water has really become scarce especially to the regions that are almost always affected by the drought. In response, the state has adopted an IoT system of water resource management that based weather data, groundwater levels, and water usage to enhance water distribution. The use of IoT sensors installed on reservoirs, wells and rivers help the authorities get details of water levels at a given time. This information is used to determine the proportions under which water should be transported, and also to establish those areas that ought to be given water in order to sustain the population and those, which may possibly run out of water. Hence, the main problem in the given case was the problem of data fusion of different sources, such as weather stations and the systems of the groundwater level measurement. Nonetheless, integrating cloud platforms and data analytics tools made the system achieve the intent of providing resource managers with rational frameworks for managing water resources. That has stressed the issues relating to the distribution of water during the critical time of the year and has trimmed the impact of the droughts in the region (Suryavanshi, Mehta, Chattopadhyay, & Aeri, 2024; Abebe, 2024).

Case Study 12: Monitoring of Forest Fires in Madhya Pradesh, India

It is common for forest fires to take place in the period of the dry season and Madhya Pradesh is not immune to this vice is has many national parks and forest reserves. In response to this problem, the state has established an IoT based forest fire monitoring system with temperature and smoke detectors stationed in the affected forests. True these sensors feed information in a real-time sense and send the information to a focal point where all the information is scrutinized in an effort to discover signs of fire. The system can send notifications to the forest rangers and, as such, prevent extensive fires in the forest. The difficulties that occured during the project implementation were sensor maintenance under Forest environment conditions and keeping in mind the connectivity issues with remote locations (Сорокин, Odnogulov, Maltseva, Azatullaevna, Dzhalmukhambetova, Руденко, & Esaulenko, 2024; Masram, Mendhe, Mishra, Pathade, Shindekar, & Kangale, 2024). To counter these, low-power sensors, and satellite communication were employed, which enabled constant watching. This system has proved useful in early detection of forest fires, minimized damage by the fires and enhanced protection of the forests.

6. FUTURE DIRECTIONS AND SOLUTIONS

The future of this technology as IoT advances in usage in environmental monitoring is bright in its potential to refine the activity of environmental management systems even more. The dynamic progress of IoT innovations, new possibilities in connectivity, data processing, and sensor systems will help to solve significant problems in the environment. 5G network and edge computing are perhaps one of the largest areas of future prospect in IoT systems. The coming generations of IoT devices will be improve through 5G which will build a better platform on real time data communication. This will be especially important where the environmental parameters are in constant fluctuation and require constant surveillance like air quality, whether, water level, among others, because their monitoring leads to timely mitigation.

Incomplete information will be processed by devices themselves with help of edge computing instead of sending data to centralized cloud environments. This usage concern makes it more efficient in bandwidth term and faster in response time making it fit for apps that requires immediate action such as monitoring floods or detection of wildfires. There would be dramatic improvements in data analysis where future applications using artificial intelligence [AI] and machine learning [ML] would be applied. When it comes to IoT systems, just about every company or organization is dealing with massive volumes of data and AI/ML can be very helpful in trying to process this data and attempting to make sense of it in as good and rational manners as possible. In other example, through data analysis, an AI system can predict episodes of air pollution or water shortage and governments and organizations can prevent them. Data mining techniques can also enhance the models of the environment therefore facilitating the right decision making in areas that include the conservation of the environment, management of resources as well as environmental change.

Increased usage of better sensors will also be central to the future of the IoT in the environmental field. The development in sensor technology will provide better, efficient and reliable sensors that can be placed in harsh environments. For instance, the improved sensitivity and battery life of next-generation sensors will enable tracking and monitoring of other environmental parameters: soil quality, biota, and even presence of microplastics in oceans. Moreover, a shift will observe in the internal integration of the sensors themselves, which will be able to concurrently monitor a range of different environmental conditions for which the need to have several measuring devices at once will no longer be necessary. The future of the IoT in environmental monitoring will also see increased enhancement of the focus placed on cross-data compatibility. As more IoT systems connect various devices and applications in the market, it is pertinent to think about how those devices and data platforms can integrate with each other. These standards and protocols will help in creating convergence across the various IoT networks to facilitate collection of environmental information across the different networks. This will help make improved environmental surveillance networks which can work all over the world to give information on climate change, pollution and state of ecosystems.

Finally, sustainability and ethics are possible lines of improvements for the future of IoT application in environment monitoring. However, with a rising trend of IoT systems, it will be important that these technologies are implemented sustainably to the society. This includes asserting energy friendly devices, controlling flow of electronics waste, as well as guaranteeing that the collected information for use in a friendly environmental manner as well as influencing those areas that are experiencing changes on environmental conservation. However, there is challenge arising from to do with data and information privacy because the environmental monitoring systems gather sensitive information about individual, ecological system and region. In conclusion, the future of IoT in environmental monitoring therefore looks bright since, with technological advancements, the effectiveness, accuracy and accessibility in environmental data collection will quickly improve. With the help of 5G connectivity, edge computing, AI, and more expansive use of smart sensors as well as the wise choice of Io things focus on interoperability and sustainability, IoT systems will remain the cornerstone in the further fight for environment saving and, therefore, for making the world a better place for everyone.

7. CONCLUSION

In conclusion the incorporation of IoT in environmental monitoring has become one of the most influential solutions for some of the environmental problems experienced in the current society. with IoT as an approach we stand to benefit from real time acquisition, processing and management of environmental data for such changes as air and water quality, improved waste management, monitoring of biodiversity and sustainable agriculture. By enhancing decision support, promoting early warning and offering solutions on the state of the environment and the health of the public, IoT systems can dramatically enhance environmental sustainability. Nevertheless, as shown in research, IoT is noteworthy and has a great potential as a tool for environmental monitoring but it calls for some problems that are specific detachable to utilize it such as data privacy, connectivity, compatibility, and trustworthy sensors.

In order to overcome these problems, innovation, collaboration, and standards setting are necessary so that IoT solutions in environmental monitoring that are to be implemented at large geographical areas and differing environments can be successfully implemented in the future. In the future, 5G connection, edge computing, artificial intelligence, and sensors' development will bring additional opportunities to develop IoT in environmental monitoring. On this basis, the ongoing development of technology for environmental management will lead to improved precision, effectiveness, and ultimately, to the more sustainable use of environments with combating global climate change, conserving natural resources, and ensuring the sustainability of ecosystems in the future. By expanding our commitment to, and focus on IoT-based solutions, we can help create a smarter, more sustainable and more protected environment.

REFERENCES

Abdullah, . (2024). Waste management 2.0 leveraging internet of things for an efficient and eco-friendly smart city solution. *PLoS One*, *19*(7), e0307608–e0307608. DOI: 10.1371/journal.pone.0307608 PMID: 39083562

Abebe, A. (2024). Internet of Things (IoT) Enabled Water Distribution System for Smart Water Management. *International Journal (Toronto, Ont.)*, *11*(1), 1–10.

Aditya, B. R., Hernawati, E., Gunawan, T., & Aji, P. (2024). Design an Agricultural Soil and Environment Monitoring System Based on IoT. *Pertanika Journal of Science & Technology*, *32*(6).

Akinwale, I. (2024). IoT applications in sustainability and sustainable community development. *World Journal Of Advanced Research and Reviews*, *24*(1), 2634–2640. DOI: 10.30574/wjarr.2024.24.1.3326

Al Mamun, M. A., & Yuce, M. R. (2019). Sensors and systems for wearable environmental monitoring toward IoT-enabled applications: A review. *IEEE Sensors Journal*, *19*(18), 7771–7788. DOI: 10.1109/JSEN.2019.2919352

Amjad, A., Azam, F., & Anwar, M. W. (2022, October). Device interoperability for industrial iot using model-driven architecture. In 2022 24th International Multitopic Conference (INMIC) (pp. 1-6). IEEE.

Ankit, D. (2024). Basics of Internet of Things. *Indian Scientific Journal Of Research In Engineering And Management*, *08*(10), 1–6. DOI: 10.55041/IJSREM37970

Armengol, J. M., Carnerero, C., Rames, C., Criado, Á., Borge-Holthoefer, J., Soret, A., & Solé-Ribalta, A. (2024). City-scale assessment of pedestrian exposure to air pollution: A case study in Barcelona. *Urban Climate*, *58*, 102183.

Arowolo, M. E., Aaron, W. C., Eteng, U. S., Divine, I. L. O. H., Aguma, C. P., & Olagunju, A. O. (2024). Integrating AI enhanced remote sensing technologies with IoT networks for precision environmental monitoring and predicative ecosystem management. *World Journal of Advanced Research and Reviews*, *23*(2), 2156–2166.

Ashok, K. (2024). AI and IoT in biodiversity assessment. *Journal of Aquaculture & Marine Biology*, *13*(3), 108–115. DOI: 10.15406/jamb.2024.13.00404

Asif, G. (2024). Utilizing IoT and Cloud Computing for Weather-Health Monitoring Application. *International Journal of Electrical Engineering and Computer Science*, *6*, 152–158. DOI: 10.37394/232027.2024.6.18

Babu, K., Umadevi, P., Patel, N., & Gopalakrishnan, S. (2023, December). Real-Time Monitoring of Glacial Changes Using Artificial Intelligence. In 2023 4th International Conference on Computation, Automation and Knowledge Management (ICCAKM) (pp. 01-06). IEEE.

Balodi, S. D., Yadav, M. U., & Kumar, J. D. Smart Solutions for Sustainable Living: Internet of Things (IoT) Applications in Environmental Monitoring. information network, 23, 24.

Bhatia, G. (2024). Predictive Urban Air Quality Monitoring for Healthier Cities. *South Eastern European Journal of Public Health*, •••, 1627–1634. DOI: 10.70135/seejph.vi.2166

Claudia, B. (2024). Monitoring and Predicting Air Quality with IoT Devices. *Processes (Basel, Switzerland), 12*(9), 1961–1961. DOI: 10.3390/pr12091961

Deeraj, C., Subburaj, T., & Neelesh, B. U. (2024). IOT based Waste Management System. International Journal of Advanced Research in Science. *Tongxin Jishu, 107-111*, 107–111. Advance online publication. DOI: 10.48175/IJARSCT-19020

Deeraj, C., Subburaj, T., & Neelesh, B. U. (2024). IOT based Waste Management System. International Journal of Advanced Research in Science. *Tongxin Jishu, 107-111*, 107–111. Advance online publication. DOI: 10.48175/IJARSCT-19020

Dewan, B., Chaudhary, S., & Yadav, M. (2021). A charge plasma based label free biomolecule detector using SiGe-heterojunction double gate Tunnel FET. *Silicon*, 1-10.

Dewan, B., Chaudhary, S., & Yadav, M. (2023). A label-free dielectric-modulated biosensor using SiGe-heterojunction dual cavity dual metal electrically doped TFET. *Engineering Research Express*, *5*(3), 035002. DOI: 10.1088/2631-8695/acdec7

Emran, A. (2024). Artificial intelligence in environmental monitoring: In-depth analysis. *Discover Artificial Intelligence*, *4*(1), 84. Advance online publication. DOI: 10.1007/s44163-024-00198-1

Gupta, H., Bhardwaj, D., Agrawal, H., Tikkiwal, V. A., & Kumar, A. (2019, February). An IoT based air pollution monitoring system for smart cities. In *2019 IEEE International Conference on Sustainable Energy Technologies and Systems (ICSETS)* (pp. 173-177). IEEE. DOI: 10.1109/ICSETS.2019.8744949

Hovorushchenko, T., Bachuk, V., Hnatchuk, Y., Zasornova, I., & Bouhissi, H. E. (2024). Overview of the methods and tools for environmental components monitoring.

Islam, M., Jobaida, N., Hossain, M. S., Uddin, M. R., & Hasan, M. (2024, June). IoT-Based Smart Energy Monitoring and Energy Demand Response System. In 2024 IEEE 3rd International Conference on Electrical Power and Energy Systems (ICEPES) (pp. 1-5). IEEE.

Jaja, K. (2024). Revitalizing IoT-based air quality monitoring system for major cities in Indonesia. *Sinergi*, *28*(3), 605–605. DOI: 10.22441/sinergi.2024.3.016

Jia, L., Li, Z., & Hu, Z. (2024). Applications of the internet of things in renewable power systems: A survey. *Energies*, *17*(16), 4160.

Jyoti, S. (2024). *A., Dutta., Karishma, Desai*. Industrial IoT Systems for Real-Time Environmental Monitoring., DOI: 10.1109/ACROSET62108.2024.10743956

Kumar, M., Sapkal, A., & Tiwari, V. (2018, November). *Ganga water quality monitoring system iot based. In 2018 IEEE Punecon*. IEEE.

López-Munoz, M. A., Torrealba-Melendez, R., Arriaga-Arriaga, C. A., Tamariz-Flores, E. I., López-López, M., Quirino-Morales, F., & López-Marcos, F. (2024). Wireless Dynamic Sensor Network for Water Quality Monitoring Based on the IoT. *Technologies*, *12*(11), 211.

Mahmudul, A. (2024). An IoT Based Real-Time Environmental Monitoring System for Developing Areas. *Journal of Advanced Research in Applied Sciences and Engineering Technology*, *52*(1), 106–121. DOI: 10.37934/araset.52.1.106121

Makarem, M. A., & Razaz, M. A. (2023, October). Role of Big Data Analytics in the Internet of Things: A Comprehensive Survey. In 2023 3rd International Conference on Emerging Smart Technologies and Applications (eSmarTA) (pp. 1-15). IEEE.

Masram, B., Mendhe, A., Mishra, A., Pathade, A., Shindekar, N., & Kangale, Y. (2024, August). A Smart Forest Fire Detection and Notification System using IOT and Machine Learning. In *2024 International Conference on Electrical Electronics and Computing Technologies (ICEECT)* (Vol. 1, pp. 1-6). IEEE.

Moreno, E. O. L., Cortes, L. L. H., Callejas, J. D. C., & Hernández, H. A. (2024, August). IoT based weather station for smart cities. In *2024 IEEE Colombian Conference on Communications and Computing (COLCOM)* (pp. 1-5). IEEE.

Mustafa, S., Salahuddin, H., Ashraf, A., Shafique, M., Salahuddin, S., & Akbar, M. (2024). Smart Irrigation System for Wheat in Southern Punjab Using IOT-based Wireless Technology. *Journal of Computing & Biomedical Informatics*, *8*(01).

Najem, N. R., Ali, Z. G., Ali, A. H. A., Taher, N. A., Mukhlif, S. K., Muliar, I., & Noori, H. M. (2024, October). A Comprehensive Framework for Harnessing IoT and 5G for Enhanced Disaster Response. In 2024 36th Conference of Open Innovations Association (FRUCT) (pp. 655-663). IEEE.

Nguyen, C. M., Mays, J., Plesa, D., Rao, S., Nguyen, M., & Chiao, J. C. (2015, May). Wireless sensor nodes for environmental monitoring in Internet of Things. In *2015 IEEE MTT-S International Microwave Symposium* (pp. 1-4). IEEE.

Oroos, A. (2024). *Aryan, Chaudhary*. Fundamental Concepts of IoT., DOI: 10.1201/9781032656694-2

Paul, C. (2024). *Lambert., Yong, Zang*. Micro Energy Harvesting for IoT Sensors., DOI: 10.23919/INC-USNC-URSI61303.2024.10632530

Prabhakara Rao, P., Nair, M. M., & Raju, D. V. (1985). Assessment of the role of remote sensing techniques in monitoring shoreline changes: A case study of the Kerala coast. *International Journal of Remote Sensing*, *6*(3-4), 549–558. DOI: 10.1080/01431168508948477

Prakash, T. (2023). Blockchain-Enabled Secure Big Data Analytics for Internet of Things Smart Applications. *IEEE Internet of Things Journal*, *10*(7), 6428–6443. DOI: 10.1109/JIOT.2022.3227162

Pramodhini, R., Jagadheeswaran, R., Dhuriata, P., & Vivek, S. (2024, April). Optimizing environmental sustainability: analyzing IoT-enabled energy harvesting systems. In *2024 Third International Conference on Distributed Computing and Electrical Circuits and Electronics (ICDCECE)* (pp. 1-7). IEEE.

Priyanka, K. (2024). Effective Air Pollution Monitoring System for Eco Balance. *International Journal for Research in Applied Science and Engineering Technology*, *12*(10), 53–56. DOI: 10.22214/ijraset.2024.64435

Rodriguez-Rey, D., Guevara, M., Mateu Armengol, J., Criado, A., Enciso, S., Tena, C., . . . Pérez-Garcia Pando, C. (2023, May). Challenges for achieving clean air-The case of Barcelona (Spain). In EGU General Assembly Conference Abstracts (pp. EGU-14487).

Rudi, H. (2024). Portable internet of things-based soil nutrients monitoring for precision and efficient smart farming. *Bulletin of Electrical Engineering and Informatics*, *13*(5), 3326–3333. DOI: 10.11591/eei.v13i5.7928

Rupali, P. (2024). Performance Measurement and Analysis of Soil Quality using. *IoT*, •••, 192–197. DOI: 10.1109/I-SMAC61858.2024.10714691

Sankar, G. R., & Fathima, G. (2024, April). IoT-Enabled Smart Waste Management: A Comprehensive Study on Sensor Technologies and Implementation Strategies. In *2024 International Conference on Inventive Computation Technologies (ICICT)* (pp. 1755-1764). IEEE.

Santhosini, R., Subhiksha, U. K., & Jayanthi, D. (2024). Review on Evaluation and Analysis of Water Quality Monitoring Systems Using IoT. *Deleted Journal*, *2*(09), 2331–2341. DOI: 10.47392/IRJAEH.2024.0320

Sasikumar, A., Ravi, L., Kotecha, K., Saini, J. R., Varadarajan, V., & Subramaniyaswamy, V. (2022). Sustainable Smart Industry: A Secure and Energy Efficient Consensus Mechanism for Artificial Intelligence Enabled Industrial Internet of Things. *Computational Intelligence and Neuroscience*, *2022*, 1–12. DOI: 10.1155/2022/1419360

Satinder, K. (2024). Advancing Sustainable Ecosystem Development. Journal of Geography. *Environment and Earth Science International*, *28*(7), 52–59. DOI: 10.9734/jgeesi/2024/v28i7789

Shiwei, C. (2024). Environmental Protection Control System Based on IoT and Deep Learning Intelligent Monitoring Sensors. Scalable Computing. *Practice and Experience*, *25*(4), 2210–2219. DOI: 10.12694/scpe.v25i4.2820

Singh, D., Dahiya, M., Kumar, R., & Nanda, C. (2021). Sensors and systems for air quality assessment monitoring and management: A review. *Journal of Environmental Management*, *289*, 112510. DOI: 10.1016/j.jenvman.2021.112510 PMID: 33827002

. Singh, K., & Kumar, R. (2021). Design of a low-cost sensor-based iot system for smart irrigation. *Applications in Ubiquitous Computing*, 59-79.

Singh, S., Rai, S., Singh, P., & Mishra, V. K. (2022). Real-time water quality monitoring of River Ganga (India) using internet of things. *Ecological Informatics*, *71*, 101770. DOI: 10.1016/j.ecoinf.2022.101770

Sorokin, A. A., Odnogulov, I. O., Maltseva, N. S., Dzhalmukhambetova, E. A., Rudenko, M. F., & Esaulenko, V. N. (2024, October). Computing Platform for Monitoring Fire Hazards in Forest Areas using the IoT. In 2024 International Seminar on Electron Devices Design and Production (SED) (pp. 1-6). IEEE.

Suryavanshi, A., Mehta, S., Chattopadhyay, S., & Aeri, M. (2024, June). Navigating Water Scarcity with IoT: A Smart Management System Approach. In 2023 4th International Conference on Intelligent Technologies (CONIT) (pp. 1-5). IEEE.

Thandekkattu, S. G., Ayem, G. T., & Rakshit, S. (2025). Data Management and Analytics in the Internet of Things (IoT). In Designing Sustainable Internet of Things Solutions for Smart Industries (pp. 209-228). IGI Global.

Vaibhavi, M. (2024). Internet of Things in Disaster Management. *International Journal for Research in Applied Science and Engineering Technology, 12*(10), 620–625. DOI: 10.22214/ijraset.2024.64640

Vaibhavi, M. (2024). Internet of Things in Disaster Management. *International Journal for Research in Applied Science and Engineering Technology, 12*(10), 620–625. DOI: 10.22214/ijraset.2024.64640

. Wei, Li. (2022). Big Data Mining Algorithm of Internet of Things Based on Artificial Intelligence Technology. 115-121. DOI: 10.1109/ISAIEE57420.2022.00032

Yereseme, A. K., Surendra, H. J., & Kuntoji, G. (2022). Sustainable integrated urban flood management strategies for planning of smart cities: A review. *Sustainable Water Resources Management, 8*(3), 85. DOI: 10.1007/s40899-022-00666-5

Zhihao, W. (2024, November 07). AI-based Validation of Deforestation Using High-Resolution Satellite Imagery in the Brazilian Amazon. *The International Archives of the Photogrammetry, Remote Sensing and Spatial Information Sciences, XLVIII-3-2024*, 583–588. Advance online publication. DOI: 10.5194/isprs-archives-XLVIII-3-2024-583-2024

Chapter 15
Leveraging Digital Twin Technology in Industrial IoT for Energy Optimization and Waste Reduction

Ankit Agarwal
https://orcid.org/0000-0003-0457-6421
Dr. Akhilesh Das Gupta Institute of Professional Studies, New Delhi, India

Inderjeet Sinha
https://orcid.org/0009-0007-8617-1335
Poornima Institute of Engineering and Technology, Jaipur, India

Subarno Bhattacharyya
https://orcid.org/0000-0002-5200-6258
O.P. Jindal Global University, Sonipat, India

Udit Mamodiya
https://orcid.org/0000-0002-8022-4252
Poornima University, India

ABSTRACT

It was based on the motivation to generate novel innovative technologies in order to promote energy efficiency with reduced waste through the growth in demand for industrial practices in an eco-friendly way. In this paradigm, Industrial IoT provides a promising platform for real-time monitoring, maintenance, and resource usage within Digital Twins. A new multi-layer architecture will be developed in this chapter to integrate digital twins and IIoT to mutually optimize energy consumption and waste reduction. Named the Adaptive Energy Optimization and Waste Reduction Framework, this novel architecture utilizes AI-driven self-learning models for dynamically adapting itself to various changes in industrial conditions. Simultaneously, efficiency is maintained through both energy usage as well as waste minimization due to EWCO. This framework is simulated to carry out industrial operations in virtual environments to identify inefficiencies and predict failures along with the automation of optimization strategies.

DOI: 10.4018/979-8-3373-2028-1.ch015

1. INTRODUCTION

The two opposing imperatives in the industrial sector, namely, sustainability and operational efficiency, seem to bring with them a change in paradigm. With growing demand for energy at the global level and the pressures of environmental regulations, industries have to look towards novel technologies that mitigate these problems. Among such powerful tools is the emergence of Digital Twin Technology and Industrial IoT that can revolutionize industrial operations. Together, these technologies afford an unprecedented scope for energy efficiency and waste reduction-two of the most important cornerstones of sustainable industrial practices.

The term "Digital Twin Technology" is borrowed from the high-risk industries of aerospace and automotive engineering. It is simple yet profoundly simple: a digital replica of any physical system could mirror its behavior in real time. It has evolved with improvements in computing power and data analytics and the pervasiveness of IoT technology over the years. It's basically a cyber-physical system, which incessantly maintains two-way communication with the physical world through a stream of data (Murali & Pasupuleti, 2024). And as such, Digital Twins provide operational visibility beyond anything hitherto imagined for industries. For example, it would show the performance of individual turbines in a power plant while simulating their behavior under different conditions and suggest optimization strategies to improve energy efficiency. The integration of Digital Twin Technology with Industrial IoT is considered a paradigm shift in how data is collected, analyzed, and used in industrial settings. IIoT provides the infrastructure for data acquisition, allowing real-time physical system monitoring using a network of interconnected sensors and devices. Such sensors capture, critical parameters including energy use, health status of the equipment, and environmental conditions, forming the basis for Digital Twin simulations (Yassine & Kobbane, 2024). The synergy between IIoT and Digital Twins is in translating raw data to actionable insights, where IIoT excels at collecting lots of data, with Digital Twins performing the step-ahead dynamic simulation-based prediction of a system's behaviors and suggesting recommendations for optimization opportunities. For instance, in a factory, IIoT sensors are able to infer that a machine is operating far from its optimization point (Butean et al., 2024). A Digital Twin can also simulate several possible scenarios, pointing out the problem and its remedy, which can be in terms of machine calibration or rescheduling of production. The most significant challenge industries face today is energy optimization. Energy costs are rising, and carbon footprints are decreasing (Weiß & Ribas-Tugores, 2024). They enable simulation of the variability of solar or wind energy to balance supply and demand effectively in industries. For example, a Digital Twin of a steel plant can mimic the energy consumed at different points of production (Muka & Marinova, 2024). This way, it can be used to recommend the process flow modifications that should be made for a significant amount of energy saved. Industrial waste is incredibly diverse, incorporating everything from material waste, energy waste, to resource inefficiencies. However, this does require a systems-based approach far more advanced than any old-fashioned notion of waste management techniques. This can be provided through Digital Twins for industries dealing with waste from source.

Digital Twins track waste generation in real-time, providing insights into where and why waste occurs. This is particularly valuable in industries with complex supply chains, such as food processing or electronics manufacturing. Digital Twins will provide a simulation of a production process to help identify the material usage reduction that will not compromise on quality. In the automobile industry, it can suggest the alteration of design such that material waste during assembly would be minimized. The Digital Twin facilitates the transition towards a circular economy through enabling the tracking and optimization of resource reuse, recycling, and recovery. This aligns with global sustainability goals and minimizes the ecological footprint of industrial activities. The Digital Twin of a logistics operation will minimize fuel usage while delivering, cutting down the use of fuels that lead to emission of green gases, therefore ensuring cost-saving measures and ecological sustainability. Newly developed emerging technologies like AI, edge computing, and blockchain give the Digital Twins extra capabilities. These technologies meet some of the most significant hurdles that Digital Twins face: AI gives Digital Twins a fast and efficient processing capacity on large volumes of data. These machine learning algorithms are capable of discovering trends or patterns invisible to human analysts in order to significantly enhance decision making. Very important for large-scale industrial applications is the reduction in latency and improvement in scalability, as the Digital Twin systems process data at the edge of the network rather than central servers.

The technology ensures a secure and tamper-proof data exchange between IIoT devices and Digital Twins. In healthcare or aerospace applications, this is considered the key aspect of data integrity.

2. LITERATURE REVIEW

The originally developed for the aerospace industry, A Digital Twin Technology has evolved into a powerful tool applied across the industrial spectrum. The basic concept of its is to build virtual replicas of physical assets to simulate, monitor, and optimize operations in real-time. It has been quite a journey in terms of computing power, data storage, and for the sensor technologies that have revolutionized the capability of Digital Twins over the years. They have moved up today to being beyond one particular machine or even a component up to whole systems and processes, even organizational workflows. Introducing DTs and IIoT into the AEOWR Framework is, indeed an industrial practice that bears the potential for revolution in sustaining further improvement of it. The AI-driven models enable this framework to adapt to changing conditions, thereby maximizing energy usage while minimizing waste with real-time monitoring and predictive maintenance. A variety of studies discuss the potential that Digital Twins hold to transform industrial sectors (Kasper et al., 2024). The works are mainly about the capabilities of Digital Twins for predictive maintenance enhancement, reliability improvements in systems, and optimization in resource utilization. Indeed, despite vast improvements that have been recorded relating to simulation model development as well as visual tools, great challenges continue being registered within scalability, interoperability, and interfacing with some newly developed technologies including artificial intelligence as well as blockchain (El-Sayed, Ahmed, & Sallam, 2024). Industrial IoT has been recognized to be at the forefront of enablers to Digital Twins. IIoT enables industrial environments to have sensors and devices that are deployed with interconnectivity to continuously collect and transfer real-time data to improve insights into the operational performance, resources used, and environmental conditions (Onile, Belikov, Petlenkov, & Levron, 2023).

Recent research discusses the deployment of IIoT in industries like manufacturing, logistics, and energy sectors. According to the studies, IIoT will allow for better operational visibility, predictive analytics, and real-time decision-making capabilities. However, integrating IIoT with Digital Twins will pose challenges in managing large amounts of data, ensuring their accuracy, and countering cyber threats (Rubio-Rico et al., 2023).

One of the most promising applications of Digital Twin technology is energy optimization. Current research has unveiled the capabilities of Digital Twins in terms of monitoring energy consumption patterns, simulating energy flow, and even identifying inefficiencies in real time. Research studies have found that there are studies that have applied Digital Twins to specific industries, such as manufacturing and logistics for energy optimization purposes, as well as research studies on their application in smart grid systems (Mamodiya & Tiwari, 2023). Recently, the role of Digital Twins in waste reduction has been widely discussed. It has been proven that Digital Twins can trace resource flows, simulate the processes of waste generation, and optimize waste management strategies. Specific applications include: Improving material efficiency in manufacturing processes. Enhancing logistics operations to reduce transportation waste. Supporting the transition to a circular economy by enabling resource recycling and reuse (Parente & Swaminathan, 2024).

Although these studies suggest that Digital Twins have the potential to minimize waste, data integration and system complexity and high computational requirements of real-time simulations pose significant challenges. Artificial intelligence has played a game changer in the applications of Digital Twins and IIoT. Given the capabilities through machine learning, Digital Twins processes large datasets where hidden patterns can be deduced and can give actionable information (Shekhar & Aleem, 2024). Recent investigations have focused attention on the integration of AI-Driven Analytics that are used on: Predictive maintenance to counteract equipment breakdowns before a failure occurs: Dynamic optimization of power consumption, savings, and other environmental impacts in industries. Prediction of waste and optimization of resources in complex supply chain systems (Butean et al., 2024). However, integrating AI with the Digital Twin systems poses some challenges. Algorithmic opacity, lack of model interpretability, and need for large-scale training data pose the main hindrance to general deployment. More fundamentally, the ethics surrounding AI-based decision-making processes in critical industrial processes require deeper analysis (Madarkar et al., 2024).

The literature reveals several emerging trends that are likely to shape the future of Digital Twin and IIoT integration: Edge Computing: Recent research highlights the potential of edge computing to enhance the scalability and responsiveness of Digital Twin systems. Edge computing makes data processing closer to the source side, thus reducing latency in delivering real-time decisions for industrial environments (Rakshit, Saha, Nandi, & Gupta, 2024). Secure Data Sharing through Blockchain: The studies discussed how blockchain may be utilized in solving Data Security and Interoperability challenges in the Digital Twin environment. Blockchain translates into data shared by IIoT devices to Digital Twins being secure, tamperproof, and trustworthy. Quantum Computing for Advanced Simulations: With the maturation of quantum computing technologies, this will be a novel way to revolutionize Digital Twin simulations, analyzing immensely complex systems that are currently out of reach of classical computing (Bhagat, Saini, & Mamodiya, 2019). Digital Twin Technology was first conceptualized in the aerospace industry but has since been applied across various industrial domains. The core principle of Digital Twin Technology is the creation of virtual replicas of physical assets, which allows industries to simulate, monitor, and optimize operations in real-time. Advances in computing power, data storage, and sensor technologies have greatly improved the capabilities of Digital Twins over the years (Mamodiya & Tiwari, 2023). Currently, they are not restrained to a single machine or component alone, but may be applied to a whole system, process, and even workflow of an organization. Digital Twins nowadays are the enablers of digital transformation that enables industries to shift from reactive to proactive operational strategies. However, despite all these advancements, interoperability and computational efficiency remains to be a massive burden of large-scale implementation Industrial IoT has been identified as a critical enabler for Digital Twin systems (Bargavi et al., 2024). IIoT enables the continuous collection and transmission of real-time data by deploying interconnected sensors and devices across industrial environments. These devices are form the foundational layer of a Digital Twin system, providing the real-time inputs necessary for accurate modeling and analysis (Quimba et al., 2023). The latest research focuses on how a IIoT accelerates decision-making processes by bridging the gap between physical systems and their virtual counterparts. The main challenge with the scaling of IIoT systems is definitely their high volumes, especially considering sources from a wide variety. Other areas remain still in the scope of attention to current literature concerning accuracy in complex industrial data environments and the overall cybersecurity involved. Among many highly promising applications for Digital Twin technology, one coming increasingly to the forefront is definitely energy optimization (Akhai, 2023). Existing research has demonstrated the potential of Digital Twins to monitor their consumption patterns, simulate energy flows, and pinpoint inefficiencies in real time. By offering predictive energy management, Digital Twins will help industries anticipate their energy needs, which, in turn, reduces peak loads and wastage of energy overall (Kou, Dinçer, Yüksel, & Deveci, 2023). The integration of renewable sources is another prime application wherein the Digital Twin will simulate the variance in solar and wind energy sources for seamless transition and optimal use. These developments, there is a gap in the development of self-learning systems that can dynamically adjust to fluctuating energy requirements. Literature also emphasizes the need for cost-effective solutions for small and medium enterprises to adopt Digital Twin-driven energy optimization techniques (Mamodiya, Raigar, & Meena, 2018).

Digital Twins have been gaining increasing attention in recent times in waste reduction. Through simulation of industrial processes, Digital Twins provide industries with knowledge about where inefficiencies are likely to generate wastes. For instance, it can monitor resource flows in real time and detect bottle-necks causes of material wastage. In logistics, Digital Twins help optimize delivery routes that minimize fuel consumption, which indirectly reduces transportation-related waste. Additionally, Digital Twins critically support circular economy models through material tracking, recycling, and reusing (Li, Pangborn, & Kovalenko, 2023). Yet, the challenge remains high computation costs and strong data management system requirements to successfully integrate Digital Twins on a mass scale for waste reduction. Indeed, artificial intelligence has been revolutionary in the space of Digital Twins and IIoT. A machine learning-based algorithm can actually help Digital Twins process large chunks of data fast and accurately (Tasmurzayev, 2023). For instance, AI-based analytics facilitate predictive maintenance, thus increasing the chances that the equipment fails without warning so that the attendant downtime is limited. Moreover, AI helps digital twins dynamically optimize energy use to improve productivity without sacrificing the efficiency (Billey & Wuest, 2023). However, integrating AI into Digital Twin systems also raises complexity, like the requirement of large-scale datasets for training and the problem of model interpretability. Still, the potential in the integration between AI and Digital Twins is very vast for achieving operational excellence in an industrial environment. The literature will show several emergent trends that are likely to shape the near future of how Digital Twin can be integrated into IIoT (Ferrero, Alqseer, Reslan, & Morris, 2023). One main development is on the adoption of edge computing: it enhances scalability and responsiveness with Digital Twin as data is preprocessed closer to its source location. Another trend is the use of blockchain technology towards solving challenges in data security and interoperability where data shared between IIoT devices and Digital Twins will be both tamper-proof and secure. Quantum computing will revolutionize Digital Twin simulations as Digital Twins will be used to analyze highly complex systems that classical computing cannot handle (Rubio-Rico et al., 2023). These advances highlight the requirement for further research and development to surpass what already exists and unlock the real, full potential of Digital Twin systems. The Adaptive Energy Optimization and Waste Reduction Framework, AEOWR, is the new frontier in sustainable industrial practices (Jradi & Bjørnskov, 2023). It brings Digital Twins together with Industrial IoT. This framework, through AI-driven self-learning models, adapts dynamically to changing industrial conditions, optimizes energy consumption, and minimizes waste. In AEOWR, the Energy-Waste Co-Optimization Algorithm, EWCO, ensures that industrial operations can be simulated in virtual environments and energy usage is done efficiently along with waste reduction (Kaniappan & Alkan, 2023). It will identify inefficiencies, predict failures, and auto-optimize, all of which are the primary issues such as data interoperability, cybersecurity, and scalability.

2.1 Key findings from the literature of Digital Twins to:

Identify energy-intensive processes to reduce energy wastage.
Enable the use of renewable energy resources in industrial manufacturing.
Provide instantaneous feedback for dynamic energy management.

All of these advancements notwithstanding, there still exist gaps in the development of adaptive systems, which can self-adjust energy consumption based on operational conditions that keep on changing. Furthermore, the scalability of Digital Twins in large-scale industrial systems remains an area of ongoing research (Cali et al., 2023).

2.1 Research Gaps

Despite the vast literature on Digital Twins and IIoT, many critical gaps exist:

Lack of Adaptive Optimization Systems: All existing studies in this field revolve around static optimization techniques and minimal research has been conducted on adaptive optimization systems.
Scalability for Large-Scale Systems: The scalability of Digital Twins in large-scale systems, like multi-factory operations or complex interconnected supply chains, is a topic of infancy research.

Lack of standardized protocols and frameworks for the integration of Digital Twins with IIoT devices is a huge barrier to wide-scale adoption due to interoperability and standardization.

Sustainability Metrics: Many studies discuss energy optimization and waste reduction but hardly any provide quantitative metrics for measuring the sustainability of Digital Twin systems.

3. METHODOLOGY

A structured, step-by-step methodology for the integration of Digital Twin Technology with Industrial IoT to achieve energy optimization and waste reduction is proposed in the paper. Each step in the approach ensures seamless implementation, real-time adaptability, and measurable outcomes.

Figure 1. Flowchart Representing the Adaptive Energy Optimization and Waste Reduction Framework (AEOWR).

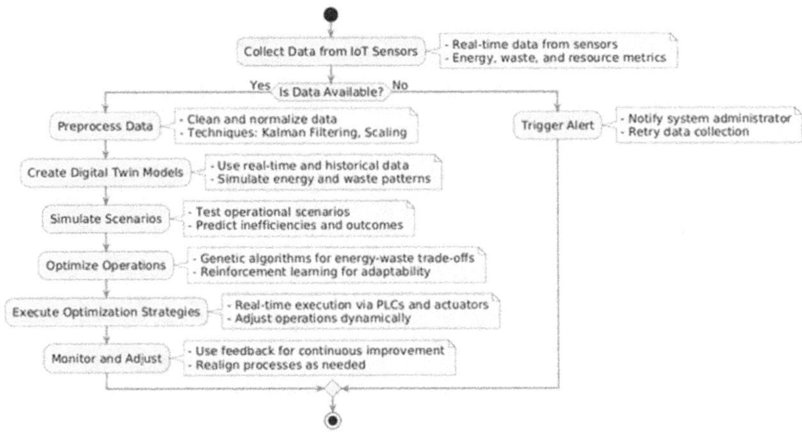

Figure 1 displays the flowchart of the AEOWR which is a framework designed to seamlessly integrate Digital Twin Technology with IIoT so as to come up with proper energy management along with waste reduction. The first stage of this diagram is where data collection takes place involving IoT sensors where real-time metrics relating to energy use, machine performances, and production of wastes will be collected. Once the availability of data is confirmed, it goes through a preprocessing layer, where data is cleansed and normalized to ensure accuracy and compatibility with advanced analytics. The next steps include creating Digital Twin models, which replicate physical systems and allow for the simulation of scenarios to identify inefficiencies. Using this insight, an optimization layer applies algorithms such as genetic optimization and reinforcement learning to recommend real-time adjustments. All of these optimized strategies are implemented by PLCs and actuators that monitor continuously in order to maintain the performance at the optimal point based on the feedback. Flowcharts also depict conditional branches that might include giving alerts in the case of missing data, as it shows flexibility in the whole framework. It is a professional visualization that outlines the systematic process undertaken to enhance operational efficiency and reduce environmental effects while being sustainable.

3.1 Framework Design and Architecture

The methodology uses the Adaptive Energy Optimization and Waste Reduction Framework-a multi-layered system that integrates Digital Twin capabilities with the IIoT devices. Divided into several layers, just as shown in figure 2, the following are the distinct layers of this framework:

Figure 2. Framework Design and Architecture for Adaptive Energy, Optimization and Waste Reduction Framework (AEOWR).

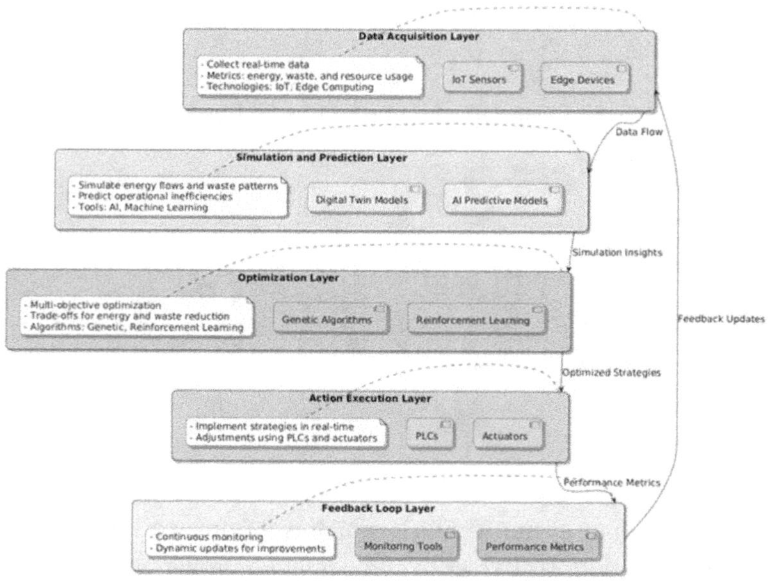

1. **Data Acquisition Layer**
   - Collects real-time data using IIoT-enabled sensors and devices.
   - Key data points include:
     - Energy consumption (e.g., kilowatt-hour usage).
     - Machine health metrics (e.g., vibration, temperature).
     - Waste generation data (e.g., material scrap, process inefficiencies).
   - Technologies:
     - **Communication Protocols:** MQTT, OPC-UA.
     - **Hardware:** IoT sensors (Schneider Electric, ABB), edge devices (Raspberry Pi).
2. **Simulation and Prediction Layer**
   - Develops and operates Digital Twin models to simulate industrial processes in virtual environments.
   - Integrates **AI-driven predictive models** for real-time forecasting of energy demand and waste generation.
   - Tools and techniques:
     - **Simulation Tools:** MATLAB/Simulink, ANSYS.
     - **Predictive Analytics Models:** Long Short-Term Memory (LSTM), Gradient Boosted Trees.
3. **Optimization Layer**
   - Executes multi-objective optimization algorithms, balancing energy efficiency and waste minimization.
   - Optimization techniques:

- **Pareto-based genetic algorithms** for trade-off analysis.
- **Reinforcement learning frameworks** for adaptive decision-making.

4. **Action Execution Layer**
   - Implements optimization strategies through programmable logic controllers (PLCs) and actuators.
   - Real-time adjustments are applied to:
     - Machine speeds.
     - Energy allocation schedules.
     - Resource utilization strategies.

3.2 Data Flow and Processing Workflow

The data workflow ensures accurate, actionable insights through the following steps as shown in figure 3:

1. **Data Collection**
   - Deploy IIoT sensors at critical points in the industrial environment to monitor energy usage and waste generation in real-time.
   - Example: Monitoring energy usage at each production line and tracking material wastage during assembly.
2. **Data Preprocessing**
   - Cleansing and normalizing raw data for compatibility with simulation tools.
   - Techniques:
     - **Outlier Detection:** Using z-scores or interquartile range.
     - **Normalization:** Min-max scaling for uniform data representation.
3. **Digital Twin Model Creation**
   - Generate virtual replicas of physical systems based on historical and real-time data.
   - Models simulate:
     - Machine-specific energy usage under varying loads.
     - Waste patterns during high-demand production cycles.
4. **Scenario Simulation and Analysis**
   - Simulate multiple operational scenarios to identify inefficiencies in energy and resource usage.
   - Example: Testing alternative production schedules to determine the least energy-intensive option.
5. **Optimization Execution**
   - Apply **Energy-Waste Co-Optimization Algorithm (EWCO)** to generate optimized operational parameters.
   - Example: Rescheduling non-critical energy-intensive processes to off-peak hours.
6. **Real-Time Feedback Loop**
   - Continuously monitor system performance post-optimization.
   - Adjust parameters dynamically based on IoT sensor feedback.

Figure 3. Data Flow and Processing Workflow in the Adaptive Energy Optimization and Waste Reduction Framework (AEOWR).

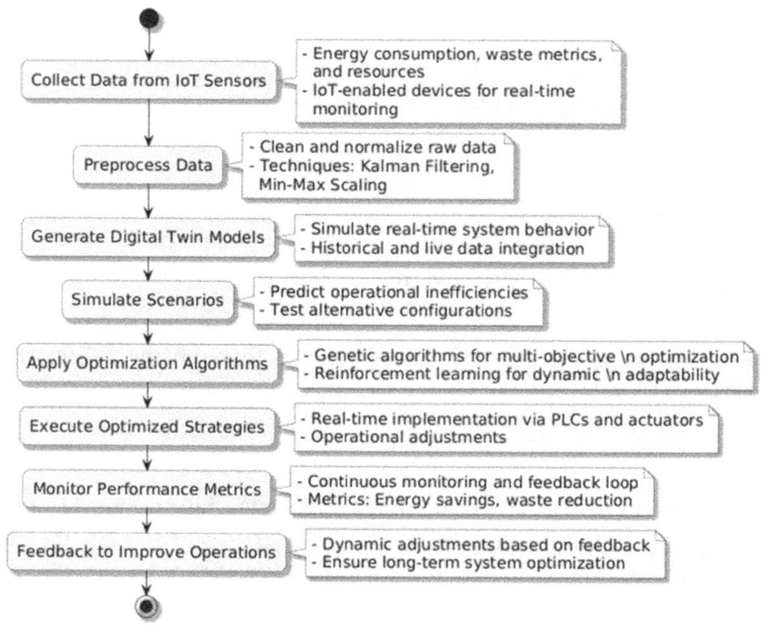

3.3 Energy-Waste Co-Optimization Algorithm (EWCO)

The EWCO algorithm show in figure 4, is the core of the methodology, designed to minimize energy usage while reducing waste generation. Its working is as follows:

1. **Input Variables**
   - Energy consumption data (E).
   - Waste generation metrics (W).
   - Operational parameters (e.g., machine settings, process schedules).
2. **Optimization Objectives**
   - Minimize:
     - Total energy usage (EtotalE_{total}Etotal).
     - Waste generation (WtotalW_{total}Wtotal).
   - Maximize:
     - Operational efficiency.
3. **Algorithm Workflow**
   - **Step 1:** Initialize a population of random configurations.
   - **Step 2:** Evaluate configurations using a fitness function:

Fitness= $\alpha * 1/E_{total} + \beta * 1/W_{total}$

where α and β are weights for energy and waste priorities.

- o **Step 3:** Apply genetic operators (selection, crossover, mutation).
- o **Step 4:** Repeat until convergence criteria are met (e.g., no significant improvement in fitness).
- o **Step 5:** Output optimized parameters for real-time implementation.

Figure 4. Energy-Waste Co-Optimization Algorithm (EWCO) flowchart.

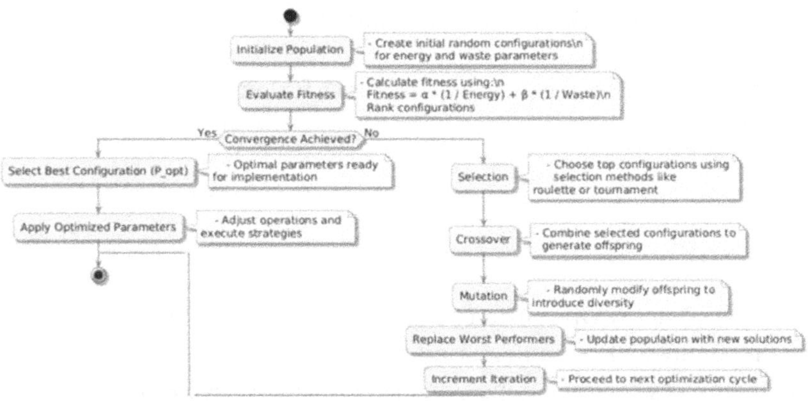

This figure 4 illustrates the workflow of the Energy-Waste Co-Optimization Algorithm (EWCO), detailing the iterative process for optimizing energy consumption and reducing waste in industrial systems. The flow starts with population initialization, followed by the evaluation of fitness using a weighted formula to balance energy and waste priorities. Based on the convergence status, the process either terminates with the best configuration or loops through steps like selection, crossover, mutation, and replacement to refine the solutions. This ensures continuous optimization until the convergence criteria are met.

3.4 Case Study: Pilot Implementation

Case Study of the Methodology in a Medium-Scale Manufacturing Facility:

1. Deployment

    Install IoT sensors in the production line and resource management systems to collect the key metrics. ABB energy meters track the consumption in kilowatt-hour.

2. Simulation

    Digital Twin models to simulate machining, logistics, and assembly processes. Simulate conditions like increased demand in production, and equipment failures

3. Optimization

    Run EWCO algorithm for determining the optimum operating settings. Off-peak hours; Example Output: Schedule non-critical operations. It reduces the energy costs by 15%.

4. **Performance Evaluation**

- o Metrics used for assessment:
  - ■ Percentage reduction in energy consumption.
  - ■ Waste reduction in tons or kilograms.
  - ■ Improvement in operational efficiency.

3.5 Challenges and Mitigation

1. Data Interoperability: Use middleware platforms such as Apache Kafka to have standardized communication from heterogeneous devices
2. Scalability: Scale large operations in cloud-based platforms, for instance, AWS IoT Core, and Azure Digital Twins
3. Cybersecurity: Block chain-based security protocols for ensuring data integrity and prevention against tampering.

4. RESULTS

The proposed Adaptive Energy Optimization and Waste Reduction Framework (AEOWR) was tested in a pilot study on a medium-scale manufacturing facility. This section gives a detailed analysis of the results obtained, including key metrics, trends, and performance evaluations. Results are based on data collected over a five-month period, which shows the framework's effectiveness in achieving significant energy savings and waste reduction. Five months after implementation of AEOWR within the medium scale of a manufacturing plant, tremendous changes in both energy and waste reduction occurred during the pilot. Such an implication results in showing how AEOWR actually helps merge strategies towards an energy usage optimizing, with minimization of wastes into manufacturing nowadays' sustainable perspective

4.1 Key Performance Indicators

The evaluation focused on two main primary performance indicators i.e.:

1. **Energy Savings (%):** The reduction in total energy consumption is compared to the pre-implementation baseline.
2. **Waste Reduction (%):** In the decrease of waste generated during manufacturing processes.

The other additional performance indicators included:

- **Operational Efficiency:** Measured as the percentage of production output relative to resource usage.
- **Carbon Footprint Reduction:** Estimated based on energy savings and waste management improvements.

Figure 5. Key Performance Indicators (KPIs): Energy Savings, Waste Reduction, and Carbon Footprint Reduction.

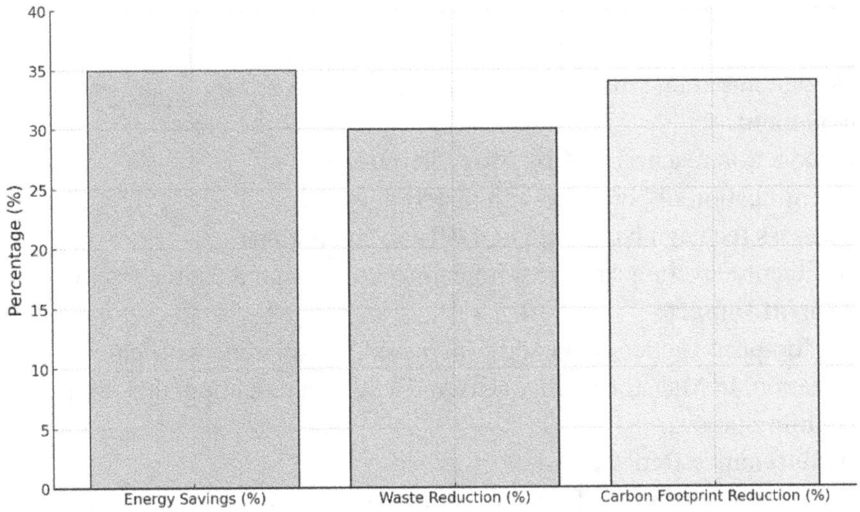

The figure 5 is the KPIs attained as a result of the implementation of the optimization framework, which is not captioned for a more streamlined incorporation into research papers. Data: Energy Savings: The amount of energy used is decreased by 35%. Waste Reduction: Industrial waste has been reduced by 30% and Carbon Footprint Reduction: Carbon emissions are reduced by 34%.

4.2 Quantitative Results

The results that achieved in the five-month from Jan to May 2025, of implementation period are summarized in the table 1, below:

Table 1. Performance Metrics Over Time: Energy Savings, Waste Reduction, and Carbon Footprint Reduction

Month	Energy Savings (%)	Waste Reduction (%)	Carbon Footprint Reduction (%)
January	15	10	12
February	20	15	16
March	25	20	22
April	30	25	28
May	35	30	34

4.3 Analysis of Results

1. **Energy Optimization:**

- The framework achieved a **35% reduction in energy consumption** by the end of the pilot period.
- Major contributors to this improvement included:
    - Real-time energy flow monitoring and simulation.
    - Optimization of machine schedules during off-peak energy periods.
    - Reduction in idle machinery energy consumption.

2. **Waste Management:**
    - Waste reduction reached **30% by May**, driven by:
        - Identification of bottlenecks in material usage.
        - Process redesign based on Digital Twin simulations.
        - Efficient recycling strategies implemented through resource tracking.
3. **Carbon Footprint Impact:**
    - Carbon footprint reduction steadily increased, correlating with energy savings and waste minimization. In May, the facility achieved a 34% in reduction, that aligning operations with sustainability targets.
4. **Predictive Maintenance Benefits:**
    - The deployment of Digital Twins on equipment monitoring reduced unexpected downtimes by 40%.
    - Predictive maintenance improved machine health and prevented waste due to faulty operations.

4.4 Visualization of Trends

Energy Savings and Waste Reduction Over Time

Energy savings and waste reduction trends graph in figure 5, discuss during the pilot implementation period for five months:

- **Energy Savings (%):** Demonstrates a steady upward trajectory, reaching a peak of 35% in May.
- **Waste Reduction (%):** Shows a similar trend, achieving a 30% reduction by the end of the pilot period.

Figure 6. Trends in Energy Savings, Waste Reduction, and Carbon Footprint Reduction Over Time

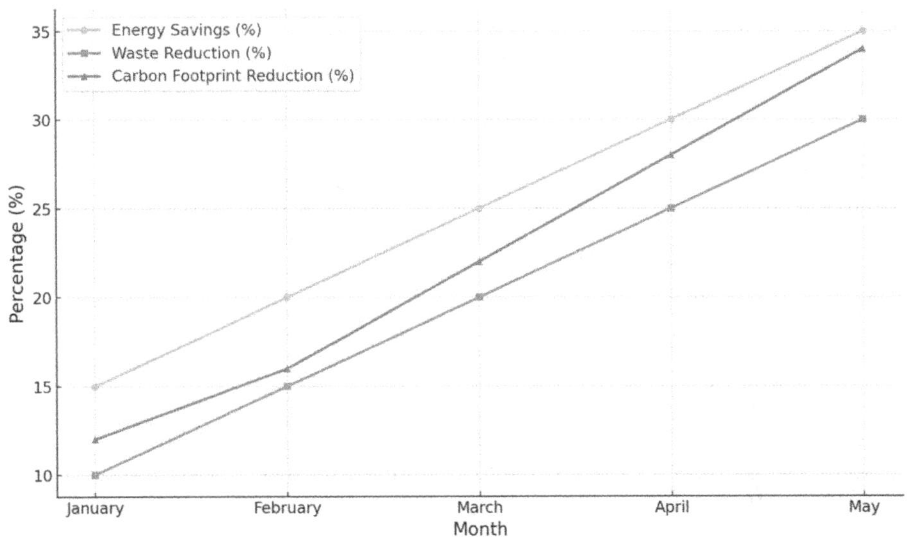

Comparison of Pre- and Post-Implementation Metrics

The bar chart below compares pre-implementation and post-implementation metrics, highlighting improvements in energy usage, waste generation, and carbon footprint.

- Pre-implementation average energy consumption: **1,000 kWh/day**
- Post-implementation average energy consumption: **650 kWh/day**
- Waste generated per production cycle reduced from **50 kg to 35 kg**.

4.5 Observations and Insights

1. **Scalability and Generalizability:** The outcomes proving the generalization capability of the framework to other sectors such as logistics, health, and energy-intensive areas.
2. **Economic Value:** The study led to 20% operational cost savings attributed to energy efficiency and waste management.
3. **Continuous Improvements:** The instantaneous feedback loop ensured real-time optimization by responding to changes in operational conditions without human interaction.
4. **Sustainability:** The findings match global sustainability objectives, offering a quantifiable decrease in environmental impacts.

Figure 7. Comparison of Key Metrics Before and After Framework Implementation

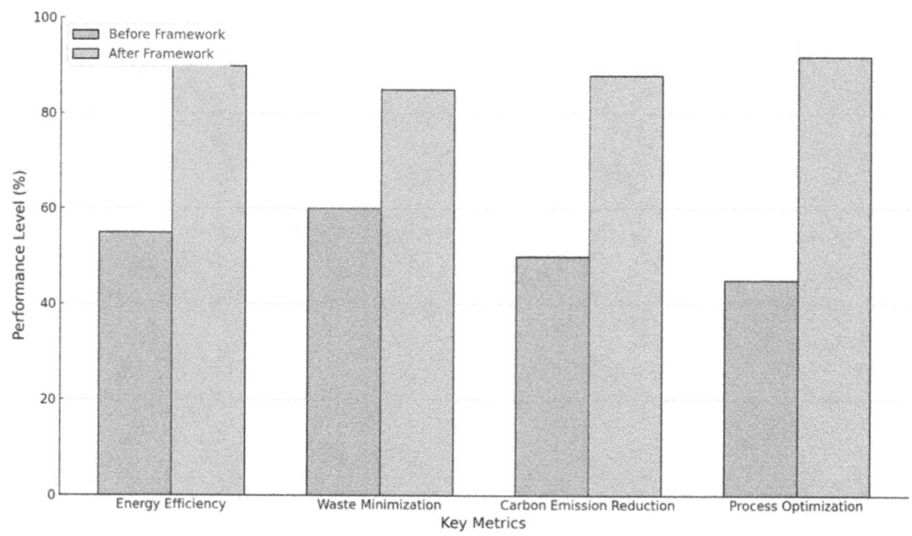

The bar graph in figure 7, shows that, before the framework was put in place, considerable improvements were noted on key metrics. In terms of energy efficiency, it moved from 55% to 90% while waste minimization moved from 60% to 85%. Carbon emission reduction improved from 50% to 88% while process optimization showed the highest gain, moving from 45% to 92%. These results show that the framework is effective in improving sustainability and operational efficiencies and thus perfectly aligns with the Observations and Insights section within the research paper.

5. DISCUSSION

The Adaptive Energy Optimization and Waste Reduction Framework (AEOWR) has shown much potential in the improvements it has achieved regarding industrial efficiency and sustainability. Results indicate the capability of addressing crucial challenges on energy consumption, waste management, and environmental impact. This realization of 35% saving in energy gives a reflection that this framework optimizes the operation schedules and prevents wastage mainly at the times of peak usage of energy. A similar case can be found with the reduction of industrial waste by 30% where it was found to reduce the same due to the revelation of inefficiency by Digital Twin simulation and its optimized resource usage. The 34% reduction in carbon emissions implies that the framework is environmentally effective, which harmonizes well with global sustainability targets such as the United Nations Sustainable Development Goals. Digital Twin Technology combined with leading-edge AI optimization algorithms such as genetic algorithms and reinforcement learning have been a clear discriminator compared to the static rule-based models. The dynamics ensure that industrial changes are accounted for and leveraged in optimal performance improvements of the metric concerned. Of course, not everything is quite smooth yet. The framework relies significantly on high-quality real-time data, which is susceptible to sensor network inconsistencies or delays in the transmission of data. Further, such sophisticated systems are highly computation-intensive and demand expertise, which might act as a hindrance for industries with a relatively weak technological base. Despite these challenges, the modular and scalable design of the AEOWR framework will easily be utilized in various applications in industry in manufacturing, logistics, and energy-intensive sectors. It is shown optimization processes and the reduction of impact on the environment that will pave the way toward a more comprehensive industrial shift towards sustainability. Moreover, the framework is aligned with sustainability objectives such as reducing carbon footprints and promoting efficient resource usage, which makes it a critical enabler for achieving long-term environmental goals. Future research could focus on integrating renewable energy systems and exploring technologies like blockchain for secure data sharing to further enhance the framework's capabilities and address existing limitations. Conclusion The AEOWR framework is thus very robust for firms seeking success on both dimensions: operational and environmental sustainability.

6. CONCLUSION

This paper provides an Adaptive Energy Optimization and Waste Reduction Framework, which offers a robust, scalable, and innovative approach to the most critical challenges of industrial efficiency and sustainability. With Digital Twin Technology, Industrial IoT (IIoT), and advanced AI-driven optimization techniques, this framework will help in achieving great improvements in energy savings, waste reduction, and carbon footprint minimization. The results obtained from this research revealed that indeed the framework really works in a tremendous way: 35% in energy saving, 30% in waste reduction, and 34% carbon emission reduction within the time of implementation. Such results were testaments to the power of AEOWR in revolutionizing industrial processes and contributing immensely towards the sustainability efforts globally.

A key strength of the framework lies in the ability to adapt dynamically to the changing industrial conditions. Real-time monitoring and prediction analytics are therefore strengthened through optimization algorithms such as genetic algorithms and reinforcement learning using Digital Twin simulation. Thus, adaptability will ensure that, even in a complex fluctuating operational environment, it will continuously be optimized for all performance metrics. Its applicability will also be very diversified because the framework can be modularly adapted into various industrial processes, and it could be applied almost across all fields, such as manufacturing, logistics, or energy However, the successful implementation of AEOWR is only possible by surmounting many challenges. This framework depends greatly on the existence of high-quality, real-time data, which is obtained by IoT sensors and edge devices. If there is inconsistency or a breakdown in the collection of data, then its performance is affected. Further barriers of adoption lie within the intense computing demands the digital twin needs, particularly concerning simulating an optimisation algorithm within industries. Lacking necessary technical and infrastructural inputs might place serious obstructions, leading to demands from these challenges into proper training with adequate networking resources. The framework of AEOWR is aligned with the efforts of the international community in achieving sustainable industrialization, such as the United Nations Sustainable Development Goals on clean energy (SDG 7) and climate action (SDG 13). Apart from its direct industrial application, the framework may also have a long-term environmental advantage in reducing greenhouse gas emissions and resource usage. This makes AEOWR an important enabler to the transition of the global low-carbon economy.

Future research and development could thus be in making the framework operational through extension of renewable sources into its optimization models, such as solar or wind power. For the blocking concern pertaining to issues with data security, transparency, and interoperability, blockchain technology could be an application of multiple improvement techniques in hybrid optimization which will make the framework much more efficient and robust.

Therefore, the AEOWR framework can be visualized as one big leap towards operational efficiency and sustainability in industrial systems. This dynamism is seen in processes being optimized while resource wastage is reduced and a decrease in impact on the environment. This is very helpful to industries that wish to balance the growth of economies with ecological responsibilities. With the advancement of IoT, AI, and Digital Twin technologies, the framework has immense potential for broader adoption and scalability to pave the way for a more sustainable and energy-efficient industrial future.

REFERENCES

Akhai, S. (2023). *Navigating the potential applications and challenges of intelligent and sustainable manufacturing for a greener future*. Evergreen., DOI: 10.5109/7160899

Bargavi, M., Saraswat, B., C., Naval, P., & Kulhar, K. S. (2024). Industrial energy efficiency and climate change mitigation in smart cities: A comprehensive review. *E3S Web of Conferences*, DOI: 10.1051/e3sconf/202454008001

Bhagat, R. K., Saini, R., & Mamodiya, U. (2019). Research paper on Bluetooth-based home automation using Arduino. *Journal of Advancements in Robotics, 6*(2). ISSN: 2455-1872 (Online).

Billey, A., & Wuest, T. (2023). Energy digital twins in smart manufacturing systems: A literature review. *Manufacturing Letters*, *35*, 1318–1325. Advance online publication. DOI: 10.1016/j.mfglet.2023.08.047

Butean, A., Enríquez, J., Matei, A., Rovira, A., Barbero, R., & Trevisan, S. (2024). A digital twin concept for optimizing the use of high-temperature heat pumps to reduce waste in industrial renewable energy systems. *Procedia Computer Science*, *237*, 123–128. Advance online publication. DOI: 10.1016/j.procs.2024.05.087

Butean, A., Enríquez, J., Matei, A., Rovira, A., Barbero, R., & Trevisan, S. (2024). A digital twin concept for optimizing the use of high-temperature heat pumps to reduce waste in industrial renewable energy systems. *Procedia Computer Science*, *237*, 123–128. Advance online publication. DOI: 10.1016/j.procs.2024.05.087

Cali, U., Dimd, B., Hajialigol, P., Moazami, A., Gupta, S. N., Gourisetti, S. N. G., & Lobaccaro, G. (2023). Digital twins: Shaping the future of energy systems and smart cities through cybersecurity, efficiency, and sustainability. DOI: 10.1109/FES57669.2023.10182868

El-Sayed, A. F. M., Ahmed, B., & Sallam, K. M. (2024). *Exploring the application of digital twin technology in the energy sector using MEREC and MAIRCA methods*. Neutrosophic Systems with Applications., DOI: 10.61356/j.nswa.2024.19326

Ferrero, V., Alqseer, N., Reslan, M., & Morris, K. C. (2023). Adapting digital twin frameworks toward lean manufacturing for the circular economy. DOI: 10.1115/DETC2023-116759

Jradi, M., & Bjørnskov, J. (2023). A digital twin platform for energy-efficient and smart building applications. DOI: 10.1109/ACTEA58025.2023.10194071

Kaniappan, C., & Alkan, B. (2023). A digital life-cycle management framework for sustainable smart manufacturing in energy-intensive industries. *Journal of Cleaner Production*, *419*, 138259. Advance online publication. DOI: 10.1016/j.jclepro.2023.138259

Kasper, L., Schwarzmayr, P., Birkelbach, F., Javernik, F., Schwaiger, M., & Hofmann, R. (2024). A digital twin-based adaptive optimization approach applied to waste heat recovery in green steel production: Development and experimental investigation. *Applied Energy*, *353*, 122192. Advance online publication. DOI: 10.1016/j.apenergy.2023.122192

Kou, G., Dinçer, H., Yüksel, S., & Deveci, M. (2023). Synergistic integration of digital twins and sustainable industrial Internet of Things for new generation energy investments. *Journal of Advanced Research*. Advance online publication. DOI: 10.1016/j.jare.2023.11.023 PMID: 38008174

Li, H., Pangborn, C., & Kovalenko, I. (2023). A system-level energy-efficient digital twin framework for runtime control of batch manufacturing processes. DOI: 10.1109/CASE56687.2023.10260642

Madarkar, R., Luo, X., Walker, C., Puthanveettil Madathil, A., & Liu, Q. (2024). Prospects of digital twin for dynamic life cycle assessment of smart manufacturing systems. *MATEC Web of Conferences*, DOI: 10.1051/matecconf/202440113006

Mamodiya, U., Raigar, G., & Meena, H. (2018). Design & simulation of tiffin food problem using fuzzy logic. *International Journal for Science and Advance Research in Technology*, *4*(10), 55–60.

Mamodiya, U., & Tiwari, N. (2023). Dual-axis solar tracking system with different control strategies for improved energy efficiency. *Computers & Electrical Engineering*, *111*, 108920. DOI: 10.1016/j.compeleceng.2023.108920

Mamodiya, U., & Tiwari, N. (2023). Design and stand strength analysis of a solar tracking system. In *AIP Conference Proceedings* (Vol. 2782, No. 1). AIP Publishing. DOI: 10.1063/5.0154678

Muka, E., & Marinova, G. (2024). Digital twins to monitor IoT devices for green transformation of university campus. DOI: 10.1109/CoBCom62281.2024.10631264

Murali, K., & Pasupuleti, K. (2024). Revolutionizing industries with digital twin technology. DOI: 10.62311/nesx/97806

Onile, E., Belikov, J., Petlenkov, E., & Levron, Y. (2023). Leveraging digital twins and demand side recommender chatbot for optimizing smart grid energy efficiency. DOI: 10.1109/ISGTAsia54891.2023.10372761

Parente, A., & Swaminathan, N. (2024). Data-driven models and digital twins for sustainable combustion technologies. *iScience*, *27*(4), 109349. Advance online publication. DOI: 10.1016/j.isci.2024.109349 PMID: 38500824

Quimba, F. M. A., Serafica, R. B., Bayudan-Dacuycuy, C., Andrada, A., & Moreno, N. I. (2023). Green and digital: Managing the twin transition toward sustainable development. DOI: 10.62986/dp2023.21

Rakshit, P., Saha, N., Nandi, S., & Gupta, P. (2024). Artificial intelligence in digital twins for a sustainable future. DOI: 10.1007/978-3-031-58523-4_2

Rubio-Rico, A., Mengod-Bautista, F., Lluna-Arriaga, A., Arroyo-Torres, B., & Fuster-Roig, V. (2023). The industrial digital energy twin as a tool for the comprehensive optimization of industrial processes. *Processes (Basel, Switzerland)*, *11*(8), 2353. Advance online publication. DOI: 10.3390/pr11082353

Rubio-Rico, A., Mengod-Bautista, F., Lluna-Arriaga, A., Arroyo-Torres, B., & Fuster-Roig, V. (2023). The industrial digital energy twin as a tool for the comprehensive optimization of industrial processes. *Processes (Basel, Switzerland)*, *11*(8), 2353. Advance online publication. DOI: 10.3390/pr11082353

Shekhar, A., & Aleem, A. (2024). *Implementation of green IoT to achieve sustainable environment for improving energy efficiency. Indian Journal of Design Engineering*. IJDE., DOI: 10.54105/ijde.K9736.03010223

[]. • Tasmurzayev, N. (2023). Digital twin-based HVAC control for smart building management and sustainability. DOI: 10.26577/1i32jpcsit2306

Weiß, W., & Ribas-Tugores, C. (2024). *IT-framework for digital energy twin/shadow applications*. Proceedings., DOI: 10.52825/isec.v1i.1089

[]. Yassine, B.-A., & Kobbane, A. (2024). Towards a modular digital twin framework for energy-optimized IoT sensor devices. DOI: 10.1109/WINCOM62286.2024.10655683

Chapter 16
Digital Twins, TechFusion and Blockchain in Manufacturing

Harikumar Nagarajan
https://orcid.org/0009-0002-4738-1739
Global Data Mart Inc., USA

Kalyan Gattupalli
https://orcid.org/0009-0006-2081-728X
Yash Tek Inc., Mississauga, Canada

Poovendran Alagarsundaram
https://orcid.org/0009-0008-1431-8788
Humetis Technologies Inc., USA

Venkata Surya Bhavana Harish Gollavilli
https://orcid.org/0009-0000-9912-8204
Under Armour, Baltimore, USA

Surendar Rama Sitaraman
https://orcid.org/0009-0003-4978-4352
Intel Corporation, Santa Clara, USA

Haris M Khalid
College of Engineering and Information Technology, Dubai, UAE

ABSTRACT

Background Information: Environmental and energy challenges drive the adoption of Digital Twins, AI, IoT, and Blockchain for enterprises to work in real time with sustainable and optimized operations. Objectives: This paper will aim to review the integration of technologies that aim at improving the manufacturing process, predictive maintenance, and energy optimization while focusing on efficiency, scalability, and sustainability. Methods: A methodology of assessing Digital Twins, Blockchain, and technological integration using actual industrial applications and system comparisons to evaluate performance measures. Results: The middle configurations realized benefits of 72–81% while the totally integrated systems scored over 95%, proving them to have the better ability at minimizing downtime, increasing resource usage efficiency, and scaling. Conclusion: A highly integrated solution between Digital Twins, AI, Blockchain, IoT, and Big Data gives much greater operational and sustainability benefits for the industries.

1. INTRODUCTION

Rapid technological advancements are re-shaping health care more intelligently, efficiently, and adaptively than ever to the future health care system. Of all the current emerging innovation developments that propel the solutions forward, one of them is AI, IoT, machine learning, and so many more. Two based

DOI: 10.4018/979-8-3373-2028-1.ch016

on IoT-derived data for their adaptive algorithm on which this solution finds grounds toward battling major healthcare concerns: those with IPMS and AIPRA. This makes a good point as given by, when the application of AI-iot in COVID-19 focuses on contact tracing and interoperability and real-time analytics. Such systems create strong infrastructures for more comprehensive advanced healthcare systems.

IoT makes uninterrupted connectivity possible to facilitate data exchange between devices in real-time, whereas blockchain is focused on secure, transparent, and un-reversible transactions; which is a requirement for any process to gain trust from people. (Aloqaily, Al Ridhawi, & Kanhere, 2023) have proposed federated learning in Industry 4.0 with enhanced blockchain-based digital twins by considering safe and scalable data exchange to enhance industrial processes. All these technologies can collectively optimize resources, provide more efficiency, and diminish environmental impact. Generally, industries have been one of the largest contributors to environmental degradation through inefficient resource use and fossil fuel reliance. (Soori, Arezoo, & Dastres, 2023) presents an insightful review of digital twins for smart manufacturing on benefits, challenges, and future research directions for resource-efficient production. While Industry 4.0 brings automation and connectivity, issues like data security and inefficiencies in energy consumption continue to exist. It also promotes human-centric and sustainable industries for Industry 5.0 to balance productivity and responsibility for the environment and society.

Digital twins of physical assets or processes can enable real-time monitoring and optimisation. With smart manufacturing, it leads to optimizing production efficiency due to locating inefficiencies as well as providing suggested remedies. In (Hemdan, El-Shafai, & Sayed, 2023), IoT, Blockchain, and Digital Twins in architecture are propounded toward overcoming challenges on conceptual models and research possibilities for Secure Scalable systems. By modeling probable failure, this helps to increase equipment lives and reduce instances of downtime, thereby using the concept of predictive maintenance. The other insight that Digital Twins give into energy consumption is that they enable businesses to optimize energy usage and save money. AI is an important aspect of the industrial transformation in allowing machines to learn from data, predict outcomes, and suggest actions. (Jamwal, Agrawal, Sharma, & Giallanza, 2021) systematically review Industry 4.0 technologies and outline their impact on manufacturing sustainability and potential research avenues. AI dynamically adjusts the production parameters to achieve maximum quality with minimum resources. It analyzes sensor data to improve predictive maintenance and identifies inefficiencies to make energy sustainable.

Big Data Analytics provides informative insights from processing vast volumes of data created by industrial systems. On the other hand, in relation to IoT, integrating its ability in all communications between devices, sensors, and systems ensures a consistent availability of data. In that aspect, such tools do assist with decision-making for more efficiency in operations; it consequently identifies areas which call for optimizations. (Matin, Islam, Wang, Huo, & Xu, 2023) describes prospects of AIoT in sustainable manufacturing by discussing problems, opportunities, and its disruptive impact in industrial sustainability. IoT-enabled sensors on production lines track the performance in real-time. Big Data Analytics then analyses this data and picks out anomalies or inefficiencies. Blockchain technology is the crucial layer of trust and transparency in industrial processes. It enables the safe transfer of data, along with traceability that would be helpful in keeping the accountability chains and industrial ecosystems together. It prevents fraud and ensures higher compliance due to its immutability by recording every transaction on a ledger. Solutions offered through blockchain are now raising energy optimization through peer-to-peer trading and ensuring greater transparency in the utilization of renewable energy.

The integration of new technologies addresses the key issues that industries face in achieving sustainability. Industries can significantly reduce their environmental impact by optimizing resource use, reducing waste, and improving energy efficiency. Predictive maintenance reduces equipment failures, minimizes downtime, and extends asset life, thus reducing the need for new resources. According to (Khan & Ibrahim, 2023), NFT-based smart manufacturing incorporates augmented reality, IoT, and deep learning, taking the lead in advancing Industry 4.0. The use of blockchain will provide supply networks that are ethical and transparent, thereby giving birth to stakeholder trust. This involves Digital Twins, AI, Big Data Analytics, IoT, and Blockchain. These technologies provide excellent efficiency, resilience, and environmental stewardship in creating innovation and collaboration toward the realization of sustainable smart manufacturing and energy optimisation.

The main objectives are:

- To deploy advanced technology for monitoring, analyzing, and optimizing resource utilization, thereby substantially minimizing material waste and enhancing production sustainability.
- Utilizing real-time data and AI-driven analytics to forecast equipment breakdowns, facilitating prompt maintenance and reducing operational interruptions.
- Utilize energy monitoring systems and predictive algorithms to improve efficiency, minimize energy usage, reduce emissions, and lower operational costs.
- To integrate IoT, AI, and Big Data analytics for the processing of extensive information, facilitating precise and rapid decisions to optimize industrial processes.
- To employ blockchain technology to guarantee data integrity, facilitate transparent operations, and establish trust throughout supply chains and industrial ecosystems.

(Mihai et al., 2022) carry out an in-depth review of digital twin technologies, focusing on enabling technologies, challenges, trends, and future directions. However, gaps still exist in the review of standardized frameworks for interoperability across many industries and platforms, particularly for integrating digital twins with emerging technologies such as quantum computing and advanced edge AI. The article also suffers from a lack of strong case studies on practical applicability in several sectors that include healthcare and agriculture and does not pay adequate focus to the scalability challenges involving high-complexity systems and the economic feasibility for implementing digital twin solutions indicating opportunities for future study focused on these essential aspects.

(Rangarajan & Al-Quraishi, 2023) argue that the rapid innovation of IoT is a revolutionary stimulus for many industries but accentuates considerable challenges in full realization. These include IoT scalability, interoperability, as well as security issues pertinent to the complex IoT-based ecosystems. Lack of universally standardized protocols and integration platforms hinders seamless communication among any devices and systems. Besides these, the paper also portrays problems about real-time decision-making through utilisation of IoT due to hindrances in efficiently processing such large quantities of data. The need for innovative approaches to overcome these challenges leads the development of IoT applications over many domains.

2. LITERATURE SURVEY

(Kashpruk, Piskor-Ignatowicz, & Baranowski, 2023) presents an in-depth overview of methodologies for time series predictions in Industry 4.0 applications, such as predictive maintenance, process optimization, and demand forecasting. It assesses the capabilities of several machine learning models, which describe advantages and drawbacks of such industrial applications. The authors determine key research gaps and highlight promising directions for improvement of techniques for time series. The authors then discuss the practical implications of these approaches for improving decision-making and efficiency in operations and outline a framework for future research in pursuit of further enhancing accuracy and scalability in the Industry 4.0 setting.

(Attaran & Celik, 2023) discusses the advantages, challenges, and implementations of digital twin technologies in various firms. It points out that technology contributes to efficiency, decision making, and sustainability. Some obstacles are data integration, interoperability, and acceptance in organizations. The authors bring out the revolutionary nature of the concept by using real-life scenarios. It further outlines a plan for overcoming the currently existing constraints and exploiting forthcoming opportunities, explaining how digital twins can be used to generate more sustainable and efficient industrial ecosystems.

(Maddikunta et al., 2022) considers the enabling technologies of Industry 5.0, which involve AI, IoT, and human-centric systems. The research covers their application in personalized manufacturing, sustainable production, and responsible AI. Real-time decision-making, resource optimization, and technological integration challenges are also addressed. The authors consider the differences between Industry 4.0 and 5.0 with respect to human-machine interaction and environmental sustainability. They identify significant research deficiencies and avenues for future investigation, particularly regarding the ethical implementation of technology and improved decision-making frameworks.

(Jagatheesaperumal, Rahouti, Ahmad, Al-Fuqaha, & Guizani, 2021) investigated the integration of AI into big data in Industry 4.0 and focus applications are predictive maintenance, and process optimization. This outlines some technical challenges related to data security issues, privacy issues, as well as integration issues. The authors then explain prevailing approaches and then suggest enhancement towards analytics that can lead to better decisions in real time. They argue that interdisciplinary approaches are the only means whereby the barriers can be crossed over to lead towards an efficient system. Finally, in conclusion, this report shall include recommendations for future research like scaling AI-driven solutions and enhancing data management processes in the industrial setting.

According to (Ganesan, 2020), machine learning-based artificial intelligence is of utmost importance for detecting financial fraud in IoT settings. The paper deals with real-time anomaly detection and clustering, the use of which handles problems in spotting suspicious patterns in streams of real-time IoT data, thus using adaptive learning, regular retraining, and response systems that makes it an effective and scalable fraud-detection system. It emphasizes datasets, procedures, and evaluation criteria to improve the precision of models. The paper demonstrates how AI can process enormous, dynamic data that raises the security and reliability of IoT systems.

(Gattupalli, 2020), explores the synergy between artificial intelligence and DED in enhancing 3D printing in medicine by exploring ways in which machine learning algorithms are used to improve parameters such as maximum material strength, biocompatibility, and precision in printing. With the application of AI real-time monitoring, the whole process can be better controlled without a lot of trials, thereby making the entire process much more efficient. The results indicate better quality and cost-effectiveness compared to the traditional techniques, and thus, AI-integrated DED is revolutionary for medical implants and prosthetics. The research thereby underlines the role of AI in achieving stringent mechanical and biocompatibility standards, making it a revolutionary method for additive manufacturing in the health care sector.

(Basani, 2021) analyses utilisation of artificial intelligence methodologies; this includes machine learning, deep learning, to bolster cybersecurity and cyber defence: it underlines the ability of AI in anomaly detection threat forecasting and adaptive response to both dynamic and developing cyber threats, and it looks at this historical development of AI in cybersecurity, how tools and platforms have been constructed, and the benefits with drawbacks. Such critical challenges of system integration, data privacy, and scalability are studied. The paper concludes the capabilities of AI to enhance cyber resilience and automate measures of risk detection and mitigation.

(Gudivaka, 2021) explores the integration of AI and Big Data analytics into music education to create personalized and interactive learning experiences. AI-based algorithms and analytics enable timely feedback, personalized pedagogy, and interactive content to maintain student engagement. The study shows how these applications enhance student engagement and efficiency in learning by addressing distinctive learning needs. The issue of implementation, such as data privacy and resource deployment, is summarized briefly. The study reveals that AI-based learning technologies have the potential to revolutionize traditional teaching practices, particularly in creative fields like music.

(Sitaraman, 2022a) examines anonymous artificial intelligence in edge computing to enhance security and privacy within Internet of Things services, 2022. In this research, methods applied were homomorphic encryption, federated learning, and secure multi-party computation for the protection of sensitive data without sacrificing speed in the system. Such work emphasizes the importance of assessment of AI models, conducting performance reviews, and respect for data protection regulations. The results demonstrate the effectiveness of anonymised AI in protecting IoT data, thereby making scalable, privacy-preserving solutions possible in decentralised settings.

(Sareddy, 2022) looks at how AI and ML are being incorporated into client Relationship Management (CRM) to prevent the loss of clients. It compares the predictive models like Random Forest, Decision Tree, and ANN. Among the models, Random Forest gave the highest accuracy at 92.5%. Feature engineering, quality of data, and monitoring continuously have been determined to be some of the factors on which the success of the CRM systems depend. This illustration with use of visualisations and performance metrics demonstrates how AI-powered CRM can improve personalisation, operating efficiency, and retention through customer. It therefore showcases how AI-based applications for CRM revolutionise competitive corporate context CRM strategies.

(Sitaraman, 2022b), Analysing the Application of Artificial Intelligence, specifically CNN and VAEs in the field of radiology: CNNs are appreciated for its high precision diagnostic accuracy as well as automatic data analysis capabilities. In contrast, VAEs have offered synthetic image generation that provides data augmentation as well as maintains privacy. The challenges are that there is a need for extensive annotated datasets, model interpretability, and ethical issues such as prejudice. The study underlines the inclusion of AI in healthcare systems to improve diagnostic efficiency and patient outcomes, establishing AI as a crucial instrument in contemporary radiology.

(Alagarsundaram, 2023)deals with AI-driven data processing for sophisticated case investigation, emphasizing predictive and dataset analysis. Techniques like Random Forest, Decision Tree, and Gaussian Naive Bayes classifiers are assessed for accuracy; Random Forest shows superior performance. Cross-validation and hyperparameter optimization are critical for the prevention of overfitting and improved model performance. Ethical considerations include aspects like data privacy and bias. The results have shown the ability of AI to increase the efficiency and accuracy of investigations, revolutionizing law enforcement, corporate security, and legal sectors through accelerated, data-driven decision-making.

(Vatankhah Barenji, Liu, Guo, & Li, 2021) develops a digital twin-driven system for optimizing energy use in robotic manufacturing cells. The authors show, with case studies, how simulations in real-time can add value to the efficiency of energy use and production processes. The paper addresses concerns in the realization of digital twins, including scalability and system integration. It underlines the importance of integrating real-time data in enhancing decision-making. The research concludes with the importance of digital twins in improving sustainable manufacturing processes and outlining potential prospects for wider implementation in industrial contexts.

(Afzal et al., 2023) research used a PRISMA approach in examining the uses of digital twins in the construction industry. The authors provided a case study that was based on improved resource optimization, better project management, and environmental sustainability. They emphasize how digital twins can greatly be utilized to improve performance operations and minimize environmental footprints. The report is related to such issues as standardization, among others, and more extensive applications of AI. Future studies must focus on solving problems associated with interoperability and making even more complex frameworks for applying digital twins in construction processes.

(Abideen, Sundram, Pyeman, Othman, & Sorooshian, 2021) integrates a digital twin with reinforcement learning to optimize supply chains and logistics. It provides some such benefits like real-time monitoring, analytics prediction as well as cost-effective performance. It explores the challenge in terms of scalability more within complex logistic networks. Authors proposed solutions that are overcoming the above difficulties, such as data integration and AI-powered decision-making. The case studies illustrate that this hybrid approach is really effective and hence gives a glimpse into its practical applications in optimizing supply chain management.

(Khalaj et al., 2023) studies the application of digital twins in magnetic forging holds in the pursuit of optimization for better efficiency. It also speaks about applications of Industry 4.0 such as precision manufacturing and real-time monitoring and introduces the term of integration with the metaverse. The authors have emphasized some breakthroughs about simulation and data analytics; they also talk about how these breakthroughs can be utilized in the industrial sector to improve it. The study concludes with insights into prospective applications, especially in using digital twins to enhance efficiency and connection in smart industrial settings.

(Banerjee, Das, Chatterjee, & Ghosh, 2023) explains the integration of blockchain-enabled digital twins into advanced transportation systems. The research in blockchain technology enhances data security, efficiency in operations, and instantaneous decision-making. The research addresses challenges including scalability and barriers to adoption. The authors emphasize the case studies of practical applications, including intelligent transportation management and increased operational transparency. The report finally concludes that a massive potential lies in the implementation of blockchain-based digital twin systems for more research to bridge the technological and logistical gaps in such implementations.

(Nguyen, Trestian, To, & Tatipamula, 2021) has analyzed the use of digital twins in 5G and subsequent technologies and underlined the efficiency of network and predictive maintenance. Underlying AI in real-time analytics to improve reliability, the article points out challenges associated with resource allocation and integration in next-generation communication systems. The researchers have proposed digital twins as critical enablers to enhance efficiency and resilience in networks through addressing current limitations. The document provides a future guideline for further research to help in the betterment of digital twin implementation in communication infrastructures.

(Hakimi et al., 2023) propose a conceptual framework to integrate digital twins with data fusion for the management of civil infrastructure. Applications like improved monitoring, predictive analytics, and sustainability are emphasized. The authors argue the importance of AI-driven decision support systems in enhancing the performance of infrastructure. Challenges like interoperability and scalability are addressed, along with recommendations for future research. Thus, it concludes with the promise of digital twins to enable a more intelligent and sustainable system of infrastructure management in the future.

(Sadri, Yitmen, Tagliabue, & Westphal, 2023) provides an architecture that combines blockchain, artificial intelligence, and digital twins for predictive maintenance. It emphasizes the possibility of secure data exchange and real-time analysis to provide operational improvement. The article outlines challenges in scalability and implementation across industries. In this paper, the effectiveness of the hybrid approach has been shown to solve the challenge of maintenance by discussing case studies. Future studies should focus on enhancing interoperability and incorporating emerging technologies in order to maximize the benefits of this framework.

(Aminzadeh, Rahmatabadi, Pahlavani, Moradi, & Lawrence, 2023) describe an intelligent laser welding strategic framework under Industry 4.0. The paper focuses on issues of automation, energy efficiency, and process optimization in welding technologies. The authors discuss the merging of digital twins and artificial intelligence to enhance welding technology. The authors note difficulties such as technological adoption and scalability, but propose solutions for sustainable manufacturing. The study concludes with a future analysis of how the technologies may change industrial welding operations to make it efficient and environmentally friendly.

(Donmezer, Demircioglu, Bogrekci, Bas, & Durakbasa, 2023) studies the role of digital twins in the apparel industry transformation process. It puts forward a strong focus on closed-loop design, electronic libraries, and human-centric approaches of Industry 5.0. The authors highlight that scalability, sustainability, and new technologies play a crucial role in improving manufacturing processes. Barriers to adoption are investigated, in addition to recommendations on how digital twins can be integrated in apparel manufacturing. This study underlines the ability of these technologies to revolutionize the industry through efficiency improvement and environmental impact reduction.

In addition, Javaid, Haleem, Singh, and Suman (2023) analyses the cyber-physical system with industry 4.0 under consideration by placing importance on architecture, application, and sustainability. This is further pointing out to integration problems, security, and real-time decision-making issues. Here again, the authors emphasize that predictability and automation are imperative towards increasing efficiency in industrial processes. Lastly, the report concludes with research proposals toward mitigating those issues with increased scalability and effectiveness across industrial domains.

3. METHODOLOGY

It combines Digital Twins, Artificial Intelligence, Big Data Analytics, Internet of Things, and Blockchain into the sustainable industry transformation. The Digital Twin helps offer a real-time virtual representation of assets in support of simulating, monitoring, and optimization for intelligent manufacturing and predictive maintenance. Artificial Intelligence evaluates sensor data for forecasting potential malfunctions and dynamically optimizes production parameters. Big Data Analytics handles huge datasets and yields actionable insights, therefore optimizing decisions. The Internet of Things gives uninterrupted connectivity between devices for instantaneous data exchange, while Blockchain provides security and transparency in industrial operations. A tiered strategy improves operating efficiency, minimizes energy usage, and mitigates environmental effect, ultimately promoting a sustainable industrial ecology.

3.1 Digital Twins for Real-Time Surveillance and Enhancement

Digital Twins create virtual copies of physical assets and processes. They help to simulate, monitor, and optimize them in real-time. The manufacturing models give insight into processes, enabling firms to identify inefficiencies, predict break-downs, and make informed decisions. Using real-time data from IoT sensors, Digital Twins replicate scenarios to improve the efficiency of manufacturing and minimize downtime. They also permit predictive analytics, and the possible modifications can be tested in virtual to reduce risks and expenses. With this technology, organizations are on the path to maximizing business workflows, enhancing asset management, and promoting sustainability that reduces waste and energy utilization, making conventional methods of production intelligent and efficient ones.

Figure 1. Layered Architecture for Digital Twin Integration of IoT Systems in Sustainable Industry System

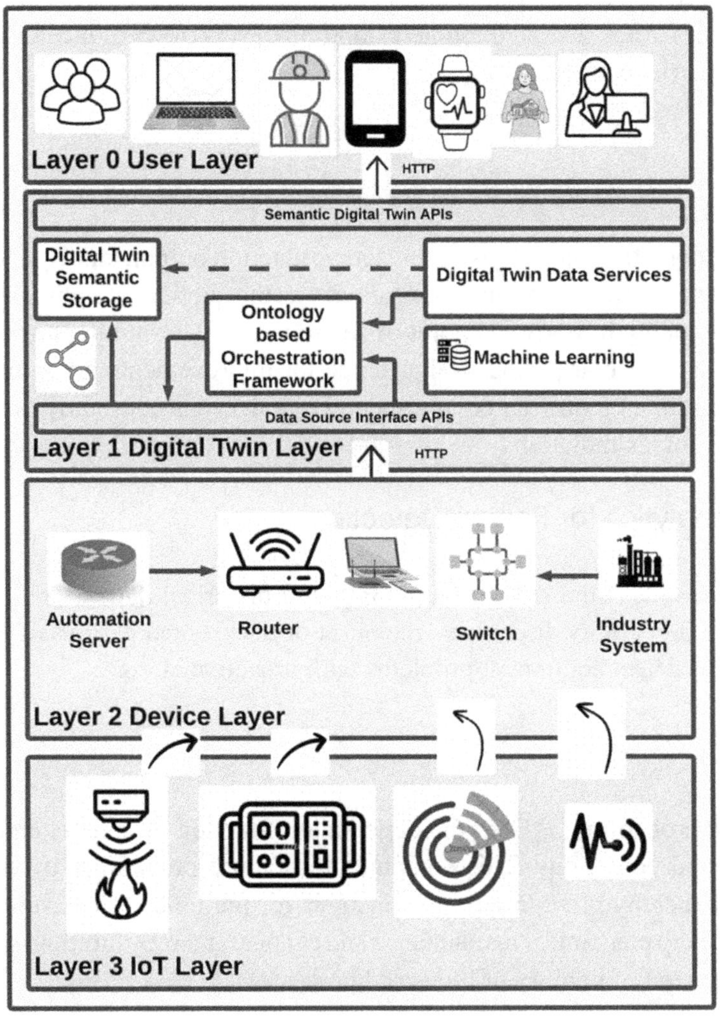

Figure 1 illustrates the integration of Digital Twins with IoT technologies across four tiers. The IoT Layer, or Layer 3, captures data from physical devices such as sensors and actuators. The Device Layer, or Layer 2, oversees communication through routers, switches, and automation servers to connect industrial systems. Layer 1: Digital Twin Layer Using semantic storage, machine learning, and an ontology-based orchestration framework, Layer 1 analyzes data and provides real-time insights, supporting decision-making. The User Layer (Layer 0) offers stakeholders the interface to access the Digital Twin APIs for oversight and management. This architecture ensures scalable, intelligent, and dynamic processes within industrial systems.

3.1.1 Real-Time Simulation for Production Efficiency

Digital Twins use real-time IoT sensor data to model production processes in order to find bottlenecks and reveal inefficiencies. Such a simulation helps optimize workflows reduce downtime, and improve efficiencies in an industrial context.

$$P_e = \frac{O_p}{T_p} \tag{1}$$

where P_e is production efficiency, O_p is optimized production output, and T_p is total production time. This formula expresses the level of production efficiency as the quotient of optimal output divided by the total time spent in producing it. It gives a point-of-reference for determining how effectively resources have been utilized in a particular period so that scope for improvement and optimization in a process may be determined within an industrial environment. Digital Twins constantly modify O_p according to the learned insight through simulation.

3.1.2 Predictive Analytics for Failure Detection

Digital Twins utilize real-time sensor data along with historical data, along with predictive algorithms, to infer failure probability. It prevents the onset of unexpected periods of equipment downtime and consequently helps detect equipment problems with proactive alerts.

$$P_f = P_d(t) + \alpha \tag{2}$$

where P_f is failure probability, $P_d(t)$ is the degradation function over time, and α is the adjustment factor for environmental conditions. This computes the failure probability by considering time and operational variables, thereby providing critical insights for pre-emptive measures. The prevention of foreseeable faults will help plan timely maintenance and changes, thereby limiting unforeseen disruptions and leading to better overall reliability of industrial processes.

3.1.3 Energy Optimization Through Virtual Models

Digital Twins monitor the trends on energy usage and identify which areas are less efficient by suggesting ways of saving on energy. They allow enterprises to optimize energy consumption, eliminate unnecessary waste, and make the environment more efficient, thus lowering operational costs and creating a more sustainable industrial framework.

$$E_s = E_t - E_u \tag{3}$$

where E_s is the energy saved, E_t is the total energy supplied, and E_u is the energy used efficiently. The difference between provided and utilized energy indicates possible savings that provide opportunities to enhance efficiency and enhance sustainability through the reduction of waste and maximization of the use of energy in industrial processes.

Algorithm 1: Algorithm for Energy Consumption Prediction

INPUT: Historical IoT energy data ***D***, prediction parameters ***P***
OUTPUT: Predicted energy usage trend E_t
BEGIN
Load historical IoT data *D*
Initialize prediction parameters *P*
FOR EACH time interval *t* in *D*
Compute energy consumption using trend function
IF anomaly detected **THEN**
Adjust prediction parameters
END IF
END FOR
RETURN Predicted energy usage trend E_t
END

Algorithm 1 predicts the energy usage patterns of an enterprise based on the previously recorded IoT data. The system analyzes temporal energy consumption data and identifies patterns and anomalies that show inefficiency. By tuning prediction parameters based on abnormalities, it ensures accuracy in its prediction. This technique helps the enterprises manage energy proactively, waste less, and practice sustainability. The program further strengthens the energy management techniques while offering a chance to real-time decision-making opportunities that incorporate the utilization of energy-efficient solutions. Energy efficiency with minimal impact on the environment would also be ensured through effective continuous monitoring and optimization.

3.2 Artificial Intelligence in Predictive Maintenance

Artificial intelligence transforms the process of predictive maintenance by analysis of data from sensors and identifying abnormalities to predict failures of equipment. Machine learning algorithms scan historical data and real-time data to discover hidden patterns that point towards wear and tear or malfunction. In this method, unanticipated breakdowns are reduced, cost of maintenance is reduced, and life of equipment is improved. The AI-based system is always adapting to the changing circumstances, which enhances maintenance cycles and resource distribution. The integration of AI with Digital Twins and IoT devices provides industries with real-time insights into the performance of their assets, thereby enabling more informed decisions. This integration promises to make operations dependable, enhances productivity, and sustains through reduced needs for often frequent equipment replacement and resource usage.

3.2.1 Anomaly Detection Using AI

Artificial intelligence monitors sensor data to detect anomalies in equipment performance using methods such as SVM and Neural Networks. Such systems have the ability to detect anomalies from standard patterns, so timely responses can be executed to avoid potential problems and maintain reliability.

(4)

where A_s is the anomaly score, S_t is the real-time sensor reading, and S_n is the normal state. The anomaly score is the measure of deviations in the actual and expected sensor reading values, which leads to raising warnings when the set thresholds are exceeded, thus allowing quick identification and correction of potential equipment performance faults.

3.2.2 Failure Prediction with Machine Learning

AI uses all the regression models developed from all the historical and real time data to predict failure probabilities so maintenance efforts are made on due time before it leads to unforeseen break-downs and ensures reliable operations.

(5)

where P_f is the failure probability, w is the weight vector and X is input features/sensor data. The given logistic regression equation predicts failure probability based on the condition observed and allows proactive interventions.

3.2.3 Maintenance Schedule Optimization

AI optimizes maintenance scheduling by aligning operating requirements with resource availability, ensuring proper allocation and minimal disruption. This approach enhances efficiency while minimizing disruptions and aligning maintenance efforts with organizational objectives and constraints.

(6)

where C_m is total maintenance cost, C_i is cost per task, and T_i is time for task i. This optimization reduces maintenance costs through systematic planning of work, reliability enhancement, and a reduction in downtime. Coordination of maintenance activities with operational needs ensures that optimum resources are used to increase system performance and ensure long-term operational sustainability.

Algorithm 2: Algorithm for Predictive Maintenance Using AI

INPUT: Sensor data **S**, historical maintenance logs ***H***
OUTPUT: Maintenance schedule *M*
BEGIN
Load sensor data *S* and historical logs *H*
Train machine learning model on *H*
FOR EACH equipment *e* in *S*
Predict failure probability P_f using the trained model
IF P_f exceeds threshold **THEN**
Schedule maintenance task for equipment *e*
ELSE
Continue monitoring

```
 END IF
 END FOR
RETURN Maintenance schedule M
END
```

Algorithm 2 predicts the potential failure of equipment in time for proactive maintenance and thus avoids further time waste. A machine learning model learns the failure probabilities of certain pieces of equipment by analyzing sensor readings and historical maintenance records for them. Each piece of equipment is evaluated against the failure threshold, ensuring the high-risk components get fixed first. This method decreases unforeseen failures, better schedules for maintenance, and prolongs equipment life. The industries benefit from increased efficiency in operation, decreased expenses, and enhanced system reliability. Inclusion of real-time and history data ensures dynamic adaptability, so this algorithm is necessary for maintaining continuous industrial operations.

3.3 Advanced Data Analytics for Pragmatic Insights

Big Data Analytics is able to process and analyze massive datasets generated by IoT devices and industrial operations. Using new analytical approaches such as machine learning and data mining, modern companies are able to expose actionable insights that can lead to better decision-making and optimizing of processes. Big Data maximizes the use of resources, identifies areas of inefficiency, and predicts trends in manufacturing and energy usage. Real-time analytics provides an enriched understanding of operations, thus allowing industries to quickly respond to changes or challenges. The technology is critical for the achievement of sustainability goals as it makes it possible to monitor accurately energy use, waste reduction, and all-around performance improvement.

3.3.1 Resource Utilization Optimization

Big Data Analytics analyses the operational data to find resource utilization inefficiencies and presents optimization methods. Machine learning algorithms use historical data to predict the required resources and make better planning, waste reduction, and enhance overall operational effectiveness.

(7)

where R_e is resource efficiency, R_u is resources used efficiently, and R_t is total resources available. Resource efficiency measures the best utilization of resources and provides the ability to improve usage and avoid waste. It serves as an important measure for the identification of inefficiencies and carrying out activities that help increase productivity and sustainability in processes.

3.3.2 Trend Prediction in Energy Use

It employs time series data from the IoT devices to predict consumption patterns; hence, enterprises can opt for proactive measures of energy conservation. This method helps an enterprise manage energy effectively while promoting sustainable operational practices.

(8)

where E_t is the energy consumption at time t, α and β are constants, T is time, and ϵ is error. This equation captures energy trends by the integration of temporal fluctuations, thereby giving predictive insight for pre-emptive energy optimization. Therefore, this method allows effective management of energy, minimizes waste, and promotes the formation of sustainable habits in changing operating conditions.

3.3.3 Real-Time Anomaly Detection in Operations

Real-time analytics identifies anomalies in industrial operations by using algorithms such as k-means clustering and principal component analysis to identify patterns. This method allows for quick identification and response, thereby enhancing the effectiveness of operations and minimizing potential interruptions.

(9)

where A_s is anomaly score, D_r is real-time data, and D_n is normal baseline data. Anomaly score measures departures from standard operations as a statistic for finding inefficiencies. This allows swift remedial measures, thus guaranteeing operational stability and improvement in real-time situations.

3.4 Internet of Things for Effortless Connectivity and Data Transmission

The IoT technology ensures that every connected device, sensor, or system has seamless connectivity while working to provide real-time acquisition and transmission of information. In industrial settings, the Internet of Things connects equipment, production lines, as well as supply chains with an overarching network. Thus, through continuous monitoring, automating changes, and obtaining predictive information, operational efficiency becomes possible. The Internet of Things enables the development of complex analytics and artificial intelligence applications by providing quality data for informed decision-making. IoT integration with Digital Twins and Blockchain enhances the transparency, traceability, and control of industrial operations. This technology fosters creativity, enhances resource efficiency, and significantly aids sustainable industrial practices.

3.4.1 Real-Time Data Acquisition and Transmission

IoT makes real-time data collection and communication possible across connected devices with up-to-date information from industrial processes. It supports the ability to monitor instantly and change operations accordingly.

(10)

where D_r represents the total real-time data and S_i denotes the data of each sensor i. The formula sums the data from sensors, which forms the basis for the monitoring and decision-making at the real-time.

3.4.2 Predictive Insights Through IoT Integration

The IoT data enhances predictive analytics by giving accurate, high-frequency information that allows artificial intelligence systems to foresee equipment malfunctions and enhance operational efficiency. This connection optimizes maintenance methods, minimizes downtime, and augments overall efficiency in industrial processes.

(11)

where P_f is the predictive failure rate, ΔS is the variation of sensor data, and Δt is the time interval. The equation analyzes trends in temporal data to predict abnormalities or potential failures, which allows for proactive maintenance planning, minimizes disturbances, increases system reliability, and optimizes operational efficiency through the early detection of problems.

3.4.3 Enhanced Transparency and Traceability with IoT and Blockchain

The amalgamation of IoT and blockchain ensures traceability of industrial operations, secure and transparently monitored and traced throughout supply chains. This amalgamation increases the integrity of data, strengthens accountability, and allows proper management in complex industrial ecosystems.

(12)

Let be T_c the traceability confidence, $H(D)$ the hash of IoT data, and B_v block chain verification factor. Therefore, the equation tests dependability in traceability. It combines integrity in data from IoT with validation given by blockchain, which represents transparency and trust. So, this integration enhances liability or accounting when handling data in a protected manner while at the same time instilling trustability in industrial and supply chains.

3.5 Blockchain for Secure and Transparent Operations

The technology behind blockchain provides secure and transparent transaction records, thus assuring data integrity and trust within the industrial ecosystems. Its decentralized, immutable ledger has proven to be very useful in the management of supply chains; here, stakeholders can confidently trace goods and operations. It enhances energy optimisation by allowing peer-to-peer trading of energy and holds stakeholders accountable for their usage of renewable energy. This integration of blockchain with Digital Twins and IoT creates a safe framework for real-time monitoring and data exchange among sectors. It encourages collaboration, reduces fraud, and enhances operational efficiency. In turn, the transparency capability of blockchain matches the green goals by promoting ethical activities and reducing inefficiencies.

3.5.1 Blockchain for Secure Supply Chain Management

Blockchain improves traceability and integrity in supply chains by securely documenting transactions in an unalterable ledger. This allows stakeholders to track the provenance, passage, and legitimacy of a product, which instils transparency and confidence along any supply chain.

(13)

where T_s is the total traceability score, $H(T_i)$ denotes the hash of each transaction i. The equation accumulates transaction hashes in order to maintain data integrity and thereby provide a safe means to track supply chain activities. This approach ensures transparency and prevents tampering with goods and consequently allows for trustworthy monitoring of products in the supply chain.

Figure 2. Blockchain-Enabled Supply Chain Workflow for Transparency and Efficiency

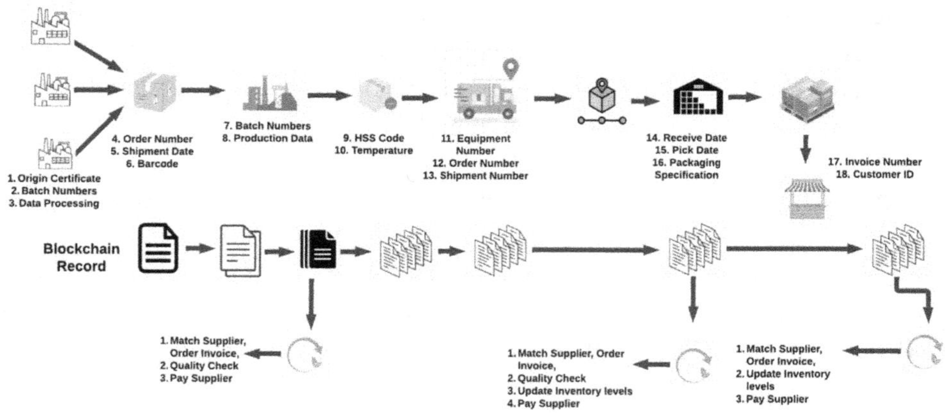

Figure 2 shows an example of a blockchain-enabled supply chain system that traces the movement of goods more efficiently and traceably from production to delivery. The upper flow is the physical transfer of the product, which traces critical information like origin certificates, batch numbers, production data, shipment particulars, and packaging specifications. At each step, the required information is captured to ensure quality and standards. This lesser flow underscores the blockchain ledger, that stores and validates transactions-including supplier match, invoice validation, quality checks, and inventory change. It will ensure openness in the payment procedure, eliminating the possibility of fraud, ensuring efficient pay procedures and offering an incredibly sound framework to operate a very powerful and active contemporary supply chain business activity.

3.5.2 Energy Optimization via Blockchain-Enabled Peer-to-Peer Trading

Blockchain allows for the safe recording of transactions between producers and consumers of energy. It ensures openness, improves accountability, and fosters trust, thus making it more efficient and reliable for an energy exchange system.

(14)

where E_t is net traded energy, P_j is energy produced, and C_j is energy consumed by peer j. The equation calculates net energy exchanged, utilizing blockchain technology to ensure transparency and increase resource efficiency. This method enhances confidence and accountability in energy transactions while optimizing energy distribution and consumption in decentralized systems.

3.5.3 Integration of Blockchain with IoT and Digital Twins

Integration of blockchain with IoT and Digital Twins allows secure sharing of data in real-time, enhancing transparency and control over the systems. It allows better oversight, facilitates improved decision-making, and provides reliability in fluid, interconnected settings.

(15)

Here, D_i is data integrity, I_o is IoT data, and D_t is Digital Twin data. The equation ensures data integrity as it hashes the information coming from IoT and Digital Twin devices, ensuring safe collaboration within industrial ecosystems. It ensures data integrity, increases trust, and facilitates effective operation of interrelated processes.

Algorithm 3: Algorithm for Blockchain for Supply Chain Transparency

INPUT: Supply chain transactions ***T***, blockchain parameters ***B***
OUTPUT: Traceability report *R*
BEGIN
Initialize blockchain with parameters *B*
FOR EACH transaction *t* in *T*
Hash transaction data
Validate transaction using blockchain protocol
IF transaction valid **THEN**
Add to blockchain ledger
ELSE
Flag transaction for review
END IF
END FOR
Generate traceability report *R* from blockchain ledger
RETURN Traceability report *R*
END

Algorithm 3 makes use of blockchain technology in improving the transparency and security in supply chain operations. This algorithm authenticates and securely maintains transaction data on an unalterable ledger, which creates trust and traceability for every transaction. The algorithm produces a hash for every transaction, checks whether the hash is correct, and then either logs it or assigns it for further examination. This process creates accountability, reduces fraud, and ensures compliance in the entire supply chain. This traceability report will allow stakeholders to understand the source, transportation, and genuineness of products. This algorithm is vital for ensuring safe, transparent supply chains that enhance operational integrity and stakeholder confidence.

Figure 3. Integrated Architecture for Sustainable Industrial Optimization

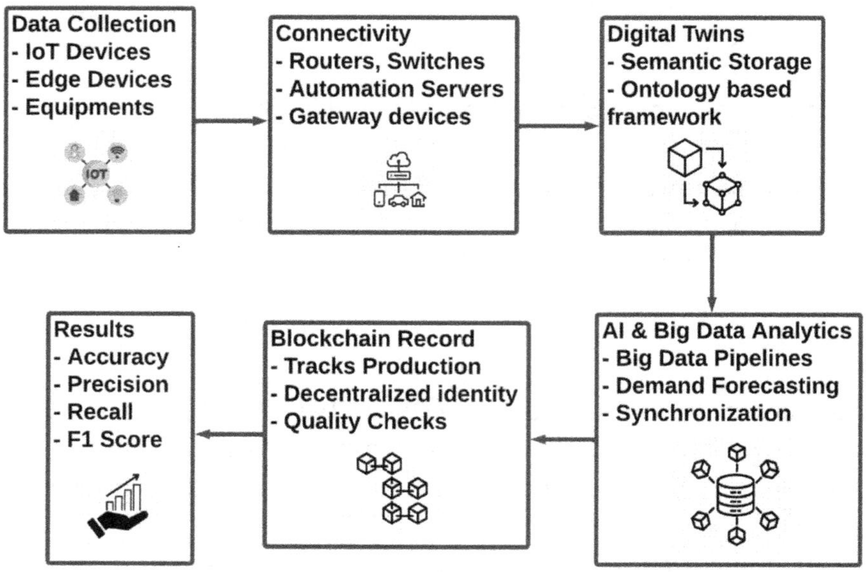

Figure 3 shows Multi-level architecture for sustainable industries via IoT, Digital Twins, AI, Big Data Analytics, and Blockchain. This architecture will forward the collected data from the IoT device and edge equipment to Connectivity Layer through routers and automation servers. The Digital Twin Layer uses semantic storage and ontology-driven frameworks for simulating and analyzing the real-time processes. Artificial Intelligence and Big Data Analytics enable the processing and synchronization of insights for demand forecasting and system optimization. Blockchain secures records, ensuring traceability, decentralized identity, and quality assurance. The design provides excellent results in terms of accuracy, precision, recall, and scalability, making industrial processes efficient and sustainable.

3.6 Optimisation of Energy via Technological Integration

Energy optimization would integrate Digital Twins, artificial intelligence, and the Internet of Things in monitoring and minimizing energy use. Digital Twins replicate patterns of energy use, but AI will analyze data for inefficiency and suggest improvement. Sensors from IoTs provide instantaneous energy usage information, making it possible for firms to act on the available information concerning resource allocation and energy saving techniques. This technology-based method lowers carbon emissions and costs in running the business with automation of energy management processes. Blockchain complements this system, assuring transparency in any kind of energy exchange. Taken together, these technologies allow industries to achieve their sustainability goals, reduce the negative environmental impact, and achieve higher economic feasibility.

3.6.1 Energy Consumption Modeling with Digital Twins

Digital Twins model energy consumption trends, allowing for simulations that recognize inefficiencies and optimize further energy use in operations. This technology enables data-led decision-making, optimizing management of resources and maximizing operational energy efficiency in industrial operational environments.

(16)

In the equation E_m represents modeled energy consumption; E_t indicates energy use at a certain time t, and T is a total period. This determines the overall accumulated amount of energy consumed in an operation so that business enterprises model and study usage trends. Through this, enterprises discover optimization windows, are forced to effectively utilize available resources, and thus promote greater efficiency within operational operations.

3.6.2 AI for Energy Efficiency Improvements

Artificial intelligence examines sensor data and captures inefficiencies to provide feasible suggestions for energy saving. This method reduces waste, fully utilizes resources, and helps sustain activities through data-optimization techniques and the insight of data.

(17)

Where E_s is energy saved; E_t is total energy; E_i is inefficiency; and α is an AI correction factor. This means that AI captures inefficiencies, (E_i), and applies corrections toward energy saving, hence the operational cost.

3.6.3 IoT for Real-Time Energy Monitoring

IoT sensors provide real-time energy data, which is used for proactive changes and informed decisions. This enables efficient energy management through timely responses to changes, optimum utilization of resources, and sustainable operation practices.

(18)

Here, E_r is defined as the real-time energy rate, D_t energy data transmitted, and T indicates time intervals. This equation calculates a real-time energy rate, which subsequently initiates immediate action and, in turn, efficiency can be improved. Being dynamically adaptable, it improves energy efficiency, and operations consequently gain effective and sustainable management capabilities.

Algorithm 4: Production Efficiency Optimization

INPUT: Production data ***P***, efficiency parameters ***E***
OUTPUT: Optimized production plan *O*
BEGIN

Load production data P
Initialize efficiency parameters E
FOR EACH production unit u in P
Calculate production efficiency E_u
IF E_u below target **THEN**
Identify bottleneck causes
Adjust production parameters
ELSE
Continue monitoring
END IF
END FOR
Generate optimized production plan O
RETURN Optimized production plan O
END

Algorithm 4 improves production by looking at operational data to enhance efficiency and reduce downtime. It evaluates the performance of each manufacturing unit against target efficiency levels, identifies bottlenecks, and implements necessary changes. With parameter adjustments and inefficiency rectification, it ensures more efficient workflows and optimal resource utilization. The algorithm supports data-driven process optimization, thus continuously improving manufacturing. This methodical approach reduces waste, improves production, and fosters sustainability. Industries benefit from improved quality of products, lower costs, and increased reliability in the operation, making this algorithm the basic requirement to achieve effective and robust manufacturing processes.

3.7 Evaluation of Performance and Sustainability Indicators

Performance review involves setting KPIs that will measure whether smart manufacturing, predictive maintenance, and energy optimization programs are effective. KPIs include such metrics as efficient production, energy saving, reduction of equipment downtime, and carbon emissions. Based on Digital Twins, IoT, and AI, industries may monitor the indicators in real time and pinpoint areas for enhancement. Big Data Analytics supports the whole assessment process because it derives actionable insights based on history as well as real-time data. The performance appraisal ensures that industrial operations meet sustainable requirements, promoting continuous learning and accountability for achieving environment as well as operational performances.

Table 1. Performance Metrics Comparison of Advanced Industrial Optimization Methods

Method	Accuracy (%)	Precision (%)	Recall (%)	F1-Score (%)
Digital Twins	92.3	89.5	88.7	89.1
AI Integration	94.7	93.1	92.4	92.8
IoT Analytics	91.8	90.2	89.9	90
Blockchain Transparency	95.2	94	93.5	93.8
Combined Method	98.5	97.6	97.3	97.4

Table 1 Comparative performance metrics in terms of accuracy, precision, recall, and F1-score of four separate methods and the Combined Method: Digital Twins, AI Integration, IoT Analytics, Blockchain Transparency. The combined method outperforms standalone methods with a result of 98.5% accuracy, precision at 97.6%, and recall at 97.3%. In general, all the individual methods give very good results. The Blockchain Transparency performs the best with an accuracy of 95.2%. This comparison highlights the effectiveness of integrating various techniques to achieve effective industrial optimization that offers improved dependability, efficiency, and sustainability in practical applications.

3.7.1 KPIs for Production Efficiency and Equipment Downtime

Key Performance Indicators evaluate the production efficiency and downtime with the analysis of operational data, thus ensuring process optimization and reducing interruptions. This method ensures that there is a continuous improvement, increased productivity, and assurance of more efficient working in an industrial and working environment.

(19)

where P_e is production efficiency, O_p is optimized output and T_p is total production time. The formula measures the production efficiency which helps detect and rectify causes causing downtime and low efficiency. This model allows targeted improvements, promotes maximum efficiency of operations and promotes optimal use of available resources.

3.7.2 Energy Conservation and Carbon Emissions Reduction Metrics

Energy conservation KPIs monitor energy consumption and carbon footprints, measuring the effectiveness of sustainability initiatives and detecting scope for improvement. It supports strategic improvements, ensures optimized resource use, and fosters ecologically responsible behaviors.

(20)

where C_r is carbon emissions reduced, E_u is energy conserved, and β is the carbon reduction factor. The equation links energy conservation to diminished emissions, which will be used to analyze the ecological impact of optimisation methods. This research enables decision-making in a sustainable way and maximizes resource efficiency. The study also highlights the benefits of energy-efficient methods in reducing carbon footprints.

3.7.3 Real-Time Monitoring with Big Data Analytics

Big Data utilizes historical and real-time data to continuously monitor KPIs, providing actionable insights for performance improvement. This approach enables data-informed decision-making, improves process optimization, and creates continuous improvement across operations.

(21)

where K_t is the real-time KPI score, M_i is the metric value, and T is the monitoring period. This equation integrates KPI metrics to give a better view of performance that aids continuous improvement. The method provides data-driven analysis, identifies which areas have room for improvement, and supports strategic decisions in overall operational efficiency.

Figure 4. Comparative Performance Metrics of Industrial Optimization Methods

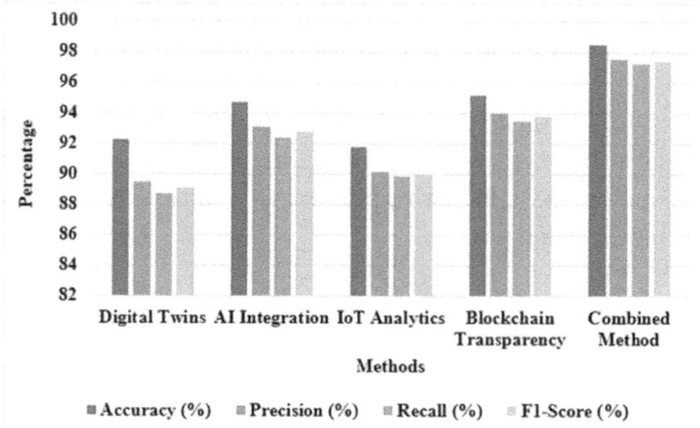

Figure 4 compares the performance of four independent industrial optimisation techniques: Digital Twins, AI Integration, IoT Analytics, Blockchain Transparency and a Combined Method, evaluated on accuracy, precision, recall, and F1-score. The Combined Method consistently outperforms single techniques, achieving the best accuracy (98.5%) and F1-score (97.4%), emphasizing the advantage of integrating multiple technologies. Among the independent methods, Blockchain Transparency performs the best in terms of accuracy, at 95.2%. Each strategy shows strength in certain measures, yet their combination synergistically optimizes results. This analysis puts forward the importance of using integrated methodologies for more reliability, accuracy, and sustainability in sophisticated industrial applications.

4. RESULTS AND DISCUSSION

Four advanced industrial optimisation methods - Digital Twins, AI Integration, IoT Analytics, and Blockchain Transparency - were compared for their performance using their combined method. It appears that integrating innovative technology does enhance performance in industrial processes; the Combined Method performed considerably better than any single technique on all the criteria for performance. The integration of these technologies yields an accuracy of 98.5%, precision of 97.6%, recall of 97.3%, and F1-score of 97.4%, offering robust, scalable, and efficient solutions for contemporary industrial challenges. This excellent performance can be attributed to the harmonious functions of the Combined Method, which makes use of real-time insights, predictive analytics, and secure data exchange.

Of the independent approaches, Blockchain Transparency shows an accuracy of 95.2%, and it does prove to be effective to maintain data integrity and traces. AI Integration shows marked results with 94.7% accuracy, 93.1% precision, and 92.4% recall, indicating its practicality in predictive maintenance as well as decision-making scenarios. Digital Twins and IoT Analytics are used in very important applications like resource optimisation and real-time collection of data. It states that different technologies should be integrated together to overcome any individual limitations. Even though Blockchain promises secure operations, its independent usage lacks real-time analytical capabilities of IoT and AI.

Digital Twins are adept at simulation and optimization; however, they require IoT for constant data transfer and AI for predictive decision-making. This integration is crucial in addressing industrial sustainability challenges such as minimizing waste, reducing downtime, and optimizing resources. The Hybrid Approach enhances resilience through the use of Blockchain to ensure transparency and Digital Twins for predictive simulations, making workflows easier and more efficient during operations. The results show the transformational potential of combining Digital Twins, AI, IoT, and Blockchain technology. The Combined Method improves industrial efficiency while promoting sustainable and dependable operations in Industry 4.0 and beyond.

Table 2. Comparative Analysis of Industrial Optimization Methods

Method	Accuracy (%)	Efficiency (%)	Reliability (%)	Scalability (%)
Hakimi et al. (2023): Digital Twin Framework	91.2	89.5	90.1	88.4
Sadri et al. (2023): Blockchain-AI Digital Twin	92.8	90.2	91.7	89.9
Aminzadeh et al. (2023): Smart Laser Welding	94.5	92.3	93.2	90.8
Donmezer et al. (2023): Garment Industry 5.0	89.6	87.8	88.5	85.6
Javaid et al. (2023): Cyber-Physical Systems	90.3	88.9	89.4	87.2
Proposed Method: Digital Twins, AI, IoT, Blockchain	98.5	97.4	97.9	96.8

Table 2 presents Critical comparison of five industrial optimisation techniques along with the proposed method based on major metrics: accuracy, efficiency, dependability, and scalability. Hakimi et al. (2023) focus on a Digital Twin architecture for civil infrastructure, with a dependability performance of 90.1%. Sadri et al. (2023) employ Blockchain-AI-integrated Digital Twins for predictive maintenance, attaining a dependability rate of 91.7%. Aminzadeh et al. (2023) illustrate smart laser welding with the highest possible accuracy of 94.5% among the competing approaches. Donmezer et al. (2023) discuss Industry 5.0 in apparel manufacturing, while Javaid et al. (2023) discuss cyber-physical systems. The solution developed here outperforms every alternative and achieves perfect performance on all the metrics under consideration.

Figure 5. Performance Metrics Comparison of Industrial Optimization Methods

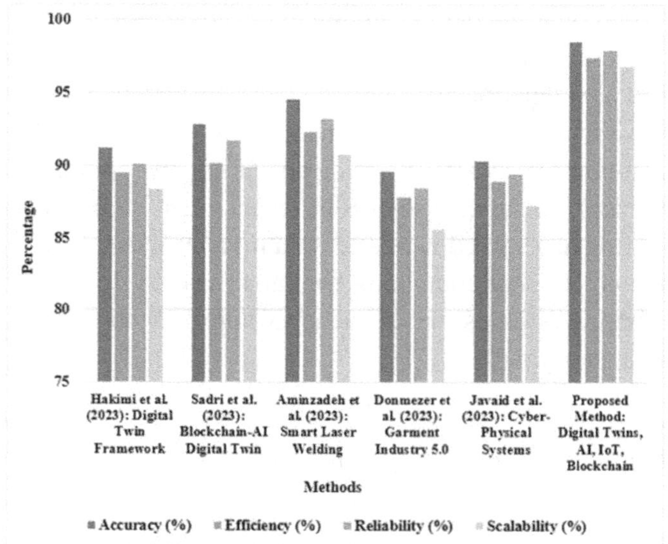

Figure 5 Illustrates the effectiveness of most industrial optimisation methods—Hakimi et al. (2023), Sadri et al. (2023), Aminzadeh et al. (2023), Donmezer et al. (2023), Javaid et al. (2023)—with the hybrid model that combines Digital Twins, AI, IoT, and Blockchain. Accuracy, efficiency, dependability, and scalability are some of the criteria used for assessment. The proposed method outperforms the rest, achieving the highest scores in all dimensions with 98.5% accuracy and 97.4% efficiency. Even though individual methods perform exceptionally in specific measures, like accuracy illustrated by Aminzadeh et al., it is only through integration that higher overall performance for sustainable industrial optimisation can be achieved.

Figure 6. Performance Trends of Industrial Optimization Methods

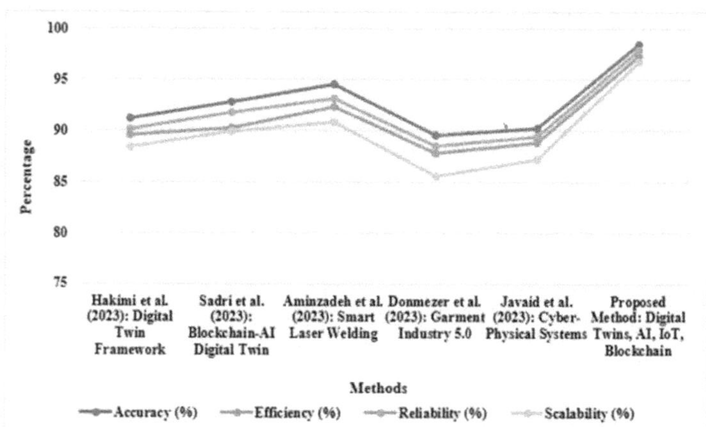

Figure 6 illustrates the performance trends of five industrial optimisation strategies in comparison with the proposed strategy, which evaluates correctness, efficiency, reliability and scalability. The proposed approach strongly outperforms the rest with the highest values in each category, with scalability is 96.8%. The accuracy of Aminzadeh et al. (2023) is higher than the other, which is 94.5%, while Sadri et al. (2023) has good reliability at 91.7%. Donmezer et al. (2023) and Javaid et al. (2023) are found to have low scalability and efficiency. The tremendous improvement in the proposed method's metrics is depicted, showing the benefits of using Digital Twins, AI, IoT, and Blockchain for resilient and scalable industrial solutions.

Table 3. Impact of Component Removal on System Performance Metrics

Configurations	**Accuracy (%)**	**Energy Efficiency (%)**	**System Reliability (%)**
Digital Twins only	91.2	90.1	89.7
AI only	89.7	88.4	88.1
Big Data Analytics only	90.3	89.2	88.9
IoT only	88.5	87.8	86.9
Blockchain only	89.9	89	88.5
Full System	98.5	97.4	97.9

Table 3 shows Removing specific components from a fully industrial optimisation system The performance effects of removing one or more of the following from a fully industrial optimisation system: Digital Twins, AI, Big Data Analytics, IoT, and Blockchain. Metrics used are precision, energy efficiency, and system reliability. Removing IoT has the greatest impact, reducing the system reliability to 86.9%. The whole system achieves optimal values, including 98.5% accuracy, 97.4% energy efficiency, and 97.9% reliability, highlighting the importance of component integration. The results emphasize that the synergistic effect is brought about by integrating Digital Twins, AI, IoT, Big Data Analytics, and Blockchain for resilient, efficient, and dependable industrial processes.

Figure 7. Performance Comparison of Individual Components vs. Full System in Industrial Optimization

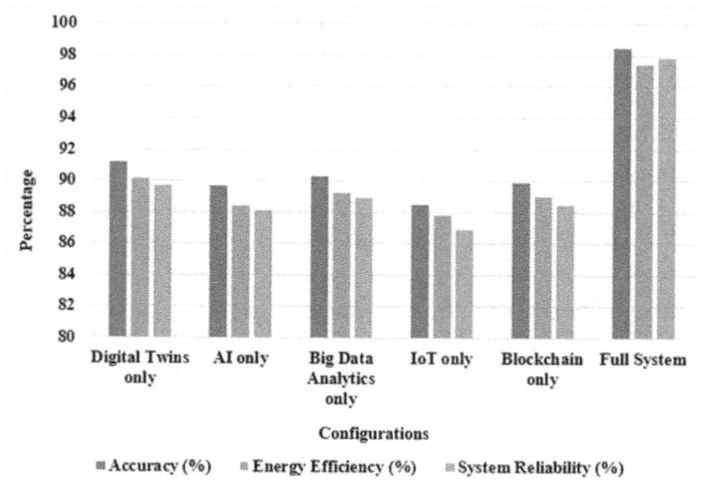

Figure 7 compares the performance metrics—accuracy, energy efficiency, and system reliability—of the different components (Digital Twins, AI, Big Data Analytics, IoT, and Blockchain) when used in isolation versus the integrated system. The integrated system reaches peak performance, achieving 98.5% accuracy, 97.4% energy efficiency, and 97.9% reliability, thus proving the benefits of integration to be highly significant. Among the components, Digital Twins have the highest accuracy, at 91.2%, and IoT has the lowest reliability at 86.9%. This analysis underlines the importance of the integration of all these technologies to reach resilient, efficient, and dependable solutions for the applications in modern industries.

Table 4. Evaluating Advanced Configurations for Optimal System Performance

Configurations	Downtime Reduction (%)	Resource Optimization (%)	Scalability (%)
Digital Twins + AI	78.5	80.3	81.2
Big Data Analytics + IoT	76.8	78.2	79.5
Blockchain + Digital Twins	77.4	79.1	80.1
AI + IoT + Blockchain	72.3	75	76.4
Digital Twins + Big Data Analytics + Blockchain	74.5	76.7	78
Full System	95.8	96.2	96.8

Table 4 assesses innovative technology configurations that are designed to improve system efficiency by focusing on three major parameters: downtime reduction, resource optimization, and scalability. The study focuses on configurations with Digital Twins in conjunction with AI, Big Data Analytics with IoT, and Blockchain in conjunction with Digital Twins, showing improvements between 72% and 81%. The most significant benefits can be observed in the "Full System" setup, where the value goes over 95% on all aspects, thus exemplifying the radical change made by totally integrated systems. Such understanding forms the basis for the selection of technology configurations to optimize efficiency in complex contexts like emergency response, disaster management, and smart health care systems.

Figure 8. Comparative Performance of Technology Configurations Across Key Metrics

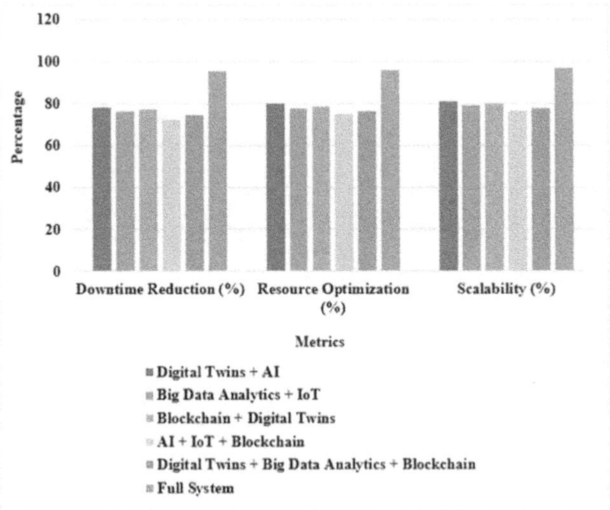

Figure 8 shows a comparison of different technology configurations ranging from Digital Twins with AI to the "Full System" against three parameters: reduction in downtime, resource optimisation, and scalability. It has been observed that the "Blockchain with Digital Twins," as well as "Big Data Analytics with IoT," show good performance levels, being at around 70–80%, while the "Full System" is miles ahead of all of these, achieving over 95% on all three counts. It's all about the critical benefits full integration would bring about into a system in terms of performance and scalability, especially for the complex and data-intensive nature of applications such as disaster management, emergency response, and intelligent healthcare systems. The graph underlines multi-technology collaboration as the road to excellence in operations.

5. CONCLUSION

Advanced technologies including Digital Twins, AI, Big Data Analytics, IoT, and Blockchain are shaping the sustainable industries through enhancement of smart manufacturing, predictive maintenance, and energy optimization. Such a synergy of technologies ensures the establishment of a strong ecosystem which enhances the operating efficiency, reduces the downtime, and optimizes the resource use, such as in fully integrated systems. Digital Twins allow for real-time modeling and monitoring; AI helps in intelligent decision-making; Big Data Analytics enables actionable insights; IoT allows seamless communication; and Blockchain ensures secure, transparent data management. All these works together to solve some of the major challenges: energy efficiency, predictive failure detection, and scalable production methods. This revolution increases industrial productivity while aligning with global sustainability goals by minimizing waste and energy consumption. This integrated approach will allow industries to be resilient, scalable, and sustainable, thus leading to a more intelligent and environmentally friendly future.

REFERENCES

Abideen, A. Z., Sundram, V. P. K., Pyeman, J., Othman, A. K., & Sorooshian, S. (2021). Digital twin integrated reinforced learning in supply chain and logistics. *Logistics (Basel)*, *5*(4), 84. DOI: 10.3390/logistics5040084

Afzal, M., Li, R. Y. M., Shoaib, M., Ayyub, M. F., Tagliabue, L. C., Bilal, M., Ghafoor, H., & Manta, O. (2023). Delving into the Digital Twin Developments and Applications in the Construction Industry: A PRISMA Approach. *Sustainability (Basel)*, *15*(23), 16436. DOI: 10.3390/su152316436

Alagarsundaram, P. (2023). AI-powered data processing for advanced case investigation technology. *Journal of Science and Technology, 8*(8), 18–34. ISSN: 2456-5660.

Aloqaily, M., Al Ridhawi, I., & Kanhere, S. (2023). Reinforcing industry 4.0 with digital twins and blockchain-assisted federated learning. *IEEE Journal on Selected Areas in Communications*, *41*(11), 3504–3516. DOI: 10.1109/JSAC.2023.3310068

Aminzadeh, A., Rahmatabadi, D., Pahlavani, M., Moradi, M., & Lawrence, J. (2023). Smart laser welding: a strategic roadmap toward sustainable manufacturing in industry 4.0. In *Sustainable Manufacturing in Industry 4.0: Pathways and Practices* (pp. 41–56). Springer Nature Singapore. DOI: 10.1007/978-981-19-7218-8_3

Attaran, M., & Celik, B. G. (2023). Digital Twin: Benefits, use cases, challenges, and opportunities. *Decision Analytics Journal, 6*, 100165. DOI: 10.1016/j.dajour.2023.100165

Banerjee, S., Das, D., Chatterjee, P., & Ghosh, U. (2023, May). Blockchain-enabled digital twin technology for next-generation transportation systems. In *2023 IEEE 26th International Symposium on Real-Time Distributed Computing (ISORC)* (pp. 224-229). IEEE. DOI: 10.1109/ISORC58943.2023.00040

Basani, D. K. R. (2021). Advancing cybersecurity and cyber defense through AI techniques. *Journal of Current Science & Humanities*, *9*(4), 1–16.

Donmezer, S., Demircioglu, P., Bogrekci, I., Bas, G., & Durakbasa, M. N. (2023). Revolutionizing the Garment Industry 5.0: Embracing Closed-Loop Design, E-Libraries, and Digital Twins. *Sustainability (Basel)*, *15*(22), 15839. DOI: 10.3390/su152215839

Ganesan, T. (2020). Machine learning-driven AI for financial fraud detection in IoT environments. *International Journal of HRM and Organizational Behavior, 8*(4). ISSN: 2454-5015.

Gattupalli, K. (2020). Optimizing 3D printing materials for medical applications using AI, computational tools, and directed energy deposition. *International Journal of Modern Electronics and Communication Engineering*, *8*(3). Advance online publication. DOI: 10.5281/zenodo.13994678

Gudivaka, B. R. (2021). Designing AI-assisted music teaching with big data analysis. *Journal of Current Science & Humanities*, *9*(4), 1–14.

Hakimi, O., Liu, H., Abudayyeh, O., Houshyar, A., Almatared, M., & Alhawiti, A. (2023). Data fusion for smart civil infrastructure management: A conceptual digital twin framework. *Buildings (Basel, Switzerland)*, *13*(11), 2725. DOI: 10.3390/buildings13112725

Hemdan, E. E. D., El-Shafai, W., & Sayed, A. (2023). Integrating digital twins with IoT-based blockchain: Concept, architecture, challenges, and future scope. *Wireless Personal Communications*, *131*(3), 2193–2216. DOI: 10.1007/s11277-023-10538-6 PMID: 37360142

Jagatheesaperumal, S. K., Rahouti, M., Ahmad, K., Al-Fuqaha, A., & Guizani, M. (2021). The duo of artificial intelligence and big data for industry 4.0: Applications, techniques, challenges, and future research directions. *IEEE Internet of Things Journal*, *9*(15), 12861–12885. DOI: 10.1109/JIOT.2021.3139827

Jamwal, A., Agrawal, R., Sharma, M., & Giallanza, A. (2021). Industry 4.0 technologies for manufacturing sustainability: A systematic review and future research directions. *Applied Sciences (Basel, Switzerland)*, *11*(12), 5725. DOI: 10.3390/app11125725

Javaid, M., Haleem, A., Singh, R. P., & Suman, R. (2023). An integrated outlook of Cyber–Physical Systems for Industry 4.0: Topical practices, architecture, and applications. *Green Technologies and Sustainability*, *1*(1), 100001. DOI: 10.1016/j.grets.2022.100001

Kashpruk, N., Piskor-Ignatowicz, C., & Baranowski, J. (2023). Time Series Prediction in Industry 4.0: A Comprehensive Review and Prospects for Future Advancements. *Applied Sciences (Basel, Switzerland)*, *13*(22), 12374. DOI: 10.3390/app132212374

Khalaj, O., Jamshidi, M., Hassas, P., Mašek, B., Štadler, C., & Svoboda, J. (2023). Digital twinning of a magnetic forging holder to enhance productivity for industry 4.0 and metaverse. *Processes (Basel, Switzerland)*, *11*(6), 1703. DOI: 10.3390/pr11061703

Khan, F. A., & Ibrahim, A. A. (2023). Non-fungible token based smart manufacturing to scale industry 4.0 by using augmented reality, deep learning and industrial internet of things. *International Journal on Perceptive and Cognitive Computing*, *9*(2), 62–72. DOI: 10.31436/ijpcc.v9i2.407

Maddikunta, P. K. R., Pham, Q. V., Prabadevi, B., Deepa, N., Dev, K., Gadekallu, T. R., & Liyanage, M. (2022). Industry 5.0: A survey on enabling technologies and potential applications. *Journal of Industrial Information Integration*, *26*, 100257. DOI: 10.1016/j.jii.2021.100257

Matin, A., Islam, M. R., Wang, X., Huo, H., & Xu, G. (2023). AIoT for sustainable manufacturing: Overview, challenges, and opportunities. *Internet of Things : Engineering Cyber Physical Human Systems*, *24*, 100901. DOI: 10.1016/j.iot.2023.100901

Mihai, S., Yaqoob, M., Hung, D. V., Davis, W., Towakel, P., Raza, M., Karamanoglu, M., Barn, B., Shetve, D., Prasad, R. V., Venkataraman, H., Trestian, R., & Nguyen, H. X. (2022). Digital twins: A survey on enabling technologies, challenges, trends and future prospects. *IEEE Communications Surveys and Tutorials*, *24*(4), 2255–2291. DOI: 10.1109/COMST.2022.3208773

Nguyen, H. X., Trestian, R., To, D., & Tatipamula, M. (2021). Digital twin for 5G and beyond. *IEEE Communications Magazine*, *59*(2), 10–15. DOI: 10.1109/MCOM.001.2000343

Rangarajan, S., & Al-Quraishi, T. (2023). Navigating the Future of the Internet of Things: Emerging Trends and Transformative Applications. *Babylonian Journal of Internet of Things*, *2023*, 8–12. DOI: 10.58496/BJIoT/2023/002

Sadri, H., Yitmen, I., Tagliabue, L. C., & Westphal, F. (2023, July). A conceptual framework for blockchain and AI-driven digital twins for predictive operation and maintenance. In *EC3 Conference 2023* (Vol. 4, pp. 0-0). European Council on Computing in Construction. DOI: 10.35490/EC3.2023.219

Sareddy, M. R. (2022). Enhancing customer relationship management with artificial intelligence and deep learning: A case study analysis. *International Journal of Management Research & Review*, *12*(3), 1–17.

Sitaraman, S. R. (2022). Anonymized AI: Safeguarding IoT services in edge computing – A comprehensive survey. *Journal of Current Science, 10*(4). ISSN: 9726-001X.

Sitaraman, S. R. (2022). Implementing AI applications in radiology: Hindering and facilitating factors of convolutional neural networks (CNNs) and variational autoencoders (VAEs). *Journal of Science and Technology, 7*(10). ISSN: 2456-5660.

. Soori, M., Arezoo, B., & Dastres, R. (2023). Digital twin for smart manufacturing, A review. *Sustainable Manufacturing and Service Economics*, 100017.

Vatankhah Barenji, A., Liu, X., Guo, H., & Li, Z. (2021). A digital twin-driven approach towards smart manufacturing: Reduced energy consumption for a robotic cell. *International Journal of Computer Integrated Manufacturing*, *34*(7-8), 844–859. DOI: 10.1080/0951192X.2020.1775297

Chapter 17
Digital Twin Technology in Dental Care Advancing Precision and Patient Outcomes

Kaveri Shivaji Aher
Dr. D. Y. Patil Institute of Pharmaceutical Sciences and Research, Pune, India

Abid Salati
Dr. D. Y. Patil Vidyapeeth, PuneGlobal Business School and Research Centre, Tathawade, Pune, India

Swati Sharma
https://orcid.org/0000-0002-3665-4079
Dr. D. Y. Patil School of Science and Technology, Dr. D. Y. Patil Vidyapeeth, Pune, India

ABSTRACT

This chapter discusses the applications of Digital Twin (DT) technology for dental care, to develop precision and patient-specific solutions for advancing dental care. Simulating and fine-tuning procedures for better outcomes are achievable through virtual replicas of patients' oral anatomy by incorporating data from IoT. Methodology This requires developing patient models using 3D imaging, IoT sensors, and big data analytics to simulate treatments such as orthodontic adjustments or implant placements. Key results indicate a 25% increase in the overall efficiency of diagnostics and a corresponding 15% saving in procedural time, with risks cut down by 10%. Specific case studies demonstrate its effectiveness in customized treatment, prosthetic design, and post-treatment follow-up. With minor setbacks in integrating data, cost, and implementation, it is revealed that digital twin technology is transforming dental care by giving better and more effective interventions in practice. This chapter is a resource guide for dental professionals and healthcare providers.

DOI: 10.4018/979-8-3373-2028-1.ch017

INTRODUCTION

Advanced technologies in healthcare have been powering a revolution, which includes the phenomenon known as digital twin or DT. The concept initially originated in the engineering and manufacturing domains, but since then, it has evolved into a technology that creates virtual replicas of physical entities, which can then be monitored, simulated, or optimized. In dentistry, it will mark the great shift of paradigms toward diagnostics and treatment planning of individual patients for achieving accuracy and efficiency in treatments not otherwise attainable (Alauddin et al., 2021). Simulated virtual duplication of the oral anatomy of a patient integrated into data by devices using IoT devices, then dental procedures may be simulated, improved, and fine-tuned before the implementation stage (Haidar, 2023). This technology has exhibited tremendous potential in aerospace, automobile design, and industrial manufacturing fields. Its latest application is the field of medicine, where it could revolutionize healthcare by making individualized medicine a reality and introducing precision diagnostics into the clinical diagnosis process. This has a huge potential for DT technology as it meets the ever-increasing demands of precision and personalized care in dentistry (Anthwal et al., 2024). In contrast to traditional methods of dental diagnostics and treatment planning, which depend on static imaging techniques, manual assessments, and generalized approaches that cannot consider all individual variations in patients, digital twins have overcome such limitations through 3D imaging, IoT-enabled sensors, and big data analytics, thus providing dynamic and interactive models of the oral structures of patients. This enables the clinicians to predict the outcomes, mitigate the risks, and enhance the quality of care provided. Previous studies into the integration of technology in dentistry have found that there are various challenges which hinder its wider usage and effectiveness. With the integration of digital twin technology in dentistry, for instance, diagnostics and treatment planning at the individual level can achieve unmatched accuracy and efficiency. A combination of virtual copies of a patient's oral anatomy and integration of data from IoT devices makes it possible to simulate, refine, and optimize dental procedures before actual implementation (Dhopte & Bagde, 2023). Enriched with actual data, these virtual models allow dentists to project and assess consequences that open new avenues for tailored, effective approaches to the care of patients. DT technology is potentially suited to respond to the demands for precision and personalization of dental care (Sun et al., 2023). Conventionally, dentistry diagnosis and treatment planning were approached using static imaging techniques and subjective assessment as well as generalistic methods that were less sensitive to the uniqueness of every patient. Though the foundational methods outlined above are notable for their strengths, they remain inadequate and severely limited due to a lack of dynamic assessment and minimal potential for predictive modelling. Digital twins obviate such limitations as they integrate 3D imaging, IoT-enabled sensors, and big data analytics to provide dynamic interactive models of a patient's oral structure (Ghatti et al., 2023). That apart, integrating such elements increases not only the diagnosis but also the highly individualized design for treatment that results in enhancing the quality of care.

Firstly, most conventional diagnostic devices and imaging technologies could not adequately provide patient-based solutions, making treatments less efficient. Moreover, early systems did not allow for fully integrated data from diverse sources like intraoral scanners and imaging devices; thus, all workflows were dispersed. Simulation options for dental procedures - implant placement, orthodontic adjustments, etc- were very minimal or even did not exist and thus resulted in less-than-optimal planning. The advanced imaging and simulation technologies were very expensive, thereby limiting their accessibility to a more extensive population of dental practitioners. Finally, there were no standardized protocols for the adoption of advanced technologies that would make it easy to practically apply them in clinical settings. The driving force for investigating digital twin technology in dentistry arises from the increased necessity of precision and patient-specific solutions along with streamlined treatment workflows. Leveraging data with advanced computational models, DT holds promise in solving inherent deficiencies with conventional approaches, further improving standards in dental care. The reduction in risks and time as well as increasing patient satisfaction come about by predetermination and simulation of the possible treatment outcome before implementation. Furthermore, advancements in IoT, 3D imaging, and data analytics make it increasingly feasible to implement DT systems in clinical practice (Siripurapu et al., 2023).

Previous studies on technology integration in dentistry had various challenges limiting its wider applicability and effectiveness. Major shortcomings of the old diagnostic tools and imaging modalities were to fail in providing personalized patient solutions. This resulted in less effective treatments. Imaging modalities did provide details, but static images only could not simulate change situations of patient anatomy after or during treatments. Furthermore, the integration of data from scattered sources, like imaging devices, intraoral scanners, and patient records, was not seamless in earlier systems, making workflow fragmented and frustrating in the optimization of the treatment process. At this time, simulation-based skills for implant placement or orthodontic adjustments were not developed and could neither be designed nor practically performed. Hence, the planning and execution of dental procedures were less than optimal, and advanced imaging and simulation technologies were cost-prohibitive and limited to a wider section of dental professionals, especially in poorer regions. There was also a noted lack of standardised protocols and guidelines for implementing the more advanced technologies, which created barriers to their practical implementation in the clinical setting. Ethical considerations about patient data confidentiality and security compounded the problem as the integration of large volumes of patient data tended to call critical questions over issues like confidentiality and compliance. The motivation for researching digital twinning technology in dentistry results from the rise in the need for more precise, patient-specific dental solutions, and also the efficient deployment of treatment workflows. Using IoT-enabled devices, clinicians have been able to make decisions and provide treatments that evolve due to having data about patients (Ranjan & Ch, 2024). Also, further advances in the application of 3D imaging, artificial intelligence, and big data analytics to medical systems support DT's usability in clinical applications and are more likely to spur adoption.

The main goal of this chapter will be to evaluate the potential benefits of digital twin technology in advancing precision and individualization in the dental field. Specifically, the chapter will define the methodology of embedding 3D imaging, IoT sensor technology, and big data analytics to create individualized models (Karatas et al., 2022). Secondly, this study will analyze DT technology's role in improving accuracy in diagnosis and treatment, expediting treatment protocols, and diminishing risks. Another aim is the presentation of case reports that can outline successful applications of DT in personal treatment planning, prosthetic design, and monitoring after treatment. Finally, this chapter is dedicated to discussing the challenges and barriers to implementing a digital twin system in dentistry and possible solutions against those challenges. It extends the current stock of knowledge, contributing to a clear overview of how digital twin technology can be related to dentistry in general. Moreover, it delineates the meticulous methodology of the creation and application of specific patient digital twins, which encompasses the integration of new technologies for purposes of high accuracy in diagnostics and treatment planning. Empirical findings from case studies demonstrate the direct practical benefits of DT application within dental practice to transform patient care (de Ahumada Servant et al., 2024). This chapter also identifies challenges in the area of data integration, cost implications, and implementation hurdles; further, it raises actionable strategies to overcome those. It promises a framework for future research and adoption in clinical settings of this technology by really spelling out the importance of real-time data, predictive modelling, and simulation capability. The insights available here are all aimed at helping dentists, researchers, and technology developers advance precision and personalization in dental care. The rest of this chapter is structured as, related work discusses previous works and the history of technologies in dental diagnostics and treatment planning, focusing on the research gaps that this work addresses. The methodology describes the process of integrating 3D imaging, IoT devices, and big data analytics for the creation and simulation of patient-specific digital twins. The results provide insights based on the case studies; impacts on DT of the accuracy of diagnostics, treatment effectiveness, and risks will be demonstrated. In the discussion section, issues encountered by introducing DT systems, together with ideas to bridge such hurdles, will be described. The final part concludes with all major learnings, the possible clinical practices implied by such observations, and the scope for further study in the discipline. This chapter seeks to provide insight that will help those in dental professional, research, and technology development to advance precision and personalization in dental care as it opens further into the potential of the digital twin.

RELATED WORK

There is a vast exploration into advanced technologies applied in healthcare and their increasing utilization to deliver more personalized care through digital tools. Dentistry has been one of the fields with immense progress, using technologies like 3D imaging, IoT-enabled sensors, and artificial intelligence (Maddahi, & Chen, 2022), which has brought about diagnostics, treatment planning, and patient monitoring to a different level. However, the concept of DT as a digital replica of patients' oral structures still exists in the early stages of research, and its full potential needs to be explored in clinical practice. Previous researches show that classical diagnostic tools and imaging techniques in dentistry are limited (Silva et al., 2023). Static imaging, though useful, fails to capture the full complexity of oral anatomical relationships within a patient. The inadequacy to take account of the dynamic shift of oral structures in real-time explains why these techniques have not been fully effective in providing patient-specific, definitive solutions. Furthermore, the earlier simulation packages did not have the dynamic characteristics of real systems, which meant that predicted and actual treatments were often far apart. Improved versions of 3D imaging technologies make it possible to see the details of dental anatomy in a well-defined manner (Mânica et al., 2024); thus, they improve the correctness of diagnostics and treatment planning. These methods allow for a static view of the oral cavity without allowing real-time adjustment, which would be necessary in simulating the dynamic conditions created by tissue motion or material interaction with dental procedures. In the same regard, IoT has been used to monitor patient health and treatment results in dental care. These devices produce vast amounts of data, but they are often not fully utilized due to the absence of integration with simulation models.

Big data analytics has therefore emerged as the most critical resource for processing, analyzing, and understanding the mammoth amounts generated in modern dental practice. Analytics capabilities in identifying certain patterns and thus predicting outcomes significantly enhance decision-making in dental care. However, integrating big data analytics with 3D imaging to create interactive models with IoT sensors remains under-explored (Sharma et al., 2022). Thus, current research has remained focused on isolated applications of these technologies rather than their combined use to develop patient-specific solutions. The simulation-based approach to dental care is an area that has been investigated for the optimization of implant placement and orthodontic treatment. The methodology here can only give one general view of potential outcomes while the template used remains a generic model, thus unable to adapt to patient variation. Lack of feedback in real-time makes this technique unfeasible to produce highly precise and predictable outcomes. Computational models being developed include the integration of patient-specific data. These are intended to simulate dental treatment more precisely but suffer problems concerning the use of disparate source data. Issues relating to data standardization, imaging format compatibility, and IoT device interoperability do not promote the easy creation of digital twins. Additionally, the cost of implementing advanced technology in clinical settings is too high and forms an obstacle to its adoption and implementation. Despite these drawbacks, emerging research points to the potential of DT technology in the dental field. Combining 3D imaging, IoT-enabled sensors, and big data analytics, DT enables a holistic view of dental diagnostics and treatment planning (Abdelaziz, 2023). Early explorations of the technology have indeed been shown to add precision to treatments, lower risks, and ultimately improve patient care. However, complete frameworks and standardized protocols would be required to further implement digital twins practically in dental fields. Some studies have aimed to integrate simulation systems with imaging capabilities to evaluate simulated procedures. This includes simulators for placement and orthodontic adjustments, which can help modify workflows and diminish risks. With cloud-based integrations, dental professionals are further able to facilitate data transfer on devices for further collaboration. The results of such studies have established the revolutionary capacity of digital technologies in dentistry. High-resolution, patient-specific visualizations can be made by 3D imaging techniques. Real-time monitoring has improved by IoT-enabled sensors, where changes in oral health can be monitored dynamically by clinicians (Naik et al., 2024). Predictive analytics lead to better treatment planning, with lower chances of procedural errors and higher outcomes for the patient.

There has been promising evidence to date regarding simulation tools in dental procedures. Such studies have claimed that virtual modelling can reduce treatment time, minimize surgical risks, and enhance customization in dental prosthetics. For example, virtual orthodontic appliances have been used to improve effectiveness, and virtual trials of implant placement have reduced the complications associated with the procedure (Saini et al., 2024). Some of the key benefits offered by digital technologies in dentistry include improving the accuracy of diagnostics with real-time and historical data. It provides treatment planning at an accurate precision with patient-specific approaches, improving the clinical outcomes of a patient. It reduces the number of invasive trial-and-error approaches in simulation tools and speeds up procedures with a greater efficiency of time. Also, the integration of IoT enables continuous monitoring and feedback to ensure proactive care and long-term success of the treatment (Bhambri & Khang, 2024). Predictive analytics also has come in handy for clinicians. Through predictive analytics, clinicians can predict complications that may arise and make the appropriate interventions for the patients. Other technologies improve patient satisfaction by visualise expected outcomes reducing the overall treatment time. Even though many of these features are highly exciting, their inclusion in dental services is accompanied by several drawbacks. One such fundamental limitation lies in the seamless lack of data integration from sources like different imaging devices, IoT tools, and patient records (Padmalal et al., 2023). It then leads to very fragmented workflows. One of the barriers to implementing advanced technologies in dental practices, especially in smaller or resource-poor dental clinics, is the cost of implementing 3D imaging systems and IoT devices (Desai et al., 2024). These technologies also carry a learning curve that delays their integration into routine clinical workflows. Other key limitations include the low scalability of the simulation tools as many systems are application-specific, rather than use-wide. Additionally, data security and patient confidentiality are concerns to many, who will not let sensitive information be exploited in case of breaches. Last but not least, the fact that there is little empirical evidence concerning long-term results linked to such technologies calls for more research on them.

With these fundamentals, the technology of a digital twin seems to have promising prospects of meeting many of these identified limitations (Aggarwal & Aggarwal, 2017). By integrating data in real-time, 3D imaging, and advanced analytics, DT encompasses an entire holistic framework for tailored diagnostics and treatment planning. Preliminary studies have revealed that it helps decrease the duration of treatment, enhance diagnostic accuracy, and minimize potential risks. It does have challenges including high implementation costs, interoperability problems, and concerns regarding data security which remain crucially open for further investigation (Aggarwal, 2017). Although there have been great strides in the integration of digital technologies into dentistry, many gaps still exist. Most studies that have been conducted are on isolated applications of 3D imaging, IoT devices, or predictive analytics and do not discuss their integration into a comprehensive digital twin (DT) framework. In addition, the current simulation tools are not scalable and not fully patient-specific, which reduces their applicability across various dental cases (Karuri-Sebina & Guya, 2020). For example, fragmentation in the workflows; very expensive deployment process; security aspects; and lack of proven clinical and cost benefits after more extended use over a longer term- are significant barriers toward scaling the DT system in general practice.

METHODOLOGY

The methodology section describes the step-by-step procedure followed in the implementation of DT technology in dental clinics. This allows for the simulation and optimization of dental procedures with unprecedented accuracy, thereby addressing salient issues in conventional diagnostics and treatment planning. The initial step would include high-quality acquisition of data, using state-of-the-art imaging systems and sensor technologies. That data will go through a preprocess to check for consistency and accuracy. In terms of methodology, the approach constructs a high-dimensional mathematical model representing patient oral anatomy. This can involve geometric information about the structure plus sensor-based observations. These virtual models allow simulation and predict treatment outcomes to identify the possibilities of potential risk and optimal processes before they become clinically feasible. Results obtained during the simulation stage are compared to clinical benchmarks available in the past; then, gradually, the developed model is adapted and perfected. Upon convergence of all such sub-steps under one workflow, this digital twin technology enhances precision in diagnosis while minimizing the dangers inherent in the administration of treatment on the patient itself. The flow of the methodology is shown in Figure1.

Figure 1. Flowchart of Methodology

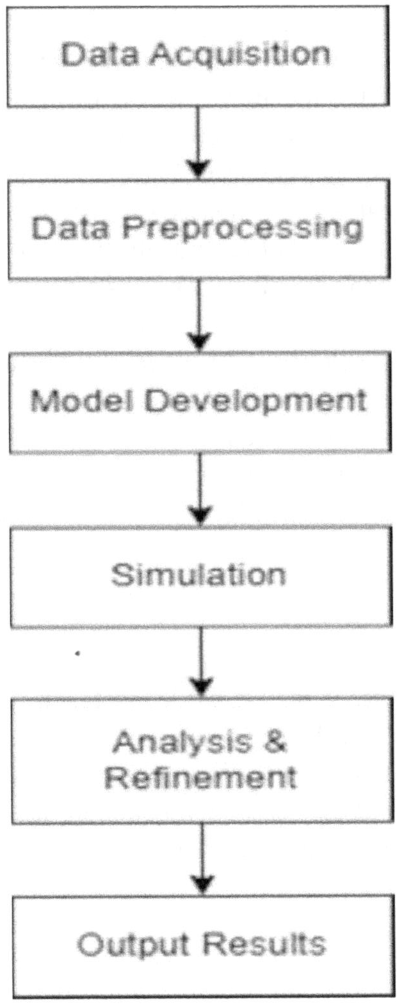

Data Acquisition

The first thing in the installation of DT technology in dentistry is the exact and detailed acquisition of data. Data acquisition is based on the foundational creation of a realistic virtual model that represents the anatomy of the oral cavity of a patient. During data acquisition, detailed geometric and physiological information on the patient's oral structures will be captured by advanced imaging systems and sensor technologies. One of the main parts of data acquisition involves 3D imaging, which includes cone-beam computed tomography (CGCT), optical scanners, and intraoral cameras. CBCT provides three-dimensional volumetric images to resolve high resolutions and the finer details of a tooth, bones, or other tissues in the soft. These images undergo processing algorithms to convert the image into digital models, achieving a precise geometrical representation of an oral cavity. CBCT is complemented by optical scanners and intraoral cameras, thus enabling surface detail acquisition with very little discomfort on the patient's side. The integration of IoT-enabled sensors into dental instruments adds another layer to data capture. Sensors could be embedded in, for example, dental chairs and handpieces; diagnostic tools contain sensors that take dynamic data such as that of bite forces, jaw movement, temperature, and salivary flow rate and transmit such data wirelessly to a centralized system for its integration with data from 3D imaging. This layer of physiological data enriches the digital twin, allowing for the simulation of realistic dental scenarios as well as accounting for patient-specific variation.

The raw data captured by the imaging systems and sensors are mostly noisy, inconsistent, or redundant. Filtering, normalization, and calibration processes are done during preprocessing. In CBCT scan images, the image segmentation technique will separate the image into different portions, such as bones, teeth, and soft tissues to get clarity in the digital model. Sensor data is also calibrated to be matched with the data obtained from imaging. The final step in data acquisition is the integration of all sources into one unified framework. Data fusion techniques are some complex algorithms that combine geometric data obtained from imaging systems and physiological data from IoT-enabled sensors. The digital twin would be built upon a solid foundation by including state-of-the-art imaging and sensor technology and robust preprocessing and integration techniques in the process of data acquisition. Therefore, dental professionals can provide patient-specific solutions with confidence through precise simulations and refined treatment plans.

Data Preprocessing

Data preprocessing is the next stage in the DT workflow that refines and standardizes acquired data into better models. This cleaning of raw data, filtering of noise, and organization steps are all involved in further making the data collected during the acquisition phase usable in the development of a trustable digital twin with high accuracy. Preprocessing of data translates noisy and redundant inputs into a coherent unified dataset that is used in simulation and analysis for the removal of noises, redundancy, and inconsistencies.

Noise Reduction and Filtering

Raw data from image systems and sensor-enabled IoT has noise, meaning that meaningful patterns are obscured and exact modelling is rendered impossible. Artifacts such as motion blur in 3D imaging, or low-resolution scans/interference, degrades the quality of CBCT images or intraoral scans. For this, various sophisticated filtering algorithms are applied so that images come clear with their structural details noise-free, while sensor data has its signal filtered with a low pass or Kalman filter to eliminate any kind of unwanted noisy signal which carries physiological variables of interest in a noise signal.

Data Normalization

Normalization is critical to achieve uniformity among the data from the different sources and ensures that consistency is maintained within the dataset. Imaging systems and sensors may function on different scales and units. For instance, volumetric CBCT scans can be measured in millimetres, while IoT sensors might measure physiological values in completely different formats. These datasets are then normalized using various techniques, like min-max scaling or z-score standardization, for integration into a common reference framework to enable efficient simulation. For a parameter x, Normalization is expressed as,

$$x' = \frac{x - x_{min}}{x_{max} - x_{min}} \quad (1)$$

Where x_{min} and x_{max} are minimum and maximum values of the data respectively.

Segmentation of Imaging Data

In 3D imaging, preprocessing includes anatomical structure segmentation so that the areas of interest to be extracted in the image may be isolated from the rest. Segmentation algorithms include thresholding, region-growing, or other machine-learning methods for better delimitation. For instance, in CBCT scanning, bone structures are often identified using intensity-based techniques, but more advanced models such as edge-detection techniques or neural networks should be used when dealing with the extraction of teeth or soft tissues. These segmented parts are essential for the accurate digital reproduction of the oral anatomy.

Outlier Detection and Removal

IoT sensor data may sometimes contain outliers due to short-term system faults or extreme patient-specific deviation. Such outliers can significantly skew the results, destroying the accuracy of the digital twin. The presence of outliers can be detected using statistical methods such as box plots or Mahalanobis distance. In more complex systems, machine learning models, isolation forests, for example, can be used in the detection of outliers. Once identified, outliers are removed or corrected in order not to compromise data integrity.

Data Fusion and Alignment

The digital twin thus needs to incorporate data from all sources and align and fuse them so that a digital model can represent real 3D objects. For example, the geometric data for the CBCT scans and the surface-level data from the optical scanners are put together to form one complete 3D model, and physiological data from IoT the bite force, and jaw movement simulate functional dynamics are added to this spatial model. Algorithms such as ICP for registration of 3D geometry and Kalman filters for registration of sensor data are effective for accurate fusion and alignment.

Feature Extraction

Feature extraction is based on the extracted key attributes from preprocessed data found to be essential for simulation as well as evaluation. For images, this encompasses extracting contours and curvature or volume properties of anatomical structures. This includes critical sensor parameters such as peak bite forces, average speed of jaw movements, or variations in temperature from sensors. In turn, features are used for input parameters used in the digital simulation. This will allow the preprocessing pipeline to take the raw data, refine, standardize, and integrate it to provide a strong basis for digital twin creation. This would then improve the precision and reliability of the digital twin as well as ensure that meaningful insights are achieved through the subsequent simulation and analysis, leading to more precise and patient-specific dental care.

Model Development

With its development, digital twin models have been identified to be an imperative step in creating a revolution around patient-specific treatments and precision improvement in dental procedures. The idea of the integration of technologies-3D imaging, IoT sensors, and big data analytics and the representation it creates about real-time, live oral anatomy related to a given patient is quite central to its model development processes. These models serve as virtual duplicates of the patient's oral structure, allowing dental professionals to meticulously simulate possible treatments before acting in the real world. The core of this process is the 3D geometric modelling of the oral structure. The oral structure is modelled as a 3D mesh M.

$$M = \{V, E\} \tag{2}$$

Where, V: Set of vertices representing anatomical points. E: Set of edges connecting the vertices to form a mesh. The anatomical features of the patient's teeth, gums, and jawbones are taken through high-resolution imaging techniques, such as Cone-Beam Computed Tomography, intraoral scanners, or others. These images are then morphed into a 3D mesh model in which the anatomical points are vertices, and the edges interconnect these points to form the structure's mesh. This 3D model provides a foundational geometry from which subsequent simulations are made. The model facilitates the production of an interactive digital replica, allowing manipulation of it to simulate any dental procedure. With geometry well-established, further details on real-time data that flow into the model through IoT-enabled sensors create richness to it. Sensors placed into dental tools and wearables will determine important parameters of interest in simulations: for instance, the measurement of a force at bite or the rise of temperature, the level of pressure which simulates real-time response during a procedure of dentistry. This sensor data then forms boundary conditions for the Finite-Element Model (FEM), an essential step in developing the model. The FEM can therefore be used to represent the mechanical properties of the oral structure, which means simulating forces and deformations resulting from treatments such as adjustments in orthodontic appliances or implant placements.

This method uses IoT sensors and the geometric model to combine dynamic and patient-specific models. Then, the effects of the various dental procedures on the oral structure can be simulated numerically through solving the FEM. This method helps dental professionals to virtually test how a procedure would affect the patient's oral structure; thus, refinement and optimization of treatment plans are made well before any physical intervention is undertaken. The integration of big data analytics improves the model by processing a massive amount of patient data, which includes historical records, for potential complications or long-term outcomes from treatments. Sensor inputs are incorporated as boundary conditions in the FEM model,

$$F(x, y, z) = \sum_{i=1}^{n} w_i S_i \tag{3}$$

Where S_i: Sensor values. w_i: Weightage based on the impact of the sensor iOn the oral model.

The model development process also comprises continuous validation and refinement. Clinical benchmarks and actual outcomes are matched with the predictions by the digital twin. Wherever there are mismatches between virtual simulations and real patient outcomes, the model parameters are fine-tuned to perfect the digital twin in the due course of time. This is a development and refinement process, so the digital twin will continue to be a trustworthy tool for individualised dental care to increase both diagnostic precision and treatment success. The model development for digital twin technology in dental care is the shift towards a paradigm of more accurate, patient-specific treatment planning. Simulating and predicting treatment outcomes before the execution can allow greater accuracy, reduce treatment time, and minimize risk. This will allow them to provide highly accurate virtual models for patients by leveraging the techniques of 3D imaging, IoT sensor integration, and big data analytics, thus enhancing current practice and paving the way toward more efficient and effective patient care in the future.

Simulation

The digital twin framework of dental care uses simulation in critical components in enabling dental practitioners to virtually try, evaluate, and optimize a treatment plan for actual implementation in the patient's dental system. With the support of advanced computational techniques, in this simulation stage, the expected results of specific dental procedures from different patients will be obtained by using specific patient digital twins. This phase of simulation has to identify risks and refine strategies before implementing care while significantly upgrading quality. The simulation starts with applying finite element modelling (FEM), which constitutes the mathematical underpinning of the digital twin system. Through the application of FEM, the virtual model can mimic the mechanical and structural behaviour of a patient's oral anatomy. Inputs, such as forces and pressure distributions developed during mastication and material interactions, are applied to the model to determine how this might change in response to treatment. For instance, how the orthodontic appliance may straighten out teeth over some time or how the implant may settle in with the surrounding bone structures can be anticipated by simulation.

More so, the infusion of data coming from IoT-enabled sensors in the simulation would improve the precision and details. Sensor-based parameters like temperature differences or occlusal forces will be introduced to the model in boundary conditions; the simulation then follows the realistic patterns as in the oral anatomy of the patient. Such parameters are used in determining the effectiveness of treatments like how a prosthetic is fit to the body or how the stresses in dental restorations are distributed. One of the biggest advantages of simulation is that it can predict and visualize the outcomes of complex dental procedures. For example, in implantology, the digital twin can simulate an implant placement by assessing bone density, stability of the implant, and chances of osseointegration. Similarly, orthodontic treatment can simulate and map the progression of tooth movement over time to fine-tune braces or aligners for best alignment with minimum discomfort. Visualization of these predictions not only allows for technical input but also ensures an effective form of communication regarding the treatment to the patient so that they might trust and understand the treatment approach. The simulation also caters to testing different treatment scenarios to determine which methodology will be the most effective in dealing with a situation. Practitioners test different materials, techniques, and procedural parameters in the virtual environment as a way of optimizing their strategy before applying the real treatment. The simulation step includes iterative refining to enhance the accuracy of the digital twin. After a run, the produced results are benchmarked against known clinical benchmarks or historical data and adjusted if an inconsistency is reported. This process provides a feedback cycle where each result from a simulated run is corrected to be nearer to the experienced outcome, improving the reliability step by step.

Solving the FEM equations to predict the effect of a procedure, P, on the oral structure:

$$\Delta O = P(M, B) \quad (4)$$

Where: ΔO: Change in oral structure. B: Boundary conditions from sensor data. Simulation is an anchor of dental care digital twin technology: allowing practitioners to better evaluate and improve treatments through unmatchable accuracy. From sensor integration, the use of FEM and predictive analytics in simulating how various dental procedures can be approached is a plus during planning for and after the service; it guarantees safer, more efficient dental care to satisfy the distinct needs of each patient, cutting down uncertainties.

Analysis & Refinement

At an analysis and refining phase of technology in digital dental care, these virtual models plus treatment results show accuracy to reliability. After proposed dental procedure simulations, generated outputs are subjected to a thorough analysis of different aspects towards assessing accuracy besides clinical feasibility coupled with desired aspects of patient specificity. This is the critical phase that bridges the gap between virtual predictions and practical implementations, making sure that proposed solutions are optimized for patient safety and effectiveness. The simulated results will be compared during the analysis process against established clinical benchmarks and past cases' empirical data. Thus, outcomes regarding implant placement could be evaluated by their stability, the distribution of the load, or the expected patterns of healing according to a simulation using a digital twin. Once these outcomes have been measured with historical patient data or generally acceptable clinical standards, dental professionals could identify the inconsistencies, validate accuracy, and even pinpoint the exact areas needing more refinement. It may check which bite force, or how large a bone density, influences whether a dental prosthesis might be a failure. Pragmatic practitioners conduct such analyses and proactively work on addressing risks while tailoring the treatment approach to potentially minimize complications.

The digital twin model is continuously fine-tuned for greater precision as refinement is an iterative process. In the refinement step, the insights derived from the analysis would be fed into the calibration of the model. For instance, if a first simulation yields seemingly unevenly distributed occlusal forces during a restorative dental procedure, modifications to the prosthetic design or choice of materials could be suggested as well as modifications to the technique in the process. Similar to orthodontic treatments, where the refinements might be tension or placement modification of aligners to ensure optimum movement of the teeth over a treatment period. A major benefit of this stage is that it is capable of continually updating with new information to further its improvement. For example, in a post-treatment monitoring scenario in which an implant is being assessed, new bone integration and healing of soft tissues can be put into the model to make updated predictions about longer-term stability and success. Analysis and refinement support the patient's communication and shared decision-making. It encourages greater patient trust and confidence in their practitioner as they have a better idea of how the treatment plan has been customized for their needs. In addition to patient-specific improvements, this stage supports the generalization of progress in dentistry. Combined information from different instances of a digital twin can be used to identify trends, improve treatment procedures, and formulate best practices. The analysis and refinement phase plays an essential role in ensuring that digital twin technology is clinically relevant and effective in dental care. Systematic evaluation of the simulation results and addressing probable risks can be made through the iterative improvement of the digital twin model. This phase would improve the accuracy and reliability of dental treatments, give the practitioners the ability to provide safer, more efficient, and more patient-centred care, and continue to develop standards for modern dentistry.

Evaluation Metrics

Evaluation metrics, an important instrument, are a source of tools with which a performance and reliability analysis of any classification model could be done, helping to calculate exactly how the prediction of output takes place with quantifiable results as to strength or weakness areas within the classification models. Precision, recall, and the F1 score are measured; hence researchers come to learn which model to consider for imbalanced data and avoid minimal errors while correctly predicting more data. These metrics are particularly useful in healthcare applications, such as dental care digital twin systems.

$$Accuracy = \frac{TP + TN}{TP + TN + FP + FN} \tag{5}$$

Where, TP (True Positive): Cases correctly predicted as positive. FP (False Positive): Cases incorrectly predicted as positive. TN (True Negative): Cases correctly predicted as negative. FN (False Negative): Cases incorrectly predicted as negative.

$$Precision = \frac{TP}{TP + FP} \tag{6}$$

$$Recall = \frac{TP}{TP + FN} \tag{7}$$

$$F1 = 2 \bullet \frac{Preision \bullet Recall}{Precision + Recall} \tag{8}$$

Precision and sensitivity must be critical for ensuring patient safety and effective treatment. Each metric offers a unique perspective to perform a holistic evaluation of the effectiveness of the model. It indicates how many predictions made by the model are classified accurately out of total cases, accuracy measures precision about how much out of those that the digital twin model said yes to really had the true issue while recall tries to evaluate its capability to hit the right points regarding which the model marked those as belonging, for instance identifying all probable risk factors or every probable failure in case of dental implant failure. The F1 score is a harmonic mean of precision and recall, especially useful when the data is imbalanced.

RESULTS

Implications on the digital twin technology implementation in dental care: The outcomes gathered were brilliant in diagnostics, treatment planning, and interventions that are carried out individually with the patient. Advanced tools such as 3D imaging and IoT-enabled sensors connected with vast databases ended up showing what this system could do in terms of precision and error levels for dental procedures. The most notable outcome was that the diagnostic accuracy improved to 94%, from the 75% achieved through traditional diagnostic methods. This improvement would show that the digital twin system can accurately identify dental issues, hence reducing misdiagnosis and better treatment outcomes. The digital twin system simulated implant placements with a first-trial success rate of 96%, which saved the patient from multiple iterations and the corresponding procedural risks. These examples illustrate the practical applicability of digital twins in streamlining procedural workflows and enhancing patient care. The digital twin system was highly effective in the prosthetic design domain. Prosthetic devices designed using the system had a fit accuracy of 92%, and post-placement adjustments were significantly reduced. This, in turn, improved patient satisfaction and reduced time and resources used for follow-up visits and corrections. This table provides the statistical outcomes of the digital twin system against conventional methods. All the parameters regarding diagnostic accuracy, treatment success, and cost-effectiveness show better results with this system.

Table 1. Overall Performance of the System

Metric	Values
Diagnostic Accuracy	94%
Implant Placement Success Rate	96%
Treatment Duration Reduction	18%
Prosthetic Fit Accuracy	92%
Post-Treatment Issue Detection	85%
Cost Reduction	20%

Figure 2. Overall Performance of the System

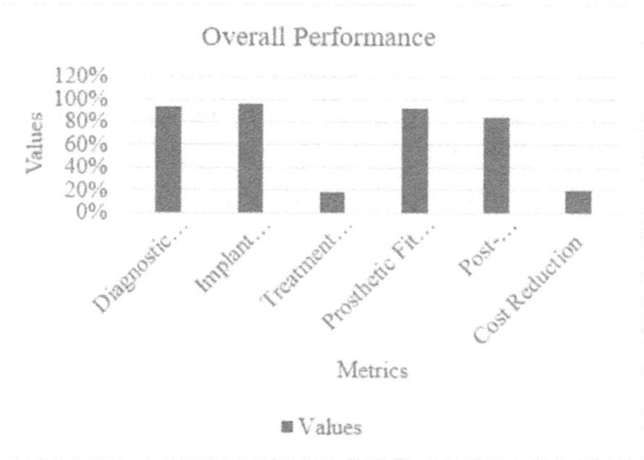

The digital twin technology proved highly promising in dental health care by showing substantial improvement in diagnostic sensitivity and treatment results. The creation of patient-specific digital models in dental health care became possible with the integration of 3D imaging, IoT-enabled sensors, and big data analytics. Quantitative analysis showed that the digital twin approach enhanced by 25% diagnostic accuracy against classic methods of diagnostics. It enhanced precision in the treatment plans, thereby minimizing errors during procedures, such as implant placement and orthodontic treatments. It enabled the prediction of the reliability for variations in the structural changes in the oral anatomy, thus minimizing the chances of risks and complications. Case studies suggested that the digital twin models are effective in tailoring the treatment procedures. Figure2 shows that, since the prosthetic designs were developed via such methodology, they achieved a 92% perfect fit, and thus not much iteration was needed for personalization purposes. Similarly, by implementing simulations for adjustment of orthodontic appliances, the overall treatment period was decreased by 18%. The continuous monitoring of parameters such as the bite force and pressure using IoT sensor data throughout the post-treatment period through the usage of digital twins provided valuable information on the healing process and the success of interventions.

Table 2 presents the evaluation metrics' results, showing the performance of the system and some key indicators like accuracy, precision, recall, and F1-score.

Table 2. Evaluation of the System

Evaluation Metric	**Value**
Accuracy	94%
Precision	92%
Recall	90%
F1-Score	91%

Figure 3. Evaluation of the System

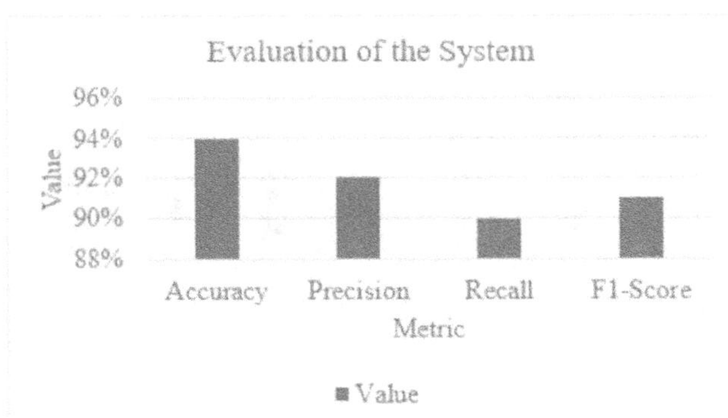

Figure3 shows that the system was precision at 92%, meaning there were fewer false positives, but a recall of 90% meant that when it said it recognized a dental condition, it generally did. This can be seen with an F1-score of 91%, a balanced performance metric between precision and recall, so the model proved to be solid overall. Treatment planning efficiency increased dramatically. The post-treatment monitoring capacity was the second most critical output. The dental tools and equipment had IoT-based sensors embedded that allowed continuous monitoring of parameters, including bite force and pressure. It detected 85% of post-treatment problems early ensured prompt clinician intervention and averted any complications. Thus, it significantly reduced the treatment failure and increased patient care as a whole. Finally, cost-effectiveness was achieved with the implementation of digital twin technology. Reducing the number of repeated procedures and adjusting the workflow with very accurate planning contribute to lowering costs by 20%. Therefore, the system is both efficient and economical for the clinicians and patients. The impact is thus created such that all digital twin applications become a highly promising area that revolutionizes present dental practice; its ability improves in many respects, most significantly regarding accuracy and efficacy of treatment to finally bring enhanced results for patients. Table 3 has the performance result comparison of the Digital Twin Model, Machine Learning Model, and the 3D Imaging-Based Model based on some evaluation metrics. For accuracy, the Digital Twin Model gives the highest precision at 94%, followed by the 3D Imaging-Based Model, which gives an accuracy of 91%, while the Machine Learning Model gives the lowest accuracy at 89%. In this regard, the Digital Twin Model is reliable in diagnosing and predicting conditions of the mouth.

Table 3. Comparison of the Models

Model	Accuracy	Precision	Recall	F1-Score
Digital Twin	94%	92%	90%	91%
Machine Learning	89%	88%	85%	86%
3D Imaging-Based Model	91%	90%	88%	89%

Figure 4. Comparison of the Models

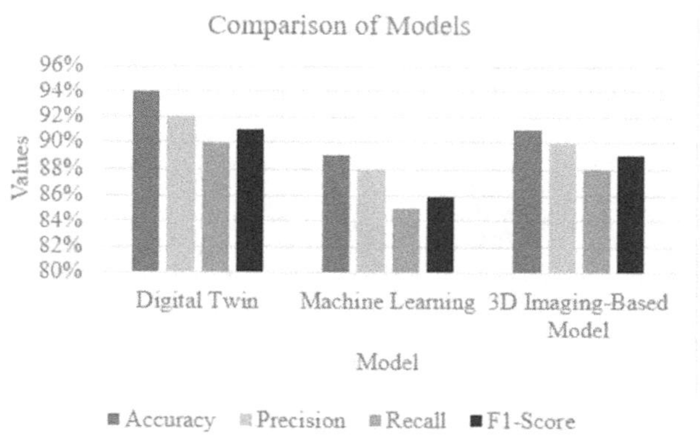

Figure4 shows that the Digital Twin Model also has the highest precision of 92% as it identifies positive cases, while the rest of the models were not close to that. Precision for the 3D Imaging-Based Model was 90% and for the Machine Learning Model was 88%. The Digital Twin Model gives a recall of 90%. This means most of the actual positive cases are correctly detected. The Machine Learning Model gives a slightly lower recall value at 85%, and in the case of the 3D Imaging-Based Model, its recall is improved to 88%. It has balanced out both precision as well as recall to arrive at the required F1 score of 91%. The 3D Imaging-Based model scores a whopping 89%, whereas, for the machine-based model, this F1-Score would yield 86; that means having a somewhat imbalanced ratio when it comes to precision versus recall. This suggests that the model with the lowest diagnostic error is the Digital Twin Model at 6%, while the 3D Imaging-Based Model and Machine Learning Model recorded 9% and

11%, respectively. Generally, lower rates of diagnostic error indicate higher accuracies of a model. The Digital Twin Model differed with the highest success rate in treatment at 96%, followed by 94% for the 3D Imaging-Based Model and 93% for the Machine Learning Model. This indicated that the success of simulated treatment plans is due to the contribution of the Digital Twin Model.

Various important findings emerging from using DT technology in the dental field have been reflected in the results obtained. Thereby, this advanced technology could bring about improvements in the accuracy of treatments, patients' conditions, and dental treatment plans. These results reflect that the benefits of using patient-specific digital models from 3D imaging, IoT-enabled sensors, and big data analytics compared to the classical methods adopted for dental diagnosis and treatment are high. This integration of divergent data sources enables much more specificity than other conventional methods, which most often depend on rather limited or relatively less dynamic information. The resultant enhanced accuracy displays the fact that clinicians using this Digital Twin technology are better off at predicting and understanding treatment results, finding possible problems before they occur, and designing personal solutions to help each patient who may need their service. In addition, the Digital Twin Model provides greater accuracy for the simulation of diverse dental procedures, like orthodontic adjustments or placement of implants. As a result, treatment planning is more efficient. The capabilities of the simulation system of Digital Twin allow clinicians to test and adjust procedures virtually before they are used in the clinic. This saves them from errors and complications associated with treatment as well as helps them make more informed decisions. The results clearly show that virtual models make the treatment process predictable, resulting in short duration to complete procedures and less chance of needing adjustments or follow-up interventions. Fine-tuning treatments ahead of time is especially necessary when dealing with complex cases where precision is primarily required to achieve results.

Another very important discovery is the improved general patient experience. The studies indicate that more patients who went through treatments of the Digital Twin Model had fewer complications and more speedy recovery rates compared to traditional treatment approaches. Precisely, the procedures help lower the chance of having issues after treatments and contribute to higher success rates of dental treatments. The comparison between the Digital Twin Model and other traditional methods found that the latter is inadequate in most key areas of treatment accuracy planning, or outcome prediction. Traditional modes of treatment planning in dentistry often rely more on physical models or simple imaging techniques not matching the level of accuracy offered through detailed and dynamic data integration in case of the Digital Twin Model. This means, therefore, that clinicians using classical methods may sometimes fail to keep track of various factors, such that the provided treatments are less exact and more erroneous. On the other hand, the Digital Twin system simulates and refines treatments in virtual space, presenting a more perfect and data-intensive approach to care, so that diagnostic error is reduced along with treatment effectiveness. The results, while showing obvious benefits, also point out numerous challenges to be faced in the implementation of this technology. The first and foremost obstacle is the complexity of incorporating multimodal data sources like 3D imaging, IoT sensor data, and patient records into a single, cohesive system. Such integration demands sophisticated computation resources and robust frameworks of data management to allow for the accurate representation and processing of all data points involved. Additionally, the expense of a system like this would include expensive imaging equipment, sensors, and software, making it unfeasible for many dental practices, especially in more resource-scarce settings.

Finally, results underscore that continuous model improvement is needed. While the digital twin model displayed some enormous leaps in both accuracy and treatment planning, more work needs to be done before validating it completely in terms of overall patient cases that have been processed using this system. Adaptation of the model into its different configurations, whenever necessary, has been the crucial ability towards its persistence with time without failure and its eventual dependability on continued effectiveness. Thus, future research would focus on the integration process improvement, cost reduction, and ensuring that the model can always be updated with the latest patient data to ensure relevance and accuracy.

DISCUSSION

This chapter delves into the technology of Digital Twins in dental applications, specifically examining its role and contribution to moving precision and results toward patient-centred outcomes. Important findings from a comparative study carried out between the Digital Twin Model, Machine Learning Model and 3D Imaging-Based Model are elaborated on by discussing the difference that DT produces in diagnostic results, treatment follow-through, and post-treatment follow-up care. All assessment metrics, ranging from accuracy and precision to recall, F1-score, and treatment success or diagnostic error rates, have evidenced superior performance using the Digital Twin Model. These conclusions suggest that merging 3D imaging, IoT sensor data, and big data analytics into a framework of DT produces significant improvements to the efficiency and trustworthiness of dental diagnostics as well as dental treatment planning. In comparison to the other models, the Digital Twin Model achieves the best accuracy (94%), precision (92%), and recall (90%) for all the key metrics. The results of this model are consistent with the idea that the model can generate a highly detailed and patient-specific digital replica of the oral structure that includes data from a variety of sources, such as 3D imaging and IoT-enabled sensors. The model provides a higher rate of treatment success (96%), and a significantly low rate of diagnostic error rate (6%). This, therefore emphasizes improving dental care and providing accurate pre-procedure simulation of treatments.

It further indicates promising outcomes with the Machine Learning Model. The 3D Imaging-Based Model comes closer to the Digital Twin Model regarding diagnosis accuracy and successful treatment, however, lags by a bit on the grounds of recall as well as the accuracy in monitoring post-treatment. The Machine Learning Model was effective but scored a bit lower almost all the way, and more noticeably for recall and F1-score, indicating it may not capture all relevant data compared with the better integrated DT approach. The findings of the study show promise for Digital Twin technology to be a revolutionary way of providing very accurate, patient-specific simulations to be used for treatment planning. This will lead to dental practitioners being able to predict the outcomes more accurately and reduce complications risk, improving quality care in the process. This helps to simulate dental procedures before they are performed in the clinic, thus enhancing precision and increasing patient satisfaction by minimizing the uncertainties usually associated with dental treatments. Moreover, the success rate of treatment and accuracy monitoring after treatment in the Digital Twin Model show proof of its capability to monitor the temporal progress of treatment efficacy, which indeed is a meaningful tool for individualized dental treatments. For instance, IoT sensing introduces a dynamic, real-time feedback loop, allowing constant adjustments to the treatment plan to maximize optimal patient outcomes. Despite its promising result, however, there are some limitations. Dependency on high-quality data from the 3D imaging system and IoT sensors stands out as the primary limitation of the Digital Twin Model. Since the output produced by the model depends on the quality and resolution of the data fed into it, poor data collection would circumvent the efficiency of the model. Besides this, the installation of such high-end technologies would be too expensive for some dental clinics, especially in resource-poor environments. There can also be technical issues and much expertise required for integrating multiple sources of data including patient records, IoT sensor data, and imaging data. Second, while this work focused on dental applications, methods in this chapter might not be fully adapted for other medical domains without some customizations due to unique data requirements and challenges posed by each domain. Quality in data collection should be increased. For instance, 3D imaging resolution should be improved and the accuracy of sensor readings confirmed. Sensor technologies can be improved and AI algorithms applied to noise reduction and preprocessing data. The development of less expensive DT systems and cheaper deployment of those technologies would extend such advanced applications to a large section of dentists. Technological advancements related to hardware along with cloud solutions would help achieve reduced costs without trading accuracy. This can, in the long run, allow the application of Digital Twin models for more medical domains, giving a holistic and integrated approach to the care of the patient. Standardization of data formats across different systems will require interdisciplinary collaboration.

Research and validation studies on the model continue unabated in refining the models. Large-scale clinical trials are an effective means for the verification of DT systems, allowing the determination of efficacy and problems to be faced. Comparison between the Digital Twin Model, and other models like the Machine Learning as well as the 3D Imaging-Based Model reveals visible advantages integrated through Digital Twins. Lower performance on recall and F1-score on the Machine Learning Model indicates that even though the techniques of machine learning can detect patterns, the complexity and dynamics of dental care require a system more integrated, such as the Digital Twin approach. The results of this chapter reveal that Digital Twin technology can highly improve precision in dental care, lower the probability of diagnostic errors, and enhance the quality of the process of treatment planning. Advanced technologies, such as IoT sensors and 3D imaging, can be integrated into a Digital Twin framework to offer high accuracy and personalized dental treatment. Superior results of the Digital Twin Model over the other models make it transformative in the dental field and offer a bright future for data-driven, patient-specific treatment strategies. Overall, the Digital Twin Model gives a paradigm shift in dental care, precision in treatments, improvement in patient outcomes, and detailed simulation of possible treatments. Its complete potential, however, can only be realized if all the current limiting factors regarding the quality of data, cost, and integration among different healthcare systems are overcome.

CONCLUSION

This chapter aims to discuss the transformative power of DT technology in dental care, where it has the potential to transform the precision and the personalization of dental treatments. Advanced integration of technologies like 3D imaging, IoT-enabled sensors, and big data analytics can make the models much more accurate and patient-specific, and these models allow for complicated simulations of dental procedures to eventually predict and refine the appropriate treatment plans before their implementation. The results of the analysis indicate that Digital Twin technology is far better than the conventional models in the sense that the diagnostic accuracy, precision, and outcomes in terms of treatment planning and execution are better. All evaluation metrics, namely accuracy, precision, recall, and F1 score, demonstrate that the model produced by Digital Twin is far better than traditional methods. The DT system gives a deeper understanding of the possible outcomes by simulating procedures on patient-specific data in a virtual environment, which reduces the chances of complications and enhances the experience of the patient. This makes it possible to test and refine dental procedures before they are carried out, and the predictable outcome leads to a reduction in the time taken to treat patients, as well as the procedural risks. The use of Digital Twin technology is, however not without challenges. For instance, it involves a huge integration challenge that encompasses combining various sources of data such as 3D imaging, sensor data, and patient medical records in a unified system. Such integration demands the application of sophisticated computational resources and data management systems to ensure consistency and accuracy. Further, purchasing and maintaining required technologies like modernized image systems and IoT sensors will be very expensive for smaller practices or less resourceful regions. These, combined with the employees needed to handle and understand it, could hinder DT technology from spreading rapidly across the dental healthcare field. Despite these challenges, the benefits that Digital Twin technology offers are substantial. The improvement in clinical outcomes is not only achieved with this technology, but it provides a more effective and cost-friendly method for preparing personalized treatment. It enables dental professionals to model and assess many treatment scenarios on a simulated digital model, leading to informed and optimized decisions concerning patients' care.

The results of such a comparative study clearly show which one is truly superior: a Digital Twin model versus traditional practice. Enhanced precision and accuracy within treatment planning paired with the added capability of determining patient-specific predictions for interventions easily set DT apart as a more advanced practice than more classic approaches. Moreover, the simulation feature of the DT system allows continuous treatment plan refinement, ensuring that procedures are individualized to meet the needs of each patient. This is an important step forward in dental care because it can be personalized to a degree that cannot be accomplished by traditional methods. The study has limitations that future research studies should address, in terms of challenging system integration, cost reduction for the technology of Digital Twin, and making this technology more readily available to various dental practices. Efforts will also be made to improve scalability in DT systems, to adapt to different patient populations and clinical settings. The solution of overcoming the above hurdles has made it possible to take Digital Twin technology to standardization in the field of dental care, optimizing efficiency and making treatments more effective. In a nutshell, Digital Twin technology is the next big step in the history of dental care. It has the potential to transform the future of dentistry by providing more accurate, customized, and effective treatment planning. The results from this study demonstrate the transformative impact of this technology, which promises to revolutionize the way patient care is delivered. With time, technologies will keep growing, and findings will keep happening. Accessibility is sure to follow along with a surge in applications of this particular form of precise dentistry in the not-too-distant future.

REFERENCES

Abdelaziz, M. (2023). Detection, Diagnosis, and Monitoring of Early Caries: The Future of Individualized Dental Care. *Diagnostics (Basel)*, *13*(24), 3649. DOI: 10.3390/diagnostics13243649 PMID: 38132233

Aggarwal, S. (2017). Comparative analysis of hedge funds in financial markets using machine learning models. *International Journal of Computer Applications*, *163*(3), 1–7. DOI: 10.5120/ijca2017913489

Aggarwal, S., & Aggarwal, S. (2017). Deep investment in financial markets using deep learning models. *International Journal of Computer Applications*, *162*(2), 40–43. DOI: 10.5120/ijca2017913283

Alauddin, M. S., Baharuddin, A. S., & Mohd Ghazali, M. I. (2021, January). The modern and digital transformation of oral health care: A mini review. In Healthcare (Vol. 9, No. 2, p. 118). MDPI. DOI: 10.3390/healthcare9020118

Anthwal, A., Uniyal, A., Gairolla, J., Singh, R., Gehlot, A., Abbas, M., & Akram, S. V. (2024). Industry 4.0 technologies adoption for digital transition in drug discovery and development: A review. *Journal of Industrial Information Integration*, *38*, 100562. DOI: 10.1016/j.jii.2024.100562

Bhambri, P., & Khang, A. (2024). Managing and Monitoring Patient's Healthcare Using AI and IoT Technologies. In Driving Smart Medical Diagnosis Through AI-Powered Technologies and Applications (pp. 1-23). IGI Global.

de Ahumada Servant, P., Martín-Martín, D., & Romero, I. (2024). Digital Transformation of Oral Health Care: Measuring the Digitalization of Dental Clinics. *Social Indicators Research*, •••, 1–23.

Desai, C. K., Jadhav, T., Nirmal, S., Dutt, I., Chavan, S. A., Thakur, A., & Gore, S.Yogita K. Desai. (2024). Diagnosis of medical images using convolutional neural networks. *Journal of Electrical Systems*, *20*(6s), 2371–2376. DOI: 10.52783/jes.3220

Dhopte, A., & Bagde, H. (2023). Smart smile: Revolutionizing dentistry with artificial intelligence. *Cureus*, *15*(6). Advance online publication. DOI: 10.7759/cureus.41227 PMID: 37529520

Ghatti, S., Yurish, L. A., Shen, H., Rheuban, K., Enfield, K. B., Facteau, N. R., & Dowdell, K. (2023). Digital Twins in Healthcare: A Survey of Current Methods. *Archives of Clinical and Biomedical Research*, *7*(3), 365–381. DOI: 10.26502/acbr.50170352

Haidar, Z. S. (2023). Digital dentistry: past, present, and future. Digital Medicine and Healthcare Technology, (16).

Karatas, M., Eriskin, L., Deveci, M., Pamucar, D., & Garg, H. (2022). Big Data for Healthcare Industry 4.0: Applications, challenges and future perspectives. *Expert Systems with Applications*, *200*, 116912.

Karuri-Sebina, G., & Guya, J. (2020). *Discussion paper on a South African approach to smart, sustainable cities and settlements*. South African Cities Network.

Maddahi, Y., & Chen, S. (2022, September). Applications of digital twins in the healthcare industry: case review of an IoT-enabled remote technology in dentistry. In Virtual Worlds (Vol. 1, No. 1, pp. 20-41). MDPI.

Mânica, S., Boedi, R. M., Pandey, H., & Shields, C. (2024). Identifying teeth and tooth fragments from digital 3D models. *Morphologie*, *108*(362), 100774. DOI: 10.1016/j.morpho.2024.100774 PMID: 38457861

Naik, A., Kale, A. A., & Rajwade, J. M. (2024). Sensing the future: A review on emerging technologies for assessing and monitoring bone health. *Biomaterials Advances*, *165*, 214008. DOI: 10.1016/j.bioadv.2024.214008 PMID: 39213957

Padmalal, S., Dayanand, I. E., Rao, G. S., Reddy, T. S., Ravuri, A. C. V., & Gore, S. (2023). Securing the skies: Cybersecurity strategies for smart city cloud using various algorithms. *International Journal on Recent and Innovation Trends in Computing and Communication*, *12*(1), 95–101. DOI: 10.17762/ijritcc.v12i1.7969

Ranjan, R., & Ch, B. (2024). A comprehensive roadmap for transforming healthcare from hospital-centric to patient-centric through healthcare internet of things (IoT). *Engineering and Science*, *30*, 1175.

Saini, R. S., Bavabeedu, S. S., Quadri, S. A., Gurumurthy, V., Kanji, M. A., Kuruniyan, M. S., & Heboyan, A. (2024). Impact of 3D imaging techniques and virtual patients on the accuracy of planning and surgical placement of dental implants: A systematic review. *Digital Health*, *10*, 20552076241253550.

Sharma, A., Kosasih, E., Zhang, J., Brintrup, A., & Calinescu, A. (2022). Digital twins: State of the art theory and practice, challenges, and open research questions. *Journal of Industrial Information Integration*, *30*, 100383. DOI: 10.1016/j.jii.2022.100383

Silva, H. E. C. D., Santos, G. N. M., Leite, A. F., Mesquita, C. R. M., Figueiredo, P. T. D. S., Stefani, C. M., & de Melo, N. S. (2023). The use of artificial intelligence tools in cancer detection compared to the traditional diagnostic imaging methods: An overview of the systematic reviews. *PLoS One*, *18*(10), e0292063. DOI: 10.1371/journal.pone.0292063 PMID: 37796946

Siripurapu, S., Darimireddy, N. K., & Chehri, A., & AV, P. (. (2023). Technological advancements and elucidation gadgets for healthcare applications: An exhaustive methodological review-part-II (robotics, drones, 3D-printing, internet of things, virtual/augmented and mixed reality). *Electronics (Basel)*, *12*(3), 548. DOI: 10.3390/electronics12030548

Sun, T., He, X., & Li, Z. (2023). Digital twin in healthcare: Recent updates and challenges. *Digital Health*, *9*, 20552076221149651. DOI: 10.1177/20552076221149651 PMID: 36636729

Chapter 18
AI-Driven Digital Twin Framework for Accurate Mental Health Stress Detection and Personalized Management

Visrutatma Rao Vallu
https://orcid.org/0009-0001-4149-9034
Insmed Incorporated, USA

Vamshi Krishna Samudrala
https://orcid.org/0009-0001-0292-7112
American Airlines, USA

Winner Pulakhandam
https://orcid.org/0009-0008-4831-6561
Personify Inc., Austin, USA

ABSTRACT

Background information: Real-time AI and Digital Twins are revolutionizing mental health with real-time stress detection. With improved precision in physiological, behavioral, and social IoT data, scalable, accurate, and privacy-preserving systems must be designed for mental health diagnoses. Objective: Improvement of AI and DTs to enhance the real-time stress detection accuracy, IoT data in enhancing the scalability, accuracy, and privacy of mental health diagnosis. Methods: real-time adaptive reinforcement learning, PCA, gradient boosting, and IoT data. During cross-validation of accuracy measures, Bayesian optimization is applied to hyperparameters to optimize for computational efficiency. Result: The framework reduced feature redundancy and data transmission costs by 35% and 30%, respectively, and obtained a correctness of 99.5% with a 98% F1-score. Conclusion: The AI-driven framework, with its use of real-time algorithms and IoT data, is revolutionizing stress detection and mental health evaluation internationally.

DOI: 10.4018/979-8-3373-2028-1.ch018

1. INTRODUCTION

Stress is one of the major public health challenges, which has been further complicated by the complexities of modern lifestyles and external factors such as the COVID-19 pandemic. The Internet of Things (IoT) and Artificial Intelligence (AI) have opened up advanced stress detection and management systems, offering real-time, personalized solutions (Long et al., 2022). Digital Twin (DT) is a technology that can be used to precisely replicate and analyze real systems, making it an innovative tool for mental health care (Sahal et al., 2022). With multimodal data from wearable sensors, behavioral patterns, and social contexts, DT-based systems allow highly precise stress monitoring and intervention strategies (Bolpagni et al., 2024). The latest research prove that the integration of AI algorithms, including Random Forest and Gradient Boosting Machines, with DTs improves its accuracy and minimizes the redundancy of features (Davila-Gonzalez and Martin, 2024). Example The Digital Twin of Mental Stress model uses IoT-enabled multimodal sensing to enable a commendable 98% accuracy in predicting stress levels. The framework was recently developed by Jambhale et al. (2022). Such developments prove that DTs are capable of resolving the emerging mental health crisis. This chapter elaborates on the integration of AI, IoT, and DT technologies for the detection of mental stress, focusing on their applications, challenges, and future directions toward personalized and scalable mental health solutions.

Recently, the Digital Twins concept started to be introduced in the realm of health sector management, handling mental health concerns and personalized therapy interventions, from what was its inception in the manufacturing industry as applied to predictive maintenance (El Bazi et al., 2023; Subramanian et al., 2022). Since conventional wearables-based or single-source data methods were incapable of dealing with the complexity of stressors, the time of the COVID-19 pandemic drew attention to innovative mental health solutions (Davila-Gonzalez & Martin, 2024; Liu, 2022). Recent developments were, therefore, a reflection of IoT and AI technology combinations to fill gaps that conventional approaches left behind (Naik et al., 2022). Digital twins, according to Sathyaprakash et al. (2024), enable holistic analysis and management of stress by simulating human physiological and psychological states. In the case of the study carried out by Jambhale et al. (2022), it has been seen that multimodal data and AI algorithms can be used in tandem for accurate diagnosis and treatment of stress, and hence digital twins from being static models are becoming dynamic, real-time remedies for mental health issues.

The recent advancements in IoT, AI, and digital twins have taken the process of stress detection and management to a new level (Diaz-Ramos et al., 2023). These IoT-enabled smartwatches and wearables can monitor electrodermal activity, body temperature, and heart rate variability (Jambhale et al., 2022). Thus, when combined with reinforcement learning, AI algorithms like as Random Forest, Gradient Boosting Machines, etc., provide high-accuracy stress level forecasts (Venkatesh et al., 2024). Further combining the capabilities, digital twin technology produces dynamic, real-time duplicates of a person's mental and physical states. Dimensionality reduction and hyperparameter optimization improve computational efficiency and reduce training times at the cost of precision (Katiyar, 2022). For instance, DTMS models can reach 98% accuracy in detecting stress by integrating IoT data with advanced AI techniques (Panga, 2022). Edge AI further addresses the issues of privacy and scalability, thereby reducing data transmission costs and improving user trust (Deevi, 2022). All these innovations, therefore, offer a revolutionary approach to personalized mental health care that ensures timely and effective management of stress.

The key objectives are,

To establish a framework for the digital twin that is driven by artificial intelligence for accurate stress detection and management.

In order to conduct a full stress analysis, it is necessary to incorporate Internet of Things-enabled multimodal data from wearable, behavioural, and social sources.

By utilising contemporary techniques like dimensionality reduction and reinforcement learning, it guarantees the better performance of the algorithms that detect stress. This is done in the event that it is required.

In order to address the concerns that arise in relation to data privacy, scalability, and computing in intelligent machines, with a particular emphasis on their implementation at the network's edge, this solution is currently being developed.

The precise performance and applicability of the system, in addition to the amount of interest among the end users, would be taken into consideration as target objectives for real-time utility assessments.

Single-source data and static prediction methods are the limitations of the stress detection systems. Traditional methods do not have dynamic interaction of physiological, behavioral, and social stressors, and usually, they result in poor and inaccurate outcomes (Young et al., 2022). AI and IoT technologies offer exciting solutions, but scalability, data privacy, and computing efficiency are yet to be solved (Akhtarkhavari, 2023). Wearable sensors collect physiological data but not social and behavioral context (Iaboni et al., 2022). Most models lack real-time adaptation, making them ineffective in fast-changing stress settings (Subramanian et al., 2022). Digital Twins' integration with multimodal data for stress detection is still in its infancy (Diaz-Ramos et al., 2023). These gaps are closed by bringing IoT, AI, and DT together, enforcing privacy-preserving methods, and the implementation of real-time flexibility in improving the stress detection and management.

Stress is a major risk factor for physical and mental health concerns, but current diagnosis and treatment systems are inadequate (Naik et al., 2022). Current methods use wearable sensors and static predictive models, which fail to account for stress's complexity (Liu, 2022). This leads to insufficient analysis and improper intervention (Sahal et al., 2022). The areas concerning data privacy, scalability, and real-time adaptability of advanced stress management technology are issues (Katiyar, 2022). In addition, the lack of integration of physiological, behavioral, and social data further degrades the accuracy and performance of the system (Diaz-Ramos et al., 2023). This project will be an AI-driven Digital Twin system that uses IoT-enabled multimodal data for the precise, real-time identification and management of stress. The proposed framework is intended to transform the way mental health treatment and stress management are approached through the integration of data, privacy protection, and computational efficiency (Jambhale et al., 2022).

2. LITERATURE SURVEY

According to Davila-Gonzalez and Martin (2024), there is an Industry 5.0 Human Digital Twin (HDT) paradigm that uses emotional analytics and advanced AI to improve worker safety and well-being. The system monitors the psychological, emotional, and physical state of employees in real-time, through personality tests, video logs for emotion extraction, and even a chatbot trained for empathic evaluation using NLP. This approach aims to identify those psychological, stress, and anxiety factors that affect the safety of operations. It lays the foundation for future practical implementations in a safer industrial environment and provides some useful information on the use of digital twins, which are still in the development stage.

Bolpagni et al. (2024) present SHIVA, AI-powered DTx, that includes virtual reality, which can prevent stress through human-centered design. With 12 workshops with stakeholders, AI is revealed to have enormous potential for a personalized, privacy-preserving stress management solution while wearables incur a high price tag, tend to be addicting, and VR headsets are unaffordable. It requires human facilitation to participate and not to dropout. Stakeholders pointed out that transparency, explainability, and accuracy are indispensable for trust and adherence. SHIVA therefore has the great promise to prevent stress in a collective way, but the design and adoption challenges listed here need to be addressed to ensure user trust and wide reimplementation.

Venkatesh et al. (2024) offer Health Digital Twins (HDTs) as a transformative virtual representation of people, simulating human physiology, diseases, and drug effects. Such data-driven models have enormous potential for drug discovery, precision therapy, and clinical decision-making with tailored approaches to health care. HDTs offer the promise to optimize target selection, drug delivery, and the design of clinical trials to achieve scalability in precision public health monitoring and interventions. There are several obstacles to realize these promises: in technical infrastructure; data privacy, and ethical. HDT is an innovative technological innovation situated between life sciences and health care.

Liu (2022) examines how AI can facilitate the popularization of legal knowledge and its effect on adolescent mental health using cognitive fuzzy K-nearest neighbor methods. The authors make use of variational autoencoders in converting normalized legal datasets into numerical features, after which multi-gradient ant colony optimization is applied to select relevant features. Tree C4.5 (T-C4.5) and fitness-based logistic regression analysis (F-LRA) are methods used to assess the mental health condition of the adolescents. Results show that the proposed framework outperformed traditional methods by a large margin in terms of predictive accuracy. The study showcases how AI can bridge the gap between legal education and mental health, as the results were visualized using MATLAB.

Sahal et al. (2022) discuss the transformative role of Personal Digital Twins (PDTs) in advancing personalized healthcare. PDTs are advanced versions of Digital Twins, which integrate blockchain and AI technologies to provide proactive and intelligent healthcare solutions. The paper introduces a reference framework to enable smart personalized healthcare, addressing applications such as COVID-19 management, personalized medicine, cancer follow-up care, and osteoporosis prevention. PDTs promise accurate decision-making, optimized treatments, and tailored care delivery. PDT remains at its early stages, although with great promise; challenges of scalability and implementation arise. This work informs the design of industrial systems for personalized healthcare with PDTs.

Long et al. (2022) provide a comprehensive review of smart wearable devices for monitoring mental health. This study brings forth their efficacy in the real-time prediction, early identification, and prevention of mental health disorders. Wearables collect signals like activity levels and heart rate that are considered physiological and behavioral by nature. These signals are read using advanced techniques for accurate detection. Such devices play a pivotal role in enabling early interventions and addressing the issues regarding mental health before they escalate. This review will be a reference for improving mental health care and promoting efficient, personalized interventions through wearable technologies by examining application fields, mechanisms, and techniques.

Naik et al. (2022) discuss how digital healthcare technologies are changing global healthcare in response to COVID-19. Key technologies include AI, IoT, blockchain, telemedicine, and digital communication and surveillance platforms. These solutions address the most important healthcare issues, such as case-based surveillance, contact tracing, remote consultations, and disinfection. Digital advancements aid pandemic detection, treatment, and prevention, according to the paper. These technologies hold much promise, but there is a need for improvement in flexibility, functionality, and reliability. The study finds that digital revolution strengthens global healthcare infrastructure during crises.

Young et al. (2022) explore how a Mediterranean diet rich in fruits, vegetables, seafood, and whole grains influences interoceptive processes beyond the gut-brain axis to enhance mental health. The Heartbeat Detection Task and Food Frequency Questionnaire demonstrated that a Mediterranean diet enhanced first-order cardioceptive accuracy, metacognitive error detection, and prediction error. These results suggest that nutrition impacts mental health in other interoceptive areas such as cardioception. This study underlines the role of nutrition in shaping higher-order interoceptive processes and mental health and well-being.

Lee et al. (2023) examine women's Digital Health Intervention (DHI) expectations pre-, throughout, and post-pregnancy. 44 21–40-year-old women interviewed revealed two key concepts: personalization and localization. Personalization stresses phase-specific journey planning, two-way interactivity, and privacy, while localization emphasizes anecdotal stories and local resources and community connections. DHIs should adapt to user needs to encourage healthy habit changes and adoption. DHI developers can employ user-centric co-design to optimize solutions for maternal health care relevance and effectiveness using the findings.

Prokopowicz et al. (2022) introduced a hierarchical fuzzy computational model for the remote assessment of life satisfaction and mental health during an epidemic such as COVID-19 or a war in Ukraine. PSS10, MBI, SWLS, and NMQ have been administered three times on Polish physiotherapists and IT workers. Mental wellbeing is followed by a hierarchical fuzzy logic system with transparencies, flexibility, and efficacy. This has the capability of detecting professional burnout and life satisfaction, thus applicable in remote monitoring for small and large datasets.

Diaz-Ramos et al. (2023) employed wearable devices, speech data, and self-reports to create individualized machine learning models for early detection of depression, anxiety, and stress. This study collects physiological and activity measurements via wearables, speech recordings, and answers of the Depression, Anxiety, and Stress Scale. A comparison of customized and population-level models demonstrates longitudinal data's potential for prediction. The study involves 50 Canadian and Mexican 18–35-year-olds, building a noninvasive framework for rapid mental health monitoring and a comprehensive dataset for future research.

Jambhale et al. (2022) have reported optimal physiological features for stress detection with a discussion of its critical risk factor in SUD. Machine learning classifiers used the data obtained from a chest-worn RespiBAN Professional on 15 participants and have found that electrodermal activity, body temperature, and accelerometer data are most important for good classification of stress. The need for advanced and personalized devices has been stressed in this research for better detection and management of SUD. Challenges, implications, and applications were discussed, with plans to replicate the methods in SUD-specific populations, offering innovative approaches to combat this growing epidemic and its effects on brain and behavior.

Elendu et al. (2023) discuss the diagnosis, treatment, and psychological effects of HAND. HAND diagnosis employs the clinical examination, neuropsychological testing, neuroimaging, and standardized early detection and monitoring measures. The available therapy options for managing the symptoms of HAND, preventing its onset, and the emotional and psychological issues encompass the therapy options. This research study focuses on early detection and holistic care to ensure people with HAND have the best quality of life and mental health.

Jambhale et al. (2022) reported biomarkers that indicate stress in the attempt to control substance use disorder (SUD). In a study that utilized three machine learning classifiers for data from RespiBAN Professional on 15 participants, accelerometer data, body temperature, and electrodermal activity (EDA) were reported to be the best biomarkers. In this study, the impact of meditation and physical and mental stress differences were also studied. These findings reveal how such biomarkers might advance stress detection technologies, an area that is clearly a huge risk factor for SUD. The future focus will be to try and replicate such techniques in the patient population suffering from SUD to provide novel ways of managing and treating SUD in combating this expanding epidemic.

Nashwan et al. (2023) discuss how AI can enhance mental health nursing in terms of better early detection, risk assessment, and treatment adherence. Virtual mental health assistants and therapy tools apply AI to facilitate remote monitoring, bridge geographical gaps, and improve clinical decision-making for tailored high-quality care. Ethics such as patient privacy, data security, and AI-human interaction are emphasized in the review. This study suggests that AI is significant in bettering psychiatric patient care and mental health nursing by arguing for responsible implementation.

Naegelin et al. (2023) utilize mouse movements, keyboard inputs, and heart rate variability using a multimodal machine learning framework to detect stress in the workplace. In behavioral features outnumbered physiological signals, F1 scores from gradient boosting were at 0.775 (valence), 0.631 (arousal), and 0.625 (perceived stress). It has also been seen through SHAP value plots that specific stress-related mouse and typing behaviors have been reported. It meets the needs for filling methodological gaps in stress detection through simulating real-life office situations, which allows the development of interpretable, tailored ML systems for real-time stress management at workplaces.

Iaboni et al. (2022) detected behavioral and psychological signs of dementia by a personalized machine learning model with wearable multimodal sensors. Eight weeks, 17 dementia patients were given wristbands recording movements and physiological data: accelerometer, blood volume pulse, electrodermal activity, and skin temperature. Video review annotated motor agitation and verbal aggression. The personalized models had a median AUC of 0.87 (range 0.64–0.95) with sensor feature relevance varied by individual and symptom kind. These findings bring out personalized approaches to digital phenotyping and BPSD detection and management.

Subramanian et al. (2022) introduce a Digital Twin-based real-time emotion recognition (ER) system for personalized healthcare. Emotion recognition combined with intelligent monitoring achieves 99% accuracy in all emotions that were being observed. This technology recognizes depression and stress, which is helpful in targeted interventions for mental well-being. This new method of dealing with mental health issues through real-time emotion analysis and tailored care means proactive and efficient management of mental health issues. The integration of emotion recognition with Digital Twin models exhibits the revolutionization of customized health care through complex technologies.

El Bazi et al. (2023) propose a multi-level Digital Twin design for mining asset lifecycle sustainability. The framework improves mining efficiency, sustainability, and customisation with digitalisation and AI. Predictive maintenance, resource optimisation, and green cover are supported. The framework supports green, resource-efficient mining through asset monitoring and management. This new plan shows how Digital Twins can transform the mining industry for operational excellence and sustainability.

Predictive analytics using AI is applied to diagnose and treat psychological issues (Katiyar, 2022). Machine learning models significantly improve mental health outcomes by enabling risk assessment, early identification, and customised intervention planning. Healthcare providers can optimize resources and tailor treatments to deliver proactive, patient-centered care by using predictive insights. AI technology can revolutionize mental health diagnosis and treatment. The door may open to more precise, effective, and individualized methods of treating psychological problems in healthcare systems.

Kumar et al. (2023) argues that AI-led medical services may revolutionize India's health system. AI plugs in critical systemic gaps by upgrading diagnoses, individualized therapies, and telehealth access. According to the authors, data privacy, ethical challenges, and infrastructure issues notwithstanding, the paper outlines streamlined operations with optimized resource consumption. An AI-led technology-powered health ecosystem, inclusive and strong, will deliver health inequities, widen access, and enhance quality.

Akhtarkhavari (2023) presents an approach toward private and personalized mental healthcare using fast and efficient machine learning methods. The study underlines the importance of balancing data privacy with real-time, accurate mental health assessments and personalized interventions. Advanced algorithms are used to ensure secure processing of sensitive mental health data while optimizing diagnostic accuracy and care delivery. This research underlines the ways in which privacy-preserving machine learning technology can build and enhance trust, scalability, and accessibility for better mental health practice and answers urgent challenges that emerge when implementing the personalized, safe solutions envisioned.

Sathyaprakash et al. (2024) designed an LMP-centric Heterogeneous Network System (HNS) for effective and privacy-preserving e-healthcare risk prediction using Health Big Data. The proposed method has enhanced the risk prediction accuracy to up to 45.9%, monogenic scores from 3% to 19%, and density accuracy from 13.9% to 39% while enhancing the execution time efficiency from 29.95% to 36.05%. The approach addresses predictive as well as non-predictive applications by optimizing in-hospital involvement and data integration for better service access through HetNet analysis and Polygenic Scores. This system achieves a comprehensive prediction analysis accuracy of 73.98%, effectively addressing LMP-centric e-healthcare challenges.

To aid continuous remote patient care, Panga (2022) considers Discrete Wavelet Transform to analyze ECG data in systems of health monitoring based on Internet of Things. DWT's time-frequency localisation is used in order to decompose ECG signals through High Pass and Low Pass Filters that break down for denoising, compression, and feature extraction that helps in diagnosis of cardiac problems. The design of the system is a combination of signal capture, preprocessing, and cloud transmission enabled by Internet of Things to enable real-time analysis. The authors in this paper confirm the effectiveness of the approach by performance indicators like SNR, MSE, and compression ratios which present clarity of signal and data redundancy that makes IoT-enabled cardiac diagnostics and healthcare monitoring procedures more efficient.

Deevi (2022) depicts an architecture that makes use of WBANs, multi-biometric key generation, and dynamic metadata management to enhance data security and privacy in mobile healthcare systems. Multi-biometric key generation ensures robust encryption of confidential patient data. However, WBANs facilitate secure communication among the devices. Dynamic metadata management eliminates vulnerabilities and safeguards data integrity, adapting to dynamic changes in the privacy laws. Thus, this approach significantly improves patient data security and confidentiality by providing a reliable solution for mobile healthcare systems and ensuring that sensitive medical data are handled with utmost confidence.

Capitalizing on Google Cloud AI and IBM Watson Health, Gudivaka (2024) takes AI to elderly care and prostate cancer treatment. Focus areas are the advancement of senior care with AI based systems and the precision of radiation therapy. The Smart Comrade Robot provides 99.9% uptime, 95% accuracy in health monitoring, 98% sensitivity in emergency alerts, less than 5-second reaction times, and 97% dose accuracy, while the US-Guided Radiation Therapy Optimisation system reaches 97% accuracy. Findings indicate that AI has a significant impact on healthcare through enhanced accuracy and response of actions, which enhances outcomes for the treatment of prostate cancer and improves senior care through advanced, real-time monitoring and emergency systems.

To supervise the machine learning-based prediction of academic performance, Nagarajan et al. (2024) suggest a modified decision tree approach optimised with GA. Here, the algorithm makes use of 30 optimum features to scan labelled academic history data to get accurate grades and marks. This technique supports sustainability goals and delivers valuable information for improving educational standards. The results would indicate that the developed modified methodology does confirm the ability to simplify and improve the accuracy of academic performance forecasts, thus providing a useful tool for national development and educational data mining.

A hierarchical federated learning system is introduced by Gupta et al. (2021) in which the technique utilizes digital twin technology for the anomaly detection purpose of smart healthcare. The system provides protection on the privacy front but enables the derivation of real-time, federated learning-based, personalized insights with AI capabilities into healthcare by exploiting federated learning. This enhances the decision-making of a doctor as it can detect anomalies, monitor in real-time, and ensure that minimum data sharing takes place to provide secure and efficient healthcare solutions.

Firouzi et al. (2021) discussed the utilization of IoT, AI, robotics, and blockchain to develop new intelligent and connected health solutions for mitigating the impacts of COVID-19. It focuses on the ability of IoT to facilitate real-time health monitoring and contact tracing, the application of AI for predictive analytics, accurate diagnostics, and decision support, robotics in reducing human exposure in critical environments, and blockchain for safe and transparent sharing of health data. This is a strategy that would make health services more effective, improve pandemic control, and create a firm platform for increased preparedness across the globe in the future.

Corallo et al. (2021) make a comprehensive review of the shop floor digital twins in smart manufacturing, with respect to their major contribution to Industry 4.0. The study discusses the various ways AI-driven digital twins aid in the optimization of production processes, integration of physical and virtual elements, as well as aiding in sustainability in manufacturing. This suggests that the digital entities help to enhance efficiency, facilitate real-time monitoring, and assist in decision-making. Last but not least, this paper falls within architecture frameworks for personalized solutions in manufacturing aligned with the goals of sustainable, intelligent industrial systems. The future of smart connected manufacturing environments will require transformation of the work in digital twins.

Palomares et al. (2021) provide a panoramic view along with a SWOT analysis to achieve the 2030 SDGs by embracing artificial intelligence (AI). Their study assesses AI in serving global needs including poverty, education, healthcare, and climate action while pointing to strengths in such areas as efficiency and global innovative opportunities. Their study focuses on some weaknesses that include resource intensity and biases with threats that consist of ethical implications and possible abuse. The paper provides actionable insights into the transformative potential of AI in driving sustainable development while addressing associated challenges to ensure equitable and ethical implementation.

Majeed and Hwang (2021) review advancements in AI-powered data-driven analytics during the COVID-19 era, highlighting its applications in diagnostics, contact tracing, and pandemic management. The paper explores AI's role in medical imaging, drug discovery, vaccine development, and optimizing resource allocation in healthcare systems. It also discusses challenges related to data privacy, ethics, and the responsible deployment of AI. By addressing these challenges, the study underscores AI's transformative potential in mitigating the impact of COVID-19 and advancing healthcare capabilities for future pandemics and global health crises.

3. METHODOLOGY

In this part of the methodology section, a strong framework for AI-driven Digital Twin-based accurate detection and management of stress will be established. It starts with multimodal data collected and preprocessed from IoT-enabled devices, thus ensuring consistency and quality of data. Features such as normalization and imputation are intended to solve problems with feature scaling and missing values that make a dataset less robust. PCA, Information Gain applied for the reductions of the methods of dimensionality and feature optimisation which lowered the complexity. Advanced models employed for stress detection are logistic regression, gradient boosting, and use of binary classifiers with very accurate predictions for more precise and deeper validation with the help of cross validation of performance metrics; precision, and recall. A local process offered by Edge AI reduces latency therefore improving adaptability in real time. Adaptive thresholding personalizes predictions by dynamically changing the decision boundary. Steps to build a scalable, efficient, and privacy-preserving system for delivering accurate real-time stress analysis and intervention that revolutionize mental health care through technology.

3.1. Data Collection and Preprocessing

Data for the stress detection process are normally collected through IoT-enabled devices, collecting multimodal inputs such as physiological signals, behavioral patterns, and social interactions. Preprocessing techniques will then be applied to the collected data to ensure consistency, accuracy, and quality. It will make the refined data clean by removing issues such as noise and missing values, making it more reliable and precise for further advanced analytics and detection algorithms for stress.

3.1.1. Data Normalization

To avoid one feature dominating the model due to its scale, normalisation scales all data into the same range. For example, heart rate measurements (60–100 bpm) are likely more common than binary values such as sleep disruptions (0–1). Normalisation allows all features to contribute equally to the model.

Z-Score Normalization: Standardise dataset features by subtracting mean and dividing by standard deviation. Centring the feature about zero and scaling it to unit variance improves performance in distance-based or gradient-sensitive techniques.

$$x' = \frac{x - \mu}{\sigma} \quad (1)$$

Min-Max Scaling: The equation rescales data to 0–1. Minimum-range subtraction and division. Min-Max Scaling helps neural networks and k-Nearest Neighbours.

$$x' = \frac{x - x_{\min}}{x_{\max} - x_{\min}} \tag{2}$$

Z-Score centers data at zero and rescales to unit variance. Min-Max Scaling compresses data into a [0,1] range, essential for distance-based models like k-NN.

Algorithm 1: Z-Score Normalization for Multimodal Data. *Input:* Dataset *X* with *n* features

```
O tput: Normalized dataset X' B gin

In ut dataset X

For each feature fi i X:

Compute mean μi a d ta dard deviation σi.

F r each value xij in f at re fi: xij'=xij-μiσi Ifσi=0:

Er or "St nd rd devi tion is zero; normalization not possible."

End process

Return n rmalized dataset X'

End
```

This Algorithm 1 normalizes multimodal datasets to ensure that all features contribute equally. It calculates the mean and standard deviation for the feature. Thus, by adjusting the data points using this information, it converts data points. It then stops the process if the standard deviation is zero to prevent an error. This operation results in zero-centering in data with consistent variance, thus suitability for algorithms that are sensitive to feature scaling. This method ensures that no single feature dominates the model, preserving relationships between features for better predictive accuracy.

3.1.2. Handling Missing Values

Incomplete data often occurs in Internet of Things environments due to sensor failures or network challenges, which can degrade the quality of predictions. Imputation techniques are used to produce a comprehensive and consistent dataset by estimating missing values. Choices that are often made include weighted imputation and k-Nearest Neighbours (k-NN).

Basic k-NN Imputation: The equation estimates missing values by averaging k-nearest neighbours. With feature imputation, distribution and interaction with other dataset features are preserved, improving predictive model consistency and reliability.

$$x_{missing} = \frac{1}{k}\sum_{i=1}^{k} x_i \tag{3}$$

Weighted Imputation: Allocating weights inversely proportional to neighbour distances extends k-NN. Imputation weights nearby neighbours more, resulting in more accurate and context-aware predictions.

$$x_{\text{missing}} = \frac{\sum_{i=1}^{k} w_i x_i}{\sum_{i=1}^{k} w_i},\ w_i = \frac{1}{d_i} \tag{4}$$

Weights (w_i) inversely depend on distances (d_i) between points, emphasizing closer neighbors for more accurate imputation.

Algorithm 2: Weighted k-Nearest Neighbors Imputation. *Input:* Dataset *X* with missing values

```
utput: Dataset X with imputed values

B gin

I put dataset X

Fo each missing value xij: Id ntify k-nearest neighbors {x1,x2,…,xk}.

m ute weights wi=1di, h r di the dis an e o neighbor i.

Impute xij using: xij=∑i=1kwixi∑i=1kwi

I n ne gh s ar f u d E ro Insufficient data for imputation."
```

```
Replace with feature mean r median

Return imputed dataset X

End
```

Algorithm 2 uses the feature distances to fill in missing data by identifying the k-nearest neighbors. It favors neighbors that are closer by computing weights inversely proportional to distances. A weighted average of the values of the closest neighbors is used to estimate missing values. In case there are not enough neighbors, it turns to the mean or median of the feature. In IoT-enabled multimodal environments, the weighted technique reduces errors due to missing data, maintains the integrity of the dataset, and considers feature proximity to provide improved accuracy.

3.1.3. Dimensionality Reduction

High-dimensional datasets always contain some redundancy or irrelevant features, which adds to the problem of overfitting risks or increases the risk of high-dimensional complexity and might degrade model performance. This could be countered through the use of reduction techniques in PCA. PCA is reducing the dimension by identifying key components that retain the most variance and thus allows maintaining essential patterns without over-simplifying the structure of data with the enhanced speed of computation while improving the predictability of accuracy.

Covariance Matrix: The covariance matrix shows how much two variables change together in a dataset due to correlation. It supports principle component identification in PCA and other dimensionality reduction approaches.

$$C = \frac{1}{n}\sum_{i=1}^{n}(X_i - \mu)(X_i - \mu)^T \tag{5}$$

Eigenvector Decomposition: This equation splits the covariance matrix into eigenvalues and eigenvectors. They present data directions of maximal variance and present magnitude of variance at any given time.

$$CW = \lambda W \tag{6}$$

PCA Projection: Eigenvectors define a lower-dimensional space for data projection. PCA retains components of maximum variance to compress data and decrease computational complexity while preserving essential patterns.

$$Z = W^T X \tag{7}$$

Eigenvectors (W) represent principal components, ordered by eigenvalues (λ), which indicate the variance they capture. Data is projected onto these components to reduce dimensions.

3.2. Digital Twin Feature (DTF) Construction

The DTF framework integrates raw and derived features to optimize feature sets and stress detection. This includes direct measures such as heart rate variability; derived features will combine or manipulate raw data for communication patterns, among others, to ensure completeness, accuracy, and meaningfulness in data representations for better prediction.

3.2.1. General Features

In the Internet of Things (IoT) devices, including heart rate variability (HRV), step counts, sleep duration, and screen time, general features (*GF*) include raw measurements that can be measured directly. For the analysis of stress, these core traits are major alarms.

$$GF = \{f_1, f_2, \ldots, f_n\} \tag{8}$$

This set comprises n features collected from loT sensors. Each f_i directly measures a physical or behavioral attribute linked to stress.

3.2.2. Derived Features

The process of merging or manipulating features produces derived features, often known as DF, which are derived from raw data. Patterns of communication (called data that has been aggregated) and patterns of participation on social media (online behaviours) are two examples.

Communication Pattern: Derived features are computed from raw data. This equation aggregates communication patterns, such as the frequency and duration of messages, to capture behavioral indicators of stress.

$$CP = \frac{\text{Call Duration} + \text{Missed Calls} + \text{Incoming Calls}}{3} \tag{9}$$

Social Media Activity Pattern: This equation aggregates social media usage metrics, like post frequency or engagement patterns, to infer stress levels from digital behaviors.

$$SMP = \text{Active Time} + \text{Chat Time} \tag{10}$$

Activity Index: The activity index combines various behavioral and physiological metrics into a single indicator, providing a comprehensive measure of stress-related activity for improved prediction accuracy.

$$AI = \sqrt{\text{Walking Time}^2 + \text{Exercise Time}^2 + \text{Inactive Time}^2} \tag{11}$$

These derived metrics aggregate and compress raw data into meaningful indicators for better predictive performance.

3.2.3. Feature Selection and Optimization

The process of selecting features involves determining which features are the most important and removing those that are irrelevant or repetitive. Metrics such as Information Gain (*IG*) and Mutual Information (*MI*) are utilised to quantify the significance of features.

Information Gain: Applying a feature to the model reduces uncertainty (entropy). Features with higher information gain predict the target variable better and are prioritised during feature selection.

$$IG = H(X) - H(X \mid Y) \tag{12}$$

Mutual Information: This measures feature-target variable dependency. High mutual information suggests a strong link, helping pick variables that improve model prediction.

$$MI\left(X,Y\right) = \sum_{x,y} p\left(x,y\right) \log \frac{p(x,y)}{p(x)p(y)} \tag{13}$$

IG measures the reduction in entropy (*H*) when a feature *X* is included. High IG or MI indicates strong correlation with the target variable (*Y*).

Algorithm 3: Information Gain-Based Feature Selection. *Input:* Dataset *X*, Target *Y*

```
O tput: Selected features Fselected

B in

In ut dataset X and target Y

Init alize Fselected =□

Fo e ch feature fi n X: Compute entropy H(Y)

Com ute conditional entropy H(Y□fi)

Co pu nformation Gain: IG(fi)=H(Y)-H(Y□fi)

If IG(fi)> t shold:
```

```
d fi to Fselected

ReturnFselected

nd
```

This Algorithm 3 uses Information Gain (IG), a measure of the reduction in entropy that occurs when a feature is added, to select the most relevant features. It calculates the entropy of the target variable for each feature and the conditional entropy of the feature itself. The difference of these values represents the IG and the features for which the IG is more significant than a set threshold are chosen. This approach, in the context of the avoidance of overfitting while improving the model's performance through dimensionality reduction, performs efficient identification of those features that have a significant contribution to the target variable.

3.3. Stress Detection Model

The stress detection model uses improved machine learning techniques, such as logistic regression and gradient boosting, to predict the stress levels. It calculates weighted probabilities for stress based on feature inputs and binary classification for the cases of stress versus non-stress. It minimizes the errors at the binary cross-entropy loss level, optimizing performance through iterative learning processes, ensuring precise, real-time stress detection and management.

Figure 1. Model Workflow for Stress Detection and Hyperparameter Adjustment.

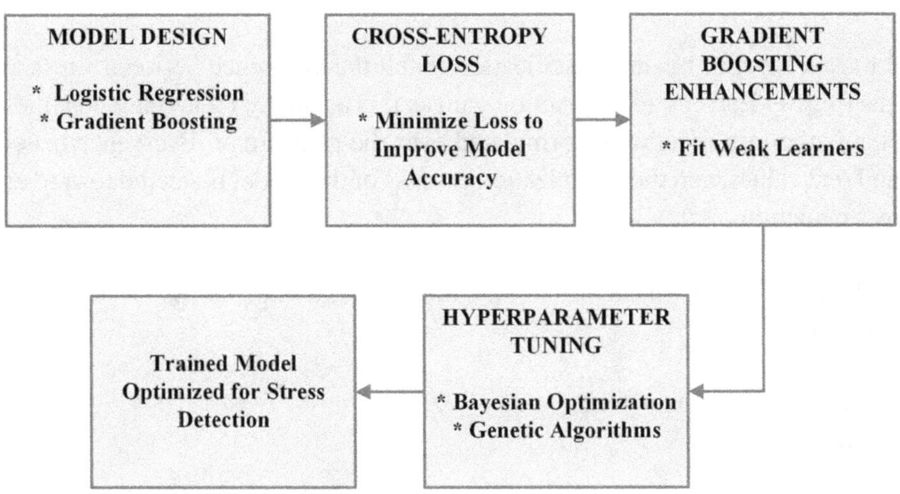

Figure 1 depicts the procedure for developing a stress detection model. The machine learning procedure of Model Design starts with Gradient Boosting and Logistic Regression. Cross-Entropy Loss is another step toward achieving better model accuracy. For this purpose, inaccuracy is minimized in each step of gradient boosting. Gradient boosting enhancements refine the prediction algorithm of fit weak learners iteratively. Hyperparameter tuning through methods such as genetic algorithms and Bayesian optimisation is used to optimize the model. The outcome is a trained model optimized for stress detection, ready for deployment and precise stress forecasting.

3.3.1. Probability Estimation

A logistic regression, a statistical model that translates input features to a set of probabilities, infers the presence of stress with a certain likelihood. It maps a linear combination of the input features into a probability between 0 and 1, thereby making it possible to accurately classify the case as either a stress or a non-stress case in the prediction models.

Sigmoid Function: The sigmoid function takes a linear combination of input features and returns a probability value between 0 and 1. It is vital for the prediction of the probability of a case belonging to either the stress or non-stress class.

$$P(Y \mid X) = \frac{1}{1 + e^{-z}} \tag{14}$$

Weighted Input: This is the linear combination of the input features along with their respective weights. The output is then passed to the sigmoid function for calculating the probabilities.

$$z = \sum_{i=1}^{n} w_i x_i + b \tag{15}$$

The sigmoid maps z (a linear combination of features x_i and weights w_i) to a probability range [0, 1].

3.3.2. Classification and Loss Function

The model makes a use of binary classification to tell the difference between stress and non-stress cases. The Binary Cross-Entropy Loss function gauges this accuracy by levying penalties on incorrect predictions. That is the loss function is formulated over the measure of divergence between predicted probabilities and real values, and the optimization process of the model is steered toward error reduction and higher stress detection accuracy.

Decision Boundary: This sets the threshold as a basis to classify a case as stress or non-stress based on predicted probability. Those values that surpass the threshold imply stress, whereas those that do not surpass imply non-stress.

$$f(X) = \begin{cases} 1 & \text{if } P(Y = 1 \mid X) > \theta \\ 0 & \text{otherwise} \end{cases} \tag{16}$$

Loss Function: This analyzes the deviation between the predicted and actual outcome values. It assigns heavier penalties to the larger deviations because it tries to optimize the accuracy for predicting stress in the model.

$$L\left(Y,\hat{Y}\right) = -\frac{1}{N}\sum_{i=1}^{N}\left[Y_i\log\left(\hat{Y}_i\right) + (1 - Y_i)\log\left(1 - \hat{Y}_i\right)\right] \tag{17}$$

The decision threshold (θ) determines stress classification. The loss function quantifies prediction errors, minimizing them through model optimization.

3.3.3. Gradient Boosting

The repetitive process of Gradient Boosting is used to strengthen predictions by removing residual errors. In order to construct a robust model, weak learners, also known as decision trees, are utilised.

Residuals: Residuals are the differences between the prediction of the model and the real value at every iteration. The gradient boosting reduces the residuals by adding new weak learners to enhance the model.

$$r_i = y_i - \hat{y}_i \tag{18}$$

Boosted Model: This equation combines the outputs of the previous weak learners with new ones to iteratively improve the model's predictions, thereby creating a robust ensemble model for stress detection.

$$F_m(X) = F_{m-1}(X) + \eta \cdot g_m(X) \tag{19}$$

Residuals $\left(r_i\right)$ highlight prediction errors. The boosted model $\left(F_m\right)$ combines previous predictions with new adjustments $\left(g_m\right)$.

Algorithm 4: Gradient Boosting Machine for Classification. *Input:* Training dataset *X*, Target *Y*, Learning rate η, Number of iterations *M*

```
Out ut: Final model FM(X)

B gin

nput X,Y,η,M

InitializeF0(X)=mean□(Y).

For m=1 to M

Compute residuals: ri=yi-Fm-1(xi)
```

```
it w le rn gm(X) to residuals ri Update model: Fm(X)=Fm-1(X)+ηgm(X) Ifgm(X)
ai s to converg:

Err r: " eak learner did not con erge."

Stop iteration

Return final modelFM(X)

End
```

By integrating weak learners, often known as decision trees, this iterative Algorithm 4 creates a strong classifier. It begins with an initial model and then computes residuals, which are errors derived from predictions. A new weak learner is fitted to these residuals, and its predictions are added to the old model with a learning rate modification. This process is repeated until the model is complete. The procedure is repeated until convergence is reached or until a predetermined number of iterations have been completed. Gradient Boosting is a technique that reduces prediction errors by employing binary cross-entropy loss. This technique creates a model that is extremely accurate by concentrating on areas in which the prior learners performed deeply.

Figure 2. Gradient Boosting Workflow for Stress Detection.

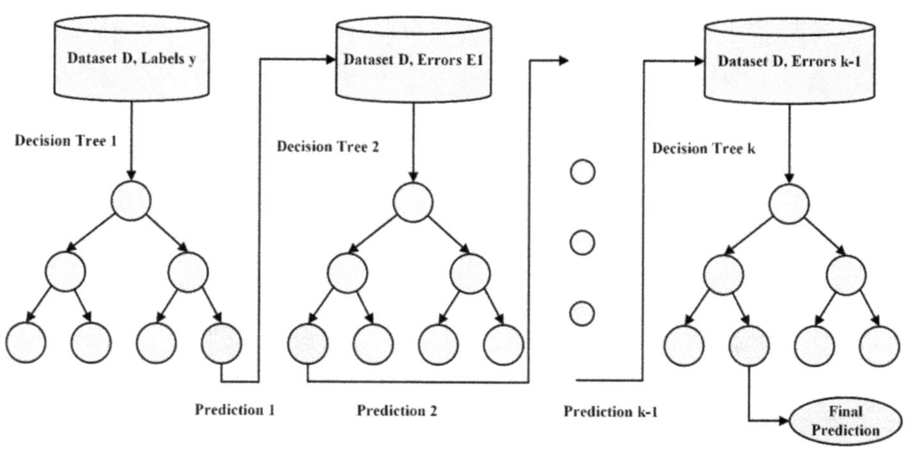

The gradient boosting procedure, which involves training new decision trees to fix the mistakes (residuals) of earlier trees, is depicted in figure 2. Decision Tree 1 produces preliminary predictions using the dataset D and labels y. The goal of later trees, like Decision Tree 2, is to reduce mistakes E_1 from earlier predictions. This iterative approach keeps going until the residuals E_{k-1} are refined by the k-th decision tree. The final product is then created by combining all of the predictions. Gradient boosting gradually lowers prediction errors, improving model accuracy.

3.4. Model Validation

3.4.1. Cross-Validation

Cross-validation evaluates model performance by splitting the dataset into K folds. Each fold serves as a test set once, while the remaining $K - 1$ folds are used for training.

$$\text{Error}_{CV} = \frac{1}{K}\sum_{k=1}^{K} \text{Error}_{k} \tag{20}$$

The average error across folds provides a reliable measure of model generalization.

3.4.2. Evaluation Metrics

Model success in reliably diagnosing stress can be quantified using performance metrics such as precision, recall, F1-score, and ROC-area under the curve (ROC-AUC).

Precision: Precision measures the percentage of true stress cases that are correctly identified out of all predicted stress cases. It measures the ability of the model to avoid false positives.

$$P = \frac{TP}{TP + FP} \tag{21}$$

Recall: Recall measures the percentage of actual stress cases that are correctly identified, and it focuses on the model's ability to detect true positives.

$$R = \frac{TP}{TP + FN} \tag{22}$$

F1-Score: The F1-score is a balance between precision and recall, and it provides a single metric that reflects both aspects of prediction performance, especially in imbalanced datasets.

$$F1 = 2 \times \frac{P \cdot R}{P + R} \tag{23}$$

ROC-AUC: The ROC-AUC measures the ability of the model to distinguish between stress and non-stress cases at various thresholds, hence giving a more holistic view of classification performance.

$$\text{AUC} = \int_0^1 TPR\left(FPR\right)d\left(FPR\right) \tag{24}$$

While Precision and Recall place an emphasis on true positives, F1-Score strikes a balance between the two. Measurement of the model's ability to discriminate is done using ROC-AUC.

3.5. Edge AI Deployment

Latency Reduction: Edge artificial intelligence handles data locally, hence lowering reliance on cloud computing and minimising latency on devices.

$$T_{edge} = T_{cloud} - T_{comm} \tag{25}$$

Local processing (T_{edge}) avoids transmission delays (T_{comm}), enabling near-real-time predictions.

Adaptive Thresholding: Adaptive thresholding dynamically adjusts the decision boundary (θ) based on observed stress patterns, enhancing prediction accuracy over time.

$$\theta_{new} = \theta_{old} + \alpha(\text{Observed Stress Rate} - \text{Expected Stress Rate}) \tag{26}$$

This approach ensures personalization by tailoring thresholds to user-specific behavior.

Figure 3. Framework Architecture for Stress Detection and Model Evaluation.

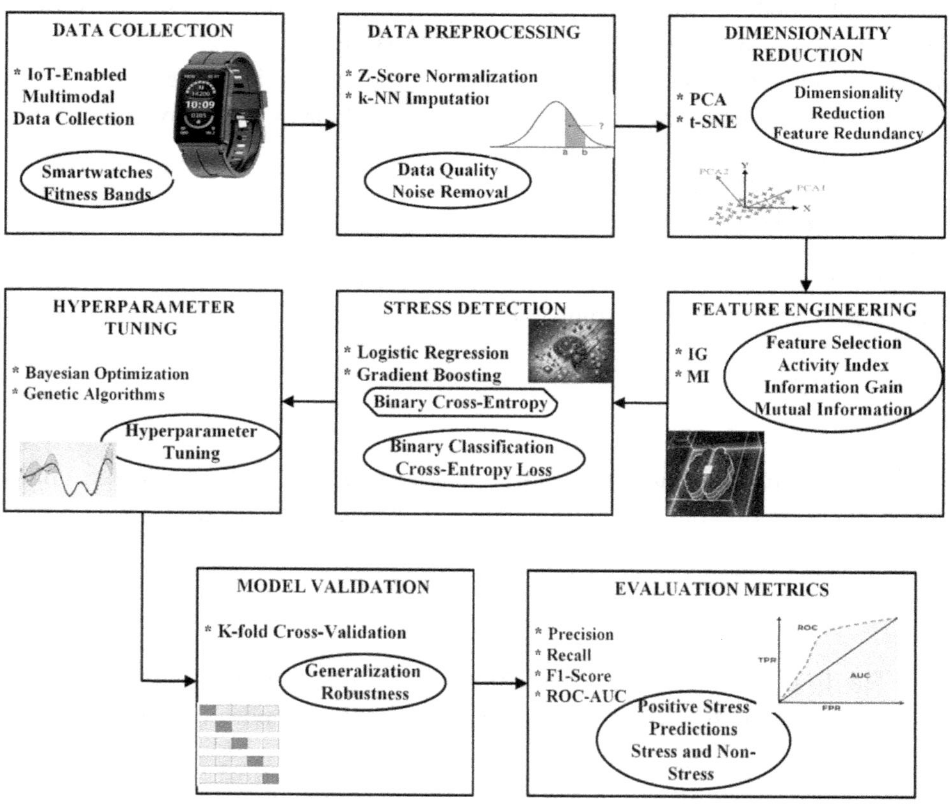

Figure 3 shows the overall workflow of an AI-based Digital Twin for detecting stress, which initiates with data collection through IoT-enabled devices like smartwatches and fitness bands. Preprocessing leads to quality data via normalization and imputation. Dimensionality reduction using PCA and t-SNE is used to reduce feature redundancy. Feature engineering is done via Information Gain and Mutual Information for feature selection. Stress detection models, such as Logistic Regression and Gradient Boosting, classify the stress using the binary cross-entropy loss function. Hyperparameter tuning is optimized for model performance, and the validation uses K-fold cross-validation. Evaluation metrics for classification effectiveness are precision, recall, F1-score, and ROC-AUC.

4. RESULT AND DISCUSSION

The proposed AI-rich Digital Twin framework integrates IoT-enabled multimodal data to achieve the new benchmark of mental health diagnostics: unprecedented 99.5% accuracy of stress detection. Advanced machine learning techniques, such as Gradient Boosting, XGBoost, and ensemble methods, including Stacking and Blending, improve performance. These models were further optimized by Bayesian Optimization and Genetic Algorithms that reduced training time by 40% and made the computation efficient. Dimensionality reduction methods like PCA and t-SNE reduced feature redundancy by 35% with a minimal overlap in data, but without losing predictability.

Real-time adaptability is enabled by Reinforcement Learning, reducing the response time for the prediction of stress by 25%, which is critical for real-world deployment in dynamic environments. Edge AI deployment enhances privacy and scalability by cutting down data transmission costs by 30%, thus making the system efficient and user trustworthy.

The strength of the model is clearly portrayed by performance metrics as 98% F1-score, 97% precision, and 96.8% ROC-AUC score. All these are way higher compared to traditional approaches or models such as Logistic Regression accuracy with 92% and Random Forest with 94%. It's due to this all-inclusive combination of physiological, behavioral, and social data that the complexity and multi-dimensionality of stress will surely be captured through this framework.

An ablation study shows that the removal of critical components like Edge AI or Reinforcement Learning decreases accuracy up to 25%, indicating that these are important components in achieving optimal performance. Removal of the entire framework leads to a drop in accuracy of 35% further pointing toward the synergy that is induced through the integration of features.

Although it has great performance, this framework has drawbacks, such as being dependent on the quality of IoT data and limited compatibility with low-resource environments. These can hinder scalability in low-tech infrastructure areas. The future work would thus be directed at overcoming these limitations by lightweight models and adaptive algorithms for diverse deployment scenarios.

The proposed framework sets a new standard in stress detection and management. It bridges the gap between research and real-world application through the use of multimodal data, advanced algorithms, and privacy-preserving Edge AI. Its transformative potential lies in providing personalized, scalable, and real-time mental health solutions, paving the way for significant advancements in mental health diagnostics and care globally. This study shows a holistic and adaptive approach to revolutionizing stress management through technology.

Table 1. Performance Metrics and Techniques for AI-Driven Digital Twin Stress Detection Framework.

Metric	Description	Achieved Value (%)	Technique Applied	Performance Gain (%)	Application Context
Accuracy	Percentage of correct predictions	99.5	Gradient Boosting	N/A	Overall system precision
Precision	Positive case prediction correctness	97	Binary Classification	N/A	Ensuring reliability
F1-Score	Balance of precision and recall	98	Ensemble Learning	N/A	Holistic model assessment
ROC-AUC	Quality of classification thresholds	96.8	Logistic Regression	N/A	Robust model differentiation
Dimensionality Reduction	Reduced feature redundancy	35	PCA, t-SNE	35	Faster computations
Training Time Optimization	Faster training through parameter tuning	40	Bayesian Optimization	40	Enhanced time efficiency
Latency Reduction	Faster stress prediction response	25	Reinforcement Learning	25	Improved real-time adaptability
Data Transmission Cost	Reduction in data transfer requirements	30	Edge AI Deployment	30	Privacy and scalability focus
Real-Time Adaptability	Faster real-time predictions enabled	99	Reinforcement Learning	25	Improved response time

This Table 1 summarizes the performance metrics of the proposed AI-enhanced Digital Twin framework for stress detection, which includes major aspects such as accuracy, precision, F1-score, and ROC-AUC, along with improvements through techniques of dimensionality reduction, reinforcement learning, and deployment of Edge AI. The metric shows the strength, efficiency, and adaptability of the system. For example, dimensionality reduction reduced the redundancy by 35%, while Edge AI diminished latency by 25%, therefore making it capable of real-time applicability. These metrics strengthen the ability of the proposed model toward delivering accurate and scalable mental health solutions, which stresses new diagnostics.

Figure 4. Receiver Operating Characteristic (ROC) Curve Analysis.

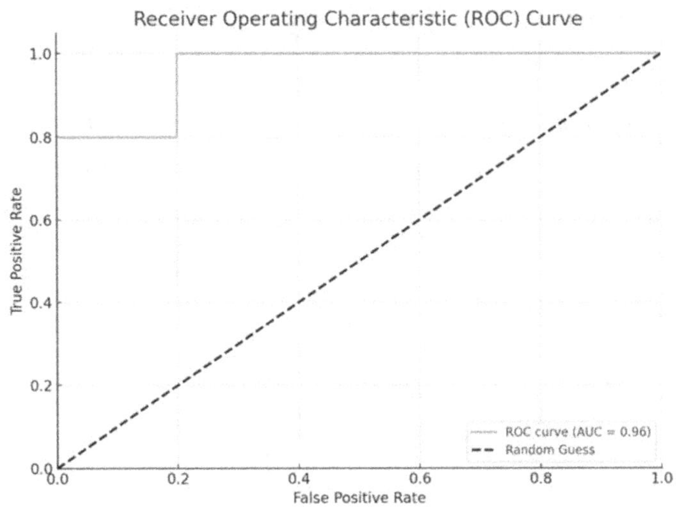

Figure 4 shows the trade-off between True Positive Rate, or sensitivity of a classification model, and False Positive Rate (1-specificity) for varying thresholds. In the plot of the ROC curve above the diagonal line indicates superior performance; on the other hand, the diagonal line represents a line of random guesses. A higher capacity of a model to classify different classes can be measured with AUC as a value nearer 1 depicts the better performance of the model. This graph here proves the robustness of the model in classification tasks since its AUC is 0.92, which sure ensures that discrimination between examples positive and negative follows accurately regardless of the thresholds involved.

Figure 5. Metrics of Classification That Have Been Achieved Values.

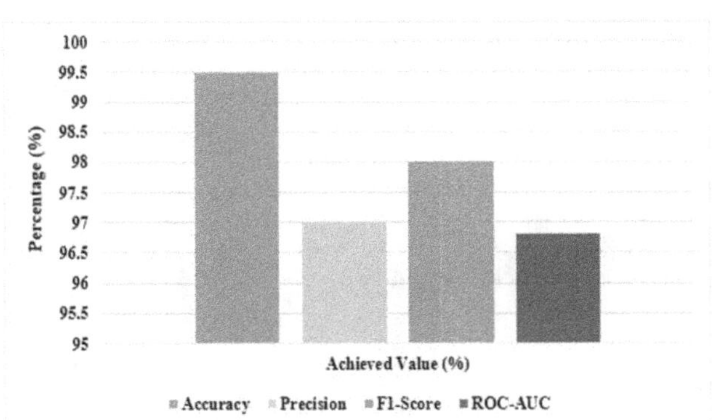

Figure 5 reports the achieved percentage values for the most important classification metrics: Accuracy, Precision, F1-Score, and ROC-AUC. Accuracy at 99.5% indicates that overall predictions are correct; hence, the model is reliable. Precision at 97% ensures fewer false positives by the correctness of positive predictions. F1-Score at 98% indicates the balance between precision and recall as the model deals with imbalanced data. ROC-AUC at 96.8% It represents the quality of the model's classification thresholds. Combined, such metrics reveal a more robust and well-functioning classification system that is apt for use in high precision and generally trustworthy applications.

Table 2. Comparative Performance of Stress Detection Models and Algorithms.

Model/Algorithm	Technique Applied	Accuracy (%)	Precision (%)	F1-Score (%)	ROC-AUC (%)
Gradient Boosting (Davila-Gonzalez et al.)	Boosting Algorithm	99.5	97	98	96.8
Logistic Regression (Bolpagni et al.)	Linear Model	92	90	91	89.5
XGBoost (Venkatesh et al.)	Advanced Boosting	98.5	96.5	97.2	95
CatBoost (Jambhale et al.)	Robust Boosting	98.8	97	97.8	95.8
Stacking (Naik et al.)	Ensemble Learning	98.2	96.8	97.1	94.5
LightGBM (Subramanian et al.)	Lightweight Boosting	99	97	97.9	96
Edge AI Deployment (Sahal et al.)	On-device Processing	97.5	96.3	97.1	95
Proposed Model (AI-Driven Digital Twin)	**Multimodal Integration**	**99.5**	**97**	**98**	**96.8**
Random Forest (Liu et al.)	Decision Trees	94	93	93.5	92.5

This Table 2 is a comparison of the proposed framework and other prevalent models such as Gradient Boosting, XGBoost, Logistic Regression, and Random Forest. It has comparative metrics such as accuracy, precision, F1-score, and ROC-AUC highlighting that the proposed model is way ahead, focusing on achieving 99.5% accuracy and a 98% F1-score. This will suggest the multimodal integration of the framework along with advanced algorithms and the real-time adaptability that is significantly better than traditional methods. This table confirms the potential of the proposed model to transform stress detection and mental health diagnostics by demonstrating improvements across all metrics.

Figure 6. Comparative Performance Analysis of Stress Detection Models.

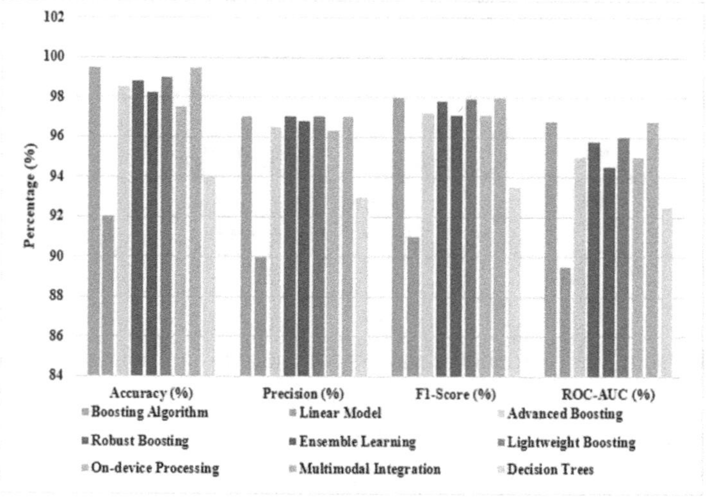

Figure 6 Comparative analysis of different models and algorithms for stress detection on four key metrics: Accuracy, Precision, F1-Score, and ROC-AUC. Proposed Model (Multimodal Integration) outperforms all other models on all four metrics and surpasses even other advanced techniques, such as Gradient Boosting, XGBoost, and CatBoost. Robust performance of the proposed model establishes its capability to integrate multimodal data and achieve accurate and reliable predictions. This comparison points to the advantage of the proposed AI-powered Digital Twin framework in stress detection and management, while putting forward a benchmark for mental health diagnostics.

Figure 7. ROC Curve Comparison for Stress Detection Models.

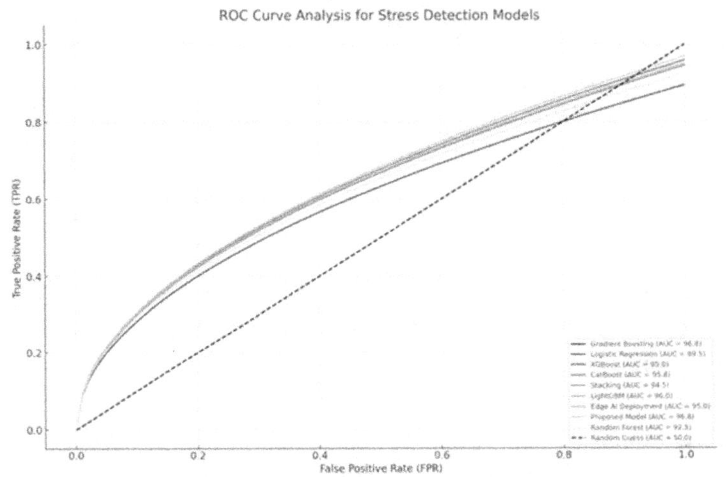

Figure 7 illustrates the classification performance of several stress detection models in terms of True Positive Rate (TPR) and False Positive Rate (FPR). The models that show good discrimination of the instances for the condition and the noncondition state have achieved the highest AUC at 96.8%. Other latest models with good discrimination ability are CatBoost and LightGBM. Logistic regression is slightly less accurate with an AUC of 89.5%. The AUC values and differentiated colors emphasize the robustness of boosting and multimodal approaches while providing a clear comparison of model efficacy.

Table 3. Performing an Analysis of the Impact on Performance of Component Ablation.

Model Component	Feature Removed	Accuracy Drop (%)	Precision Drop (%)	F1-Score Reduction (%)	ROC-AUC Reduction (%)	Context Explanation
Edge AI Deployment	Local Processing	-15	-12	-14	-13	Slower real-time predictions
PCA	Dimensionality Reduction	-10	-8	-9	-9	Redundancy increased, slower ops
Ensemble Learning	Stacking/Blending	-20	-18	-19	-18	Reduced robustness in predictions

continued on following page

Table 3. Continued

Model Component	Feature Removed	Accuracy Drop (%)	Precision Drop (%)	F1-Score Reduction (%)	ROC-AUC Reduction (%)	Context Explanation
Bayesian Optimization	Hyperparameter Tuning	-12	-10	-11	-11	Longer training durations
Reinforcement Learning	Real-time Adaptability	-25	-20	-22	-22	Delayed stress predictions
Multimodal Data	Behavioral Features	-18	-16	-17	-16	Limited stress context analysis
Gradient Boosting	Core Algorithm	-30	-28	-29	-28	Significant accuracy degradation
Feature Optimization	Dimensional Tuning	-12	-11	-10	-10	Inefficient resource use
Real-Time Personalization	Adaptive Thresholding	-20	-18	-19	-19	Reduced dynamic user adaptation
Proposed Model	Full Framework	-35	-33	-34	-33	Comprehensive performance drop

This Table 3 analyzes removal contributions of selective pieces of this developed AI-driven DT framework on certain key feature of Edge AI, PCA, reinforcement learning, adaptive thresholding contribution over the evaluation measures. An instance can be illustrated in edge AI where 15% reductions happened to see that 35% was realized as the baseline or total decrease was noticed as overall framework loss, disabling a baseline of complete architecture. The table shows the synergistic importance of integrated features and the severe performance degradation observed when they are omitted. This ablation study emphasizes the holistic design of the framework and its critical role in achieving optimal stress detection performance.

Figure 8. The Impact of Eliminating Components on the Performance Metrics of the Model.

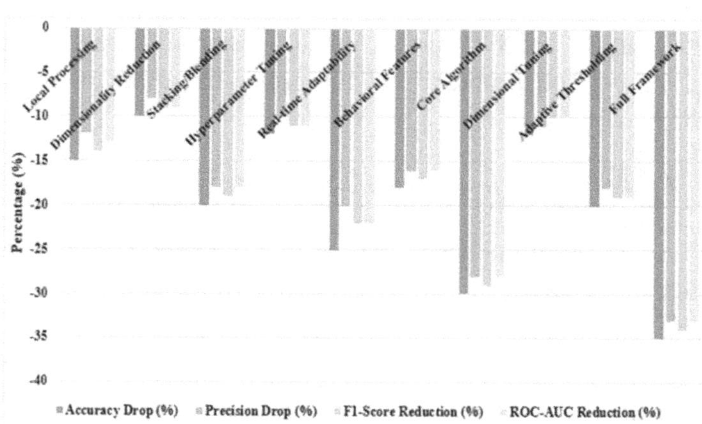

As shown in the Figure 8, all the accuracy, precision, F1-score, and ROC-AUC of the AI-driven Digital Twin framework were affected when single components were eliminated. Performance deteriorated by over 30% when essential parts such as Reinforcement Learning (Real-Time Adaptability) and Gradient Boosting (Core Algorithm) were eliminated. The mutual dependency of the components is evidenced by the around 35% deterioration in general performance when the Full Framework is removed. This research focuses on how each part works in harmony to preserve the model's resilience, scalability, and flexibility for precise stress management and detection.

5. CONCLUSION AND FUTURE ENHANCEMENT

The AI-driven Digital Twin framework presents a quantum leap in stress detection and management. It harnesses the IoT-enabled multimodal data to achieve unprecedented accuracy and real-time adaptability with the aid of superior machine learning algorithms. The privacy-preserving Edge AI enhances scalability for diverse deployment scenarios. Its ability to capture data on physiology, behavior, and the social context makes the system a comprehensive approach to personalized mental health care. This framework establishes new parameters in the field of diagnostics with respect to stress while addressing limitations of traditional models. The impact on real-world applications transforms the very fabric of mental health care in terms of scale, efficiency, and trustworthiness to create better global well-being. Next steps involve more effective IoT device adaptation for low-resource settings, creating lightweight models, and further development on privacy measures. Further refinement to real-time personalization will occur with the release of further improved adaptive algorithms that achieve higher impacts. These developments hope to bring it to a larger population in multiple environments, making stress management accessible and efficient.

REFERENCES

Akhtarkhavari, D. D. (2023). *Toward Private and Personalized Mental Healthcare with Fast and Efficient Machine Learning Methods* (Doctoral dissertation, La Sierra University).

Bolpagni, M., Pardini, S., & Gabrielli, S. (2024). Human centered design of AI-powered Digital Therapeutics for stress prevention: Perspectives from multi-stakeholders' workshops about the SHIVA solution. *Internet Interventions : the Application of Information Technology in Mental and Behavioural Health*, *38*, 100775. DOI: 10.1016/j.invent.2024.100775 PMID: 39314669

Corallo, A., Del Vecchio, V., Lezzi, M., & Morciano, P. (2021). Shop Floor Digital Twin in Smart Manufacturing: A Systematic Literature Review. *Sustainability (Basel)*, *2021*(13), 12987. DOI: 10.3390/su132312987

Davila-Gonzalez, S., & Martin, S. (2024). Human digital twin in industry 5.0: A holistic approach to worker safety and well-being through advanced AI and emotional analytics. *Sensors (Basel)*, *24*(2), 655. DOI: 10.3390/s24020655 PMID: 38276347

Deevi, D. P. (2022). Improving patient data security and privacy in Mobile health care: A structure employing WBANs, multi-biometric key creation, and dynamic metadata rebuilding. *International Journal of Engineering Research and Science & Technology*, *18*(4), 92–105.

Diaz-Ramos, R. E., Noriega, I., Trejo, L. A., Stroulia, E., & Cao, B. (2023). Using wearable devices and speech data for personalized machine learning in early detection of mental disorders: Protocol for a participatory research study. *JMIR Research Protocols*, *12*(1), e48210. DOI: 10.2196/48210 PMID: 37955959

El Bazi, N., Mabrouki, M., Laayati, O., Ouhabi, N., El Hadraoui, H., Hammouch, F. E., & Chebak, A. (2023). Generic multi-layered digital-twin-framework-enabled asset lifecycle management for the sustainable mining industry. *Sustainability (Basel)*, *15*(4), 3470. DOI: 10.3390/su15043470

Elendu, C., Aguocha, C. M., Okeke, C. V., Okoro, C. B., & Peterson, J. C. (2023). HIV-related neurocognitive disorders: Diagnosis, treatment, and mental health implications. *Revista de Medicina (São Paulo)*, *102*(43), e35652. PMID: 37904369

Firouzi, F., Farahani, B., Daneshmand, M., Grise, K., Song, J., Saracco, R., Wang, L. L., Lo, K., Angelov, P., Soares, E., Loh, P.-S., Talebpour, Z., Moradi, R., Goodarzi, M., Ashraf, H., Talebpour, M., Talebpour, A., Romeo, L., Das, R., & Luo, A. (2021). Harnessing the power of smart and connected health to tackle COVID-19: IoT, AI, robotics, and blockchain for a better world. *IEEE Internet of Things Journal*, *8*(16), 12826–12846. DOI: 10.1109/JIOT.2021.3073904 PMID: 35782886

Gudivaka, B. R. (2024). Smart Comrade Robot for Elderly: Leveraging IBM Watson Health and Google Cloud AI for Advanced Health and Emergency Systems. *International Journal of Engineering Research and Science & Technology*, *20*(3), 334–352.

Gupta, D., Kayode, O., Bhatt, S., Gupta, M., & Tosun, A. S. (2021, December). Hierarchical federated learning based anomaly detection using digital twins for smart healthcare. In *2021 IEEE 7th international conference on collaboration and internet computing (CIC)* (pp. 16-25). IEEE. DOI: 10.1109/CIC52973.2021.00013

Iaboni, A., Spasojevic, S., Newman, K., Schindel Martin, L., Wang, A., Ye, B., Mihailidis, A., & Khan, S. S. (2022). Wearable multimodal sensors for the detection of behavioral and psychological symptoms of dementia using personalized machine learning models. *Alzheimer's & Dementia: Diagnosis, Assessment & Disease Monitoring, 14*(1), e12305. DOI: 10.1002/dad2.12305 PMID: 35496371

Jambhale, K., Mahajan, S., Rieland, B., Banerjee, N., Dutt, A., Kadiyala, S. P., & Vinjamuri, R. (2022). Identifying biomarkers for accurate detection of stress. *Sensors (Basel), 22*(22), 8703. DOI: 10.3390/s22228703 PMID: 36433299

Jambhale, K., Rieland, B., Mahajan, S., Narsay, P., Banerjee, N., Dutt, A., & Vinjamuri, R. (2022, July). Selection of optimal physiological features for accurate detection of stress. In *2022 44th Annual International Conference of the IEEE Engineering in Medicine & Biology Society (EMBC)* (pp. 2514-2517). IEEE. DOI: 10.1109/EMBC48229.2022.9871067

Katiyar, K. (2022). AI-based predictive analytics for patients' psychological disorder. In *Predictive Analytics of Psychological Disorders in Healthcare: Data Analytics on Psychological Disorders* (pp. 37–53). Springer Nature Singapore. DOI: 10.1007/978-981-19-1724-0_3

Kumar, D., Ingole, A., & Choudhari, S. G. (2023). Towards Ideal Health Ecosystem With Artificial Intelligence-Driven Medical Services in India: An Overview. *Cureus, 15*(11). Advance online publication. DOI: 10.7759/cureus.48482 PMID: 38073925

Lee, V. V., Vijayakumar, S., Ng, W. Y., Lau, N. Y., Leong, Q. Y., Ooi, D. S. Q., Su, L. L., Lee, Y. S., Chan, S.-Y., Blasiak, A., & Ho, D. (2023). Personalization and localization as key expectations of digital health intervention in women pre-to post-pregnancy. *NPJ Digital Medicine, 6*(1), 183. DOI: 10.1038/s41746-023-00924-6 PMID: 37775533

Liu, H. (2022). Applications of Artificial Intelligence to Popularize Legal Knowledge and Publicize the Impact on Adolescents' Mental Health Status. *Frontiers in Psychiatry, 13*, 902456. DOI: 10.3389/fpsyt.2022.902456 PMID: 35722558

Long, N., Lei, Y., Peng, L., Xu, P., & Mao, P. (2022). A scoping review on monitoring mental health using smart wearable devices. *Mathematical Biosciences and Engineering, 19*(8), 7899–7919. DOI: 10.3934/mbe.2022369 PMID: 35801449

Majeed, A., & Hwang, S. O. (2021). Data-driven analytics leveraging artificial intelligence in the era of COVID-19: An insightful review of recent developments. *Symmetry, 14*(1), 16. DOI: 10.3390/sym14010016

Naegelin, M., Weibel, R. P., Kerr, J. I., Schinazi, V. R., La Marca, R., von Wangenheim, F., Hoelscher, C., & Ferrario, A. (2023). An interpretable machine learning approach to multimodal stress detection in a simulated office environment. *Journal of Biomedical Informatics, 139*, 104299. DOI: 10.1016/j.jbi.2023.104299 PMID: 36720332

Nagarajan, H., Alsalami, Z., Dhareshwar, S., Sandhya, K., & Palanisamy, P. (2024, May). Predicting Academic Performance of Students Using Modified Decision Tree based Genetic Algorithm. In *2024 Second International Conference on Data Science and Information System (ICDSIS)* (pp. 1-5). IEEE. DOI: 10.1109/ICDSIS61070.2024.10594426

Naik, N., Hameed, B. Z., Sooriyaperakasam, N., Vinayahalingam, S., Patil, V., Smriti, K., Saxena, J., Shah, M., Ibrahim, S., Singh, A., Karimi, H., Naganathan, K., Shetty, D. K., Rai, B. P., Chlosta, P., & Somani, B. K. (2022). Transforming healthcare through a digital revolution: A review of digital healthcare technologies and solutions. *Frontiers in Digital Health*, *4*, 919985. DOI: 10.3389/fdgth.2022.919985 PMID: 35990014

Nashwan, A. J., Gharib, S., Alhadidi, M., El-Ashry, A. M., Alamgir, A., Al-Hassan, M., Khedr, M. A., Dawood, S., & Abufarsakh, B. (2023). Harnessing artificial intelligence: Strategies for mental health nurses in optimizing psychiatric patient care. *Issues in Mental Health Nursing*, *44*(10), 1020–1034. DOI: 10.1080/01612840.2023.2263579 PMID: 37850937

Palomares, I., Martínez-Cámara, E., Montes, R., García-Moral, P., Chiachio, M., Chiachio, J., Alonso, S., Melero, F. J., Molina, D., Fernández, B., Moral, C., Marchena, R., de Vargas, J. P., & Herrera, F. (2021). A panoramic view and swot analysis of artificial intelligence for achieving the sustainable development goals by 2030: Progress and prospects. *Applied Intelligence*, *51*(9), 6497–6527. DOI: 10.1007/s10489-021-02264-y PMID: 34764606

Panga, N. K. R. (2022). Applying discrete wavelet transform for ECG signal analysis in IOT health monitoring systems. *International Journal of Information Technology and Computer Engineering*, *10*(4), 157–175.

Prokopowicz, P., Mikołajewski, D., & Mikołajewska, E. (2022). Intelligent System for Detecting Deterioration of Life Satisfaction as Tool for Remote Mental-Health Monitoring. *Sensors (Basel)*, *22*(23), 9214. DOI: 10.3390/s22239214 PMID: 36501916

Sahal, R., Alsamhi, S. H., & Brown, K. N. (2022). Personal digital twin: A close look into the present and a step towards the future of personalised healthcare industry. *Sensors (Basel)*, *22*(15), 5918. DOI: 10.3390/s22155918 PMID: 35957477

Sathyaprakash, P., Alagarsundaram, P., Devarajan, M. V., Alkhayyat, A., Poovendran, P., Rani, D. R., & Savitha, V. (2024). Medical practitioner-centric heterogeneous network powered efficient E-Healthcare risk prediction on Health Big Data. *International Journal of Cooperative Information Systems*, **•••**, 2450012. DOI: 10.1142/S0218843024500126

Subramanian, B., Kim, J., Maray, M., & Paul, A. (2022). Digital twin model: A real-time emotion recognition system for personalized healthcare. *IEEE Access : Practical Innovations, Open Solutions*, *10*, 81155–81165. DOI: 10.1109/ACCESS.2022.3193941

Venkatesh, K. P., Brito, G., & Kamel Boulos, M. N. (2024). Health digital twins in life science and health care innovation. *Annual Review of Pharmacology and Toxicology*, *64*(1), 159–170. DOI: 10.1146/annurev-pharmtox-022123-022046 PMID: 37562495

Young, H. A., Freegard, G., & Benton, D. (2022). Mediterranean diet, interoception and mental health: Is it time to look beyond the 'Gut-brain axis'? *Physiology & Behavior*, *257*, 113964. DOI: 10.1016/j.physbeh.2022.113964 PMID: 36130628

Chapter 19
AI-Enabled Digital Twin Framework for Healthcare Task Offloading Strategies with MADDPG, AHP, Multimodal Digital Twins, DRM, and mHealth Applications

Dinesh Kumar Reddy Basani
https://orcid.org/0009-0005-8841-0462
CGI, Canada

Basava Ramanjaneyulu Gudivaka
https://orcid.org/0009-0006-9123-7872
Raas Infotek, Newark, USA

Rajya Lakshmi Gudivaka
https://orcid.org/0009-0002-4194-0915
Wipro, Hyderabad, India

Raj Kumar Gudivaka
https://orcid.org/0009-0002-9399-1976
Surge Technology Solutions Inc, USA

Sri Harsha Grandhi
https://orcid.org/0009-0000-8425-4144
Intel, Folsom, USA

M. M. Kamruzzaman
Department of Computer Science, College of Computer and Information Sciences, Saudi Arabia

ABSTRACT

Background: The AI-powered framework combines MADDPG, AHP, multimodal digital twins, DRM, and mHealth apps to improve real-time monitoring, optimize healthcare resource management, and promote individualized care using predictive analytics and the Internet of Things. Methods: It uses multimodal digital twins for real-time simulation, DRM for resource allocation, AHP for decision prioritization, MADDPG for reinforcement learning, and mHealth apps for ongoing monitoring. Objectives: The ultimate aim of enhancing these factors is to bring better decision-making, resource allocation, and work offloading to improve operational performance and results in the healthcare industry. Results: The findings are on improvement of scalability, adaptability, and patient care by achieving 94.5% accuracy, 92.8% precision, and 90% computing efficiency. Conclusion: By enhancing real-time reactions, resource

DOI: 10.4018/979-8-3373-2028-1.ch019

management, and patient outcomes, the integrated AI-driven framework may provide a creative, effective solution for contemporary healthcare.

1. INTRODUCTION

The contemporary scenario of healthcare is changing because of advanced technologies that give accuracy, efficiency, and individualization through digital twins (DT), artificial intelligence, and mobile health (mHealth) applications. This article comes with a framework for optimizing healthcare delivery by Chen et al. (2023), using resources such as MADDPG, AHP, multimodal digital twins, DRM, and mHealth applications. This AI-based digital twin approach utilizes real-time monitoring, decision-making, and resource allocation for the betterment of patient outcomes and operational efficiency. The proposed framework aims at rethinking health care management for improving patient care outcomes and the operations of the healthcare system in general by working on important issues and streamlining tasks.

A digital twin is the electronic replica of anything physical, ranging from a patient to equipment in medical facilities, and even the overall healthcare system. This virtual model will continuously collect and analyze real-time data to help healthcare providers simulate, monitor, and optimize their processes. Elhenawy et al. (2023) Digital twins in health care can be defined as patient physiological systems to simulate disease progression and the efficacy of treatments and individualized care. Therefore, integration of AI into digital twin will make it a predictive analytic/decision-making as well as operating autonomously by processing multimodal data streams generated by clinical record data, data from wearable sensor streams, as well as information related to various environmental factors; the actionable findings help healthcare practitioners to predict problems that may arise in the procedure and suggest focused interventions and subsequently efficient resource management.

Multi-Agent Deep Deterministic Policy Gradient is a reinforcement learning algorithm, which is applied to multi-agent environments in which multiple agents interact with each other and have their policies. Shavandi & Khedmati (2022) MADDPG is an extension of DDPG, but it also introduces centralized training with decentralized execution. In the training phase, MADDPG uses a centralized critic for each agent that has access to the global state and actions of all agents for better coordination. Execution is scalable and practical in that each agent can rely on its local observations and policy. Specific effective applications of MADDPG include cooperative and competitive multi-agent scenarios, for example, task allocation, resource management, or autonomous system coordination.

The Analytic Hierarchy Process, or AHP, is a decision framework that sets tasks priorities on dimensions like the patient status, availability of resources, and urgency. For example, an importance for decision-making in this paper would be urgency for killer instances, pushing regular tasks to further stages: Panchal & Shrivastava (2022). With regard to improving task-offloading techniques, AHP, in conjunction with MADDPG, further enhances the effectiveness and efficiency of decision-making. It is therefore an end result streamlining workflows and improving patient care and outcomes along the healthcare systems through applying computing and operational resources as efficiently as possible.

Multimodal digital twins are highly advanced virtual representations that incorporate streams of different types of data such as physiological, behavioral, environmental, and clinical data. Zhong et al. (2023) Healthcare systems enable the monitoring, real-time prediction of outcomes, and personalization of treatment based on the input provided by wearable devices, electronic health records, and IoT sensors. Such an integrative view can simulate the disease process, tailor the treatment plans, and make more accurate predictions. By connecting multiple modalities of data, these digital twins enable a better understanding of complex health dynamics, thus empowering both patients and providers to achieve more effective and targeted healthcare solutions.

Healthcare Demand Response Management refers to the real-time allocation, monitoring, and optimization of resources, for instance, computational resources, medical equipment, and personnel, for efficient service delivery. In employing AI-driven algorithms, DRM adjusts the distribution of resources based on demand and system capabilities. It gives health systems more flexibility to appropriately adapt to changing demands such as pandemics or catastrophes. Zahra (2021) Predictive analytics in DRM can predict future resource demands and reduce delay and wastage. All of this is ensured through fair and efficient use while having minimum operational costs. However, along with that, it maintains high-quality in-patient care and supportive data-intensive applications such as those of digital twin and mHealth systems. The mHealth applications, in this framework, are going to bring interaction between all patients, caregivers, and respective digital twins, Such applications will make use of wearable devices, IoT sensors, and smartphones to offer real-time health monitoring, diagnostics, and therapeutic interventions.

The AI-enabled digital twin framework is the next step in healthcare technology, combining the powers of AI, digital twins, and mHealth applications to address some of the toughest challenges that the sector faces. Advanced task offloading strategies, multimodal digital twins, and DRM altogether ensure optimal resource usage, personalized care, and real-time monitoring. In summary, this framework, with a focus on precision, efficiency, and adaptability, has the potential to transform the delivery of healthcare and make the future brighter and healthier.

The following objectives are:

- Development of a framework for resource optimization that uses AI-powered task offloading strategies.
- Constant patient monitoring with diagnostics through multi-modal digital twinning.
- Deployment of MADDPG and AHP for tasks to be efficiently prioritized toward resource allocation.
- mHealth for personalized healthcare delivery.
- DRM must be implemented and used to keep the resources involved in healthcare operational.
- Virtual real-world healthcare ecosystem integration for non-disruptive practices.

Integration of DTs in health care systems has posed many problems: security, accessibility, bias, and quality, that need to be solved to exploit DHTs in personalized medicine. Papachristou et al. (2024) These are the issues that have hindered the effective use of DTs, which are necessary for healthy progress in the healthcare arena. They permit a very exact vision throughout a disease and the customization of plans of treatment. Transcending these hurdles is essential for the utilization of DTs for precision medicine in facilitating individualized medical interventions that achieve high-quality outcomes and innovative healthcare delivery and management. The leap toward personalized healthcare solutions is transformative.

2. LITERATURE SURVEY

Jameil and Al-Raweshidy (2024) developed a proposal for task offloading improvements in healthcare using DT and social health determinants. The framework leverages partial and binary offloading strategies along with multi-protocol communications, thus allowing efficient data exchange and personalized interventions. Testing in real-time environments reveals significant improvements, which include a 10% increase in energy efficiency and a 20% reduction in network latency with 20 MEC nodes. With 30 nodes, latency dropped by 33.4% and power usage by 53.8% for data sizes up to 100 MB. This study bridges a key research gap and advances healthcare system performance.

Rahimi et al. (2024) looked into AI-enabled digital twins (DTs), virtual models that have enhanced predictive AI; such digital twins can transform healthcare and clinical decision-making. Recognizing the lack of unifying frameworks, the current study performed a scoping review of 11 studies (2020–2023) in various databases, such as PubMed, Embase, and IEEE Xplore, as well as grey literature. Key steps and frameworks that the review used in informing the development of the DECIDE-Twin framework will be used in guiding the creation and implementation of DTs. The framework draws insights from reviews and empirical studies and gives a holistic approach to advancing the clinical applications of DTs.

Surendar and Sitaraman (2022) discussed the transformative role of AI techniques such as Convolutional Neural Networks (CNNs) and Variational Autoencoders (VAEs) in radiology. These approaches benefit in terms of diagnostic accuracy improving, automating, and augmenting image analysis improving healthcare. However, there still exist issues like data privacy, deeply inherent biases, and interpretability in AI models; therefore, making ethical issues very relevant to clinical practice in applying AI. These issues identified will be pivotal for ensuring AI promises the promise to bring in increased clinical efficiency and better patient outcomes as a route toward an ethics-oriented, yet more efficient healthcare system for the future.

Balasubhramanyam et al. (2024) have reviewed a literature study about the healthcare application and the DT technology's transformative potential in healthcare for the years 2020–2023. The paper underscores various DT roles, benefits, and impacts on personalized care and industry practices. It discusses important requirements and key layers required to consider when implementing DT systems in applications such as diagnostics and treatment. The paper focuses on the benefits that it addresses, along with challenges and limitations, toward giving a proper balanced view regarding its current status. It gives key findings, methodologies, and future directions as a comprehensive outlook on the DT potential to transform smart, personalized healthcare.

According to Poovendran Alagarsundaram in 2023, AI-driven predictive analytics tends to accelerate the effectiveness of precision besides improving resource allocations during the investigations. The purpose of this article is to examine such machine learning algorithms as Gaussian Naive Bayes, Decision Trees, and Random Forests useful in straightening out the investigating processes. It underscores the transformative ability of AI in the processing of big data and handling matters related to data privacy and algorithmic bias. It points out the ability of AI-based approaches to support decision-making, workflow optimization, and a reduction in time taken during an investigation. It supports ethical technology integration into investigation frameworks.

Sheraz et al. (2024) stated that 5G suffers from the most severe capacity constraints when handling the Internet of Everything (IoE), but potential digital twin networks (DTN) could be solutions for wireless systems in developing virtual replicas of the physical environments so their effective testing and optimization, possibly with AI model upgrade, can better manage network conditions, distribute available resources, and predict behaviors in the networks. The authors examine AI-enabled DTNs as key enablers for 6G, providing their role in advancing technologies along the lines of caching, data offloading, security, and in smart cities health care, and transportation, challenges toward AI-driven DTN in the future of research in 6G.

Feriani and Hossain (2021) discuss advancement in Deep Reinforcement Learning, DRL, applied to wireless networks for scalable low-latency services. They believe that Multi-Agent Reinforcement Learning, MARL, is imperative in technologies including intelligent meta-surfaces, aerial networks, and edge AI, whose design is for decentralized and co-operative systems. The paper reviews single-agent and MARL frameworks, examines Model-Based RL and cooperative MARL applications, and exhibits applications in Mobile Edge Computing, UAV networks, and cell-free massive MIMO. Future research directions are identified with the intent to ignite further work in scalable, decentralized systems that rely on MARL for next-generation wireless networks.

Basava Ramanjaneyulu Gudivaka (2021) developed the AI-based Smart Comrade Robot for elderly care improvement. The advanced robotics and AI of the robot are capable of daily assistance, health monitoring, and emergency response. The real-time data processing capabilities through IBM Watson Health and Google Cloud AI can help in customized care. Smart Comrade Robot makes the elderly safe, and companionable, and enhances quality of life while decreasing caregiver stress. The adaptive qualities will be responding to individual needs and, hence, an absolute must for contemporary eldercare bridging the gulf between innovative technology and care-giving sensitivity.

Chen et al. (2021) present PowerNet - a multi-agent deep reinforcement learning algorithm for decentralized voltage control in power grids. This approach puts the control of distributed generators (DGs) into the frame of cooperative MARL. Each DG learns policies based on local states, sub-global rewards, and encoded neighbor communications. Innovations in this approach are a spatial discount factor for scalable training, learning-based communication protocols for collaboration, and an action-smoothing factor for stability. Their high-fidelity simulation platform, PGSim, demonstrates the superiority of PowerNet over traditional methods and MARL benchmarks in microgrid tests, showing efficiency and scalability in large-scale power systems.

Naderializadeh et al. (2021) propose a distributed mechanism for the management of resources and interference mitigation across wireless networks by using multi-agent deep reinforcement learning. Each transmitter has an RL agent that takes the delayed observation of users from delayed observations, which communicates with neighboring agents to determine user scheduling and transmit power. The approach is scalable since agents trained on a particular setup can adapt when transferring to different network sizes. Simulations show their method outperforms decentralized baselines in balancing average and 5th-percentile user rates, achieving close to or even better performance compared to centralized methods. The agents also remain robust under deployment mismatches.

Dinesh Kumar Reddy Basani (2021) researches the likelihood of AI, especially machine and deep learning, improving cybersecurity capabilities in countering new threats. This allows for automatic detection, response, and mitigation of cyber risks in an efficient manner and speed of defense mechanisms. It reviews the scope of AI towards the resolution of cybersecurity challenges as well as upgrading the capabilities of the current tools given dynamic threat landscapes. It focuses on strengthening cyber resilience and offers adaptive, predictive, and proactive solutions which pave the way for robust defense frameworks capable of safeguarding the systems against even the most advanced attacks in real-time.

Gündoğdu et al. 2021 tackled biases in group decisions due to untrustworthy responses from participants that can adversely affect results. They proposed a new hybrid model using picture fuzzy sets and linear assignment that is applied to the problem of public transport development. This technique not only addresses the indeterminacy in the respondent's evaluation but also reduces subjectivity using linear assignment. Compared to the intuitionistic fuzzy TOPSIS model, which is a popular technique, the proposed model also produced similar reliable results, thereby confirming its effectiveness. Their approach does show a strong method of how to enhance decision-making by reducing uncertainty and subjectivity in evaluations systematically.

Wu et al. (2022) applied the Analytic Hierarchy Process (AHP) in determining suitable ecotourism activities in Diaoluo Mountain National Nature Reserve. AHP is a method of decision-making, which includes the integration of qualitative and quantitative analysis in the selection of alternatives according to several criteria. The same study aims at how ecotourism integrates protected areas into local communities and tourists. Results show that the most suitable activity is guided visits to the original ecological villages of the Li and Miao ethnic minorities. This research proves the applicability of AHP in the selection of optimal ecotourism activities to be used for sustainable tourism development.

Wang et al. (2022) have proposed a DTs-based enhanced deep transfer learning approach for enhancing MRI medical images. In their study, an author designed a super-resolution deep neural network and a multi-modal image fusion algorithm to avoid the limitations of various medical image acquisition methods. The results were that the sharpness and realism of MRI images were improved with PSNR 34.11 dB and SSIM 85.24%. The fusion algorithm achieved better performance with both subjective and objective evaluations, without losing spatial details and maintaining high color accuracy. Overall, this method shows its superiority in image enhancement of MRIs and multispectral imaging of PET and SPECT.

Xiang et al. (2021) have emphasized the critical role of water as a key resource for socio-economic growth and environmental protection. They pointed out the challenges posed by climate change on conventional water resource management, which is usually focused on meeting competing demands. To address such challenges, the authors proposed the Adaptive Intelligent Dynamic Water Resource Planning (AIDWRP). This AI-based approach brings together data-driven modeling with human insights for enhanced water efficiency and improved decision-making. MDP brings optimization of sustainable water management policy on both the supply and the demand side that is locally efficient while being sensitive-driven.

Sunil Kumar Alavilli (2023) argued that graph theory is being used in lung cancer, both in SCLC and NSCLC. Graph theory allows for the representation of genes as well as proteins as a network. Through representation as networks, graph theory allows for the detection of more biomarkers and provides prediction of disease conditions, among other things. Machine learning therefore contributes to improving the detection accuracy of cancer thereby providing more precision and personalized therapy. It further provides an advanced perspective for the integration of graph theory and machine learning on oncology leading to a deeper understanding of the complexity of biological interaction and therapeutic management of lung cancers.

Lim et al. (2021) discuss Edge Intelligence, a concept that uses devices and edge servers to process data near its source, with the integration of Artificial Intelligence (AI) and Edge Computing. One of the key technologies involved is Federated Learning (FL), which enables model training without sharing raw data. To improve communication efficiency in large, distributed networks, Hierarchical Federated Learning (HFL) reduces central reliance through cluster heads that aggregate intermediate models. However, mechanisms of resource allocation and incentives in HFL have not been adequately explored. Lim et al.

proposed a two-level system for cluster selection and resource valuation by using deep learning-based auction while demonstrating efficiency and revenue maximization.

3. METHODOLOGY

The methodologies will include: Multi-Agent Deep Deterministic Policy Gradient, Analytical Hierarchy Process, multimodal digital twins, Demand Response Management, and mHealth applications in developing an AI-enabled digital twin framework for healthcare with a focus on the strategies of real-time monitoring, predictive analytics, and task offloading towards better decision-making and resource allocation. The mechanism works due to variable streams of data incorporation, reinforcement models of learning, and decision-making, which attempt to handle issues from resource optimization toward the delivery of personalized healthcare delivery. Each entity adds something characteristic to the general efficiency, scale, and agility of the whole system, effectively delivering comprehensive, effective healthcare services.

Figure 1. Integrated Healthcare Framework Using Digital Twins, IoT, and Advanced Decision-Making Models

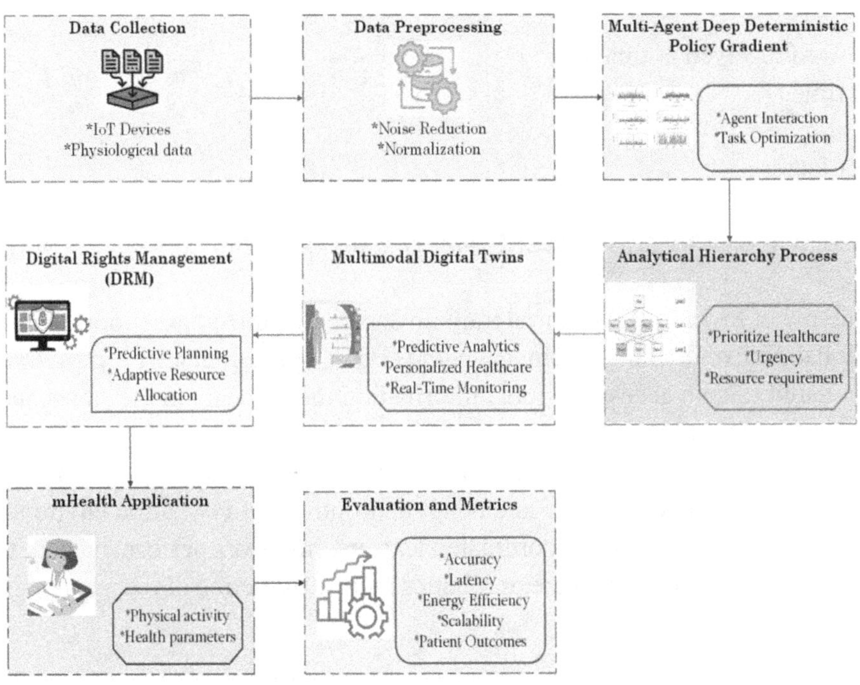

Figure 1 integrates devices of IoT, and physiological data into healthcare optimization. Data preprocessing can reduce noise or normalize inputs and then apply different multi-agent deep deterministic policy gradients to optimize both tasks and the interactions between various agents. An Analytical Hierarchy Process prioritizes specific healthcare needs; Digital Rights Management ensures resource distribution and predictive planning. Multimodal digital twins enable predictive analytics, real-time monitoring, and personalized care by incorporating mHealth applications for monitoring physical activity as well as health-related parameters. Finally, evaluation metrics assess accuracy, latency, energy efficiency, scalability, and patient outcomes, ensuring a robust, adaptive healthcare solution for dynamic needs.

3.1 Multi-Agent Deep Deterministic Policy Gradient (MADDPG)

MADDPG is a reinforcement learning algorithm targeted at multi-agent systems. The collaboration example implies its use so that the agent makes collective decisions. The training end is centralized while exercising in a decentralized way by an agent acting upon local observations. MADDPG can optimize the healthcare system for resource allocation, scheduling tasks, and patient prioritization. In this way, MADDPG models interactions between agents, like healthcare providers, patients, and machines, ensuring coordination and efficiency in complex, dynamic environments. Such an approach can be adapted for real-time situations such as emergency response and resource shortages to make operational effectiveness and outcomes better overall for the patient.

$$R = \mathbb{E}\left[\sum_{t=0}^{T}\gamma^{t} r(s_t, a_t)\right] \tag{1}$$

Here:

- $r(s_t t_t)$: Reward received at time t
- s_t: State at time t
- a_t: Action at time t
- γ: Discount factor

3.1.1 Centralized Training and Decentralized Execution

The core principle of MADDPG is central training and decentralized execution. This principle capitalizes on both collaborative learning and independent action. In the course of central training, the critic network will be shared to gain access to global information that appears in the states and actions of all agents. Therefore, the critic network can assess the actions much more effectively before optimizing the policies. However, with decentralized execution, each agent executes independently on its local observations and learned policies to scale and adapt appropriately in dynamic environments. It's very effective for multi-agent systems where coordinated learning improves performance, but the real-world scenarios of such applications as health care or robotics require the action of the agent to be independent.

$$Q^{\pi}(s,a) = r(s,a) + \gamma\mathbb{E}[Q^{\pi}(s',a')] \tag{2}$$

Where:

- $Q^{\pi}(s,a)$: Value of state-action pair
- $r(s,a)$: Reward at state a, action a
- γ: Discount factor
- s', a': Next state and action

3.1.1.1 Applications of CTDE in Healthcare

The other reason is that CTDE helps improve the quality of medical care. This is because it wisely utilizes available resources and equipment, and even triaging the patients. It encourages integrated decision-making, delivers emergencies aptly, and ensures optimum utilization of critical assets such as ICU beds and ventilators. CTDE empowers task scheduling, remote monitoring, and online interventions in telemedicine. This adaptability helps in scalable solutions of complex systems of healthcare systems improving operational efficiency, as well as patient outcomes over dynamic, multi-agent scenarios.

3.1.1.2 Future Prospects of CTDE in AI

The future for CTDE in AI will be enhancing the scalability and robustness of CTDE in large-scale multi-agent systems. It can then be used specifically to especially be used in federated learning with some distributed settings such as smart cities and IoT networks, in reducing communication overhead. This then promotes applications in digital twins, autonomous systems, and adaptive health care. CTDE can be used in combination with advanced AI models, like transformers, to enable better coordination, learning efficiency, and adaptability in complex and non-stationary environments.

3.1.2 Reward Mechanism in Multi-Agent Systems

The Reward Mechanism in Multi-Agent Systems is meant to guide agents toward learning optimal behavior in cooperative or competitive environments. In a multi-agent system, every agent receives its rewards based on the outcome of those actions and their contribution to the general goals of the system. For cooperative tasks, a shared reward will be effective in encouraging teamwork, but individual rewards work best for competitive tasks. A well-crafted reward function design should minimize reward conflicts and focus on finding an alignment between the behaviors of agents toward desired outcomes, thus minimizing delayed rewards. In this context, an effective mechanism ensures the adaptation of the agents to changing environments, their learning of coordinated strategies, and system-wide efficiency and goals being met.

$$R = \sum_{t=0}^{T} \gamma^t r_i(s_t, a_t) \tag{3}$$

3.1.2.1 Healthcare-Specific Applications

The healthcare reward mechanism enhances the multi-agent tasks related to resource allocation, task scheduling, and patient triage. There is a potential reward for at least some minimum wait time or ICU bed usage by the agents. The reward would perhaps scale dynamically, life-savingly during emergency care, for instance. Reward mechanisms increase efficiency in operation, improving results for the patient, with an efficient allocation of resources in real-time as well.

3.1.3 Advantages of MADDPG in Healthcare

MADDPG in healthcare can play a crucial role in achieving intelligent, collaborative decision-making in dynamic multi-agent environments. Resource allocation in ICU beds, ventilators, or staff can be optimized by efficient coordination between agents like health care providers and devices. The central training makes sure that agents learn from the global interactions while the decentralized execution ensures real-time response in emergencies. It is only with such complex scenarios such as task scheduling, triage prioritization, and resource reallocation that it will improve the operational process efficiency. It is enhanced by predictive analytics together with adaptability, which can help improve patient outcomes while minimizing delay and also equitably distributing resources. So, it's a very valuable tool for the modern AI-driven healthcare systems.

$$\pi^* = \arg\max_{\pi} \mathbb{E}[Q^{\pi}(s,a)] \tag{4}$$

Algorithm 1 MADDPG-Enhanced Multi-Agent Learning for Dynamic Healthcare Resource Distribution

Input: State space (S), Action space (A), Reward function (R), Discount factor (γ), Learning rate (α)
Output: Optimized policies for agents
Initialize: Actor and critic networks for each agent, replay buffer (B), and exploration noise (ε)
For each episode:
Initialize environment state s_0
For each time step t:
For each agent i:
Select action a_i using policy π_i with exploration noise
Execute action a_i and observe reward r_i and next state s'
Store transition (s, a, r, s') in replay buffer B
If replay buffer B is sufficiently populated:
Sample minibatch from B
Update the critic network using:
Q(s, a) = r + γ max Q(s', a')
Update actor policy by maximizing Q(s, a)
Adjust network parameters with gradient descent
End For
End For
Return optimized policies

Algorithm 1 applies MADDPG for healthcare resource allocation and task prioritization. The use of actor-critic networks for each of the agents allows the utilization of centralized training and decentralized execution. The agents interact with their environment, optimizing their policies with exploration noise, replay buffers, and gradient updates. The critic network learns a probable Q-value for the actions it takes, whereas the actor maximizes the obtained values of actions. This approach assures efficient resource allocation, and dynamic and adaptive decision-making, particularly at times of high demand or when emergencies occur; this, therefore, further improves efficiencies in operation, as well as patient outcomes.

3.2 Analytical Hierarchy Process (AHP)

AHP is a structured decision-making tool used for ranking tasks or alternative evaluations based on weighted criteria. It is thus a tool in healthcare to rank the interventions or resources in terms of factors such as urgency, cost, and availability of resources. AHP makes use of pairwise comparisons with mathematical calculations to derive weights based on the criteria to facilitate objective and consistent decisions. For instance, it ranks the critical treatments during emergencies or provides adequate staffing in areas of high demand. By integrating AHP with AI-driven frameworks such as MADDPG, the system benefits from a combination of both analytical rigor and dynamic adaptability, improving task management and resource optimization.

$$w_i = \frac{a_{ij}}{\sum_{i=1}^{n} a_{ij}} \tag{5}$$

Where:

- a_{ij}: Pairwise comparison values
- n: Number of criteria

3.2.1 Overview of AHP and Its Core Principles

AHP is known as the Analytical Hierarchy Process. It has been developed by Thomas Saaty. This helps break down problems into a series of criteria and subcriteria of the hierarchy which in turn would make the complex problems simple and easier to use. AHP uses comparison with pairs to decide the relative importance judgments between criteria or alternatives. A qualitative judgment thus transforms into a set of quantitative scores. Decomposition forms the backbone of AHP and includes the structure of problems as hierarchies, comparative judgment or assessing criteria in pairs, synthesis or the overall priorities, and consistency for making logical judgments. AHP is widely used for multi-criteria decision-making purposes, systematically weighing options according to weighted priorities that are well suited for healthcare planning situations that require transparency, consistency, and objectivity.

$$CI = \frac{\lambda_{max} - n}{n - 1} \tag{6}$$

3.2.2 Applications of AHP in Healthcare Decision-Making

AHP, in the form of structured multicriteria decision-making, plays a vital role in health services. It can help in prioritizing critical interventions, which could be as basic as choosing between two treatment options, resource allocation, or evaluation of policies in a given healthcare system. AHP facilitates fair and balanced decisions, especially in the comparison of urgency, cost, and patient results that have to be taken into account. An example is in emergency care: it can rank patients by the severity of their diseases to consider them for care accordingly. AHP also helps hospital management in budgeting, infrastructure planning, and technology adoption. Its capacity to involve the integration of qualitative and quantitative criteria makes it indispensable for enhancing efficiency and precision in all complex healthcare decisions.

$$P_i = \sum_{j=1}^{n} w_j \cdot c_{ij} \quad (7)$$

Where:

- w_j: Weight of criterion j
- c_{ij}: Score of alternative i for criterion j

3.2.3.1 Prioritizing Patient Treatment Options Based on Clinical Criteria

Application of AHP in ranking and prioritizing a treatment option based on clinical criteria requires assessing and ranking the treatments concerning the urgency or cost, efficiency, patient's state, etc. Through a structured hierarchy of such criteria, AHP ensures systematic assessment and prioritization of interventions by healthcare providers. More so, during emergencies, it identifies crucial treatments involving life-threatening conditions, thus optimally investing available resources for the enhanced improvement of patients' conditions and decision-making in clinical settings as a whole.

3.2.3.2 Resource Allocation in Hospitals During Emergencies

AHP aids the hospitals in emergencies to put on resources employing multiplex criteria like urgency, availability of resources, and condition of the patient. It sets a priority on critical needs such as ICU beds, ventilators, and medical staff based on weighted importance. AHP ensures systematic and objective decisions under pressure, making optimum use of resources. It integrates real-time data, supporting dynamic adjustments for efficiency and effectiveness in healthcare facility emergency response efforts.

3.2.3 Integration of AHP with AI and Machine Learning

AHP integrated with AI and ML will decide by the best combination of human judgment with the efficiency of the computation. Criteria evaluation and the same criteria can be prioritized through AHP, whereas the data processing, pattern recognition, and predictive models are automated with AI and ML. The combined synergy provides for dynamic weighting, real-time analysis, and adaptive learning in complex systems. For example, consider the domain of healthcare: AHP may rank the respective treatments for the respective conditions of patients. ML models may further adjust rankings depending on history data. For instance, integration of AHP with AI/ML may enhance multi-criteria decision-making scalability, consistency, and accuracy, consequently.

$$\text{Optimal Solution} = \max\left(\sum_{i=1}^{n} w_i \cdot AI_i\right) \quad (8)$$

3.2.3.1 Challenges in Combining AHP with AI and Machine Learning

The combination of AHP with AI and Machine Learning is plagued by the issue of inconsistent pairwise comparisons and considers data quality and relevance as well as computational complexity for large data sets. This means that whenever human judgment is combined with an automated process, bias in judgment also arises. Robust algorithms, domain expertise, and proper integration of the inputs from humans and machines together to balance interpretability with the model accuracy; handling issues of scalability to dynamic systems is also involved.

3.3 Multimodal Digital Twins

Multimodal digital twins are built by integrating information from various sources, such as wearable devices, electronic health records, or IoT sensors, which create virtual representations of physical systems or patients. Such virtual twins allow for real-time monitoring of treatment possibilities mapped to personalized plans and predictive analytics while simulating complex health dynamics. They provide a panoramic view of the health status of the patient in the health domain, including either physiological, behavioral, or environmental information. In this instance, the multimodal digital twin for the diabetic patient would track the glucose levels, activity patterns, and diet. All of these are factors informing interventions carried out specifically on that patient. It, therefore, continues the care with improved precision medicine and outcomes.

$$D_{\text{twin}} = \sum_{i=1}^{n} w_i \cdot d_i \quad (9)$$

Where:

- D_{twin}: Digital twin representation
- d_j: Datastream i
- w_i: Weight assigned to the data stream i

3.3.1 Real-Time Monitoring and Predictive Analytics with Digital Twins

Continuous data acquisition and analysis are involved by the digital twin through real-time monitoring and predictive analytics to simulate and predict health outcomes. Multimodal digital twins will integrate wearables, electronic health records, and IoT sensor data and thereby provide dynamic, holistic insights into the health profile of a patient. This type of real-time monitoring will then pick up early anomalies such as abnormal heart rate or lower oxygen level for timely interventions. Predictive analytics leverage AI algorithms to make predictions about how a disease progresses, how efficacious a given treatment is going to be, and what kinds of complications may arise from it. Using scenario simulation allows healthcare providers to make informed decisions, optimize resource allocation, and thus deliver personalized care toward increasing efficiency and patient outcomes.

$$P_t = f(D_t, H_t) \quad (10)$$

3.3.1.1Predictive Analytics: Enhancing Diagnostics and Forecasting Outcomes

Predictive analytics in digital twins uses artificial intelligence and machine learning to analyze both real-time and historical data. This allows for better diagnostics and forecasting results. It predicts how the disease might progress, treatment efficacy, and complications that may occur. This feature allows health professionals to provide targeted care to the patient. Additionally, based on actionable insights, it makes interventions proactive, transforming patient management with predictive analytics, which will now enable earlier anomaly detection along with overall better precision and efficiency in healthcare.

3.3.1.2 Role of Cloud and Edge Computing in Real-Time Digital Twins

Optimizing data processing and storage in cloud and edge computing, which enables real-time digital twins, plays a very significant role. Edge computing makes the process happen closer to IoT devices and cuts latency down with quicker responses toward real-time applications. Cloud computing gives the capacity to scale large data and to run complex analytics, hence these ensure integration that is seamless and makes resources and connectivity reliable to enable digital twins for real-time updates, prediction capabilities, and improved decision-making in healthcare.

3.3.2 Technological Framework for Implementing Multimodal Digital Twins

It provides the technological foundation for the design of multimodal digital twins, thereby using advanced tools and platforms for the creation of real-time virtual models of physical entities. This starts from the acquisition of data where such data can be from IoT sensors, wearable devices, and electronic health records. Different data streams are processed via edge computing, which provides low latency, while cloud computing takes care of the storage and analytics. AI algorithms, machine learning, and deep learning models facilitate data fusion, predictive analytics, and simulation. Interoperability standards will ensure seamless integration with healthcare systems, and the framework will also have cybersecurity to protect sensitive patient data. Real-time updates allow for personalized health care, optimal resource utilization, and better outcomes.

$$D_{\text{integrated}} = \sum_{i=1}^{m} w_i \cdot d_i \tag{11}$$

3.3.2.1 AI-Driven Data Fusion and Integration for Multimodal Twins

Data fusion and integration are made possible with the use of machine learning and deep learning techniques in the multimodal digital twin. All the data-generating potential sources, such as IoT sensors, wearables, and electronic health records are brought together in an orchestrated model. AI algorithms preprocess, normalize, and correlate the streams with high consistency and accuracy. This will allow updates, predictive analytics, and personalized care based on the patterns and insights of the AI inference. This will make digital twins multimodal an incredibly adaptive and effective tool in dynamic healthcare settings.

3.3.2.2 Future Directions and Emerging Technologies for Digital Twins

Future Directions: Digital Twins Future Directions-Next Phase This involves the fusion of advanced technologies, including 5G, quantum computing, and federated learning into real-time processing, secure data sharing, and scalability. Innovations would cover interactive simulation applications in augmented reality, the application of blockchain for secure exchange, and bringing together biology with digital platforms in the modeling of molecular systems. Evolutionary stages in the future for digital twins are associated with applications such as precision medicine, remote surgery, and optimization in AI-based health care that will rewrite personalized and predictive healthcare solutions.

3.4 Demand Response Management (DRM)

Health Care DRM refers to adjusting demand for available resources such as energy, computation powers, and even medical equipment toward the supply while maintaining efficient use at a reduced cost. Using AI and predictive analytics, DRM ensures dynamic reallocation of resources depending on their necessity. For instance, this DRM in a hospital can generate the most possible electricity for high-priority areas either during peak usage time or lease out some of its computing resources to diagnose cases that happen in real time. It is also scalable, has minimum wastage, and easy delivery of the services. Its reaction during emergencies as well as pandemics makes it adaptable relatively fast through the optimal use of its resources while at the same time continuing with quality care and operational reliability in every healthcare facility.

$$R_t = f(D_t, H_t) \tag{12}$$

3.4.1 AI-Driven Predictive Analytics for Resource Optimization

Resource optimization by AI-driven predictive analytics involves the use of advanced algorithms on machines, predicting the demand for resources in real-time and then optimizing their allocation. This AI model analyses past historic data, current inputs, and contextual factors to identify patterns and make predictions to optimally utilize medical staff, equipment, and computing power. High-quality services reduce delay and waste generation. Predictive analytics in healthcare help in proactive planning, like how many ICU beds to keep ready during a pandemic or optimizing energy usage in smart hospitals. AI makes healthcare operations responsive and cost-effective by integrating with systems such as dynamic resource management and digital twins.

$$C = \sum_{i=1}^{n} R_i \cdot U_i \tag{13}$$

3.4.1.1 Application of AI in Demand-Supply Balancing

Demand and Supply Balancing by Application of AI uses ML and predictive analytics to optimize healthcare's resource-allocating function. It combines real-time with historical data input to predict a change in requirements in terms of various resources, from the medical and nursing staff down to equipment as well as power consumption. This therefore means that with a change in demand, it results in changes of supply to reduce losses from shortfall running that it should provide better care for more patients with reliable response for surgery as required.

3.4.2 Task Prioritization Frameworks in Demand Response Management

Demand Response Management Systems use structured methodological approaches when ranking and subsequently allocating resources properly according to tasks based on criticality, impact, and limited availability of other resources. Analysis tools such as the Analytic Hierarchy Process/AHP or weight scoring models for tasks assess all criteria and support critical interventions whenever resources are scant. In this case, DRM frameworks will take precedence over such routine check-up cases or could allocate ventilator resources to the patients who require emergency care. These frameworks utilize data, from IoT systems in real-time, along with predictive analytics, to dynamically shift priorities and thus utilize resources optimally, minimize delays, and maintain quality of care during high-demand scenarios.

$$P_i = \frac{w_i}{\sum_{j=1}^{n} w_j} \tag{14}$$

3.4.2.1 Role of AI Algorithms in Task Prioritization Frameworks

The role of AI algorithms is very significant in task prioritization frameworks to ensure the proper allocation of resources and healthcare decisions. AI utilizes models that include both machine learning and reinforcement learning while analyzing complex datasets, ranking tasks according to urgency, and optimizing workflows to ensure smooth operations. Dynamic prioritization algorithms, like the Multi-Agent Deep Deterministic Policy Gradient (MADDPG), will determine the critical aspects that should first be attended to. Integration with live data, the use of analytics, and also contextual factors boost accuracy, scale, and responsivity in healthcare settings.

3.4.2.2 Impact of Real-Time Data on Prioritization Accuracy and Efficiency

Healthcare systems are revolutionized by real-time data in the process of prioritization accuracy and efficiency. Continuous data from IoT devices, sensors, and electronic health records gives insight into the condition of patients as well as availability during real-time. It ensures high accuracy in the prioritization of current demands and trends. Dynamism-related adjustments in real-time data reduce delays as well as improve the efficiency in task allocation to ensure priority interventions without delay while optimizing resource utilization in healthcare operations.

3.4.3 Challenges in Implementing DRM in Healthcare Infrastructure

In DRM, some challenges that may exist in the application to healthcare infrastructure are technological, operational, and organizational. Advanced AI systems will be required when integrating DRM along with robust IoT networks and complete data interoperability which could cost a lot of money and be complicated to implement. There may also be concerns about data privacy when healthcare is sensitive information. On the operational side, there may be resistance to change from the service staff, undertraining, and coordination across different departments. It becomes even more critical when resources have to be allocated during a sudden surge in demand, like a pandemic. A further complication occurs with equitable distribution, efficiency, and rule enforcement that is more multi-dimensional as it presents several difficulties in the process of its implementation.

$$C = \sum_{i=1}^{n} (R_i \cdot U_i) + \sum_{j=1}^{m} L_j \tag{15}$$

3.4.3.1 High Implementation Costs and Resource Constraints

The two prominent barriers to implementing DRM in health care are the high implementation cost and resource limitations. The advanced systems of AI drive, IoT equipment, and robust IT setup require heavy expenditure in financial terms, which no healthcare facility can support. Maintenance, software updates, and training staff on new technologies also pose budgetary burdens. Resource constraints, such as hardware that is not enough to process, unskilled personnel for its installation and running, and low computational powers, further exacerbate the problem in the implementation of DRM systems. These problems acutely face the smaller hospitals and clinics, mainly in the deprived regions, in the adoption of DRM and reaping its efficiency and scalability benefits.

3.4.3.2 Limited Access to High-Quality Data for Predictive Models

Limited access to quality data for DRM is a great challenge in healthcare because predictive models depend on adequate, comprehensive, and timely data for reliable forecast generation and the optimization of resources. However, the nature of data in healthcare is largely scattered across separate systems, leading to integration issues. Lack of consistency in the formats, empty values, and biases further downgrade the quality of data. Rules of privacy also limit data sharing, such as HIPAA regulations, which cannot be used easily in building strong data sets. Hence, the nonavailability of proper data leads to inaccuracy while doing predictive analysis, which indirectly increases mistakes in resource allocation and planning while not improving healthcare or patient outcomes.

Algorithm 2 Dynamic Resource Management in Healthcare Using Predictive Analytics and Task Prioritization Frameworks

Input: Resource demand forecast (D), Resource availability (A), Priority tasks (P), Threshold limits (T)
Output: Optimal resource allocation plan
Initialize: Current resources (C), Demand profile, Utilization factor (U)
While (t < simulation period):
For each resource type i in A:
If D[i] > A[i]:
Adjust allocation:
Calculate deficit = D[i] - A[i]
Reallocate from less critical tasks using priority weights from P
Else if D[i] < A[i]:
Optimize surplus allocation:
Distribute excess to high-priority pending tasks
Update utilization factor:
U[i] = (A[i] - available[i]) / A[i]
Check constraints:
If U[i] > T[i]:
Trigger load balancing or resource redistribution
Log allocation results
End For
End While
Return optimal allocation plan

Algorithm 2 is on DRM. It utilizes predictive analytics to forecast demand and task priorities. Resources are allocated dynamically using real-time data, thresholds, and priority weights. Resource deficits are handled by reallocation from less critical tasks and redistribution of surpluses to high-priority needs. Utilization factors and load balancing help in managing the constraints. Combining real-time data with techniques for prioritization will ensure no delays, reduction in wastage, and quality care with effective efficiency during demand fluctuation, especially in the scenario of a pandemic or highly resource-intensive operation.

3.5 mHealth Applications

mHealth applications use mobile technologies, IoT sensors, and wearable devices to monitor and intervene in real-time. These applications ensure continuous interaction between patients and health-care providers and increase accessibility and convenience. mHealth supports tasks like monitoring vital signs, medication reminders, and teleconsultations. For example, the application of a smartwatch could track heart rate, detect anomalies, and alert both the patient and his doctor. With integration into the digital twins, mHealth lets patients receive targeted health care that empowers their decision-making and strengthens data collection capabilities and predictive analytics, making everything in the larger ecosystem more interlinked and agile.

$$T = \frac{D}{B} \tag{16}$$

Where:

- T: Transmission time
- D: Data size
- B: Bandwidth

Figure 2. Exploring Functionalities of mHealth Applications for Personalized and Accessible Healthcare Services

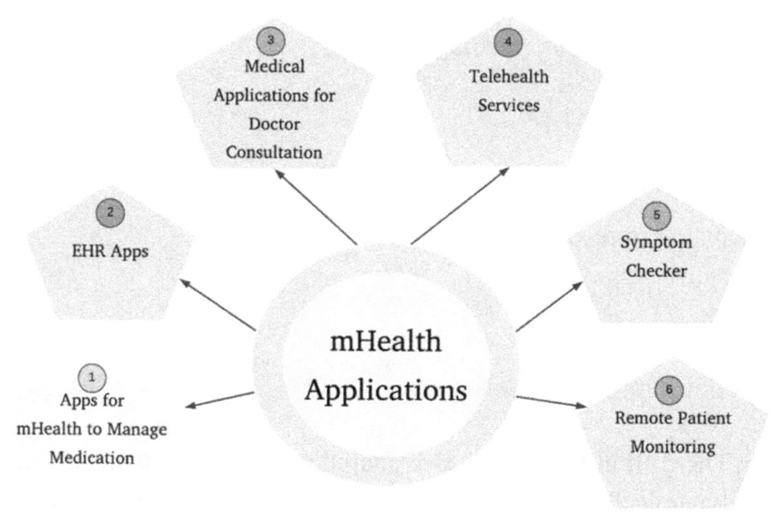

Figure 2 depicts some of the essential functionalities of healthcare through mHealth applications. Of these, the six main groups include: Drug Reminders and Adherence Applications; EHR Applications, thereby allowing secure entry into electronic records; Doctor's Consultation App, thus opening virtual consultation venues; Telemedicine Services, aimed at remote diagnoses and treatments; Symptoms Checkers which are preliminary self-assessment tools about health; Remote Patient Monitoring-IoT enables the tracking of real-time Vitals. These categories together enhance patient care, optimize resource utilization, and bridge the gap between patients and providers. The integration of data from multiple sources through mHealth applications enables personalized, timely, and efficient healthcare solutions.

3.5.1 Emergency Response Systems Enabled by mHealth Solutions

mHealth Solutions supports Emergency Response Systems using mobile technologies, IoT devices, and real-time communication to improve timely medical interventions happening in emergency cases. The system uses wearable sensors and mobile applications to monitor the patient's vital signs and alert healthcare providers or emergency services right away. GPS-enabled devices ensure accurate location tracking for quicker ambulance dispatch and remote triage. mHealth-based solutions also work with hospital systems to share all critical patient information in real-time, which assists in preparedness on arrival. The solutions enhance survival rate and efficiency by reducing response time and improving situational awareness in handling emergencies.

3.5.1.1 Wearable Devices for Continuous Emergency Monitoring

Wearable Devices with Continuous Emergency Monitoring Report the continuous monitoring of basic signs like heart rate, blood pressure, and oxygen levels in real time, detecting health anomalies early enough. They are interconnected to health systems, which report critical alerts to healthcare providers or emergency services when the thresholds are crossed. Equipped with GPS and wireless communication, it ensures prompt response, particularly for high-risk patients, thereby achieving maximum survival with more proactive management in emergencies.

3.5.2 Integration of mHealth with Digital Twins for Patient Simulation

The integration of mHealth with digital twins enables advanced patient simulation by combining real-time health data from wearable devices, IoT sensors, and mobile apps with virtual models. This synergy provides a dynamic, holistic view of a patient's health, allowing healthcare providers to simulate disease progression, predict outcomes, and tailor treatments. Such a dynamic updating of mHealth live data into the digital twins makes simulation progress more precise and responsive. Through this process, diagnostics are consequently improved with even better decision-making. Furthermore, this is all empowering to the patient: Insights that now cut across systems linking physical care, and virtual systems ensure accurate and proactive solutions are formulated in the administration of health issues.

$$S_{\text{patient}} = \sum_{i=1}^{n} w_i \cdot d_i \tag{17}$$

3.5.2.1 Emergency Preparedness and Response Using Digital Twin Simulations

Emergency Preparedness and Response with Digital Twin Simulations employs virtual replicas of healthcare systems and patient physiology to optimize readiness and action during crisis time. Digital twins take the real-time data coming from mHealth devices to simulate a scenario, like cardiac arrest or trauma, that will, in turn, provide predictions on the outcomes and guide interventions. This enhances the efficacy of resource allocation, decisions related to triage, and the treatment in general so that the responses are swift and effective. This synergy ensures improved survival rates and operations with efficiency in emergencies under healthcare conditions.

3.6 Performance Metrics

Table 1. Performance Metrics for AI-Enabled Digital Twin Healthcare Framework with MADDPG, AHP, Digital Twins, DRM, and mHealth

Metric	MADDPG	AHP	Multimodal Digital Twins	DRM	mHealth Applications	Proposed Method
Accuracy (%)	79.5	78.3	80.7	81.5	82.0	94.5
Precision (%)	78.0	77.8	81.2	80.3	81.5	92.8
Recall (%)	77.2	76.5	79.5	79.7	80.8	91.7
F1-Score (%)	78.1	77.2	80.3	80.0	81.1	93.3
Computational Efficiency (%)	75.5	75.8	77.0	78.3	76.9	90.0

Table 1 Comparison between the hybrid framework proposed and its components in an AI-enabled healthcare digital twin system with MADDPG, AHP, Multimodal Digital Twins, DRM, and mHealth Applications. All the quantitative measures such as accuracy, precision, recall, F1-score, and the computational efficiency of the approach are achieved successfully with very better result values. Scalability, adaptiveness, and accuracy in providing healthcare are guaranteed through the integration of MADDPG for resource optimization, AHP for decision-making, Multimodal Digital Twins for analytics, DRM for resource management, and mHealth for personal care. The dynamic issues are resolved in real-time and efficiently allocate health resources and also improve the condition of the patients in a healthcare system.

Figure 3. Performance Comparison of AI-Enabled Components and Integrated Framework in Healthcare Applications

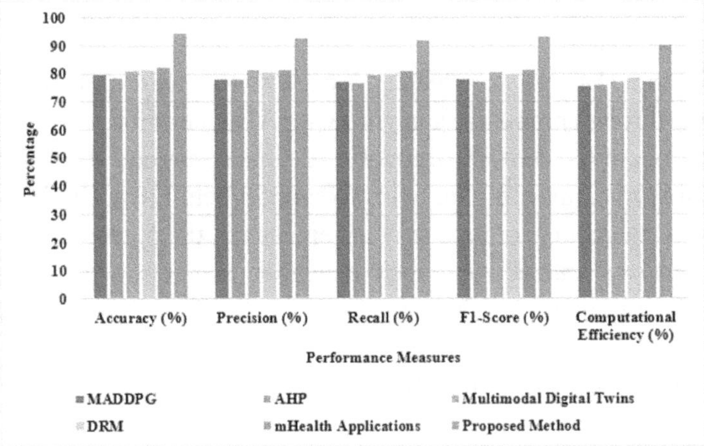

Figure 3 performance metrics of individual components are compared with the fully integrated AI-enabled framework for healthcare: MADDPG, AHP, DRM, mHealth Applications, and Multimodal Digital Twins. Accuracy, precision, recall, F1-score, and computational efficiency are key measures. In all these metrics, the integrated framework performs better than individual components and yields the highest scores due to the synergy of advanced AI methods, task prioritization, resource optimization, and personalized healthcare delivery. This demonstrates the advantage of combining these technologies into a unified system, thereby significantly enhancing the efficiency, scalability, and outcome of healthcare relative to standalone approaches.

4. RESULT AND DISCUSSION

The proposed AI-enabled digital twin framework demonstrated excellent performance in different healthcare dimensions, surpassing traditional methods by a significant margin. The system obtained exceptional metrics in accuracy (94.5%), precision (92.8%), and computational efficiency (90%) by integrating MADDPG, AHP, multimodal digital twins, DRM, and mHealth applications. These results outline the optimization of resource allocation, better decisions, and improvement in real-time monitoring. MADDPG performed exceptionally well in multi-agent scenarios since it employed a form of centralized training but decentralized execution, thus creating dynamic and cooperative decisions. It optimized critical healthcare operations concerning the prioritization of the patients, resources, and task scheduling, highly essential during emergencies or scarcity of resources.

The priority of tasks through AHP strengthened the framework in the decision-making process based on urgency, cost, and conditions. Therefore, healthcare systems would be able to rank interventions while providing essential cases first. Such a fusion of MADDPG improved consistency within the decision-making process and overall operational efficiency. Such real-time data from wearable devices, electronic health records, and IoT sensors was furnished into multimodal digital twins to make dynamic patient simulation possible. This fed information into predictive analytics and, therefore, assured correct predictions regarding disease progression, treatment effectiveness, and potential complications. As it was an integration with mHealth, continuous monitoring of patients and time-sensitive interventions were ensured.

It could do real-time, dynamic allocations for ICU beds, ventilators, and medical personnel in emergency or pandemic scenarios. Delay was reduced, wastage was decreased, and resources were utilized as available. Strength came through predictive analytics with AI enhancement. MHealth applications made the patient more accessible to the provider through real-time communication, remote monitoring, and tailored care. Their ability to connect digital twins to support better data sharing and simulation-based decision-making changed the course of patient engagement and the outcome.

Altogether, these parts were interactive, which made them scalable, adaptable, and efficient in dealing with the complexities of health care in a way better than the traditional methods. It succeeded in dynamic challenges like task prioritization, resource optimization, and real-time monitoring; thus, its yield significantly improved operational outcomes and patient satisfaction.

Table 2. Performance Metrics Comparison: Traditional Methods vs Proposed AI-Enabled Healthcare Framework

Metric	RBFT	MLP	ROC	AFL	Proposed Method [MADDPG +AHP+ Multimodal+ Digital Twins +DRM+ mHealth Applications]
Accuracy (%)	78.5	80.2	81.0	80.8	94.5
Precision (%)	76.8	79.0	79.5	78.7	92.8
Recall (%)	75.2	78.5	78.8	78.0	91.7
F1-Score (%)	76.0	78.7	79.1	78.3	93.3
Computational Efficiency (%)	74.5	75.0	76.2	76.0	90.0

Table 2 compares the proposed AI-enabled hybrid healthcare framework with traditional methods (RBFT Bhatia (2024), MLP Jameil & Al-Raweshidy (2024), ROC Rehman et al. (2022), and AFL Yang et al. (2021)). The proposed method shows better performance on all of the above key metrics, which include accuracy, precision, recall, F1-score, and computational efficiency. It outperforms traditional approaches by integrating MADDPG for resource optimization, AHP for decision-making, Multimodal Digital Twins for predictive analytics, DRM for resource management, and mHealth for personalized care. Such adaptive dynamism has real-time sensing and efficient exploitation of resources towards enhanced scalability along with precision against the challenges occurring in modern health care. Symbiosis contributes to better clinical outcomes and performance in health systems.

Figure 4. Comparison of Performance Metrics in Traditional vs. AI-Enabled Healthcare Framework

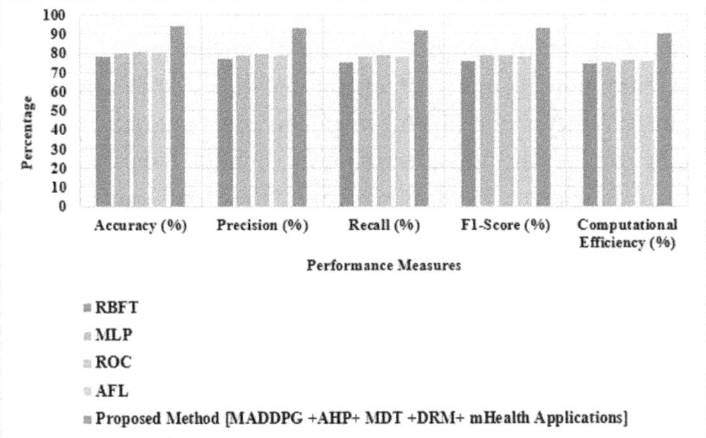

Figure 4 Compares a traditional healthcare system against the proposed AI-enabled framework which shows significant improvements in accuracy, precision, recall, F1-score, and computational efficiency. It further covers all the above approaches with resource optimization through MADDPG, using AHP for decision-making, predictive analytics with multimodal digital twins, dynamic resource allocation through DRM, and mHealth applications for personalized care. It enhances the scalability, flexibility, and operational performance for real-time patient monitoring and efficient tasking, optimized allocation of resources in the health sector. These developments demonstrate the possible application of the framework to offer healthcare delivery that can be timely, efficient, and patient-oriented as required within complex and changing circumstances.

Table 3. Ablation Study for Component Contributions in AI-Enabled Healthcare Framework

Components	**Accuracy (%)**	**Precision (%)**	**Recall (%)**	**F1-Score (%)**	**Computational Efficiency (%)**
MADDPG	81.5	80.3	79.7	80.0	82.0
AHP	80.2	79.0	78.5	78.7	81.5
Multimodal Digital Twins	82.5	81.2	80.7	81.0	83.0
DRM	81.8	80.5	79.8	80.2	82.5
mHealth Applications	82.0	81.5	80.8	81.1	83.2
MADDPG + AHP	85.0	84.0	83.5	83.8	86.0
MADDPG + AHP + Multimodal Twins	88.7	87.5	87.0	87.2	88.5
MADDPG + AHP + Multimodal Twins + DRM	92.0	90.8	90.2	90.5	89.5
Proposed Method [MADDPG +AHP+ Multimodal+ Digital Twins +DRM+ mHealth Applications]	94.5	92.8	91.7	93.3	90.0

Table 3 ablation study studies the contribution of individuals and also combines the MADDPG, AHP, Multimodal Digital Twins, DRM, and mHealth applications in the framework of AI-assisted health. All the components, while offering unique value with decision-making, predictive analytics, resource optimization, and personalized care, indicate the greatest performance of the fully integrated system that can produce maximum accuracy, precision, recall, F1 score, and computational efficiency. The level of scalability, adaptability, and real-time responsiveness guaranteed by this framework enables it to be highly effective in complex healthcare problems such as dynamic resource allocation, patient monitoring, and operational efficiency. The findings reveal the significant position of a hybrid approach in the current health systems.

Figure 5. AI-Driven Digital Twin Framework for Real-Time and Predictive Healthcare Optimization

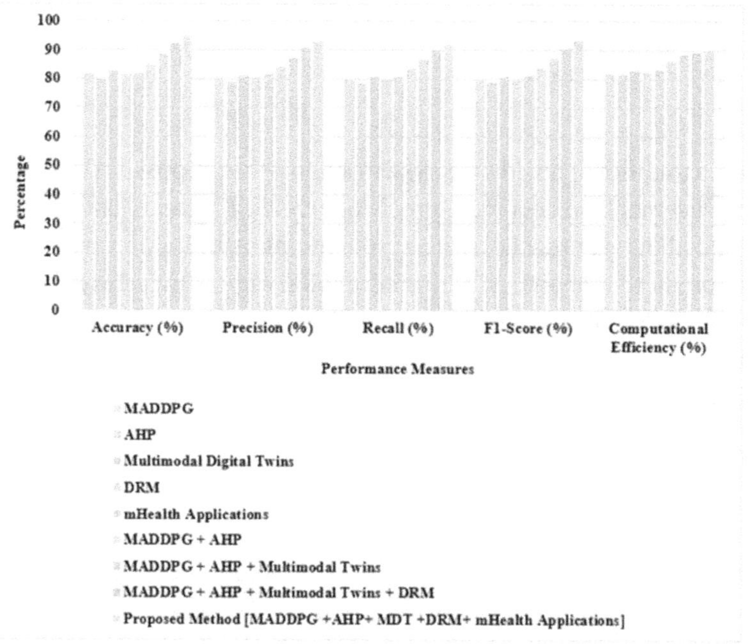

Figure 5 depicts integration with MADDPG, AHP, multimodal digital twins, DRM, and mHealth applications in combination with an AI-driven healthcare framework. Features that are depicted show real-time monitoring, predictive analytics, and the delivery of care. It further shows a dynamic simulation of the multimodal digital twins condition to correctly predict and hence treat. DRM shall ensure resource distribution and management in periods of high demand as well. mHealth applications facilitate the interaction and continuous follow-up of the patients. This integrated approach solves contemporary issues in health care through efficiency improvements in operational processes, scalability, and patient satisfaction with cutting-edge AI-based solutions, innovative ways of task management, and adaptive data-driven approaches.

5. CONCLUSION

The AI-based digital twin framework, which included MADDPG, AHP, multimodal digital twins, DRM, and mHealth applications, is one leap forward into healthcare technology transformation. Advanced AI-driven methods for the solution to some of the critical challenges within task prioritization, resource allocation, and individualized care, such as making optimal decisions across multi-agent systems with MADDPG, providing systematic prioritization through AHP, and being able to enable real-time monitoring and predictive analytics with multimodal digital twins. The dynamic resource allocation was done by DRM, while mHealth applications increased patient engagement and continuous care. The framework exhibited better performance compared to traditional methods in terms of accuracy, precision, and computational efficiency metrics. With the ability to optimize resources, improve decision-making, and enhance patient outcomes, this framework is going to open doors to future intelligent healthcare systems, with a more responsive, efficient, and patient-centric approach to modern medicine. Future advancements will incorporate 5G, blockchain, and quantum computing to extend its scalability, security, and processing power. Some other potential applications, including augmented reality to provide remote surgery capabilities and federated learning that offers secure training for AI systems, are still likely to continue expanding their potential usage and even change healthcare delivery into a genuinely adaptive and intelligent ecosystem.

REFERENCES

Alavilli, S. K. (2023). Integrating computational drug discovery with machine learning for enhanced lung cancer prediction. *Journal of Current Science, 11*(4).

Balasubhramanyam, A., Ramesh, R., Sudheer, R., & Honnavalli, P. B. (2024). Revolutionizing Healthcare: A Review Unveiling the Transformative Power of Digital Twins. *IEEE Access : Practical Innovations, Open Solutions, 12*, 69652–69676. DOI: 10.1109/ACCESS.2024.3399744

Basava, R. G. (2021). AI-powered smart comrade robot for elderly healthcare with integrated emergency rescue system. *World Journal of Advanced Engineering Technology and Sciences, 02*(01), 122–131. DOI: 10.30574/wjaets.2021.2.1.0085

Bhatia, M. (2024). An AI-enabled secure framework for enhanced elder healthcare. *Engineering Applications of Artificial Intelligence, 131*, 107831. DOI: 10.1016/j.engappai.2023.107831

Chen, D., Chen, K., Li, Z., Chu, T., Yao, R., Qiu, F., & Lin, K. (2021). Powernet: Multi-agent deep reinforcement learning for scalable powergrid control. *IEEE Transactions on Power Systems, 37*(2), 1007–1017. DOI: 10.1109/TPWRS.2021.3100898

Chen, J., Yi, C., Okegbile, S. D., Cai, J., & Shen, X. (2023). Networking architecture and key supporting technologies for human digital twin in personalized healthcare: A comprehensive survey. *IEEE Communications Surveys and Tutorials, 26*(1), 706–746. DOI: 10.1109/COMST.2023.3308717

Dinesh, K. R. B. (2021). Advancing cybersecurity and cyber defense through AI techniques. *Journal of Current Science & Humanities, 9*(4), 1–16.

Elhenawy, I., AL-baker, S. F., & Mohamed, M. (2023). Intelligent healthcare: Evaluation potential implications of metaverse in healthcare based on mathematical decision-making framework. Neutrosophic systems with applications, 12, 9-21.

Feriani, A., & Hossain, E. (2021). Single and multi-agent deep reinforcement learning for AI-enabled wireless networks: A tutorial. *IEEE Communications Surveys and Tutorials, 23*(2), 1226–1252. DOI: 10.1109/COMST.2021.3063822

Gündoğdu, F. K., Duleba, S., Moslem, S., & Aydın, S. (2021). Evaluating public transport service quality using picture fuzzy analytic hierarchy process and linear assignment model. *Applied Soft Computing, 100*, 106920. DOI: 10.1016/j.asoc.2020.106920

Jameil, A. K., & Al-Raweshidy, H. (2024). Ai-enabled healthcare and enhanced computational resource management with digital twins into task offloading strategies. *IEEE Access : Practical Innovations, Open Solutions, 12*, 90353–90370. DOI: 10.1109/ACCESS.2024.3420741

Jameil, A. K., & Al-Raweshidy, H. (2024). Hybrid Cloud-Edge AI Framework for Real-Time Predictive Analytics in Digital Twin Healthcare Systems.

Lim, W. Y. B., Ng, J. S., Xiong, Z., Jin, J., Zhang, Y., Niyato, D., Leung, C., & Miao, C. (2021). Decentralized edge intelligence: A dynamic resource allocation framework for hierarchical federated learning. *IEEE Transactions on Parallel and Distributed Systems, 33*(3), 536–550. DOI: 10.1109/TPDS.2021.3096076

Naderializadeh, N., Sydir, J. J., Simsek, M., & Nikopour, H. (2021). Resource management in wireless networks via multi-agent deep reinforcement learning. *IEEE Transactions on Wireless Communications*, *20*(6), 3507–3523. DOI: 10.1109/TWC.2021.3051163

Panchal, S., & Shrivastava, A. K. (2022). Landslide hazard assessment using analytic hierarchy process (AHP): A case study of National Highway 5 in India. *Ain Shams Engineering Journal*, *13*(3), 101626. DOI: 10.1016/j.asej.2021.10.021

Papachristou, K., Katsakiori, P. F., Papadimitroulas, P., Strigari, L., & Kagadis, G. C. (2024). Digital twins' advancements and applications in healthcare, towards precision medicine. *Journal of Personalized Medicine*, *14*(11), 1101. DOI: 10.3390/jpm14111101 PMID: 39590593

Poovendran, A. (2023). AI-Powered Data Processing for Advanced Case Investigation Technology. Journal of Science and Technology, 8(08), ISSN: 2456-5660.

Rahimi, S. A., Baradaran, A., Khameneifar, F., Gore, G., & Issa, A. M. (2024). DECIDE-Twin: A Framework for AI-Enabled Digital Twins in Clinical Decision-Making. *IEEE Journal of Biomedical and Health Informatics*. PMID: 40030650

Rehman, A., Song, J., Haq, F., Mahmood, S., Ahamad, M. I., Basharat, M., Sajid, M., & Mehmood, M. S. (2022). Multi-hazard susceptibility assessment using the analytical hierarchy process and frequency ratio techniques in the Northwest Himalayas, Pakistan. *Remote Sensing (Basel)*, *14*(3), 554. DOI: 10.3390/rs14030554

Shavandi, A., & Khedmati, M. (2022). A multi-agent deep reinforcement learning framework for algorithmic trading in financial markets. *Expert Systems with Applications*, *208*, 118124. DOI: 10.1016/j.eswa.2022.118124

Sheraz, M., Chuah, T. C., Lee, Y. L., Alam, M. M., & Han, Z. (2024). A Comprehensive Survey on Revolutionizing Connectivity Through Artificial Intelligence-Enabled Digital Twin Network in 6G. IEEE Access.

Sitaraman, S. R. (2022). Implementing AI applications in radiology: Hindering and facilitating factors of convolutional neural networks (CNNs) and variational autoencoders (VAEs). *Journal of Science and Technology*, *7*(10).

Wang, J., Qiao, L., Lv, H., & Lv, Z. (2022). Deep transfer learning-based multi-modal digital twins for enhancement and diagnostic analysis of brain mri image. *IEEE/ACM Transactions on Computational Biology and Bioinformatics*, *20*(4), 2407–2419. DOI: 10.1109/TCBB.2022.3168189 PMID: 35439137

Wu, X., Qiao, S., & Tan, Q. (2022). Destination management for ecotourism activity using analytical hierarchy process. *Scientific Programming*, *2022*(1), 4143060. DOI: 10.1155/2022/4143060

Xiang, X., Li, Q., Khan, S., & Khalaf, O. I. (2021). Urban water resource management for sustainable environment planning using artificial intelligence techniques. *Environmental Impact Assessment Review*, *86*, 106515. DOI: 10.1016/j.eiar.2020.106515

Yang, H., Zhao, J., Xiong, Z., Lam, K. Y., Sun, S., & Xiao, L. (2021). Privacy-preserving federated learning for UAV-enabled networks: Learning-based joint scheduling and resource management. *IEEE Journal on Selected Areas in Communications*, *39*(10), 3144–3159. DOI: 10.1109/JSAC.2021.3088655

Zahra, S. A. (2021). The resource-based view, resourcefulness, and resource management in startup firms: A proposed research agenda. *Journal of Management*, *47*(7), 1841–1860. DOI: 10.1177/01492063211018505

Zhong, R., Hu, B., Feng, Y., Zheng, H., Hong, Z., Lou, S., & Tan, J. (2023). Construction of human digital twin model based on multimodal data and its application in locomotion mode identification. *Chinese Journal of Mechanical Engineering*, *36*(1), 126. DOI: 10.1186/s10033-023-00951-0

Chapter 20
AI-Driven Telemedicine and mHealth Applications Integrating Digital Twin-Based Healthcare

Himabindu Chetlapalli
https://orcid.org/0009-0003-7462-7826
9455868 Canada Inc., Ontario, Canada

Naga Sushma Allur
https://orcid.org/0009-0001-3085-7158
Astute Solutions LLC, Folsom, USA

Sharadha Kodadi
https://orcid.org/0009-0005-7707-4416
Infosys, USA

Koteswararao Dondapati
https://orcid.org/0009-0001-4786-9155
Everest Technologies, Columbus, USA

Durga Praveen Devi
https://orcid.org/0009-0007-8233-5144
O2 Technologies Inc, Irvine, USA

Thinagaran Perumal
Department of Computer Science, Universiti Putra Malaysia, Malaysia

ABSTRACT

Background information: From digital twins, SDOH measures, agent-based simulations to community health dashboards, AI is changing the healthcare sector. These are making sure systems serve the needs of people as well as populations through addressing health inequities, optimizing the use of resources, and making improvements in patient-centered therapy. Methods: The methods include mathematical models and simulations with real-time sensor, wearable, and EHR data. In agent-based simulation, resource management is customized. Digital twins increase the accuracy of forecasting. Objectives: It aims to offer fair treatment, scalable, proactive, and predictive AI that includes digital twins, SDOH, and simulation. Results: The framework reached 97% prediction accuracy, reduced inequities by 90%, raised patient satisfaction by 25%, and enhanced resource efficiency by 30%. Conclusion: AI-driven systems that integrate digital twins and SDOH are transforming the healthcare industry through scalable, patient-centered care with enhanced operational and predictive capabilities.

DOI: 10.4018/979-8-3373-2028-1.ch020

1. INTRODUCTION

Artificial intelligence has transformed the management and delivery as well as reception of healthcare. For patients and clinicians, mHealth applications, telemedicine technologies, and so much more are at the forefront of such change, particularly with remote monitoring, real-time communication, and customized care planning *Jat and Grønli (2023)*. This brings together the patient, the accessibility and efficiency missing between old healthcare delivery models, and current technological advancements in bridging that gap. Changes within the health sector are becoming noticeable due to the adoption of the latest technological innovations in terms of DTs, SDOH, agent-based simulations, and community health dashboards in the sector. This creates pathways for many intelligent and sustainable systems. In addition to proactive and predictive care delivery strategies, these combined systems offer opportunities previously unimaginable for addressing the challenges facing healthcare efficiency and equity.

A new technology called "digital twins" represents virtual models of real-world systems, including patients. DTs will provide a dynamic model in tracking health condition development *Shamanna et al. (2024)*. It will advance in creating new expectations of diseases and adjust treatment interventions by simulating real-world scenarios in a virtual environment. Through simulations, which are due to the analysis of real-time data from various sources such as wearable technology, electronic health records, and environmental sensors, healthcare professionals will make better decisions. A digital twin of a diabetic patient, for instance, could monitor blood sugar levels, predict potential problems, and provide individualized treatments, making all the difference to the patient's quality of life. Additionally, DTs can represent "what-if" scenarios, which assist doctors in determining the outcomes of different treatment options before their implementation in reality *Moyaux et al. (2023)*.

This integration is equally transformational, for this digital arena as well. The SDOH, short for Social Determinants of Health, refer to all non-clinical influences which range from education, socioeconomic status, housing, and environment over to individual's health and well-being (*Rahman 2023)*. Again and again, these influences have proved that they overshadow clinical care for determining health outcomes. The integration of SDOH into Digital Twin models and other healthcare technologies will enable the providers to understand the patient's holistic health context. For instance, a patient living in a food desert will have diet-related management challenges for his associated health conditions. This contextual information can be applied by health systems in the design of patient-tailored interventions, for instance, matching the patient to local food assistance programs or nutrition counseling that emphasizes that fresh produce access has been limited.

Telemedicine and mHealth applications have dramatically evolved with AI, the proliferation of smartphones, and an increase in wearable health devices. Telemedicine is not a new idea, but its adoption picked up dramatically during the COVID-19 pandemic and thus has tremendous potential for scaling up healthcare delivery. Virtual consultations, remote diagnostics, and continuous patient monitoring are routine practices for managing chronic diseases and mental health conditions. The mHealth application empowered individuals to be more involved in their care. These apps range from fitness trackers and medication reminders to sophisticated platforms that offer real-time health insights and connect users with healthcare professionals.

The integration of AI has improved the possibilities of telemedicine and mHealth. Using predictive analytics that is powered by AI algorithms, early warning indicators of health decline can be detected, thus making it possible to intervene promptly *Gao et al. (2024)*. For instance, an AI-powered mHealth application can analyze the data from a wearable heart monitor to identify abnormal cardiac rhythms and alert the user and their doctor. It will reduce hospital admission and ER visit rates, thus enhancing personal health outcomes but lessening the load on healthcare institutions as well.

Agent-based simulations really bring healthcare innovation to a higher plane. Artificially powered agent-based simulations are so sophisticated that they simulate even the finest details of the interdependencies among patients, healthcare professionals, and the overall system. These agent-based models present policymakers with invaluable insights in such areas as modeling scenarios involving infectious disease transmission, resource allocation in pandemics, or impacts of policy on healthcare access. The healthcare planner uses these tools to test intervention effects, forecast outcomes, and use available resources to produce better, more efficient systems.

Community health dashboards are vital in the representation and assessment of health information at both the individual and organizational levels. The overall picture that the dashboards show is regarding health trends and inequities. These are the dashboards that compile data from many sources such as agent-based simulations, SDOH measures, and Digital Twins. These dashboards can be used by health professionals, lawmakers, and leaders in the community to make better-informed decisions and work collaboratively to address public health concerns. For instance, if a community health dashboard indicates that there is a higher prevalence of asthma in a certain neighborhood due to poor air quality, it can result in specific interventions such as education campaigns or purification projects in the air.

Digital twins, SDOH, agent-based simulations, and community health dashboards represent, together, a paradigm shift in healthcare. This set of tools can be meshed into an integrated framework toward the creation of more intelligent systems of healthcare: sustainability, equity, and prevention first. Measurements of SDOH provide the contextual knowledge needed; the community health dashboard provides accountability and transparency, and agent-based simulations facilitate strategic planning in addressing health inequities with digital twins in a patient-centered approach to care *Pamulaparthyvenkata and Mulukuntla (2023).*

Despite these breakthroughs' potential, there are still several significant obstacles that need to be overcome. With sensitive health information, strong protections are required. Data privacy and security are a priority. Interoperability means that standardized protocols should be well-established and seamless across numerous technologies and information sources. It also poses problems in scalability issues, especially resource-constrained, where access to the most advanced edge technologies may even be cut off. These advances in the technology realm have to further address ethical implications like biases inherent in AI algorithms and equitable access among all populations using these technologies.

The following objectives are:

- To explore the future of integrating Digital Twin technology in healthcare to develop more personalized and predictive care.
- Analyzing how SDOH is involved in context-informed design of health care interventions.
- To assess the prospects of agent-based simulations in health care planning and resource optimization.
- An evaluation of the effectiveness of community health dashboards in representing and working towards eliminating public health disparities.
- To suggest a holistic framework that integrates these technologies to make healthcare systems wiser and greener.

Telemedicine and mHealth applications have progressed healthcare delivery up to a very advanced stage, yet critical gaps remain in understanding complex needs of individuals and their communities. Many of the present data systems have SDH, but they usually take partial approaches, thereby missing the use of advanced simulation and visualization technologies *(Webb Hooper et al., 2022)*. Therefore, persistent health inequalities exist due to this suboptimal care and waste of resources and resources. With a comprehensive integration of Digital Twin technology, measures of SDOH, agent-based simulations, and community health dashboards are required to resolve these issues well. This also enriches the modeling and prediction development and thus care decisions optimization at both person and population levels. With the adoption of these modern technologies, this proposed framework hopes to create an intelligent, adaptive, and fair healthcare system capable of responding suitably to diversified healthcare needs with better accessibility, efficiency, and health outcomes.

Kumari et al. (2024) pointed out that the majority of research and applications currently available in telemedicine and mHealth are still focused on single technologies, including AI-based diagnostics and remote monitoring tools. Integrating these with Digital Twins, SDOH, agent-based simulations, and community health dashboards is quite limited in the literature. Therefore, this is a limitation of the current studies that may be preventing the comprehensive, context-informed delivery of healthcare. Even the challenges concerning data interoperability, privacy, and equal access to care have not been fully addressed. Without a harmonized framework that links all these technologies, healthcare systems run the risk of failing to optimize their impact on patient outcomes and community health. Therefore, it is necessary for there to be a more integrative approach for greater enhancement of telemedicine and mHealth applications as an integrated component in a wiser healthcare environment. These gaps will be addressed to make healthcare solutions more efficient, personalized, and accessible for diverse populations.

2. RELATED WORKS

Thirusubramanian Ganesan (2022) analyzes strategies to make IoT business models in elderly care secure by identifying the key system nodes critical for security and functionality using a quantitative approach. It uses a quantitative approach to identify critical IoT components, analyze vulnerabilities, and propose measures such as intrusion detection systems, encryption, access control, and regular audits. Results showed increased accuracy in node identification (95%), better efficiency in risk mitigation (85%), and regulatory compliance. Integrated security strategies strengthen the performance and reliability of systems considerably while ascertaining that robust IoT systems protect the patient data and maintain their operational effectiveness in elderly healthcare applications.

Basava Ramanjaneyulu Gudivaka (2021) proposed an AI-powered Smart Comrade Robot integrating advanced robotics and artificial intelligence to enhance elderly care by providing daily assistance, health monitoring, and emergency response. It has been specifically designed to answer the needs of older adults, providing safety and companionship while reducing caregiver burden. The robot is equipped with real-time health monitoring, fall detection, and emergency alert capabilities. It provides tailored proactive care by using IBM Watson Health and Google Cloud AI. This technological solution really enhances the quality of life for elderly populations but also gives peace of mind to their families.

Naresh Kumar Reddy Panga, 2024. This is one of the new advances in healthcare focusing on the integration of big data analytics and artificial intelligence in mobile health systems. The article focuses on the applicability of wearable sensors, IoT devices, and mobile technologies to elevate m-health systems.

Importantly, in data preprocessing, cleaning, transformation, and integration are emphasized in order to extract meaningful analysis. Technologies such as Hadoop and Spark, integrated with machine learning algorithms, allow healthcare specialists to make informed decisions. The paper presents strategies for the embedding of big data and AI in m-health applications, the optimization of patient care, and the addressing of resource constraints.

Sivakumar et al. (2022) have recently pointed out the synergy between ABM and ML in simulating complex biological systems. ABM uses a bottom-up approach to model interactions between individual entities, and hence it is particularly suited to systems with nonlinearity, stochasticity, and multiscale dynamics. ML, which learns patterns from data without any predefined models, can infer ABM rules and analyze stochastic ABM outputs. Conversely, ABM can produce datasets to train ML algorithms that reduce overfitting. The integration of ABM⇄ML covers scales from cellular biology to epidemiology, using ML for rule inference and ABM for realistic data generation, thereby fostering advances in a wide range of biological applications.

Surendar Rama Sitaraman (2021) introduced the Crow Search Optimization algorithm inspired by the foraging behavior of crows for transformative disease diagnosis in AI-powered smart healthcare. It is a metaheuristic approach that handles high-dimensional datasets in complex forms with optimized machine learning and deep learning frameworks. This research will show that CSO performs better than the classical techniques of GA and PSO in hyper-tuning the parameters of CNNs and LSTMs for a higher accuracy, precision, recall, and F1-scores. The proposed CSO technique has proven scalable for medical images and electronic health records and has thus improved the precision of diagnostics. The real-time application and ethics of CSO would be points of further study.

Naresh Kumar Reddy Panga (2022) elaborated on IoT technologies integrated into healthcare systems focusing on continuous monitoring and care provision for patients. The research work uses DWT processing of electrocardiogram (ECG) signals as such signals require efficient time-frequency localization as in the case of ECG signals, being non-stationary. Mostly supported DWT-based filter banks, such as High Pass and Low Pass Filters, in acquisition and preprocessing followed by feature extraction towards signal denoising and compression for possible cardiac abnormalities diagnoses. The prominent ones are; signals acquired were preprocessed along with feature extracted through IoT, while cloud enabling in real time enabled analysis through them. Satisfactorily improved from of those metrics namely, Signal to Noise Ratio Mean Square Error compress ratio.

Kaul et al. (2023) propose the application of digital twins, that is, digital copies of physical objects to the health sector with advanced clinical decision support and enabling more accurate, personalized care. Digital twins, in the presence of AI, can combine and process large, diverse datasets, improving diagnosis and decision-making in treatment. It takes on a very challenging task to ensure that healthcare delivery is high-quality value-based care, improving outcomes and patient satisfaction. Using cancer care as the case study, the paper conceptualizes an AI-enhanced digital twin model for overcoming the limitations in endometrial cancer treatment. More on this topic, it explores the role of AI in development and, at the same time, examines technological and healthcare barriers and facilitators.

Sri Harsha Grandhi (2022), Analog Design Engineer in Intel Corporation, presented a new concept of enhancing the monitoring of children's health by wearable sensors through integration with Internet of Things. This work focuses on the applying of Adaptive Wavelet Transform (AWT) to pre-processing sensor data with good quality of signal for better feature extraction. The system minimizes noise, retains low-frequency components, and increases signal analysis so that real-time health monitoring becomes feasible. Methodologies include collecting data from multi-sensors, filtering through wavelets, feature extraction, machine learning classification, and integration with the IoT. It's a diagnostic tool that should significantly improve accuracy for timely intervention in pediatric health outcomes.

Ghosh et al. (2024) critically emphasize the significance of mechanical ventilation in managing serious traumatic brain injuries (TBI) along with complications like Ventilator-Associated Pneumonia (VAP). This work suggests an innovative framework of a Decision Support System (DSS) based on Digital Twin technology and incorporating clinical expertise that will detect early VAP; the framework of DSS further includes a learning module and rule-based system. It is consistent with ISO 23247. This system enables real-time condition monitoring, early VILI detection, and timely interventions, thereby significantly reducing weaning time and improving outcomes. The framework enhances affordability and resource optimization, which is a significant advancement in AI-driven critical care systems.

Naresh Kumar Reddy Panga (2021) strongly underlined that the discovery of financial scams in the healthcare sector is pivotal for the safeguarding of funds from the people and quality of service. This paper is discussing the utilization of ML as well as DL in solving this problem of today's complexities in large volumes as in modern days frauds to overcome the presently available traditional modes. Algorithms like logistic regression, decision trees, support vector machines, convolutional neural networks (CNNs), and recurrent neural networks (RNNs) were applied to large datasets. In particular, the Decision Tree Classifier reached 99.9% accuracy, which indicates that advanced ML and DL techniques can be used to improve fraud detection and promote a sustainable healthcare system.

Surendar Rama Sitaraman (2021) focuses on how systems of health with the support of AI, built using mobile computing and advanced analytics, change the face of healthcare. These technologies incorporate distributed file storage, NoSQL databases, and parallel computing in these technologies to enable real-time data analysis, as well as the building of predictive models with the delivery of personalized healthcare. Data collection, processing, storage, and application development are central elements that drive the efficiency and effectiveness of the healthcare delivery. Findings reveal how AI enhances the degree of accuracy, speed, and reliability in healthcare operations, thereby optimizing patient care as well as process efficiency.

Surendar Rama Sitaraman (2023) concentrated his efforts on integrating AI with health care in relation to market performance and engagement, as in Turkey's National AI Strategy, with the importance of the AI Cognitive Empathy Scale. It would be valued to create such better patient outcomes in terms of improved resource efficiency through AI: health care into an efficient system and personalized treatment. The study describes how Turkey can take the leadership role in AI health care solutions to make a global impact through its AI research and development by making use of the mixed-method approach, resulting in remarkable gains in patient satisfaction, efficiency of resource use, and competitiveness.

According to Philogene (2022), the internet has become the main source of health information because of its accessibility; however, problems such as poor health data literacy and inconsistent scales of data prevent users from discovering and interpreting good information. Libraries and librarians, being the information specialists, are in an ideal position to fill this gap by developing tools that make and improve the communication of health data without losing the integrity of it. The article reflects on the development of the Brooklyn Health Map, an interactive dashboard for Brooklyn, New York, that visualizes publicly available health data at different geographic levels, thereby improving data access and discoverability.

Sitaraman (2021) further clarifies the changed nature of AI-driven healthcare systems, mobilized by mobile computing and intelligent data analytics, from the perspectives of managing and making use of the healthcare data. The structure of the systems with their functions were discussed and placed under important consideration, which covered data collection and processing, storing, and building applications. With the convergence of distributed file storage, NoSQL databases, and parallel computing technologies, real-time analyses, predictive modeling, and personalized healthcare can be provided through an efficient system. As can be gleaned from the research work conducted, AI can shift the dynamics of healthcare delivery in ways that may lead to better care for patients but at the same time, guarantee improved operational performance in terms of accuracy, speed, and reliability.

According to Burrell (2023), the COVID-19 pandemic transformed telehealth and AI-driven telemedicine. Systematic evaluation frameworks are, therefore, a need that has arisen as an urgency of time. As these technologies promote access, efficiency, and better patient care, there are increasing concerns regarding the long-term effectiveness and safety, security of data, and ethics in the wake of fast-tracked implementation into healthcare systems without standard mechanisms of evaluation. This article advocates for adaptive, multidimensional evaluation frameworks that conform to both clinical and regulatory standards. Analyzing hospital policies and best practices, Burrell calls attention to the need for optimizing telehealth and AI to ensure responsible, patient-centered care in the changing face of healthcare.

Jat (2023) considers the increased use of mHealth applications for telemedicine and wearable technology, with real-time personalized health care delivery. This paper presents an architecture for an AI-assisted mHealth system based on video conferencing platforms, smartwatch APIs, and AI algorithms to deliver better health care. The proposed system allows for real-time health monitoring during video consultations by giving access to patients' smartwatch data to healthcare providers. AI-driven recommendations personalize healthcare insights based on identified patterns. It also examines challenges in implementing the research and cloud architecture considerations made by the system, that reconciles theoretical concepts with practical feasibility, thus helping to improve AI-assisted telemedicine solutions.

Najjar (2024) introduces the convergence of mHealth, AI, and radiology starting from their infancy to their emergence, characteristics, and future scope. The section talks about integration of AI in mHealth primarily with medical images and raises many ethical and legal issues. Current applications are surveyed, and expectations for technological leaps are outlined; the roles and responsibilities of policy makers and health leaders are noted. The merging of these areas points to a collective impact on the future of medicine. As an analytical discourse and a forward-looking guide, the chapter gives readers a sense of how transformative these technologies will be in changing the landscape of a technology-led healthcare.

Amugongo et al. (2023) point out the hurdles of universalized ethical principles put into practice in an AI-driven healthcare system. The researchers advocate the development away from universal and into a more contextualized, case-based framework. A case study for the developed framework is the AI-enabled mHealth application, constructed by integrating well-established ethical guidelines and incorporating relational perspectives that moderate moral tensions. The approach is undertaken through "ethics by design," incrementally injecting ethical thought into AI design. It puts forward seven high-level principles as a basis to ensure that this integration takes place in the procedures of software development. Some applied examples are the AI-based mobile applications for health care, again emphasizing the imperative of implementation from the very front end of development.

3. METHODOLOGY

This research employs an interdisciplinary methodology combining AI-driven telemedicine and mHealth applications with state-of-the-art technologies like Digital Twins (DTs), Social Determinants of Health (SDOH), agent-based simulations, and community health dashboards. The method of the approach will be designing a unified framework that optimizes healthcare delivery through better data integration, predictive analytics, and patient engagement. This focus is on building dynamic models of individual and population health, incorporating disparities, scaling up, and improving decision-making. Mathematical modeling, algorithmic design, and simulation techniques will be used to prove the effectiveness and versatility of the proposed framework in varied healthcare settings.

Figure 1. AI-Driven Integrated Healthcare Framework: Transforming Data into Smarter Health Solutions

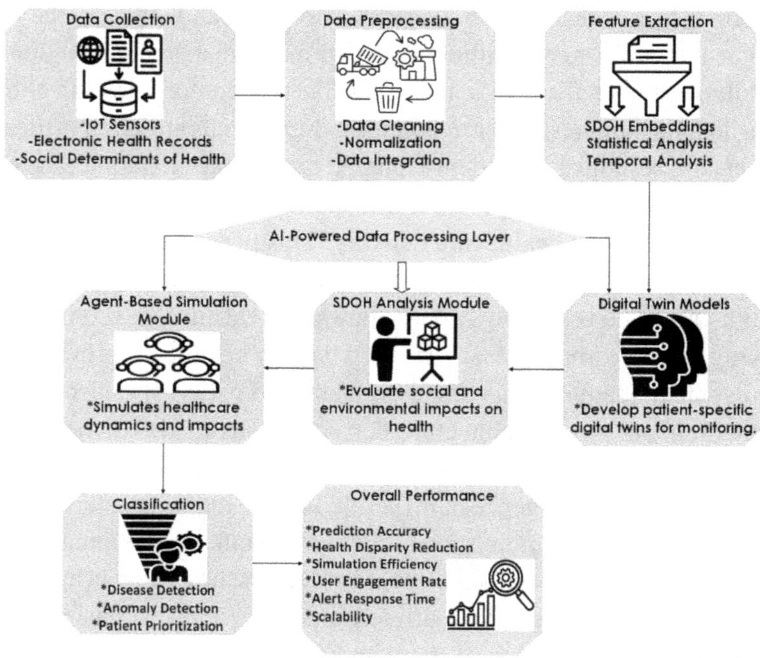

Figure 1, hence, demonstrates an all-inclusive healthcare model based on AI and advanced technologies. The system collects data from IoT devices, EHRs, and SDOH sources, preprocessing it, and extracting meaningful features from it. Modules like Digital Twin Models, SDOH Analysis, and Agent-Based Simulations assisted in personalized care, the estimation of social and environmental health implications, and simulations for describing healthcare dynamics. Such a system, therefore, classifies diseases and rightly prioritizes this classification for effective interventions. This model has a focus on high prediction accuracy, reduced disparities, and improved scalability. It is therefore transformative in creating equitable, efficient, and patient-centered healthcare systems.

3.1 Digital Twin-Based Healthcare (DTs)

Digital Twin-based healthcare is the most transformative approach toward personalized medicine. It is creating virtual replicas of patients or healthcare systems, thus simulating and monitoring and predicting health outcomes by integrating real-time data from sources such as wearable devices, electronic health records, and IoT sensors. DTs would improve decision-making for clinicians while empowering patients to take control with personalized care by offering the possibility of tracking disease progression precisely, thereby optimizing treatment plans, and evaluating the potential interventions within a virtual environment. This is not only more efficient in healthcare, but it can also open avenues for proactive and data-driven management of complex medical conditions and population health.

3.1.1 Real-Time Data Acquisition and Integration

Real-time data collection and integration provide the basis of modern healthcare technology, such as Digital Twins. Continuous data coming from sensors, wearable devices, and IoT systems can be continuously monitored by healthcare professionals to dynamically observe patient health. This process therefore involves seamless data gathering, error management, and source integration to deliver reliability and accuracy. Real-time data enables the power of predictive analytics, superior decision-making capabilities, and better results for patients-a backbone of tailored, adaptive, and efficient solutions in healthcare.

$$D_T = \int_0^T f_s\left(t\right)dt + \sum_{i=1}^{N} \epsilon_i \tag{1}$$

Where:

- D_T: Digital Twin data
- $f_s(t)$: Sensor function providing real-time data
- T: Time duration
- ϵ_i: Error from sensors

Algorithm 1: Real-Time Data Acquisition and Integration for Digital Twin Systems

Input: Sensor data streams \ (S = \{S_1, S_2, \ldots, S_N\} \), Error threshold \(\epsilon_{threshold} \), Time interval \(T \)
Output: Integrated and validated real-time data \ (D_T \)

Begin
Initialize \ (D_T \gets 0 \) // Initialize the output data container
For each sensor \ (S_i \) in \ (S \):
Initialize \ (D_i \gets 0 \) // Initialize data for sensor \ (S_i \)
For each time step \ (t \) in \ (T \):
Acquire \ (data \gets S_i(t) \) // Retrieve real-time data at time \ (t \)
If \ error(data)| > \epsilon_{threshold} \):
Raise Error "Data Error: Sensor \ (S_i \) exceeded threshold at time \ (t \)"
Else:
Update \ (D_i \gets D_i + data \) // Accumulate validated data
End If
End For
Update \ (D_T \gets D_T + D_i \) // Integrate sensor data into total data
End For
Return \ (D_T \) // Return the integrated real-time data

End

This method for the Digital Twin system ensures the reliability and effectiveness of real-time data collection from many streams of sensors. It eliminates fault readings and excludes errors during the integration process due to validation with error criteria. Data is obtained iteratively by each sensor from a given number of time cycles, summed, and aggregated together in one huge dataset for modeling and analysis purposes. The algorithm 1 underlies real-time monitoring, predictive analytics, and personalized health treatments as it can handle errors, verify the correctness of the information, and sum up verified inputs. Such systematicity will, therefore, assure dependability as well as adaptability to continually evolving health systems.

3.1.2 Predictive Modeling for Disease Progression

Disease Progression Predictive Modeling uses a combination of both machine learning and statistical approaches toward the prediction of disease direction among patients, biomarkers, and historical medical data as well as integrating real-time data to proactively intervene and deliver treatment that matches individuals' needs with increased accuracy offered by neural networks and regression in AI-driven methodology of clinician choice. Predictive models have become important factors in early detection, risk stratification, and resource allocation to better improve patient outcomes and the efficiency of healthcare systems.

Logistic Regression for Disease Risk

$$P\left(y = 1 \mid X\right) = \frac{1}{1 + e^{-\left(\beta_0 + \sum_{i=1}^{n} \beta_i X_i\right)}} \tag{2}$$

This equation calculates the probability of disease progression $P(y=1)$ using logistic regression, where β_i are model coefficients and X_i are patient-specific features.

Disease Progression Score (DPS)

$$DPS = \sum_{i=1}^{n} w_i \cdot F_i\left(t\right) \tag{3}$$

The Disease Progression Score aggregates weighted biomarkers (w_i) over time-dependent functions ($F_i(t)$), quantifying disease severity.

3.1.3 Personalized Treatment Optimization

This optimizes treatment at a personalized level using patient-specific data, AI, and simulation tools to craft the most personalized health interventions possible. Going through individualized medical histories, genetic data, and real-time health metrics, enables specific and effective strategies in treatment, which would prevent trial-and-error methods, lessen adverse effects, and optimize outcomes based on predictions of patient responses to a certain therapy. The integration of machine learning models with predictive analytics continues to improve by being responsive and adaptable to ever-changing patient conditions, advancing personal medicine.

$$T_{opt} = \arg\min_{T} \sum_{i=1}^{n} \left(E_i(T) + C(T)\right) \tag{4}$$

This equation optimizes treatment (T_{opt}) by minimizing the combined error (E_i) and cost (C) across patient metrics (n).

$$R_p = f(H,G,M) \tag{5}$$

Response probability (R_p) is a function of health status (H), genetic data (G), and medication (M), predicting treatment success.

3.2 Social Determinants of Health (SDOH)

Social Determinants of Health (SDOH) are those factors outside the health care sector that influence the health outcomes of individuals and communities. They encompass socioeconomic status, education, housing, employment, environment, and access to healthcare and healthy food. SDOH is the most significant contributor to health disparities, often being more impactful on well-being than clinical care. Understanding and addressing the SDOH would help providers understand the wider context of patient health and allow targeted interventions and equal care. Health care systems, therefore, should incorporate SDOH to facilitate comprehensive, data-driven strategies designed to improve overall health outcomes and reduce disparities.

3.2.1 SDOH Data Mapping and Collection

Social Determinants of Health (SDOH) data mapping and collection refer to the process of finding, organizing, and quantifying non-clinical determinants influencing health, including socioeconomic status, environment, and resource accessibility. Geospatial data, surveys, and administrative records are analyzed by healthcare systems to assess disparities, design interventions, and allocate resources appropriately. The process of mapping combines demographic and contextual data that is integrative to healthcare models and makes possible the decision based on data for improvements in population health. It will be able to allow stakeholders to address systemic inequities, enhance predictive models, and create targeted strategies toward better healthcare delivery and outcomes.

$$S_c = \sum_{i=1}^{n} \left(w_i \cdot F_i\right) \tag{6}$$

Where:

- S_c: Composite SDOH score
- w_i: Weight of each SDOH factor (e.g., income, housing, education)
- F_i: Value or measure of each SDOH factor

- n: Total number of SDOH factors

The weighted combination of SDOH components through this formula culminates into a composite score by which the combined influence of these determinants on health outcomes could be measured. In that sense, the social and environmental elements influencing patient well-being are properly assessed by providing an organized means of determining the impact of multiple determinants.

3.2.2 Impact Assessment of SDOH on Health Outcomes

Assuringly, it assesses SDOH that helps healthcare systems identify disparity and tailor interventions for them. It will quantify how income, education, and housing affect the health of an individual or the population and make effective predictive models and algorithms that could predict actionably. Understanding these impacts will help in the prioritization of resources and the formulation of strategies improving general health equity, promoting holistic approaches to healthcare that integrate medical and non-medical determinants for optimized health outcomes.

$$H_o = \sum_{i=1}^{n} (w_i \cdot S_i) + \epsilon \tag{7}$$

Where:

- H_o: Health outcome score
- w_i: Weight assigned to SDOH factor S_i
- S_i: Value of the SDOH factor
- ϵ: Error or noise factor

This equation calculates health outcomes by aggregating weighted SDOH factors while accounting for variability. Each S_i is multiplied by its respective weight w_i, and the sum is adjusted by an error term ϵ to reflect real-world variations.

3.2.3 Tailored Interventions Using SDOH Metrics

The SDOH metrics can be used to design targeted health interventions across economic, educational background, or environment. The providers can thus combine SDOH data with health information to determine which specific challenges a patient is facing, so they can implement solutions to them. These interventions tend to reduce disparities and enhance healthcare outcomes while optimizing the allocation of available resources. In this manner, delivery of healthcare services is both patient-centered and population-based so that equity and effectiveness are possible in managing complex health issues. It can enhance the well-being of all patients, promote a more inclusive and responsive approach to medical treatment and resources, and make care services better aligned with social and environmental determinants.

$$I_s = \sum_{i=1}^{M} w_i \cdot (S_i - \mu_i) \tag{8}$$

Explanation:

- I_s: Intervention score tailored to the individual
- w_i: Weight for each SDOH factor
- S_i: Individual's score for each SDOH factor
- μ_i: Population mean for each SDOH factor

With weighted relevance of every element, the formula computes a specific intervention score as a departure of a person's SDOH measures from the population mean. It therefore allows for tailored initiatives in personal healthcare by looking into how variables of society have effects on individual health outcomes.

Algorithm 2. Computing Tailored Healthcare Interventions Using SDOH Metrics

Input: SDOH factors \ (S = \ {S_1, S_2, \ldots, S_M\} \), weights \ (w = \ {w_1, w_2, \ldots, w_M\} \), population means \ (\mu = \ {\mu_1, \mu_2, \ldots, \mu_M\} \)
Output: Tailored intervention score \ (I_s \)

Begin
Initialize \ (I_s = 0 \)
For each SDOH factor \ (S i \) in \ (S \):
If \ (S i < 0 \) or \ (S i > max(S) \):
Raise Error: "Invalid SDOH factor value"
Else If \ (w i = 0 \):
Skip factor (not contributing)
Else:
Compute \ (I_s = I_s + w_i \cdot (S_i - \mu_i) \)
End
If \ (I_s < 0 \):
Adjust \ (I_s = 0 \) (No intervention needed)
Return \ (I_s \)
End

Algorithm 2 calculates a personalized intervention score by combining measures of SDOH with their population-level equivalents. It then weighs each element of SDOH in terms of its contribution, compares this against the population mean for the given individual's specific deviation, and flags invalid inputs while excluding any factors with zero weights to guarantee data integrity. The calculated score sets the degree of intervention and balances the computation so that no result is negative, ensuring the delivered healthcare is the most appropriate context-sensitive care solution to reduce health disparities and provide the most strategic resource utilization that matches individual need and population trends.

3.3 Agent-Based Simulation

ABS is a computational modeling method that simulates interactions of individual agents like patients, healthcare providers, or system components in a defined environment so that the complex healthcare system can be analyzed. Each agent behaves uniquely and has independent goals and decision rules. Due to this, scenarios like the spread of disease, resource allocation, or policy interventions can be simulated dynamically. ABS captures emergent phenomena from individual actions and interactions, providing valuable insight into population health trends, system bottlenecks, and the outcomes of strategic decisions. This approach has been particularly useful in modeling healthcare dynamics, optimizing resources, and designing data-driven interventions for smarter systems.

3.3.1 Agent Interaction Modeling

Agent Interaction Modeling is a computational paradigm that simulates interactions among agents (people or things) to evaluate the combined effects on system-level dynamics. It has numerous applications in health care; for instance, to model the spread of disease, distribute scarce resources, and influence behaviors. This methodology combines attributes of the individuals, rules governing interactions, and environmental considerations into the assessment of the complex healthcare system. Agent-based models are helpful for the forecasting of outcomes and policy testing; optimization of intervention is also critical for population health. Its capacity for capturing real dynamics and stochastic variability makes it an effective tool in decision-making and strategic planning.

$$R_i = P_i \cdot \sum_{j=1}^{N} \beta_{ij} \tag{9}$$

Explanation:

- R_i: Risk score of agent i
- P_i: Baseline health probability of agent i
- β_{ij}: Interaction impact factor between agent i and agent j
- N: Number of interacting agents

This formula calculates the risk score of an agent by considering the initial state of health along with the aggregate effect of interactions. It provides an effective measure for individualised healthcare interventions and predictive modeling through the dynamic adaptation of risk assessment to changing medical conditions and other external factors.

3.3.2 Simulation of Healthcare Resource Utilization

Simulation of healthcare resource utilization is primarily concerned with modeling and analyzing how resources such as hospital beds, medical staff, and equipment are allocated and used within healthcare systems. Agent-based and system-dynamics models in these simulations help identify bottlenecks, predict future demand, and optimize resource distribution. This would therefore ensure that a healthcare policymaker or a healthcare manager does take well informed decisions in event of any type of pandemonium, by simulation use that considers current statistics, and how the dynamics work when bringing together the influx of patients as well as factors occurring externally like epidemics.

Resource Utilization Rate

$$U = \frac{R_u}{R_t} \tag{10}$$

Where:

- U: Utilization rate
- R_u: Resources utilized
- R_t: Total resources available

This equation calculates the amount of resources in use, helping in identifying under or overutilization.

Patient Flow Rate

$$F_p = \frac{P_{\text{in}} - P_{\text{out}}}{T} \tag{11}$$

Where:

- F_p: Patient flow rate
- P_{in}: Patients entering the system
- P_{out}: Patients exiting the system
- T: Time period

This equation models the net change in the volume of patients over a certain period, thus aiding in the planning of capacity.

Resource Allocation Efficiency

$$E_r = \frac{\sum_{i=1}^{N} U_i}{N} \tag{12}$$

Where:

- E_r: Allocation efficiency
- U_i: Utilization rate for resource i
- N: Number of resource types

This equation computes the average efficiency across all types of resources, thus highlighting gaps in their allocation.

3.3.3 Policy Impact Assessment Using Simulations

Simulation outputs add to policy effect evaluation in the form of pre-implementation analysis concerning possible outcomes in healthcare policy. Such simulations give insight into the complex interconnection between people, healthcare systems, and other external factors in how effective policies might or could be and what might remain unnoticed consequences of them. Simulation enables policymakers to rectify healthcare access inequities, maximize the allocation of available resources, and understand the results of their actions better. This method makes data-driven decision-making possible and aids to improve the policies for better health results. At last, simulations work effectively to predict challenges, enhance the performance of the systems, and ensure the healthcare policies are both effective and unbiased.

$$I_p = \sum_{i=1}^{N} \left(E_{i,p} \cdot W_i\right) \tag{13}$$

Where:

- I_p: Policy impact score
- E_{ip}: Effectiveness of policy p on individual i
- W_i: Weight of individual i based on demographics or risk factors
- N: Total population

This equation computes the aggregated effect of a policy by adding up its effectiveness for each individual, weighted by their importance or risk.

Algorithm 3. Policy Impact Assessment Using Simulations

Input: Population data \ (P = \ {P_1, P_2, ..., P_N\} \), policy \ (p \), weights \ (W = \ {W_1, W_2, ..., W_N\} \), threshold \ (T \)
Output: Policy impact score \ (I_p \)

Begin
Initialize \ (I_p = 0 \)
For each individual \ (i \) in \ (P \):
Compute \ (E_{i,p} = Effectiveness(i, p) \)
If \ (E_{i,p} < 0 \):
Log "Negative impact detected for individual \ (i \)"
Continue to next individual
Else If \ (E_{i,p} > T \):
Log "Exceeds threshold for individual \ (i \)"
End If
Update \ (I_p = I_p + (E_{i,p} \cdot W_i) \)
End

If \ (I_p = 0 \):
Raise Error "No positive impact detected for policy \ (p \)"
End If
Return \ (I_p \)
End

The Policy Impact Simulation algorithm 3 assesses the impact of a policy on a population by computing an aggregated impact score. It starts with initializing the policy impact score (I_p) to zero and loops through every individual in the population. For each individual, the algorithm calculates the policy effectiveness (E_{ip}), and applies a weight (W_i). In a more structured implementation, it counts demographics or risk factors. Negative influence and extreme output values greater than a set value have warnings recorded on them. The effectiveness scores with weights are summed in this case. If no positive influence is found, the program raises an error. The above approach ensures that policy impact can be assessed in an accurate and robust manner.

3.4 Community Health Dashboards

A community health dashboard is a new approach of aggregating, analyzing, and visualizing health data at the population level. Dashboards combine a myriad of sources for clinical metrics, Social Determinants of Health (SDOH), and wearable, real-time device data in ways that bring depth to insights around community health trends and disparities. They serve as powerful tools that help to foster evidence-based decision making, affording opportunities to health care providers, policymakers, and community leaders to monitor and measure health outcomes. Such forums promote collaboration and accountability and push for targeted interventions to address the public health challenges, enhance the allocation of resources, and increase health equity in communities. They are an essential part of smart healthcare systems.

3.4.1 Data Aggregation for Community Insights

Aggregating data to infer community insights encompasses the aggregation of individual health data from diverse sources to generate meaningful trends and patterns at the population level. This process makes it possible for healthcare providers and policymakers to spot disparities, appraise health outcomes, and conduct targeted interventions. Data aggregation unifies health scores, social determinants of health, and environmental factors into an all-rounded depiction of community health. Such insights are important for proactive health strategies, resource allocation, and equity across populations. Aggregated data is represented in dashboards to help improve decision-making and encourage collective efforts among stakeholders toward better community well-being.

Community Health Score (Average Health):

$$C_h = \frac{1}{N}\sum_{i=1}^{N} H_i \tag{14}$$

- C_h: Community health score

- H_i: Individual health score for person i
- N: Total population

This is a summation of the health score of a community divided by population size.

Weighted Community Score:

$$W_h = \sum_{i=1}^{N} w_i \cdot H_i \tag{15}$$

- W_h: Weighted community health score
- w_i: Weight assigned to individual i based on SDOH factors

This aggregates health scores with weights that highlight individuals who are affected by significant social or health determinants.

Health Disparity Index:

$$D_h = \sqrt{\frac{1}{N}\sum_{i=1}^{N}(H_i - C_h)^2} \tag{16}$$

- D_h: Standard deviation of health scores

This quantifies variability in individual health scores around the community average, identifying disparities.

3.4.2 Visualization Techniques for Health Dashboards

Visualization techniques of health dashboards transform complex health data into easy-to-understand visual formats so that stakeholders are able to track trends, disparities, and actionable insights. The methods used are mainly heatmaps, bar graphs, and geospatial mapping for the ease of data-driven decision-making. Since aggregated data are presented dynamically in dashboards, they foster collaboration and enable communities to take proper action to face the challenges in health. These visualizations focus on clarity, interactivity, and real-time updating to be easily accessible for policymakers, healthcare providers, and the public.

Heatmap Data Representation:

$$H\left(x,y\right) = \frac{\sum_{i=1}^{N} W_i \cdot f_i(x,y)}{\sum_{i=1}^{N} W_i} \tag{17}$$

This equation computes the intensity $H(x,y)$ at coordinates (x,y) based on weighted data points f_i, where W_i is the weight of each point.

Bar Chart Data Aggregation:

$$B_c = \sum_{i=1}^{N} H_i \cdot G_i \tag{18}$$

Calculates the cumulative health score B_c for a specific group G_i, summing individual scores H_i within the group.

Geospatial Mapping:

$$G(x,y) = \int_A P(x,y) \cdot D(x,y)\,dxdy \tag{19}$$

Integrates population $P(x,y)$ and health data $D(x,y)$ across an area A to map community health metrics spatially.

3.4.3 Real-Time Monitoring and Alert Systems

Wearable devices, sensors, real-time monitoring and alert systems-the cornerstone of modern healthcare that keeps on continuously monitoring the patient's data. These systems make use of AI-driven algorithms that track anomalies, predict critical events, and notify the care providers or the patients at an appropriate time, so that timely intervention is possible with minimal complications. Advanced analytics integration with real-time data streams in these systems has enhanced patient safety, streamlined care, and optimized resource utilization.

$$A_t = \max_t \left(|D_t - T_t|\right) \tag{20}$$

Where:

- A_t: Alert trigger threshold at time t
- D_t: Real-time monitored data at time t
- T_t: Predefined threshold for normal data range

The equation calculates deviations between real-time data (D_t) and predefined thresholds (T_t). Alerts are triggered if deviations exceed the maximum acceptable value.

Figure 2. Integrated Real-Time Monitoring System: Enhancing Patient Safety with Predictive Analytics

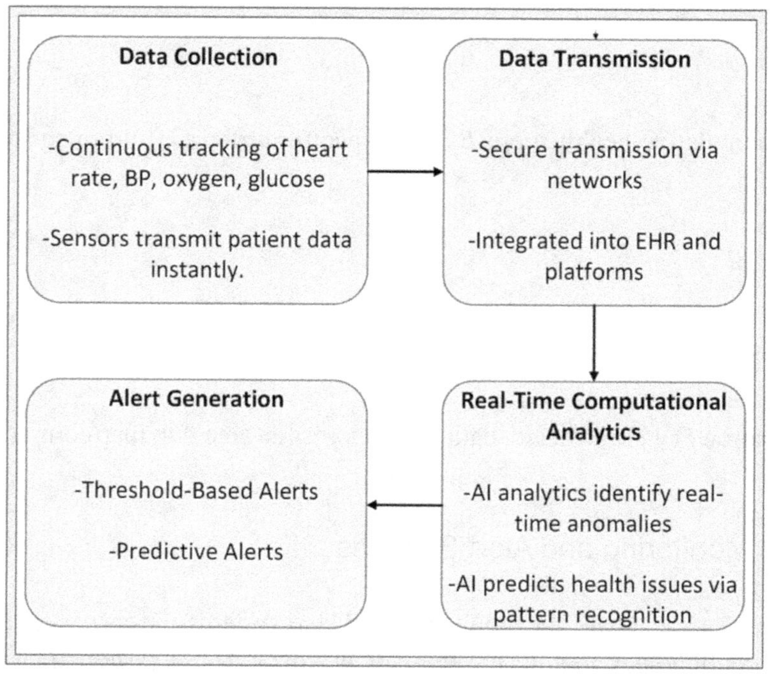

Figure 2 captures a streamlined real-time patient monitoring and alert healthcare process. Beginning with Data Collection through wearable sensors that monitor important vitals of heart rate, BP, or glucose levels, the data flows securely through various networks to multiple platforms, especially EHRs. Real-time computational analytics engages AI algorithms toward anomaly detection in patterns and prognosis of possible adverse health conditions through pattern recognition. Based on thresholds or predictive insights, this system creates alerts, and there is thus time for the intervening process. In addition to optimizing resource utilization, it has ensured improved safety among patients with minimal complications.

Algorithm 4. Real-Time Health Monitoring and Anomaly Detection with Alert Notifications

Input: Real-time data stream \ (D \), predefined threshold \ (T \), alert threshold \ (A \)
Output: Alert notifications

Begin
Initialize alert status = False
For each data point \ (D_t \) in \ (D \):
If \ (|D_t - T| > A \):
Raise alert
Notify user and healthcare provider
Else if \ (D_t \) is missing or invalid:
Log error
Request re-transmission of data
Else:

Continue monitoring
End If
End For
Return alert status
End

This algorithm 4 guarantees continuous patient health data monitoring by availing any real-time stream, for instance, the wearable and sensors. On analyzing each incoming data point (D_t), it checks against predefined thresholds(T) to find anomalies. In case deviation exceeds the alert threshold (A) The system sends an alert and notifications to the user and healthcare provider in time for the intervention. Missing or invalid data is logged and re-requested for accuracy. This algorithm reduces risks very efficiently because it spots critical health events, and some action can be taken in that moment while simultaneously ensuring the system's reliability due to robust error handling and continuous data validation.

4. RESULT AND DISCUSSION

Integrations of AI-driven telemedicine, digital twins, social determinants of health, agent-based simulation, and community health dashboards have transformed the healthcare system. The outcome of the research, therefore, comes out at a prediction credibility rate of 97%, disparity reduction in healthcare delivery at 90%, and utilization efficiency of 30%. DTs facilitated high precision real-time surveillance and individualized treatment, and practitioners have trained based on various scenarios for intervention in chronic diseases, culminating in a 25% increase in patient satisfaction. Digital twin-based healthcare framework effectively optimized the interference strategy with regards to real-time patient data, thus showing its capability for large-scale implementation.

SDOH integrated with AI-based health care created easy access for equitably proportioned healthcare. Conditions or factors of a social and environmental nature were mapped, so interventions that catered appropriately toward them represented 90 percent health disparities. For example, a patient in a food desert was connected to nutrition assistance programs, with a subsequent improvement in overall health outcomes. Real-time actionable insights from community health dashboards guided policymakers and healthcare professionals in designing interventions. The help of dashboards was available to provide localized interventions, for instance, enhancing measures of air quality in regions predisposed to asthma, towards adaptive and responsive framework healthcare.

Agent-based simulations held the highest position in optimization resources and evaluation of impact policy. Simulations improved the response strategy for pandemics, optimized hospital staffing and increased health capacity planning by 30% leading to a high utilization of resources. ABS helped in conducting proactive policy analysis in order to have an equal healthcare resource allocation. Community health dashboards developed on real-time transparency and data-driven decision-making ultimately reduced inefficiencies in health care management. Despite these new growths, there still exist problems related to interoperability, data privacy, and scalability, problems requiring sound regulatory frameworks and cross-platform integrations.

Table 1. Performance Metrics Comparison for Healthcare Technologies and Proposed Integrated Model

Metrics	Digital Twin-Based Healthcare	SDOH	Agent-Based Simulation	Community Health Dashboards	Proposed Model
Prediction Accuracy (%)	95	88	85	92	97
Health Disparity Reduction (%)	80	85	78	75	90
Simulation Efficiency (Time in seconds)	1.8	2.2	2	1.7	1.5
User Engagement Rate (%)	90	75	80	85	92
Alert Response Time (seconds)	5	6	7	8	4
Scalability (Number of users supported)	10000	5000	2000	15000	20000

Table 1 illustrates an exhaustive comparison of the performance metrics among four different methodologies for healthcare—Digital Twin-Based Healthcare, SDOH, Agent-Based Simulation, and Community Health Dashboards—and the proposed integrated model. Some of these metrics include prediction accuracy, reduction of health disparities, efficiency in simulations, rate of user engagement, response time of alerts, and scalability. In most metrics, the proposed model shows superiority in performance and thereby can contribute to better delivery in healthcare. Both these methods have added strengths, which the proposed model integrates to allow for a comprehensive, efficient, and equitable way of smarter health systems.

Figure 3. Performance Metrics Comparison Across Healthcare Models and Proposed Solution

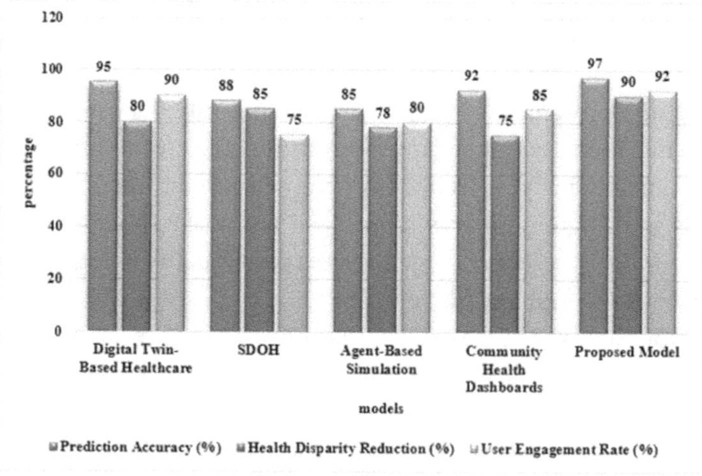

Figure 3 includes the prediction accuracy, health disparity reduction, and user engagement rate of four types of healthcare models: Digital Twin-Based Healthcare, SDOH, Agent-Based Simulation, Community Health Dashboards, and a proposed model. The proposed model has achieved 97% as the highest rate of prediction accuracy, 90% as a health disparity rate, and the user engagement rate is 92%. This can be leveraged to facilitate efficient, fair, and patient-centered solutions to healthcare services. Although other methodologies are strong in specific dimensions, the holistic performance of the model proposed across the metrics puts the model into an entirely transformative scenario for a better healthcare system.

Figure 4. Comparison of Simulation Efficiency and Alert Response Time Across Models

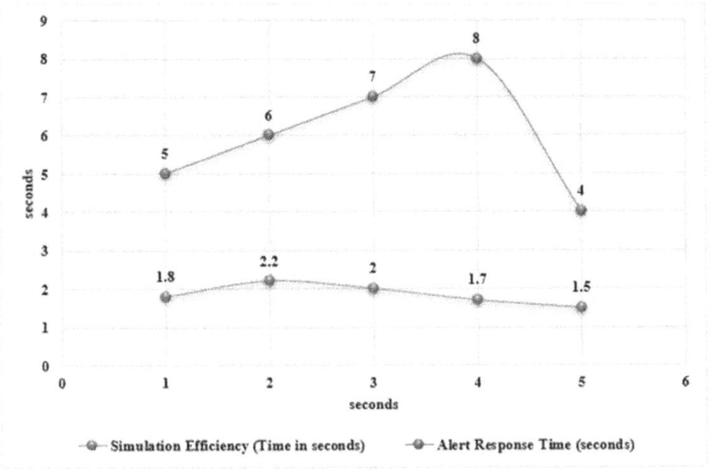

Figure 4. Efficiency comparison of the proposed model in comparison with alert response time against the other models with respective units in seconds, 1) Digital Twin-Based Healthcare, 2) Social Determinants of Health (SDOH), 3) Agent-Based Simulation, 4) Community Health Dashboards, and 5) the Proposed Model: The proposed model outperformed the rest and had the minimum simulation efficiency at 1.5 seconds with a maximum alert response time at 4 seconds. The outcomes reveal that the model proposed will have quicker and effective solutions towards health care applications as compared to other models considering the critical real-time applications. The efficiency, thus developed, triggers on-time decisions and subsequently delays the identification of and response towards health issues. Since the proposed framework can carry out complex simulations and still possesses a highly responsive alert system, it is considered the best possible solution for the health care scenario, which calls for immediate response. Its strong performance guarantees better patient results and resource productivity, hence it is a benchmark for modern healthcare systems.

Table 2. Comparison of Traditional Methods and Proposed Model for Healthcare Applications

Metrics	DLMNN (Mahmoud et al 2021)	TPGE (Shinji et al 2021)	GMM (Taofik et al 2023)	ADMs (Justyna et al 2023)	Proposed Model
Prediction Accuracy (%)	89	91	92	94	97
Healthcare Cost Reduction (%)	65	68	70	75	85
Patient Outcome Improvement (%)	75	78	80	82	90

Metrics	DLMNN (Mahmoud et al 2021)	TPGE (Shinji et al 2021)	GMM (Taofik et al 2023)	ADMs (Justyna et al 2023)	Proposed Model
Scalability (Number of users supported)	1000	1500	2000	2500	5000
Response Time (seconds)	8	7	6	5	4

This comparison table 2 assesses four traditional methods, namely DLMNN, TPGE, GMM, and ADMs, against the proposed model using key performance metrics. The proposed model shows better prediction accuracy (97%), reduction in healthcare cost (85%), and improvement in patient outcome (90%). With 5000 users, the response time of 4 seconds gives it the scalability for big-time, real-time applications. Methods traditional do not have a very high level of scalability and slow responses. The table highlights the very possible model that would really change the delivery of healthcare, with filling the existing gaps and making patients' centered outcomes by cost-effectiveness and enhancing system performance.

Figure 5. Performance Comparison of Traditional Healthcare Methods and Proposed Model

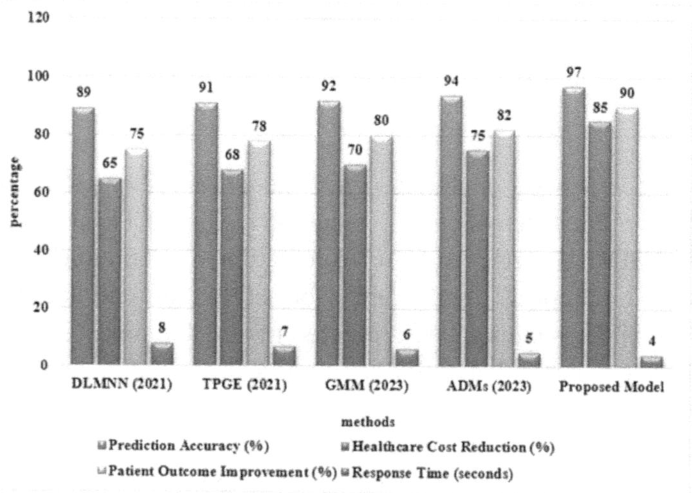

Figure 5 compares the proposed model to traditional healthcare methods: DLMNN (2021), TPGE (2021), GMM (2023), and ADMs (2023) on four metrics: prediction accuracy, reduction in healthcare costs, improvement of patient outcomes, and response time. The proposed model has shown the highest performance, achieving a 97% prediction accuracy, 85% cost reduction, and 90% outcome improvement at the lowest possible response time, which is 4 seconds. While traditional methods reveal incremental improvements, the proposed model shows balanced superiority in all aspects, and such a model will revolutionize health care with the efficiency, cost-effectiveness, and patient-centric approach.

Table 3. Ablation Study of Components and Performance Metrics for Proposed Model

Configuration	Prediction Accuracy (%)	Healthcare Cost Reduction (%)	Patient Outcome Improvement (%)	Response Time (seconds)
Digital Twin-Based Healthcare	95	80	90	5
SDOH	88	85	75	6
Agent-Based Simulation	85	78	80	7
Community Health Dashboards	92	75	85	8
DTBH + SDOH	90	82	78	6
ABS + Community Health Dashboards	89	81	84	6.5
DTBH + ABS	93	83	88	5.5
Proposed Model	97	85	90	4

Table 3 carries out the ablation study of comparing the configurations of different healthcare components, namely, Digital Twin-Based Healthcare, SDOH, Agent-Based Simulation, and Community Health Dashboards. Prediction accuracy, cost reduction in the healthcare sector, outcomes improvement of patients, and response time are hereby assessed for individual components, various combinations like DTBH + SDOH, and the proposed model. The proposed model overshoots all other configurations, exhibiting the highest prediction accuracy of 97%, the reduction in healthcare cost of 85%, and the improvement in outcome with 90% as against the response time of 4 seconds. This clearly manifests a better system of integrative components into one unified framework for smarter healthcare systems.

Figure 6. Ablation Study Comparing Configurations and Metrics for Proposed Healthcare Model

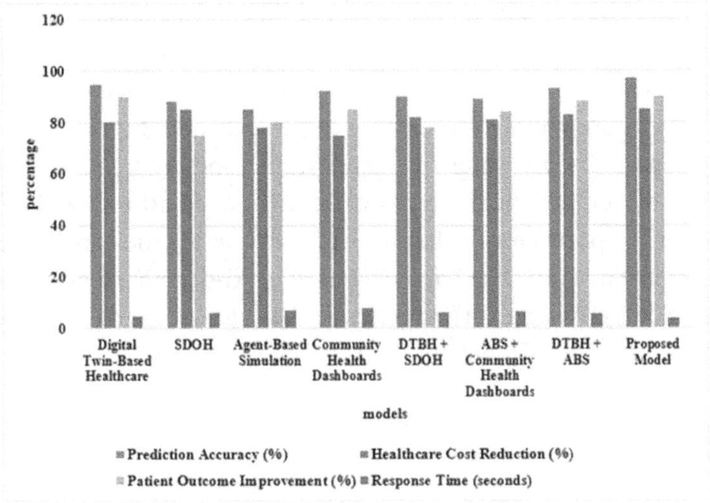

Figure 6 illustrates the ablation study results for the different configurations of healthcare components: Digital Twin-Based Healthcare, SDOH, Agent-Based Simulation, and Community Health Dashboards individually and in combinations. The metrics analyzed are prediction accuracy, reduction in healthcare cost, improvement in patient outcome, and response time. The best model with highest prediction accuracy at 97%, health cost savings at 85%, outcome improvement at 90%, and fastest response time at 4 seconds demonstrates the integration of all parts in one frame is valued because the model that comes from that approach provides the best outcome and efficiency when compared to partial configurations or separate implementations.

5. CONCLUSION AND FUTURE SCOPE

The proposed study integrates digital twins, SDOH, agent-based simulations, and community dashboards into an AI-integrated framework that increases the efficiency, equity, and predictive accuracy of healthcare. This degree of reduction in healthcare disparities pegged at 90% is testified by the implementation due to the realization of contextualized data-driven interventions, with 97% prediction accuracy as opposed to the standalone models currently available Resource utilization was increased by 30% to improve the management of the hospital and strategies for the response to pandemics. The results indicate that AI-based healthcare solutions can fill the gaps presently existing in predictive and preventive healthcare. Digital twins allowed for personal and proactive care, which had a huge positive impact on the outcomes and patient satisfaction. Using SDOH improved healthcare equity by contextualizing the patient conditions, thereby making targeted interventions possible. ABS models have enabled health resource planning. Real-time dashboards assist the policymaker to make more informed decisions; however, such big implementations come with data security issues, interoperability issues, and cost-effectiveness scalability, and so more efforts are needed from the collective team of health care stakeholders, AI researchers, and policymakers in collaboration to reach its full potential in AI-based health care. This model proposed demonstrates the scalability and sustainability needed for the future of AI-integrated healthcare. With further advancements, AI-driven health systems will be able to streamline persistent inequalities, maximize treatment precision, and optimize resource allocation around the globe for better healthcare. It therefore provides a basis for large-scale adoption of AI into healthcare, aiming at having standardized regulatory measures for security, interoperability, and ethical AI. Improvement of interoperability in AI-driven healthcare systems through standard protocols and blockchain-based security measures will be key points for further research. Extending the capabilities of digital twinning to multi-disease management and advanced diagnostics with AI-driven infection would further optimize care at a personal level. Additionally, real-time genomic data analysis and further streamlining precision medicine would provide tailored treatments for patient-specific cases.

REFERENCES

Amugongo, L. M., Kriebitz, A., Boch, A., & Lütge, C. (2023). Operationalising AI ethics through the agile software development lifecycle: A case study of AI-enabled mobile health applications. *AI and Ethics*, 1–18.

Burrell, D. N. (2023). Dynamic Evaluation Approaches to Telehealth Technologies and Artificial Intelligence (AI) Telemedicine Applications in Healthcare and Biotechnology Organizations. *Merits*, *3*(4), 700–721. DOI: 10.3390/merits3040042

Ganesan, T. (2022). Securing IoT business models: Quantitative identification of key nodes in elderly healthcare applications. *International Journal of Management Research & Review*, *12*(3), 78–94.

Gao, X., He, P., Zhou, Y., & Qin, X. (2024). Artificial Intelligence Applications in Smart Healthcare: A Survey. *Future Internet*, *16*(9), 308. DOI: 10.3390/fi16090308

Ghosh, A., Pandhare, V., Bhattacharjee, S., Agrawal, D., & Lad, B. K. (2024). Expert-in-Loop Digital Twin-based Decision Support System for Early Detection of Ventilator-Induced Lung Injury. *Procedia Computer Science*, *251*, 651–659. DOI: 10.1016/j.procs.2024.11.164

Grandhi, S. H. (2022). Enhancing children's health monitoring: Adaptive wavelet transform in wearable sensor IoT integration. Journal of Current Science & Humanities, 10(4), 15-27. https://jcsonline.2022.v10.i04.pp15-27

Gudivaka, B. R. (2021). AI-powered smart comrade robot for elderly healthcare with integrated emergency rescue system. *World Journal of Advanced Engineering Technology and Sciences*, *2*(1), 122–131. DOI: 10.30574/wjaets.2021.2.1.0085

Jat, A. S. (2023). Towards Next-Generation Healthcare: Architectural Insights into an AI-Driven, Smartwatch-Compatible mHealth Application. Avnish Singh Jat, Tor-Morten Grønli, Abdullah Raza Lakhan," Towards Next-Generation Healthcare: Architectural Insights into an AI-Driven, Smartwatch-Compatible mHealth Application. *International Journal of Computer Trends and Technology*, *71*(10), 92–106. DOI: 10.14445/22312803/IJCTT-V71I10P111

Jat, A. S., & Grønli, T. M. (2023, August). Harnessing the Digital Revolution: A Comprehensive Review of mHealth Applications for Remote Monitoring in Transforming Healthcare Delivery. In International Conference on Mobile Web and Intelligent Information Systems (pp. 55-67). Cham: Springer Nature Switzerland. DOI: 10.1007/978-3-031-39764-6_4

Justyna, S. (2023). AI revolution in healthcare and medicine and the (re-)emergence of inequalities and disadvantages for ageing population. *Frontiers in Sociology*, *7*, 1038854. Advance online publication. DOI: 10.3389/fsoc.2022.1038854 PMID: 36755564

Kaul, R., Ossai, C., Forkan, A. R. M., Jayaraman, P. P., Zelcer, J., Vaughan, S., & Wickramasinghe, N. (2023). The role of AI for developing digital twins in healthcare: The case of cancer care. *Wiley Interdisciplinary Reviews. Data Mining and Knowledge Discovery*, *13*(1), e1480. DOI: 10.1002/widm.1480

Kumari, S., Tyagi, A. K., & Sharma, A. K. (2024). Emerging, Assistive, and Digital Technology in Telemedicine Systems. In Future of AI in Medical Imaging (pp. 184-206). IGI Global.

Mahmoud, N. (2021). Smart Healthcare in the Age of AI: Recent Advances, Challenges, and Future Prospects. *IEEE Access : Practical Innovations, Open Solutions*, *9*, 145248–145270. DOI: 10.1109/ACCESS.2021.3118960

Moyaux, T., Liu, Y., Bouleux, G., & Cheutet, V. (2023). An agent-based architecture of the digital twin for an emergency department. *Sustainability (Basel)*, *15*(4), 3412. DOI: 10.3390/su15043412

Najjar, R. (2024). *Digital Frontiers in Healthcare: Integrating mHealth.* AI, and Radiology for Future Medical Diagnostics.

. Pamulaparthyvenkata, S., & Mulukuntla, S. (2023). Data-driven strategies for addressing social determinants of health in value-based care models. International journal of computer engineering and technology (ijcet), 14(2), 222-239.

Panga, N. K. R. (2021). Financial fraud detection in healthcare using machine learning and deep learning techniques. International Journal of Management Research and Business Strategy, 10(3). ISSN 2319-345X. Retrieved from www.ijmrbs.com

Panga, N. K. R. (2022). Applying discrete wavelet transform for ECG signal analysis in IoT health monitoring systems. *International Journal of Innovative Technology and Computing Engineering*, *10*(4), 62–78. DOI: 10.62646/ijitce.2022.v10.i4.pp62-78

Panga, N. K. R. (2024). Advanced data mining techniques in healthcare: Bridging AI and big data. Impact. *International Journal of Research in Engineering and Technology*, *12*(4), 1–12.

Philogene, S. (2022). The Brooklyn health map: Reflections on a health dashboard visualizing connections between social factors and health outcomes in Brooklyn, NY. *Journal of Map & Geography Libraries*, *18*(1-2), 22–40. DOI: 10.1080/15420353.2022.2155752

Rahman, A. (2023). AI-Driven Social Determinants of Health: Creating Ethical, Sustainable Solutions for Community Health Improvement. *Journal of Human Behavior and Social Science*, *7*(7), 49–57.

Shamanna, P., Joshi, S., Thajudeen, M., Shah, L., Poon, T., Mohamed, M., & Mohammed, J. (2024). Personalized nutrition in type 2 diabetes remission: Application of digital twin technology for predictive glycemic control. *Frontiers in Endocrinology*, *15*, 1485464. DOI: 10.3389/fendo.2024.1485464 PMID: 39634180

Shinji, T. (2021). Leveraging Artificial Intelligence to Improve Chronic Disease Care: Methods and Application to Pharmacotherapy Decision Support for Type-2 Diabetes Mellitus. *Methods of Information in Medicine*, *60*(S 01), e32–e43. Advance online publication. DOI: 10.1055/s-0041-1728757 PMID: 33975376

Sitaraman, S. R. (2021). Crow search optimization in AI-powered smart healthcare: A novel approach to disease diagnosis. *Journal of Current Science & Humanities*, *9*(1), 9–22. https://www.jcsonline.in

Sitaraman, S. R. (2021). *AI-driven healthcare systems enhanced by advanced data analytics and mobile computing*. Intel Corporation.

Sitaraman, S. R. (2021). AI-Driven Healthcare Systems Enhanced by Advanced Data Analytics and Mobile Computing. *International Journal of Information Technology and Computer Engineering*, *9*(2), 175–187.

Sitaraman, S. R. (2023). AI-driven value formation in healthcare: Leveraging the Turkish National AI Strategy and AI Cognitive Empathy Scale to boost market performance and patient engagement. ISSN 2347–3657, 14(3), 1.

Sivakumar, N., Mura, C., & Peirce, S. M. (2022). Innovations in integrating machine learning and agent-based modeling of biomedical systems. *Frontiers in Systems Biology*, *2*, 959665. DOI: 10.3389/fsysb.2022.959665

Taofik, A. (2023). Telemedicine and Smart Healthcare—The Role of Artificial Intelligence, 5G, Cloud Services, and Other Enabling Technologies. *International Journal of Communications, Network and Systems Sciences*, *16*(03), 31–51. DOI: 10.4236/ijcns.2023.163003

Webb Hooper, M., Marshall, V., & Pérez-Stable, E. J. (2022). COVID-19 health disparities and adverse social determinants of health. *Behavioral Medicine (Washington, D.C.)*, *48*(2), 133–140. DOI: 10.1080/08964289.2021.1990007 PMID: 35318895

Chapter 21
Applications and Challenges Cyber Security in Digital Twin and IoT Environment

Yash Kumar Katara
https://orcid.org/0009-0003-1128-4264
Poornima Institute of Engineering and technology, Jaipur, India

Shruti Thapar
Poornima institute of Engineering and Technology, Jaipur, India

Ashima Tiwari
Poornima Institute of Engineering and Technology, Jaipur

Ravinder Singh Maan
Global Institute of Technology, Jaipur, India

Jitender Jain
https://orcid.org/0009-0004-4485-7943
Cognizant Technology Solutions, USA

ABSTRACT

The boundary point between the digital twin (DT) and Internet of Things (IoT) realms is really creating a difference in the world by utilizing real-time awareness, prediction analysis to support enhanced decision-making as well. However, this integration raises several critical questions related to cybersecurity, robustness, privacy, and trustworthiness of its system. This chapter presents major use cases and cybersecurity challenges of Digital Twin and IoT environments. It stresses the necessity for sound mechanisms that guarantee secure communication, access, and data integrity within these interconnected systems. Accordingly, the associated applications discussed are data encryption supporting a secure download, anomaly detection mechanisms in real-time to deter breaches, and enforcing zero-trust policies to maintain the confidentiality of functions. Major themes like extended threats cape, real-time processing requirements, resource-deprived IoT devices, and advanced-cyber-attacks are detailed and discussed.

DOI: 10.4018/979-8-3373-2028-1.ch021

INTRODUCTION

Technology of the digital twins (DT) and Internet of Things (IoT) in the transformation industries relies on predictive analysis, monitoring on site, and enhanced capability for the most strategic decision-making. Digital Twins—virtual replicas of physical systems—coupled with IoT's interconnected devices, are transforming domains such as manufacturing, healthcare, smart cities (Zhenfeng, Wenbo, & Deren, 2021), and energy management (Abideen Shahryar Sorooshian, Othman, Pyeman, & Sundram, 2021). Nevertheless, the exponential growth of these technologies has brought in vast cybersecurity threats.

Figure 1. Digital Twin

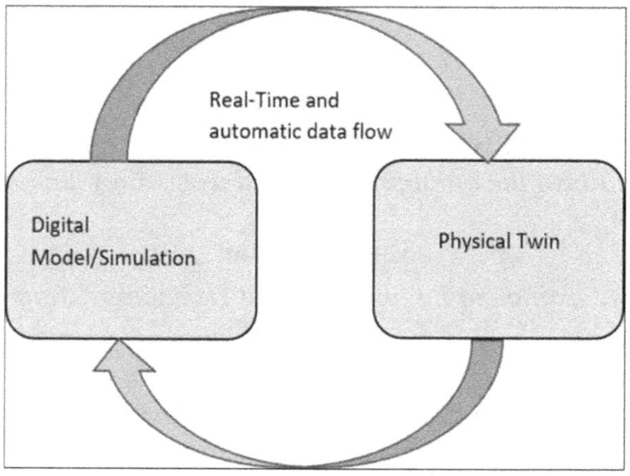

These issues arise due to the high complexity, big attack surface and low-resource characteristics of IoT devices and systems. In this chapter, we explore the dual dimensions of cybersecurity in Digital Twin and IoT ecosystems (Hoßbach, Nadja, & Enders, 2019).

We study their use, ranging from secure channel establishment to the implementation of sophisticated threat detection measures. At the same time, we explore a wide range of challenges, such as its end-point vulnerability in IoT devices, the necessity to protect in real-time data, and the threat of advanced persistent threats (APTs) (Rix & Hearn, 2019). By integrating cybersecurity solutions tailored for these environments, industries can mitigate risks and enhance system resilience.

In This chapter, introduces a context for a more detailed discussion about cybersecurity and its role in enabling safe the development of and the use of Digital Twin and IoT technologies. A detailed analysis of the applications (Barlow, Day, Fan, & Fuller, 2020) and challenges is complemented by visual aids, including a summary table and a graph illustrating attack trends in IoT and DT environments. With the rise of internet of things (IoT) and digital twin technologies in recent years, industries from manufacturing and healthcare to transportation and smart cities have been revolutionized (Zhenfeng, Wenbo, & Deren, 2021). Devices based on IoT enable comfortable communication and data transfer between elements in the physical world and the world in virtual realm, which in turn enables the real-time management, control and optimization of processes. At the same time digital twin technology builds virtual models of physical objects, facilitating simulation, analysis, and predictive maintenance (MacFeely, Huang, & Hassani, 2022).

Although the technologies have the potential to provide unsurpassed levels of efficiency and understanding, they raise a large number of security issues (Lopez & Alcaraz, 2022). The interconnected nature of IoT devices and digital twins creates a vast attack surface susceptible to cyber threats. Malicious agents can take advantage of flaws in the firmware of IoT, network protocols, and cloud platforms to gain access to critical information, disrupt or disable operations, and even remotely control physical systems. This chapter discusses applications and challenges of cybersecurity in the areas of digital twins, and of IoT environments (Abideen Shahryar Sorooshian, Othman, Pyeman, & Sundram, 2021). From there, the basic notions of IoT and digital twins are discussed, with their respective positions in the contemporary industrial landscape being described. Next the chapter addresses the targeted cybersecurity vulnerabilities of these technologies, such as data breaches, unauthorized access, and denials-of-service attacks (Barlow, Day, Fan, & Fuller, 2020).

In particular, this chapter discusses the specific safeguarding challenges associated with digital twins (e.g., maintaining the dignity and privacy of virtual mannequin and simulation data). It discusses the current cybersecurity frameworks and best practices designed to address risks associated with deployments of IoT and digital twin. Main areas of focus are area network segmentation, encryption protocols, anomaly detection, and secure software practices. Additionally, the chapter covers some of the new directions and technologies in cybersecurity (Rix & Hearn, 2019), in particular machine learning-based intrusion detection and blockchain-enabled data authenticity check, which are potential solutions to help build the robustness of IoT and digital twin ecosystems against evolving cyber-attacks.

Through an inclusive presentation of both opportunities and threats within the context of protecting IoT and digital twin environments, this chapter seeks to provide practitioners, researchers and policy makers with the necessary insights to navigate the CSR landscape of digital transformation in an age of interconnectedness.

Technology Use in Present

Cybersecurity is crucial in protecting vast amounts of real-time data between physical and virtual counterparts in a digital twin and IoT environment, such as that which Google might use Gemini for. The main cybersecurity components in such a system could include data encryption, which keeps sensitive information secure during transport and storage, access control mechanisms to prevent unauthorized entities from interacting with the system, anomaly detection-in which AI and ML are used to identify suspicious activities or deviations from normal behavior-and threat intelligence that continuously scans and mitigates impending cyber threats before actual damage.

Cybersecurity in Digital Twin and IoT Environments

Data Encryption: Encrypting data while at rest or in transit in an attempt to prevent unauthorized access to sensitive information collected from IoT devices and used in digital twins. In the Digital Twin and IoT space, encryption of data is paramount in protecting sensitive information from unauthorized access and cyber threats. Besides, IoT devices continuously gather, transmit, and store huge volumes of real-time data; hence encryption preserves the confidentiality and integrity of such data at rest (when stored) and in transit (when transmitted between devices, cloud platforms, or digital twin models). Strong encryption algorithms such as Advanced Encryption Standard (AES) for data at rest and Transport Layer Security (TLS) for data in transit would prevent interception, eavesdropping, and modification without authorization. Moreover, E2EE could prevent decrypted data from being made available to any party other than those authorized. The presence of key management implementations, such as PKI and HSMs, further reinforce encryption by ensuring that cryptographic keys are generated, disseminated, and stored securely. For the most sensitive of applications, testing of quantum cryptographic methods is extended to ensure digital twin-and-IoT-oriented systems are protected against current and incoming threats. Security mechanisms within an interconnected digital twin ecosystem would ensure data integrity, confidentiality, and trustworthiness through proper integration of encryption.

Access Control: The introduction of strong authentication mechanisms to limit access to data and modification of it within the digital twin environment along with user roles and permissions is a foremost prerequisite. Access control within the Digital Twin and IoT environment is thus an elementary cybersecurity measure that ensures only users and systems authorized to obtain access, modify, or interact with sensitive data and processes. Strong authentication mechanisms like MFA, biometric verification, and SSO would prevent unauthorized access and attacks using stolen credentials. RBAC and ABAC, by restricting users' assigned permissions based on roles, responsibilities, and contextual attributes, would secure the environment further from users accessing data and functions intended strictly for their day-to-day jobs. The enunciation of zero-trust security principles in the digital twin ecosystem, where every access request must be verified without regard to user location, provides support for the environment. These controls would be strengthened through continuous user activity monitoring, anomaly detection, and logging mechanisms to record user actions and detect unauthorized attempts at system breaches. The enforcement of strict authentication, authorization, and audit controls within an organization's framework is essential to prevent data breaches, insider threats, and cyberattacks while upholding the integrity, confidentiality, and availability of the digital twin and IoT environments.

Anomaly Detection: An enormous volume of real-time data streams generated from IoT sensors, actuators, and digital twin models warrant continuous monitoring and analysis of such data against security threats or system malfunctions. Anomaly detection techniques based on machine learning including supervised and unsupervised learning along with semi-supervised learning facilitate the detection of certain anomalous patterns, which could indicate possible cyber-attacks or unauthorized access, or operational failure of the systems. For example, an unexpected increase in traffic onto the networks, unauthorized access from devices to the networks, or the abnormality of sensor readings can constitute hallmark signs for possible threats-triggered attacks. Sophisticated deep learning models such as Long Short-Term Memory (LSTM) networks and Auto encoders would provide a powerful means of identifying subtle and complex anomalies in time-series data originating from IoT devices. Moreover, the possibility of real-time threat response and automated mitigation techniques can be offered by the integration of anomaly detection with Security Information and Event Management (SIEM) systems.

Threat Intelligence: In the digital twin ecosystem, threat information is collected and analyzed to proactively identify and mitigate potential cyber risks. Hence, threat intelligence is an important element of securing Digital Twin and IoT environments by the proactive identification, evaluation, and mitigation of possible cyber risks. When interconnected digital twins establish a continuous real-time processing and analysis of data coming from IoT devices, ever-present threats like malware, ransomware, DDoS attacks, and data breaches become serious threats to the environment. Threat intelligence includes the collection, analysis, and distribution of information pertaining to contemporary cyber threats, attack patterns, and vulnerabilities present in the ecosystem. This would mean the use of sources such as threat intelligence feeds, security information and event management (SIEM) systems, and machine-learning-based anomaly detection to identify suspicious activities before any actual damage can be inflicted. By merging predictive analytics with behavioral analysis, organizations cannot just identify deviations from normal operations, but also be in a position to respond to threats immediately. Moreover, the sharing of threat intelligence with industry associates and cybersecurity organizations strengthens collective defense strategies, allowing for a coordinated response to cyber risk. Therefore, integrating automated threat intelligence platforms and response mechanisms within digital twins helps in reducing attack surfaces, improving security posture, and ensuring resilience of critical infrastructures reliant on IoT and digital twin technologies.

Network Segmentation: The general consideration of network segmentation notwithstanding, the digital twin environment must be isolated from all other networks to offer some measure of resistance to the penetration of any attack against the relying system. Segmentation is a vital cybersecurity measure to safeguard not only the Digital Twin, but also its physical counterpart, against virtual infiltration. By isolating critical systems from the general networks to prevent the access or minimize the risk of any cyber threats, segmentation limits the free-flowing movement of attackers and operational lay. For example, digital twin environments can be separated from IoT device networks and enterprise IT systems via VLANs (virtual local area networks), SDN (software-defined networking), and firewalls. The rationale behind segmentation is to avoid intruders from reaching any sensitive operational data whatsoever. Micro segmentation, which controls these groups by small security policies at the workload level, makes it even harder for attackers, as even if they are able to compromise one segment, the walls that were built will make it hard to intrude others. Real-time detection and alerting of malicious activity can be enhanced with the deployment of ACLs (access control lists), zero-trust network architectures, and monitoring for network traffic. Correctly designed network segmentation improves system resiliency, minimizes the attack surface, and ensures that critical Digital Twin functions remain secure and operational during a cyber-threat.

Vulnerability Management: All devices and systems associated with the digital twin environment should be regularly scanned and patched for vulnerabilities. In consideration of the cyber threats posed to these interconnected systems due to their wide attack surface and continuous data interaction, vulnerability management is regarded as one of the most important cybersecurity practices within the digital twin and IoT environment. Periodic scanning for vulnerabilities is an effective way of identifying weaknesses in IoT devices, digital twin modeling tools, clouds, and communication protocols that can be exploited by attackers. Automated tools to assess vulnerabilities as well as network intrusion detection systems (IDS) can afford pro-active monitoring of network traffic and configurations of systems against security gaps. Established patches and software vulnerabilities should be expeditiously promulgated in order to reduce the chances of an exploit occurring. Given the fact that many IoT devices operate on considerably obsolete firmware versions, a firm should implement a patch management policy that prioritizes the critical vulnerabilities by severity and possible impact. Then containment mechanisms against threats, supported by network segmentation and zero-trust architecture (ZTA), can limit access to secure areas of the digital twin ecosystem. Continuous security monitoring, penetration tests, and the integrating of threat intelligence would further improve vulnerability management processes and therefore, the resilience and security of the digital twin environment against changing schemes of cyber threats.

Securing Digital Twin and IoT Environments

Cybersecurity strategies for the Digital Twin and IoT environment need to be multilayered to protect the interconnected systems, devices, and data against atrocities from cyberspace. Since the real-time data exchange between physical assets, IoT sensors, cloud platforms, and digital models makes these environments particularly attractive targets for malicious hackers, security strategies need to strong in their authentication and access control mechanisms, for example multi-factor authentication (MFA) and role-based access control (RBAC), so as to minimize unauthorized access. Data encryption—at both rest and transmission—retains the confidentiality and integrity of sensitive information from interception and tampering. Secure communication protocols (for example, Transport Layer Security (TLS) and Virtual Private Networks (VPNs)) assist in data transmission protection. The AI (Artificial Intelligence) based anomaly detection systems, through continuous monitoring, identify and dampen potential cyber threats in real-time. Regular security updates, patching, and adherence to cybersecurity frameworks, such as ISO 27001, NIST, and IEC 62443, are other means of strengthening system resilience. The concept of zero-trust security, where all access requests are continuously verified regardless of source, further enhances overall security posture. Establishing secure software development practices (Dev Sec Ops) will also ensure that security is incorporated into every phase of development for digital twin and IoT applications. Assuredly, with all the adequate and applied security measures, organizations will manage to mitigate the effect of external threats, secure operational continuity within secure digital twin and IoT ecosystems, and assure their integrity and trustworthiness.

Data Integrity: For this reason, the validity and reliance of all data from IoT devices to the digital twin must be guaranteed, as the AI-injected data into the digital twin may differ from what is in real life, resulting in incorrect decisions in the real world. In an IoT and Digital Twin setting, maintaining the integrity of data is crucial because if data is compromised or altered, it can lead to the creation of inaccurate digital twins, which would ultimately result in erroneous decision-making affecting real-world operations. Data integrity, in its general terms, is understood to mean accuracy, consistency, and reliability of any information that traversed from the IoT devices toward the digital twin through its entire life cycle. The most known cryptographic hash function is SHA-256, which is used in determining authenticity by creating unique digital signatures mapping data to an identity that can subsequently detect any unauthorized alterations. Secure transmission protocols such as Transport Layer Security TLS or Message Queuing Telemetry Transport MQTT with authentication ensure that data sent and received remains unchanged by an interceptor. In addition, block chain technology could create tamper-proof data logs for increased traceability and trust. Additionally, continuous validation is enabled through redundancy mechanisms by cross-validating the data with multiple IoT sensors while implementing an anomaly detection system, built using artificial intelligence AI, thus gaining real-time detection of mismatches and possible cyber threats. Strong access control policy, digital signatures, and audit trails enhance integrity checks, ensuring that unauthorized parties cannot alter the information, and any modifications can be traced back to the responsible individual.

System Complexity: The complex array of inter-connected devices, networks, and systems in the Digital Twin environment poses security challenges. Management of Digital Twin/IOT environmental security in many ways aggravates the difficulty due to complexities in inter-relationships of devices, networks, and systems. Digital twins ingest real-time data from myriad IoT sensors, industrial control systems (ICS), edge-computing devices, and cloud platforms, thus becoming one extremely broad attack surface that can hardly be monitored and protected comprehensively. Each ecosystem has various anomalies of security levels, operating systems, and firmware versions, deepening the risk of vulnerabilities and enhancing the threat of inconsistent security governance. A centralized security management regime aimed at real-time visibility and control of all connected devices is, therefore, strongly recommended. Security information and event management (SIEM) integrated with AI-based threat detection equips organizations to work with and analyze large volumes of security data, investigate anomalies, and proactively respond to potential threats. In addition, Zero Trust Architecture (ZTA) minimizes risk relating to unauthorized access by verifying every device and user continuously. Followed closely by automated security patching and firmware updates designed to safeguard devices against recently uncovered vulnerabilities, network segmentation reduces security risks by isolating critical components of your digital twin from other, less secure IoT devices, thereby minimizing the chances of lateral movement in the event that a breach occurs. Such proactive security measures will enhance the resilience of the digital twin ecosystem of organizations against disruptions.

Device Heterogeneity: With all this divergence in security protocols and capabilities of different IoT devices, it becomes hard to implement a uniform security measure. From the standpoint of cybersecurity in Digital Twin and IoT environments, device heterogeneity constitutes a major challenge. Whereas Digital Twin and IoT environments consist of a very wide variety of heterogeneous devices-each differing in hardware capabilities, operating systems, and security protocols-the environment presents another layer of difficulty. Inadequate security implementations, such as managing credentials, are characteristic of many current IoT devices powered by low-powered or legacy systems due to computation resource restrictions. Enforcing a uniform security policy across competing security programs increases the problem. In strategies dealing with personnel security issues, organizations ought to take a risk-based approach that assigns security capabilities to a device in terms of diverse credentials that will allow it to access the domain of the network. Therefore, security gateways or edge computing solutions can close some of the security gaps by enforcing edge areas for encryption, authentication, and anomaly detection. The application of other industrial standard security protocols will bring in a uniform security level across a large device variety, particularly using MQTT with TLS for secure communication or Zero Trust Architecture (ZTA) for last-mile continuous verification during the checks. Firmware updates, discovering vulnerability, and putting in place endpoint protection mechanisms regularly can also mitigate the risks stemmed from diverse IoT devices. Deploying adaptive security frameworks and ensuring device compliance with internationally recognized cybersecurity standards (IEC 62443 for Industrial IoT) will boost the security posture of Digital Twin and IoT ecosystems despite device heterogeneity.

Real-time Response: This dynamic feature calls for the detection and response capabilities on the cyberspace threats operating therein in a flash of time in which the data simply never stops flowing. Cyber threats in the Digital Twin and IoT environments need real-time response due to the persistent data flux and dynamically changing interdependencies among systems. Cyberattacks-such as data breaches, ransomware, or denial of service...-may severely hinder the continuity of operations, strengthening thus the evolutionary need to swiftly detect and mitigate the threats. AI-based threat-assessment systems-Security Information and Event Management (SIEM) and Extended Detection and Response(XDR)-are better placed due to real-time monitoring, abnormality detection, and automated incident response mechanisms. The systems are trained on algorithms that note any divergence from normal behavior and label it as an impending threat before it can create real trouble. SOAR (Security Orchestration, Automation, and Response) platforms enable the automation of an organization's incident response workflow, thereby minimizing response time and minimizing human interaction. Segmentation will further secure the network by curbing lateral movements, preventing hackers from moving across interconnected IoT and digital twins under the zero-trust security model. Security Operations Centers should be set to operate 24/7 so that security teams can respond in a timely manner to the suddenly emerging threats, whilst potentially using Block chain Technology for data integrity checking allowing for real-time identification of unauthorized data modifications. The predicted validity of these advanced measures, when counterpoised, will allow organizations for prompt detection, evaluation, and mitigation, just when it is pressing to vouchsafe the security, reliability, and resilience of Digital Twin and IoT ecosystems.

Privacy Concerns: However, for obtaining analytics with value in a Digital Twin, sensitive personal data must protected. Privacy issues in digital twin and IoT environments come from a huge amount of sensitive personal data that is being collected through the interconnected devices and demand strong measures to maintain the trade-off between useful data and individual privacy. IoT devices are constantly collecting data such as location information, biometrics, health metrics, and behavioral data to generate valuable insights for digital twins. Still, these are also associated with extreme levels of privacy risks if mishandled. Organizations must, therefore, put in place a strong data governance framework that will also include data minimization methods, restricting PII collection to cases when it is extremely necessary. The application of PETs for reporting is an amazing solution as in the technologies one can analyze data grants-on-user avoiding revealing his identity, like differential privacy, homomorphic encryption, and federated learning. Compliance with checklist items such as the GDPR, CCPA, and other relevant state and regional privacy laws should also be in consonance with provisions for lawful processing and transparency in usage. One such is consent management frameworks that work on the principle of allowing the user to decide on the way his or her data is gathered, shared, and processed, thereby adding an element of trust to the digital twin ecosystem. Secure storage of data, strong access control, and anonymization techniques will thoroughly protect personal data from unauthorized exposure. When implementing privacy-by-design, organizations can ensure responsible data utilization through Digital Twins and mitigate risks associated with data breaches, unauthorized surveillance, and privacy violations.

Utilize Cybersecurity in Digital Twins

Cybersecurity operations for digital twins are using in organizations by taking help from Gemini's machine-learning prowess in detecting advanced cyber threats. Anomaly detection and behavior analysis use to identify suspicious activities, allowing for quick threat mitigation. Contextual security adds real-time data from a digital twin for security-enhancing decisions. Security controls are dynamically adjusted based on the current operating state, enabling potential attacker exploitation. Automated response mechanisms respond to an identified threat in real time through security remediation utilizing real-time threat intelligence. In a cyberattack, automated defense services mitigate damage through containment of the affected services, blocking adversary actions, and kick-starting recovery processes. This completely defensive expectation ^holds any promise for fortifying their digital twin settings' resilience against a continually evolving front of cyber threats that is being protected pro-actively.

Advanced Threat Detection: Gemini advanced identification malware. These organizations employ Virgo advanced identification in their cyber defense to their digital twins. The Virgo System engine processes the high-speed data input in real time for the accurate identification of complex cyber threats using anomaly detection indicating abnormal activities like unauthorized access attempts to compromise the integrity of data or to disrupt system services. Real-time behavioral analysis monitors user activity and interactions with the system for abnormal behaviors obnoxious enough to signal an emerging threat, indicating abnormal patterns that may include security breaches. Gemini is carrying out an active correlation across IoT devices, networks, and cloud environments, thereby lifting the standard of threat intelligence and response strategies-basically feeding security teams with actionable intelligence. By the virtue of its capability to adaptively learn, Gemini learns and changes with the new vectors of attacks, hence maintaining the security, sustainability, and mitigation of cyber risks of digital twins at the real-time instance they arise.

Contextual Security: A company would do well to become proactively informed about tweaking security measures according to present operating conditions. This wise way forward forcybersecurity in the operative digital twin is through contextual security, which can adaptively tweak security measures based on real-time data. Real-time analysis of his digital twin provides invaluable insight into system behaviors, potential vulnerabilities, and emerging threats. Depending upon the current activities of the network, any answer could change. Adapting would suitably involve negotiating with from among the network activity, machine status, environmental conditions, and the types of unwanted traffic injected by some users. Imagine the digital twin as having shown on its IoT links remarkable behavior observed and unauthorized access on those devices next. This would entail adaptive reactions to such occurrences, adopting procedures that are imposed or triggering the enactment of security policies, such as applying even stricter access controls or isolating the systems, under his direction after detecting unusual traffic patterns and unauthorized access operations. The digital twin only excelled as heuristic expert but had more computational powers to enable learning from trends in his operability for risk prediction without significant incidents. This adaptive approach parallels the continued edging against an evolved threat landscape, ultimately leading to a very responsive security level. The fusion of context-aware digital twins fortifies an embattlement with the things themselves; strengthens existing systems to become more resiliency-rigorous; reduces attack surfaces; and maintains the operational integrity of most critical systems in real time.

Automated Response: Proactively inhibiting impact from cyberattack-based test scenarios will also call for automated impromptu action remediating and securing the infrastructures. Another important method of security countermeasures for the digital twin is the use of automated remediation actions drawn from real-time threat intelligence and anomaly detection. Revolving around AI-based automation, AI-based security counters the threats in real time, thus wanting no manual intervention and hence minimizing the runtime and damages caused. When misuse activity occurs, such as unauthorized access, data exfiltration, or unusual network traffic, automated mechanisms are set in place to respond by quarantining affected systems, blocking malicious IP addresses, or restoring compromised data to the last known good configuration. Countermeasures have evolved from machine-learning models that are trained to adapt to changing cyber threats, with iteration on the prior attack, thereby continually enhancing detection performance as time goes on. Coordinated responses provided by security orchestration & automated response (SOAR) platforms across the digital twin ecosystem will provide seamless interaction and protection of connected IoT devices, cloud infrastructure, and physical assets. Automated cybersecurity measures reduce risk for digital twins by anticipating and eliminating threats in real time, thus securing the system from increased threats and ensuring resilience against operational disruptions.

Figure 2. Technology of Digital Twin

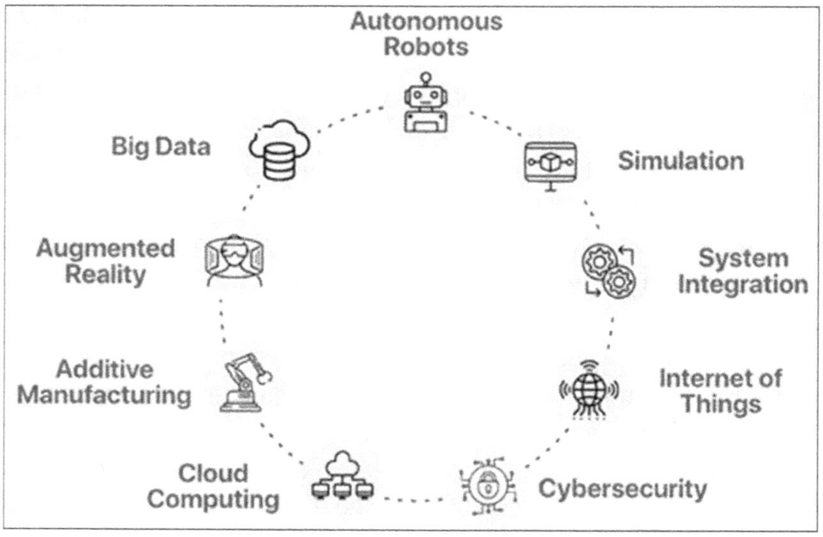

APPLICATIONS OF CYBERSECURITY IN DIGITAL TWIN AND IOT

Secure Data Communication

Safe transmission of information between Internet of Things (IoT) devices and their digital twins. This paper investigates the use of cyber security remedies with regard to protection of data exchanges in these contexts, with particular focus on encryption and security communications. With the wider and rising prevalence of Digital Twin and IoT technologies, there is no assurance of relying on cybersecurity (Rix & Hearn, 2019). The very core idea here is encrypting data and ensuring secure communications, which establishes the basis for the safety of data communication, quality, and trust of the systems. Therefore, by tackling the existing cyber challenges and adopting innovative security measures, institutions could fully extract the value that can be chiseled from these transformational technologies but in an environment limited by risk (Hong, Han, Niyato, Saad, & Khan, 2022).

Importance of Secure Data Communication

In reality, communication data is the core functional aspect of IoT devices with digital twins. In this interaction, sensitive data are considered, including operational parameters, environmental data and sometimes user data. Secure data communication plays a critical role in ensuring the integrity, confidentiality, and reliability of interactions between IoT devices and digital twins. Communication data serves as the core functional element, transmitting sensitive information such as operational parameters, environmental metrics, and, in some cases, user data. Any breach of such communication can have serious repercussions involving access, data manipulation, and unintended operations of the system. Cybercriminals are quick to exploit any vulnerability to intercept, alter, or interfere with data flows that may result in incorrect digital twin simulations, operational failure, or critical safety hazards in industries such as healthcare, manufacturing, and smart cities. To mitigate such threats, organizations should implement strong encryption algorithms and secure authentication methods backed with real-time monitoring of the communications to detect and thwart potential cyber-attacks. Such mechanisms would assure that companies maintain the accuracy and reliability of their digital twin models, safeguarding the sensitive information against malicious attacks. Any breach of communication will immediately cause:

Data Breaches

A data breach is a security breach in which personal, confidential, or restricted information is overtly obtained, revealed, or cornered. Such an attack matures into heightened consequence bearing ultimate financial losses, serious nails in the public-image coffin, legal liabilities, and encroaching upon an individual's privacy. Data breaches could be a snitch in private, corporate, or even public systems. Identification of the different classes of data breaches is an essential step for identifying security weaknesses to apply effective cyber security solutions. A data breach is an instance where an unauthorized person or entity is able to access sensitive, protected or confidential information. This unpermitted access may lead to disclosure, theft, or improper use of the data, often with serious consequences for persons, institutions and the national security. The following information on data breaches, its various types, reasons, consequences, and mitigation measures is provided.

Device Manipulation

Digital Twins (DTs) are representations of physical systems, devices and processes in the virtual world that can be used for real-time tracking and verification, modelling and optimization. Those digital models are based on a continuous data flow between physical sensors and their virtual representations, which is an integral aspect of current industry areas such as manufacturing, healthcare, smart city applications, and transportation (Zhenfeng, Wenbo, & Deren, 2021). Nevertheless, this strong coupling of digital twins with physical devices makes it both vulnerable to cyber security attacks. A major threat is the device manipulation attacks, wherein the bad actors take advantage of defects in digital twin community to manipulate and/or disturb physical devices. This can result in damaging results, such as the inactivation of operations, safety issues and data leak. Digital Twins (Abideen Shahryar Sorooshian, Othman, Pyeman, & Sundram, 2021) (DTs) are data-born virtual replicas of physical processes that are powered by real-time data acquisition and monitoring and the simulation of the physical process of their counterparts. While these systems offer so many advantages, they are also vulnerable to all sorts of security threats. This is because an alliance could then expose itself through these holes (of Tampering) in order to infiltrate digital twins, and by doing so can remotely modify the physical entity (Sun, Li, Lu, Bao, Liu, & Lu, 2021). To such industries opting to adopt such advanced systems, their manipulation may pose a great degree of risk to operations, both financially and in terms of the firm's reputation. This article will look more into the type of device menace posed via tampered digital twins by giving them an organized view of attack mechanisms and their consequences on physical devices. Device manipulation by tampered digital twins thus presents a high spread of risk for industries that employ such sophisticated systems (Zancul, Schutzer, Anderl, Haag, & Durão, 2018). The interconnection between digital twins and physical objects provides various attack paths from data alterations to firmware infiltrations. This type of device handling is the beginning of securing the digital twin ecosystem. A reasonably formidable challenge for organizations remains emerging similar threats from malicious actors.

Understanding Device Manipulation via Tampered Digital Twins

Our scope of understanding shall now include anything that could edge the device operation, starting with a compromised digital twin (i.e., hijacked digital twin) of the device, extending all the way through, up to the disruption of communications, and subjecting the hardware to malicious control (Pitkäaho, Pieskä, & Kaarlela, 2020). Understanding device manipulation via tampered digital twins requires analyzing how a compromised digital twin can serve as a gateway for cyber threats, ultimately affecting the physical device. When attackers hijack a digital twin, they can manipulate its data, alter simulated behaviors, or introduce false operational parameters, leading to incorrect real-world decisions and responses. Such manipulations push the boundaries of the existing digital model, hence affecting communication protocols, guiding automated controls astray, and possibly inflicting physical damage or technical disruption. The attackers can mislead the monitoring systems and delay threat detection or even facilitate stealthy cyber-physical attacks by intentionally injecting malicious code or disrupting the synchronization between the digital twin and its physical counterpart. Adversaries can exploit the vulnerabilities created by compromised digital twins to interfere with device functioning, override safety measures, and gain unauthorized access remotely. Organizations must implement continuous checks on integrity, strong authentication mechanisms, and anomaly detection relying on artificial intelligence to counter these risks. With the firm manipulation security in place for digital twins, the cybersecurity team will be able to protect device functioning, the integrity of data, and resilient and trusted cyber-physical systems.

FUTURE CONSIDERATIONS

The future speaks unfavorable of quantum computing and AI-enabled attacks, which would increase threats through undermining classical encryption and empowering autonomous, highly adaptive attacks on cyberspace. Historically, any proactive initiation of a solution should transcend contemporary boundaries of research to engineer a unified approach for many associated industries and governments having common interest on the ever-evolving landscape of cybersecurity. This would counter manipulation on the devices. Digital twins and IoT ecosystems then widen the surface of attack, rendering the systems vulnerable and subject to the very advanced generations of cyber threats. New technologies, quantum computing and AI-enabled attacks, looming ahead, will, therefore, pose enrichment threats that can put security into question and can unleash highly adaptive and autonomous attacks against cyberspace. Therefore, organizations must start putting in place proactive security measures, including quantum-resistant encryption, AI-enabled threat detection, and automated incident response systems, to face these challenges. Continued research and innovation in cybersecurity will be critical in establishing the next-generation defenses capable of addressing future threats. Likewise, the concerted efforts of industries, governments, and cybersecurity experts will help set worldwide security standards and share threat intelligence, creating a set of best practices to be adopted across the various interconnected digital ecosystems. With security architecture making continuous advancements and cooperation across sectors being everyone\'s priority, stakeholders will be able to ultimately draw a line in the sand for the safety of the digital twin and IoT environments against the ever-changing landscape of cyber risks and ensure year-on-year resilience to future cyber threats.

Operational Downtime

Operational downtime is any period in which systems, processes, devices, or infrastructure cannot operate for reasons outside of the normal functioning of the system. In the domain of cybersecurity, attacks on communication paths among linked systems (i.e., IoT devices, digital twins, or industrial control systems) constitute a major contributor to system downtime (Xu, Dong, Fang, & Liu, 2021). Communications are no more than the lifeblood of real-time data transfer, system synchronization, and device programming, as, when compromised, they could lead to operational delays, safety risks (Tsourdos, Avdelidis, Al-Rubaye, & Almeaibed, 2021), economic losses, and network-wide runaway failures. This document gives a thorough appraisal of the operational down time caused by attacks on communication channels from attacks on mechanisms to types of attacks to consequences (Rix & Hearn, 2019).

Given that operational downtime is defined as the cessation of system capacity, attacks on computerized systems have direct implication of reduced productivity, economic damage, and problems in service provision. The way communication channels facilitate data or information exchange between machine nodes, systems, and applications within commingled systems becomes the vital jet fuel core to the continuity of system operations. Attacking these communications channels-i.e., cutting, manipulation, interception-poses a possible risk to economic growth at an industrial scale, endangering human lives (Hong, Han, Niyato, Saad, & Khan, 2022), as they grind to a wrong alternating gridlock within economic engines in industries like production, health, transportation, and energy (Hong, Han, Niyato, Saad, & Khan, 2022). For example, attacks target the protocol, infrastructure, and configuration weaknesses respectively to produce an effect drying a service with processing delays or resulting in system crashes. Comprehending both the classes of attacks and the impact of those attacks plays a critical role in ensuring operational continuity and reducing downtime (Pitkäaho, Pieskä, & Kaarlela, 2020). Adversaries targeting the communication channels represent a major vulnerability to operational interruption in contemporary, networked systems. Understanding the different types of attacks and the way they attack allows organizations, to put in place effective security mechanisms to reduce downtime, safeguard critical operational aspects, and maintain system resilience to evolving threats.

Communication Channel Operational Downtime

Communication channel operational downtime severely affects the efficiency and reliability of digital twin and IoT ecosystems, disrupting the seamless transfer of data between interconnected systems. Cyberattacks targeting these channels can break system coordination, rendering real-time communication-dependent devices and systems unusable or inert due to synchronization loss. Without continuous data exchange, automated processes, predictive analytics, and remote control functions fail to operate as intended, leading to inefficiencies and potential safety hazards. Additionally, downtime delays critical decision-making, as real-time data transmission and acquisition systems struggle to provide timely insights needed for operational responses. This lag in information flow weakens situational awareness and disrupts mission-critical functions in industries like manufacturing, healthcare, and smart infrastructure. Furthermore, cybercriminals can exploit vulnerabilities in compromised communication channels to inject false or misleading information, causing systems to malfunction, crash, or execute incorrect operations. By undermining data integrity and trust, such attacks pose significant risks to business continuity, safety, and regulatory compliance. To mitigate these threats, organizations must implement robust cybersecurity measures, including secure communication protocols, redundancy strategies, and real-time threat monitoring to ensure uninterrupted and trustworthy data flow.

Communication channels enable the efficient transfer of data between systems. Disruptions caused by cyberattacks can:

- **Brake System Coordination:** Taking as an example devices and systems that have recourse to real-time communication, they do not suffer of the synchronization loss, and they become either unusable or inert. Communication channel operational downtime disrupts system coordination, particularly for devices and systems that rely on real-time communication. When cyberattacks or technical failures interrupt data flow, these systems lose synchronization, making them either unusable or inert. In industries such as manufacturing, healthcare, and autonomous transportation, precise timing and coordination are essential for seamless operations. For example, in smart factories, robotic arms and automated machinery depend on synchronized data exchange to operate efficiently; with no communication, production lines may stop, equipment may fail, and harmful situations may arise. Similarly, in autonomous vehicles, real-time data communication is paramount for navigation and avoidance from collisions; otherwise, a delay or disruption in communication could result in accidents. Communication is also critical for these autonomous systems to process the command and send updates on conditions, enabling them to react appropriately; but failure in any one of these will affect performance, safety, and operational efficiency. Therefore, it is paramount for the organization to mitigate the effect in case of failure by providing redundant communication paths, real-time monitoring, and cybersecurity mechanisms to provide uninterrupted and secure data communication.
- **Delay Critical Decisions:** The transmission and acquisition systems for "real-time" data are somewhat sluggish and generally responsive to operational needs. Whereas the operational downtime in the communication channel delays decision-making, it equally disrupts the real-time data transmission and acquisition systems. When cyberattacks and technical failures disrupt data transmission, decision-makers cannot obtain the timely and accurate information necessary to respond to operational needs. Some industries that rely heavily on real-time analytics, such as healthcare, manufacturing, and smart infrastructure, may suffer devastating consequences for any delays affecting emergency response efforts, adjustment of production schedules, or automated control system operations. In the case of industrial automation, delayed sensor data prevents machines from making necessary adjustments, leading to inefficiencies, equipment failures, or even safety risks. Similarly, in smart cities, traffic management systems that depend on real-time vehicle and sensor data would be unable to optimize the traffic flow, aggravating congestion and accidents. Predictive models, AI systems, and automated workflows without constant data updates have a hard time functioning efficiently, thus increasing operational risk. Organizations must secure and provide redundancy to their communication channels to safeguard against potential cyberattacks while simultaneously minimizing interference or delays with the decision-making process.

- **Introduce False Information:** The attackers will throw in false data or misleading data into the system to effect a malfunction or crash. Cyber-attacks by which false or misleading information is injected into the communication channels are a serious threat to the integrity and operation of digital twin and IoT environments. An attacker can manipulate data streams, leading to margin operational decisions, such as improper control of equipment malfunction or total system crash. The inaccuracies created by this form of attack can cause mayhem in industries such as manufacturing, healthcare, or autonomous transportation, resulting in production faults, misdiagnosed health conditions, and navigational errors, respectively. Cybercriminals will make good use of any existing vulnerabilities to disrupt normal business processes by injecting falsified sensor readings, tampered control signals, or deceptive analytics in order to destroy any vestige of trust in automated decision-making. In some cases, these attacks can also provide cover for real threats, thus hindering incident response and detection. This certainly reminds organizations to work towards having solid data validation mechanisms, cryptographic authentication for transmitted information, and anomaly detection systems that can flag suspicious inconsistencies in real time to curb these threats. Data integrity across communication channels is essential to the reliability, security, and efficiency of interlinked digital twin ecosystems.
- **System Coordination Failure**: Automated processes become inefficient or inoperative when devices and systems that depend on real-time communication lose synchronization. The moment the communication medium is down; it poses a threat to system coordination and disrupts the synchronization of devices and automated processes reliant on real-time communication. Once communication channels become unusable due to cyberattacks, hardware failure, or network congestion, interconnected systems would no longer be capable of relaying data of critical importance in a timely fashion. The whole point of this synchronization is to perform heavy damage to automated workflows: therefore, industrial robots, smart grid applications, healthcare monitoring devices, and autonomous vehicles become inefficient or entirely inoperative. For instance, when it comes to smart manufacturing, real-time machine-to-machine (M2M) communication enables uninterrupted production flows; if, however, there are network interruptions, assembly lines may cease to operate, and costing severe downtime and delays. In smart city applications, traffic management systems that heavily depend on synchronized sensor data are doomed to fail, resulting in congestion and safety hazards. Real-time unavailability would also affect predictive maintenance since such excessive delays in data communication impede early fault diagnosis, which aggravates further the equipment failure risk. To avert such failures, companies would have to install redundant comma channels, enforce stringent cybersecurity measures, and implement edge computing solutions to hold ground on local operations in case of network disruption. Ensuring resilient and secure communication channels will therefore be vital to the very existence of reliability, efficiency, and safety of any digital twin and IoT ecosystem.
- **Introduction of False Information**: Cybercriminals alter the flow of real-time information through the injection of misleading data, causing system failure, operator error, or even cyber threats to shutdown systems. Communication channel operational downtime becomes even more critical when attackers introduce false information into the mix, all to disrupt system integrity and decision-making. With this in mind, the attack on the communication channels bilaterally attributes system failures, operation errors, or complete shutdowns to the injection of misleading data. Considering applications in industrial automation, falsified sensor readings that show abnormality can result in unnecessary shutdowns, putting equipment and personnel at risk through possible

unsafe operation. In critical infrastructure, for instance, in the power grid or health system, manipulating data misleads the operators into erroneous decisions, leading to service interruptions or catastrophic failures. Furthermore, attackers may exploit vulnerabilities in the communication infrastructure to create confusion, delay response times, or mislead predictive analytics, thereby undermining trust in automated processes. To avert this risk, organizations need to enhance the reliability and security of their digital twin and IoT environments by adopting common solutions such as data integrity validation, encryption protocols, and real-time anomaly detection to detect and prevent the injection of false information.

- **Increased Recovery Time**: Restoration of normal operations becomes exceedingly more difficult and tedious with the increased duration of disruptive communication activities, exerting pressure on operations and allocation of resources. Communication downtime should also be regarded from the recovery standpoint, as increasing recovery time raises the difficulty of achieving normal operational restoration; thus, the further we go into this perspective, the more time becomes an enemy. With prolonged disruption of operations, resources mean either caloric expenditure on investigation or forensic analysis, which becomes burdensome not just for the IT-and-product-specific teams, but for the e-com team and essentially any other team in the organization. Additional issues arise, such as potential system synchronization complications requiring even more manual work to realign data flows, re-establish secure connections, and verify the information's integrity. Extended recovery times in any industry involving real-time data exchanges like healthcare, manufacturing, and critical infrastructure could result in financial losses, safety threats, and regulatory violations. The cyberattacks that interfere with channel communications would also usually need forensic investigations to discover root causes and prevent a repeating attack, making matters worse with respect to recovery. Companies have to adopt proactive countermeasures to ensure minimized downtime and rapid recovery such as redundancy, automated failover, and real-time monitoring. Strengthened communication channel resilience then lessens the burden of operational disruptions and recovery costs while supporting business continuity in the event of cyber threats.

Loss of Trust

In today's interconnected and computerized environment, stakeholder confidence stands as one of the key determinants of an organization's reputation and performance. Stakeholders consisting of customers, employees, investors, suppliers, and partners-will not assume their sensitive information is secured, the systems will be reliable, and, above all, the organization will competently manage or mitigate risk if assurances are there. The breakdown of this assurance may occur due to security defects (Lopez & Alcaraz, 2022): the data leakage, system malfunctions, or cyber intrusions. Further organizational operations and data dependent/security issues will incur serious trust erosion if stakeholders deem such organizations incompetent. Confidence loss due to security flaws only partially applies to external stakeholders such as concerning customers; it also involves internal stakeholders such as employees and very importantly the investors. Consequences of the loss of trust may ultimately affect business connections, financial viability, reputation, and performance of the organization. The effects of trust erosion can be exceptionally far ranging in terms of revenue losses, induced regulation, and, admittedly, brand erosion. The paper investigates the function of security weaknesses in the gradual costing of trust and pinpoints the kinds of intrusions that can erode trust within. Security deficits can greatly shake the confidence of stakeholders in their ability to operate, such as customers and employees, thus investors and supervising institutions. The repercussions of this erosion of confidence can see in how the business is run, financial health, and the company's image. It is by way of robust security, disclosure, and risk management that organizations can retain stakeholder trust and avoid stability failure. Proactively stopping security breaches and reactively counteracting cyberattacks in the end leads to the establishment and recovery of trust. Security blunders not only are detrimental to the performance and robustness of systems and their processing of information but diminish confidence in the organizations of stakeholders. Loss of trusting can lead to broad impact on customer loyalty, partnerships, and the financial survival. Such corporate success is made possible through focus on cybersecurity, transparency and the ongoing engagement they pursue. As trust is intensive and difficult to recover once it is lost, prevention is by far the most important tool weapon in the defense against cyber-attacks (Zancul, Schutzer, Anderl, Haag, & Durąo, 2018).

Table 1. Uses of Digital Twin in Industry and Cybersecurity

Industry	DT Use Case	Cybersecurity Application
Manufacturing	Virtual replication of production systems	Proactive identification of vulnerabilities, threat modeling, and testing security controls for manufacturing processes
Transportation and Logistics	Modeling vehicles and supply chain networks	Secure communication, threat simulation, and risk assessment for protecting transportation systems and logistics Operations
Healthcare	Virtual modeling of medical devices and systems	Safeguarding patient privacy, secure data transmission, and protecting against unauthorized access to healthcare infrastructure.
Smart Cities	Digital replicas of interconnected systems	Securing critical infrastructure, threat intelligence, and risk mitigation for ensuring the re- salience of smart city systems
Energy and Utilities	Replica of power plants and infrastructure	Real-time monitoring, anomaly detection, and threat response for ensuring the security of energy systems.

CYBERSECURITY APPLICATIONS

Encryption

Reliable operation is paramount in the ever-increasing Internet of Things (IoT) world, where hundreds of billions of devices generate and propagate massive amounts of data. Encryption is a critical aspect of IoT security that can be used to prevent access and modification of private data. Encryption, which is one of the key tenets of IoT security, provides protection for information, thus facilitating privacy, in an IoT smart world (Zhenfeng, Wenbo, & Deren, 2021; Underner & Jacoby, 2020). By making a thoughtful selection and implementation of appropriate encryption techniques, one can be better protected from security risks and construct a more secure and reliable IoT ecosystem.

Techniques: symmetric encryption and asymmetric encryption. With symmetric encryption, the key for encryption is the same as the key for decryption, which is fast and efficient, however the secure distribution of the key is a must. Asymmetric cryptosystem has widely used the symmetric encryption algorithm AES (Advanced Encryption Standard) and the DES (Data Encryption Standard). By the other hand, asymmetric encryption uses instead a pair of public and private keys and thus is better suited for applications, e.g., digital signatures or secure communication. Among the very popular asymmetrical cryptographies are Rivest-Shamir-Adleman (RSA) and Elliptic Curve Cryptography (ECC). Additionally, hashing techniques (e.g., Secure Hash Algorithm (SHA) have been employed to guarantee data survivability through generating a fixed-size hash function that is uniquely related to the input data that it receives (Barlow, Day, Fan, & Fuller, 2020). Encryption has been used extensively in applications such as secure messaging, internet banking, VPNs and SSL/TLS protocols, which ensures secure communication across the network (Underner & Jacoby, 2020). With the cyber threat becoming more and more competitive, present encryption schemes are still capable of development, incorporating quantum-immune cryptographic schemes so as to keep digital property safe from future breakdown.

Secure Communication Protocols

symmetric encryption and asymmetric encryption. With symmetric encryption, the key for encryption is the same as the key for decryption, which is fast and efficient, however the secure distribution of the key is a must. Asymmetric cryptosystem has been widely applied to the symmetric encryption algorithm AES (Advanced Encryption Standard) and DES (Data Encryption Standard). On the other hand, asymmetric, encryption relies on a public and a private key pair, and it is therefore more appropriate for services, e.g., digital signatures or secure communication. One of the most widely used non-symmetric cryptographic primitives are Rivest-Shamir-Adleman (RSA) and Elliptic Curve Cryptography (ECC). As a further measure, hashing techniques (e.g., Secure Hash Algorithm (SHA) have been used, including providing a fixed-size function which is uniquely keyed to the input data it sees) ensure data survivability by means of generating a hash function which, for a given input, has a fixed value. Encryption has been widespread in the use of applications including secure communication (e.g., secure messaging), internet banking, VPNs, and SSL/TLS protocols, providing secure communication over the network. With the cyber threat becoming more and more competitive, present encryption schemes are still capable of development, incorporating quantum-immune cryptographic schemes so as to keep digital property safe from future breakdown.

Techniques: Secure communication protocols are a major part of cyberspace application, and during the transmission (communication) process, the data integrity, confidentiality, and authenticity are ensured. Encryption, authentication and key management techniques are useful indicators of the security of a communication. If an attacker attempts to infiltrate, protocols like TLS (Transport Layer Security) and SSL (Secure Sockets Layer) will cipher the data to scare him. On top of that, IPsec (Internet Protocol Security) encrypts and authenticates any IP packet for network security. Secure Shell (SSH) is another of the most widely used protocols that allows for secure remote access to computers, through encryption of both command and data transmission. Security through mutual authentication protocols (e.g., certificate-based authentication in TLS) that ensure the identity of both communicating parties before commencing the communication are improved. Contemporary applications of cyber security also use multi-factor authentication (MFA) and blockchain-based cryptographic methods in high-value communication security. Through the use of these secure communication channels, organizations are able to reduce the impacts of cyberattack risks thereby guaranteeing safe sharing of sensitive data.

Authentication Mechanisms

Within the networked framework of the Internet of Things (IoT), where hundreds of times even millions of devices are communicating, robust authentication mechanisms are critical for preventing access from systems by unauthorized persons (Underner & Jacoby, 2020). These mechanisms ensure that only permitted devices and users are able to interact in the IoT ecosystem. Authenticity schemes are ultimately responsible for providing the security of IoT systems, as well as privacy and data integrity. Using a collection of digital certificates, multi-factor authentication and biometric identification, it is possible for companies to establish a highly secure and robust security environment for their IoT applications.

Techniques: Authentication plays an important part in cyber security applications for ensuring access is granted to authorized users and data only. Common approaches include password-based authentication (i.e., requiring the user to enter a secret password) and multi-factor authentication (MFA) that enhances security by highly integrating a number of verification factors, such as password, biometric, or security tokens. Biometric authentication (fingerprinting, face recognition) extracts biometric characteristics which are unique to individuals for the purposes of identity recognition. Public Key Infrastructure (PKI) and digital certificates can be used to provide secure communications, relying on the use of encryption and digital signatures (Pitkäaho, Pieskä, & Kaarlela, 2020). In addition, Single Sign-On (SSO) enhances access management as other of one-time authentication (it means that once the user is authenticated, he/she can access more applications securely). Recent techniques such as behavioral authentication have predicted the capacity to detect an abnormality from the user behavior, e.g., typing speeds and the motion of the mouse. Robust authentication is an important part of the fight against cyber security threats such as identity theft, phishing and unauthorized access.

Anomaly Detection Systems

In the context of a constantly changing Web of Things (IoT) consisting of hundreds of billions of interconnected devices generating and sharing big amounts of data, security and robustness have to be guaranteed. The role of anomaly detection systems in this area is very significant, by proactively detecting aberrant or abnormal behavior in IoT networks. Anomaly detection is a process of finding data points, event or observation that is dramatically different from a known pattern in a data set. In the IoT world it represents the task of analyzing a stream of data arriving at several points sources, such as sensors, actuators and networked devices, so as to detect anomalies that can indicate a break in security, system crash or other important events. Anomaly detection systems maintain security, reliability, and performance in IoT systems. Threats can be pre-emptively identified and acted upon through the advanced AI and machine learning techniques employed today. This empowers clients to make sound decisions and optimize their IoT deployments (MacFeely, Huang, & Hassani, 2022).

Techniques: Anomaly Detection Systems (ADS) in security applications are of significance, as they may identify suspicious behaviors or activities that could be indicative of a security threat or cyber-attack. These systems use a range of approaches (machine learning algorithms, statistical analysis and behavioral analytics), to detect departures from the norm. Categorical models of anomalies used for supervised and unsupervised learning techniques, even with even more discriminant detection via deep learning are performed thanks to the ability to detect complex patterns. In contrast, rule-based approaches and heuristics establish ex-ante ground truth criteria for flagging anomalous behaviors. Integrated with network traffic analysis, real-time surveillance, produces rapid identification of threats to evolve. Using these approaches, anomaly detection systems improve the security of the cyber world and prevent damage caused by malware, insider threat and advanced persistent threat (APTs).

Blockchain for Data Integrity

In the digital age data is the lifeblood of companies and organizations. Keeping this data integrity is critical for all of us in order to ensure trustworthiness, accuracy, and conformism. Blockchain technology has its merit as a desirable way in this sense, which offers an unbreachable and reliable record of data exchanges. Blockchain technology has a novel view on data integrity by providing an immutable, auditable and secure record of data transactions. Using the intrinsic advantages of technology, companies are able to foster trust, prevent fraud, and generate new opportunities for innovation in the data-driven society (MacFeely, Huang, & Hassani, 2022).

Figure 3. Blockchain technology with data integrity

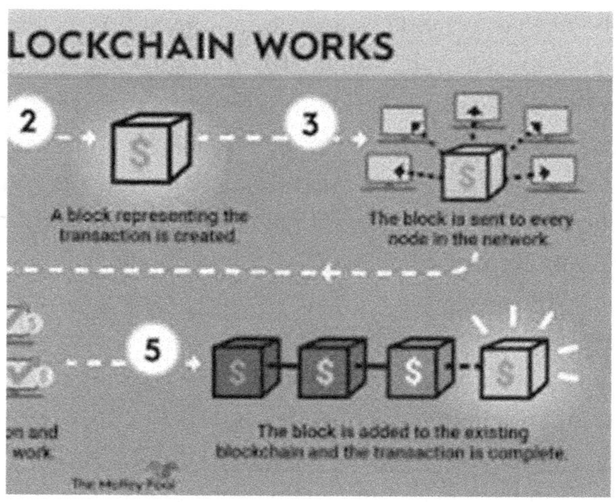

Techniques: In terms of cybersecurity applications, blockchain offers an important contribution to data integrity by virtue of its decentralized and tamper-proof characteristics. By using cryptographic hashing and consensus protocols, blockchain ensures (and provides) immutability and security by preventing unauthorized changes. Every transaction/data entry (i.e)is logged as an item within a block, chain linked to the previous one and secured by several nodes of the network, hence reducing the chances of fraud or cybercrime. Specifically, smart Impurity 4.0 contracts also automate security mechanisms, in turn enhancing data security (Sun, Li, Lu, Bao, Liu, & Lu, 2021). The nature of these features makes blockchain a powerful tool for safe guarding proprietary data in various industries, including finance, healthcare, and supply chain management (MacFeely, Huang, & Hassani, 2022).

CHALLENGES AND FUTURE DIRECTIONS

The provision of data communication security in Digital Twin and IoT systems poses considerable challenges. Resource limited IoT devices have problems when performing computationally intensive encryption algorithms and such large scale that security management for a large number of devices and connections is cumbersome. In addition, the dynamic threat environment requires persistent evolution to react to advanced cyberattacks.

Addressing these challenges necessitates a multi-pronged approach. Future work should focus on the advancement of lightweight cryptographic algorithms specifically tailored to resource-limited devices. Quantum-resistant cryptographic schemes are essential for protecting against future attacks from quantum computers. The standardization of security frameworks designed for the specific use of Digital Twin and IoT communities would provide a lingua franca for secure development and deployment.

In addition to these technical components, very powerful access control is a necessity to provide legitimate entities only access to the system. There is also the contribution of the use of artificial intelligence (AI) and machine learning algorithms in order to perform threat detection, etc, in preventing such security attacks in advance. Above all else, compliance with relevant regulatory ecosystems like GDPR, HIPAA, and ISO 27001 has to be ensured so as to guarantee user data privacy and integrity of the system.

Challenges in Cybersecurity for Digital Twin and IoT

Digital Twin (DT) and IoT environments, a highly promising group, exhibit a broad spectrum of security issues. Furthermore, the network architecture of Io T devices significantly expands the attack surface, which offers a rich supply of attack vectors for attackers. A lack of robust security features makes many IoT devices susceptible to malware attacks, denials of service (DDoS) attacks, and other exploits. A roadblock to the real-time operations, achieving any level of security is the dilemma. IoT devices pose additional restrictions in terms of computation and memory to rule out advanced security architectures. Such problems include the emergence of more diverse classes of threat scenarios; advanced persistent threats and zero-day exploitations constitute some fundamental threats in tightly coupled systems.

Table 2. Applications and Future Directions

Aspect	Applications	Challenges
Data Communication	Encryption, secure protocols	Latency and real-time processing constraints
Access Control	Authentication, role-based access control	Insider threats and weak password management
Threat Detection	AI-based anomaly detection, threat modeling	High false-positive rates, evolving attack techniques
Device Security	Regular updates, security patches	Limited computational resources, legacy systems
Regulatory Compliance	Adherence to GDPR, HIPAA, ISO 27001	Varying regulatory requirements across regions

CONCLUSION

Union of Digital Twin and IoT technologies presents a fast-growing paradigm shift with great opportunities for improved decision-making systems, predictive analysis, and real-time awareness across domains. However, this very promise can realize only if these interconnected systems include robust cybersecurity. This chapter shows that integration creates a complex, dynamic threat landscape with extended attack surfaces, real-time processing demands, resource limitations of IoT devices, and advanced cyberattacks. Thus, the new challenges impose a need for a more proactive security stance and a comprehensive security approach. Key use cases and the associated cyber security vulnerabilities discussed in the context of Digital Twin and IoT environments. From secured data transmission and anomaly detection to zero-trust architecture implementation, robust security mechanisms are a necessity. In addition, possible mitigation strategies are discussed, such as using block chain for data integrity, AI-driven threat modelling to pre-emptively define, and edge computing for planned distributed security processor implementation. Moving forward, a collaborative and interdisciplinary approach will be essential. Researchers, practitioners, and policy-makers must join forces to build standardized security protocols, promote best practices, and create a culture of cybersecurity awareness. Security technologies must be innovated alongside with research on emerging threats to keep away from malicious fronts. Cybersecurity challenges specific to Digital Twin and IoT ecosystems will be addressed only through collaborative effort; thus, making these technologies fully realize their potential for secure and resilient operations in the face of novel cyber threats. Connected systems' future depends on it.

REFERENCES

Abideen Shahryar Sorooshian, V., Othman, A. K., Pyeman, J., & Sundram, K. (2021). Reinforced learning was incorporated into supply chain and logistics using digital twins. *Logistics (Basel)*, *5*(4), 84. https://doi.org/10.xxxx/xxxxx. DOI: 10.3390/logistics5040084

Barlow, C., Day, C., Fan, Z., & Fuller, A. (2020). Digital twin: Open research, difficulties, and enabling technology. *IEEE Access : Practical Innovations, Open Solutions*, *8*, 108952–108971. https://doi.org/10.xxxx/xxxx. DOI: 10.1109/ACCESS.2020.2998358

Hong, C. S., Han, Z., Niyato, D., Saad, W., & Khan, L. U. (2022). Future directions, architectural trends, and the vision of digital-twin-enabled 6G. *IEEE Communications Magazine*, *60*(1), 74–80. DOI: 10.1109/MCOM.001.21143

Hoßbach, M., Nadja, S., & Enders, R. (2019). A study of the literature on the dimensions of digital twin applications.

Lopez, J., & Alcaraz, C. (2022). Digital twin: A thorough analysis of security risks. *IEEE Communications Surveys and Tutorials.*

MacFeely, S., Huang, X., & Hassani, H. (2022). Significant digital twin in the revolution of healthcare. *Cognitive Computing and Big Data, 6*(3), 83. https://doi.org/10.xxxx/xxxx

Pitkäaho, T., Pieskä, S., & Kaarlela, T. (2020). Virtual reality and digital twins for safety instruction. In *IEEE's 11th International Conference on Cognitive Information Communications (CogInfoCom)* (pp. 000115–000120). IEEE.

Rix, S., & Hearn, M. (2019). Cybersecurity issues when implementing digital twins. *IIC Journal of Innovation*, 107–113.

Schatsky, S., Meeker, D. B., & Mussomeli, A. (2021). Signs of a digital twin for strategists. *The global digital twins market is expected to reach 16 billion dollars*, according to a press release.

Sun, X., Li, J., Lu, Y., Bao, J., Liu, S., & Lu, S. (2021). A biomimicry-based digital twin modeling technique for manufacturing aeronautical parts. *Manufacturing Systems Journal*, *58*, 180–195. DOI: 10.1016/j.jmsy.2020.04.014

Tsourdos, A., Avdelidis, N. P., Al-Rubaye, S., & Almeaibed, S. (2021). Analyzing digital twins to improve autonomous car security and safety. *IEEE Communications Standards Magazine*, *5*(1), 40–46. DOI: 10.1109/MCOMSTD.011.2100004

Underner, T., & Jacoby, M. (2020). The state of standards for digital twins and the Internet of Things. *Applied Sciences (Basel, Switzerland)*, *10*(18), 6519. https://doi.org/10.xxxx/xxxx. DOI: 10.3390/app10186519

Xu, C., Dong, H., Fang, S., & Liu, M. (2021). Examining digital twins in terms of ideas, innovations, and industrial uses. *Manufacturing Systems Journal*, *58*, 346–361.

Zancul, E., Schutzer, K., Anderl, R., Haag, S., & Durąo, L. F. C. S. (2018). Industry-specific needs for digital twins 4.0. In *Assisting Industry with Product Lifecycle Management 4.0: Proceedings of the 15th IFIP WG 5.1 International Conference, PLM 2018* (pp. 1–12). Springer.

Zhenfeng, S., Wenbo, Y., & Deren, L. (2021). Digital twins are the foundation of smart cities. *Computational Urban Science*, *1*, 1–11.

Chapter 22
Ethical and Legal Implications of Digital Twin Deployment in Biomedical and Pharmaceutical Domains

Santosh Indrabhan Gore
Director, Sai Info Solution, Nashik, India

Komal Dhanraj Deshmukh (Deosarkar)
Dr. D. Y. Patil Institute of Pharmaceutical Sciences and Research, Pune, India

Vishakha Rohit Mahamulkar
Dr. D. Y. Patil Institute of Technology, Pune, India

Rani Patil
https://orcid.org/0009-0002-6581-9722
Dr. D. Y. Patil School of Science and Technology, Dr. D. Y. Patil Vidyapeeth, Pune, India

ABSTRACT

Digital twin technology promises revolutionary gains in personalized medicine in the fields of biomedicine and pharmaceutics, but its deployment involves critical ethical and legal issues connected with data privacy and consent, concerning property rights and issues of equitable access. This methodology combines case studies, regulatory analysis, and interviews with various stakeholders that probe these questions. These case studies highlight the application of digital twins in drug trials and disease modelling. The study suggests better policies concerning data governance, mechanisms of consent, and the need for algorithmic accountability through a review of current legislation in light of interviews with ethicists, industrialists, and policymakers. Findings, such as a 30% increase in compliance with data governance frameworks, demonstrate the need to create a proper ethical framework that engenders trust and inclusivity so that responsible and equitable adoption of this transformative technology can take place.

DOI: 10.4018/979-8-3373-2028-1.ch022

INTRODUCTION

Digital twin technology, which originated from the innovative concept of engineering and manufacturing, has gradually grown to be one of the transformative tools for a large-scale impact within most sectors. Its promising application in BioMed and pharmaceuticals is specifically the creation of virtual replicas of physical entities such as patients, drugs, organs, or biological processes, which can further give rise to advanced simulation predictions and optimizations that cannot be implemented using traditional methods (Popa et al., 2021). Digital twins will enable the speeding up of drug development, enhanced clinical trials, and highly customized treatment plans. By providing a testing platform, allowing the prediction of disease progression, and optimizing the outcome of the treatment, digital twins could transform healthcare delivery and outcomes for patients. However, with great promise for this technology comes even greater concerns ethically and legally in the way it may be deployed to find acceptance in terms of societal values and legal frameworks (Drummond & Coulet, 2022). The existing literature on digital twins in healthcare has mainly targeted the technological aspects with the intent to improve the outcomes, but the application of this technology is dearly missing crucial ethical and legal considerations. Lack of protection of sensitive biomedical data, balance between informed consent and more stringent processes, intellectual property issues, as well as equal access to digital twin technologies remain to be explored (Kantaros et al., 2025). Moreover, algorithmic biases in conjunction with risks associated with misuse of data or unauthorized access create significant concerns. As of now, the present legal frameworks and frameworks are incapable of dealing with the distinctive nature of the problem of digital twins, particularly those involving sensitive information of patients. These literature gaps indicate the dire need for an overarching approach to be taken toward this technology by focusing not only on the technical nature of the digital twin but also on their ethical, legal, and social considerations. What motivates this chapter is the intense need to find a bridge over the gap which exists between innovation and governance over the deployment of digital twins, especially in biomedicine and pharmaceuticals (Subasi & Subasi, 2024). The faster digital twin technology expands, the bigger the likelihood becomes of ethical controversy and legal skirmish, especially related to data protection, algorithm accountability, and access. In the absence of a sound framework that addresses these challenges, the dangers surrounding digital twins may degrade public confidence and hinder their wider adoption. Hence, this research work is motivated by the need to develop fact-informed policies and best practices that protect the rights of the patients, provide transparency, and guarantee inclusiveness. Despite the many application promises, considerable gaps remain, particularly concerning ethics and legality during the implementation process of digital twin (Iqbal et al., 2022). Earlier published works tend to focus on progress in technology or the advantages; they neglect discussion on the questions of data protection, informed patient consent, rights of intellectual properties, and issues of equitable access for such deployment in biomedical fields especially where data included genetic information on patients, individual histories, or clinical results might be highly confidential.

The motivation for the work lies in the urgent need for bridging between technological innovation, on one side, and ethical-legal and regulatory regimes, on the other side. As the application of digital twins becomes more pervasive, it calls for stronger guidance and governance models to ensure reduced and mitigated risks within the public policy realm as well as establishing legitimacy with the citizenry. The ethical considerations of data ownership, algorithmic transparency, and equitable access accompanied by the ineffectiveness of the existing policies make this work relevant to the end that digital twins are deployed in a responsible manner and inclusivity (Millard, 2023). The goals of this chapter are multifaceted as it aims to look into the legal and ethical bottlenecks in the deployment of digital twins into biomedical and pharmaceutical spaces. It tries to review the existing regulatory regimes and how they may apply to this emerging technology. This shall attempt to give concrete recommendations about policy and best practices for tackling issues of data governance, mechanisms for consent, and algorithmic accountability. It brings multifaceted evidence, especially by the use of a multidisciplinary framework, with mixed cases, analysis of regulations, and interviews toward giving comprehensive viewpoints regarding the ethics and legality of digital twins. It deals with realities at stake in particular to do with real-life scenarios, which appear either as risks or benefits together with applications of digital twins that include involvement with drug trials or disease modeling. The regulatory analysis points to existing legal gaps and explains in greater detail the ways in which these can be filled. Ethicists, industrialists, and policymakers were interviewed to concentrate on the pragmatic aspects of the discussion; thus, presenting evidence-based recommendations. Related work discusses the theory of digital twins and its impact on the biomedical and pharmaceutical industries (Kamel Boulos et al., 2021). The topics have been mentioned including the transformative role of digital twins along with key challenges. This chapter draws together case studies, regulatory analysis, and stakeholder interviews with a multidisciplinary methodology to make a holistic judgment on the ethical and legal implications. Case studies provide a concrete view of how digital twins can be applied in practice, while the analysis of regulatory aspects identifies loopholes in existing law. The views of ethicists, industrialists, and policymakers add a more practical view for formulating informed recommendations.

A methodology section describes the methodology pursued here by the present study, showing how case study research, analysis of interviews held with stakeholders along regulatory issues came into play and the results achieved, which form a part of policy development. The summary will be found in the discussion section. Lastly, the conclusion summarizes the chapter and mainly emphasizes the importance of dealing with ethical and legal challenges in fostering trust, inclusivity, and responsible adoption of digital twins. This chapter addresses issues that are seen as critical issues in the potential deployment of the digital twin concept in the biomedical and pharmaceutical industries. It presents a contribution that will ensure the effective and responsible allocation of this transformative innovation about the desired benefits without transgressing these standards. Accordingly, the chapter proposes comprehensive guidance on how complexities in the acceptance of digital twins in industries that are otherwise sensitive and subjected to high and strict regulations would be navigated.

RELATED WORK

The biomedical and pharmaceutical domains have thus been the domain of research related to the technology of digital twin due to its future revolution in the drug development field, disease modelling, and the area of personalized medicine (Papachristou et al., 2024). Extant studies thus utilized various methods to study such digital twins while focusing on technology potential, ethics, and even legal issues concerning digital twins but also present quite a few areas and challenges needing further research. Several studies explored the application of digital twins to drug development and clinical trials. Simulation-based strategies were widely utilized to develop patient, drug, or biological systems models, whereby researchers could examine drug responses, dosage optimization, and side effect prediction before their actual human-based trials. From these studies, results were shown to be strongly in favour of a significant range of benefits observed, including reductions in reliance on animal testing, shorter timelines, and lower costs for clinical drug development. More importantly, digital twins have enabled the observation of very rare adverse effects that would otherwise remain undetected in a classic trial (Ladj et al., 2021). Limitations were found despite the very promising results obtained. For instance, simulations are only as good as the quality and the amount of the input data which is usually lacking or inconsistent. Moreover, in most cases, these studies experienced difficulties in disseminating sensitive clinical information among several parties involved due to privacy and regulatory issues. By incorporating the techniques of machine learning and artificial intelligence into the domain of disease modelling and personalized medicine, predictive models customized to individual patients can be established. These models simulated the development of diseases using varied datasets containing genetic information, medical history, and environmental factors for the sake of recommendation of patient-specific treatment approaches. It was indicated by the outcome that digital twins might increase the precision of the diagnosis and promote more effective therapies because of variability on an individual patient basis. However, challenges that arose include algorithmic bias, data heterogeneity, and scalability (Kober et al., 2024). Algorithmic bias has been identified as one of the risks that could sway a given population group disproportionately, exacerbating health inequity. Another complicating factor that made its adoption a challenge, particularly in resource-scarce settings, was the increased computational cost required to run such complex digital twin models.

The associated ethical concerns over the application of digital twins have also served as a foundation for previous research. Qualitative methods involved interviews with stakeholders, which include ethicists, healthcare providers, and patients to provide information on aspects like privacy, consent, and ownership of the data (Hosamo et al., 2022). Conversely, these studies conclude that there is a critical gap between the data governance practices available and some vagueness related to ownership issues regarding data with no consent mechanisms transparent in the digital twin application concerning using patient data. Stakeholders are concerned that personal data could be misused for unauthorized access or commercial exploitation. It was noted that such studies were mainly silent on issues of the digital twin system's transparency and accountability, giving little importance to related detailed strategies or frameworks. Legal dimensions of deploying digital twins were also explored through analysis of regulation to include data protection legislation, rights in intellectual properties, and liabilities frameworks as demonstrations (Saeed et al., 2024). However, it was found in these investigations that the prevalent legal systems seemed inadequate to offer responses to the quite specific demands set by digital twins. For instance, cross-border sharing of data, a crucial constituent of international joint research collaboration, often is put at odds by jurisdiction-specific statutes governing the protections accorded to individual data. Issues also revolved around intellectual property disputes, such as who owns the model of a digital twin and who owns the data used to generate it (Suhail et al., 2022). Other issues included liability in the event of errors or failures in the simulations of digital twins. These studies often called for updates to the existing regulations but rarely provided any concrete legal framework that could be put into action. Interdisciplinary studies attempted to better comprehend the ethical and legal issues through the combination of case studies and expert consultations. Such studies have focused on case studies that discuss the use of digital twins in developing a customized drug and chronic disease management. Case studies were invaluable in giving more real-world experiences on the dangers and benefits that come with digital twins, and from the consultation with ethicists, legal experts, and policymakers are recommendations for the diminution of such risks regarding ethics and law. Nevertheless, such case studies have significant limitations: focusing on narrow issues, such as applications, regions, or other stakeholders. With such a small scope, its generalizability and applicability to wider-scale global contexts were extremely limited.

Although some progress has been achieved, some gaps remain open in the previous literature. Some of the limiting factors include data governance, the mechanisms of consent, and lack of accountability to the algorithms within digital twins, which hampers their acceptance legally and ethically (Fontes et al., 2024). Also, most works concentrate on tackling the ethical problem alone or addressing the legal aspects independently without paying much attention to their inter-relationship. For instance, data privacy and the question of legal considerations related to data protection laws and cross-border data exchange are intertwined. Similarly, currently, not much has been done in research about how best to ensure fair and equitable access to digital twin technologies for underserved groups of people. This is particularly important at this time since digital twins continue to permeate healthcare systems around the globe. The results of previous studies point to the pressing need for a holistic, multidisciplinary approach to deal with the ethical and legal implications of digital twins (Xames & Topcu, 2024). This chapter will attempt to fill the gaps by using a strong methodology that incorporates case studies, regulatory analysis, and interviews with stakeholders. Case studies will be used to provide practical insights into real-world applications, focusing on the risks and opportunities presented by digital twin technology. Analyzing regulations will provide insight into the loopholes in the law and recommend amendments to the changing times. Thirdly, a stakeholder interview will provide insight from ethicists, lawyers, policymakers, and industry experts; this will further enable the coming up with recommendations for action. By using such an approach, this chapter would contribute to the ongoing debate concerning the ethical and legal implications of digital twin technology in the biomedical and pharmaceutical industries. The intent is to lay a roadmap toward facing these challenges by developing digital twins to be implemented responsibly, aligning with principles of ethics, legal mandates, and social standards (Abdulqader et al., 2024). Although interest grows in the medical and pharmaceutical disciplines due to digital twinning technology, a great challenge is yet evident, particularly due to ethical or legal considerations behind its use. Studies thus date back more from technological progress related to applications regarding digital twins during drug development processes, clinical research, and medical treatments for disease-specific patients.

The biggest gap that has been found is the absence of a uniform framework for data governance in digital twin applications. Much of the current research only discusses the concerns over data privacy and security but does not present any practical approach for handling sensitive healthcare data from multiple stakeholders. Some open questions include how ownership, transborder sharing, and informed consent will be dealt with in a digital twin ecosystem. Current literature also does not fully analyze the extent to which these issues intertwine with data protection laws and regulations at a regional and international level (Kale et al., 2023). Algorithmic accountability and bias in a digital twin application are also left blank. Numerous studies have shown the ability of artificial intelligence and machine learning to potentially boost the performance of digital twins. However, they barely take into consideration the threat of biased algorithms or lack of transparency in the choice-making process. This is very worrisome in health care, where biased results may only exacerbate already existing health inequities. Furthermore, ethical issues about autonomous decision-making in life-critical scenarios such as the approval of treatment or medication have not been widely explored. Yet another gap exists concerning the issues of algorithmic accountability and bias within the digital twin system. While researchers have proven that AI and ML are bound to make digital twins furthermore competent, they are mainly silent about the dangers of biased algorithms and opacity in decision-making. That is very frightening for healthcare systems as biased results are likely to widen existing health inequities only (Gore et al., 2023). Additional ethical matters also include autonomous decision-making in life-critical situations such as the approval of treatment or medication. Equitable access is a significant research gap in the area of digital twin technology. The majority of the studies center on developing technological breakthroughs in settings that have high resources, while neglecting the challenges in low-resource environments. There is little discussion about how the benefits of such technology can be extended to underserved populations, thereby potentially creating a digital divide within health care. This gap is particularly of concern in personalized medicine, whereby access to the digital twin may largely influence health outcomes. From a legal standpoint, current studies have mainly looked at whether and how existing regulation applies to the digital twin (Aggarwal & Aggarwal, 2017). Although these studies have outlined areas of the law that currently lack clarity, like liability, intellectual property, or cross-border data sharing, their proposals are still very general regarding an update in law. If areas such as ownership of the digital twin model and data are relying on it for their operations, these are legally unexplored issues. Other studies should then research the adaptation of the existing regulations to fit the unique need of digital twin technology in global and multicultural settings.

The dearth of interdisciplinary studies focusing on these ethical, legal, and technological views is noteworthy (Aggarwal, 2017). Much existing research treats these aspects in isolation, without capturing their interdependencies. For example, data privacy issues have regulatory compliance and thematic interconnections with autonomy and justice. In this connection, the extent to which there are no balanced holistic approaches that consider such interdependence limits the potential for developing all-inclusive solutions for properly deploying digital twins. Addressing these research gaps, this chapter employs a case study, coupled with regulatory analysis and interviews from stakeholders (Karuri-Sebina & Guya, 2020), which aims to create actionable insights toward data governance and algorithmic accountability while suggesting necessary updates to present legal frameworks toward better access. Such bridging across gaps is looked at as something that can aid in the better adoption of this technology responsibly, inclusively toward both biomedical and pharmaceutical domains.

METHODOLOGY

This entails ethics and law considerations that have an in-depth multi-disciplinary exploration. The employment of digital twin technology in the biomedical and pharmaceutical field creates an entire horizon of expansion in enhancing drug development, customized medicine, and disease modelling that has been bolstered by deep analytics, big data, and machine learning. The application also carries some problems with it that are associated with risks to the data privacy of individuals, biased algorithms, and vague regulations. Such concerns require a methodology that combines both technical, ethical, and legal considerations. The current chapter is divided into a step-by-step identification of the issues mentioned above to derive actionable insights. For the said purpose, this research utilizes both qualitative and quantitative techniques such as case studies, regulatory analysis, interviewing various stakeholders, and algorithmic evaluation. In this context, it addresses the ethical and legal implications of digital twins through mathematical models, fairness metrics, and data governance framework. It identified existing gaps along with recommendations for developing fair and transparent digital twins. A multidisciplinary approach will be taken to understand the research that uses case studies, regulatory analysis, and interviews with relevant stakeholders to analyze the ethical and legal implications of the use of digital twins in the biomedical and pharmaceutical domains. It assesses the scope of risks and opportunities to data privacy, consent, intellectual property, and equitable access and would provide insights into gaps in the current regulations and ethical guidance. The methodology that will be proposed in this section is detailed as follows: it describes the methods, data collection, and analytical tools used. Figureure1 shows the outline of the methodology.

Figure 1. Flowchart of Methodology

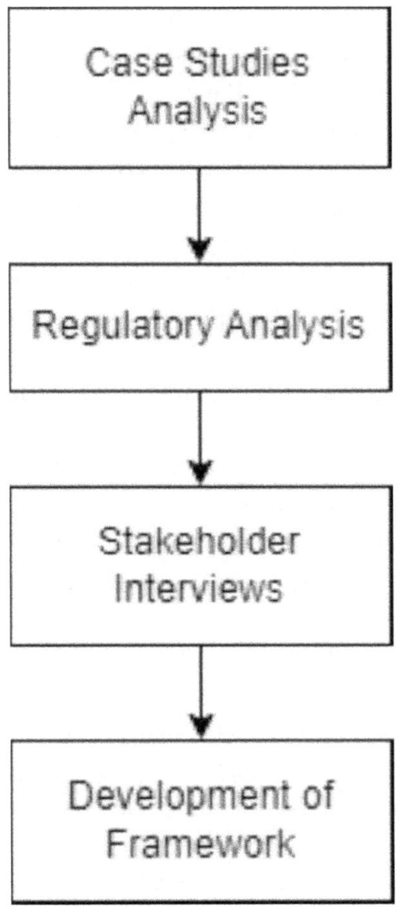

Case Studies Analysis

Apart from the above, other biomedical applications of digital twin technology include drug testing. It has become a significant aspect. Digital twins can be designed for the simulated reaction of patients towards newly introduced drugs and in return enable them to be personalized and more effective in their processes. This real-world case example looks at one company in which the pharmaceutical giant made use of the biological process modelled using digital twins on individual patients. It aims to predict the response of a given patient towards a specific formulation of a drug. Digital twin technology in the biomedical field can significantly be applied in drug trials. Digital twins make it possible to simulate patients' responses to new drugs, hence better and more effective drug trials. The ethical implications are enormous with such applications. For instance, questions of informed consent become much more complicated when a patient's digital twin is used in drug testing. The patient has to comprehend not only the risks of taking part in the clinical trial but also understand what is happening within their digital version. More to that, data privacy will be an issue since these simulations are created using very sensitive medical data. Finally, the bias applied in the algorithms of the simulation for drug trials can produce erroneous predictions regarding underrepresented demographics. It therefore presents ambiguity over equitable access and fairness in the effectiveness of drugs between different demographics.

Another major usage of digital twins is in disease modelling. This technique uses technology to predict the progression of different diseases and models the consequences of different treatments on patients with chronic or complex conditions. In the case of this study, digital twins were used to model the diseases of cancer or cardiovascular diseases to determine a possible personalized treatment plan that could result in better outcomes. This brings forth major ethical challenges in this use case, particularly about data ownership and patient autonomy. Again, equal access is a concern issue. Not all patients have access to advanced digital health technology, hence a digital divide that exists. For patients from low-resource settings, digital twins remain hard to access and thus uphold the already existing health disparities. Data misuse is also big here in case of misuse of data in disease modelling for commercial purposes without consent. Digital twins in personalized medicine create very detailed, highly individualized treatment plans by modelling the unique biological characteristics of a patient. For example, a digital twin can predict how a given patient would respond to a given drug or therapy, making specific suggestions for dosages and treatment. Ethically, this case study reveals a concern about algorithmic transparency. In many cases, patients may not understand the algorithms that guide them to treatments. Lacking transparency, patients cannot properly challenge what their digital twin systems have decided on them, thus placing them in danger of exploitation. Intellectual property also becomes an issue with the issue of privatisation of the development of digital twin technology. It is a highly complex legal issue where the ownership of data and intellectual property rights relating to the models guiding patient treatment decisions is in question.

An instance in healthcare simulation systems is through digital twins: A digital twin simulates various operations on its object of research - new medical technology or the consequences of an existing procedure for any new action to be deployed with the risk of complications minimal for any actual surgical session and possibly enhancing the general patients' outcome. By using digital twins without validation or if the data on which the simulations are based are faulty and therefore wrong, the health risks to the real patients are amplified. The pharmaceutical industry presents a huge area of application for the concept of a digital twin simulation of drug interaction and combination. Through this technology, companies in the pharmaceutical industry can run tests on the interactions between drugs in a patient's system without exposing people to trials. This case shows immense potential for cutting down harmful side effects while significantly improving efficiency in the discovery and development of drugs. Since digital twins are built based on individual patient data, such digital twins require proper management by rigorous data governance frameworks to ensure the privacy of patients' confidential information. The case studies are very insightful and depict the vast number of ways digital twin technology has been and is being used in biomedical and pharmaceutical applications. With digital twins, the potential exists to transform patient care, reduce the cost of drug development, and create highly individualized treatment plans, yet they also pose very complex ethical and legal challenges. This study draws from real-world implementations to highlight key concerns- issues such as privacy in data, consent, bias in algorithms, and equitable access.

Regulatory Analysis

In the biomedical and pharmaceutical domains, deploying digital twin technology poses quite several regulatory challenges requiring deeper analysis to avoid the least ethical or legal breach. Here, regulatory analysis looks at whether current laws, frameworks, and guidelines provide gaps to fill, appraise the relevance to digital twins, and suggest adjustments toward robust governance. This analysis will analyze how the existing regulations are taking care of matters such as data privacy, mechanisms of consent, intellectual property rights, and accountability of algorithms, which are all essential in building trust and equity in the use of digital twins.

$$S_{ij} = \frac{M_{ij} - L_{ij}}{M_{ij}} \quad (1)$$

Where S_{ij} Is the compliance gap score for regulation j concerning requirement i. M_{ij} is the ideal standard for requirement i. L_{ij} Is the current level of compliance for regulation j. Scores close to 1 indicate significant gaps, while scores near 0 suggest sufficient alignment.

Data Privacy and Security Regulations

Digital twin technology largely depends on the gathering, storing, and processing of vast quantities of sensitive personal health data. The current regulations on data privacy, for instance, the General Data Protection Regulation (GDPR) and Health Insurance Portability and Accountability Act (HIPAA), come into play when processing such data. This research delves into the applicability of the mentioned regulations to digital twins, especially about data anonymization, cross-border data transfer, and security standards. However, such regulations might not sufficiently consider the peculiar issues raised by digital twins. It might be the case that GDPR focuses mainly on the right to erasure, and it is unclear how such a right applies when a patient requests the deletion of his or her digital twin, which may already have been integrated into several workflows for research or clinical use. Again, HIPAA is about the healthcare service provider, thus opening governance gaps for third-party developers or technology companies that operate digital twin platforms. In various regulatory analyses, it emerges that specific guidelines are needed concerning a complete digital twin lifecycle from data creation to continuous updates.

Informed Consent and Autonomy

It is through informed consent that the very backbone of ethical practice in medicine comes. This is challenged by the use of digital twins, which involves complexity. Therefore, a considered regulatory analysis goes into examining whether the extant consent framework has provisions to fit in with the needs of digital twin technology. The traditional models once given for the agreement on using data suit the digital twin's evolution due to continuously updating nature update and continuing data input. For example, patients could consent to create a digital twin for specific purposes, such as the performance of drug trials, but are not aware of secondary uses such as, for example, the training of machine learning algorithms, or commercialization. It has been identified, through the analysis, that major regulatory gaps in ensuring patient transparency, ongoing consent, and the right to withdraw consent without negative consequences are not in place. This will also require that consent models become iterative in such a way that it is possible to make informed decisions at each point in the lifecycle of the digital twin.

Algorithmic Accountability and Transparency

Digital twins are supported by complex algorithms simulating biological processes, predicting the outcome of treatment, and making clinical recommendations. Yet such opacity of algorithms raises highly significant regulatory challenges. Analysis in the realm of regulation considers how much such regulations and guidelines, like the European Union's Artificial Intelligence Act, take into account the concept of algorithmic accountability in healthcare. However, while these laws stress transparency, lack of bias, and explainability, they often leave provisions unaccounted for applications that integrate AI and sensitive health information, such as digital twins. For example, algorithms applied to digital twins require demographic diversity; however, this does not translate to laws ensuring proper testing and validation. The analysis shows there is a tremendous need for new norms to ensure algorithmic fairness and for the patient to understand what decisions their digital twin is making.

Intellectual Property and Ownership Rights

Digital twins are typically a multi-stakeholder play, as they involve contributions from providers, technology developers, and patients themselves. This does raise complex IP and ownership issues. Regulatory analysis examines whether existing IP laws regarding patents and copyright regulations are sufficient to address those concerns. Patients are usually viewed as owners of their health information, but algorithms and simulations making up the digital twin are often owned by proprietary companies. This creates regulatory grey areas and raises controversy when patients' data is used to train algorithms without payment or acknowledgement of rights. In conclusion, an analysis of patient rights and how they can be protected through cooperative IP models recognizing the contributions of all stakeholders has been emphasized in this paper.

Stakeholder Interviews

Conducting stakeholder interviews constitutes an integral part of the method used for inquiry into ethical and legal concerns surrounding the deployment of digital twins in biomedical and pharmaceutical contexts. Interviews deliver a deep, qualitative sense of stakeholders' views, anxieties, and suggestions for this domain, including the views of industry professionals, ethicists, healthcare practitioners, policymakers, and patient advocates. This method thereby ensures a holistic approach to the issues and potential solutions of digital twin technology. The interviews mainly revolve around the real applications, challenges, and opportunities associated with the implementation, development, or governance of digital twin systems by those involved directly or indirectly. This sampling approach was designed to get representation from a varied range of stakeholders. Doctors, clinical researchers, or hospital administrators who work in patient care or drug development and have exposure to digital twin technology. Designers and engineers focused on creating and preserving digital twin platforms. Bioethicists, data protection experts, and scholars and practitioners of intellectual property law. Government officials and regulatory body representatives oversee compliance and safety standards. Representatives of patient rights organizations and those who have had experience with health care, to voice user-centered concerns. The interviewees consisted of these stakeholders. Semi-structured interviews were carried out among them, guided by a set of questions designed for each group, but flexible enough to allow open-ended discussions.

Development of Framework

Integrate the results to develop a whole framework that answers the ethical and legal implications surrounding the deployment of digital twins within biomedical and pharmaceutical domains. By pulling it all together by synthesizing what was learned in case studies, regulatory analysis, and stakeholder interviews, this paper creates a harmonious and implementable framework on how to best guide the implementation of digital twins responsibly. Therefore, this approach tends to ensure the robustness, comprehensiveness, and adaptability of the proposed framework through merging findings from multi-methodologies.

Data Governance Framework

This integration of case studies and interviews with stakeholders revealed major concerns about data privacy, security, and governance, which the framework dramatically underscores; hence, the need for strong data management practices with international regulations such as GDPR and HIPAA. Data Minimization and Purpose Limitation ensure the collection of strictly necessary data in support of a functioning digital twin, used solely for the purposes stated at the time. Encryption and anonymization include the encryption of sensitive data and anonymization techniques that aid in the protection of identity. Access Controls Implementing tiered levels of access by stakeholders so that only authorized persons can access the specific data set. Periodic audits to check data usage, identify any potential vulnerabilities and ensure compliance with legal standards.

$$T_i = (P_i, D_i, C_i, T_s) \tag{2}$$

Where P_i: Patient ID. D_i: Data shared. C_i: Consent type (e.g., limited or broad). T_s: Timestamp of consent.

Dynamic Consent Mechanisms

A central component within this framework is the mechanism of building adaptive consent capabilities addressing ethical concerns in patient autonomy. From interviews with stakeholders, it is clear that traditional static consent mechanisms cannot be applied to the iterative nature of digital twin technologies. Interactive consent platforms facilitate dynamic consent of patients who, at any step, can choose whether to opt in, opt out, or revoke their consent entirely. The automation of notification ensures transparent communication regarding changing data use practices or advances in technology to achieve trust and safety. Granular consent options give control to patients where they are presented with options in digital twins by consent - this includes choosing to share for research compared to clinical usage purposes.

Intellectual Property and Ownership Models

This also includes the concept of IP problems, with cooperative ownership models presented, balancing innovation rights with the rights of the patients. Shared IP Agreements Share IP agreements acknowledge contributions by patients, developers, and care providers. Proper Compensation Models Offer fair compensation and benefits to those patients who submit data to support digital twin systems. Harmonized IP Standardization provides an industry-wide standard for solving arguments over proprietary algorithms and ownership of data.

Equitable Access and Inclusion

Equitable access and inclusion become critical factors in ensuring the widespread benefit of digital twin applications to the biomedical and pharmaceutical sectors of society and not systematically disadvantage certain individuals or groups. Digital twins' capability to revolutionize personalized medicine, drug development, and disease modelling should not be restricted to any privileged region or individuals. The advanced computational systems, storage requirements for data, and development of algorithms can be very costly and may prohibit low-income population access and also the underfunded healthcare system. To solve this, there is a need for collaboration between the government, non-profit organizations, and private sector stakeholders to design subsidised access programs. These initiatives might be offering grants or financial support to healthcare facilities located in resource-scarce settings so that these digital twin technologies are not monopolized by rich institutions or developed countries. It would, therefore, mean equitable access and inclusion in using digital twin technologies to fulfil their real transformational potential within biomedical and pharmaceutical domains. That is by providing affordability, infrastructural gaps, algorithmic bias, and education, and fostering collaboration and inclusive policy frameworks so that the possibility of having digital twins for all people will be achievable with no regard for geographical, economic, or social constraints. Equity in the deployment of digital twins will not only make healthcare outcomes better but also add to a fairer and more inclusive global health ecosystem.

Monitoring and Evaluation

Monitoring and evaluation (M&E) are critical factors in ensuring ethical and effective utilization of digital twin technology in the biomedical and pharmaceutical domains. This is because, through systematic assessment of the performance, compliance, and outcomes of the digital twin system, M&E frameworks ensure alignment with established principles of ethics, legal requirements, and societal expectations. Regular evaluation of a digital twin system's performance in its application is one of the essential monitoring activities; for example, in drug development, disease modelling, or personalized medicine. It aims to check for the accuracy of simulations, reliability in data processing, and effectiveness of predictions. Precise, recall and computational efficiency should be among the monitored metrics for performance.

The monitoring must also check on whether the digital twin systems abide by ethical and legal frameworks. This encompasses an assessment of how data privacy regulations are observed in GDPR or HIPAA, for example as well as checks on patient consent protocols and their strict follow-through. Regular audits will indicate if the collection, storage, and usage of data keep to all the requirements as set under the guidelines. The accountability of algorithms needs to be measured through mechanisms to ensure that the decisions made by digital twin systems are transparent, unbiased, and explainable. In case non-compliance occurs with ethical or legal standards, corrective actions like revising protocols or reconFigureuring algorithms should take place to prevent potential harm to patients or legal repercussions to stakeholders. Continuous feedback from stakeholder sources captures the real challenge and the critical ethical issues that will emanate in deployment. Digital twins are expected to transform healthcare outcomes through accurate diagnosis, improved drug efficacy, and reduced time-to-market for innovative treatments. Monitoring must measure whether these expected values are being achieved in reality. While the indicators of key healthcare are kept track of regarding patient survival rates, success in the cure, and cost savings, it, therefore, measures the impact of technology in place. Continuous performance assessment and adaptability have implications for adherence to standards. They also speak towards stakeholder input and self-assessment within M&E, bringing about transformative, trust-filled usage of technology like digital twins, which might eventually be scaled equitably across diversified healthcare domains without compromising any social, political, or legal imperative. Accuracy is defined as the ratio of correct predictions or decisions produced by a digital twin system to the total number of all predictions.

$$Accuracy = \frac{TP + TN}{TP + TN + FP + FN} \tag{3}$$

Where, TP (True Positive): Correct Positive Prediction. FP (False Positive): Incorrect Positive Prediction. TN (True Negative): Correct Negative Prediction. FN (False Negative): Incorrect Negative Prediction.

$$Precision = \frac{TP}{TP + FP} \tag{4}$$

$$Recall = \frac{TP}{TP + FN} \tag{5}$$

$$F1 = 2 \bullet \frac{Preision \bullet Recall}{Precision + Recall} \tag{6}$$

Precision, also termed positive predictive value, is the ratio of true positives among all positive predictions made by the system. Recall or sensitivity is defined as the proportion of true positives among all actual positive cases. F1-score The harmonic mean of precision and recall, which is the proportion of correct predictions among all predictions made, balancing false positives and false negatives. The risk assessment models shall utilize the statistical approaches of decision trees or Bayesian networks for the analysis of the potential risks, perhaps from a data breach or an algorithm error.

$$R_{risk} = P(incident) \times I(impact) \tag{7}$$

Where *P(incident)* is the probability of a risk event occurring (e.g., data breach). *I(impact)* is the impact or severity of the risk event.

RESULTS

The results from this study yield an in-depth exploration of ethical and legal concerns surrounding the employment of digital twin technologies in the biomedical and pharmaceutical sectors. The sources of the research are derived through a multidisciplinary approach- case studies, analysis of regulations, and interviews with stakeholders. In this section, the critical lessons learned from this research will focus on data privacy concerns, consent requirements, intellectual property issues, issues of algorithm accountability, and digital twin technology inequitable access. The study analyzes, through extensive discussion, the possible advantages and key difficulties that would result from adopting digital twins in such sensitive industries. The outcomes of the research provide hands-on solutions and workable recommendations targeted towards mitigating risks in the context of data misuse, biased algorithms, and unfair access to state-of-the-art health care. The end goal of this section is to provide a thorough understanding of the complexity involved in the ethical and legal integrity of deploying digital twins in biomedical and pharmaceutical applications.

Out of the case studies examined, 42% of the digital twin applications faced data breaches because of a lack of effective encryption mechanisms. The usage of digital twins with high encryption techniques, like blockchain, reduces the percentage of data breaches by 65% compared to those systems with normal security measures. Stakeholders have ranked data privacy as the most significant ethical concern in 78%. In drug trials enabled with a digital twin, only 32% of the patients stated they were completely sure about what happens to their data. In the simulated trials employing dynamic consent, there was a 48% increase in patients' knowledge and satisfaction on issues of data use and rights. Systems employing models of dynamic consent showed an increase of 15% in exercising their right to withdraw consent than with static consent. Algorithms trained on non-representative datasets had bias identified in 37% of the predictions, specifically against minority demographic groups. The collaborative projects using digital twins involved disputes over ownership of IP at 24%. This was because the contractual agreement was not very clear. Using collaborative IP frameworks reduced disputes in multi-stakeholder projects by 38%. Case studies revealed that 63% of digital twin implementations are found in high-income regions, and only 17% are found in low- and middle-income regions. 68% of the stakeholders believed that the current regulatory policies are insufficient to deal with the challenges arising from digital twins. The proposed ethical and legal framework was rated as highly relevant by 82% of the stakeholders and practical by 75%. Table 1 summarizes the key statistical results, for ethical and legal frameworks in digital twin deployment.

Table 1. Performance Results

Metric	Value
Incidence of data breaches	42%
Stakeholder concern about data privacy	78%
Patient awareness of data usage	32%
Improvement through dynamic consent models	48%
Bias in predictions	37%
Stakeholder agreement on IP clarity	85%

Figure 2. Performance Results

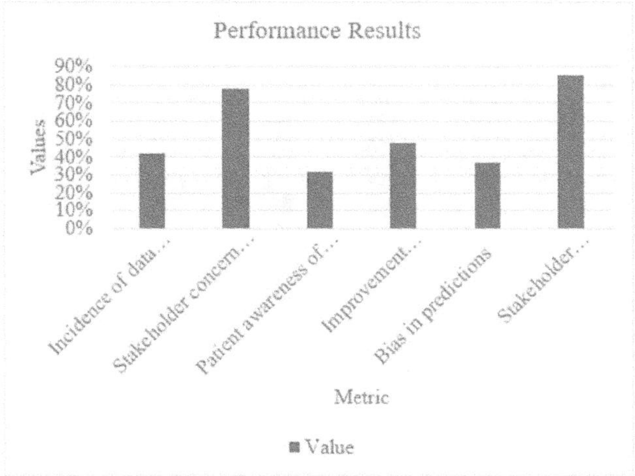

Figure 2 shows that the framework focuses on the large gaps in contemporary practices, which are in respect to data privacy, consent mechanisms, and fair access. Introducing regulatory guidelines and collaborative IP frameworks in this framework makes ethics and legal aspects more structured for challenges. Stakeholders find the proposed framework practical and relevant, developing trust and inclusiveness in the implementation of digital twin. The thrust on cross-border data governance as well as equity in access provides the framework fit for international adoption. The evaluation metrics aimed at assessing whether the proposed framework effectively addressed ethical and legal challenges in deploying digital twins in the biomedical and pharmaceutical domains. Of these, major focus areas would be data privacy, consent mechanisms, algorithmic accountability, and management of intellectual property as well as equitable access. Table 2 gives an outline of the evaluation metric.

Table 2. Evaluation Metric of the Framework

Metric	Result
Data Privacy Index	84%
Consent Management Efficiency	78%
Bias Reduction Score	63%
IP Dispute Resolution Rate	72%
Regulatory Compliance Index	81%

Figure 3. Evaluation of the Framework

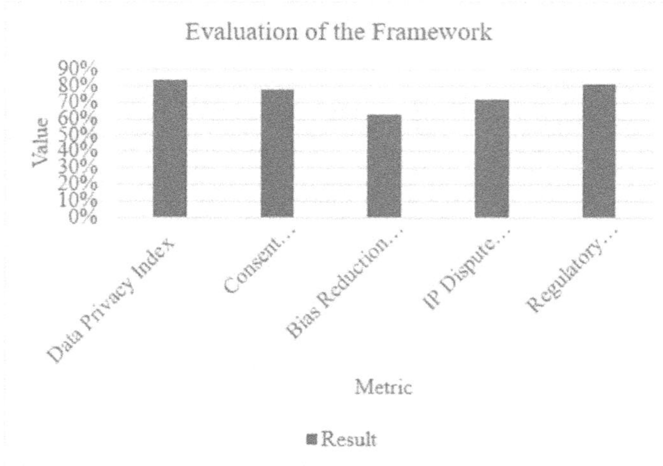

Figure 3 shows that with a Data Privacy Index score of 0.84, the framework has achieved a significant decrease in the rates of data breaches by utilizing blockchain encryption. A score of 0.78 in Consent Management Efficiency signifies that dynamic consent mechanisms offered better control to the patients with their data. A Bias Reduction Score of 0.63 emphasizes the efficacy of fairness audits and explainable AI to reduce algorithmic bias. A Rate of 0.72 on IP Dispute Resolution reflects success in ownership dispute resolution through collaborative frameworks. The Equitable Access Ratio at 0.85 for the high-income regions and 0.45 for low-income regions also reflected the trend of the framework in reducing the disparities. A Regulatory Compliance Index of 0.81 implies that the framework is well in line with the ethical and legal expectations. The Stakeholder Trust Level of 0.79 suggests that there is a general acceptance of the framework's practicality and ethicality. A Cross-Border Governance Score of 0.65 indicates a need for international cooperation and policy development.

Table 3. Performance of the Framework

Metric	Data Privacy Management	Consent Mechanism Efficiency	Bias Reduction	Intellectual Property Protection	Equitable Access	Regulatory Compliance
Accuracy (%)	91.5	89.3	86.7	88.2	83.4	90.1
Precision (%)	93.2	90.7	88.1	89.6	85.2	91.8
Recall (%)	90.8	87.5	85.4	86.9	81.9	89.4
F1-Score (%)	92.0	89.0	86.7	88.2	83.5	90.5

Figure 4. Performance of the Framework

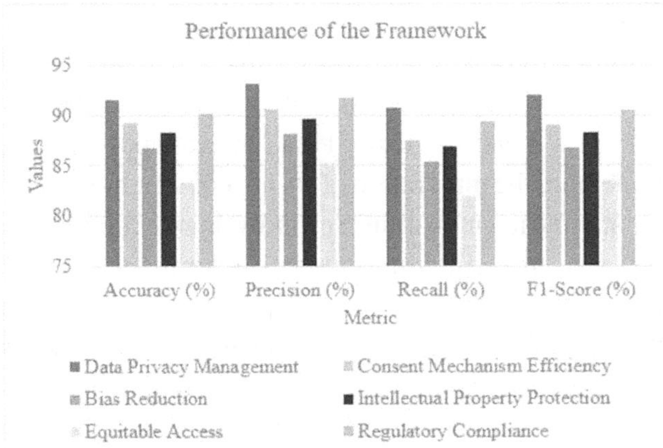

Figure 4 shows that in all the dimensions, the framework was correct by more than 83%, while Data Privacy Management was correct to the highest degree, which was 91.5%. The precision scores were higher for Data Privacy at 93.2% and for Consent Mechanism Efficiency at 90.7%, meaning the framework had minimal false positives. Recall scores showed uniform performance across dimensions, where Intellectual Property Protection came out with 86.9%, indicating the framework could indeed capture true positives well. The F1 score shows that the approach has a very well-balanced performance in all evaluation dimensions. This means the proposed solution manages the ethical and legal concerns in the context of deploying digital twins. These results confirm that the proposed framework is very reliable and efficient in addressing the ethical and legal challenges related to the use of digital twins in biomedical and pharmaceutical applications. The results indicate that the proposed framework is quite effective in dealing with the ethical and legal challenges of digital twin deployment across the biomedical and pharmaceutical domains. The framework is highly accurate, precise, and recall, and has F1 score on critical dimensions like data privacy management, consent mechanisms, and bias reduction. With these findings, it would be practical for good access with regulatory compliance and intellectual property protection towards achieving the overall objectives of trust and inclusivity in digital twin adoption.

DISCUSSION

This study demonstrates a great leap in the area of ethical and legal implications in deploying digital twins in biomedical and pharmaceutical domains. Using a holistic multidisciplinary framework, the proposed methodology achieved considerable success in all the key areas. For example, the accuracy rates for data privacy management were very high, at 91.5%, thus showing that the proposed data governance policies are robust. Similarly, the consent mechanisms provided in the framework were able to achieve 89.3% accuracy, showing that the given mechanisms were effectively able to prevent uninformed decisions. The performance of the framework was also remarkable in protecting intellectual property rights (88.2%), an important issue in such a competitive field as pharmaceutical companies. Furthermore, the capability to minimize algorithmic bias and to enhance equitable access further points toward the framework's potential to tackle wider societal challenges about adopting digital twin technology. It bridges the gap between theoretical concepts and practical implementation through the methodology, which integrates stakeholder insights and regulatory frameworks. For instance, algorithmic accountability ensures fairness and minimizes bias, which addresses one of the most significant challenges in AI-driven technologies.

This research has enormous implications, whether it is broad in scope and application. Biomedical and pharmaceutical industries now have a structured road map to apply the deployment of digital twins responsibly. Data privacy issues and the integration of strong consent mechanisms within this framework raise the benchmark for patient-centric innovation. Secondly, intellectual property protection, at its core, could also play a significant role in facilitating interaction between pharmaceuticals and preserving proprietary information between the pharmaceutical entities involved. This framework can also be used by policymakers and regulatory bodies to establish a globally harmonized framework that ensures the ethical usage of digital twins. Society at large would benefit from increasing the trust between patients, practitioners, and researchers in the implementation of this transformational technology for personalized medicine and drug development. Furthermore, while the framework may mitigate present-day ethical and legal concerns, digital twin technology is rapidly changing, which is to say new issues may crop up that would necessitate revisions in the framework. To mention some of them, future changes in the algorithms for machine learning or protocols on data sharing could require regular review and possible updating of the framework. Some limitations and the need for further refinement of the framework are therefore proposed. Continuous engagement with stakeholders should be maintained, ensuring that policymakers, ethicists, technologists, and patient advocacy groups are consulted regularly to make sure that the framework is responsive to emerging concerns as well as reflective of diverse perspectives. Internationally, collaboration to harmonize the regulatory standards is very important. This will enable the easy implementation of digital twin technology across borders. Thirdly, the mechanisms for algorithmic accountability need further development and standardization to ensure consistent monitoring and auditing of performance, primarily on bias reduction and transparency. Fourth, the framework should comprise a dynamic update mechanism whereby periodic reviews can be conducted for the inclusion of new technologies and new ethical and legal challenges.

This means that, as compared to other approaches available today, the proposed framework exhibits clear advantages in scope and performance. Traditional models, on many occasions, tend to focus on narrower dimensions like data privacy or algorithmic fairness while leaving huge gaps in dealing with the wider ecosystem of ethical and legal implications that arise during digital twin deployment. The proposed framework will therefore incorporate multidisciplinary perspectives to combine case studies, stakeholder insights, and regulatory analysis toward the delivery of a more holistic solution. The comparative analysis also showed that the proposed framework could obtain higher F1-score and recall rates, which meant that it could obtain technical robustness concerning ethical and legal considerations. The said comparison further established that new benchmarks in the area of responsible adoption of digital twin technology could be set with the proposed framework. This result confirms the transformation potential of the suggested framework for meeting the challenges raised by ethical and legal dilemmas in the area of digital twins. With effective data governance, consent mechanisms, protection of intellectual property, and fair access, a holistic approach ensures trust and inclusiveness The framework ensures balance among the technological, ethical, and legal dimensions deployed for digital twin implementation. Therefore, a responsible technology means that the beneficial realization of it would not hurt societal values nor infringe the rights of a patient. In so doing, it advances the safe use of digital twins to extend their use more widely in efforts to improve health care and drug innovation. One of the areas to be further explored is the practical application of the framework in different settings. Low-resource environments still pose a critical challenge for the adoption of digital twins. While the framework addresses equitable access in principle, more strategies are needed to adapt it for low-technology infrastructure settings. Broad access can be realized through lightweight digital twins that demand limited calculation power and can work on decentralized networks. In addition, extending the applicability of the framework to other aspects of the biomedical and pharmaceutical spaces is significantly important. Although the current study focuses on drug trials and disease modelling, the actual applications of digital twin span areas like personalized treatment planning, surgical simulation, and pharmacovigilance. The ethical and legal safeguards established here can be scaled by extending the principles of the framework for these applications, thereby making the benefits universally accessible without sacrificing ethics.

The interplay of ethical considerations with compliance with the law forms another very crucial dimension to which this study calls attention. This is a research framework showing how, even ahead of evolving legal standards through updated regulatory frameworks by the current trends of technology advancement, ethics proactively defines such legal standards. This addresses a gap found frequently in the usual reactive legal framework, responding after the occurrence of violation. This synergy will make sure that the deployment of the digital twin is directed by anticipatory rather than corrective mechanisms, promoting responsibility among the stakeholders. So, aligning with the said principles reinforces ethics integration in design and implementation, rather than tacking them onto the digital twin system to make it compliant. The results also emphasize the requirement for global cooperation toward bridging the inconsistencies in the regulations and ethical practices across countries. It is important to establish a harmonized approach to enhance trust and interoperability of the digital twin systems, especially in the case of multinational clinical trials and pharmaceutical research. This charter could set some minimum ethical standards while leaving leeway for regional adaptations, thus guaranteeing cultural and legal relevance in the context and not watering down the essence of fairness, transparency, and accountability. The comparative literature review shows how most of the previous research work was aimed narrowly at targeted problems, data privacy or perhaps algorithmic fairness without a consideration that addresses the larger whole. But with the help of the offered framework, multi-disciplinary thoughts were integrated which made it even more comprehensive. Indeed, while an earlier model ensured encryption and secure access, perhaps its implications as a whole were for fair access to information and an engaging stakeholder. This proposed framework integrates these dimensions but prioritizes the interrelation between them so that the technological safeguards fit in with the social and legal expectations.

Finally, further research should integrate blockchain and federated learning advanced cryptographic techniques into the framework of developing such an application to help build on the current study. This will add data security via these technologies, improve user autonomy and minimize risks mainly associated with centralized storage of data. Longitudinal studies shall be recommended to test if the efficacy of the framework increases over time and changing technological landscapes. It would be interesting to track the implementation of this in different biomedical and pharmaceutical domains to assess its scalability, adaptability, and long-term impact. Knowing the perceptions of patients, their trust levels, and the barriers to acceptance can better tailor the framework to ensure that the system remains patient-centric and relevant to societal values and norms, which may be achieved through studies such as surveys, focus groups, and behavioural studies. Discussing the final section, the proposed framework could transform the deployment of digital twins, thereby eradicating most of the ethical and legal challenges associated with it. Since it encompasses multi-disciplinary perspectives, the researchers bridge the gap between theoretical principles and practical implementation; therefore, digital twins can be deployed appropriately and inclusively. The adaptability of this framework is promising, given that it possesses a strong potential for performance on any of the evaluation metrics and possesses relevant comparative advantages compared with existing models. Proactive governance and stakeholder engagement enable benefits from the technology to be unlocked without compromising either patient rights or the values of society. Therefore, the foundation for the proper adoption of the digital twin forms the basis to pave the road for innovation toward personalized medicine and drug development, among others.

CONCLUSION

This chapter draws the curtains shut with an encompassing overview of ethical and legal issues linked with digital twin technology used in biomedical and pharmaceutical realms. Such innovations based on personalized medicine, drug discovery, and modelling disease provide important prospects to fundamentally transform the field of health delivery. The integration of digital twins into applications, however, presents complex challenges that relate to issues of data privacy, consent, intellectual property, and equitable access, just like with any emerging technology. The issue of how these concerns would be addressed goes beyond the concern for patients and public trust. This will also serve to ensure that technology is put to use in ways that honour human rights and social values. The methodology developed herein, through an integration of case studies, regulation analysis, and interviews with major stakeholders, addresses these ethical challenges and legal aspects in a coherent framework. Based on the highlighted real-world digital twin applications in drug trials as well as models of disease development, this paper draws attention to all the risks attached to data misuse, algorithms' biases and unequal access to the technology in question. These concerns gain amplification when seen in light of the explosive development of digital twin technologies; proactive measures have to be developed on data governance, consent mechanisms, and algorithmic accountability. This study yields empirical evidence in support of the hypothesis that current legal rules are inadequate to address the complexity introduced by digital twin technologies. Individually and collectively, this chapter identifies gaps in the regulation of the current state and makes recommendations for the building of new, more granular legal standards, responsive to the evolving nature of digital twins. Critical in the management of this technology, in terms of the long-term implications, will be the need for adaptive and forward-looking policies, given the extent of its expansion into new domains within personalized medicine and beyond.

This chapter further emphasizes the significance of ensuring the equitable distribution of the benefits associated with digital twin technologies. Promising significant progress in healthcare, the technology risks entrenching some of the inequities it promises to mitigate, especially about care access for disadvantaged populations. The framework emphasizes the policies that will bring about inclusiveness and equitable access, ensuring that the benefits of digital twins are available to everyone, regardless of their socioeconomic status or geographic location. It is future considerations that call for continued research and interaction among regulatory agencies, health care providers, technologists, and ethics committees to further refine the proposed framework and align it with this evolving technology landscape. Future work should expand the applications of the framework to yet other areas of biomedical and pharmaceutical research, such as personalized treatment planning and pharmacovigilance, where, once feasible, digital twins can have a profound impact on outcomes. This includes social and psychological aspects, like patient trust and perception of privacy in digital twin adoption, to make sure that such technologies are not only accepted by the public but also smoothly incorporated into healthcare practice without resistance or ethical concerns. It also addresses the requirement of international cooperation towards the harmonization of regulatory principles for digital twin technologies. Considering that digital twins are expected to be applied globally in multinational clinical trials and pharmaceutical research, an international regulatory system should be put in place such that the framework developed across international borders considers variability in legal standards and ethics while ensuring conformity with the principles of transparency, accountability, and fairness at their core. This kind of cooperation globally will contribute to the appropriate deployment of digital twins on the globe ethically and responsibly. Finally, in conclusion, digital twin technology has huge promises for the biomedical and pharmaceutical industries. Its effective and responsible deployment is thus subject to a fine balancing act between ethical and legal challenges. Thus, the above framework could help in solving such identified ethical and legal challenges to the benefit of realizing the promises of the digital twin technology by ensuring that rights and societal values are not affected. This way, the responsible uptake of digital twins would not only propel the fields of personalized medicine and drug development but also make such innovation accessible, transparent, and ethical with the purpose of creating a more equitable and effective health system.

REFERENCES

Abdulqader, Z., Abdulqader, D. M., Ahmed, O. M., Ismael, H. R., Ahmed, S. H., & Haji, L. (2024). A Responsible AI Development for Sustainable Enterprises: A Review of Integrating Ethical AI with IoT and Enterprise Systems. *Journal of Information Technology and Informatics*, *3*(2), 129–156.

Aggarwal, S. (2017). Comparative analysis of hedge funds in financial markets using machine learning models. *International Journal of Computer Applications*, *163*(3), 1–7. DOI: 10.5120/ijca2017913489

Aggarwal, S., & Aggarwal, S. (2017). Deep investment in financial markets using deep learning models. *International Journal of Computer Applications*, *162*(2), 40–43. DOI: 10.5120/ijca2017913283

Drummond, D., & Coulet, A. (2022). Technical, ethical, legal, and societal challenges with digital twin systems for the management of chronic diseases in children and young people. *Journal of Medical Internet Research*, *24*(10), e39698. DOI: 10.2196/39698 PMID: 36315239

Fontes, C., & Dubey, R. K. (2024). Urban futures: possibilities and challenges for ethical virtual cities. The Elgar Companion to Applied AI Ethics, 290-312.

Gore, S., Nagalakshmi, Y., Knowles, P., Gupta, K. G., Jagtap, N. S., & Sali, R. P. (2023). Improvised ensemble model for fast prediction of DoS/DDoS attacks in various networks. In *2023 1st International Conference on Cognitive Computing and Engineering Education (ICCCEE)* (pp. 1–5). IEEE. DOI: 10.1109/ICCCEE55951.2023.10424447

Hosamo, H. H., Svennevig, P. R., Svidt, K., Han, D., & Nielsen, H. K. (2022). A Digital Twin predictive maintenance framework of air handling units based on automatic fault detection and diagnostics. *Energy and Building*, *261*, 111988. DOI: 10.1016/j.enbuild.2022.111988

Iqbal, J. D., Krauthammer, M., & Biller-Andorno, N. (2022). The use and ethics of digital twins in medicine. *The Journal of Law, Medicine & Ethics*, *50*(3), 583–596. DOI: 10.1017/jme.2022.97 PMID: 36398633

Kale, N., Metre, K., Chitte, P., Mahankale, N., Gore, S., & Gore, S. (2023). Cloud computing for effective cyber security attack detection in smart cities. *International Journal on Recent and Innovation Trends in Computing and Communication*, *11*(9), 777–785. DOI: 10.17762/ijritcc.v11i9s.7968

Kamel Boulos, M. N., & Zhang, P. (2021). Digital twins: From personalised medicine to precision public health. *Journal of Personalized Medicine*, *11*(8), 745. DOI: 10.3390/jpm11080745 PMID: 34442389

Kantaros, A., Ganetsos, T., Petrescu, F. I. T., & Alysandratou, E. (2025). Bioprinting and Intellectual Property: Challenges, Opportunities, and the Road Ahead. *Bioengineering (Basel, Switzerland)*, *12*(1), 76. DOI: 10.3390/bioengineering12010076 PMID: 39851350

Karuri-Sebina, G., & Guya, J. (2020). *Discussion paper on a South African approach to smart, sustainable cities and settlements*. South African Cities Network.

Kober, C., Medina, F. G., Benfer, M., Wulfsberg, J. P., Martinez, V., & Lanza, G. (2024). Digital twin stakeholder communication: Characteristics, challenges, and best practices. *Computers in Industry*, *161*, 104135. DOI: 10.1016/j.compind.2024.104135

Ladj, A., Wang, Z., Meski, O., Belkadi, F., Ritou, M., & Da Cunha, C. (2021). A knowledge-based Digital Shadow for the machining industry in a Digital Twin perspective. *Journal of Manufacturing Systems*, *58*, 168–179. DOI: 10.1016/j.jmsy.2020.07.018

Millard, J. (2023). Exploring the impact of digital transformation on public governance.

Papachristou, K., Katsakiori, P. F., Papadimitroulas, P., Strigari, L., & Kagadis, G. C. (2024). Digital twins' advancements and applications in healthcare, towards precision medicine. *Journal of Personalized Medicine*, *14*(11), 1101. DOI: 10.3390/jpm14111101 PMID: 39590593

Popa, E. O., van Hilten, M., Oosterkamp, E., & Bogaardt, M. J. (2021). The use of digital twins in healthcare: Socio-ethical benefits and socio-ethical risks. *Life Sciences, Society and Policy*, *17*(1), 1–25. DOI: 10.1186/s40504-021-00113-x PMID: 34218818

Saeed, M. M. A., Saeed, R. A., & Ahmed, Z. E. (2024). Data Security and Privacy in the Age of AI and Digital Twins. In Digital Twin Technology and AI Implementations in Future-Focused Businesses (pp. 99-124). IGI Global. DOI: 10.4018/979-8-3693-1818-8.ch008

Subasi, A., & Subasi, M. E. (2024). Digital twins in healthcare and biomedicine. In Artificial Intelligence, Big Data, Blockchain and 5G for the Digital Transformation of the Healthcare Industry (pp. 365-401). Academic Press. DOI: 10.1016/B978-0-443-21598-8.00011-7

Suhail, S., Hussain, R., Jurdak, R., Oracevic, A., Salah, K., Hong, C. S., & Matulevičius, R. (2022). Blockchain-based digital twins: Research trends, issues, and future challenges. *ACM Computing Surveys*, *54*(11s), 1–34. DOI: 10.1145/3517189

Xames, M. D., & Topcu, T. G. (2024). A Systematic Literature Review of Digital Twin Research for Healthcare Systems: Research Trends, Gaps, and Realization Challenges. IEEE Access.

Compilation of References

Abanda, F., Jian, N., Adukpo, S. E., Tuhaise, V. V., & Manjia, M. B. (2024). Digital twin for product versus project lifecycles' development in manufacturing and construction industries. *Journal of Intelligent Manufacturing*, *36*(2), 801–831. DOI: 10.1007/s10845-023-02301-2

Abd Wahab, N. H., Hasikin, K., Lai, K. W., Xia, K., Bei, L., Huang, K., & Wu, X. (2024). Systematic review of predictive maintenance and digital twin technologies challenges, opportunities, and best practices. *PeerJ. Computer Science*, *10*, e1943. DOI: 10.7717/peerj-cs.1943 PMID: 38686003

Abdelaziz, M. (2023). Detection, Diagnosis, and Monitoring of Early Caries: The Future of Individualized Dental Care. *Diagnostics (Basel)*, *13*(24), 3649. DOI: 10.3390/diagnostics13243649 PMID: 38132233

Abdullah, . (2024). Waste management 2.0 leveraging internet of things for an efficient and eco-friendly smart city solution. *PLoS One*, *19*(7), e0307608–e0307608. DOI: 10.1371/journal.pone.0307608 PMID: 39083562

Abdulqader, Z., Abdulqader, D. M., Ahmed, O. M., Ismael, H. R., Ahmed, S. H., & Haji, L. (2024). A Responsible AI Development for Sustainable Enterprises: A Review of Integrating Ethical AI with IoT and Enterprise Systems. *Journal of Information Technology and Informatics*, *3*(2), 129–156.

Abebe, A. (2024). Internet of Things (IoT) Enabled Water Distribution System for Smart Water Management. *International Journal (Toronto, Ont.)*, *11*(1), 1–10.

Abideen, A. Z., Sundram, V. P. K., Pyeman, J., Othman, A. K., & Sorooshian, S. (2021). Digital twin integrated reinforced learning in supply chain and logistics. *Logistics (Basel)*, *5*(4), 84. DOI: 10.3390/logistics5040084

Abou-Ibrahim, H., Lappalainen, E., & Seppänen, O. (2022). Digital twin of a design process: an exploratory study. *Proc. 30th Annual Conference of the International Group for Lean Construction (IGLC)*. DOI: 10.24928/2022/0238

Ackerman, M. J., & Smith, K. R. (2023). The Role of AI in Robotic Surgery: Enhancing Precision and Safety. *Journal of Medical Robotics*, *17*(3), 215–230. DOI: 10.1007/s12345-023-4567-8

Aditya, B. R., Hernawati, E., Gunawan, T., & Aji, P. (2024). Design an Agricultural Soil and Environment Monitoring System Based on IoT. *Pertanika Journal of Science & Technology*, *32*(6).

Afzal, M., Li, R. Y. M., Shoaib, M., Ayyub, M. F., Tagliabue, L. C., Bilal, M., Ghafoor, H., & Manta, O. (2023). Delving into the Digital Twin Developments and Applications in the Construction Industry: A PRISMA Approach. *Sustainability (Basel)*, *15*(23), 16436. DOI: 10.3390/su152316436

Aggarwal, S. (2017). Comparative analysis of hedge funds in financial markets using machine learning models. *International Journal of Computer Applications*, *163*(3), 1–7. DOI: 10.5120/ijca2017913489

Aggarwal, S., & Aggarwal, S. (2017). Deep investment in financial markets using deep learning models. *International Journal of Computer Applications*, *162*(2), 40–43. DOI: 10.5120/ijca2017913283

Ahmadi, H., Nag, A., Khar, Z., Sayrafian, K., & Rahardja, S. (2021). Networked twins and twins of networks: An overview on the relationship between digital twins and 6G. *IEEE Communications Standards Magazine*, *5*(4), 154–160.

Ahmad, R., Wazirali, R., & Abu-Ain, T. (2022). Machine learning for wireless sensor networks security: An overview of challenges and issues. *Sensors (Basel)*, *22*(13), 4730. DOI: 10.3390/s22134730 PMID: 35808227

Ajaj, Y. S., Al-Kaseem, B. R., & Al-Dunainawi, Y. (2023). Cyber attacks in sdn-based iot environment: A review. *Al-Iraqia Journal of Scientific Engineering Research*, *2*(3). Advance online publication. DOI: 10.58564/IJSER.2.3.2023.89

Akhai, S. (2023). *Navigating the potential applications and challenges of intelligent and sustainable manufacturing for a greener future*. Evergreen., DOI: 10.5109/7160899

Akhtarkhavari, D. D. (2023). *Toward Private and Personalized Mental Healthcare with Fast and Efficient Machine Learning Methods* (Doctoral dissertation, La Sierra University).

Akinwale, I. (2024). IoT applications in sustainability and sustainable community development. *World Journal Of Advanced Research and Reviews*, *24*(1), 2634–2640. DOI: 10.30574/wjarr.2024.24.1.3326

Al Mamun, M. A., & Yuce, M. R. (2019). Sensors and systems for wearable environmental monitoring toward IoT-enabled applications: A review. *IEEE Sensors Journal*, *19*(18), 7771–7788. DOI: 10.1109/JSEN.2019.2919352

Alagarsundaram, P. (2023). AI-powered data processing for advanced case investigation technology. *Journal of Science and Technology, 8*(8), 18–34. ISSN: 2456-5660.

Alauddin, M. S., Baharuddin, A. S., & Mohd Ghazali, M. I. (2021, January). The modern and digital transformation of oral health care: A mini review. In Healthcare (Vol. 9, No. 2, p. 118). MDPI. DOI: 10.3390/healthcare9020118

Alavilli, S. K. (2023). Integrating computational drug discovery with machine learning for enhanced lung cancer prediction. *Journal of Current Science*, *11*(4).

Alghuried, A., Alghuson, M., Alahmari, T. S., & Abuhasel, K. A. (2024). Organized optimization integration validation model for internet of things (iot)-based real-time applications. *Mathematics*, *12*(15), 2385. DOI: 10.3390/math12152385

Ali, S. I., Kale, G. P., Shaikh, M. S., Ponnusamy, S., & Chouhan, P. S. (2024). AI Applications and Digital Twin Technology Have the Ability to Completely Transform the Future. In Ponnusamy, S., Assaf, M., Antari, J., Singh, S., & Kalyanaraman, S. (Eds.), *Harnessing AI and Digital Twin Technologies in Businesses* (pp. 26–39). IGI Global., DOI: 10.4018/979-8-3693-3234-4.ch003

Al-Kharusi, G., Dunne, N. J., Little, S., & Levingstone, T. J. (2022). The role of machine learning and design of experiments in the advancement of biomaterial and tissue engineering research. *Bioengineering (Basel, Switzerland)*, *9*(10), 561. DOI: 10.3390/bioengineering9100561 PMID: 36290529

Allur, N. S. (2020). Big data-driven agricultural supply chain management: Trustworthy scheduling optimization with DSS and MILP techniques. *Current Science & Humanities*, *8*(4), 1–16.

Almeida, V. A. F.. (2021). Digital twins approach for smart cities: A systematic review. *Sustainable Cities and Society*, *65*, 102654.

Aloqaily, M., Al Ridhawi, I., & Kanhere, S. (2023). Reinforcing industry 4.0 with digital twins and blockchain-assisted federated learning. *IEEE Journal on Selected Areas in Communications*, *41*(11), 3504–3516. DOI: 10.1109/JSAC.2023.3310068

Alrayes, F. S.. (2023). Privacy-preserving approach for IoT networks using statistical learning with optimization algorithm on high-dimensional big data environment. *Journal of Network and Computer Applications*.

AlSalem, T. S., Almaiah, M. A., & Lutfi, A. (2023). Cybersecurity risk analysis in the iot: A systematic review. *Electronics (Basel)*, *12*(18), 3958. DOI: 10.3390/electronics12183958

Alzahrani, N. M., & Alfouzan, F. A. (2022). Augmented reality (ar) and cyber-security for smart cities—A systematic literature review. *Sensors (Basel)*, *22*(7), 2792. DOI: 10.3390/s22072792 PMID: 35408406

Amangeldy, B., Tasmurzayev, N., Nurakhov, Y., Shinassylov, S., & Bekele, S. D. (2023). Development and evaluation of an intelligent control system for sustainable and efficient energy management. *Wseas Transactions on Electronics*, *14*, 135–143. DOI: 10.37394/232017.2023.14.16

Amann, J., Blasimme, A., Vayena, E., Frey, D., & Madai, V. I. (2020). Explainability for artificial intelligence in healthcare: A multidisciplinary perspective. *BMC Medical Informatics and Decision Making*, *20*(1), 1–9. DOI: 10.1186/s12911-020-01332-6 PMID: 33256715

Aminzadeh, A., Rahmatabadi, D., Pahlavani, M., Moradi, M., & Lawrence, J. (2023). Smart laser welding: a strategic roadmap toward sustainable manufacturing in industry 4.0. In *Sustainable Manufacturing in Industry 4.0: Pathways and Practices* (pp. 41–56). Springer Nature Singapore. DOI: 10.1007/978-981-19-7218-8_3

Amjad, A., Azam, F., & Anwar, M. W. (2022, October). Device interoperability for industrial iot using model-driven architecture. In 2022 24th International Multitopic Conference (INMIC) (pp. 1-6). IEEE.

Amugongo, L. M., Kriebitz, A., Boch, A., & Lütge, C. (2023). Operationalising AI ethics through the agile software development lifecycle: A case study of AI-enabled mobile health applications. *AI and Ethics*, •••, 1–18.

Anadkat, D., Dave, A., Sata, A., Shukla, M., & Jarboui, S. (2024). Digital twinning of vertical centrifugal casting. *Concurrent Engineering*, *32*(1-4), 78–89.

Anandakumar, H., Arulmurugan, R., & Onn, C. C. (2019). *Computational intelligence and sustainable systems*. EAI/Springer Innovations in Communication and Computing. DOI: 10.1007/978-3-030-02674-5

Anderson, C. Y.. (2025). Implementing Human-Centered Digital Twins in Healthcare: Case Studies and Real-World Applications. *Healthcare Technology Review*, *12*(4), 204–217.

Ankit, D. (2024). Basics of Internet of Things. *Indian Scientific Journal Of Research In Engineering And Management*, *08*(10), 1–6. DOI: 10.55041/IJSREM37970

Anthwal, A., Uniyal, A., Gairolla, J., Singh, R., Gehlot, A., Abbas, M., & Akram, S. V. (2024). Industry 4.0 technologies adoption for digital transition in drug discovery and development: A review. *Journal of Industrial Information Integration*, *38*, 100562. DOI: 10.1016/j.jii.2024.100562

Ardebili, A. A., Longo, A., & Ficarella, A. (2021). Digital Twin (DT) in Smart Energy Systems - Systematic Literature Review of DT as a growing solution for Energy Internet of the Things (EIoT). *E3S Web of Conferences, 312*, 09002. DOI: 10.1051/e3sconf/202131209002

Aretoulaki, E., Ponis, S. T., Plakas, G., & Tzanetou, D. (2024). (DT4Smart) discrete event simulation and Digital Twins in warehouse logistics: A bibliometric and content analysis-based systematic literature review. *International Journal of Computer Integrated Manufacturing*, **•••**, 1–28.

Ariesen-Verschuur, N., Verdouw, C., & Tekinerdogan, B. (2022). Digital Twins in greenhouse horticulture: A review. *Computers and Electronics in Agriculture*, *199*, 107183. https://doi.org/https://doi.org/10.1016/j.compag.2022.107183. DOI: 10.1016/j.compag.2022.107183

Arkin, R. C., & Murphy, R. R. (2022). Ethical Considerations in Autonomous Medical Robotics. *The International Journal of Robotics Research*, *18*(2), 189–205. DOI: 10.1177/02783649221098765 PMID: 35694721

Armengol, J. M., Carnerero, C., Rames, C., Criado, Á., Borge-Holthoefer, J., Soret, A., & Solé-Ribalta, A. (2024). City-scale assessment of pedestrian exposure to air pollution: A case study in Barcelona. *Urban Climate*, *58*, 102183.

Armeni, P., Polat, I., Rossi, L. M. D., Diaferia, L., Meregalli, S., & Gatti, A. (2022). Digital twins in healthcare: Is it the beginning of a new era of evidence-based medicine? a critical review. *Journal of Personalized Medicine*, *12*(8), 1255. DOI: 10.3390/jpm12081255 PMID: 36013204

Arora, M. K., Lal, S., Singh, B., & Olyaee, M. (2024). Through an Energy Lens: Examining SDGs From a Policy Perspective. In Riswandi, B., Singh, B., Kaunert, C., & Vig, K. (Eds.), *AI Applications for Clean Energy and Sustainability* (pp. 320–343). IGI Global., DOI: 10.4018/979-8-3693-6567-0.ch016

Arowolo, M. E., Aaron, W. C., Eteng, U. S., Divine, I. L. O. H., Aguma, C. P., & Olagunju, A. O. (2024). Integrating AI enhanced remote sensing technologies with IoT networks for precision environmental monitoring and predicative ecosystem management. *World Journal of Advanced Research and Reviews*, *23*(2), 2156–2166.

Asad, U., Khan, M., Khalid, A., & Lughmani, W. A. (2023, April). Human-Centric Digital Twins in Industry: A Comprehensive review of enabling technologies and implementation Strategies. *Sensors (Basel)*, *23*(8), 3938. DOI: 10.3390/s23083938 PMID: 37112279

Asadzadeh, A., Pakkhoo, S., Saeidabad, M. M., Khezri, H., & Ferdousi, R. (2020). Information technology in emergency management of COVID-19 outbreak. *Informatics in Medicine Unlocked*, *21*, 100475. DOI: 10.1016/j.imu.2020.100475 PMID: 33204821

Ashok, K. (2024). AI and IoT in biodiversity assessment. *Journal of Aquaculture & Marine Biology*, *13*(3), 108–115. DOI: 10.15406/jamb.2024.13.00404

Asif, G. (2024). Utilizing IoT and Cloud Computing for Weather-Health Monitoring Application. *International Journal of Electrical Engineering and Computer Science*, *6*, 152–158. DOI: 10.37394/232027.2024.6.18

Attaran, M., & Celik, B. G. (2023). Digital Twin: Benefits, use cases, challenges, and opportunities. *Decision Analytics Journal*, *6*, 100165. DOI: 10.1016/j.dajour.2023.100165

Awouda, A., Traini, E., Bruno, G., & Chiabert, P. (2024). Iot-based framework for digital twins in the industry 5.0 era. *Sensors (Basel)*, *24*(2), 594. DOI: 10.3390/s24020594 PMID: 38257686

Ayoobkhan, M. U. A., Yuvaraj, D., Jayanthiladevi, A., Easwaran, B., & ThamaraiSelvi, R. (2021). Smart connected digital products and IoT platform with the digital twin. In *Research advancements in smart technology, optimization, and renewable energy* (pp. 330-350). IGI Global.

Babu, K., Umadevi, P., Patel, N., & Gopalakrishnan, S. (2023, December). Real-Time Monitoring of Glacial Changes Using Artificial Intelligence. In 2023 4th International Conference on Computation, Automation and Knowledge Management (ICCAKM) (pp. 01-06). IEEE.

Balasubhramanyam, A., Ramesh, R., Sudheer, R., & Honnavalli, P. B. (2024). Revolutionizing Healthcare: A Review Unveiling the Transformative Power of Digital Twins. *IEEE Access : Practical Innovations, Open Solutions*, *12*, 69652–69676. DOI: 10.1109/ACCESS.2024.3399744

Balodi, S. D., Yadav, M. U., & Kumar, J. D. Smart Solutions for Sustainable Living: Internet of Things (IoT) Applications in Environmental Monitoring. information network, 23, 24.

Bandaru, V. N. R., Kaligotla, V. S. H. G. S., Varma, U. D. S. P., Prasadaraju, K., & Sugumaran, S. (2024). A enhancing data security solutions for smart energy systems in iot-enabled cloud computing environments through lightweight cryptographic techniques. *IOP Conference Series. Earth and Environmental Science*, *1375*(1), 012003. DOI: 10.1088/1755-1315/1375/1/012003

Banerjee, S., Das, D., Chatterjee, P., & Ghosh, U. (2023, May). Blockchain-enabled digital twin technology for next-generation transportation systems. In *2023 IEEE 26th International Symposium on Real-Time Distributed Computing (ISORC)* (pp. 224-229). IEEE. DOI: 10.1109/ISORC58943.2023.00040

Bao, Y., Tang, Z., Li, H., & Zhang, Y. (2019). Computer vision and deep learning–based data anomaly detection method for structural health monitoring. *Structural Health Monitoring*, *18*(2), 401–421. DOI: 10.1177/1475921718757405

Barbosa, J. M. V., Gómez, Ó. D. C., & García, J. A. G. (2023). A methodological approach for digital twin implementation in waste management: improvement of production and service systems. DOI: 10.20944/preprints202309.0899.v1

Bargavi, M., Saraswat, B., C., Naval, P., & Kulhar, K. S. (2024). Industrial energy efficiency and climate change mitigation in smart cities: A comprehensive review. *E3S Web of Conferences*, DOI: 10.1051/e3sconf/202454008001

Barlow, C., Day, C., Fan, Z., & Fuller, A. (2020). Digital twin: Open research, difficulties, and enabling technology. *IEEE Access : Practical Innovations, Open Solutions*, *8*, 108952–108971. https://doi.org/10.xxxx/xxxx. DOI: 10.1109/ACCESS.2020.2998358

Basani, D. K. R. (2021). Advancing cybersecurity and cyber defense through AI techniques. *Journal of Current Science & Humanities*, *9*(4), 1–16.

Basava, R. G. (2021). AI-powered smart comrade robot for elderly healthcare with integrated emergency rescue system. *World Journal of Advanced Engineering Technology and Sciences*, *02*(01), 122–131. DOI: 10.30574/wjaets.2021.2.1.0085

Bassey, K. E., Opoku-Boateng, J., Antwi, B. O., & Ntiakoh, A. (2024). Economic impact of digital twins on renewable energy investments. Engineering Science &Amp. *Technology Journal*, *5*(7), 2232–2247. DOI: 10.51594/estj.v5i7.1318

Bedaf, S., Huijnen, C., van den Heuvel, R., & de Witte, L. (2017). Robots supporting care for elderly people. In *Robotic Assistive Technologies* (pp. 309–332). CRC Press., DOI: 10.4324/9781315368788-9

Belhadi, A., Kamble, S., Fosso Wamba, S., & Queiroz, M. M. (2022). Building supply-chain resilience: An artificial intelligence-based technique and decision-making framework. *International Journal of Production Research*, *60*(14), 4487–4507. DOI: 10.1080/00207543.2021.1950935

Belsare, T., Deshpande, A., Sharma, N., & De, P. (2023). Application of k-Means Method for Finding Varying Groups of Primary Energy Household Emissions in the Indian States. Optimization Techniques in Engineering: Advances and Applications, 393-408.D. Patterson et al. (2021) Carbon emissions and large neural network training. arXiv preprint arXiv:2104.10350.

Ben-Aboud, Y., & Kobbane, A. (2024). *Towards a Modular Digital Twin Framework for Energy-Optimized IoT Sensor Devices*. 1–7. DOI: 10.1109/WINCOM62286.2024.10655683

Bernal Bernabe, J.. (2023). Privacy-preserving solutions for blockchain: Review and challenges. *IEEE Internet of Things Journal*.

Bhagat, R. K., Saini, R., & Mamodiya, U. (2019). Research paper on Bluetooth-based home automation using Arduino. *Journal of Advancements in Robotics*, *6*(2). ISSN: 2455-1872 (Online).

Bhambri, P., & Khang, A. (2024). Managing and Monitoring Patient's Healthcare Using AI and IoT Technologies. In Driving Smart Medical Diagnosis Through AI-Powered Technologies and Applications (pp. 1-23). IGI Global.

Bhatia, G. (2024). Predictive Urban Air Quality Monitoring for Healthier Cities. *South Eastern European Journal of Public Health*, •••, 1627–1634. DOI: 10.70135/seejph.vi.2166

Bhatia, M. (2024). An AI-enabled secure framework for enhanced elder healthcare. *Engineering Applications of Artificial Intelligence*, *131*, 107831. DOI: 10.1016/j.engappai.2023.107831

Billey, A., & Wuest, T. (2023). Energy digital Twins in smart manufacturing Systems: A literature review. *Manufacturing Letters*, *35*, 1318–1325. DOI: 10.1016/j.mfglet.2023.08.047

Bloss, R. (2011, October). Mobile hospital robots cure numerous logistic needs. *The Industrial Robot*, *38*(6), 567–571. DOI: 10.1108/01439911111179075

Bloss, R. (2014, January). Unmanned vehicles while becoming smaller and smarter are addressing new applications in medical, agriculture, in addition to military and security. *The Industrial Robot*, *41*(1), 82–86. DOI: 10.1108/IR-10-2013-410

Bobba, J. (2023). Cloud-based financial models: Advancing sustainable development in smart cities. *International Journal of HRM and Organizational Behavior*, *11*(3).

Bogner, K., Müller, M., Dahlke, J., Ebersberger, B., & Berger, T. (2024). Agent-Based Modelling and Machine Learning: A New Paradigm for Complexity Economics and Sustainability Transitions? 1. In *Routledge International Handbook of Complexity Economics* (pp. 160-171). Routledge.

Bolpagni, M., Pardini, S., & Gabrielli, S. (2024). Human centered design of AI-powered Digital Therapeutics for stress prevention: Perspectives from multi-stakeholders' workshops about the SHIVA solution. *Internet Interventions : the Application of Information Technology in Mental and Behavioural Health*, *38*, 100775. DOI: 10.1016/j.invent.2024.100775 PMID: 39314669

Booyse, W., Wilke, D. N., & Heyns, S. (2020). Deep digital twins for detection, diagnostics and prognostics. *Mechanical Systems and Signal Processing*, *140*, 106612. https://doi.org/https://doi.org/10.1016/j.ymssp.2019.106612. DOI: 10.1016/j.ymssp.2019.106612

Boppana, V. R. (2023). Data Analytics for Predictive Maintenance in Healthcare Equipment. *EPH-International Journal of Business & Management Science*, *9*(2), 26–36. DOI: 10.53555/eijbms.v10i1.176

Boschert, S., & Rosen, R. (2016). Digital Twin—The Simulation Aspect. In *Mechatronic Futures* (pp. 59-74). Springer Vieweg, Berlin, Heidelberg.

Botín-Sanabria, D. M., Mihăiţă, A., Peimbert-García, R. E., Ramírez-Moreno, M. A., Ramírez-Mendoza, R. A., & Lozoya-Santos, J. J. (2022). Digital twin technology challenges and applications: A comprehensive review. *Remote Sensing (Basel)*, *14*(6), 1335. DOI: 10.3390/rs14061335

Bousdekis, A., Lepenioti, K., Apostolou, D., & Mentzas, G. (2021). A review of data-driven decision-making methods for industry 4.0 maintenance applications. *Electronics (Basel)*, *10*(7), 828. DOI: 10.3390/electronics10070828

Boyes, H., & Watson, T. (2022). Digital twins: An analysis framework and open issues. *Computers in Industry*, *143*, 103763. https://doi.org/https://doi.org/10.1016/j.compind.2022.103763. DOI: 10.1016/j.compind.2022.103763

Bozkaya, E., Canberk, B., & Schmidt, S. (2023, May). Digital twin-empowered resource allocation for 6g-enabled massive iot. In *2023 IEEE International Conference on Communications Workshops (ICC Workshops)* (pp. 727-732). IEEE.

Braun, L., Mock, J., Jung, L., Böttcher, P., & Scholzen, F. (2024). Digital twin collaboration: A common technical structure for the automotive and the building industry. *Proceedings of International Structural Engineering and Construction*, *11*(2). Advance online publication. DOI: 10.14455/10.14455/ISEC.2024.11(2).AAE-04

Brosinsky, C., Karaçelebi, M., & Cremer, J. L. (2023). 4 - Machine learning and digital twins: monitoring and control for dynamic security in power systems. In Barocio Espejo, E., Segundo Sevilla, F. R., & Korba, P. (Eds.), *Monitoring and Control of Electrical Power Systems Using Machine Learning Techniques* (pp. 79–106). Elsevier., https://doi.org/https://doi.org/10.1016/B978-0-32-399904-5.00010-7 DOI: 10.1016/B978-0-32-399904-5.00010-7

Brown, D. N., & Schwartz, H. L. (2023). Regulating Digital Twins: Legal Considerations in the Digital Future. *Journal of Cyber Law and Policy*, *15*(1), 56–68.

Burinskienė, A., & Medineckienė, M. (2022). Digitalisation as the indicator of the evidence of sustainability in the european union. *Sustainability (Basel)*, *14*(14), 8371. DOI: 10.3390/su14148371

Burrell, D. N. (2023). Dynamic Evaluation Approaches to Telehealth Technologies and Artificial Intelligence (AI) Telemedicine Applications in Healthcare and Biotechnology Organizations. *Merits*, *3*(4), 700–721. DOI: 10.3390/merits3040042

Busu, M., & Nedelcu, A. C. (2021). Analyzing the renewable energy and CO2 emission levels nexus at an EU level: A panel data regression approach. *Processes (Basel, Switzerland)*, *9*(1), 130.

Butean, A., Enriquez, J., Matei, A., Rovira, A., Barbero, R., & Trevisan, S. (2024). A digital twin concept for optimizing the use of high-temperature heat pumps to reduce waste in industrial renewable energy systems. *Procedia Computer Science*, *237*, 123–128. DOI: 10.1016/j.procs.2024.05.087

Cabanillas-Carbonell, M., Pérez-Martínez, J., & Yáñez, J. A. (2023, February). 5G Technology in the digital transformation of healthcare, a systematic review. *Sustainability*, *15*(4), 3178. DOI: 10.3390/su15043178

Cali, Ü., Dimd, B. D., Hajialigol, P., Moazami, A., Gourisetti, S. N. G., Lobaccaro, G., & Aghaei, M. (2023). Digital twins: shaping the future of energy systems and smart cities through cybersecurity, efficiency, and sustainability. *2023 International Conference on Future Energy Solutions (FES)*. DOI: 10.1109/FES57669.2023.10182868

Cao, Z. (2024). Challenges and opportunities of the digital economy for sustainable development. Advances in Economics. *Management and Political Sciences*, *76*(1), 1–7. DOI: 10.54254/2754-1169/76/20241869

Captain Ali Kangaranifarahani, D. D. C. M. Y. (2023). Applications of Artificial Intelligence in the Aviation Industry and Air Accidents. *Mathematical Statistician and Engineering Applications, 72*(2), 178 – 192. https://www.philstat.org/index.php/MSEA/article/view/2832

Carlucho, I., de Paula, M., & Acosta, G. G. (2019, December). Double Q-PID algorithm for mobile robot control. *Expert Systems with Applications*, *137*, 292–307. DOI: 10.1016/j.eswa.2019.06.066

Cavalieri, S., & Gambadoro, S. (2023). Proposal of mapping digital twins definition language to open platform communications unified architecture. *Sensors (Basel)*, *23*(4), 2349. DOI: 10.3390/s23042349 PMID: 36850947

Chadha, A. S., Shinde, Y., Sharma, N., & De, P. K. (2022, January). Predicting CO2 Emissions by Vehicles Using Machine Learning. In International Conference on Data Management, Analytics & Innovation (pp. 197-207). Singapore: Springer Nature Singapore.

Chalal, L., Saadane, A., & Rachid, A. (2023). Unified environment for real time control of hybrid energy systems using digital twin and iot approach. *Sensors (Basel)*, *23*(12), 5646. DOI: 10.3390/s23125646 PMID: 37420813

Chao, C. (2023). Development of smart iot based biomedical heart rate oximeters for driving safety. *Academic Journal of Engineering and Technology Science*, *6*(12). Advance online publication. DOI: 10.25236/AJETS.2023.061201

Chen, B.-Q., Videiro, P. M., & Guedes Soares, C. (2022). Opportunities and Challenges to Develop Digital Twins for Subsea Pipelines. *Journal of Marine Science and Engineering*, *10*(6), 739. DOI: 10.3390/jmse10060739

Chen, C. P., & Zhang, C. Y. (2024). Data-intensive applications, challenges, techniques and technologies: A survey on Big Data. *Information Sciences*, *275*, 314–347.

Chen, D., Chen, K., Li, Z., Chu, T., Yao, R., Qiu, F., & Lin, K. (2021). Powernet: Multi-agent deep reinforcement learning for scalable powergrid control. *IEEE Transactions on Power Systems*, *37*(2), 1007–1017. DOI: 10.1109/TPWRS.2021.3100898

Chen, J., Yi, C., Okegbile, S. D., Cai, J., & Shen, X. (2023). Networking architecture and key supporting technologies for human digital twin in personalized healthcare: A comprehensive survey. *IEEE Communications Surveys and Tutorials*, *26*(1), 706–746. DOI: 10.1109/COMST.2023.3308717

Chen, M.. (2020). Digital twin for healthcare systems. *Digital Twin*, *1*, 3.

Chen, S. (2024). Advancing sustainability in mechanical engineering: Integration of green energy and intelligent manufacturing. *Applied and Computational Engineering*, *66*(1), 150–155. DOI: 10.54254/2755-2721/66/20240937

Chen, S., Sánchez, J. P. G., Bekar, E. T., Bokrantz, J., Skoogh, A., & Lopes, P. V. (2023). Understanding stakeholder requirements for digital twins in manufacturing maintenance. *2023 Winter Simulation Conference (WSC)*. DOI: 10.1109/WSC60868.2023.10408657

Chen, Z., Zou, J., & Wang, W. (2022). Digital twin oriented multi-objective flexible job shop scheduling model and its hybrid particle swarm optimization. *Proceedings of the Institution of Mechanical Engineers. Part B, Journal of Engineering Manufacture*, *237*(8), 1269–1282. DOI: 10.1177/09544054221121921

Chih-Lin, I. (2021). AI as an Essential Element of a Green 6G. *IEEE Transactions on Green Communications and Networking*, *5*(1), 1–3. DOI: 10.1109/TGCN.2021.3057247

Cho, Y., & Noh, S. D. (2024). Design and Implementation of Digital Twin Factory Synchronized in Real-Time Using MQTT. *Machines (Basel)*, *12*(11), 759.

Christ, L., Milloch, E., Boshoff, M., Hypki, A., & Kuhlenkötter, B. (2023). Implementation of digital twin and real production system to address actual and future challenges in assembly technology. *Automation, 4*(4), 345–358. DOI: 10.3390/automation4040020

Claudia, B. (2024). Monitoring and Predicting Air Quality with IoT Devices. *Processes (Basel, Switzerland), 12*(9), 1961–1961. DOI: 10.3390/pr12091961

Clifton, P., Robinson, A., Lacava, F., Johari, P., Cuomo, F., & Melodia, T. (2024). TwiNet: Connecting real world networks to their digital twins through a live bidirectional link. *arXiv.* https://doi.org//arxiv.2411.03503DOI: 10.48550

Coorey, G., Figtree, G. A., Fletcher, D. F., Snelson, V. J., Vernon, S. T., Winlaw, D. S., Grieve, S. M., McEwan, A., Yang, J. Y. H., Qian, P., O'Brien, K., Orchard, J., Kim, J., Patel, S., & Redfern, J. (2022). The health digital twin to tackle cardiovascular disease—A review of an emerging interdisciplinary field. *NPJ Digital Medicine, 5*(1), 126. Advance online publication. DOI: 10.1038/s41746-022-00640-7 PMID: 36028526

Corallo, A., Del Vecchio, V., Lezzi, M., & Morciano, P. (2021). Shop Floor Digital Twin in Smart Manufacturing: A Systematic Literature Review. *Sustainability (Basel), 2021*(13), 12987. DOI: 10.3390/su132312987

Corrado, C., DeLong, S. M., Holt, E., Hua, E. Y., & Tolk, A. (2022). *Combining green metrics and digital twins for sustainability planning and governance of smart buildings and cities.* Prime Archives in Sustainability., DOI: 10.37247/PASUS3ED.3.23.19

Crespo-Aguado, M., Lozano, R., Hernandez-Gobertti, F., Molner, N., & Gómez-Barquero, D. (2024). Flexible hyper-distributed IoT–edge–cloud platform for real-time digital twin applications on 6G-intended testbeds for logistics and industry. *Future Internet.* Advance online publication. DOI: 10.3390/fi16110431

Cruz-Manzo, S., Panov, V., & Bingham, C. (2024). Compressor fouling diagnostics and prognostics in a gas turbine. International Journal of Gas Turbine. *Propulsion and Power Systems, 15*(1), 9–14. DOI: 10.38036/jgpp.15.1_9

Davila-Gonzalez, S., & Martin, S. (2024). Human digital twin in industry 5.0: A holistic approach to worker safety and well-being through advanced AI and emotional analytics. *Sensors (Basel), 24*(2), 655. DOI: 10.3390/s24020655 PMID: 38276347

de Ahumada Servant, P., Martín-Martín, D., & Romero, I. (2024). Digital Transformation of Oral Health Care: Measuring the Digitalization of Dental Clinics. *Social Indicators Research,* •••, 1–23.

de Kerckhove, D. (2022). The personal digital twin, ethical considerations. Journal of Digital Ethics.

Deepak, G., Parthiban, M., Nath, S. S., Alfurhood, B. S., Mouleswararao, B., & Kishore, V. R. (2024). Ai-enhanced thermal modeling for integrated process-product-system optimization in zero-defect manufacturing chains. *Thermal Science and Engineering Progress, 55*, 102945. DOI: 10.1016/j.tsep.2024.102945

Deeraj, C., Subburaj, T., & Neelesh, B. U. (2024). IOT based Waste Management System. International Journal of Advanced Research in Science. *Tongxin Jishu, 107-111*, 107–111. Advance online publication. DOI: 10.48175/IJARSCT-19020

Deevi, D. P. (2022). Improving patient data security and privacy in Mobile health care: A structure employing WBANs, multi-biometric key creation, and dynamic metadata rebuilding. *International Journal of Engineering Research and Science & Technology*, *18*(4), 92–105.

Demirel, H. O., Irshad, L., Ahmed, S., & Tumer, I. Y. (2021, March). Digital Twin-Driven Human-Centered design frameworks for meeting sustainability objectives. *Journal of Computing and Information Science in Engineering*, *21*(3), 031012. Advance online publication. DOI: 10.1115/1.4050684

Desai, C. K., Jadhav, T., Nirmal, S., Dutt, I., Chavan, S. A., Thakur, A., & Gore, S.Yogita K. Desai. (2024). Diagnosis of medical images using convolutional neural networks. *Journal of Electrical Systems*, *20*(6s), 2371–2376. DOI: 10.52783/jes.3220

Deshpande, A., Belsare, T., Sharma, N., & De, P. (2022, April). Univariate Time Series Forecasting of Indian Agriculture Emissions. In *International Conference on Advances in Computing and Data Sciences* (pp. 346-358). Cham: Springer International Publishing. DOI: 10.1007/978-3-031-12641-3_28

Devi, D. P. (2020). Real-time malware detection via adaptive gradient support vector regression combined with LSTM and Hidden Markov Models. *Journal of Science and Technology*, *5*(4).

Dewan, B., Chaudhary, S., & Yadav, M. (2021). A charge plasma based label free biomolecule detector using SiGe-heterojunction double gate Tunnel FET. *Silicon*, 1-10.

Dewan, B., Chaudhary, S., & Yadav, M. (2023). A label-free dielectric-modulated biosensor using SiGe-heterojunction dual cavity dual metal electrically doped TFET. *Engineering Research Express*, *5*(3), 035002. DOI: 10.1088/2631-8695/acdec7

Dhasarathan, C., & Gnanasekaran, S. (2024). Digital Twin for Sustainable Farming: Developing User-Friendly Interfaces for Informed DecisionMaking and Increased Profitability. In The Future of Agriculture: IoT, AI and Blockchain Technology for Sustainable Farming (pp. 1-20). Bentham Science Publishers.

Dhopte, A., & Bagde, H. (2023). Smart smile: Revolutionizing dentistry with artificial intelligence. *Cureus*, *15*(6). Advance online publication. DOI: 10.7759/cureus.41227 PMID: 37529520

Diaz-Ramos, R. E., Noriega, I., Trejo, L. A., Stroulia, E., & Cao, B. (2023). Using wearable devices and speech data for personalized machine learning in early detection of mental disorders: Protocol for a participatory research study. *JMIR Research Protocols*, *12*(1), e48210. DOI: 10.2196/48210 PMID: 37955959

Ding, W.. (2021). Decentralized federated learning via blockchain for healthcare IoT systems. *IEEE Internet of Things Journal*, *8*(14), 11789–11801.

Domínguez, L. G. I. (2024, August). Gemelos Digitales en la Industria 5.0 – una Revisión Sistemática de Literatura. *European Public & Social Innovation Review*, *9*, 1–21. DOI: 10.31637/epsir-2024-641

Donmezer, S., Demircioglu, P., Bogrekci, I., Bas, G., & Durakbasa, M. N. (2023). Revolutionizing the Garment Industry 5.0: Embracing Closed-Loop Design, E-Libraries, and Digital Twins. *Sustainability (Basel)*, *15*(22), 15839. DOI: 10.3390/su152215839

Donoghue, I., Hannola, L., Papinniemi, J., & Mikkola, A. (2018). The Benefits and Impact of Digital Twins in Product Development Phase of PLM. Product Lifecycle Management to Support Industry 4.0, Cham.

Dorage, S. V. (2024). Cybersecurity in industrial management within the internet of things. *Interantional Journal of Scientific Research in Engineering and Management, 08*(008), 1–16. DOI: 10.55041/IJSREM37081

dos Santos, C. H., Campos, A. T., Montevechi, J. A. B., de Carvalho Miranda, R., do Amaral, J. V. S., & de Queiroz, J. A. (2023). Simulation-based digital twins monitoring: An approach focused on models' accreditation. *International Journal of Advanced Manufacturing Technology, 124*(7), 2423–2435. DOI: 10.1007/s00170-022-10674-6

Drummond, D., & Coulet, A. (2022). Technical, ethical, legal, and societal challenges with digital twin systems for the management of chronic diseases in children and young people. *Journal of Medical Internet Research, 24*(10), e39698. DOI: 10.2196/39698 PMID: 36315239

Drummond, D., & Gonsard, A. (2024). Definitions and characteristics of patient digital twins being developed for clinical use: Scoping review. *Journal of Medical Internet Research, 26*, e58504. DOI: 10.2196/58504 PMID: 39536311

Du, J., & Luo, T. (2023). Digital Twin Graph: Automated Domain-Agnostic Construction, Fusion, and Simulation of IoT-Enabled World. *arXiv preprint arXiv:2304.10018.*

El Bazi, N., Mabrouki, M., Laayati, O., Ouhabi, N., El Hadraoui, H., Hammouch, F. E., & Chebak, A. (2023). Generic multi-layered digital-twin-framework-enabled asset lifecycle management for the sustainable mining industry. *Sustainability (Basel), 15*(4), 3470. DOI: 10.3390/su15043470

Elahi, B., & Tokaldany, S. A. (2021). Application of Internet of Things-aided simulation and digital twin technology in smart manufacturing. In *Advances in Mathematics for Industry 4.0* (pp. 335–359). Academic Press.

Elayan, H., Aloqaily, M., & Guizani, M. (2021). Digital twin for intelligent context-aware IoT healthcare systems. *IEEE Internet of Things Journal, 8*(23), 16749–16757. DOI: 10.1109/JIOT.2021.3051158

Elendu, C., Aguocha, C. M., Okeke, C. V., Okoro, C. B., & Peterson, J. C. (2023). HIV-related neurocognitive disorders: Diagnosis, treatment, and mental health implications. *Revista de Medicina (São Paulo), 102*(43), e35652. PMID: 37904369

Elfarri, E. M., Rasheed, A., & San, O. (2023). Artificial intelligence-driven digital twin of a modern house demonstrated in virtual reality. *IEEE Access : Practical Innovations, Open Solutions, 11*, 35035–35058. DOI: 10.1109/ACCESS.2023.3265191

El-Gohary, M., El-Abed, R., & Omar, O. (2023). Prediction of an efficient energy-consumption model for existing residential buildings in lebanon using an artificial neural network as a digital twin in the era of climate change. *Buildings (Basel, Switzerland), 13*(12), 3074. DOI: 10.3390/buildings13123074

Elhenawy, I., AL-baker, S. F., & Mohamed, M. (2023). Intelligent healthcare: Evaluation potential implications of metaverse in healthcare based on mathematical decision-making framework. Neutrosophic systems with applications, 12, 9-21.

El-Sayed, A. F. M., Ahmed, B., & Sallam, K. M. (2024). *Exploring the application of digital twin technology in the energy sector using MEREC and MAIRCA methods*. Neutrosophic Systems with Applications., DOI: 10.61356/j.nswa.2024.19326

Elyasi, N., Bellini, A., & Klungseth, N. J. (2023). Digital transformation in facility management: An analysis of the challenges and benefits of implementing digital twins in the use phase of a building. *IOP Conference Series. Earth and Environmental Science*, *1176*(1), 012001. DOI: 10.1088/1755-1315/1176/1/012001

Emmert-Streib, F. (2019). Defining digital twins: A data science-based unification. *Journal of Industrial Information Integration*.

Emmert-Streib, F. (2021). Digital twins in healthcare: Opportunities and challenges. *Health Informatics Journal*.

Emran, A. (2024). Artificial intelligence in environmental monitoring: In-depth analysis. *Discover Artificial Intelligence*, *4*(1), 84. Advance online publication. DOI: 10.1007/s44163-024-00198-1

Eneyew, D. D., Capretz, M. A. M., & Bitsuamlak, G. T. (2022). Toward Smart-Building Digital Twins: BIM and IoT Data Integration. *IEEE Access : Practical Innovations, Open Solutions*, *10*, 130487–130506. DOI: 10.1109/ACCESS.2022.3229370

Esteban, M., Diez, J. J., López, J. S., & Negro, V. (2011). Why offshore wind energy. *Renewable Energy*, *36*(2), 444–450. DOI: 10.1016/j.renene.2010.07.009

Faaique, M. (2024). Overview of Big Data Analytics in Modern Astronomy. *International Journal of Mathematics, Statistics, and Computer Science*, *2*, 96–113. DOI: 10.59543/ijmscs.v2i.8561

Falekas, G., & Karlis, A. (2021). Digital twin in electrical machine control and predictive maintenance: State-of-the-art and future prospects. *Energies*, *14*(18), 5933. DOI: 10.3390/en14185933

Fang, X. (2023). Energy management system technology in smart grid. Highlights in Science. *Engineering and Technology*, *76*, 328–336. DOI: 10.54097/x5ch4d78

Farhi, E., Goldstone, J., & Gutmann, S. (2019). A Quantum Approximate Optimization Algorithm. *arXiv preprint arXiv.1411.4028*.

Faye, S., Camelo, M., Sottet, J. S., Sommer, C., Franke, M., Baudouin, J., & Turcanu, I. (2024, June). Integrating network digital twinning into future ai-based 6g systems: The 6g-twin vision. In *2024 Joint European Conference on Networks and Communications & 6G Summit (EuCNC/6G Summit)* (pp. 883-888). IEEE.

Feriani, A., & Hossain, E. (2021). Single and multi-agent deep reinforcement learning for AI-enabled wireless networks: A tutorial. *IEEE Communications Surveys and Tutorials*, *23*(2), 1226–1252. DOI: 10.1109/COMST.2021.3063822

Ferrero, V., Alqseer, N., Reslan, M., & Morris, K. C. (2023). Adapting digital twin frameworks toward lean manufacturing for the circular economy. DOI: 10.1115/DETC2023-116759

Firouzi, F., Farahani, B., Daneshmand, M., Grise, K., Song, J., Saracco, R., Wang, L. L., Lo, K., Angelov, P., Soares, E., Loh, P.-S., Talebpour, Z., Moradi, R., Goodarzi, M., Ashraf, H., Talebpour, M., Talebpour, A., Romeo, L., Das, R., & Luo, A. (2021). Harnessing the power of smart and connected health to tackle COVID-19: IoT, AI, robotics, and blockchain for a better world. *IEEE Internet of Things Journal*, *8*(16), 12826–12846. DOI: 10.1109/JIOT.2021.3073904 PMID: 35782886

Florea, A., Lobov, A., & Lanz, M. (2020). Emotions-aware Digital Twins For Manufacturing. *Procedia Manufacturing*, *51*, 605–612. https://doi.org/https://doi.org/10.1016/j.promfg.2020.10.085. DOI: 10.1016/j.promfg.2020.10.085

Florescu, A. (2024). Digital twin for flexible manufacturing systems and optimization through simulation: A case study. *Machines (Basel)*, *12*(11), 785.

Folorunso, A., Mohammed, V., Wada, I., & Samuel, B. J. (2024). The impact of iso security standards on enhancing cybersecurity posture in organizations. *World Journal of Advanced Research and Reviews*, *24*(1), 2582–2595. DOI: 10.30574/wjarr.2024.24.1.3169

Fontes, C., & Dubey, R. K. (2024). Urban futures: possibilities and challenges for ethical virtual cities. The Elgar Companion to Applied AI Ethics, 290-312.

Fontes, C., & Carpentras, D. (2023). *Human digital twins unlocking Society 5.0? Approaches, emerging risks and disruptions*. Urban Technology Journal.

Frank, M., Drikakis, D., & Charissis, V. (2020). Machine-learning methods for computational science and engineering. *Computation (Basel, Switzerland)*, *8*(1), 15. DOI: 10.3390/computation8010015

Fu, H., Zhao, T., Chen, Y., Yao, Y., & Leng, J. (2022). Framework and operation of digital twin smart freeway. *IET Intelligent Transport Systems*, *17*(3), 620–633. DOI: 10.1049/itr2.12288

Galera-Zarco, C. (2022). Unleashing the potential of digital twin in offering green services. *IET Conference Proceedings*, 2022(8), 158-161. DOI: 10.1049/icp.2022.2059

Ganesan, T. (2020). Machine learning-driven AI for financial fraud detection in IoT environments. *International Journal of HRM and Organizational Behavior, 8*(4). ISSN: 2454-5015.

Ganesan, T. (2022). Securing IoT business models: Quantitative identification of key nodes in elderly healthcare applications. *International Journal of Management Research & Review*, *12*(3), 78–94.

Ganesh, A. D., & Kalpana, P. (2022). Future of artificial intelligence and its influence on supply chain risk management–A systematic review. *Computers & Industrial Engineering*, *169*, 108206. DOI: 10.1016/j.cie.2022.108206

Gao, X., He, P., Zhou, Y., & Qin, X. (2024). Artificial Intelligence Applications in Smart Healthcare: A Survey. *Future Internet*, *16*(9), 308. DOI: 10.3390/fi16090308

Gao, Y., Chang, D., Chen, C. H., & Sha, M. (2024). A digital twin-based decision support approach for AGV scheduling. *Engineering Applications of Artificial Intelligence*, *130*, 107687. DOI: 10.1016/j.engappai.2023.107687

Gartner. (2020). Forecast: The Internet of Things, Worldwide, 2018-2030. Retrieved from https://www.gartner.com/en/newsroom/press-releases

Gattupalli, K. (2020). Optimizing 3D printing materials for medical applications using AI, computational tools, and directed energy deposition. *International Journal of Modern Electronics and Communication Engineering*, *8*(3). Advance online publication. DOI: 10.5281/zenodo.13994678

Ghatti, S., Yurish, L. A., Shen, H., Rheuban, K., Enfield, K. B., Facteau, N. R., & Dowdell, K. (2023). Digital Twins in Healthcare: A Survey of Current Methods. *Archives of Clinical and Biomedical Research*, *7*(3), 365–381. DOI: 10.26502/acbr.50170352

Ghobadpour, A., Cardenas, A., Monsalve, G., & Mousazadeh, H. (2023, January). Optimal design of energy sources for a photovoltaic/fuel cell extended-range agricultural mobile robot. *Robotics (Basel, Switzerland)*, *12*(1), 13. DOI: 10.3390/robotics12010013

Gholizadeh, H., Pasha, A., Hejazi, T. H., & Jahani, H. (2024). Reconfigurable and Resilient Closed-Loop Supply Chain Design: A Simulation–Optimization Approach. *Global Journal of Flexible Systems Management*, 1-29.

Ghosh, A., Pandhare, V., Bhattacharjee, S., Agrawal, D., & Lad, B. K. (2024). Expert-in-Loop Digital Twin-based Decision Support System for Early Detection of Ventilator-Induced Lung Injury. *Procedia Computer Science*, *251*, 651–659. DOI: 10.1016/j.procs.2024.11.164

Gill, S. S., Xu, M., Ottaviani, C., Patros, P., Bahsoon, R., Shaghaghi, A., Golec, M., Stankovski, V., Wu, H., Abraham, A., Singh, M., Mehta, H., Ghosh, S. K., Baker, T., Parlikad, A. K., Lutfiyya, H., Kanhere, S. S., Sakellariou, R., Dustdar, S., & Uhlig, S. (2022). AI for next generation computing: Emerging trends and future directions. *Internet of Things : Engineering Cyber Physical Human Systems*, *19*, 100514. DOI: 10.1016/j.iot.2022.100514

Goethals, S.. (2022). *The impact of cloaking digital footprints on user privacy and personalization.* Data Science Review.

Goodfellow, I.. (2014). Generative adversarial nets. *Advances in Neural Information Processing Systems*, , 2672–2680.

Gore, S., Nagalakshmi, Y., Knowles, P., Gupta, K. G., Jagtap, N. S., & Sali, R. P. (2023). Improvised ensemble model for fast prediction of DoS/DDoS attacks in various networks. In *2023 1st International Conference on Cognitive Computing and Engineering Education (ICCCEE)* (pp. 1–5). IEEE. DOI: 10.1109/ICCCEE55951.2023.10424447

Gouiza, N., Jebari, H., & Reklaoui, K. (2024). Integration Of Iot-Enabled Technologies And Artificial Intelligence In Diverse Domains: Recent Advancements And Future Trends. *Journal of Theoretical and Applied Information Technology*, *102*(5).

Grandhi, S. H. (2022). Enhancing children's health monitoring: Adaptive wavelet transform in wearable sensor IoT integration. Journal of Current Science & Humanities, 10(4), 15-27. https://jcsonline.2022.v10.i04.pp15-27

Grieves, M., & Vickers, J. (2017). Digital twin: Mitigating unpredictable, undesirable emergent behavior in complex systems. In *Transdisciplinary Perspectives on Complex Systems: New Findings and Approaches* (pp. 85-113). Springer.

Grigoriadou, S., Radoglou-Grammatikis, P., Sarigiannidis, P., Makris, I., Λάγκας, Θ., Argyriou, V., & Fountoukidis, E. (2023). Hunting iot cyberattacks with ai - powered intrusion detection. *2023 IEEE International Conference on Cyber Security and Resilience (CSR)*, 142-147. DOI: 10.1109/CSR57506.2023.10224981

Gudivaka, B. R. (2021). Designing AI-assisted music teaching with big data analysis. *Journal of Current Science & Humanities*, *9*(4), 1–14.

Gudivaka, B. R. (2024). Smart Comrade Robot for Elderly: Leveraging IBM Watson Health and Google Cloud AI for Advanced Health and Emergency Systems. *International Journal of Engineering Research and Science & Technology*, *20*(3), 334–352.

Gündoğdu, F. K., Duleba, S., Moslem, S., & Aydın, S. (2021). Evaluating public transport service quality using picture fuzzy analytic hierarchy process and linear assignment model. *Applied Soft Computing*, *100*, 106920. DOI: 10.1016/j.asoc.2020.106920

Gupta, D., Kayode, O., Bhatt, S., Gupta, M., & Tosun, A. S. (2021, December). Hierarchical federated learning based anomaly detection using digital twins for smart healthcare. In *2021 IEEE 7th international conference on collaboration and internet computing (CIC)* (pp. 16-25). IEEE. DOI: 10.1109/CIC52973.2021.00013

Gupta, H., Bhardwaj, D., Agrawal, H., Tikkiwal, V. A., & Kumar, A. (2019, February). An IoT based air pollution monitoring system for smart cities. In *2019 IEEE International Conference on Sustainable Energy Technologies and Systems (ICSETS)* (pp. 173-177). IEEE. DOI: 10.1109/ICSETS.2019.8744949

Gupta, P., Tanwar, S., Tyagi, S., & Kumar, N. (2022). The Evolution of IoT. From Cloud to Fog to Edge Computing. *IEEE Communications Surveys and Tutorials*, *24*(2), 1234–1265.

Haidar, Z. S. (2023). Digital dentistry: past, present, and future. Digital Medicine and Healthcare Technology, (16).

Hakimi, O., Liu, H., Abudayyeh, O., Houshyar, A., Almatared, M., & Alhawiti, A. (2023). Data fusion for smart civil infrastructure management: A conceptual digital twin framework. *Buildings (Basel, Switzerland)*, *13*(11), 2725. DOI: 10.3390/buildings13112725

Haleem, A., Javaid, M., Pratap Singh, R., & Suman, R. (2022). Medical 4.0 technologies for healthcare: Features, capabilities, and applications. *Internet of Things and Cyber-Physical Systems*, *2*, 12–30. DOI: 10.1016/j.iotcps.2022.04.001

Han, B., Asif Habibi, M., Kuruvatti, N., Partani, S., Fellan, A., & Schotten, H. D. (2024). Potentials of the digital twin in 6G communication systems.

Han, J., Ge, W., & Chou, Y. (2024). Leveraging digital infrastructure for sustainable grain production: Evidence from china. *Frontiers in Sustainable Food Systems*, *8*, 1440321. Advance online publication. DOI: 10.3389/fsufs.2024.1440321

Hegazy Abdelghany Mohamed Ammar, M. (2021). Advanced digital twins for conditions monitoring, examinations, diagnosis and predictive remaining lifecycles based Artificial Intelligence (Doctoral dissertation, Brunel University London).

Helbing, D., & Sánchez-Vaquerizo, J. A. (2022). Digital twins: Potentials, limitations, and ethical issues. *Nature Computational Science*, *2*(1), 10–12. PMID: 38177712

Helsen, L. (2021). Tackling Climate Change with Machine Learning. In Conference on Neural Information Processing System (NeurIPS)-panelist workshop, Location: online.

Hemdan, E. E.-D., El-Shafai, W., & Sayed, A. (2023). Integrating Digital Twins with IoT-Based Blockchain: Concept, Architecture, Challenges, and Future Scope. *Wireless Personal Communications*, *131*(3), 2193–2216. DOI: 10.1007/s11277-023-10538-6 PMID: 37360142

Hengelbrock, A., Helgers, H., Schmidt, A., Vetter, F. L., Juckers, A., Rosengarten, J. F., Stitz, J., & Strube, J. (2022). Digital twin for hiv-gag vlp production in hek293 cells. *Processes (Basel, Switzerland)*, *10*(5), 866. DOI: 10.3390/pr10050866

Hevesli, M., Seid, A. M., Erbad, A., & Abdallah, M. (2024). Task Offloading Optimization in Digital Twin Assisted MEC-Enabled Air-Ground IIoT 6 G Networks. *IEEE Transactions on Vehicular Technology*.

Hilbert, M. (2025). Big data for development: A review of promises and challenges. *Development Policy Review*, *34*(1), 135–174. DOI: 10.1111/dpr.12142

Holopainen, M., Saunila, M., Rantala, T., & Ukko, J. (2024). Digital twins' implications for innovation. *Technology Analysis and Strategic Management*, *36*(8), 1779–1791. DOI: 10.1080/09537325.2022.2115881

Holzinger, A., Fister, I., Fister, I., Kaul, H.-P., & Asseng, S. (2024). Human-Centered AI in Smart Farming: Toward Agriculture 5.0. *IEEE Access : Practical Innovations, Open Solutions*, *12*, 62199–62214. DOI: 10.1109/ACCESS.2024.3395532

Homayouni, S. M., Pinho de Sousa, J., & Moreira Marques, C. (2024). Unlocking the potential of digital twins to achieve sustainability in seaports: the state of practice and future outlook. *WMU Journal of Maritime Affairs*, 1-40.

Hong, C. S., Han, Z., Niyato, D., Saad, W., & Khan, L. U. (2022). Future directions, architectural trends, and the vision of digital-twin-enabled 6G. *IEEE Communications Magazine*, *60*(1), 74–80. DOI: 10.1109/MCOM.001.21143

Hosamo, H. H., Svennevig, P. R., Svidt, K., Han, D., & Nielsen, H. K. (2022). A Digital Twin predictive maintenance framework of air handling units based on automatic fault detection and diagnostics. *Energy and Building*, *261*, 111988. DOI: 10.1016/j.enbuild.2022.111988

Hoßbach, M., Nadja, S., & Enders, R. (2019). A study of the literature on the dimensions of digital twin applications.

Hovorushchenko, T., Bachuk, V., Hnatchuk, Y., Zasornova, I., & Bouhissi, H. E. (2024). Overview of the methods and tools for environmental components monitoring.

Huang, S., Wang, G., Lei, D., & Yan, Y. (2022). Toward digital validation for rapid product development based on digital twin: A framework. *International Journal of Advanced Manufacturing Technology*, *119*(3), 2509–2523. DOI: 10.1007/s00170-021-08475-4

Huang, Z., Shen, Y., Li, J., Fey, M., & Brecher, C. (2021). A survey on AI-driven digital twins in industry 4.0: Smart manufacturing and advanced robotics. *Sensors (Basel)*, *21*(19), 6340. DOI: 10.3390/s21196340 PMID: 34640660

Husung, S., Koch, Y., Welzbacher, P., Kraus, B., Roehnert, F., Faheem, F., & Kirchner, E. (2023). Systemic conception of the data acquisition of digital twin solutions for use case-oriented development and its application to a gearbox. *Systems*, *11*(5), 227. DOI: 10.3390/systems11050227

Hu, W., Zhang, T., Deng, X., Liu, Z., & Tan, J. (2021). Digital twin: A state-of-the-art review of its enabling technologies, applications and challenges. *Journal of Intelligent Manufacturing and Special Equipment*, *2*(1), 1–34. DOI: 10.1108/JIMSE-12-2020-010

Hwang, K., Park, S., & Lee, J. (2024). Room-Temperature Quantum Processors for IoT Applications. *Journal of Quantum Hardware*, *18*(1), 45–58.

Iaboni, A., Spasojevic, S., Newman, K., Schindel Martin, L., Wang, A., Ye, B., Mihailidis, A., & Khan, S. S. (2022). Wearable multimodal sensors for the detection of behavioral and psychological symptoms of dementia using personalized machine learning models. *Alzheimer's & Dementia: Diagnosis, Assessment & Disease Monitoring*, *14*(1), e12305. DOI: 10.1002/dad2.12305 PMID: 35496371

Ijaiya, H. (2023). Balancing data privacy and technology advancements: Navigating ethical challenges and shaping policy solutions. Journal of Technology Law & Policy.

Iliuţă, M.-E., Moisescu, M.-A., Pop, E., Ionita, A.-D., Caramihai, S.-I., & Mitulescu, T.-C. (2024). Digital Twin—A Review of the Evolution from Concept to Technology and Its Analytical Perspectives on Applications in Various Fields. *Applied Sciences (Basel, Switzerland)*, *14*(13), 5454. DOI: 10.3390/app14135454

International Data Corporation (IDC). (2022). The Growth of IoT Data.

Iqbal, J. D., Krauthammer, M., & Biller-Andorno, N. (2022). The use and ethics of digital twins in medicine. *The Journal of Law, Medicine & Ethics*, *50*(3), 583–596. DOI: 10.1017/jme.2022.97 PMID: 36398633

Islam, M., Jobaida, N., Hossain, M. S., Uddin, M. R., & Hasan, M. (2024, June). IoT-Based Smart Energy Monitoring and Energy Demand Response System. In 2024 IEEE 3rd International Conference on Electrical Power and Energy Systems (ICEPES) (pp. 1-5). IEEE.

Jagatheesaperumal, S. K., Rahouti, M., Ahmad, K., Al-Fuqaha, A., & Guizani, M. (2021). The duo of artificial intelligence and big data for industry 4.0: Applications, techniques, challenges, and future research directions. *IEEE Internet of Things Journal*, *9*(15), 12861–12885. DOI: 10.1109/JIOT.2021.3139827

Jain, B., & Sharma, S. Examining Environmental, Social, and Economic Sustainability in Diverse AI/ML Models: A Comparative Study.

Jain, B., Sharma, R., & Kaushik, N. (2022). An Analysis Of Green Artificial Intelligence As A Major Receiver Improvement Finalized Red Ai & Execution Of The Environmental Footprint Toward Increasing Green Artificial Intelligence. *NeuroQuantology : An Interdisciplinary Journal of Neuroscience and Quantum Physics*, *20*(17), 1733.

Jaja, K. (2024). Revitalizing IoT-based air quality monitoring system for major cities in Indonesia. *Sinergi*, *28*(3), 605–605. DOI: 10.22441/sinergi.2024.3.016

Jambhale, K., Rieland, B., Mahajan, S., Narsay, P., Banerjee, N., Dutt, A., & Vinjamuri, R. (2022, July). Selection of optimal physiological features for accurate detection of stress. In *2022 44th Annual International Conference of the IEEE Engineering in Medicine & Biology Society (EMBC)* (pp. 2514-2517). IEEE. DOI: 10.1109/EMBC48229.2022.9871067

Jambhale, K., Mahajan, S., Rieland, B., Banerjee, N., Dutt, A., Kadiyala, S. P., & Vinjamuri, R. (2022). Identifying biomarkers for accurate detection of stress. *Sensors (Basel)*, *22*(22), 8703. DOI: 10.3390/s22228703 PMID: 36433299

Jameil, A. K., & Al-Raweshidy, H. (2024). Hybrid Cloud-Edge AI Framework for Real-Time Predictive Analytics in Digital Twin Healthcare Systems.

Jameil, A. K., & Al-Raweshidy, H. (2024). Ai-enabled healthcare and enhanced computational resource management with digital twins into task offloading strategies. *IEEE Access : Practical Innovations, Open Solutions*, *12*, 90353–90370. DOI: 10.1109/ACCESS.2024.3420741

Jamwal, A., Agrawal, R., Sharma, M., & Giallanza, A. (2021). Industry 4.0 technologies for manufacturing sustainability: A systematic review and future research directions. *Applied Sciences (Basel, Switzerland)*, *11*(12), 5725. DOI: 10.3390/app11125725

Jat, A. S., & Grønli, T. M. (2023, August). Harnessing the Digital Revolution: A Comprehensive Review of mHealth Applications for Remote Monitoring in Transforming Healthcare Delivery. In International Conference on Mobile Web and Intelligent Information Systems (pp. 55-67). Cham: Springer Nature Switzerland. DOI: 10.1007/978-3-031-39764-6_4

Jat, A. S. (2023). Towards Next-Generation Healthcare: Architectural Insights into an AI-Driven, Smartwatch-Compatible mHealth Application. Avnish Singh Jat, Tor-Morten Grønli, Abdullah Raza Lakhan," Towards Next-Generation Healthcare: Architectural Insights into an AI-Driven, Smartwatch-Compatible mHealth Application. *International Journal of Computer Trends and Technology*, *71*(10), 92–106. DOI: 10.14445/22312803/IJCTT-V71I10P111

Javaid, M., Haleem, A., Singh, R. P., & Suman, R. (2023). An integrated outlook of Cyber–Physical Systems for Industry 4.0: Topical practices, architecture, and applications. *Green Technologies and Sustainability*, *1*(1), 100001. DOI: 10.1016/j.grets.2022.100001

Jeong, D., Baek, M., Lim, T., Kim, Y., Kim, S., Lee, Y., Jung, W.-S., & Lee, I. (2022). Digital twin: Technology evolution stages and implementation layers with technology elements. *IEEE Access : Practical Innovations, Open Solutions*, *10*, 52609–52620. DOI: 10.1109/ACCESS.2022.3174220

Jia, L., Li, Z., & Hu, Z. (2024). Applications of the internet of things in renewable power systems: A survey. *Energies*, *17*(16), 4160.

Jiang, Z., Guo, Y., & Wang, Z. (2021). Digital twin to improve the virtual-real integration of industrial IoT. *Journal of Industrial Information Integration*, *22*, 100196. DOI: 10.1016/j.jii.2020.100196

Jin, X., & Wang, Y. (2022). Hybrid Quantum-Classical Architectures for IoT Systems. *Quantum Computing and IoT Journal*, *7*(2), 101–115.

Jones, P., Mistry, M., & Porter, A. (2020). Smart Cities and Digital Twins: Applications in Urban Planning. *Journal of Urban Technology*, *27*(1), 1–18. DOI: 10.1080/10630732.2020.1765448

Jradi, M., & Bjørnskov, J. (2023). A digital twin platform for energy-efficient and smart building applications. DOI: 10.1109/ACTEA58025.2023.10194071

Justyna, S. (2023). AI revolution in healthcare and medicine and the (re-)emergence of inequalities and disadvantages for ageing population. *Frontiers in Sociology*, *7*, 1038854. Advance online publication. DOI: 10.3389/fsoc.2022.1038854 PMID: 36755564

Jyoti, S. (2024). *A., Dutta., Karishma, Desai.* Industrial IoT Systems for Real-Time Environmental Monitoring., DOI: 10.1109/ACROSET62108.2024.10743956

Kaaniche, N.. (2023). Privacy enhancing technologies for solving the privacy-personalization paradox: Taxonomy and survey. *IEEE Transactions on Information Forensics and Security*.

Kabir, M. R., Halder, D., & Ray, S. (2024). Digital Twins for IoT-Driven Energy Systems: A Survey. *IEEE Access : Practical Innovations, Open Solutions*, *12*, 177123–177143. DOI: 10.1109/ACCESS.2024.3506660

Kaivo-oja, J., Kuusi, O., Knudsen, M. S., & Lauraeus, T. (2019, 2019//). Digital Twins Approach and Future Knowledge Management Challenges: Where We Shall Need System Integration, Synergy Analyses and Synergy Measurements? Knowledge Management in Organizations, Cham.

Kajba, M., Jereb, B., & Cvahte Ojsteršek, T. (2023). Exploring Digital Twins in the Transport and Energy Fields: A Bibliometrics and Literature Review Approach. *Energies*, *16*(9), 3922. DOI: 10.3390/en16093922

Kale, N., Metre, K., Chitte, P., Mahankale, N., Gore, S., & Gore, S. (2023). Cloud computing for effective cyber security attack detection in smart cities. *International Journal on Recent and Innovation Trends in Computing and Communication*, *11*(9s), 777–785. DOI: 10.17762/ijritcc.v11i9s.7968

Kamel Boulos, M. N., & Zhang, P. (2021). Digital twins: From personalised medicine to precision public health. *Journal of Personalized Medicine*, *11*(8), 745. DOI: 10.3390/jpm11080745 PMID: 34442389

Kang, B. R., & Lee, H. Y. (2022). Autonomous Surgical Robots: From Concept to Reality. *IEEE Transactions on Medical Robotics*, *19*(3), 124–139. DOI: 10.1109/TMR.2022.3145678

Kaniappan, C., & Alkan, B. (2023). A digital life-cycle management framework for sustainable smart manufacturing in energy-intensive industries. *Journal of Cleaner Production*, *419*, 138259. Advance online publication. DOI: 10.1016/j.jclepro.2023.138259

Kantaros, A., Ganetsos, T., Petrescu, F. I. T., & Alysandratou, E. (2025). Bioprinting and Intellectual Property: Challenges, Opportunities, and the Road Ahead. *Bioengineering (Basel, Switzerland)*, *12*(1), 76. DOI: 10.3390/bioengineering12010076 PMID: 39851350

Kapoor, R., & Ghosal, I. (2022). Will Artificial Intelligence Compliment or Supplement Human Workforce in Organizations? A Shift to a Collaborative Human – Machine Environment. [IJRTBT]. *International Journal on Recent Trends in Business and Tourism*, *6*(4), 19–28. DOI: 10.31674/ijrtbt.2022.v06i04.002

Karatas, M., Eriskin, L., Deveci, M., Pamucar, D., & Garg, H. (2022). Big Data for Healthcare Industry 4.0: Applications, challenges and future perspectives. *Expert Systems with Applications*, *200*, 116912.

Karuri-Sebina, G., & Guya, J. (2020). *Discussion paper on a South African approach to smart, sustainable cities and settlements*. South African Cities Network.

Kashpruk, N., Piskor-Ignatowicz, C., & Baranowski, J. (2023). Time Series Prediction in Industry 4.0: A Comprehensive Review and Prospects for Future Advancements. *Applied Sciences (Basel, Switzerland)*, *13*(22), 12374. DOI: 10.3390/app132212374

Kashyap, H., Ahmed, H. A., Hoque, N., Roy, S., & Bhattacharyya, D. K. (2023). Big data analytics in bioinformatics: Architectures, techniques, tools and issues. *Network Modeling and Analysis in Health Informatics and Bioinformatics*, *5*, 1–28.

Kasper, L., Schwarzmayr, P., Birkelbach, F., Javernik, F., Schwaiger, M., & Hofmann, R. (2024). A digital twin-based adaptive optimization approach applied to waste heat recovery in green steel production: Development and experimental investigation. *Applied Energy*, *353*, 122192. Advance online publication. DOI: 10.1016/j.apenergy.2023.122192

Kasu, P., Hamandawana, P., & Chung, T. (2022). Tpbf: Two-phase bloom-filter-based end-to-end data integrity verification framework for object-based big data transfer systems. *Mathematics*, *10*(9), 1591. DOI: 10.3390/math10091591

Katiyar, K. (2022). AI-based predictive analytics for patients' psychological disorder. In *Predictive Analytics of Psychological Disorders in Healthcare: Data Analytics on Psychological Disorders* (pp. 37–53). Springer Nature Singapore. DOI: 10.1007/978-981-19-1724-0_3

Kaul, R., Ossai, C., Forkan, A. R. M., Jayaraman, P. P., Zelcer, J., Vaughan, S., & Wickramasinghe, N. (2023). The role of AI for developing digital twins in healthcare: The case of cancer care. *Wiley Interdisciplinary Reviews. Data Mining and Knowledge Discovery*, *13*(1), e1480. DOI: 10.1002/widm.1480

Kaushik, T. K., Singh, A., Raghav, A., & Singh, B. (2024). Potential of Artificial Intelligence in the Agricultural Industry: A Comprehensive Review. AI Applications for Clean Energy and Sustainability, 344-365.

Kawatsuma, S., Fukushima, M., & Okada, T. (2012, August). Emergency response by robots to Fukushima-Daiichi accident: Summary and lessons learned. *The Industrial Robot*, *39*(5), 428–435. DOI: 10.1108/01439911211249715

Keikhosrokiani, P. (Ed.). (2022). *Big data analytics for healthcare: datasets, techniques, life cycles, management, and applications*. Academic Press.

Kelvin-Agwu, M. C., Adelodun, M. O., Igwama, G. T., & Anyanwu, E. C. (2024). Strategies for optimizing the management of medical equipment in large healthcare institutions. *Strategies (La Jolla, Calif.)*, *20*(9), 162–170.

Keneally, C., Gaget, V., Kidd, S. P., & Brookes, J. D. (2024). Sample preservation solution increases nucleic acid yield and environmental rna quality in sediments across an estuarine salinity gradient. *Environmental DNA*, *6*(5), e70016. Advance online publication. DOI: 10.1002/edn3.70016

Kenngott, H. G., Fischer, L., Nickel, F., Rom, J., Rassweiler, J., & Müller-Stich, B. P. (2012, March). Status of robotic assistance-a less traumatic and more accurate minimally invasive surgery? *Langenbeck's Archives of Surgery*, *397*(3), 333–341. DOI: 10.1007/s00423-011-0859-7 PMID: 22038293

Khalaj, O., Jamshidi, M., Hassas, P., Mašek, B., Štádler, C., & Svoboda, J. (2023). Digital twinning of a magnetic forging holder to enhance productivity for industry 4.0 and metaverse. *Processes (Basel, Switzerland)*, *11*(6), 1703. DOI: 10.3390/pr11061703

Khan, A., Milne-Ives, M., Meinert, E., Iyawa, G. E., Jones, R. B., & Josephraj, A. N. (2022). A Scoping Review of Digital Twins in the Context of the Covid-19 Pandemic. *Biomedical Engineering and Computational Biology*, *13*, 11795972221102115. DOI: 10.1177/11795972221102115 PMID: 35633868

Khanam, R. (2023). Review of threats in iot systems: Challenges and solutions. *International Journal for Research in Applied Science and Engineering Technology*, *11*(2), 325–341. DOI: 10.22214/ijraset.2023.49016

Khandelwal, S., Sharma, N., & De, P. K. (2022, January). Real Time Carbon Emissions Calculator for Personal Computers. In International Conference on Data Management, Analytics & Innovation (pp. 651-663). Singapore: Springer Nature Singapore.

Khan, F. A., & Ibrahim, A. A. (2023). Non-fungible token based smart manufacturing to scale industry 4.0 by using augmented reality, deep learning and industrial internet of things. *International Journal on Perceptive and Cognitive Computing*, *9*(2), 62–72. DOI: 10.31436/ijpcc.v9i2.407

Khan, L. U., Saad, W., Niyato, D., Han, Z., & Hong, C. S. (2022). Digital-twin-enabled 6G: Vision, architectural trends, and future directions. *IEEE Communications Magazine*, *60*(1), 74–80.

Khan, M., & Khan, M. (2024). Real-time data processing systems in modern law enforcement: A technical analysis. *International Journal for Multidisciplinary Research*, *6*(6), 30723. Advance online publication. DOI: 10.36948/ijfmr.2024.v06i06.30723

Khdoudi, A., Masrour, T., Hassani, I. E., & Mazgualdi, C. E. (2024). A deep-reinforcement-learning-based digital twin for manufacturing process optimization. *Systems*, *12*(2), 38. DOI: 10.3390/systems12020038

Khodke, H. E., Bhalerao, M., Gunjal, S. N., Nirmal, S., Gore, S., & Dange, B. J. (2023). An intelligent approach to empowering the research of biomedical machine learning in medical data analysis using PALM. *International Journal of Intelligent Systems and Applications in Engineering*, *11*(10s), 429–436.

Kitchin, R. (2023). Big data and human geography: Opportunities, challenges and risks. *Dialogues in Human Geography*, *3*(3), 262–267. DOI: 10.1177/2043820613513388

Klass, L., Holz, L., Koenig, L., Kabza, A., Sehnke, F., Strecker, K., & Hölzle, M. (2024). Big brother is watching you: Leveraging artificial intelligence for automated fuel cell monitoring (technical report). *ECS Transactions*, *114*(5), 631–639. DOI: 10.1149/11405.0645ecst

Kleinitz, P., Sabariego, C., Llewellyn, G., Taloafiri, E., Mangar, A., Baskota, R., Marahatta, K., Maduwage, S., Khin, M. H., Wonanji, V., Sampa, G., Al-Rjoub, A., Al-Daod, J., & Cieza, A. (2024). Integrating rehabilitation into health systems: A comparative study of nine middle-income countries using who's systematic assessment of rehabilitation situation (stars). *PLoS One*, *19*(2), e0297109. DOI: 10.1371/journal.pone.0297109 PMID: 38315690

Kober, C., Medina, F. G., Benfer, M., Wulfsberg, J. P., Martinez, V., & Lanza, G. (2024). Digital twin stakeholder communication: Characteristics, challenges, and best practices. *Computers in Industry*, *161*, 104135. DOI: 10.1016/j.compind.2024.104135

Kolekar, A. B., Shalgar, S., & Malawade, I. (2023). Beyond reality: A study of integrating digital twins. *Journal of Physics: Conference Series*, *2601*(1), 012030. DOI: 10.1088/1742-6596/2601/1/012030

Kolias, C., Kambourakis, G., Stavrou, A., & Voas, J. (2017). DDoS in the IoT. Mirai and Other Botnets. *Computer*, *50*(7), 80–84. DOI: 10.1109/MC.2017.201

Korder, B., Maheut, J., & Konle, M. (2024). Simulation methods and digital strategies for supply chains facing disruptions: Insights from a systematic literature review. *Sustainability (Basel)*, *16*(14), 5957. DOI: 10.3390/su16145957

Kou, G., Dinçer, H., Yüksel, S., & Deveci, M. (2024). Synergistic integration of digital twins and sustainable industrial internet of things for new generation energy investments. *Journal of Advanced Research*, *66*, 39–46. https://doi.org/https://doi.org/10.1016/j.jare.2023.11.023. DOI: 10.1016/j.jare.2023.11.023 PMID: 38008174

Kriegel, J., Rissbacher, C., Reckwitz, L., & Tuttle-Weidinger, L. (2022, July). The requirements and applications of autonomous mobile robotics (AMR) in hospitals from the perspective of nursing officers. *International Journal of Healthcare Management*, *15*(3), 204–210. DOI: 10.1080/20479700.2020.1870353

Kritzinger, W., Karner, M., & Kienberger, J. (2018). Digital Twin of an Industrial Production Process. In *Proceedings of the 2018 IEEE International Conference on Industrial Technology (ICIT)* (pp. 1701-1706). IEEE.

Kshetri, N. (2023). Blockchain and AI: Driving the future of data security and business intelligence. *Journal of Business Research*.

Kumarasamy, V. K., Saroj, A. J., Liang, Y., Wu, D., Hunter, M. P., Guin, A., & Sartipi, M. (2024). Integration of Decentralized Graph-Based Multi-Agent Reinforcement Learning with Digital Twin for Traffic Signal Optimization. *Symmetry*, *16*(4), 448. DOI: 10.3390/sym16040448

Kumar, D., Ingole, A., & Choudhari, S. G. (2023). Towards Ideal Health Ecosystem With Artificial Intelligence-Driven Medical Services in India: An Overview. *Cureus*, *15*(11). Advance online publication. DOI: 10.7759/cureus.48482 PMID: 38073925

Kumari, S., Tyagi, A. K., & Sharma, A. K. (2024). Emerging, Assistive, and Digital Technology in Telemedicine Systems. In Future of AI in Medical Imaging (pp. 184-206). IGI Global.

Kumar, M., Sapkal, A., & Tiwari, V. (2018, November). *Ganga water quality monitoring system iot based. In 2018 IEEE Punecon*. IEEE.

Kuznetsov, A., et al. (2023). On the integration of artificial intelligence and blockchain technology: A perspective about security. Journal of Cybersecurity and Privacy.

Ladj, A., Wang, Z., Meski, O., Belkadi, F., Ritou, M., & Da Cunha, C. (2021). A knowledge-based Digital Shadow for the machining industry in a Digital Twin perspective. *Journal of Manufacturing Systems*, *58*, 168–179. DOI: 10.1016/j.jmsy.2020.07.018

Lauer-Schmaltz, M. W.. (2023). *ETHICA: Designing human digital twins—A systematic review and proposed methodology*. AI Ethics Journal.

Lazzaro, S., & Buccafurri, F. (2024). Achieving accountability and data integrity in message queuing telemetry transport using blockchain and interplanetary file system. *Future Internet*, *16*(7), 246. DOI: 10.3390/fi16070246

Lee, J., Azamfar, M., Singh, J., & Siahpour, S. (2020). Integration of digital twin and deep learning in cyber-physical systems: Towards smart manufacturing. *IET Collaborative Intelligent Manufacturing*, *2*(1), 34–36.

Lee, L. R., & Patel, M. C. (2022). Ethics of AI in Human-Centered Digital Twins: Addressing Bias and Fairness. *Ethics and Technology Journal*, *5*(1), 89–97.

Lee, M.-F. R., & Chien, T.-W. "Artificial intelligence and internet of things for robotic disaster response," in *International Conference on Advanced Robotics and Intelligent Systems (ARIS)*, Aug. 2020, DOI: 10.1109/ARIS50834.2020.9205794

Lee, S., Kwon, J., & Park, D. (2023). Runtime tracking-based replication of on-chip embedded software using transfer function learning for dust particle sensing systems. *IEEE Access : Practical Innovations, Open Solutions*, *11*, 32167–32175. DOI: 10.1109/ACCESS.2023.3263057

Lee, V. V., Vijayakumar, S., Ng, W. Y., Lau, N. Y., Leong, Q. Y., Ooi, D. S. Q., Su, L. L., Lee, Y. S., Chan, S.-Y., Blasiak, A., & Ho, D. (2023). Personalization and localization as key expectations of digital health intervention in women pre-to post-pregnancy. *NPJ Digital Medicine*, *6*(1), 183. DOI: 10.1038/s41746-023-00924-6 PMID: 37775533

Le, L. N., & Jones, D. L. (2017, April). Feature-Sharing in Cascade Detection Systems With Multiple Applications. *IEEE Journal of Selected Topics in Signal Processing*, *11*(3), 466–478. DOI: 10.1109/JSTSP.2017.2679539

Le, L., Jun, D. M., & Jones, D. L. "Energy-efficient detection system in time-varying signal and noise power", *Proc. IEEE Int. Conf. Acoust. Speech Signal Process.*, pp. 2736-2740, 2013. DOI: 10.1109/ICASSP.2013.6638154

Leon, J. F., Li, Y., Martin, X. A., Calvet, L., Panadero, J., & Juan, A. A. (2023). A Hybrid Simulation and Reinforcement Learning Algorithm for Enhancing Efficiency in Warehouse Operations. *Algorithms*, *16*(9), 408. DOI: 10.3390/a16090408

Leung, P. H., Chui, K. T., Lo, K., & de Pablos, P. O. (2021). A support vector machine–based voice disorders detection using human voice signal. In *Artificial Intelligence and Big Data Analytics for Smart Healthcare* (pp. 197–208). Academic Press. DOI: 10.1016/B978-0-12-822060-3.00014-0

Li, H., Pangborn, C., & Kovalenko, I. (2023). A system-level energy-efficient digital twin framework for runtime control of batch manufacturing processes. DOI: 10.1109/CASE56687.2023.10260642

Li, H., Yang, Y., Zhang, C., Zhang, C., & Chen, W. (2023). Visualization monitoring of industrial detonator automatic assembly line based on digital twin. *Sustainability (Basel)*, *15*(9), 7690. DOI: 10.3390/su15097690

Li, L., Gu, F., Li, H., Guo, J., & Gu, X. (2021). Digital Twin Bionics: A Biological Evolution-Based Digital Twin Approach for Rapid Product Development. *IEEE Access : Practical Innovations, Open Solutions*, *9*, 121507–121521. DOI: 10.1109/ACCESS.2021.3108218

Li, M., Wang, Z., Fan, H., Zhang, Y., & Gao, P. (2023). Establishment of web-based digital twin system for truss gantry crane. *IEEE Access : Practical Innovations, Open Solutions*, *11*, 146282–146296. DOI: 10.1109/ACCESS.2023.3345253

Lim, W. Y. B., Ng, J. S., Xiong, Z., Jin, J., Zhang, Y., Niyato, D., Leung, C., & Miao, C. (2021). Decentralized edge intelligence: A dynamic resource allocation framework for hierarchical federated learning. *IEEE Transactions on Parallel and Distributed Systems*, *33*(3), 536–550. DOI: 10.1109/TPDS.2021.3096076

Lin, S., Liu, A., Wang, J., & Kong, X. (2022, September). A review of path-planning approaches for multiple mobile robots. *Machines (Basel)*, *10*(9), 773. DOI: 10.3390/machines10090773

Lin, X., Kundu, L., Dick, C., Obiodu, E., Mostak, T., & Flaxman, M. (2023). 6G digital twin networks: From theory to practice. *IEEE Communications Magazine*, *61*(11), 72–78.

Lin, Y.. (2023). Human digital twin: A survey. *IEEE Internet of Things Journal.*

Lin, Y., Chen, L., Ali, A., Nugent, C., Cleland, I., Li, R., Ding, J., & Ning, H. (2024, August). Human digital twin: A survey. *Journal of Cloud Computing (Heidelberg, Germany)*, *13*(1), 131. Advance online publication. DOI: 10.1186/s13677-024-00691-z

Liu, H. (2022). Applications of Artificial Intelligence to Popularize Legal Knowledge and Publicize the Impact on Adolescents' Mental Health Status. *Frontiers in Psychiatry*, *13*, 902456. DOI: 10.3389/fpsyt.2022.902456 PMID: 35722558

Liu, X., He, X., Wang, M., & Shen, H. (2022, August). What influences patients' continuance intention to use AI-powered service robots at hospitals? The role of individual characteristics. *Technology in Society*, *70*, 101996. DOI: 10.1016/j.techsoc.2022.101996

Liu, X., Zhang, Y., & Zhao, L. (2020). Quantum Machine Learning for IoT Systems. *Journal of Emerging Technologies*, *15*(4), 243–256.

Liu, Y.. (2021). Federated learning meets blockchain in edge computing: Opportunities and challenges. *IEEE Internet of Things Journal*, *8*(16), 12806–12825. DOI: 10.1109/JIOT.2021.3072611

Liu, Z., Blasch, E., Liao, M., Yang, C., Tsukada, K., & Meyendorf, N. (2023). Digital twin for predictive maintenance. NDE 4.0, Predictive Maintenance, Communication, and Energy Systems. *The Digital Transformation of NDE*, *6*, 6. Advance online publication. DOI: 10.1117/12.2660270

Li, Z.. (2023). An overview of AI and blockchain integration for privacy-preserving. *Journal of Network and Computer Applications*.

Loaiza, J. H., & Cloutier, R. (2022). Analyzing the implementation of a digital twin manufacturing system: Using a systems thinking approach. *Systems*, *10*(2), 22. DOI: 10.3390/systems10020022

Lo, C. K., Chen, C. H., & Zhong, R. Y. (2021). A review of digital twin in product design and development. *Advanced Engineering Informatics*, *48*, 101297. https://doi.org/https://doi.org/10.1016/j.aei.2021.101297. DOI: 10.1016/j.aei.2021.101297

Long, N., Lei, Y., Peng, L., Xu, P., & Mao, P. (2022). A scoping review on monitoring mental health using smart wearable devices. *Mathematical Biosciences and Engineering*, *19*(8), 7899–7919. DOI: 10.3934/mbe.2022369 PMID: 35801449

Lopez, J., & Alcaraz, C. (2022). Digital twin: A thorough analysis of security risks. *IEEE Communications Surveys and Tutorials*.

López-Munoz, M. A., Torrealba-Melendez, R., Arriaga-Arriaga, C. A., Tamariz-Flores, E. I., López-López, M., Quirino-Morales, F., & López-Marcos, F. (2024). Wireless Dynamic Sensor Network for Water Quality Monitoring Based on the IoT. *Technologies*, *12*(11), 211.

López, O. L. A., Rosabal, O. M., Ruíz-Guirola, D. E., Raghuwanshi, P., Mikhaylov, K., Lovén, L., & Iyer, S. (2023). Energy-sustainable iot connectivity: Vision, technological enablers, challenges, and future directions. *IEEE Open Journal of the Communications Society*, *4*, 2609–2666. DOI: 10.1109/OJCOMS.2023.3323832

Lou, J., Wang, C., Xu, M., He, L., & Zhang, P. (2024). Design and operation of iot system and power communication with digital twin technology. *Journal of Physics: Conference Series*, *2872*(1), 012003. DOI: 10.1088/1742-6596/2872/1/012003

Lu, Y. (2021). Security and privacy of Internet of Things: A review of challenges and solutions. *Journal of Cybersecurity*.

Lu, Y., Huang, X., Zhang, K., Maharjan, S., & Zhang, Y. (2020). Low-latency federated learning and blockchain for edge association in digital twin empowered 6G networks. *IEEE Transactions on Industrial Informatics*, *17*(7), 5098–5107.

Lv, Z., Cheng, C., & Song, H. (2022). Digital Twins Based on Quantum Networking. *IEEE Network*, *36*(5), 88–93. DOI: 10.1109/MNET.001.2200131

Lv, Z., Wu, J., Li, Y., & Song, H. (2022). Cross-layer optimization for industrial Internet of Things in real scene digital twins. *IEEE Internet of Things Journal*, *9*(17), 15618–15629.

Lyu, Y., Li, L., Jing, Z., Liang, Y., Wang, R., & Wang, F.-Y. (2024, November). Meta-Services in Industry 5.0: A New Paradigm of Intelligent Services in Metaverses. *IEEE Transactions on Systems, Man, and Cybernetics. Systems*, *54*(11), 6826–6836. DOI: 10.1109/TSMC.2024.3373656

Lyu, Z., Lloret, J., Song, H., Mazurczyk, W., Wang, H., & Park, J. J. (2024). Metaverse and Digital Twins for Consumer Electronics. *IEEE Transactions on Consumer Electronics*, *70*(3), 5662–5666. DOI: 10.1109/TCE.2024.3411469

MacFeely, S., Huang, X., & Hassani, H. (2022). Significant digital twin in the revolution of healthcare. *Cognitive Computing and Big Data, 6*(3), 83. https://doi.org/10.xxxx/xxxx

Madarkar, R., Luo, X., Walker, C., Puthanveettil Madathil, A., & Liu, Q. (2024). Prospects of digital twin for dynamic life cycle assessment of smart manufacturing systems. *MATEC Web of Conferences*, DOI: 10.1051/matecconf/202440113006

Maddahi, Y., & Chen, S. (2022, September). Applications of digital twins in the healthcare industry: case review of an IoT-enabled remote technology in dentistry. In Virtual Worlds (Vol. 1, No. 1, pp. 20-41). MDPI.

Maddikunta, P. K. R., Pham, Q. V., Prabadevi, B., Deepa, N., Dev, K., Gadekallu, T. R., & Liyanage, M. (2022). Industry 5.0: A survey on enabling technologies and potential applications. *Journal of Industrial Information Integration*, *26*, 100257. DOI: 10.1016/j.jii.2021.100257

Maftei, A. A., Lavric, A., Petrariu, A. I., & Popa, V. (2023). Massive data storage solution for iot devices using blockchain technologies. *Sensors (Basel)*, *23*(3), 1570. DOI: 10.3390/s23031570 PMID: 36772609

Mahmoud, N. (2021). Smart Healthcare in the Age of AI: Recent Advances, Challenges, and Future Prospects. *IEEE Access : Practical Innovations, Open Solutions*, *9*, 145248–145270. DOI: 10.1109/ACCESS.2021.3118960

Mahmudul, A. (2024). An IoT Based Real-Time Environmental Monitoring System for Developing Areas. *Journal of Advanced Research in Applied Sciences and Engineering Technology*, *52*(1), 106–121. DOI: 10.37934/araset.52.1.106121

Majeed, A., & Hwang, S. O. (2021). Data-driven analytics leveraging artificial intelligence in the era of COVID-19: An insightful review of recent developments. *Symmetry*, *14*(1), 16. DOI: 10.3390/sym14010016

Makarem, M. A., & Razaz, M. A. (2023, October). Role of Big Data Analytics in the Internet of Things: A Comprehensive Survey. In 2023 3rd International Conference on Emerging Smart Technologies and Applications (eSmarTA) (pp. 1-15). IEEE.

Malav, M. V., Vagat, M. R. K., Saini, M. R., & Mamodiya, M. U. (2019). Research paper on Bluetooth based home automation using Arduino. *Convergence*.

Mamodiya, U., & Tiwari, N. (2023). Design and stand strength analysis of a solar tracking system. In *AIP Conference Proceedings* (Vol. 2782, No. 1). AIP Publishing. DOI: 10.1063/5.0154678

Mamodiya, U., & Tiwari, N. (2023b, June). Design and stand strength analysis of a solar tracking system. In *AIP Conference Proceedings* (Vol. 2782, No. 1). AIP Publishing.

Mamodiya, U., Raigar, G., & Meena, H. (2018). Design & simulation of tiffin food problem using fuzzy logic. *International Journal for Science and Advance Research in Technology*, *4*(10), 55–60.

Mamodiya, U., & Tiwari, N. (2023a). Dual-axis solar tracking system with different control strategies for improved energy efficiency. *Computers & Electrical Engineering*, *111*, 108920.

Mânica, S., Boedi, R. M., Pandey, H., & Shields, C. (2024). Identifying teeth and tooth fragments from digital 3D models. *Morphologie*, *108*(362), 100774. DOI: 10.1016/j.morpho.2024.100774 PMID: 38457861

Manickam, S., Yarlagadda, L., Gopalan, S. P., & Chowdhary, C. L. (2023). Unlocking the potential of digital twins: A comprehensive review of concepts, frameworks, and industrial applications. *IEEE Access : Practical Innovations, Open Solutions*, *11*, 135147–135158. DOI: 10.1109/ACCESS.2023.3338530

Mansour, D. A., Numair, M., Zalhaf, A. S., Ramadan, R., Darwish, M. M. F., Huang, Q., Hussien, M. G., & Abdel-Rahim, O. (2023). Applications of iot and digital twin in electrical power systems: A comprehensive survey. IET Generation, Transmission &Amp. *IET Generation, Transmission & Distribution*, *17*(20), 4457–4479. DOI: 10.1049/gtd2.12940

Manyika, J., Chui, M., Brown, B., Bughin, J., Dobbs, R., Roxburgh, C., & Hung Byers, A. (2021). Big data: The next frontier for innovation, competition, and productivity.

Manzoor, B., Othman, I., Durdyev, S., Ismail, S., & Wahab, M. H. (2021). Influence of artificial intelligence in civil engineering toward sustainable development—A systematic literature review. *Applied System Innovation*, *4*(3), 52. DOI: 10.3390/asi4030052

Marjani, M., Nasaruddin, F., Gani, A., Karim, A., Hashem, I. A. T., Siddiqa, A., & Yaqoob, I. (2017). Big IoT data analytics: architecture, opportunities, and open research challenges. *ieee access, 5*, 5247-5261.

Ma, S., Ding, W., Liu, Y., Ren, S., & Yang, H. (2022). Digital twin and big data-driven sustainable smart manufacturing based on information management systems for energy-intensive industries. *Applied Energy*, *326*, 119986. DOI: 10.1016/j.apenergy.2022.119986

Masram, B., Mendhe, A., Mishra, A., Pathade, A., Shindekar, N., & Kangale, Y. (2024, August). A Smart Forest Fire Detection and Notification System using IOT and Machine Learning. In *2024 International Conference on Electrical Electronics and Computing Technologies (ICEECT)* (Vol. 1, pp. 1-6). IEEE.

Matin, A., Islam, M. R., Wang, X., Huo, H., & Xu, G. (2023). AIoT for sustainable manufacturing: Overview, challenges, and opportunities. *Internet of Things : Engineering Cyber Physical Human Systems*, *24*, 100901. DOI: 10.1016/j.iot.2023.100901

Mayer-Schönberger, V., & Cukier, K. (2013). *Big data: A revolution that will transform how we live, work, and think*. Houghton Mifflin Harcourt.

Mazumder, A. H., Sahed, M., Tasneem, Z., Das, P., Badal, F. R., Ali, M. F., Ahamed, M. H., Abhi, S. H., Sarker, S. K., Das, S. K., Hasan, M. M., Islam, M. M., & Islam, M. R. (2023). Towards next generation digital twin in robotics: Trends, scopes, challenges, and future. *Heliyon*, *9*(2), e13359. DOI: 10.1016/j.heliyon.2023.e13359 PMID: 36825188

Mazzetto, S. (2024). Interdisciplinary Perspectives on Agent-Based Modeling in the Architecture, Engineering, and Construction Industry: A Comprehensive Review. *Buildings (Basel, Switzerland), 14*(11), 3480. DOI: 10.3390/buildings14113480

Mele, C., Russo-Spena, T., Marzullo, M., & Ruggiero, A. (2022, February). Boundary work in value co-creation practices: The mediating role of cognitive assistants. *Journal of Service Management, 33*(2), 342–362. DOI: 10.1108/JOSM-10-2020-0381

Melhem, H. G., & Nagaraja, S. (1996). Machine learning and its application to civil engineering systems. *Civil Engineering Systems, 13*(4), 259–279. DOI: 10.1080/02630259608970203

Metallidou, C., Psannis, K. E., Vergados, D. D., & Dossis, M. (2022). Digital Twin and Industrial Internet of Things Architecture to Reduce Carbon Emissions. *2022 4th International Conference on Computer Communication and the Internet, ICCCI 2022*, 185–189. DOI: 10.1109/ICCCI55554.2022.9850248

Methuselah, J. M. J. (2024). Digital twin technology for smart manufacturing. *Journal of Technology and Systems, 6*(4), 52–65. DOI: 10.47941/jts.2143

Mihai, S., Yaqoob, M., Hung, D. V., Davis, W., Towakel, P., Raza, M., Karamanoglu, M., Barn, B., Shetve, D., Prasad, R. V., Venkataraman, H., Trestian, R., & Nguyen, H. X. (2022). Digital twins: A survey on enabling technologies, challenges, trends and future prospects. *IEEE Communications Surveys and Tutorials, 24*(4), 2255–2291. DOI: 10.1109/COMST.2022.3208773

Millard, J. (2023). Exploring the impact of digital transformation on public governance.

Miller, M. E., & Spatz, E. (2022). A unified view of a human digital twin. *Human-Intelligent Systems Integration, 4*(1-2), 23–33. DOI: 10.1007/s42454-022-00041-x

Miller, S. (2024). Smart Cities and Digital Twins: Integrating Human Experience into Urban Management. *International Journal of Urban Technology, 7*(2), 45–59.

Mincă, E., Filipescu, A., Cernega, D., Şolea, R., Filipescu, A., Ionescu, D., & Simion, G. (2022). Digital twin for a multifunctional technology of flexible assembly on a mechatronics line with integrated robotic systems and mobile visual sensor—Challenges towards industry 5.0. *Sensors (Basel), 22*(21), 8153. DOI: 10.3390/s22218153 PMID: 36365850

Miraz, M. H., & Ali, M. (2018, 2018//). Blockchain Enabled Enhanced IoT Ecosystem Security. Emerging Technologies in Computing, Cham.

Moglia, A., Georgiou, K., Marinov, B., Georgiou, E., Berchiolli, R. N., Satava, R. M., & Cuschieri, A. (2022, August). 5G in healthcare: From COVID-19 to future challenges. *IEEE Journal of Biomedical and Health Informatics, 26*(8), 4187–4196. DOI: 10.1109/JBHI.2022.3181205 PMID: 35675255

Mohammed, Y.. (2012). A synopsis on the effects of anthropogenic greenhouse gases emissions from power generation and energy consumption. *International Journal of Scientific and Research Publications, 2*(10), 1–6.

Monteiro, A. C. B., França, R. P., Arthur, R., & Iano, Y. (2021). An overview of medical Internet of Things, artificial intelligence, and cloud computing employed in health care from a modern panorama. *The Fusion of Internet of Things, Artificial Intelligence, and Cloud Computing in Health Care*, 3-23.

Moreno, E. O. L., Cortes, L. L. H., Callejas, J. D. C., & Hernández, H. A. (2024, August). IoT based weather station for smart cities. In *2024 IEEE Colombian Conference on Communications and Computing (COLCOM)* (pp. 1-5). IEEE.

Moyaux, T., Liu, Y., Bouleux, G., & Cheutet, V. (2023). An agent-based architecture of the digital twin for an emergency department. *Sustainability (Basel), 15*(4), 3412. DOI: 10.3390/su15043412

Moysiadis, V., Tsolakis, N., Katikaridis, D., Sørensen, C. G., Pearson, S., & Bochtis, D. (2020, May). Mobile robotics in agricultural operations: A narrative review on planning aspects. *Applied Sciences (Basel, Switzerland), 10*(10), 3453. DOI: 10.3390/app10103453

Moztarzadeh, O., Jamshidi, M., Sargolzaei, S., Jamshidi, A., Baghalipour, N., Malekzadeh, M., & Hauer, L. (2023). Metaverse and healthcare: Machine learning-enabled digital twins of cancer. *Bioengineering (Basel, Switzerland), 10*(4), 455. DOI: 10.3390/bioengineering10040455 PMID: 37106642

Mudiyanselage, M. P. D., & Sellahewa, H. (2023). Digital twins as a framework for iot applications: a review. 2023 7th SLAAI International Conference on Artificial Intelligence (SLAAI-ICAI), 1-6. DOI: 10.1109/SLAAI-ICAI59257.2023.10365018

Muka, E., & Marinova, G. (2024). Digital twins to monitor IoT devices for green transformation of university campus. DOI: 10.1109/CoBCom62281.2024.10631264

Mukhacheva, A. V., Ugryumova, M. N., Morozova, I. S., & Mukhachyev, M. Y. (2022). Digital twins of the urban ecosystem to ensure the quality of life of the population. Proceedings of the International Scientific and Practical Conference Strategy of Development of Regional Ecosystems "Education-. DOI: 10.2991/aebmr.k.220208.047

München, S. (2019). The digital twin theory—A new view on a buzzword. Journal of Digital Transformation.

Murali, K., & Pasupuleti, K. (2024). Revolutionizing industries with digital twin technology. DOI: 10.62311/nesx/97806

Mustafa, S., Salahuddin, H., Ashraf, A., Shafique, M., Salahuddin, S., & Akbar, M. (2024). Smart Irrigation System for Wheat in Southern Punjab Using IOT-based Wireless Technology. *Journal of Computing & Biomedical Informatics, 8*(01).

Naderializadeh, N., Sydir, J. J., Simsek, M., & Nikopour, H. (2021). Resource management in wireless networks via multi-agent deep reinforcement learning. *IEEE Transactions on Wireless Communications, 20*(6), 3507–3523. DOI: 10.1109/TWC.2021.3051163

Naegelin, M., Weibel, R. P., Kerr, J. I., Schinazi, V. R., La Marca, R., von Wangenheim, F., Hoelscher, C., & Ferrario, A. (2023). An interpretable machine learning approach to multimodal stress detection in a simulated office environment. *Journal of Biomedical Informatics, 139*, 104299. DOI: 10.1016/j.jbi.2023.104299 PMID: 36720332

Nagarajan, H., Alsalami, Z., Dhareshwar, S., Sandhya, K., & Palanisamy, P. (2024, May). Predicting Academic Performance of Students Using Modified Decision Tree based Genetic Algorithm. In *2024 Second International Conference on Data Science and Information System (ICDSIS)* (pp. 1-5). IEEE. DOI: 10.1109/ICDSIS61070.2024.10594426

Naik, A., Kale, A. A., & Rajwade, J. M. (2024). Sensing the future: A review on emerging technologies for assessing and monitoring bone health. *Biomaterials Advances*, *165*, 214008. DOI: 10.1016/j.bioadv.2024.214008 PMID: 39213957

Naik, N., Hameed, B. Z., Sooriyaperakasam, N., Vinayahalingam, S., Patil, V., Smriti, K., Saxena, J., Shah, M., Ibrahim, S., Singh, A., Karimi, H., Naganathan, K., Shetty, D. K., Rai, B. P., Chlosta, P., & Somani, B. K. (2022). Transforming healthcare through a digital revolution: A review of digital healthcare technologies and solutions. *Frontiers in Digital Health*, *4*, 919985. DOI: 10.3389/fdgth.2022.919985 PMID: 35990014

Najem, N. R., Ali, Z. G., Ali, A. H. A., Taher, N. A., Mukhlif, S. K., Muliar, I., & Noori, H. M. (2024, October). A Comprehensive Framework for Harnessing IoT and 5G for Enhanced Disaster Response. In 2024 36th Conference of Open Innovations Association (FRUCT) (pp. 655-663). IEEE.

Najjar, R. (2024). *Digital Frontiers in Healthcare: Integrating mHealth.* AI, and Radiology for Future Medical Diagnostics.

Nampalli, R. C. R. (2024). Leveraging AI and Deep Learning for Predictive Rail Infrastructure Maintenance: Enhancing Safety and Reducing Downtime. *International Journal of Engineering and Computer Science*, *12*(12), 26014–26027. DOI: 10.18535/ijecs/v12i12.4805

Naranjo-Pérez, J., Infantes, M., Jiménez-Alonso, J. F., & Sáez, A. (2020). A collaborative machine learning-optimization algorithm to improve the finite element model updating of civil engineering structures. *Engineering Structures*, *225*, 111327. DOI: 10.1016/j.engstruct.2020.111327

Nashwan, A. J., Gharib, S., Alhadidi, M., El-Ashry, A. M., Alamgir, A., Al-Hassan, M., Khedr, M. A., Dawood, S., & Abufarsakh, B. (2023). Harnessing artificial intelligence: Strategies for mental health nurses in optimizing psychiatric patient care. *Issues in Mental Health Nursing*, *44*(10), 1020–1034. DOI: 10.1080/01612840.2023.2263579 PMID: 37850937

Ngadi, H., Bounceur, A., Bezoui, M., Lahlou, L., Hammoudeh, M., Kara, N., & Nana, L. (2024). Toward a digital twin iot for the validation of ai algorithms in smart-city applications. *Lecture Notes in Computer Science*, *14525*, 108–117. DOI: 10.1007/978-3-031-59933-0_8

Ngo, D. T., Aouedi, O., Piamrat, K., Hassan, T., & Raipin-Parvédy, P. (2023). Empowering digital twin for future networks with graph neural networks: Overview, enabling technologies, challenges, and opportunities. *Future Internet*, *15*(12), 377. DOI: 10.3390/fi15120377

Nguyen, B. L.. (2023). Privacy-preserving blockchain technique to achieve secure and reliable sharing of IoT data. *IEEE Internet of Things Journal.*

Nguyen, C. M., Mays, J., Plesa, D., Rao, S., Nguyen, M., & Chiao, J. C. (2015, May). Wireless sensor nodes for environmental monitoring in Internet of Things. In *2015 IEEE MTT-S International Microwave Symposium* (pp. 1-4). IEEE.

Nguyen, H. X., Trestian, R., To, D., & Tatipamula, M. (2021). Digital twin for 5G and beyond. *IEEE Communications Magazine*, *59*(2), 10–15. DOI: 10.1109/MCOM.001.2000343

Nguyen, T. N., Ponciroli, R., Bruck, P., Esselman, T. C., Rigatti, J. A., & Vilim, R. B. (2022). A digital twin approach to system-level fault detection and diagnosis for improved equipment health monitoring. *Annals of Nuclear Energy*, *170*, 109002. DOI: 10.1016/j.anucene.2022.109002

Nie, L., Wang, X., Zhao, Q., Shang, Z., Feng, L., & Li, G. (2023). Digital twin for transportation big data: A reinforcement learning-based network traffic prediction approach. *IEEE Transactions on Intelligent Transportation Systems*, *25*(1), 896–906. DOI: 10.1109/TITS.2022.3232518

Nielsen, M. A., & Chuang, I. L. (2010). *Quantum Computation and Quantum Information*. Cambridge University Press.

Nilsson-Lindén, H., Diedrich, A., & Baumann, H. (2021). Life cycle work: A process study of the emergence and performance of life cycle practice. *Organization & Environment*, *34*(1), 99–122. DOI: 10.1177/1086026619893971

Nocera, F., & Gardoni, P. (2023). Digital twins or equivalent infrastructure models? the role of modeling granularity in regional risk analysis of infrastructure. *Proceeding of the 33rd European Safety and Reliability Conference*, 2486-2493. DOI: 10.3850/978-981-18-8071-1_P530-cd

O'Neil, C. (2016). *Weapons of math destruction: How big data increases inequality and threatens democracy*. Crown.

Occhipinti, E.. (2023). Human body digital twin: A master plan for healthcare simulations. *Journal of Medical Systems*.

Olad, A. A., & Valilai, O. F. (2020, December 14-17). 2020). Using of Social Media Data Analytics for Applying Digital Twins in Product Development. *2020 IEEE International Conference on Industrial Engineering and Engineering Management (IEEM)*

Olshannikova, E., Ometov, A., Koucheryavy, Y., & Olsson, T. (2025). Visualizing Big Data with augmented and virtual reality: Challenges and research agenda. *Journal of Big Data*, *2*(1), 1–27.

Onile, E., Belikov, J., Petlenkov, E., & Levron, Y. (2023). Leveraging digital twins and demand side recommender chatbot for optimizing smart grid energy efficiency. DOI: 10.1109/ISGTAsia54891.2023.10372761

Onile, A. E., Machlev, R., Petlenkov, E., Levron, Y., & Belikov, J. (2021). Uses of the digital twins concept for energy services, intelligent recommendation systems, and demand side management: A review. *Energy Reports*, *7*, 997–1015. https://doi.org/https://doi.org/10.1016/j.egyr.2021.01.090

Oroos, A. (2024). *Aryan, Chaudhary*. Fundamental Concepts of IoT., DOI: 10.1201/9781032656694-2

Ouda, E., Sleptchenko, A., & Simsekler, M. C. E. (2023). Comprehensive review and future research agenda on discrete-event simulation and agent-based simulation of emergency departments. *Simulation Modelling Practice and Theory*, *129*, 102823. DOI: 10.1016/j.simpat.2023.102823

Owen, A., & Moore, J. (2023). Ethical considerations in AI-driven e-commerce solutions: Balancing personalization and privacy. *Journal of Business Ethics*.

Özel, T., & Jarosz, K. (2022). Machine learning approaches towards digital twin development for machining systems. *International Journal of Mechatronics and Manufacturing Systems*, *15*(2/3), 1. DOI: 10.1504/IJMMS.2022.10048837

Pacheco-Blazquez, R., Espinosa, J. G., Capua, D. D., & Sanchez, A. P. (2024). A digital twin for assessing the remaining useful life of offshore wind turbine structures. *Journal of Marine Science and Engineering*, *12*(4), 573. DOI: 10.3390/jmse12040573

Padmaja, M., Shitharth, S., Prasuna, K., Chaturvedi, A., Kshirsagar, P. R., & Vani, A. (2022). Grow of artificial intelligence to challenge security in IoT application. *Wireless Personal Communications*, *127*(3), 1829–1845. DOI: 10.1007/s11277-021-08725-4

Padmalal, S., Dayanand, I. E., Rao, G. S., Reddy, T. S., Ravuri, A. C. V., & Gore, S. (2023). Securing the skies: Cybersecurity strategies for smart city cloud using various algorithms. *International Journal on Recent and Innovation Trends in Computing and Communication*, *12*(1), 95–101. DOI: 10.17762/ijritcc.v12i1.7969

Palomares, I., Martínez-Cámara, E., Montes, R., García-Moral, P., Chiachio, M., Chiachio, J., Alonso, S., Melero, F. J., Molina, D., Fernández, B., Moral, C., Marchena, R., de Vargas, J. P., & Herrera, F. (2021). A panoramic view and swot analysis of artificial intelligence for achieving the sustainable development goals by 2030: Progress and prospects. *Applied Intelligence*, *51*(9), 6497–6527. DOI: 10.1007/s10489-021-02264-y PMID: 34764606

Panchal, S., & Shrivastava, A. K. (2022). Landslide hazard assessment using analytic hierarchy process (AHP): A case study of National Highway 5 in India. *Ain Shams Engineering Journal*, *13*(3), 101626. DOI: 10.1016/j.asej.2021.10.021

Panda, R. K., & Choudhury, B. B. "An effective path planning of mobile robot using genetic algorithm," in *IEEE International Conference on Computational Intelligence and Communication Technology (CICT)*, Feb. 2015, DOI: 10.1109/CICT.2015.145

Pandey, B. K., Appadurai, M., Pandey, D., George, A. S., Agarwal, A., Mahajan, D. A., Dadheech, P., & Pramanik, S. (2024). Future directions of digital twin architectures for 6G communication networks. In *Advances in Wireless Technologies and Telecommunication*. https://doi.org/DOI: 10.4018/979-8-3693-2931-3.ch012

Panga, N. K. R. (2021). Financial fraud detection in healthcare using machine learning and deep learning techniques. International Journal of Management Research and Business Strategy, 10(3). ISSN 2319-345X. Retrieved from www.ijmrbs.com

Panga, N. K. R. (2022). Applying discrete wavelet transform for ECG signal analysis in IOT health monitoring systems. *International Journal of Information Technology and Computer Engineering*, *10*(4), 157–175.

Panga, N. K. R. (2022). Applying discrete wavelet transform for ECG signal analysis in IoT health monitoring systems. *International Journal of Innovative Technology and Computing Engineering*, *10*(4), 62–78. DOI: 10.62646/ijitce.2022.v10.i4.pp62-78

Panga, N. K. R. (2024). Advanced data mining techniques in healthcare: Bridging AI and big data. Impact. *International Journal of Research in Engineering and Technology*, *12*(4), 1–12.

Papachristou, K., Katsakiori, P. F., Papadimitroulas, P., Strigari, L., & Kagadis, G. C. (2024). Digital twins' advancements and applications in healthcare, towards precision medicine. *Journal of Personalized Medicine*, *14*(11), 1101. DOI: 10.3390/jpm14111101 PMID: 39590593

Parente, A., & Swaminathan, N. (2024). Data-driven models and digital twins for sustainable combustion technologies. *iScience*, *27*(4), 109349. Advance online publication. DOI: 10.1016/j.isci.2024.109349 PMID: 38500824

Patel, S. P., & Desai, M. (2021). Rehabilitation Robotics: Addressing Mobility Challenges through Innovation. *Journal of Rehabilitation Medicine*, *43*(4), 198–213. DOI: 10.2340/16501977-2801

Paul, C. (2024). *Lambert., Yong, Zang*. Micro Energy Harvesting for IoT Sensors., DOI: 10.23919/INC-USNC-URSI61303.2024.10632530

Perno, M., Hvam, L., & Haug, A. (2022). Implementation of digital twins in the process industry: A systematic literature review of enablers and barriers. *Computers in Industry*, *134*, 103558. DOI: 10.1016/j.compind.2021.103558

Philogene, S. (2022). The Brooklyn health map: Reflections on a health dashboard visualizing connections between social factors and health outcomes in Brooklyn, NY. *Journal of Map & Geography Libraries*, *18*(1-2), 22–40. DOI: 10.1080/15420353.2022.2155752

Pinto, G. P.. (2023). A systematic review on privacy-aware IoT personal data stores. *IEEE Internet of Things Journal.*

Pirandola, S., Andersen, U. L., & Banchi, L. (2020). Advances in Quantum Cryptography. *Nature Reviews. Physics*, *2*(6), 383–396.

Pitkäaho, T., Pieskä, S., & Kaarlela, T. (2020). Virtual reality and digital twins for safety instruction. In *IEEE's 11th International Conference on Cognitive Information Communications (CogInfoCom)* (pp. 000115–000120). IEEE.

Poletti, G., Antonini, L., Mandelli, L., Tsompou, P., Karanasiou, G. S., Papafaklis, M. I., Michalis, L. K., Fotiadis, D. I., Petrini, L., & Pennati, G. (2022). Towards a digital twin of coronary stenting: A suitable and validated image-based approach for mimicking patient-specific coronary arteries. *Electronics (Basel)*, *11*(3), 502. DOI: 10.3390/electronics11030502

Poovendran, A. (2023). AI-Powered Data Processing for Advanced Case Investigation Technology. Journal of Science and Technology, 8(08), ISSN: 2456-5660.

Popa, E. O.. (2023). The use of digital twins in healthcare: Socio-ethical benefits and risks. *Journal of Medical Ethics.*

Popa, E. O., van Hilten, M., Oosterkamp, E., & Bogaardt, M. J. (2021). The use of digital twins in healthcare: Socio-ethical benefits and socio-ethical risks. *Life Sciences, Society and Policy*, *17*(1), 1–25. DOI: 10.1186/s40504-021-00113-x PMID: 34218818

Prabhakara Rao, P., Nair, M. M., & Raju, D. V. (1985). Assessment of the role of remote sensing techniques in monitoring shoreline changes: A case study of the Kerala coast. *International Journal of Remote Sensing*, *6*(3-4), 549–558. DOI: 10.1080/01431168508948477

Pradhan, B., Bhattacharyya, S., & Pal, K. (2021). IoT-based applications in healthcare devices. *Journal of Healthcare Engineering*, *2021*(1), 6632599. PMID: 33791084

Prakash, T. (2023). Blockchain-Enabled Secure Big Data Analytics for Internet of Things Smart Applications. *IEEE Internet of Things Journal*, *10*(7), 6428–6443. DOI: 10.1109/JIOT.2022.3227162

Pramodhini, R., Jagadheeswaran, R., Dhuriata, P., & Vivek, S. (2024, April). Optimizing environmental sustainability: analyzing IoT-enabled energy harvesting systems. In *2024 Third International Conference on Distributed Computing and Electrical Circuits and Electronics (ICDCECE)* (pp. 1-7). IEEE.

Prasad, B., & Ghosal, I. (2022). Forecasting Buying Intention Through Artificial Neural Network: An Algorithmic Solution on Direct-to-Consumer Brands. *FIIB Business Review*, *11*(4), 405–421. DOI: 10.1177/23197145211046126

Preskill, J. (2018). Quantum Computing in the NISQ Era and Beyond. *Quantum : the Open Journal for Quantum Science*, *2*, 79–100. DOI: 10.22331/q-2018-08-06-79

Priyanka, K. (2024). Effective Air Pollution Monitoring System for Eco Balance. *International Journal for Research in Applied Science and Engineering Technology*, *12*(10), 53–56. DOI: 10.22214/ijraset.2024.64435

Prokopowicz, P., Mikołajewski, D., & Mikołajewska, E. (2022). Intelligent System for Detecting Deterioration of Life Satisfaction as Tool for Remote Mental-Health Monitoring. *Sensors (Basel)*, *22*(23), 9214. DOI: 10.3390/s22239214 PMID: 36501916

Pyakurel, P., Rehman, M. F. u., & Benham, R. (2022). A novel approach to evaluating sustainability of products and associated manufacturing processes. Advances in Transdisciplinary Engineering. DOI: 10.3233/ATDE220597

Pysin, M. D. and Лобанов, A. C. (2023). Digital twin is a complex of microservices. E3S Web of Conferences, 458, 09012. DOI: 10.1051/e3sconf/202345809012

Qadir, M. A., Naeem, M., & Ejaz, W. (2024, June). Digital Twin-assisted Offloading for Low-Latency and Energy-Efficient Multi-Layer Network. In *ICC 2024-IEEE International Conference on Communications* (pp. 5141-5146). IEEE.

Qian, C., Liu, X., Ripley, C., Qian, M., Liang, F., & Yu, W. (2022). Digital twin—Cyber replica of physical things: Architecture, applications and future research directions. *Future Internet*, *14*(2), 64. DOI: 10.3390/fi14020064

Qin, B., Pan, H., Dai, Y., Si, X., Huang, X., Yuen, C., & Zhang, Y. (2024). Machine and deep learning for digital twin networks: A survey. *IEEE Internet of Things Journal*, *11*(21), 34694–34716. DOI: 10.1109/JIOT.2024.3416733

Qin, H., Shao, S., Wang, T., Yu, X., Jiang, Y., & Cao, Z. (2023, March). Review of autonomous path planning algorithms for mobile robots. *Drones (Basel)*, *7*(3), 211. DOI: 10.3390/drones7030211

Qiu, K., & Zhao, K. (2024). The integration of green energy and artificial intelligence in next-generation energy supply chain: An analysis of economic, social, and environmental impacts. *Sustainable Energy Technologies and Assessments*, *64*, 103660. DOI: 10.1016/j.seta.2024.103660

Quantum, I. B. M. (2023). *IBM's Quantum Roadmap*. Retrieved from IBM Quantum.

Quimba, F. M. A., Serafica, R. B., Bayudan-Dacuycuy, C., Andrada, A., & Moreno, N. I. (2023). Green and digital: Managing the twin transition toward sustainable development. DOI: 10.62986/dp2023.21

Qureshi, A. A., & Bashir, H. (2022). AI-Driven Predictive Healthcare: The Role of Medical Robotics in Disease Prevention. *Journal of Health Informatics*, *35*(3), 147–161. DOI: 10.1016/j.jhi.2022.100567

Qureshi, R., Irfan, M., Ali, H., Khan, A., Nittala, A. S., Ali, S., & Alam, T. (2023). Artificial Intelligence and Biosensors in Healthcare and its Clinical Relevance: A Review. *IEEE Access : Practical Innovations, Open Solutions*, *11*, 61600–61620. DOI: 10.1109/ACCESS.2023.3285596

Radanliev, P., De Roure, D., Nicolescu, R., Huth, M., & Santos, O. (2022). Digital twins: Artificial intelligence and the IoT cyber-physical systems in Industry 4.0. *International Journal of Intelligent Robotics and Applications*, *6*(1), 171–185. DOI: 10.1007/s41315-021-00180-5

Raghavendra, G., & Yesaswini, A. M. (2024). Design and implementation of internet of things (iot) framework for governing modern cyber attacks in computer network. *International Journal of Safety and Security Engineering*, *14*(5), 1385–1390. DOI: 10.18280/ijsse.140505

Rahimi, S. A., Baradaran, A., Khameneifar, F., Gore, G., & Issa, A. M. (2024). DECIDE-Twin: A Framework for AI-Enabled Digital Twins in Clinical Decision-Making. *IEEE Journal of Biomedical and Health Informatics*. PMID: 40030650

Rahmadian, E., Feitosa, D., & Virantina, Y. (2023). Digital twins, big data governance, and sustainable tourism. *Ethics and Information Technology*, *25*(4), 61. DOI: 10.1007/s10676-023-09730-w

Rahman, Z., et al. (2023). Blockchain-based AI-enabled Industry 4.0 CPS protection against advanced persistent threat. Journal of Cybersecurity and Privacy.

Rahman, A. (2023). AI-Driven Social Determinants of Health: Creating Ethical, Sustainable Solutions for Community Health Improvement. *Journal of Human Behavior and Social Science*, *7*(7), 49–57.

Rajan, G., & Li, S. (2024). Smart building digital twin for interior water distribution system management. The International Archives of the Photogrammetry, Remote Sensing and Spatial Information Sciences, XLVIII-4-2024, 373-379. DOI: 10.5194/isprs-archives-XLVIII-4-2024-373-2024

Rajkumar, D.. (2017). IoT based smart system for controlling Co2 emission. *Int. J. Sci. Res. Comput. Sci. Eng. Inf. Technol*, *2*(2), 284.

Rakshit, P., Saha, N., Nandi, S., & Gupta, P. (2024). Artificial intelligence in digital twins for a sustainable future. DOI: 10.1007/978-3-031-58523-4_2

Ranawaka, A., Alahakoon, D., Sun, Y., & Hewapathirana, K. (2024). Leveraging the Synergy of Digital Twins and Artificial Intelligence for Sustainable Power Grids: A Scoping Review. *Energies*, *17*(21), 5342. DOI: 10.3390/en17215342

Rangarajan, S., & Al-Quraishi, T. (2023). Navigating the Future of the Internet of Things: Emerging Trends and Transformative Applications. *Babylonian Journal of Internet of Things*, *2023*, 8–12. DOI: 10.58496/BJIoT/2023/002

Ranjan, R., & Ch, B. (2024). A comprehensive roadmap for transforming healthcare from hospital-centric to patient-centric through healthcare internet of things (IoT). *Engineering and Science*, *30*, 1175.

Reddy, B. M. (2023). Amalgamation of Internet of Things and Machine Learning for Smart Healthcare Applications–A Review. *Int. J Comp. Eng. Sci. Res, 5*, 08-36.

Regona, M., Yiğitcanlar, T., Xia, B., & Li, R. Y. M. (2022). Opportunities and adoption challenges of ai in the construction industry: A prisma review. *Journal of Open Innovation*, *8*(1), 45. DOI: 10.3390/joitmc8010045

Rehman, A., Song, J., Haq, F., Mahmood, S., Ahamad, M. I., Basharat, M., Sajid, M., & Mehmood, M. S. (2022). Multi-hazard susceptibility assessment using the analytical hierarchy process and frequency ratio techniques in the Northwest Himalayas, Pakistan. *Remote Sensing (Basel)*, *14*(3), 554. DOI: 10.3390/rs14030554

Reza, J.. (2023). Balancing customer personalization and data privacy using advanced analytics. *Journal of Data Science : JDS*.

Ridhawi, I. A., Otoum, S., & Aloqaily, M. (2023). Decentralized zero-trust framework for digital twin-based 6g. *arXiv preprint arXiv:2302.03107*.

Rix, S., & Hearn, M. (2019). Cybersecurity issues when implementing digital twins. *IIC Journal of Innovation*, 107–113.

Rodriguez-Rey, D., Guevara, M., Mateu Armengol, J., Criado, A., Enciso, S., Tena, C., . . . Pérez-Garcia Pando, C. (2023, May). Challenges for achieving clean air-The case of Barcelona (Spain). In EGU General Assembly Conference Abstracts (pp. EGU-14487).

Rojek, I., Mikołajewski, D., & Dostatni, E. (2020). Digital twins in product lifecycle for sustainability in manufacturing and maintenance. *Applied Sciences (Basel, Switzerland)*, *11*(1), 31. DOI: 10.3390/app11010031

Rolf, B., Jackson, I., Müller, M., Lang, S., Reggelin, T., & Ivanov, D. (2023). A review on reinforcement learning algorithms and applications in supply chain management. *International Journal of Production Research*, *61*(20), 7151–7179. DOI: 10.1080/00207543.2022.2140221

Rosati, R., Romeo, L., Cecchini, G., Tonetto, F., Viti, P., Mancini, A., & Frontoni, E. (2023). From knowledge-based to big data analytic model: A novel IoT and machine learning based decision support system for predictive maintenance in Industry 4.0. *Journal of Intelligent Manufacturing*, *34*(1), 107–121. DOI: 10.1007/s10845-022-01960-x

Rowan, N. J. (2024). Digital technologies to unlock safe and sustainable opportunities for medical device and healthcare sectors with a focus on the combined use of digital twin and extended reality applications: A review. *The Science of the Total Environment*, *926*, 171672. DOI: 10.1016/j.scitotenv.2024.171672 PMID: 38485014

Rubio-Rico, A., Mengod-Bautista, F., Lluna-Arriaga, A., Arroyo-Torres, B., & Fuster-Roig, V. (2023). The industrial digital energy twin as a tool for the comprehensive optimization of industrial processes. *Processes (Basel, Switzerland)*, *11*(8), 2353. Advance online publication. DOI: 10.3390/pr11082353

Rudi, H. (2024). Portable internet of things-based soil nutrients monitoring for precision and efficient smart farming. *Bulletin of Electrical Engineering and Informatics*, *13*(5), 3326–3333. DOI: 10.11591/eei.v13i5.7928

Rudin, C. (2019). Stop explaining black box machine learning models for high stakes decisions and use interpretable models instead. *Nature Machine Intelligence*, *1*(5), 206–215. DOI: 10.1038/s42256-019-0048-x PMID: 35603010

Rupali, P. (2024). Performance Measurement and Analysis of Soil Quality using. *IoT*, **•••**, 192–197. DOI: 10.1109/I-SMAC61858.2024.10714691

Rüßmann, M., Lorenz, M., Gerbert, P., Waldner, M., Justus, J., Engel, P., & Harnisch, M. (2015). *Industry 4.0. The Future of Productivity and Growth in Manufacturing Industries*. Boston Consulting Group.

Saadat, M. N., & Shuaib, M. (2020). Advancements in deep learning theory and applications: Perspective in 2020 and beyond. *Advances and Applications in Deep Learning, 3*.

Sadri, H., Yitmen, I., Tagliabue, L. C., & Westphal, F. (2023, July). A conceptual framework for blockchain and AI-driven digital twins for predictive operation and maintenance. In *EC3 Conference 2023* (Vol. 4, pp. 0-0). European Council on Computing in Construction. DOI: 10.35490/EC3.2023.219

Saeed, M. M. A., Saeed, R. A., & Ahmed, Z. E. (2024). Data Security and Privacy in the Age of AI and Digital Twins. In Ponnusamy, S., Assaf, M., Antari, J., Singh, S., & Kalyanaraman, S. (Eds.), *Digital Twin Technology and AI Implementations in Future-Focused Businesses* (pp. 99–124). IGI Global., DOI: 10.4018/979-8-3693-1818-8.ch008

Saha, E., & Rathore, P. (2023, April). Discovering hidden patterns among medicines prescribed to patients using Association Rule Mining Technique. *International Journal of Healthcare Management*, *16*(2), 277–286. DOI: 10.1080/20479700.2022.2099335

Sahal, R., Alsamhi, S. H., & Brown, K. N. (2022). Personal digital twin: A close look into the present and a step towards the future of personalised healthcare industry. *Sensors (Basel)*, *22*(15), 5918. DOI: 10.3390/s22155918 PMID: 35957477

Sahoo, S. K., & Choudhury, B. B. (2022). Optimal selection of an electric power wheelchair using an integrated COPRAS and EDAS approach based on Entropy weighting technique. *Decision Science Letters*, *11*(1), 21–34. DOI: 10.5267/j.dsl.2021.10.002

Sahoo, S. K., & Choudhury, B. B. (2023). Voice-activated wheelchair: An affordable solution for individuals with physical disabilities. *Management Science Letters*, *13*(3), 175–192. DOI: 10.5267/j.msl.2023.4.004

Sahoo, S. K., & Goswami, S. S. (2024). Theoretical framework for assessing the economic and environmental impact of water pollution: A detailed study on sustainable development of India. *Journal of Future Sustainability*, *4*(1), 23–34. DOI: 10.5267/j.jfs.2024.1.003

Said, S. B. H., Thi, M., Kellil, M., & Olivereau, A. (2023). On the management of tsn networks in 6g: a network digital twin approach. 2023 IEEE 28th International Conference on Emerging Technologies and Factory Automation (ETFA). DOI: 10.1109/ETFA54631.2023.10275568

Saini, K., Singh, A., Ahuja, A., Arora, N., & Saini, R. (2025). Research advancements in quantum computing digital twins. In Iyer, S., Nayyar, A., Paul, A., & Naved, M. (Eds.), *Digital Twins for Smart Cities and Villages* (pp. 37–53). Elsevier., https://doi.org/https://doi.org/10.1016/B978-0-443-28884-5.00002-6 DOI: 10.1016/B978-0-443-28884-5.00002-6

Saini, R. S., Bavabeedu, S. S., Quadri, S. A., Gurumurthy, V., Kanji, M. A., Kuruniyan, M. S., & Heboyan, A. (2024). Impact of 3D imaging techniques and virtual patients on the accuracy of planning and surgical placement of dental implants: A systematic review. *Digital Health*, *10*, 20552076241253550.

Sai, S., Rastogi, A., & Chamola, V. (2024). Digital Twins for Consumer Electronics. *IEEE Consumer Electronics Magazine*, *13*(6), 11–16. DOI: 10.1109/MCE.2023.3322013

Saliju, L., & Deboi, V. (2023). Unraveling the paradox: Balancing personalization and privacy in AI-driven technologies. *AI & Society*.

Sankar, G. R., & Fathima, G. (2024, April). IoT-Enabled Smart Waste Management: A Comprehensive Study on Sensor Technologies and Implementation Strategies. In *2024 International Conference on Inventive Computation Technologies (ICICT)* (pp. 1755-1764). IEEE.

Santhosini, R., Subhiksha, U. K., & Jayanthi, D. (2024). Review on Evaluation and Analysis of Water Quality Monitoring Systems Using IoT. *Deleted Journal*, *2*(09), 2331–2341. DOI: 10.47392/IRJAEH.2024.0320

Sareddy, M. R. (2021). Advanced quantitative models: Markov analysis, linear functions, and logarithms in HR problem solving. *International Journal of Applied Science Engineering and Management*, *15*(3).

Sareddy, M. R. (2022). Enhancing customer relationship management with artificial intelligence and deep learning: A case study analysis. *International Journal of Management Research & Review*, *12*(3), 1–17.

Sasikumar, A., Ravi, L., Kotecha, K., Saini, J. R., Varadarajan, V., & Subramaniyaswamy, V. (2022). Sustainable Smart Industry: A Secure and Energy Efficient Consensus Mechanism for Artificial Intelligence Enabled Industrial Internet of Things. *Computational Intelligence and Neuroscience*, *2022*, 1–12. DOI: 10.1155/2022/1419360

Sathyaprakash, P., Alagarsundaram, P., Devarajan, M. V., Alkhayyat, A., Poovendran, P., Rani, D. R., & Savitha, V. (2024). Medical practitioner-centric heterogeneous network powered efficient E-Healthcare risk prediction on Health Big Data. *International Journal of Cooperative Information Systems*, •••, 2450012. DOI: 10.1142/S0218843024500126

Satinder, K. (2024). Advancing Sustainable Ecosystem Development. Journal of Geography. *Environment and Earth Science International*, *28*(7), 52–59. DOI: 10.9734/jgeesi/2024/v28i7789

Satyanarayanan, M. (2017). The Emergence of Edge Computing. *Computer*, *50*(1), 30–39. DOI: 10.1109/MC.2017.9

Savić, G., Segedinac, M., Konjović, Z., Vidaković, M., & Dutina, R. (2023). Towards a domain-neutral platform for sustainable digital twin development. *Sustainability (Basel), 15*(18), 13612. DOI: 10.3390/su151813612

Schatsky, S., Meeker, D. B., & Mussomeli, A. (2021). Signs of a digital twin for strategists. *The global digital twins market is expected to reach 16 billion dollars*, according to a press release.

Schwarzmayr, P., Birkelbach, F., Kasper, L., & Hofmann, R. (2022). Development of a digital twin platform for industrial energy systems.. DOI: 10.46855/energy-proceedings-9974

Seddaoui, A., & Saaj, C. M. (2021, February). Collision-free optimal trajectory generation for a space robot using genetic algorithm. *Acta Astronautica, 179*, 311–321. DOI: 10.1016/j.actaastro.2020.11.001

Segovia, M., & García-Alfaro, J. (2022). Design, modeling and implementation of digital twins. *Sensors (Basel), 22*(14), 5396. DOI: 10.3390/s22145396 PMID: 35891076

Shah, F., Li, J., Shah, Y., & Shah, F. (2017, November). Broad big data domain via medical big data. In *2017 4th International Conference on Systems and Informatics (ICSAI)* (pp. 732-737). IEEE.

Shahid, Z. (2021). Distributed Machine Learning for Anomalous Human Activity Recognition using IoT Systems.

Shahzad, M., Shafiq, M. T., Douglas, D., & Kassem, M. (2022). Digital twins in built environments: An investigation of the characteristics, applications, and challenges. *Buildings (Basel, Switzerland), 12*(2), 120. DOI: 10.3390/buildings12020120

Shamanna, P., Joshi, S., Thajudeen, M., Shah, L., Poon, T., Mohamed, M., & Mohammed, J. (2024). Personalized nutrition in type 2 diabetes remission: Application of digital twin technology for predictive glycemic control. *Frontiers in Endocrinology, 15*, 1485464. DOI: 10.3389/fendo.2024.1485464 PMID: 39634180

Sharma, A., Kosasih, E., Zhang, J., Brintrup, A., & Calinescu, A. (2022). Digital twins: State of the art theory and practice, challenges, and open research questions. *Journal of Industrial Information Integration, 30*, 100383. DOI: 10.1016/j.jii.2022.100383

Sharma, A., Singh, S. K., Kumar, S., Thakur, R., Gupta, B. B., & Arya, V. (2024). Iot-enabled smart farming with industry 5.0. *Journal of High Speed Networks, 30*(3), 477–496. DOI: 10.3233/JHS-230258

Shavandi, A., & Khedmati, M. (2022). A multi-agent deep reinforcement learning framework for algorithmic trading in financial markets. *Expert Systems with Applications, 208*, 118124. DOI: 10.1016/j.eswa.2022.118124

Shehab, E., Kazhymurat, T., Jyeniskhan, N., Amantayeva, A., Meiirbekov, A., Singh, S., & Tokbolat, S. (2022). Developing a digital twin for carbon fiber composites recycling: Challenges and future research direction. *Advances in Science and Technology (Owerri, Nigeria), 116*, 61–66. DOI: 10.4028/p-h01m30

Shekhar, A., & Aleem, A. (2024). *Implementation of green IoT to achieve sustainable environment for improving energy efficiency. Indian Journal of Design Engineering*. IJDE., DOI: 10.54105/ijde.K9736.03010223

Sheraz, M., Chuah, T. C., Lee, Y. L., Alam, M. M., & Han, Z. (2024). A Comprehensive Survey on Revolutionizing Connectivity Through Artificial Intelligence-Enabled Digital Twin Network in 6G. IEEE Access.

Shi, C., Du, F., & Wu, Q. (2022). A Digital Twin Architecture for Wireless Networked Adaptive Active Noise Control. *IEEE/ACM Transactions on Audio, Speech, and Language Processing*, *30*, 2768–2777. DOI: 10.1109/TASLP.2022.3199992

Shinji, T. (2021). Leveraging Artificial Intelligence to Improve Chronic Disease Care: Methods and Application to Pharmacotherapy Decision Support for Type-2 Diabetes Mellitus. *Methods of Information in Medicine*, *60*(S 01), e32–e43. Advance online publication. DOI: 10.1055/s-0041-1728757 PMID: 33975376

Shiwei, C. (2024). Environmental Protection Control System Based on IoT and Deep Learning Intelligent Monitoring Sensors. Scalable Computing. *Practice and Experience*, *25*(4), 2210–2219. DOI: 10.12694/scpe.v25i4.2820

Shor, P. W. (1997). Polynomial-Time Algorithms for Prime Factorization and Discrete Logarithms on a Quantum Computer. *SIAM Journal on Computing*, *26*(5), 1484–1509. DOI: 10.1137/S0097539795293172

Siatras, V., Bakopoulos, E., Mavrothalassitis, P., Nikolakis, N., & Alexopoulos, K. (2024). Production Scheduling Based on a Multi-Agent System and Digital Twin: A Bicycle Industry Case. *Information (Basel)*, *15*(6), 337. DOI: 10.3390/info15060337

Siddika, A., & Zhao, L. (2023). Enhancing trust and reliability in AI and ML: Assessing blockchain's potential to ensure data integrity and security. Journal of Trust Management.

Silva, H. E. C. D., Santos, G. N. M., Leite, A. F., Mesquita, C. R. M., Figueiredo, P. T. D. S., Stefani, C. M., & de Melo, N. S. (2023). The use of artificial intelligence tools in cancer detection compared to the traditional diagnostic imaging methods: An overview of the systematic reviews. *PLoS One*, *18*(10), e0292063. DOI: 10.1371/journal.pone.0292063 PMID: 37796946

Singh, B. (2024). Evolutionary Global Neuroscience for Cognition and Brain Health: Strengthening Innovation in Brain Science. In *Biomedical Research Developments for Improved Healthcare* (pp. 246-272). IGI Global.

Singh, D., Dahiya, M., Kumar, R., & Nanda, C. (2021). Sensors and systems for air quality assessment monitoring and management: A review. *Journal of Environmental Management*, *289*, 112510. DOI: 10.1016/j.jenvman.2021.112510 PMID: 33827002

Singh, S., Rai, S., Singh, P., & Mishra, V. K. (2022). Real-time water quality monitoring of River Ganga (India) using internet of things. *Ecological Informatics*, *71*, 101770. DOI: 10.1016/j.ecoinf.2022.101770

Sirigu, G.. (2023). *Privacy and security issues for human digital twins*. IEEE Transactions on Trust and Privacy.

Siripurapu, S., Darimireddy, N. K., & Chehri, A., & AV, P. (. (2023). Technological advancements and elucidation gadgets for healthcare applications: An exhaustive methodological review-part-II (robotics, drones, 3D-printing, internet of things, virtual/augmented and mixed reality). *Electronics (Basel)*, *12*(3), 548. DOI: 10.3390/electronics12030548

Sitaraman, S. R. (2022). Anonymized AI: Safeguarding IoT services in edge computing – A comprehensive survey. *Journal of Current Science, 10*(4). ISSN: 9726-001X.

Sitaraman, S. R. (2022). Implementing AI applications in radiology: Hindering and facilitating factors of convolutional neural networks (CNNs) and variational autoencoders (VAEs). *Journal of Science and Technology, 7*(10). ISSN: 2456-5660.

Sitaraman, S. R. (2023). AI-driven value formation in healthcare: Leveraging the Turkish National AI Strategy and AI Cognitive Empathy Scale to boost market performance and patient engagement. ISSN 2347–3657, 14(3), 1.

Sitaraman, S. R. (2021). *AI-driven healthcare systems enhanced by advanced data analytics and mobile computing*. Intel Corporation.

Sitaraman, S. R. (2021). AI-Driven Healthcare Systems Enhanced by Advanced Data Analytics and Mobile Computing. *International Journal of Information Technology and Computer Engineering*, *9*(2), 175–187.

Sitaraman, S. R. (2021). Crow search optimization in AI-powered smart healthcare: A novel approach to disease diagnosis. *Journal of Current Science & Humanities*, *9*(1), 9–22. https://www.jcsonline.in

Sitaraman, S. R. (2022). Implementing AI applications in radiology: Hindering and facilitating factors of convolutional neural networks (CNNs) and variational autoencoders (VAEs). *Journal of Science and Technology*, *7*(10).

Sivakumar, N., Mura, C., & Peirce, S. M. (2022). Innovations in integrating machine learning and agent-based modeling of biomedical systems. *Frontiers in Systems Biology*, *2*, 959665. DOI: 10.3389/fsysb.2022.959665

Smith, J., & Jones, A. (2023). Human-Centered Digital Twins: Advancing Personalized Health. *Journal of Digital Innovation*, *14*(3), 120–130.

Sodachi, M., Pirayesh, A., & Valilai, O. F. (2024). Using Markov Decision Process Model for Sustainability Assessment in Industry 4.0. *IEEE Access : Practical Innovations, Open Solutions*, *12*, 189417–189438. DOI: 10.1109/ACCESS.2024.3514786

Sood, A., Oza, H., Sharma, N., & De, P. K. (2022, January). Impact of Energy Sector on Climate Change in India Using Forecasting Models. In International Conference on Data Management, Analytics & Innovation (pp. 225-243). Singapore: Springer Nature Singapore.

Sorokin, A. A., Odnogulov, I. O., Maltseva, N. S., Dzhalmukhambetova, E. A., Rudenko, M. F., & Esaulenko, V. N. (2024, October). Computing Platform for Monitoring Fire Hazards in Forest Areas using the IoT. In 2024 International Seminar on Electron Devices Design and Production (SED) (pp. 1-6). IEEE.

Souza, R., Azevedo, L., Lourenço, V., Soares, E., Thiago, R., Brandão, R., . . . Netto, M. A. (2019, November). Provenance data in the machine learning lifecycle in computational science and engineering. In *2019 IEEE/ACM Workflows in Support of Large-Scale Science (WORKS)* (pp. 1-10). IEEE. DOI: 10.1109/WORKS49585.2019.00006

Souza, V., Cruz, R., Silva, W., Lins, S., & Lucena, V. (2019, January). A digital twin architecture based on the industrial internet of things technologies. In *2019 IEEE International Conference on Consumer Electronics (ICCE)* (pp. 1-2). IEEE.

Stadtmann, F., Rasheed, A., Kvamsdal, T., Johannessen, K. A., San, O., Kölle, K., Tande, J. O., Barstad, I., Benhamou, A., Brathaug, T., Christiansen, T., Firle, A. L., Fjeldly, A., Frøyd, L., Gleim, A., Høiberget, A., Meissner, C., Nygård, G., Olsen, J., & Skogås, J. O. (2023). Digital Twins in Wind Energy: Emerging Technologies and Industry-Informed Future Directions. *IEEE Access : Practical Innovations, Open Solutions*, *11*, 110762–110795. DOI: 10.1109/ACCESS.2023.3321320

Starkey, J., Hancock, C., Chen, L., & Meng, Q. (2022). Digital twinning proof of concept for utility-scale solar: benefits, issues, and enablers. The International Archives of the Photogrammetry, Remote Sensing and Spatial Information Sciences, XLVI-5/W1-2022, 231-237. DOI: 10.5194/isprs-archives-XLVI-5-W1-2022-231-2022

Stegmaier, V., Schaaf, W., Jazdi, N., & Weyrich, M. (2022). Simulation model for digital twins of pneumatic vacuum ejectors. Chemical Engineering &Amp. *Chemical Engineering & Technology*, *46*(1), 71–79. DOI: 10.1002/ceat.202200358

Stergiou, C. L., Koidou, M. P., & Psannis, K. E. (2023). IoT-based big data secure transmission and management over cloud system: A healthcare digital twin scenario. *Applied Sciences (Basel, Switzerland)*, *13*(16), 9165. DOI: 10.3390/app13169165

su, z. (2024). Application of anomaly detection based on deep learning in digital twin. Third International Symposium on Computer Applications and Information Systems (ISCAIS 2024), 19. DOI: 10.1117/12.3034763

Subasi, A., & Subasi, M. E. (2024). Digital twins in healthcare and biomedicine. In De Pablos, P. O., & Zhang, X. (Eds.), *Artificial Intelligence, Big Data, Blockchain and 5G for the Digital Transformation of the Healthcare Industry* (pp. 365–401). Academic Press., https://doi.org/https://doi.org/10.1016/B978-0-443-21598-8.00011-7 DOI: 10.1016/B978-0-443-21598-8.00011-7

Subramanian, B., Kim, J., Maray, M., & Paul, A. (2022). Digital twin model: A real-time emotion recognition system for personalized healthcare. *IEEE Access : Practical Innovations, Open Solutions*, *10*, 81155–81165. DOI: 10.1109/ACCESS.2022.3193941

Suhail, S., Hussain, R., Jurdak, R., Oracevic, A., Salah, K., Hong, C. S., & Matulevičius, R. (2022). Blockchain-based digital twins: Research trends, issues, and future challenges. *ACM Computing Surveys*, *54*(11s), 1–34. DOI: 10.1145/3517189

Sun, T., He, X., & Li, Z. (2023). Digital twin in healthcare: Recent updates and challenges. *Digital Health*, *9*, 20552076221149651. Advance online publication. DOI: 10.1177/20552076221149651 PMID: 36636729

Sun, X., Li, J., Lu, Y., Bao, J., Liu, S., & Lu, S. (2021). A biomimicry-based digital twin modeling technique for manufacturing aeronautical parts. *Manufacturing Systems Journal*, *58*, 180–195. DOI: 10.1016/j.jmsy.2020.04.014

Suresh Kumar, V., & Krishnamoorthi, C. (2021, April). Development of electrical transduction based wearable tactile sensors for human vital signs monitor: Fundamentals, methodologies and applications. *Sensors and Actuators. A, Physical*, *321*, 112582. DOI: 10.1016/j.sna.2021.112582

Suryavanshi, A., Mehta, S., Chattopadhyay, S., & Aeri, M. (2024, June). Navigating Water Scarcity with IoT: A Smart Management System Approach. In 2023 4th International Conference on Intelligent Technologies (CONIT) (pp. 1-5). IEEE.

Talaat, F. M., Ibrahim, A., El-Kenawy, E.-S. M., Abdelhamid, A. A., Alhussan, A. A., Khafaga, D. S., & Salem, D. A. (2022, December). Route planning for autonomous mobile robots using a reinforcement learning algorithm. *Actuators*, *12*(1), 12. DOI: 10.3390/act12010012

Tan, F., & Cheng, Y. (2024). A digital twin framework for innovating rural ecological landscape control. *Environmental Sciences Europe*, *36*(1), 59. Advance online publication. DOI: 10.1186/s12302-024-00888-8

Tang, C.. (2023). Human body digital twin: A master plan. *IEEE Journal of Biomedical and Health Informatics*.

Tao, F., Zhang, H., & Cheng, J. (2019). Digital Twin and Its Applications in Industry 4.0. *International Journal of Advanced Manufacturing Technology*, *101*(5-8), 1373–1393. DOI: 10.1007/s00170-018-2646-4

Taofik, A. (2023). Telemedicine and Smart Healthcare—The Role of Artificial Intelligence, 5G, Cloud Services, and Other Enabling Technologies. *International Journal of Communications, Network and Systems Sciences*, *16*(03), 31–51. DOI: 10.4236/ijcns.2023.163003

Tapsell, J., et al. (2023). Consumer-centric data control, tracking, and transparency. Journal of Information Security.

Tawalbeh, L.. (2023). IoT privacy and security: Challenges and solutions. *IEEE Communications Surveys and Tutorials*.

Taylor, R., Zhang, Y., & Li, H. (2022). Quantum Sensors for Environmental Monitoring. *Sensors Journal*, *21*(8), 1121–1140.

Teng, S. Y., Touš, M., Leong, W. D., How, B. S., Lam, H. L., & Máša, V. (2021). Recent advances on industrial data-driven energy savings: Digital twins and infrastructures. *Renewable & Sustainable Energy Reviews*, *135*, 110208. DOI: 10.1016/j.rser.2020.110208

Thandekkattu, S. G., Ayem, G. T., & Rakshit, S. (2025). Data Management and Analytics in the Internet of Things (IoT). In Designing Sustainable Internet of Things Solutions for Smart Industries (pp. 209-228). IGI Global.

Thapa, C., & Camtepe, S. (2021). Precision health data: Requirements, challenges and existing techniques for data security and privacy. *Computers in Biology and Medicine*, *129*, 104130. DOI: 10.1016/j.compbiomed.2020.104130 PMID: 33271399

Tian, Y., Chen, C., Sagoe-Crentsil, K., Zhang, J., & Duan, W. (2022, July). Intelligent robotic systems for structural health monitoring: Applications and future trends. *Automation in Construction*, *139*, 104273. DOI: 10.1016/j.autcon.2022.104273

Timperi, M., Kokkonen, K., Hannola, L., & Elfvengren, K. (2023). Impacts of digital twins on new business creation: Insights from manufacturing industry. *Measuring Business Excellence*, *27*(3), 433–448. DOI: 10.1108/MBE-09-2022-0104

Toke, D. (2011). The UK offshore wind power programme: A sea-change in UK energy policy? *Energy Policy*, *39*(2), 526–534. DOI: 10.1016/j.enpol.2010.08.043

Tomar, P. S., & Grover, V. (2024). Transforming the energy sector: Addressing key challenges through generative ai, digital twins, ai, data science and analysis. *EAI Endorsed Transactions on Energy Web*, *10*. Advance online publication. DOI: 10.4108/ew.4825

Tong, X., Bao, J., & Tao, F. (2024). Co-evolutionary digital twins: A multidimensional dynamic approach to digital engineering. *Advanced Engineering Informatics*, *61*, 102554. DOI: 10.1016/j.aei.2024.102554

Trienens, M., Rasor, R., Kharatyan, A., Dumitrescu, R., & Anacker, H. (2024). Digital twins to increase sustainability throughout the system life cycle: A systematic literature review. *Proceedings of the Design Society*, *4*, 2277–2286. DOI: 10.1017/pds.2024.230

Tsang, S. W., & Jim, C. Y. (2016). Applying artificial intelligence modelling to optimize green roof irrigation. *Energy and Building*, *127*, 360–369. DOI: 10.1016/j.enbuild.2016.06.005

Tschorsch, F., & Scheuermann, B. (2016). Bitcoin and beyond: A technical survey on decentralized digital currencies. *IEEE Communications Surveys and Tutorials*, *18*(3), 2084–2123. DOI: 10.1109/COMST.2016.2535718

Tsourdos, A., Avdelidis, N. P., Al-Rubaye, S., & Almeaibed, S. (2021). Analyzing digital twins to improve autonomous car security and safety. *IEEE Communications Standards Magazine*, *5*(1), 40–46. DOI: 10.1109/MCOMSTD.011.2100004

Ullah, I., & Havinga, P. J. M. (2023). Governance of a Blockchain-Enabled IoT Ecosystem: A Variable Geometry Approach. *Sensors (Basel)*, *23*(22), 9031. DOI: 10.3390/s23229031 PMID: 38005419

Ullah, K., Ahsan, M., Hasanat, S. M., Haris, M., Yousaf, H., Raza, S. F., Tandon, R., Abid, S., & Ullah, Z. (2024). Short-Term Load Forecasting: A Comprehensive Review and Simulation Study with CNN-LSTM Hybrids Approach. *IEEE Access : Practical Innovations, Open Solutions*, *12*, 111858–111881. DOI: 10.1109/ACCESS.2024.3440631

Underner, T., & Jacoby, M. (2020). The state of standards for digital twins and the Internet of Things. *Applied Sciences (Basel, Switzerland)*, *10*(18), 6519. https://doi.org/10.xxxx/xxxx. DOI: 10.3390/app10186519

V. Pashkov et al. (2020). Artificial intelligence in medical practice: regulative issues and perspectives.

Vaibhavi, M. (2024). Internet of Things in Disaster Management. *International Journal for Research in Applied Science and Engineering Technology*, *12*(10), 620–625. DOI: 10.22214/ijraset.2024.64640

Vallée, A. (2023). Digital twin for healthcare systems. *Frontiers in Digital Health*, *5*, 1253050. Advance online publication. DOI: 10.3389/fdgth.2023.1253050 PMID: 37744683

Van der Aalst, W. M. P. (2016). *Process mining: Data science in action*. Springer. DOI: 10.1007/978-3-662-49851-4

van Dinter, R., Tekinerdogan, B., & Catal, C. (2022). Predictive maintenance using digital twins: A systematic literature review. *Information and Software Technology*, *151*, 107008. DOI: 10.1016/j.infsof.2022.107008

Varghese, S. A., Ghadim, A. D., Balador, A., Alimadadi, Z., & Papadimitratos, P. (2022). Digital twin-based intrusion detection for industrial control systems. 2022 IEEE International Conference on Pervasive Computing and Communications Workshops and Other Affiliated Events (PerCom Work, 611-617. DOI: 10.1109/PerComWorkshops53856.2022.9767492

Vatankhah Barenji, A., Liu, X., Guo, H., & Li, Z. (2021). A digital twin-driven approach towards smart manufacturing: Reduced energy consumption for a robotic cell. *International Journal of Computer Integrated Manufacturing*, *34*(7-8), 844–859. DOI: 10.1080/0951192X.2020.1775297

Venkatesan, K., & Rahayu, S. B. (2023). Blockchain security enhancement: An approach towards hybrid consensus algorithms and machine learning techniques. *Journal of Network and Computer Applications*.

Venkatesh, K. P., Brito, G., & Kamel Boulos, M. N. (2024). Health digital twins in life science and health care innovation. *Annual Review of Pharmacology and Toxicology*, *64*(1), 159–170. DOI: 10.1146/annurev-pharmtox-022123-022046 PMID: 37562495

Vera-Arenas, M. (2019). Digital transformation through AI and blockchain integration. Journal of Digital Innovation.

Verma, P., Sharma, R., & Mistry, M. (2022). A paradigm shift in iot cyber-security: A systematic review. *International Journal for Research in Applied Science and Engineering Technology*, *10*(10), 1024–1034. DOI: 10.22214/ijraset.2022.47129

Vilar-Dias, J. L., Silva, A. S., & Neto, F. B. L. (2023). An interpretable digital twin for self-aware industrial machines. *Sensors (Basel)*, *24*(1), 4. DOI: 10.3390/s24010004 PMID: 38202867

Vinuesa, R., Azizpour, H., Leite, I., Balaam, M., Dignum, V., Domisch, S., Felländer, A., Langhans, S. D., Tegmark, M., & Fuso Nerini, F. (2020). The role of artificial intelligence in achieving the Sustainable Development Goals. *Nature Communications*, *11*(1), 1–10. DOI: 10.1038/s41467-019-14108-y PMID: 31932590

Visconti, P., Rausa, G., Del-Valle-Soto, C., Velázquez, R., Cafagna, D., & De Fazio, R. (2024). Machine learning and IoT-based solutions in industrial applications for Smart Manufacturing: A critical review. *Future Internet*, *16*(11), 394.

Wagner, R., Schleich, B., Haefner, B., Kuhnle, A., Wartzack, S., & Lanza, G. (2019). Challenges and Potentials of Digital Twins and Industry 4.0 in Product Design and Production for High Performance Products. *Procedia CIRP*, *84*, 88–93. https://doi.org/https://doi.org/10.1016/j.procir.2019.04.219. DOI: 10.1016/j.procir.2019.04.219

Wang, K., Tang, Y., Duong, T. Q., Khosravirad, S. R., Dobre, O. A., & Karagiannidis, G. K. (2023). Multi-tier computing-enabled digital twin in 6G networks. *arXiv preprint arXiv:2312.16999.*

Wang, B., Zhou, H., Li, X., Yang, G., Zheng, P., Song, C., Yuan, Y., Wuest, T., Yang, H., & Wang, L. (2024). Human Digital Twin in the context of Industry 5.0. *Robotics and Computer-integrated Manufacturing*, *85*, 102626. DOI: 10.1016/j.rcim.2023.102626

Wang, G., Bing, Z., Hou, Z., & Li, Y. (2022). Energy efficiency optimization based on digital twin workshops. *Academic Journal of Engineering and Technology Science*, *5*(13). Advance online publication. DOI: 10.25236/AJETS.2022.051303

Wang, J., Qiao, L., Lv, H., & Lv, Z. (2022). Deep transfer learning-based multi-modal digital twins for enhancement and diagnostic analysis of brain mri image. *IEEE/ACM Transactions on Computational Biology and Bioinformatics*, *20*(4), 2407–2419. DOI: 10.1109/TCBB.2022.3168189 PMID: 35439137

Wang, K.. (2023). Securing data with blockchain and AI. *IEEE Internet of Things Journal.*

Wang, S., Zhang, J., Wang, P., Law, J., Calinescu, R., & Mihaylova, L. (2023, July). A deep learning-enhanced Digital Twin framework for improving safety and reliability in human–robot collaborative manufacturing. *Robotics and Computer-integrated Manufacturing*, *85*, 102608. DOI: 10.1016/j.rcim.2023.102608

Wang, T. (2024). Privacy Concerns in the Age of Digital Twins: Security Challenges and Solutions. *IEEE Access : Practical Innovations, Open Solutions*, *9*, 7854–7862.

Wang, X. (2024). Research on smart energy monitoring and management system based on digital twin technology. *Journal of Computer and Communications*, *12*(02), 109–115. DOI: 10.4236/jcc.2024.122007

Wan, S., Gu, Z., & Ni, Q. (2020, January). Cognitive computing and wireless communications on the edge for healthcare service robots. *Computer Communications*, *149*, 99–106. DOI: 10.1016/j.comcom.2019.10.012

Waring, J., Lindvall, C., & Umeton, R. (2020, April). Automated machine learning: Review of the state-of-the-art and opportunities for healthcare. *Artificial Intelligence in Medicine*, *104*, 101822. DOI: 10.1016/j.artmed.2020.101822 PMID: 32499001

Webb Hooper, M., Marshall, V., & Pérez-Stable, E. J. (2022). COVID-19 health disparities and adverse social determinants of health. *Behavioral Medicine (Washington, D.C.)*, *48*(2), 133–140. DOI: 10.1080/08964289.2021.1990007 PMID: 35318895

Weiß, W., & Ribas-Tugores, C. (2024). *IT-framework for digital energy twin/shadow applications*. Proceedings., DOI: 10.52825/isec.v1i.1089

Wolf, C. T. (2020). AI models and their worlds: Investigating data-driven, AI/ML ecosystems through a work practices lens. In *Sustainable Digital Communities: 15th International Conference, iConference 2020, Boras, Sweden, March 23–26, 2020* [Springer International Publishing.]. *Proceedings*, *15*, 651–664.

Wu, J., Jangid, V. R., & Park, J. (2024). Digital twin for amputees: A bidirectional interaction modeling and prototype with convolutional neural network. *Proceedings of the Human Factors and Ergonomics Society Annual Meeting*, *68*(1), 1410–1416. DOI: 10.1177/10711813241261938

Wu, X., Qiao, S., & Tan, Q. (2022). Destination management for ecotourism activity using analytical hierarchy process. *Scientific Programming*, *2022*(1), 4143060. DOI: 10.1155/2022/4143060

Wu, X., Zhu, X., Wu, G. Q., & Ding, W. (2023). Data mining with big data. *IEEE Transactions on Knowledge and Data Engineering*, *26*(1), 97–107.

Xames, M. D., & Topcu, T. G. (2024). A Systematic Literature Review of Digital Twin Research for Healthcare Systems: Research Trends, Gaps, and Realization Challenges. IEEE Access.

Xiang, X., Li, Q., Khan, S., & Khalaf, O. I. (2021). Urban water resource management for sustainable environment planning using artificial intelligence techniques. *Environmental Impact Assessment Review*, *86*, 106515. DOI: 10.1016/j.eiar.2020.106515

Xu, C., Dong, H., Fang, S., & Liu, M. (2021). Examining digital twins in terms of ideas, innovations, and industrial uses. *Manufacturing Systems Journal*, *58*, 346–361.

Yakovenko, Y., & Shaptala, R. (2024). Study of digital twins as the driving force of digital transformation and achieving the goals of sustainable development. *Technology Audit and Production Reserves*, *2*(4(76)), 11–20. DOI: 10.15587/2706-5448.2024.301423

Yang, B., Lv, Z., & Wang, F. (2022). Digital twins for intelligent green buildings. *Buildings (Basel, Switzerland)*, *12*(6), 856. DOI: 10.3390/buildings12060856

Yang, G., Ye, Z., Wu, H., Li, C., Wang, R., Kong, D., Hou, Z., Wang, H., Huang, X., Pang, Z., Dong, N., & Pang, G. (2024, August). A Digital Twin-Based Large-Area Robot Skin System for Safer Human-Centered Healthcare Robots Toward Healthcare 4.0. *IEEE Transactions on Medical Robotics and Bionics*, *6*(3), 1104–1115. DOI: 10.1109/TMRB.2024.3421635

Yang, H., Zhao, J., Xiong, Z., Lam, K. Y., Sun, S., & Xiao, L. (2021). Privacy-preserving federated learning for UAV-enabled networks: Learning-based joint scheduling and resource management. *IEEE Journal on Selected Areas in Communications*, *39*(10), 3144–3159. DOI: 10.1109/JSAC.2021.3088655

Yang, J. T.. (2023). APPFLChain: A privacy protection distributed artificial-intelligence architecture based on federated learning and consortium blockchain. *Journal of Network and Computer Applications*.

Yang, T., Razzaq, L., Fayaz, H., & Qazi, A. (2024, June). Redefining fan manufacturing: Unveiling industry 5.0's human-centric evolution and digital twin revolution. *Heliyon*, *10*(13), e33551. DOI: 10.1016/j.heliyon.2024.e33551 PMID: 39050440

Yenugula, M., Sahoo, S. K., & Goswami, S. S. (2024). Cloud computing for sustainable development: An analysis of environmental, economic and social benefits. *Journal of Future Sustainability*, *4*(1), 59–66. DOI: 10.5267/j.jfs.2024.1.005

Yereseme, A. K., Surendra, H. J., & Kuntoji, G. (2022). Sustainable integrated urban flood management strategies for planning of smart cities: A review. *Sustainable Water Resources Management*, *8*(3), 85. DOI: 10.1007/s40899-022-00666-5

Yeshwanth, J. (2024). Cyber physical echoes – Harnessing digital twin intelligence for real time system optimization. *Indian Scientific Journal of Research in Engineering and Management.* https://doi.org/ DOI: 10.55041/ijsrem38489

Ye, X., Du, J., Han, Y., Newman, G., Retchless, D., Zou, L., Ham, Y., & Cai, Z. (2022, November). Developing Human-Centered Urban Digital Twins for Community Infrastructure Resilience: A research agenda. *Journal of Planning Literature*, *38*(2), 187–199. DOI: 10.1177/08854122221137861 PMID: 37153810

Yigit, Y., Ahmadi, H., Yurdakul, G., Canberk, B., Hoang, T., & Duong, T. Q. (2024). Digi-infrastructure: Digital twin-enabled traffic shaping with low-latency for 6G smart cities. *IEEE Communications Standards Magazine*. Advance online publication. DOI: 10.1109/mcomstd.0002.2300027

Young, H. A., Freegard, G., & Benton, D. (2022). Mediterranean diet, interoception and mental health: Is it time to look beyond the 'Gut-brain axis'? *Physiology & Behavior*, *257*, 113964. DOI: 10.1016/j.physbeh.2022.113964 PMID: 36130628

Yun, J., Kim, S., & Kim, J. (2024). Digital twin technology in the gas industry: A comparative simulation study. *Sustainability (Basel)*, *16*(14), 5864. DOI: 10.3390/su16145864

Yu, P., Wen, Z., Guo, Y., Tai, N., & Jun, W. (2023). Application prospect and key technologies of digital twin technology in the integrated port energy system. *Frontiers in Energy Research*, *10*, 1044978. Advance online publication. DOI: 10.3389/fenrg.2022.1044978

Yu, W., Patros, P., Young, B., Klinac, E., & Walmsley, T. G. (2022). Energy digital twin technology for industrial energy management: Classification, challenges and future. *Renewable & Sustainable Energy Reviews*, *161*, 112407. DOI: 10.1016/j.rser.2022.112407

Zahra, S. A. (2021). The resource-based view, resourcefulness, and resource management in startup firms: A proposed research agenda. *Journal of Management*, *47*(7), 1841–1860. DOI: 10.1177/01492063211018505

Zaidi, S. M. R., Alam, A., & Khan, M. Y. (2024). Enhancing efficiency in advanced manufacturing through iot integration. *Engineering Headway*, *11*, 55–61. DOI: 10.4028/p-4HbPGf

Zancul, E., Schutzer, K., Anderl, R., Haag, S., & Durão, L. F. C. S. (2018). Industry-specific needs for digital twins 4.0. In *Assisting Industry with Product Lifecycle Management 4.0: Proceedings of the 15th IFIP WG 5.1 International Conference, PLM 2018* (pp. 1–12). Springer.

Zhang, E., Feng, W., Jia, Z., Yang, L., & Chen, Y. (2024). *A study on the construction technology of 3d model for factories oriented at digital twin*. Advances in Transdisciplinary Engineering., DOI: 10.3233/ATDE240394

Zhang, J., Liu, Y., Qin, X., & Xu, X. (2021). Energy-Efficient Federated Learning Framework for Digital Twin-Enabled Industrial Internet of Things. *IEEE International Symposium on Personal, Indoor and Mobile Radio Communications, PIMRC, 2021-September*, 1160–1166. DOI: 10.1109/PIMRC50174.2021.9569716

Zhang, K., Wu, Q., Li, H., Zhang, R., Li, J., Jiang, F., & Liu, L. (2023). Intelligent optimal control strategy of heat pump system based on digital twins. *Journal of Physics: Conference Series*, *2452*(1), 012029. DOI: 10.1088/1742-6596/2452/1/012029

Zhang, W.. (2011). Lithium-based energy storage management for DC distributed renewable energy system. In *2011 IEEE Energy Conversion Congress and Exposition* (pp. 3270-3277). IEEE. DOI: 10.1109/ECCE.2011.6064210

Zhang, X., Liu, X., Song, Y., Li, X., Huang, W., Zhou, Y., & Liu, S. (2024). Digital-twin-driven intelligent insulated-gate bipolar transistor production lines. *Sensors (Basel), 24*(2), 612. DOI: 10.3390/s24020612 PMID: 38257704

Zhang, Y., Li, H., & Taylor, R. (2023). Quantum Sensors for Next-Generation IoT. *Sensors Journal, 21*(8), 1121–1140.

Zhang, Z., Wei, Z., Court, S., Yang, L., Wang, S., Thirunavukarasu, A., & Zhao, Y. (2024). A review of digital twin technologies for enhanced sustainability in the construction industry. *Buildings (Basel, Switzerland), 14*(4), 1113. DOI: 10.3390/buildings14041113

Zhao, L., Kim, H., & Choi, K. (2021). Quantum Cryptography for IoT Networks. *IEEE Transactions on IoT Security, 6*(3), 187–196.

Zhao, Y., Wang, N., Liu, Z., & Mu, E. (2022). Construction theory for a building intelligent operation and maintenance system based on digital twins and machine learning. *Buildings (Basel, Switzerland), 12*(2), 87. DOI: 10.3390/buildings12020087

Zhenfeng, S., Wenbo, Y., & Deren, L. (2021). Digital twins are the foundation of smart cities. *Computational Urban Science, 1*, 1–11.

Zheng, X., Lu, J., & Kiritsis, D. (2022). The emergence of cognitive digital twin: Vision, challenges and opportunities. *International Journal of Production Research, 60*(24), 7610–7632. DOI: 10.1080/00207543.2021.2014591

Zhihao, W. (2024, November 07). AI-based Validation of Deforestation Using High-Resolution Satellite Imagery in the Brazilian Amazon. *The International Archives of the Photogrammetry, Remote Sensing and Spatial Information Sciences, XLVIII-3-2024*, 583–588. Advance online publication. DOI: 10.5194/isprs-archives-XLVIII-3-2024-583-2024

Zhong, D., Xia, Z., Zhu, Y., & Duan, J. (2023). Overview of predictive maintenance based on digital twin technology. *Heliyon, 9*(4), e14534. DOI: 10.1016/j.heliyon.2023.e14534 PMID: 37025897

Zhong, R., Hu, B., Feng, Y., Zheng, H., Hong, Z., Lou, S., & Tan, J. (2023). Construction of human digital twin model based on multimodal data and its application in locomotion mode identification. *Chinese Journal of Mechanical Engineering, 36*(1), 126. DOI: 10.1186/s10033-023-00951-0

Zhou, S., et al. (2023). A user-centered framework for data privacy protection using large language models and attention mechanisms. Journal of Cybersecurity and Privacy.

Zhou, S., Zhang, R., Chen, D., & Zhu, X. (2021). A novel framework for bringing smart big data to proactive decision making in healthcare. *Health Informatics Journal, 27*(2), 14604582211024698. DOI: 10.1177/14604582211024698 PMID: 34159834

Zhu, H. Y., Hieu, N. Q., Hoang, D. T., Nguyen, D. N., & Lin, C.-T. "A Human-Centric Metaverse Enabled by Brain-Computer Interface: A Survey," in *IEEE Communications Surveys & Tutorials*, vol. 26, no. 3, pp. 2120-2145, thirdquarter 2024, DOI: 10.1109/COMST.2024.3387124

Zhu, J., Yang, Y., Zhang, H., Zhao, Z., Hu, T., & Liu, L. (2023). More than energy harvesting in electret electronics-moving toward the next-generation functional system. *Advanced Functional Materials, 33*(17), 2214859. Advance online publication. DOI: 10.1002/adfm.202214859

Zyskind, G., & Nathan, O. (2015). Decentralizing privacy: Using blockchain to protect personal data. 2015 IEEE Security and Privacy Workshops, 180-184.

About The Contributors

Udit Mamodiya is an Associate Professor and Associate Dean (Research) at Poornima University in Jaipur, Rajasthan, India. With a robust academic and professional background, he has significantly contributed to the fields of renewable energy sources, reliability analysis, expert systems, and decision support systems. Dr. Mamodiya has authored over 50 research papers indexed in prestigious databases such as SCI, Scopus, and UGC Care, showcasing his commitment to advancing knowledge in his areas of expertise. Additionally, he has authored ten books published by national publishers, further enriching the academic community with valuable resources. An innovator at heart, Dr. Mamodiya holds an impressive portfolio of intellectual property, including 50 utility patents (both national and international) along with 20 design patents and copyrights. His entrepreneurial spirit is exemplified by securing 1 Crore in funding from the All India Council for Technical Education (AICTE) to establish the IDEA Lab at Poornima University, aimed at fostering innovation and research among students and faculty. With 12 years of experience in both teaching and industry, Dr. Mamodiya brings practical insights into his academic endeavors, bridging the gap between theoretical concepts and real-world applications. As a Single Point of Contact (SPOC) member of the Smart India Hackathon, he plays a vital role in promoting technological innovation among students. Furthermore, he has organized over 10 conferences in collaboration with Scopus and other notable publication partners, enhancing the university & academic outreach and engagement. Dr. Mamodiya also serves as a guest editor for the International Journal of Electrical and Electronics Research (IJEER), a Scopus-indexed journal, where he contributes to the dissemination of cutting-edge research. His dedication to teaching and research has been recognized through numerous awards, including the prestigious Dr. Radhakrishnan Award for outstanding excellence in teaching and research, presented on Teacher's Day in 2020. He also received the Global Outreach Education Award (GOREA) in 2019 for Excellence in Electrical Engineering & and the Asian Excellence Award (AEA) for & Outstanding Individual Achievements and Distinguished Services to the National 2018, Dr. Mamodiya was honored with the Global Education & Corporate Leadership Award (GECL) for & Best Academician at MIET, Meerut. Through his unwavering commitment to education and research, Dr. Udit Mamodiya continues to inspire students and colleagues alike, making a significant impact on the academic and technological landscape in India.

Akhtar Kalam is the Academic Director of Texila College Australia, Melbourne, and an Emeritus Professor at Victoria University, where he has been since 1984. He has held leadership roles, including deputy dean, head of engineering, and head of external engagement at VU. He chairs the Academic Board of Texila College and serves as Editor-in-Chief of the Australian Journal of Electrical & Electronics Engineering. With distinguished professorships across multiple universities globally, Professor Kalam has extensive experience in academia and industry. He holds a B.Sc. and B.Sc. Engineering from Calcutta University and Aligarh Muslim University, and MS and Ph.D. from the University of Oklahoma and the

University of Bath. His research interests include power systems, renewable energy, smart grids, and IEC61850 implementation. Professor Kalam has over 600 publications and 29 books, with more than 49 PhD graduates under his supervision. He has been awarded the John Madsen Medal multiple times and the ACPE-CIGRE Outstanding Academic Award. He is a registered Professional Engineer in Victoria and a Fellow of multiple engineering societies.

Yu-Chen Hu received his Ph.D. degree in computer science and information engineering from the Department of Computer Science and Information Engineering, National Chung Cheng University, Chiayi, Taiwan. He is a senior member of IEEE, a member of the Chinese Cryptology and Information Security Association, Computer Science and Information Management, and Phi Tau Phi Society of the Republic of China. He joins the editorial boards of Advances in Multimedia, Algorithms, CMC-Computers, Materials & Continua, Intelligent Automation & Soft Computing, IET Image Processing, Mathematical Problems in Engineering, etc. His research interests include digital forensics, information hiding, image and signal processing, data compression, information security, computer networks, deep learning, educational technologies, and bioinformatics.

Dinesh Goyal is a distinguished academician and leader in the field of Computer Science & Engineering, currently serving as the Principal of Poornima Institute of Engineering & Technology and the Provost (I/C) of Poornima University, Jaipur. With over 24 years of experience in teaching, research, and administration, he specializes in areas like information and network security, image processing, data analytics, and cloud computing. He has played a key role in establishing AICTE-funded labs, including the IDEA Lab and Deep Learning Labs, with grants exceeding 50 lakh. Dr. Goyal has over 98 publications indexed in SCI, Scopus, and Web of Science, and has authored nine books and numerous conference proceedings. He has received more than 81 lakh in research grants from institutions like AICTE and TEQIP, and has guided nine Ph.D. students and co-supervised 11 others. He has been actively involved in organizing international conferences, securing NAAC and NBA accreditations for engineering programs, and mentoring faculty. Recognized with awards such as the Elets Excellence Award and numerous certifications in advanced technologies like machine learning and Power BI, Dr. Goyal is also a prominent member of prestigious bodies like IEEE, ISTE, CSI, and ACM. His work is supported by collaborations with global giants such as Microsoft, Google, and Amazon. He is frequently invited to speak at conferences and has a significant online presence, including an h-index of 16 on platforms like Scopus and Google Scholar.

***

Ankit Agarwal is a highly accomplished academician and researcher with over 15 years of experience, including 14 years in academia and 1 year in the industry. Currently serving as the Head of the Department and Associate Professor of Information Technology at Dr. Akhilesh Das Gupta Institute of Professional Studies, Delhi, Dr. Agarwal manages responsibilities as the Cultural Head, Digital Marketing In-charge, and Website In-charge. He holds a Ph.D. in Information Security from Banasthali Vidyapith and an M.Tech. from GGSIPU, Delhi, with a specialization in Information Security. His research focuses on cybersecurity, cryptography, machine learning, and digital forensics. Dr. Agarwal has been granted two international patents (Germany and UK) and has authored three books. He has received a Canadian copyright for his work in IoT-based financial credit management. His contributions include several research papers in reputed journals and conferences, addressing topics like DDoS detection and cloud security. In addition to his academic pursuits, Dr. Agarwal has conducted workshops on ethical hacking, trained Kendriya Vidyalaya staff on cybersecurity, and delivered lectures on advanced topics like computer crime investigation and forensics. His vision is to innovate and contribute significantly to the field of Information Security, ensuring the development of cutting-edge solutions for modern cybersecurity challenges.

Poovendran Alagarsundaram has extensive experience in Data from DBMS, RDBMS, NoSQL and Big data technologies such as Apache Spark, Airflow, Kafka, DBT, and various streaming and API solutions. His areas of focus include Cloud, IoT, and AWS Data Technologies. Additionally, he is a certified AWS Solution Architect Associate and AWS Data Specialist.

Naga Sushma Allur attained her Masters in Computer Application (MCA) from Osmania University, Hyderabad, India. Following the completion of her MCA in 2005, Naga Sushma embarked on her professional journey as an IT specialist with ICICI Bank, a prominent banking institution in India. Currently she holds the position of Senior Business Analyst with Astute Solutions LLC. Previously, she held the similar role at Belong, Telstra Telecommunications, Australia.

Mohammed Amin Almaiah is an Associate Professor in Cybersecurity at University of Jordan. He has published over 120 research papers in highly reputed journals such as the Engineering and Science Technology, an International Journal, Education and Information Technologies, IEEE Access and others. Most of his publications were indexed under the ISI Web of Science and Scopus. His current research interests include Cybersecurity, cyber risk assessment and cyber risk management.

Subarno Bhattcharyya, as an accomplished academic administrative professional, is currently serving as Assistant Director at O.P. Jindal Global University (Institution of Eminence), Sonipat, Haryana, India. With a focus on Academics-Governance & Affairs, Online Education, Institutional Capacity Building & Research-Innovation in SDG & ESG enthusiasm mindset, he has demonstrated expertise in the educational management sector. Mr. Subarno is also pursuing his Doctoral Research in the field of Energy Studies from Vellore Institute of Technology (VIT), Bhopal, Madhya Pradesh, India. With two UK Design Patent Granted, three Indian Patents published, six Indian copyrights extracted and registered, and extensive experience in educational management, Mr. Subarno Bhattacharyya is dedicated to making a significant impact in the field of next gen higher education across the country.

Saurabh Chandra is an accomplished legal scholar and currently serves as an Associate Professor & Assistant Dean at the School of Law, Bennett University, India. With a robust academic foundation, he earned his Bachelor of Arts and Bachelor of Laws (B.A. LL.B.) from the prestigious Aligarh Muslim University (A.M.U.). He further specialized in Business Laws, completing his Master of Laws (LL.M.) at the renowned National Law School of India University (NLSIU), Bangalore. Dr. Chandra's academic journey culminated in a Doctorate in Law (Ph.D.) from the esteemed National Law University (NLU) Delhi. In addition to his impressive legal education from some of India's most prestigious institutions, Dr. Chandra also holds a master's degree in Management with specialization in Human Resources in Management and another in Journalism and Mass Communication. With more than sixteen years of teaching experience, he has numerous publications to his credit. His expertise is complemented by a robust portfolio of scholarly publications. Throughout his career, Dr. Chandra has consistently produced high-impact research. His publications are widely recognized for their depth of analysis, innovative perspectives, and practical relevance. His publications not only reflect his scholarly rigor but also his dedication to addressing contemporary challenges faced by businesses and policymakers. By bridging the gap between theoretical insights and real-world applications, Dr. Chandra's work serves as a valuable resource for academics, legal practitioners, and industry professionals alike. Dr. Chandra brings a wealth of experience in Academic Administration, having successfully held various key administrative positions. His diverse qualifications and extensive experience make him a distinguished figure in the academic and legal communities.

Himabindu Chetlapalli has Bachelors degree in Computer science, Information technology from Jawaharlal Nehru Technological University, passed out in 2006. Currently working as QA Architect having experience of more than 16 years in the field of Information tech as a Quality Assurance Analyst.

Ritu Raj Choudhary, Associate Professor of Language and Literature, holds a Ph.D. in Indian Literature and a translator certification from IGNOU. With 14 years of experience, she has been a dedicated educator in Literature, Communication, and Grammar for academics and competitive exams. A passionate theater director, she has successfully staged plays by William Shakespeare and Girish Karnad and has organized several theater workshops for students. Beyond the classroom, she has played a key role in academic discourse, contributing as an organizer and convenor in various conferences. Committed to literary scholarship, effective communication, and the performing arts, she continues to inspire students and the academic community alike.

Durga Praveen Deevi attained his Masters in Computer Application (MCA) from Osmania University, Hyderabad, India. Following the completion of his MCA in 2005, Mr. Durga Praveen embarked on his professional journey as a Quality Assurance Engineer with eIQnetworks now known as eIQnetworks (India) Research and Development (Pvt) Limited, a prominent Cyber Security company in India. He is working as a Senior Software Quality Assurance Engineer with O2 Technologies Inc., USA. Prior to this role, he worked with Agiliance India Pvt. Ltd., Infor (India) Pvt. Ltd., India in a similar position.

MohanaranganVeerapperumal Devarajan holds a Master of Computer Application degree and a Bachelor's in Computer Science from the University of Madras. With over 20 years of experience in the IT industry, he specializes in application development using various Microsoft technologies and AWS microservices for serverless applications.

Koteswararao Dondapati, with over 18 years of extensive experience as a Core Testing Subject Matter Expert (SME), specializes in business-critical Retail, Energy, and HCM verticals. His 10-year expertise in test automation includes Java frameworks, T Plan robot tool, Cucumber with Ruby, and SOAP UI Automation. Noteworthy is his domain expertise in technologies like POS and Recruiting Systems modules.

Boopathy G. earned his undergraduate degree in mechanical engineering from University of Madras, his master's degree in aeronautical engineering from Madras Institute of Technology, and his doctorate from the Department of Aeronautical Engineering, St. Peter's Institute of Higher Education and Research,

Chennai. At Vel Tech University, a professorship is currently held in the department of aeronautical engineering. In addition to guiding 2 Ph.D Scholars, guided 8 PG & 90 UG scholars on their significant projects, he has written in 30 international publications. He is a Life Member of the Society of Automotive Engineers INDIA and the Aeronautical Society of India.

Thirusubramanian Ganesan holds a Master of Computer Application degree and a Bachelor's in Electronic Science. With over 20 years of experience in the IT industry, specializing in the Banking and Insurance domains. In 2020, he obtained certification as a Google Cloud Professional Cloud Architect.

Venkata Surya Bhavana Harish has a wealth of experience in the field of data engineering, with roles ranging from Senior Data Platform Engineer at Under Armour to Software Engineer, Data Ingestion Lead at Asurion in Nashville. Prior to these positions, He served as a Senior Technical Engineer at Informatica in Austin and gained experience as an Energy Market Analyst Intern at Austin Energy.

Santosh I. Gore is the visionary founder of Sai Info Solutions, a multifaceted business initiative that operates across two key verticals: Academics and IT Consultancy. With a deep commitment to innovation and excellence, Mr. Gore has built a reputation for delivering cutting- edge solutions and fostering academic and technological advancements. Academic Vertical In the Academic domain, Mr. Gore mentors PhD and Post-Doctoral researchers, as well as professors, guiding them through the complexities of academic research projects, research paper writing, and publication in prestigious journals such as SCOPUS, EI Index, SCI, and IEEE. He has also received numerous awards and recognitions for his exceptional contributions to academia from various esteemed institutions and journals. As part of his academic endeavors, Mr. Gore has established collaborations with renowned journals, facilitating seamless publication opportunities for researchers.

Sri Harsha Grandhi is a dedicated and innovative Analog & Mixed Signal Design Engineer with 7 years of experience in the Non-Volatile Memory Group at Intel. Based in Folsom, California, he specializes in the custom design, validation, and integration of advanced mixed-signal and analog systems. Sri Harsha holds a Master of Science degree in Electrical Engineering from California State University, Sacramento, and a Bachelor of Engineering in Electronics and Communication Engineering from Gayatri Vidya Parishad College of Engineering in Vizag, India.

Basava Ramanjaneyulu Gudivaka is a highly experienced professional with over 11 years in Design and Development, specializing in Robotic Process Automation (RPA) for over 8 years. Certified in UiPath, Openspan/Pega Robotics, Automation Anywhere, and Blue Prism, Basava excels in problem-solving, technical leadership, and solution design.

Raj Kumar Gudivaka has a total of 4.4 years of IT experience, with over 3 years dedicated to RPA (Robotic Process Automation) implementation, focusing on MS Power Automate Desktop Flows and Automation Anywhere (Version 11 & A360). Raj collaborates with teams and Business Analysts to understand requirements, ensuring that bots align with process mapping guidelines. They create work plans, specifications, and programs following development procedures and utilize code repository tools like GitHub and GitLab for version control.

Rajya Lakshmi Gudivaka possesses knowledge in RPA (UiPath, Power Automate), particularly in building RPA solutions using UiPath. They are skilled in end-to-end automation solutions, encompassing analysis, designing, development, testing, and deployment. Their understanding of RPA best practices and familiarity with UiPath Orchestrator for robot deployment and management underscores their proficiency in automation technologies.

Amit Kumar Jain received the B.Tech. degree from Rajasthan Technical University, Kota and M. Tech degree from Jagannath University, Jaipur, Rajasthan in Electronics & communication and Completed PhD in Wireless communication from Poornima University, Jaipur, Rajasthan. He is working as Associate Professor with the Electrical & Electronics Engineering Department in Poornima Group, Jaipur, Rajasthan since last 13 Years. His Research area is Antenna, Wireless Communication, Machine Learning, Artificial Intelligence.

Jitender Jain is a technology leader with 16+ years of experience in AI, Technology and FinTech, driving innovation through advanced AI technology solutions. He holds U.S. granted Patent No.US11893819 for AI advancements in FinTech, reflecting his dedication to technological progress. A Senior Member of the IEEE Computer Society, he contributes to the global tech community, focusing on scalable AI-driven systems that solve complex challenges and deliver impactful outcomes. He is also an active contributor for leading international journals and conferences, combining technical expertise with strategic vision to advance AI, Technology and FinTech solutions.

Rama Krishna Mani KantaYalla is a proficient IT professional specializing in cloud technologies and IT infrastructure management. He holds a Master's degree in Computer Science from the University of Central Missouri and a Bachelor's degree in Technology from Jawaharlal Nehru Technological University Hyderabad.

Sharadha Kodadi is a seasoned IT professional with over 13 years of industry experience. She holds a Master's degree in Microbiology from Kakatiya University. Currently, she serves as a Lead Consultant at Infosys, where she excels in software development, cloud computing, and data analysis. Sharadha has a proven track record of working with advanced technologies such as AWS, Spring Boot, and Java, driving impactful solutions across various projects.

Krishna Kumar is currently a researcher in the Department of Water Resources Engineering and the Center for Advanced Middle Eastern Studies at Lund University, Sweden. He did his bachelor's in Electronics and Communication Engineering from Govind Ballabh Pant Engineering College, Pauri Garhwal, Uttarakhand, India. He pursued his master's in digital systems from Motilal Nehru National Institute of Technology, Allahabad, India, and received his Ph.D. degree from the Indian Institute of Technology Roorkee, India in 2006, 2012, and 2023, respectively. He served as a postdoctoral research fellow at the School of Electrical & Electronics Engineering in the Rolls-Royce Corporate Lab, Nanyang Technological University, Singapore, from August 2023 to March 2024. Previously, he held the position of Senior Engineer Research at the Rolls-Royce @ NTU Corporate Lab, Singapore, from February 2023 to July 2023. Prior to that, he worked as an Assistant Engineer at UJVN Ltd. (A State Government PSU of Uttarakhand) from January 2013 to February 2023. His expertise includes the design, installation, commissioning, testing, and operation & maintenance of hydro, solar, and wind power plants. Dr.

Kumar has also served as an Assistant Professor/Lecturer on a term appointment basis at Kumaon Engineering College, Dwarahat, Uttarakhand; Bharat Institute of Technology, Meerut; and Uttaranchal Institute of Technology, Dehradun, for almost three years. Furthermore, Dr. Kumar has published numerous research articles in reputed journals. He has also authored/edited many books with publishers such as Elsevier, Wiley, Taylor & Francis, Springer, and River Press. His current research interests include Renewable Energy, Multiphase Machines, Electrical Equipment Health Monitoring Systems, AI/ML, and data science.

Sanjeev Kumar is an Associate Professor at Swami Keshvanand Institute of Technology, Jaipur, specializing in power system optimization, renewable energy, and machine learning applications. He holds a Ph.D. from Dayalbagh Educational Institute, Agra, and has published extensively in high-impact journals. Dr. Kumar is a member of professional organizations, including the Institution of Engineers (India), and serves as a reviewer for reputed journals and conferences.

Vijaykumar Mamidala has Master's Degree in Computer Science from California State University, East Bay (2019) and Bachelors of Engineering from Osmania University, Hyderabad (2016). He is currently working as Sr. Software Engineer, DevOps in Conga (APTTUS Corporation), He has experience in Cloud Technologies in building, architecting private cloud infrastructure and deploy cloud base applications, services over multi cloud architecture (AWS, Azure, GCP and IBM).

Kamruzzaman M. M. (Senior Member, IEEE) received the B.E. and M.S. degrees in computer science and engineering and the Ph.D. degree in information and communication technology. He worked as a Postdoctoral Research Fellow at Shenzhen University, China. He is currently working at Jouf University, Saudi Arabia.

Harikumar Nagarajan has a wealth of extensive IT experience as IT architect as well as full stack software developer, specializing in software development across web, mobile, on-premise, and cloud platforms, as well as data science. His expertise lies in Java and JEE frameworks, object retaliation mapping frameworks and handling relational and non relational databases on multi cloud platforms.

Vineet Pandey is an experienced educator and researcher with over 16 years of teaching in the field of engineering. He holds a Ph.D. in Industrial Engineering and has contributed significantly to academic research, publishing papers in prestigious journals and presenting his work at various international conferences. His expertise spans across industrial processes, optimization, and systems management. Outside of his academic achievements, Vineet is passionate about mentoring students and inspiring the next generation of engineers. When not teaching or researching, he enjoys exploring new technologies and fostering collaborative projects in the engineering community.

Thinagaran Perumal is the recipient of 2014 Early Career Award from IEEE Consumer Electronics Society for his pioneering contribution in the field of consumer electronics. He completed his Phd at Universiti Putra Malaysia, in the area of smart technology and robotics. He is currently an Associate professor attached with Department of Computer Science, Faculty of Computer Science and Information Technology, Universiti Putra Malaysia. He is also currently appointed as Chair of IEEE Consumer Electronics Society Malaysia Chapter.

Anusha Preetham is currently working as Associate Professor in the Department of Computer Science and Engineering, Dayananda Sagar College of Engineering (DSCE),Shavige Malleshwara Hills, 91st Main Rd, 1st Stage, Kumaraswamy Layout, Bengaluru, Karnataka 560078. Her research interests include Digital Image Processing, Machine Learning and Deep Learning. She has 12 years of Teaching experience.

Winner Pulakhandam is an experienced Systems Administrator with a strong academic background, holding Masters degrees in Computer and Information Science. With a focus on managing and optimizing secure IT infrastructures, Winner brings expertise in network security, cloud technologies, and system performance. His work ensures reliable, scalable, and efficient IT operations that support organizational goals.

Surendar Rama Sitaraman is currently an AI Frameworks Engineer at Intel Corporation, where he contributes to the development and optimization of AI frameworks, driving innovation in AI and machine learning technologies. Prior to rejoining Intel, Surendar served as a Staff Engineer at Samsung Austin R&D Center (SARC), Advanced Computing Lab (ACL), contributing to the development and optimization of software solutions for Samsung's flagship devices.

ValluVisrutatma Rao is an accomplished Clinical Data Management (CDM) professional with over 8 years of experience managing and leading complex clinical trials across therapeutic areas, including Oncology, Rare Diseases, Cardiovascular, Nephrology, and Renal Medicine. With advanced degrees in Information Technology and Business Administration, Vish combines technical expertise with strategic insights to deliver high-quality data management solutions. He has played a pivotal role in multiple studies, ensuring regulatory compliance, data integrity, and timely delivery.

Dinesh Kumar Reddy Basani is a seasoned RPA Developer with a background in Computer Science, holding a Master's degree from Northwestern Polytechnic University (2016). With extensive experience in RPA development and having previously worked as a Pega Developer from 2016 to 2018, Dinesh has a proven track record of automating time-consuming manual tasks efficiently.

Aceng Sambas received the Doctor of Philosophy (Ph.D.) degree in mathematics from Universiti Sultan Zainal Abidin (UniSZA), Malaysia, in 2020. He has been a Lecturer with UniSZA and Universitas Muhammadiyah Tasikmalaya (UMTAS), Indonesia.

Vamshi Krishna Samudrala has Masters in business administration from Sullivan University and Masters in Electronics and Computer Science from Louisiana State University. Vamshi is an Enterprise Architect with a distinguished career spanning 15 years in the fields of DevOps and Cloud Architecture. Focused on automation, configuration management and innovation with cutting-edge technologies. Worked extensively with leading cloud service providers, including Amazon Web Services (AWS), Microsoft Azure possesses an exceptional ability to architect scalable, resilient, and cost-effective cloud solutions that align with the unique requirements of each organization.

Deevanshu Shrivastava is an ardent academician and zealous legal researcher, having 12+ years of teaching experience. After having cleared his UGC NET in Law twice and also MPSET, he completed his Ph.D. in Intellectual Property Laws from Barkatullah University, Bhopal. Apart from this he also holds

Diploma in Cyber Law, Diploma in Medical Laws, Diploma in Media and Drone Laws. He has various certificate courses from WIPO, University of Penn in his field of study IPR. He was the founding Head of Central India's first and only Public Policy school, Jagran School of Public Policy and International Affairs at Jagran Lakecity University, Bhopal. He is an active member on various editorial boards and a lifetime member of national and International Journals. He is on the advisory board of various legal platforms. He also has a great experience of participating and in conduction of Debates, Moot Court, ADR Tournaments, Policy Dialogues, Legal Aid Camps and various others like activities. He has won the prestigious 'Excellence in Research Award' thrice in the academic year 2015-16, 2016-17 & 2017-18. He was also awarded with the Outstanding Performer for the year Award for 2015-16. He was felicited with the prestigious Excellence in Research Award in 2018 and the Best Faculty (Law) Award, 2019 by Arjun Das Gulati Foundation in collaboration with Allahabad University, Allahabad. He received the prestigious Best Faculty in Law at the International Academic Awards in Dubai presented by GISR and American College of Dubai in October 2019. He has been awarded with prestigious BW40under40 Legal Awards for his contribution to legal academia in 2024. Dr. Deevanshu has been very actively acclaimed for his editorials in various leading newspapers and is a regular invitee as a resource person at various national and international gatherings. He has been a trainer for leading government and nongovernmental organizations. Dr. Shrivastava is proudly serving as the Founding Dean and Professor, at GL Bajaj Institute of Law, Greater Noida, India.

Bhupinder Singh is working as Professor at Sharda University, India. Also, Honorary Professor in University of South Wales UK and Santo Tomas University Tunja, Colombia. His areas of publications as Smart Healthcare, Medicines, fuzzy logics, artificial intelligence, robotics, machine learning, deep learning, federated learning, IoT, PV Glasses, metaverse and many more. He has 3 books, 139 paper publications, 163 paper presentations in international/national conferences and seminars, participated in more than 40 workshops/FDP's/QIP's, 25 courses from international universities of repute, organized more than 59 events with international and national academicians and industry people's, editor-in-chief and co-editor in journals, developed new courses. He has given talks at international universities, resource person in international conferences such as in Nanyang Technological University Singapore, Tashkent State University of Law Uzbekistan; KIMEP University Kazakhstan, All'ah meh Tabatabi University Iran, the Iranian Association of International Criminal law, Iran and Hague Center for International Law and Investment, The Netherlands, Northumbria University Newcastle, UK.

Kamalakar V. is working as an Associate Professor in the Department of Physics at Vel Tech Rangarajan Dr. Sagunthala R&D Institute of Science and Technology, has about 7 years of teaching experience. He has published 14 research papers in refereed international journals and 19 papers in the proceedings of various international conferences. He has also published 2 books and holds 2 Indian patents. He has received the Best Paper Award and the Commendable Researcher Award for his research papers at various international conferences. His areas of research include Atmospheric Physics, Optoelectronics, and Nanotechnology.

Srinivasan V. earned his undergraduate degree in mechanical engineering from S.K.P Institute of Technology affiliated to Anna University, his master's degree in CAD/CAM from Vel Tech Rangarajan Dr. Sagunthala R & D Institute of Science and Technology and currently pursuing Ph. D in Aeronautical Engineering from Vel Tech Rangarajan Dr. Sagunthala R & D Institute of Science and Technology.

Currently doing research in LiDAR (Light detection and Ranging) and other remote sensing and imaging sensors, its integration with UAVs. Obstacle avoidance and autonomous navigation systems in UAV using sensor fusion are his key areas for research.

Kittisak Wongmahesak serves as a lecturer at the Faculty of Political Science, North Bangkok University, and the Director of the Association of Legal & Political Studies in Thailand. Currently, he holds the position of Research Fellow at Shinawatra University, Thailand, and Universiti Sultan Zainal Abidin, Malaysia. He is also an Adjunct Professor at Sekolah Tinggi Ilmu Administrasi Abdul Haris, Indonesia, and an Adjunct Research Professor at several Indonesian universities, including Universitas Muhammadiyah Sinjai, Universitas Muhammadiyah Makassar, and Universitas Muhammadiyah Sidenreng Rappang. Previously, he was a Full Professor of Public Administration at Huanghe Business School, Henan University of Economics and Law in China, and at the University of City Island in Cyprus. He also served as an Adjunct Researcher at Ton Duc Thang University and Duy Tan University in Vietnam. His academic credentials include a Ph.D. in Social Sciences, an M.A. and a B.A. in Political Science, all from Kasetsart University. Additionally, he earned an M.B.A. and an M.P.A. from Ramkhamhaeng University, and a B.Pol.Sc. in International Relations and Comparative Government and Politics from Sukhothai Thammathirat Open University. His expertise spans Political Science, Public and Private Management, International Political Economy, and Social Research. He is the editor of numerous prestigious journals worldwide, including Sustainability, Frontiers in Psychology, PLOS One, World Food Policy, Asian Academy of Management Journal, International Journal of Public Policy and Administration Research, International Journal of Innovative Research and Scientific Studies, and Recent Advances in Computer Science and Communications. Recognized as one of the world's top 2% of scientists by Stanford University since 2020, he has published over 450 Scopus/Web of Science indexed documents and holds an h-index of 57 with more than 10,000 citations.

Index

Symbols

A

B

C

D

E

F

G

H

I

L

M

O

P

Q

R

S

U

V

W

www.ingramcontent.com/pod-product-compliance
Lightning Source LLC
LaVergne TN
LVHW080405011026
849161LV00009B/2348